second edition

Introduction to Clinical Psychology

Michael T. Nietzel
University of Kentucky

Douglas A. Bernstein
University of Illinois

PRENTICE-HALL, INC. Englewood Cliffs, New Jersey 07632

Library of Congress Cataloging-in-Publication Data

BERNSTEIN, DOUGLAS A.
  Introduction to clinical psychology.

  Authors' names reversed on t.p. of earlier ed.
  Bibliography: p.
  Includes indexes.
  1. Clinical psychology. I. Nietzel, Michael T.
II. Title. [DNLM: 1. Psychology, Clinical.
WM 105 B531i]
RC467.B47 1987   616.89   86-25198
ISBN 0-13-479411-7

Editorial/production supervision
  and interior design: Arthur Maisel
Cover design: Ben Santora
Manufacturing buyer: Barbara Kittle

© 1987 by Prentice-Hall, Inc.
A Division of Simon & Schuster, Inc.
Englewood Cliffs, New Jersey 07632

Printed in the United States of America

10 9 8 7 6 5 4 3 2 1

ISBN 0-13-479411-7 01

Prentice-Hall International (UK) Limited, *London*
Prentice-Hall of Australia Pty. Limited, *Sydney*
Prentice-Hall Canada Inc., *Toronto*
Prentice-Hall Hispanoamericana, S.A., *Mexico*
Prentice-Hall of India Private Limited, *New Delhi*
Prentice-Hall of Japan, Inc., *Tokyo*
Prentice-Hall of Southeast Asia Pte. Ltd., *Singapore*
Editora Prentice-Hall do Brasil, Ltda., *Rio de Janeiro*

Contents

Preface

In the first edition of this book, we tried to accomplish three goals. First, we wanted a book that, while it was appropriate for graduate students, was written especially with sophisticated undergraduates in mind. We believed this was important because many undergraduate psychology majors express an interest in clinical psychology without having a clear understanding of what the field involves and requires. An even larger number of nonmajors also wish to know more about clinical psychology. We felt that both groups of undergraduates would benefit from a thorough survey of the field which does not go into all the details typically found in "graduate students only" texts.

Second, we wanted to present a scholarly portrayal of the history of clinical psychology, its scope, functions, and future that stressed the value of different theoretical perspectives. For this reason, we did not limit ourselves to our own preferences for cognitive-behavioral theory but instead described three theoretical systems—psychoanalytic, behavioral, and phenomenological—in as neutral a manner as possible. We do champion the empirical research tradition of clinical psychology throughout the book because we believe it is a necessary and useful perspective for all clinicians to follow, regardless of their theoretical orientation.

Third, we wanted to write a book that would be interesting and enjoyable to read. Because we like being clinical psychologists and because we enjoy teaching students about the field, we tried to create a book that would pass that enthusiasm on to others.

In this revised edition, our goals are the same, but we have made some changes that we believe strengthen the book. We have streamlined the writing to make the text even more accessible to undergraduates, but we have also aimed for coverage which is sufficiently comprehensive to make it useful to graduate students. We have updated all the chapters and rearranged several in order to capture the many developments that have occurred in clinical psychology in the first half of the 1980s. New material has been added on diagnostic advances (DSM-III), research strategies (meta-analysis), innovative treatments (the cognitive therapies), specialized assessment instruments (especially testing of children), and developing professional issues (alternative systems for financing mental health care). Finally, because new biological discoveries have become so important to the field, we have added an entirely new chapter on biological contributions to clinical psychology, as illustrated in health psychology, neuropsychology, and psychopathology.

Acknowledgments

We want to thank several people for their valuable contributions to this book. Our colleagues, Doug Snyder, Rich Milich, David Berrry, Art Nonneman, Ruth Baer, Robert Russell, and Tom Widiger carefully read parts of the manuscript and offered many valuable suggestions for its improvement. Kelly Hemmings provided excellent library research and tireless commitment to completing the references and indexes. Countless undergraduate and graduate students asked the questions, raised the controversies, and argued opposing positions that have found their way into the text; they are really the people who stimulated this book. Now, we hope they read it. We also owe deep thanks to Shirley Jacobs who was single-handedly responsible for producing the manuscript, a task that required skill, patience, and perseverance, all of which she showed in amounts that were simply amazing. Finally, we want to thank our wives, Geri and Luann, for understanding what it takes to finish a project like this.

Michael T. Nietzel

Douglas A. Bernstein

chapter 1

Clinical Psychology: Definitions and History

At many universities in the United States, more Ph.D.'s are awarded in psychology than in any other discipline: At the beginning of the 1980s, between 3000 and 3300 doctoral degrees in psychology were granted each year. The largest group of them (about 40 percent) was earned by students studying clinical psychology (Stapp, Fulcher & Wicherski, 1984). During the 1960s and 1970s one indicator of the popularity of clinical psychology was the claim that it was easier to be admitted to medical school than to be accepted into a Ph.D. program in clinical psychology. Nyman (1973) concluded that during that era 80 percent of the applicants to doctoral programs in clinical psychology were rejected. Although clinical psychology remains a popular career, the odds for acceptance into its graduate programs have shifted in recent years in favor of applicants. It is now estimated that approximately 60 percent are accepted (Korn, 1984), although others claim that the odds are not that good (Hovancik, 1985). A decline in the number of college-aged persons in the population, some shifts in the career aspirations of these persons, and an increase in the number of training programs have improved the prospects for admission.

The appeal of clinical psychology is reflected in the membership of the American Psychological Association (APA), the national organization of psychologists in the United States, and in a recent census of all psychologists (Stapp, Tucker & VandenBos 1985). About 40 percent of all psychologists list clinical psychology as their major field, representing the single largest interest area in psychology. Obviously, then, clinical psychology remains an immensely popular educational and occupational field, a remarkable fact considering that it is only about eighty-five years old and did not begin to grow rapidly until after World War II. What is it that a clinical psychologist does that makes so many people want to become one? Or, to put it more generally, what is clinical psychology? The answer to this question is not simple, but in this book we shall attempt to describe the field in a way that will allow you to draw your own conclusions. In the process, we shall look at the history, current status, and future of the field; its areas of uniqueness and its overlap with other fields; the training and activities of its members; the factors that unite it and the issues that threaten to divide it.

SOME ATTEMPTS AT DEFINITION

We would like to provide a commonly accepted and easily remembered definition of clinical psychology from which the rest of the material in this book would logically flow. However, no such definition exists. In recent years the field has been expanding in so many different directions that any attempt to capture it in a sentence or two is bound to be too vague or too narrow and, in any case, soon outdated. This lack of definition has caused confusion in the public's mind over what clinical psychology is all about. The same problem exists to a certain extent among clinical psychologists themselves: "We are running in so many directions and we are doing so many things, that we may fall into the danger of not knowing who we are as a profession" (L'Abate, 1964). In spite of a continual process of self-examination within the field, there is a set of factors underlying most definitions of clinical psychology which provides a workable definition of the discipline.

Box 1-1 presents a sampling of definitions which reveals, first, that clinical psychology is a specialty within the larger discipline of psychology. Clinical psychologists, like all other psychologists, are concerned with the study and understanding of *behavior.* Unlike some psychologists, however, clinicians are concerned almost entirely with

human behavior; they study animals mainly when the use of human subjects is impractical or unsafe and when the behavior of animals can illuminate general behavioral principles and relationships that are relevant at the human level.

As shown in Box 1-1, clinical psychologists do *research* on human behavior. Clinical psychology also applies the knowledge and principles gained from research in a practical way, but this alone does not make the field unique; other specialties, such as industrial and educational psychology, are also noted for their applied orientation.

Another aspect of clinical psychology is *assessment or measurement* of the abilities and characteristics of individual human beings. The clinician collects information that will be analyzed and used to support conclusions about the person observed. While such information might be collected from large groups as part of a clinical research project, it is more frequently employed by the clinician as a means of understanding the particular individual at hand. However, many nonclinicians (e.g., personality researchers and industrial psychologists) administer and score tests of various kinds. Assessment activities alone cannot fully define clinical psychology or account for its distinctiveness.

Another important characteristic of clinical psychology is that contemporary clinicians are involved in *helping* people who are psychologically distressed. Therapeutic work is the most recently evolved aspect of the field, but it clearly rivals assessment activities in the general public's image of the clinical psychologist. Nevertheless, providing therapy is not unique to clinical psychology: Psychiatrists, family physicians, social workers, counselors, nurses, educators, and the clergy also perform interventions aimed at the alleviation of psychological problems. Clinical treatment thus joins the other functions we have discussed as one aspect of clinical psychology.

Where does all this leave us? Clinical psychology is a subarea of psychology. It applies psychological knowledge (as do other

BOX 1-1   Some definitions of clinical psychology

1. [Clinical psychology] "is the application of psychological principles and techniques to the problems of an individual. The body of knowledge on which it is based stems from the findings of psychology, personality theory, psychiatry, psychoanalysis, and anthropology." (Watson, 1951, p. 5)

2. "Clinical psychology is concerned with the psychological adjustment problems of the individual—more specifically, with the determination and evaluation of capacities and characteristics relating to adjustment and the study of psychological techniques for improving adjustment." (Shakow, 1969, p. 14)

3. "Broadly stated, clinical psychology is the field of application of psychological principles that is primarily concerned with the psychological adjustment of individuals." (Rotter, 1971, p. 1)

4. "The specialty of clinical psychology may be defined as that branch of psychology which deals with the search for and application of psychological principles aimed at understanding the uniqueness of the individual client or patient, reducing his personal distress, and helping him to function more meaningfully and effectively." (Goldenberg, 1973, p. 1)

5. "Clinical psychology is concerned with understanding and improving human function. . . . As a clinical field it is dedicated to improving the lot of individuals in distress, using the best knowledge and techniques available, while striving through research to increase the knowledge and sharpen the techniques needed for improved intervention in the future." (Korchin, 1976, p. 3)

6. Several clinicians have surveyed the ever-expanding boundaries of clinical psychology and have argued that some new name would better capture the diversity of the field. Levy (1984) has coined the term *human services psychology* to define "that sector of professional psychology concerned with the promotion of human well-being through the acquisition and application of psychological knowledge about the treatment and prevention of psychological and physical disorders."

subareas); and its members generate research about human behavior, engage in individual assessment, and provide various forms of psychological assistance. However, the defining characteristic that distinguishes clinical psychology from the other branches of psychology is what has been called the *clinical attitude* or the *clinical approach* (Korchin, 1976). This term means that clinical psychologists combine knowledge generated by clinical and other research with their own efforts at individual assessment in order to understand and help a particular person. The very word *clinical* is derived from the Greek for *bed* or *pertaining to a bed* and reflects the clinician's concern for helping distressed persons on an individual basis.

The clinical attitude sets clinicians apart from other psychologists whose interests, though often related to clinical psychology, tend to be more abstract in that they involve a search for principles and relationships that apply to human behavior problems on a general, or *nomothetic*, level. Clinical psychologists are interested in research of this kind, but they are more concerned with how general principles shape lives, problems, and treatments on an individual, or *idiographic*, level.

The clinical attitude is distinctive with respect to the helping professions outside psychology as well. Psychiatrists, social workers, and others assist people in psychological distress, but their fields are not traditionally noted for research into or systematic assessment of the problematic conditions they seek to alleviate. Their involvement with a given case is more likely to focus upon treatment.

The clinical attitude and the ways it contrasts with related approaches are most obvious with respect to a given case. For example, in reading a description of the problems of a person just admitted to a mental institution, the psychopathologist is likely to search for psychological or biological relationships which might explain the "disorder," while the psychiatrist (a medical doctor who specializes in psychological problems) might weigh the potential benefits of psychological, medical, or combined treatment. The clinical psychologist, however, would probably plan a strategy for further assessment of the problem and, depending upon the outcome of the assessment process, develop an intervention for dealing with the person's distress. The research evidence that guides the clinical psychologist in these pursuits (and which also aids other helping professions) often comes from the work of fellow clinical psychologists.

So it is not the research, the individual assessment, the treatment, or any of the other activities that makes clinical psychology unique. Rather, it is the clinical attitude, the idea of not only learning about behavior (particularly problematic behavior) but also doing something about it that is indigenous to clinical psychology (Wyatt, 1968, p. 235). It is this combination *within a single discipline* of reasearch, assessment, and intervention, all aimed at understanding human behavior and distress on an individual basis, that provides the substance of clinical psychology.

CLINICAL PSYCHOLOGISTS AT WORK

Now that we have outlined the nature of clinical psychology, it becomes easier to consider the range of things that clinical psychologists do, the variety of places in which they are found, and the array of clients and problems with which they work. Our examples of clinical activities, work settings, clients, and problems are only a small sample; it is always possible to find others. On the other hand, our coverage is so broad that it

is unlikely any given clinical psychologist will be associated with all the functions, locations, clients, and problems listed.

Let us look first at some isolated examples of clinical activities, settings, clients, and problems. Later we shall see how these dimensions are combined for individual clinicians.

The Activities of Clinical Psychologists

The popular stereotypes of the clinician as mind reader, hypnotist, psychotherapist, or mental tester are, like most stereotypes, only partly accurate at best. The research activity of clinical psychologists is, as already mentioned, a vital though underpublicized aspect of the field. In addition, clinicians often engage in teaching, consultation, and administrative functions which are even less well known. It is probably fair to say that 95 percent of all clinical psychologists spend their working lives engaged in some combination of six activities: *assessment, treatment, research, teaching, consultation,* and *administration.*

Assessment. Assessment involves the collection of information about people: their behavior, their problems, their unique characteristics, their abilities, and their intellectual functioning. This information may be used to diagnose problematic behavior, to assist in guiding a client toward an optimal vocational choice, to facilitate selection of job candidates, to describe a client's personality characteristics, to guide selection of treatment techniques, to aid legel decisions regarding the commitment of individuals to institutions, to provide a more complete picture of a client's problems, to screen potential participants in a psychological research project, to establish pretreatment baseline levels of behavior against which to measure posttreatment improvement, and for literally hundreds of other purposes. Most clinical assessment devices fall into one of three categories: *tests, interviews,* and *observations.*

Tests, interviews, and observations are

not always totally separate means of assessment. For example, a clinician may observe the nonverbal behavior of a client during a testing session or an interview in order to estimate the client's level of discomfort in social situations. Further, a test may be embedded in the context of an interview, as when the client is asked to provide specific information whose accuracy provides clues to reality contact.

Various modes of assessment are combined in assessment *batteries* and *multiple assessment* strategies. Here, information necessary for the clinician's work is collected through a series of procedures sometimes including simply a variety of tests, but often encompassing a more elaborate combination of tests, interviews, and observations that focus not only on the client but also on significant others who can provide additional relevant information.

Treatment. This function of the clinical psychologist involves helping people solve distressing psychological problems. The intervention may be called psychotherapy, behavior modification, psychological counseling, or other names, depending upon the orientation of the clinician, and may involve many combinations of clients and therapists. Though one-to-one treatment has been traditional and is the single most frequent activity of clinicians today (Peterson, 1985), it is now common for one psychologist to deal with groups of clients (e.g., family members, co-workers, hospital ward residents). Sometimes two or more clinicians work as a team to deal with the problems of an individual, couple, or group. The emphasis of treatment may be on alleviating the distress and/or problematic behavior of one or more troubled individuals, or may include prevention of psychological problems before they appear by altering the institutions, the social or environmental situation, or the behavioral skills of persons "at risk" (e.g., teenage parents) or of an entire community. Herink (1980) lists more than 250 different "brand names" of therapy ranging literally

from A (Aikido) to Z (Zaraleya psychoenergetic technique).

Treatment by a clinical psychologist may be on an outpatient basis (the client lives in the community) or may be part of the services offered to residents (inpatients) of an institution. It may be as brief as one session or extend over several years. Treatment sessions may consist of anything from client or therapist monologues to painstaking construction of new behavioral skills to episodes of intense emotional drama, and may range from highly structured to totally spontaneous interactions. The goals of clinician and client may be quite limited (as when a solution to a specific problem is sought), very ambitious (as when a complete analysis and reconstruction of the client's personality is planned), or may fall somewhere between these extremes. Therapy may be conducted free of charge, on a sliding scale based on client income, or in return for very large fees, and may, in given cases, result in anything from worsening of client problems to no change to vast improvement.

Research. By training and by tradition, clinical psychologists are research-oriented. This research activity makes them notable among other helping professions; some would assert that it is in this area that clinicians make their greatest contribution. In the realm of psychotherapy, for example, theory and practice were once based mainly upon case study evidence, subjective impressions of treatment efficacy, and rather poorly designed research. This "prescientific" era (Paul, 1969a) in the history of psychotherapy research has now evolved into an "experimental" era in which the quality of research has improved greatly and the conclusions we can draw about the effects of therapy are much stronger (Smith, Glass & Miller, 1980). This development is due in large measure to the research of clinical psychologists.

In recent years there has been some shift away from the research emphasis in the training of clinicians. This change is due in

*"I can tell you one thing right off—you
can't solve your problems by running away."*

FIGURE 1-1. Drawing by Richter;
© 1947, 1975, The New Yorker
Magazine, Inc.

part to an erosion of the number of academic-research jobs available and in part to students' greater interests in careers that emphasize clinical service. We discuss this issue more extensively in Chapter 12, but for now we want to point out that clinical psychology will risk its special identity as a mental health profession if it neglects research training in favor of purely professional objectives (Schneider, 1985).

The areas commonly investigated by clinicians include neuropsychology, behavioral medicine, stress and social support, social problems, childhood problems, community development, psychopharmacology, developmental problems, geriatrics, test construction and validation, personality diagnosis and adjustment, psychoanalytic theory, therapeutic processes, brain damage and mental retardation, behavior disorders, marriage and family problems, outcomes of various forms of psychological treatment, the design and analysis of experiments, and the value and training of nonprofessionals as therapeutic agents. A journal called *Psychological Abstracts* contains brief summaries of clinical and other psychological research; a glance at a few issues will document the diversity and intensity of the clinician's involvement in research. Another journal, *Clinical Psychology Review*, first published in 1981, includes longer reviews of topics germane to clinical psychology.

Clinical investigations vary greatly with respect to their setting and scope. Some are conducted in the controlled confines of a laboratory, while others are run in the more naturalistic but often uncontrollable circumstances of the real world. Some projects are carried out by clinicians who are aided by paid research assistants and clerical personnel and supported by funds from governmental or private sources, but a great deal of research is generated by clinicians whose budgets are limited and who depend on volunteer help and their own ability to scrounge for space, equipment, and subjects.

Teaching. A considerable portion of many clinical psychologists' time is spent in educational activities. Clinicians who hold full- or part-time academic positions conduct graduate and undergraduate courses in such areas as personality, abnormal psychology, introductory clinical psychology, psychotherapy, behavior modification, interviewing, psychological testing, research design, and clinical assessment.

Clinicians often conduct specialized graduate seminars on various advanced topics; frequently they supervise the work of graduate students who are learning assessment and therapy skills in the context of practicum courses. Supervision of a practicum is a special kind of teaching that combines the use of research evidence and other didactic material with the clinician's own experience to guide students' assessment and treatment of actual clients. Practicum teaching usually involves a model in which the student sees a client on a regular basis and, between assessment or treatment sessions, also meets with the supervisor (the client is aware of the student's status and of the participation of the supervisor). Supervision may occur on an individual basis or may be part of a meeting with a small group of practicum students, all of whom maintain the confidentiality of any material discussed.

The clinician's teaching task is particularly delicate in practica since a balance must be struck between directing the student and allowing for independence. The therapist-in-training may feel stifled if supervision is too heavy-handed. At the same time, the supervisor is ultimately responsible for the case and thus cannot allow the student to make serious errors that would be detrimental to client welfare.

A good deal of teaching is also done by clinical psychologists who supervise undergraduate and graduate students' research efforts. This kind of teaching begins when a student comes to the supervisor with a vaguely defined research topic and asks for advice and a list of relevant readings. In addition to providing the reading list, most research supervisors help the student frame appropriate research questions, apply basic principles of research design in answering those questions, and use various tricks of the trade relevant to the problem at hand. These tasks require considerable teaching skill if the supervisor is to avoid giving the student so much guidance and direction that the student really becomes an assistant who, instead of wrestling with and learning from research problems, merely carries out orders.

Much of the teaching done by clinical psychologists involves in-service (i.e., on-the-job) training of psychological, medical, or other interns, as well as social workers, nurses, institutional aides, ministers, police officers, suicide prevention and other hotline personnel, prison guards, teachers, administrators, business executives, day-care workers, lawyers, probation officers, dentists, and many other groups whose vocational skills might be enhanced by increased psychological sophistication. Some clinical psychologists also do a lot of teaching in the context of therapy (particularly those who adopt a behavioral approach to treatment; see Chapter 9) since part of therapy involves helping people learn new and more adaptive ways of behaving.

One last point about clinical psychologists as teachers: They are often not formally trained for the job. The same might be said, of course, about other psychologists (and many other Ph.D.'s, for that matter), but the lack of attention to teaching in clinical training programs is unfortunate because educational activities are such an integral part of clinicians' work. This significant omission is due at least in part to the fact that clinical training time is so precious that most of it is taken up with research, assessment, and treatment functions.

Consultation. Clinical psychologists often temporarily leave their regular jobs to provide advice to various organizations about a variety of problems. This activity is called consultation; it combines research, assessment, treatment, and teaching. Perhaps this is why some clinicians find consultation satisfying and lucrative enough that they engage in it full-time. Organizations that benefit from consultants' expertise range in size and scope from one-person medical practices to huge government agencies and multinational corporations. The consultant may also work with neighborhood associations, walk-in treatment centers, and many other community-based organizations.

Rather than cataloging all the consulting activities in which a clinical psychologist might engage, let us look at some basic dimensions of the consulting function. The first of these is the *orientation* or *goal* of the consultation. When consulting is *case*-oriented, the clinician is expected to focus attention on a case and either deal with it directly or offer advice as to how it might be handled. An example would be providing treatment for a problem case in a mental health agency, medical facility, penal institution, business, or other organization. When consultation is *program-* or *administration*-oriented, it focuses not on case-level problems but on those aspects of organizational function or structure that are causing trouble. For example, the consultant may develop new procedures for screening candidates for various jobs within an organization, set up criteria for identifying promotable personnel, or reduce staff turnover rates by increasing administrators' awareness of the psychological impact of their decisions on employees.

A second dimension of clinical consulting work is *locus of responsibility*. In some cases, responsibility for the solution to an organi-

zation's problem is transferred to the consultant, as when a mental health clinic contracts for the psychological assessment of suspected cases of brain damage among new clients. In such instances, responsibility for the cases rests with the clinician; giving some advice and then going home is not appropriate. More commonly, however, the responsibility for problem resolution remains with the organization served. A clinician may participate in decisions about which treatment approach would be of greatest benefit to a client, but if the client gets worse instead of better, the consultant is not held culpable. The ultimate burden of responsibility remains with the clinic.

A third major consulting dimension involves *functions*. A partial account of what a consultant could do for an organization might include education (e.g., familiarizing staff with relevant reading materials), advice (e.g., about cases or programs), direct service (e.g., assessment, treatment, and evaluation), and reduction of intraorganizational conflict (e.g., eliminating sources of trouble by altering personnel assignments).

Successful consultation is not easy. The clinician must be aware of his or her role as an outsider and of the implications of that role. The consultant's presence might be resented and resisted by rank-and-file personnel if they see it as a threat to their jobs. Interpersonal rivalries may color the information the consultant receives about a problem. Consultants make great scapegoats. Administrators often blame them for ideas and strategies that later prove unpopular. (For further reading on consulting, see Caplan, 1970; Gallessich, 1982; and Schulberg & Jerrell, 1983).

Administration and Management. This function, involving the management or day-to-day running of an organization, might be named by most clinical psychologists as their least-preferred activity. The reasons given would include aversion to paperwork, lack of interest in routine details of business and budget, impatience with conflicts among employees, reluctance to deal with the time-consuming and often acrimonious process of hiring and firing, and the frustration that sometimes attends dealing with other administrators. Nevertheless, clinical psychologists sometimes find themselves in administrative roles by choice. They may be asked to take on administrative jobs because of the sensitivity, interpersonal skill, research expertise, and organizational abilities associated with their field. On the other hand, some of the clinician's skills can be liabilities in administration because they may lead to overanalysis of problems and to conflicts between helping and managerial roles. Whatever the circumstances, many clinicians find it satisfying to guide an organization toward reaching its goals and improving its services.

Examples of the administrative posts held by clinical psychologists include: head of a university psychology department, director of a graduate training program in clinical psychology, director of a student counseling center, head of a consulting firm or testing center, superintendent of a school system, chief psychologist at a hospital or clinic, director of a mental hospital, director of a community mental health center, manager of a governmental agency, and director of the psychology service at a Veterans Administration (VA) hospital.

Administration and management have become increasingly popular professional activities for clinical, counseling, and industrial-organizational psychologists. Kilburg (1984) contends that management is now the third most important job market for psychologists behind direct clinical services and academic jobs, accounting for 8.4 percent of clinicians' primary employment positions. The expanding career opportunities for psychologists in management are highlighted in the October 1984 issue of *Professional Psychology: Research and Practice,* which includes articles on (1) the key knowledge and skills used by psychologist-managers, (2) an overview of the type of management positions available, and (3) the special problems faced by psychologists in managerial jobs.

Distribution of Clinical Functions

Not all clinical psychologists perform each of the six functions we have discussed. Some spend nearly all their time at one task, while others spread themselves around. To many clinicians, the potential for distributing their time among several functions is one of the most attractive aspects of their field, and the data from several surveys conducted over the last twenty years provide some idea of the work pattern that results. Unfortunately, each survey asked about clinical functions in a somewhat different way, but the variety of a given clinician's work is still discernible. Garfield and Kurtz (1976) reported that over 50 percent of the clinicians they surveyed held two jobs; some held three or more. Further, the majority of those who have only one job still participate in a variety of functions within it (Goldschmid, Stein, Weissman & Sorrels, 1969). Clinicians spend more time in service of various kinds than in research; Garfield and Kurtz (1976) found that 58.7 percent of their respondents identified themselves primarily as clinical practitioners, while only 4.7 percent called themselves researchers. As we have mentioned, data like these have caused concern in the field over what some see as an erosion of the traditionally strong research contributions of clinical psychologists. There also has been a trend over the years toward more involvement in treatment and a corresponding movement away from assessment activities (Garfield & Kurtz, 1976; Kelly, 1961). One other striking finding is that, across the five surveys reported in Box 1-2, the percentage of clinicians engaged in private practice has almost doubled.

Work Settings for Clinical Psychology

There was a time when most clinical psychologists worked in a single type of facility: child clinics or guidance centers; however,

BOX 1-2 Percentage of clinicians employed in various work settings

Type	Kelly (1961) (N = 1024)	Goldschmid et al. (1969) (N = 241)	Cuca (1975) (N = 8447)	Garfield and Kurtz (1976) (N = 855)	Stapp and Fulcher (1983) (N = 2436)
Academic	20%	17%	38%	29%	17.9%
Direct service[a]	50%	28%	c	35%	39.8%
Research	d	d	c	d	d
Community agency	d	16%	c	c	e
Schools	3%	d	c	c	1.3%
Private practice	17	28%	16%	23.3%	31.1%
Industry	3%	d	c	c	8.6%[e]
Military	1.5%	d	c	c	d
Other	5.5%	11%	45%	12.7%	d

[a] Includes hospitals, clinics, medical schools, mental health centers, etc.

[b] Includes business, government, and others.

[c] Included under "other."

[d] Not included.

[e] Included under "direct service."

the settings in which clinicians now function are expanding in all directions (Stapp, Tucker & VandenBos, 1985).

Clinical psychologists are now found in college and university psychology departments; law schools; public and private medical and psychiatric hospitals; city, county, and private mental health clinics; community mental health centers; student health and counseling centers; medical schools; the military; university psychological clinics; child treatment centers; public and private schools; institutions for the mentally retarded; prisons; juvenile offender facilities; business and industrial firms; probation departments; rehabilitation centers for the handicapped; nursing homes and other geriatric facilities; orphanages; alcoholism treatment centers; health maintenance organizations; and many other places. Further, a significant number of clinicians function independently in full- or part-time private practice.

The number of psychologists involved in private practice has grown dramatically. Almost a third of clinicians now list independent practice as their primary employment (Stapp & Fulcher, 1983), and almost two

thirds of clinicians whose primary position is not in private practice engage in part-time private work (Norcross & Prochaska, 1982). In addition, in one study, private practitioners reported greater satisfaction with their career than did clinicians working in institutional settings (Norcross & Prochaska, 1983). If you suspect that this greater satisfaction might be associated with larger financial rewards, you're right. The median 1984 salary for full-time private therapists was $47,360 (Turkington, 1985), while the 1985–86 median salary for full professors in departments awarding the Ph.D. ranged from $37,350 to $46,550 (*APA Monitor*, March 1986).

Determination of just how many clinical psychologists are employed in each type of setting is difficult, partly because new jobs are evolving all the time, but the surveys summarized earlier have addressed the question. Their results, summarized in Box 1-2, focus on broad types of employment rather than specific locations. There are problems in combining the data from these surveys because each of them used a different system for categorizing work settings. Still, it is clear that direct-service facilities (e.g., hospitals and clinics) are among the most common places of employment for clinical psychologists, along with private practice and academic institutions.

Clients and Problems

Within the limits imposed by their areas of expertise, clinical psychologists may work on almost any kind of human behavior problem. Clinical contacts may be voluntarily arranged by the client (or the client's family), prescribed by a court or other legal agency, or take place as a function of the clinician's entry into the client's hospital ward, school, or community.

Having already considered the problems the clinician deals with as teacher, re-searcher, consultant, and administrator, one should also be aware of the problems she or he faces in the assessment and treatment areas. Client complaints are often very complex and frequently stem from a combination of biological, psychological, and social factors, with the result that the clinical psychologist does not always work independently. A given case is sometimes referred to other professionals (e.g., a psychiatrist or social worker) or dealt with through formation of an assessment and treatment team composed of experts from several related helping professions.

The clinician encounters a wide range of client problems. According to one recent survey of more than 6500 psychologists (VandenBos & Stapp, 1983), the most com-

FIGURE 1-2. Drawing by Modell; © 1972, The New Yorker Magazine, Inc.

"And when did it first occur to you that perhaps life is not a cabaret?"

BOX 1-3 Percentage of academic clinicians devoting various amounts of time to professional activities

	% Time Spent in Activity		
Activity	*<10%*	*10%–20%*	*>30%*
Graduate courses	7	77	16
Undergraduate courses	29	58	13
Own research	21	63	15
Supervising research	26	67	5
Own clinical work	53	39	8
Clinical supervision	38	55	7
Administration	35	55	10

Note: All percentages are rounded to the nearest whole number. Based on Shemberg and Leventhal (1978, Table 2).

monly treated problems are, in order of frequency: (1) anxiety and depression, (2) difficulties in interpersonal relations, (3) marital problems, (4) school difficulties, (5) psychosomatic and physical symptoms, (6) job-related difficulties, (7) alcohol and/or drug abuse, (8) psychoses, and (9) mental retardation.

Work Schedules and Specific Illustrations

Let us now pull together what we have been saying about clinical functions, settings, clients, and problems by considering some examples of how and where various clinicians actually spend their time.

A Professor's Day. Shemberg and Leventhal (1978) surveyed 244 full-time faculty members in 120 doctoral clinical programs to determine how clinicians in academia spent their time. The results are summarized in Box 1-3. They confirm the fact that clinical faculty members spend less time than other clinicians in direct clinical work and devote most of their time to graduate and undergraduate teaching, research, and supervision of research.

The Work of Other Clinicians. Harrower (1961) asked seventy clinical psychologists in New York City to provide a sketch of their day or week. Some of their responses, presented in edited form below, give a clear picture of the endless variety of clinical work outside of academics (Harrower, 1965, pp. 1149–1454).

1. I spend about eight hours a week with a private agency where I give seminars for fellows in psychology and trainees in psychiatry and social work. I also test infants several hours a week for two adoption agencies. The balance of my time is given over to private work in diagnosis and therapy.
   2. Two afternoons and one evening a week are devoted to community clinic work. In one clinic I conduct group psychotherapy. In the other I coordinate and supervise a group psychotherapy program. At least six to eight hours a week are devoted to teaching at a local university. Three afternoons and three mornings a week are spent in my private office practicing both individual and group therapy.
   3. My private practice is exclusively assessment-oriented, and when self-referred patients are seen it is with the understanding that they will be referred to a therapist if indicated. I see an average of six patients a week. Three-quarters of my week are devoted to teaching and training activities (six hours of lectures and seminars with psychologists and psychiatric residents and fellows). Outside activities include consultation work with the VA, public speaking, and participation in community activities by serving on boards and committees.
   4. Most of my work involves long-term psychotherapy. My work day, Monday through Fri-

day, is from nine to six, with some variation. One evening is devoted to teaching a graduate course in psychology, and one evening to attending a therapy group. I am at the college, doing counseling and administrative work about four hours each day, and see patients for about the same average amount of time.

5. Half-time consultant to the United Epilepsy Association as director of program (administration and planning public education and community service programs in epilepsy). Private practice limited to psychotherapy.

6. Administration and supervision of psychology department at a hospital; individual assessment and therapy consultations; lead two therapy seminars, consultation and writing in relation to two research projects; average of four to five therapy patients four evenings a week in private office; administration of clinical psychology teaching program for medical students; lecture one hour per week to psychiatric residents.

7. Director and clinical psychologist of mental retardation diagnostic clinic. About 20 percent of time in assessment, 10 percent in parent counseling, 70 percent in administration and supervision. Also about ten hours per week in private practice (assessment and therapy).

8. I see about thirty patients a week for from one to two hours each, for marriage counseling. In addition, I teach one or more classes a week on preparation for marriage, and conduct seminars for ministers and adult community leaders in marital counseling techniques and sex education.

9. Three mornings a week are currently devoted to work in two private schools. In one, I serve as "coordinator" of the interdisciplinary guidance department, in another as consultant to teachers and parents about children's problems. Remainder of time is devoted to therapy with adults.

The combination of clients, settings, and clinical functions represented in these examples comes about partly as a function of each clinical psychologist's interests and expertise and partly through the influence of larger social factors. For example, a clinician could not work in a community mental health center or VA hospital unless legislation had been passed creating such settings. Similarly, much clinical research depends upon grants from federal agencies like The National Institute of Mental Health, whose existence depends upon continued congressional appropriations. Participation in various clinical functions or work with certain types of clients is legitimized by the perceptions of other professions and the general public. If no one saw the clinician as capable of doing effective therapy, that function would soon disappear from the field. Thus, the current state and future development of clinical psychology depend largely on the society in which it is embedded. The history of clinical psychology illustrates this point well.

THE ROOTS OF CLINICAL PSYCHOLOGY

Anyone born in the United States since World War II might assume that the field of clinical psychology has always existed. Such an assumption would be false, however, since clinical psychology as we now know it is a child of the postwar era, and, like a confused adolescent, is filled with conflict over what it should be as it continues to develop. However, clinical psychology is also old in the sense that its roots extend back to periods before the field was ever named and to prewar years when it appeared only in embryonic form.

Just as full understanding of clients' problems is easier when their social, cultural, educational, and vocational backgrounds are known, it is easier to understand the current dimensions, new developments, and critical issues in clinical psychology when its historical background is reviewed. In the rest of this chapter we provide that review by looking first at the factors that were most influential in the formal birth of clinical psychology in 1896, and then following the growth of the new field to the present. Many of the details mentioned here are drawn from Reisman (1976) and Watson (1953), to which the interested reader should turn for more intensive historical coverage. Box 1-4 provides a general

BOX 1-4   Some significant dates and events in the history of clinical psychology

1879	Wilhelm Wundt establishes first formal psychology laboratory at the University at Leipzig.
1885	Sir Francis Galton establishes first mental testing center at the South Kensington Museum, London.
1890	James McKeen Cattell coins term "mental test."
1892	American Psychological Association (APA) founded (first president: G. Stanley Hall).
1895	Breuer and Freud publish *Studies in Hysteria*.
1896	Lightner Witmer founds first psychological clinic, University of Pennsylvania.
1905	Binet-Simon intelligence scale published in France.
	Freud publishes *Three Essays on the Theory of Sexuality*.
1907	First clinical journal, *Psychological Clinic*, founded by Witmer.
1908	First clinical internship offered at Vineland Training School.
1909	William Healy founds first child-guidance center, the Juvenile Psychopathic Institute, Chicago.
	National Committee for Mental Hygiene founded.
	Freud lectures at Clark University.
1910	Goddard's English translation of the 1908 revision of the Binet-Simon intelligence scale published.
1912	J. B. Watson publishes *Psychology as a Behaviorist Views It*.
1916	Terman's Stanford-Binet intelligence test published.
1917	Clinicians break away from APA to form American Association of Clinical Psychology (AACP).
1919	AACP rejoins APA as its clinical section.
1920	Watson and Rayner demonstrate that a child's fear can be learned.
1921	James McKeen Cattell forms Psychological Corporation.
1924	David Levy introduces Rorschach Inkblot Test to America.

1924	Mary Cover Jones employs learning principles to remove children's fears.
1931	Clinical section of APA appoints committee on training standards.
1935	Murray's Thematic Apperception Test (TAT) published.
1936	First clinical text, *Clinical Psychology*, published by Louttit.
1937	Clinical section of APA breaks away to form American Association for Applied Psychology (AAAP).
1938	First Buros *Mental Measurement Yearbook* published.
1939	Wechsler-Bellevue Intelligence Test published.
1942	Carl Rogers publishes *Counseling and Psychotherapy*.
1943	Minnesota Multiphasic Personality Inventory (MMPI) published.
1945	AAAP rejoins APA.
1946	Veterans Administration and National Institute of Mental Health begin support for training of clinical psychologists.
1947	American Board of Examiners in Professional Psychology organized.
1949	Boulder, Colorado, conference on training in clinical psychology convenes.
1953	APA *Ethical Standards for Psychologists* published.
1956	Stanford Training Conference.
1958	Miami Training Conference.
1965	Chicago Training Conference.
1968	Psy.D. training program begun at the University of Illinois.
1969	California School of Professional Psychology founded.
1973	Vail, Colorado, Training Conference.
1980	Third edition of American Psychiatric Association's *Diagnostic and Statistical Manual (DSM-III)* published.
	Smith, Glass, and Miller publish *The Benefits of Psychotherapy*.
1981	APA publishes its revised *Ethical Principles of Psychologists*.

chronology of some events that have been important in the development of clinical psychology.

In order to understand modern clinical psychology, one must be aware of three sets of social and historical factors that initially shaped the field and which continue to influence it to this day. They include: (1) the use of scientific methods by psychology in general, (2) the development of interest in human individual differences, and (3) the ways in which human behavior disorders have been viewed and treated over the years.

1   The research tradition in psychology. From its nineteenth-century beginnings in the psychophysics of Fechner and Weber, the experimental physiology of Helmholtz, and the work of the first "real" psychologist, Wilhelm Wundt, psychology sought to establish itself as a science that employed the methods and procedures of natural sciences like biology and physics. Though the roots of psychology were partly in philosophy, and though many early psychologists were preoccupied with philosophical questions, the discipline was determined to approach human behavior by conducting *research* that employed two powerful tools of science, observation and experiment. Thus, the early history of psychology, which began "officially" in Wundt's psychological laboratory at the University at Leipzig in 1879, is primarily the history of *experimental* psychology (Boring, 1950; Leahey, 1980).

By the time clinical psychology began to emerge, seventeen years after the founding of Wundt's laboratory, the experimental research tradition in psychology was well established. Psychology laboratories had been set up at major universities in Europe and the United States, and early psychologists were experimenting on many basic aspects of human behavior. The first clinicians, already trained to think in scientific terms and use laboratory methods, also applied research methods to clinical problems. The research tradition they brought to their work

took root and grew in the new field until clinical psychologists attained special recognition among the helping professions as experts in various research activities.

To some, the scientific orientation and the skill that forms the basis of clinicians' continuing reputation for research expertise also form the strongest link between clinical psychology and psychology itself. The question of whether this link should be maintained, intensified, or deemphasized in the training and daily activities of clinical psychologists has been one of the liveliest issues in the field. We shall consider this point in more detail later.

The research tradition of experimental psychology has strongly shaped clinical psychology. It has provided a methodology for approaching clinical subject matter, engendered empirical evaluation of clinical functions, and acted as a point of contention that keeps clinicians engaged in the healthy process of self-examination.

2   Attention to individual differences. Because clinical psychology deals with the individual, it could not appear as a discipline until differences among human beings began to be recognized and measured. There would be little impetus for learning about individuals in a world where everyone is thought to be about the same.

Differences among people have always been noticed and sometimes assessed. In his *Republic,* Plato pointed out that people should do work for which they are best suited; he suggested specifically that prospective soldiers be tested for military ability prior to their acceptance in the army. Du-Bois (1970) and McReynolds (1975) refer to Pythagoras (sixth century B.C.) selecting members of his brotherhood on the basis of facial characteristics, apparent intelligence, and emotionality, and to the 4000-year-old Chinese system of ability testing for prospective government employees. However, it was not until the early 1800s that the idea of paying systematic attention to subtle psychological differences really caught on. Until then, people were thought of as falling into a few broad categories such as male-female, good-evil, sane-insane, wise-foolish.

The earliest developments in the scientific measurement of differences among individuals came from astronomy and anatomy. The astronomical story began in 1796, when Nevil Maskelyne was Astronomer Royal at the Greenwich (England) Observatory. He had an assistant named Kinnebrook whose recordings of the moment at which various stars and planets crossed a certain point in the sky consistently differed from those of his boss by five- to eight-tenths of a second. Maskelyne assumed that his readings were correct and that Kinnebrook was in error. Result: Kinnebrook lost his job.

This incident drew the attention of F. W. Bessel, an astronomer at the University of Konigsberg (Germany) observatory. Bessel wondered whether Kinnebrook's "error" might reflect something about the characteristics of various observers, and, during the next several years, he compared his own observations with those of other experienced astronomers. Bessel found that discrepancies appeared regularly and that the size of the differences depended upon the person with whom he compared notes. The differences associated with each observer became known as the "personal equation," since it allowed for correction of calculations based upon personal characteristics. Bessel's work led to later research by psychologists on the speed of and individual differences in reaction time.

The second source of interest in variations among individuals began with the study of phrenology by the anatomist Franz Gall and his pupil, Johann Spurzheim, at the beginning of the nineteenth century. As a child in Germany, Gall thought he saw a relationship between the shape of his schoolmates' heads and their mental characteristics. This idea later became the basis for phrenology, which assumes (1) that each area of the brain is associated with a different faculty or function (like self-esteem, language, or reverence); (2) that the better developed each of these areas is, the more strongly that faculty or function will manifest itself in behavior; and (3) that the pattern of over- or underdevelopment of each faculty will be reflected in corresponding bumps or depressions in the skull.

Although the brain plays the major role in determining behavior, and although its functions are localized to a certain extent, Gall's theory was mostly fallacious. The conclusions he drew and the procedures he used to test them were scorned by the scientists of his day. Nevertheless, Gall went around Europe locating and measuring the bumps on people's heads. He began with prisoners and mental patients whose behavioral characteristics seemed well established (he thought the "acquisitiveness" bump was especially strong among pickpockets). Later, under Spurzheim's influence, phrenology was applied to more respectable segments of society, and an elaborate map of the brain was developed which showed the thirty-seven "powers" or "organs" of the mind.

The importance for clinical psychology of the now discredited field of phrenology lies in its orientation toward assessment of individual characteristics. The phrenologists specialized in feeling heads and providing the owners with a profile of mental makeup. This process may be the origin of the expression "having your head examined"; it certainly anticipated one of the purposes (though not the procedures) of assessment in clinical psychology.

Measuring individual mental or behavioral characteristics through physical dimensions survived in the 1876 work of Cesare Lombroso, an Italian psychiatrist who correlated facial features with criminal behavior, and in the twentieth-century body-type systems of Ernst Kretschmer and William Sheldon. Today these approaches are not taken seriously by scientists, but they remain a part of our folklore.

It was not until later in the nineteenth century that the procedures began to appear that were to form the foundation of

BOX 1-5   A sample from Galton's questionnaire

Think of some definite object—suppose it is your breakfast-table as you sat down to it this morning—and consider carefully the picture that rises before your mind's eye.

1. Illumination—Is the image dim or fairly clear? Is its brightness comparable to that of the actual scene?
2. Definition—Are all the objects pretty well defined at the same time, or is the place of sharpest definition at any one moment more contracted than it is in a real scene?
3. Colouring—Are the colours of the china, of the toast, bread-crust, mustard, meat, parsley, or whatever may have been on the table, quite distinct and natural?

Source: Galton, 1883, in Dennis, 1948, p. 279.

clinical psychology's assessment function. These procedures differed from those we have discussed so far in that rather than measuring physical dimensions or observing differences in performance among a few selected individuals, they consisted of systematically collecting *samples of behavior* from large groups of individuals responding to standard sets of stimuli. Such behavior samples were first used to make general statements about individual mental characteristics; later, as statistical sophistication increased, they were used to establish group norms against which a person could be evaluated quantitatively. By 1890 these procedures had been named *mental tests*. The story of their origin began some thirty years earlier.

In 1859 Charles Darwin published his momentous work, *The Origin of Species,* in which he proposed two important ideas: (1) variation of individual characteristics occurred within and between species (including humans), and (2) natural selection took place based in part upon those characteristics. Darwin's cousin, Sir Francis Galton, was fascinated by these ideas, and explored Darwin's notions as they applied to the inheritance of individual differences.

Galton's tests were aimed at measuring the relatively fixed capacities, structures, and functions which he thought comprised the mind. Many of these tests focused on sensorimotor capacity. For example, Galton tried to discriminate high from low intelligence on the basis of individuals' ability to make fine discriminations among objects of differing weight and among varying intensities of heat, cold, and pain. He sought to measure individual differences in vividness of mental imagery; for this purpose, he invented the questionnaire (see Box 1-5). Galton's interests also extended to associative processes, so he developed the word association test to explore this phenomenon. Galton set up a laboratory in London where, for a small fee, anyone could take a battery of tests and receive a copy of the results. This operation comprised the world's first *mental* testing center;[1] and it appeared as part of the health exhibition in the 1884 International Exhibition (an early world's fair).

By the late 1880s some psychologists began to show interest in the measurement of individual differences in mental functioning. The person usually credited with merging individual mental measurement with the new science of psychology is James McKeen Cattell, an American who in 1886 took his doctorate in psychology under Wundt in Leipzig. Cattell's interest in the application of psychological methods to the study of individual differences, already evident in his

---

[1] The world's first organized *human* testing centers appeared in China in the fourteenth century (DuBois, 1970).

doctoral dissertation on individual variation in reaction time, was intensified by his contact with Galton while lecturing at Cambridge University in 1887. In 1888 Cattell founded the third psychological laboratory in the United States,[2] and in 1890 he coined the term "mental test." Cattell was one of the first psychologists to appreciate the practical uses of tests for selection and diagnosis of people. This recognition of the applied potential of mental tests foreshadowed the emergence of clinical psychology.

His experience in Wundt's laboratory taught Cattell that "psychology cannot attain the certainty and exactness of the physical sciences unless it rests on a foundation of experiment and measurement" (Dennis, 1948, p. 347), so one of his first tasks was to construct a standard battery of mental tests for use by all researchers interested in individual differences. He chose ten tests that reflected his orientation toward using sensorimotor functioning as an index of mental capacity. Cattell also collected less systematic information from subjects about personal qualities such as dreams, diseases, preferences, recreational activities, and future plans (Shaffer & Lazarus, 1952).

In spite of their popularity at other universities like Wisconsin, Clark, and Yale, sensorimotor mental tests were criticized because of their low correlations with most criteria (e.g., Sharp, 1899, cited in Reisman, 1976). By this time, however, an alternative approach to testing had evolved from several quarters. In 1891 Hugo Munsterberg, a psychologist at the University of Freiburg (Germany) who later came to Harvard, constructed a set of fourteen tests to assess children's mental ability. These tests went beyond Galton-Cattell tasks to include more complex functions like reading, classification of objects, and mathematical operations. The German psychiatrist Emil Kraepelin (originator of an early classifica-

tion system for behavior disorders) also designed tests aimed at more complex mental functions such as memory, fatigue, and attention.

Finally, and most important, in 1895 a French lawyer and scientist by the name of Alfred Binet began to develop measures of complex mental ability in normal and defective children. Binet's involvement in this kind of testing grew out of the recognition that retarded children (who had been distinguished from psychotics only as late as 1838) might be helped if they could be identified and given special educational attention. By 1896 Binet and his colleague Victor Henri had described a battery of tests that measured not just "simple part processes" such as space judgment, motor skill, muscular effort, and memory, but also comprehension, attention, suggestibility, aesthetic appreciation, and moral values.

Thus, by 1896 psychology was involved in the measurement of individual differences in mental functioning. It also hosted two overlapping approaches to the task: (1) the Cattell-Galton sensorimotor tests, aimed at assessing relatively fixed mental *structures*, and (2) the instruments of Binet and others, which emphasized complex mental *functions*. Each of these approaches was important to the development of clinical psychology, the former because it fostered the appearance of the first psychological clinic and the latter because it provided a mental test which was to give the new field its first clear identity.

The rest of this story must wait, however, until we examine a third major influence on clinical psychology: changing views of behavior disorder and its treatment.

3   Conceptions of behavior disorder. From the beginning of recorded history, human beings have been faced with the problem of how to explain and deal with behavior that is bizarre or apparently irrational. The explanations and procedures that have appeared over the centuries to handle this problem make stimulating read-

---

[2] The first two labs were set up by William James at Harvard in 1879 and G. Stanley Hall at Johns Hopkins in 1883.

FIGURE 1-3. James McKeen Cattell (1860–1944). (From *Scientific Monthly*, 1929, *28*, 25. Reprinted by permission of the American Association for the Advancement of Science.)

Hippocrates
1st Medical Model

ing (e.g., Davison & Neale, 1986; Ullmann & Krasner, 1975; Zilboorg & Henry, 1941); rather than covering that material in detail here, we shall merely outline the historical progression of ideas about behavior disorder in order to show how they have influenced various professions, including clinical psychology.

The earliest explanations of disordered behavior involved supernatural agents. Persons who acted "crazy" were thought to be possessed by demons or spirits, and treatment often involved various forms of exorcism (including *trephining*, or boring small holes in the skull to provide evil spirits with an exit).[3] In Greece before Hippocrates, these ideas continued in revised form: Disordered behavior was attributed to the influence of one or more of the gods. In early cultures that practiced monotheism, God was seen as a possible source of behavior problems. In the Old Testament, for example, we are told that "the Lord shall smite thee with madness, and blindness, and astonishment of heart" (Deuteronomy 28:28).

As long as supernatural approaches to behavior disorders were prevalent, philosophy and religion were dominant in explaining and dealing with them. Sometimes the practitioners in these fields came from the ranks of the "disturbed." In some primitive groups the shamans, or healers, were those who had themselves been possessed or influenced by supernatural beings.

Supernatural explanations of behavior disorders were still strong when, in about the fourth century B.C., the Greek physician Hippocrates suggested that these aberrations were due to natural causes. Hippocrates argued that behavior disorders, like other behaviors, are a function of the bodily distribution of four fluids, or humors: blood, black bile, yellow bile, and phlegm.

This theory, generally acknowledged as the first medical model of behavioral problems, paved the way for the concept of mental illness and legitimized the involvement of the medical profession in its treatment. From Hippocrates until the fall of Rome in A.D. 476, physicians provided the dominant approach to behavior disorders.

In the Middle Ages, naturalistic explanations were swept away and replaced by a return to demonological explanations of behavior problems. The church became the primary social and legal institution in Europe, and religious personnel again took over responsibility for understanding and dealing with unusual behavior. Physicians were expected to confine their ministrations to physical illnesses only. Many medical men solved this problem by becoming priests.

The church began treating the "insane" by exorcising spirits. For example, Zilboorg and Henry (1941, pp. 131–132) quote from a tenth-century invocation designed to alleviate hysteria, then believed to be a female disorder caused by a wandering uterus under demonic control.

O womb, womb, womb, cylindrical womb, red womb, white womb, fleshy womb, bleeding womb, large womb, neufredic womb, bloated womb, O demoniacal one! . . . I conjure thee, O womb, in the name of the Holy Trinity to come back to the place from which thou shouldst neither move nor turn away . . . and to return, without anger, to the place where the Lord has put thee originally. . . . I conjure thee not to harm that maid of God, N., not to occupy her head, throat, neck, chest, ears, teeth, eyes, nostrils, shoulderblades, arms, hands, heart, stomach, spleen, kidneys, back, sides, joints, navel, intestines, bladder, thighs, shins, heels, nails, but to lie down quietly in the place which God chose for thee, so that this maid of God N. be restored to health.

People suspected of showing deviant behavior were treated as heretics who were under the control of the devil. Physician-priests "diagnosed" such cases by looking for signs of the devil (*stigmata diaboli*) on the skin (Spanos, 1978). Demon possession was

---

[3] This idea continues today in some primitive cultures and parts of Western society. The popularity of *The Exorcist*, the tenets of certain fundamentalist religions, and scattered reports of modern-day demon possession and antidevil procedures all point to the tenacity of demonological notions.

FIGURE 1-4. The inhumane treatment of the hospitalized "insane" did not deter tourists from buying tickets to gawk at them. (Reprinted by permission of Hoffman-LaRoche, Inc., Nutley, New Jersey.)

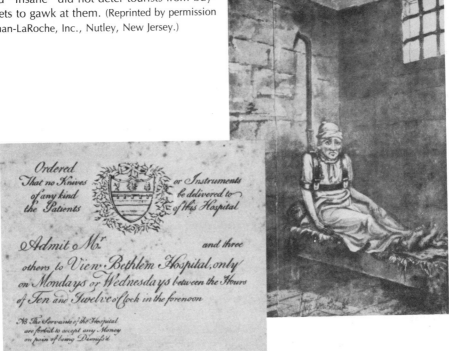

also diagnosed by "dead spots" or local anesthesias which were disclosed by pricking the body with sharp instruments. Once a "diagnosis" of possession was made (and it usually was), "treatment" began. This consisted of torture to produce confessions of heresy, or burning at the stake. These practices continued in varying forms in Europe and in America until the eighteenth century.

However, long before these atrocities finally ended, the demonological model of disorder was questioned by some physicians and scholars, and treatment of deviant individuals gradually began to take the form of confinement in newly established hospitals and asylums such as London's St. Mary of Bethlehem (organized in 1547 and referred to by locals in contracted form as "bedlam"). The hospital movement grew and saved many lives, but it did not necessarily make them worth living. Even though many eighteenth-century scholars agreed that the "insane" were suffering from mental illness (not possession), the medical profession, which was now back in charge of the problem, had little to offer in the way of treatment. Because of fear and misunderstanding by the general public, the "insane" became little more than prisoners who lived under abominable conditions and received mainly custodial care. The doctors who treated them thought mental illness resulted from brain damage or from an overabundance of blood in the brain. At St. Mary of Bethlehem

A physician would visit once a year to prescribe treatment: bleeding of all patients in April, purges and "vomits" of surviving patients in May, and once again bleeding all patients in October. At smaller private institutions . . . a physician might visit once in ten years to prescribe a regime of treatment for the next decade. As a continuing feature of institutionalization, patients were chained to posts in dungeons, whipped, beaten, ridiculed, and fed only the coarsest of slops (Reisman, 1976, p. 10).

Thanks to the efforts of European and American reformers of the eighteenth and early nineteenth centuries (Philippe Pinel, William Tuke, Benjamin Rush, and Eli Todd), improved living conditions and more humane treatment aimed at improving patient behavior were instituted. Pinel ushered in the Moral Era of treatment with the following comment: "It is my conviction that these mentally ill are intractable only because they are deprived of fresh air and liberty" (quoted in Ullmann & Krasner, 1975, p. 135). Thus began a new awareness of the possibility that deviates from society's norms could be helped, rather than simply hidden.

During this period physicians retained the major responsibility for treatment. Late in the nineteenth century, syphilis was identified as the organic cause of general paresis, a deteriorative brain syndrome that had once been treated as a form of insanity. This event bolstered the view that all behavior disorder was organically based and that other disease entities awaited discovery by doctors. The notion that there could be "no twisted thought without a twisted molecule" (Gerard, 1956, quoted in Abood, 1960), along with the crusading of Dorothea Dix to enlarge and improve the medical aspects of mental hospitals in the United States, hastened the decline of the short-lived (but effective) "moral treatment" era. These factors further established medical doctors as the only legitimate agents for the treatment of mental illness.

The search by doctors for organic causes and physical treatment of mental illness resulted in what Zilboorg and Henry (1941) called a "psychiatric revolution." It started when a few French physicians of the mid-nineteenth century began to explore what Franz Anton Mesmer had called "animal magnetism" and which James Braid, an English surgeon, later termed "hypnotism." Research and demonstrations of the rela-

tionship between hypnosis and behavior disorders (particularly hysteria) by Jean-Martin Charcot, Hippolyte Bernheim, and Pierre Janet sparked interest in the possibility that mental illness might be partially psychological in nature and thus might respond to psychological as opposed to organic treatment.

The issue attracted the attention of a young Viennese neurologist named Sigmund Freud who by 1896 had proposed the first stage of a theory that saw behavior disorders not as a result of fixed organic conditions, but as a consequence of the dynamic struggle of the human mind to satisfy instinctual (mainly sexual) desires, while at the same time coping with the rules and restrictions of the outside world. Freud's theory brought a less-than-enthusiastic reaction from his medical colleagues. One doctor called Freud's idea "a scientific fairy tale" (Krafft-Ebing, quoted in Reisman 1976, p. 41). Nevertheless, the idea grew to become a comprehensive theory of the dynamic nature of behavior and behavior disorder, and it ultimately redirected the entire course of the mental health professions, including clinical psychology.

Freud's influence on clinical psychology was slight at first because his theory was so controversial and because it dealt with the problem of mental illness, therefore remaining within the province of the medical profession. Psychologists laid no claim to a treatment function at this time, but we shall see that dynamic approaches to behavior pioneered by Freud and his followers shaped the activities of clinical psychologists in other areas and ultimately provided the foundation for their involvement in therapy.

THE BIRTH OF CLINICAL PSYCHOLOGY: 1896–1917

We have now examined the three main roots of clinical psychology, and it should be clear that by the end of the nineteenth century, the ground had been prepared for its appearance. Psychology had been identified as a science; psychologists had begun to apply scientific methods to the study of individual differences; and Freud's dynamic approach to behavior disorder was about to open up vast new areas of subject matter for psychologists interested in understanding deviance.

It was in this historical context that the first recognized clinical psychologist appeared, an American named Lightner Witmer. Following graduation from the University of Pennsylvania in 1888, Witmer studied for his Ph.D. in psychology with Wundt at the University in Leipzig. Upon completion of his doctorate in 1892, Witmer was appointed director of the University of Pennsylvania psychology laboratory.

In March of 1896 a schoolteacher named Margaret Maguire asked Witmer to help one of her students who was a "chronic bad speller." When Witmer took the case, he became the first clinical psychologist and be-

FIGURE 1-5. Lightner Witmer (1867–1956). (Courtesy of George Eastman House. Reproduced by permission.)

gan an enterprise that became the world's first psychological clinic. The willingness of a psychologist to work with a child's scholastic problem may not now seem significant enough to mark the founding of a profession, but remember that until this point, psychology had dealt with people only to study their behavior in general, not to become concerned about them as individuals. Witmer's decision was as unusual then as would be an attempt by a modern astronomer to determine the "best" orbit for the moon in order to alter its path.

Witmer's approach was to assess the nature of the child's problem and then facilitate appropriate remedial procedures. For example, he found that Ms. Maguire's bad speller had a vision problem. Witmer saw to it that glasses were fitted and that the child received tutoring.

Though not all Witmer did was to be equally influential later, there were several aspects of his new clinic that came to characterize subsequent clinical work for some time.

1. The clients were children, a natural development since Witmer had been offering a course on child psychology and had attracted the attention of teachers concerned about their students.
2. Recommendations for helping clients were preceded by some kind of diagnostic assessment.
3. Witmer did not work alone. He used a team approach whereby members of various professions would consult and collaborate on a given case.
4. There was a clear interest in preventing future problems through early diagnosis and remediation.

At the 1896 meeting of the four-year-old American Psychological Association, Witmer described his new brand of psychology to his colleagues. His friend Joseph Collins recounted the scene as follows:

[Witmer said] that clinical psychology is derived from the results of an examination of many human beings, one at a time, and that the analytic method of discriminating mental abilities and defects develops an ordered classification of observed behavior, by means of postanalytic generalizations. He put forth the claim that the psychological clinic is an institution for social and public service, for original research, and for the instruction of students in psychological orthogenics which includes vocational, educational, correctional, hygienic, industrial, and social guidance. The only reaction he got from his audience was a slight elevation of the eyebrows on the part of a few of the older members. (Quoted in Brotemarkle, 1947, p. 65)

The lead-balloon reception accorded Witmer's talk was based on four factors summarized by Reisman:

For *one*, the majority of psychologists considered themselves scientists and probably did not regard the role described by Witmer as appropriate for them. *Two*, even if they had considered his suggestions admirable, few psychologists were prepared by training or experience to perform the functions he proposed. *Three*, they were not about to jeopardize their identification as scientists, which was tenuous enough in those early years, by plunging their profession into what they felt were premature applications. *Four*, aside from any prevalent skeptical and conservative attitude, Witmer had an unfortunate talent for antagonizing his colleagues. (Reisman, 1976, p. 46)

These objections provided the first clue that a conflict would arise between psychology as a science and psychology as an applied profession. As noted earlier, this issue is as active today as it was in 1896.

In spite of objections, Witmer continued his work and expanded his clinic in order to deal with the increasing caseload, which at first consisted mainly of "slow" or retarded children. Later, the clinic accepted other kinds of cases: speech disorders, sensory problems, and learning disabilities. Consistent with his orthogenic (preventive guidance) orientation, Witmer also worked with "normal" and intellectually superior children, providing guidance and advice to parents and teachers.

In 1897 the new clinic began offering a four-week summer course in child psychology. It consisted of case presentations, instruction in diagnostic testing, and demonstrations of remedial techniques. By 1900 three children were being seen per day and the clinic staff had grown to eleven members. Under Witmer's influence, the University of Pennsylvania began offering formal courses in clinical psychology during the 1904–1905 academic year. In 1907 Witmer set up a residential school for training retarded children and founded and edited the first clinical journal, *The Psychological Clinic*. By 1909 over 450 cases had been handled in Witmer's facilities. Clinical psychology was on its way.

However, the influence of Witmer's clinic, school, journal, and training courses was limited. Witmer got clinical psychology rolling but had little to do with steering it, mainly because Witmer ignored most of the developments that would later become prominent in clinical psychology.

The things Witmer ignored included, first, the introduction in the United States of Alfred Binet's new intelligence test, the Binet-Simon scale. Like Binet's earlier tests, this instrument dealt with complex mental processes rather than the fixed mental structures with which Witmer was concerned. Binet and Simon had developed their test to identify school children whose mental abilities were too low to include them in regular classes. In spite of Binet's warning that it did not provide a wholly objective measure of intelligence, the Binet-Simon gained wide attention. Henry H. Goddard of the Vineland (New Jersey) Training School heard about the Binet-Simon scale while in Europe in 1908 and brought it to the United States for use in assessing the intelligence of "feebleminded" children in the clinic he had set up two years earlier.

The popularity of Goddard's translation of the Binet-Simon scale and Lewis Terman's 1916 American revision of it (known as the Stanford-Binet) grew so rapidly in the United States that they overshadowed other tests of intelligence, including those used by Witmer. The Binet scales provided a focus for clinical assessment activities which, until 1910, had been diffuse and disorganized. All over the country, new university psychological clinics (more than twenty of them by 1914) and institutions for the retarded were adopting the Binet approach while deemphasizing Witmer's "old-fashioned" methods.

Another early development that Witmer ignored was the clinical assessment of adults, initially designed to aid psychiatrists diagnose and plan treatment for brain damage and other problems. After 1907, psychological examination of mental patients in some hospitals became routine. Similar assessments began in prisons to assist staff in identifying disturbed convicts or planning rehabilitation programs.

Finally, Witmer did not join other clinically oriented psychologists in adopting the Freudian approach to behavior disorder. Freud's approach became known to clinical psychology through close association with psychiatry in mental hospitals and also through child-guidance clinics which, though often run by psychiatrists, routinely employed psychologists.

The child-guidance movement in America was stimulated by the National Committee for Mental Hygiene, a group founded by former mental patient, Clifford Beers, and supported by William James, a Harvard psychologist, and Adolf Meyer, the country's most prominent psychiatrist. With funds from philanthropist Henry Phipps, the committee (which ultimately became the National Association for Mental Health) worked to improve treatment of the mentally ill and to prevent psychological disorders. Guidance clinics for children were very much in line with the ideal of prevention. The first of them was founded in Chicago in 1909 by an English-born psychiatrist names William Healy.

Like Witmer, Healy worked with children, employed a team approach, and emphasized prevention, but otherwise his ori-

entation was quite different. Instead of dealing mainly with learning disabilities or other educational difficulties, Healy focused on cases of child misbehavior that required the attention of school authorities, the police, or the courts. Healy's clinic operated on the assumption that juvenile offenders were suffering from some form of mental illness that could be prevented from causing more serious problems later. Finally, Freud's ideas influenced the tone of Healy's Chicago clinic (first called the Juvenile Psychopathic Institute and later the Institute for Juvenile Research).

This dynamic, motivational approach differed from Witmer's and it received a huge boost in popularity when, in the same year Healy opened his clinic, G. Stanley Hall, a psychologist, arranged for Sigmund Freud and two of his followers, Carl Jung and Sandor Ferenczi, to speak at the twentieth anniversary celebration of Clark University in Worcester, Massachusetts. This event and the lectures associated with it "sold" psychoanalysis to American psychologists. Freud's theory was compatible with their interest in the way the mind deals with its environment (the functionalism of William James and G. Stanley Hall) as opposed to what it is made of (the structuralism of Wundt). It also appealed to the emphasis on pragmatism in the United States.

One of the results of this excitement over Freud was that psychological and child-guidance clinics followed Healy's model, not Witmer's. This fact, coupled with the spreading use of Binet intelligence tests, left Witmer in the background. He stayed involved with activities and clients that have since become more strongly associated with school psychologists, vocational counselors, speech therapists, and remedial teachers than with clinical psychologists.

After clinical psychology adopted the Binet-Simon scales it became identified primarily with the testing of problematic children in clinics and guidance centers. This image led critics to argue that clinicians spent too much time diagnosing hopeless cases and that they were not sufficiently psychoanalytic in orientation. At the same time, schools and other institutions that dealt with children were desperately searching for clinical psychologists to do the testing which was fast becoming fashionable.

The need for clinicians' services outweighed the effects of their critics, and the field continued its slow advance during the 1910–1917 period. Its practitioners gave established tests, constructed new ones, and conducted evaluative research on the reliability and validity of them all. Most of the new instruments were aimed at measuring intelligence, but a few began to focus on the assessment of personality through word associations or questionnaire items.

Training for clinical psychology was a problem during this period. A few internships were available at places like the Vineland Training School, and courses in intelligence testing and related subjects were taught here and there, but training was not formalized. Virtually anyone could use the title of clinical psychologist. The science-conscious APA was little help in this regard. It took no official notice of the problems of the new field except to pass a 1915 resolution discouraging the use of mental tests by unqualified persons, then appointing a committee to consider what "unqualified" meant.

A group of disgruntled clinicians agreed that they could best advance the interests of their new profession by forming a separate organization; so in December 1917, the American Association of Clinical Psychologists (AACP) was established. This step did not help much, and, after the APA promised to give more consideration to professional issues and problems, the AACP rejoined the APA as its clinical section in 1919.

BETWEEN THE WARS: 1918–1941

When America became involved in World War I, large numbers of adult men had to be classified in terms of their intellectual prowess and psychological stability. No techniques existed to do this, so the Army asked Robert Yerkes (then APA president) to head a committee of assessment-oriented experimental psychologists who were to develop appropriate measures.[4] This group produced the Army Alpha and Army Beta intelligence tests, which could be administered to groups of literate or nonliterate adults. To help detect behavior disorders among the recruits, Yerkes's committee recommended Robert Woodworth's Psychoneurotic Inventory (when given to soldiers, it was more politely titled "personal data sheet"; see Yerkes, 1921, in Dennis, 1948). By 1918 psychologists had evaluated nearly two million men for the army.

After the war, clinical psychologists still assessed children, but they began to find increased employment as testers in adult-oriented facilities as well. Clinicians were also using a wider variety of intelligence tests for children and adults and adding new measures of personality, interests, specific abilities, emotions, and traits. They developed many of these tests themselves, while adopting others from the psychoanalytically oriented psychiatrists of Europe. Some of the more familiar instruments of this period include the Seashore Musical Ability Test (1919), Jung's Word Association Test (1919), the Rorschach Inkblot Test (1921), the Miller Analogies Test (1926), the Goodenough Draw-A-Man Test (1926), the Strong Vocational Interest Test (1927), the Thematic Apperception Test (1935), the Bender-Gestalt Test (1938), and the Wechsler-Bellevue Intelligence Scale (1939).

So many psychological tests appeared (over 500 by 1940) that a *Mental Measurements Yearbook* was needed to catalog them (Buros, 1938). The development, administration, and evaluation of these instruments continued to stimulate clinicians' assessment

---

[4] The group included Henry Goddard of the Vineland School; Guy Whipple, publisher of a 1910 *Manual of Mental and Physical Tests;* and Lewis Terman, developer of the Stanford-Binet scales.

and research functions. In 1921 Cattell formed the Psychological Corporation to sell tests and provide consultation and research to business and industry. Clinical psychologists of this period also researched and theorized on such topics as the nature of personality, the source of human intelligence (i.e., heredity or environment), the causes of behavior disorders, the nature and application of hypnosis, and the relationship between learning principles and deviance.

By the mid-1930s there were fifty psychological clinics and at least a dozen child-guidance clinics in the United States. Clinical psychologists in these settings "perceived themselves as dealing with educational, not psychiatric problems. But this distinction was growing increasingly difficult to maintain" (Reisman, 1976, pp. 176–177). Slowly, clinicians began to add a treatment function to their assessment, training, and research roles. By the late thirties a few had even gone into private practice.

Therapy focused initially on children and was a natural outgrowth of clinicians' involvement in diagnostic and remedial work with children. It also stemmed from the prestige associated with clinicians' use of personality tests, such as the Rorschach and the TAT. These somewhat mysterious techniques provided a common language for diagnostician (psychologist) and therapist (psychiatrist) to discuss child and adult patients, thus increasing the clinician's association with treatment. Engaging in treatment also allowed clinical psychologists to obtain better-paying, more responsible jobs, to be less dependent on testing as a means of dealing with people, and to become involved with the "whole patient."

Even though its settings, clients, and functions were beginning to expand, clinical psychology was not a fully recognized profession in the 1930s. At the beginning of World War II there were still no official training programs for clinicians. Few of them held Ph.D.'s, some had M.A.'s, and many had B.A.'s or less. To get a job as a clinical psychologist, all one needed was a few courses in testing, abnormal psychology, and child development, along with an "interest in people."

While clinicians did not like their second-class reputation as mental testers, they received little help from their university colleagues or the APA in upgrading that image through standardized training programs or official certification. Discomfort on the part of academic psychologists over the appropriateness of "applied" psychology, combined with the cost of clinical training, led to a slow response by university psychology departments to develop graduate programs in clinical psychology.

Although the APA had appointed committees on clinical training at various times during the twenties and thirties (and had even set up a short-lived certification program), its involvement was halfhearted. For example, in 1935 the APA Committee on Standards of Training in Clinical Psychology suggested that a Ph.D. plus one year of supervised experience was necessary to qualify a person as a clinical psychologist, but after issuing its report the committee disbanded; little came of its efforts.

The discontent of clinical and other non-academic psychologists erupted in 1937, and they again broke away from APA to form a separate organization, this time called the American Association of Applied Psychology (AAAP). It contained divisions of consulting, clinical, educational, and industrial psychology and remained independent for eight years before rejoining APA.

By the end of the 1930s all the ingredients for the modern field of clinical psychology had been assembled: Its six functions (assessment, treatment, research, teaching, consultation, and administration) had appeared. Clinical psychology had expanded beyond its original clinics into hospitals, prisons, and other settings. It worked with adults as well as children, and was motivated to stand on its own; only the support of its parent discipline and the society it served was still needed. This support came as the result of World War II.

THE POSTWAR EXPLOSION

America's entry into World War II again necessitated mass testing of military personnel on intelligence, ability, and personality dimensions, and again a committee of psychologists was formed to help with the task. Because psychometric and clinical sophistication had increased greatly since the time of the Yerkes committee, this new group of psychologists produced a correspondingly wider range of military-oriented tests, including the Army General Classification Test (a group intelligence instrument), a psychiatric screening questionnaire called the Personal Inventory, brief measures of intelligence, short forms of the Rorschach and the TAT, and several ability tests for selection of officers, pilots, and the like.[5]

The involvement of psychology in World War II was far greater than in World War I. For example, about 1500 psychologists (nearly 25 percent of those available) served in World War II, and Reisman (1976) reports that in 1944 alone, over sixty million psychological tests were given to twenty million soldiers and civilians. In addition to giving tests, psychologists conducted interviews, wrote psychological reports, and because of the overwhelming case load of psychological casualties, performed psychoanalytically oriented therapy. For those who had been clinicians before the war, military life meant an opportunity to consolidate and expand their clinical functions, but such individuals were a minority. Most wartime psychologists came from academic settings. For them, the army's desperate need

for applied psychological services meant taking on clinical responsibilities for the first time.

These converted clinicians found that they were able to handle their new jobs remarkably well, and many of them began to like the work. Authorities in the military and civilian establishment were impressed with the clinical skills of psychologists. Psychologists became commissioned military officers, just like physicians. By the end of the war, many clinicians were hooked on therapy with adults, and former experimentalists became enamored of clinical functions. Their wartime testing and therapeutic activities brought psychologists increasing public attention and prestige.

This awakening of interest in clinical work might have come to nothing if there had not been so much of it to do. The war left over 40,000 men in VA neuropsychiatric hospitals, and there were not enough clinical psychologists and psychiatrists to deal adequately with these patients. Where the APA and university psychology departments had vacillated over the education and roles of clinicians, the needs of the VA prompted clear and immediate action. A 1946 VA circular defined clinical psychology as a profession that engaged in diagnosis, treatment, and research relating to adult disorders; it described clinicians as holders of the Ph.D. More important, the VA said it needed 4700 of these individuals to fill lucrative, high-prestige jobs and that it would help pay for clinical training. Hathaway (1958, p. 107) said, "This document, more than any other single thing, has served to guide the development of clinical psychology."

Here was the support clinical psychology had been waiting for. Early in 1946 the chief medical director of the VA met with representatives of major universities to ask them to start formal clinical training programs; by that fall, 200 graduate students became VA clinical trainees at 22 institutions (Peck & Ash, 1964). By 1951 the VA had become the

---

[5] Some of the latter techniques included behavioral measures that required candidates to perform various tasks under frustrating or stressful conditions. Such "real-life" observation is now a popular clinical assessment strategy (see Chapter 6).

largest single employer of psychologists in the United States.

Not all psychology departments that began clinical training programs after the war were enthusiastic about doing so. Faculty members who were sympathetic to clinical work saw governmental support as a boon, while others who were devoted to psychology as a pure science objected to the intrusion of professional training which, to their way of thinking, was begun merely because the government (first through the VA and then through the United States Public Health Service, USPHS) was willing to pay for it. Shakow (1965) characterized this as a conflict between the "virgins" and the "prostitutes." Whatever one calls it, it was a continuation of the same "science versus profession" issue that had been brewing ever since 1896.

Nevertheless, the VA and USPHS went ahead with their funding plans and turned to the APA for guidance as to which university clinical programs merited federal support. Accordingly, an initial evaluation of existing programs was provided by a Committee on Graduate and Professional Training in 1947 (Kelly, 1961). Later that year, a more extensive report came from David Shakow's Committee on Training in Clinical Psychology, which had been appointed by the APA to (1) recommend the content of clinical programs, (2) set up training standards to be followed by universities and internship facilities, and (3) report on current programs (Shakow, 1978, presents details of the history and composition of this committee).

This Shakow report was meant only to provide training guidelines, but since it was so intimately tied to the dispensation of federal money to individual students and whole departments, the "guidelines" were adopted as policy "and soon became the 'bible' of all departments of psychology desirous of having their programs evaluated and reported on favorably by the APA" (Kelly, 1961, p. 110). Shakow felt that this reaction tended

to crystallize prematurely the nature of clinical training, and that, if things had gone a bit more slowly, the resulting programs might have been better.

The Shakow report laid the groundwork for later controversy over how clinicians should be trained, an issue that related directly to the science-profession problem. The recommendations of greatest contemporary importance include the following (APA, 1947):

1. Clinical psychologists should be trained first as psychologists (i.e., as scientists) and second as practicing professionals.
2. Clinical training should be as rigorous as that given to nonclinicians and thus should consist of a four-year doctorate, including a year of supervised clinical internship experience.
3. Clinical training should focus on the "holy trinity" (assessment, research, and treatment) by offering courses in general psychology, psychodynamics, assessment techniques, research methods, and therapy (see Shakow, 1978, for a succinct summary of the full report).

Thus began "what later came to be recognized as something of an educational experiment: the training of persons both as scientists and as practitioners, not in a separate professional school [as is the case in medicine or law], but in the graduate schools of our universities" (Kelly, 1961, p. 112). This experiment continued with the support of the APA, the federal government, internship facilities, and universities. Two years after the Shakow report appeared, a national conference on clinical training at Boulder, Colorado, formally adopted its recommendations. In addition, APA created an Education and Training Board to evaluate and publish lists of accredited doctoral-level clinical programs and internship settings.

The scientist-professional training package described in the Shakow report and adopted at Boulder in 1949 came to be known as the "Boulder model"; it set the pattern for clinical training for at least the next twenty-five years. Nevertheless, not everyone in the field was enthusiastic about it, and though its official APA status was reaffirmed at subsequent training conferences in 1955, 1958, 1962, 1965, and 1973, discontent remained. In Chapter 12 we consider the details of these conferences and the modifications of the Boulder model that have ensued. Suffice it to say here that psychologists committed to professional practice felt that the model emphasized research training at the expense of preparation for applied work, while more academically oriented psychologists failed to see the need for so much emphasis on application.

In spite of such problems, government support of university-based Boulder model training contributed to the explosive growth of clinical psychology. By 1948 there were 22 APA-approved clinical training programs, 60 by 1962, 83 by 1973, and 131 by 1985. Postwar personality and intelligence assessment mushroomed following the introduction of tests like the Minnesota Multiphasic Personality Inventory (MMPI), new scoring procedures for projectives like the Rorshach, and new adult intelligence scales. The clinician's treatment function, now recognized by the government and by the public, blossomed as well. Three times as many clinical psychologists engaged in therapy after the war as before it, and the emphasis swung toward work with adults rather than children. The clinician in private practice became a more common phenomenon as practitioners sought to pattern themselves after physicians.

Legal recognition of clinical psychology as a profession was growing as well. In the postwar years, states passed laws providing for licensure or certification of qualified clinicians, and the APA set up an independent certification group to identify individuals who had attained particularly high levels of clinical experience and expertise. The APA also developed a code of ethics governing the behavior of all its members, but focusing on those engaged in applied activities.

These and other aspects of clinical psychology as a profession are discussed more fully in Chapter 12.

Clinical research also expanded after World War II and produced some disturbingly negative conclusions on the usefulness of some personality tests (see, e.g., Magaret, 1952), the value of clinicians' diagnostic judgments when compared to statistically based decisions (Meehl, 1954), and the effectiveness of traditional (e.g., mainly Freudian) forms of psychotherapy (Eysenck, 1952). Such research influenced a shift away from standard clinical assessment and the development of many new treatment approaches, including those of Carl Rogers and Joseph Wolpe.

By the 1980s, almost everything that could have been said about clinical psychology before World War II had changed. The clinical psychologist before the war was primarily a diagnostician whose clients were usually children. Since 1945 the functions, settings, and clients of clinical psychology have expanded dramatically. Today's clinician enjoys a wider range of theoretical approaches and practical tools for dealing with the problems of assessing and altering human behavior.

Although the field has advanced in spectacular fashion during the last forty years, neither its development nor its self-examination has been completed. Clinicians are an introspective and self-critical group. The issues clinical psychologists continue to debate include society's needs for psychological service, the value of clinical assessment and psychotherapy, the problems and prospects of private practice, the prevention of psychological problems, and ways of providing services to segments of the population (such as the poor) who do not usually receive them.

Above all, clinicians focus on the scientist-professional issue: How can the clinician be a scientifically minded psychologist who waits for carefully validated evidence before diagnosing a condition or proceeding with treatment and, at the same time, function as a "front-line" practitioner who must take immediate action in order to help distressed people with complex problems about which little knowledge may be available? Some observers feel that the scientific and professional roles are basically incompatible, and that a psychologist must choose one or the other. Accordingly, some clinical students become subjective, intuitive practitioners to whom "data" is a nasty word, while others work as full-time researchers in hopes of generating empirical findings that will someday make clinical practice scientific.

This "either-or" polarization has unfortunate consequences. It isolates the practitioner from research that may be useful in applied work, and it may place the researcher in a laboratory that is so artificial that results apply only to other laboratory settings or situations where the most interesting and important clinical problems may not appear. The cumulative result of this polarization could be a reduction in the mutual stimulation between clinic and laboratory that most careful thinkers in the field consider to be vital to the future of clinical psychology (see Cohen, Sargent & Sechrest, 1986).

In spite of suggestions that would formalize the distinction between the scientific and applied aspects of psychology (through totally separate training programs, for example), a difficult though potentially more fruitful alternative has remained attractive.

This involves steering a moderate course that seeks to avoid exclusive identification as scientist *or* professional, and which attempts to generate and utilize both scientific knowledge and clinically derived experience so that they may nourish rather than compete with one another.

If the past is any indicator of the future, those who take varying positions on the scientist-professional issue will remain in contact and in contention. Those who see clinical psychology as an art and have little use for laboratory approaches to it line up on one side of the question, while those who discount the value of subjective judgment and other apparently nonscientific aspects of clinical work are found on the other. Less predictable are the individuals who conceptualize clinical psychology as a field which at present has certain artistic characteristics, a scientific base, and a capability to exploit both.

As the size and stature of clinical psychology have grown, concern over self-preservation has decreased, leaving the field less conservative and more tolerant of divergent ideas, not only about clinical roles and training, but about more basic issues like the development of human problems and the means through which they can best be alleviated. Our task in the next chapter is to review the most influential of these ideas and illustrate their importance for the day-to-day functioning of clinicians.

chapter 2

Models of Clinical Psychology

To appreciate fully the dimensions of an object, one must examine it from several angles; this is why sculpture is often displayed in a place where the viewer can walk around it. Events are also subject to multiple interpretations, depending on one's point of view. This phenomenon is so reliable that instructors often stage sudden and unusual classroom events (such as the attempted "murder" of the professor by a "disgruntled former student") in order to demonstrate the inevitable variability in observer recollection.

Listening to differing accounts of the same occurrence from varying points of view can be confusing, but may also be illuminating in the sense that, as with a statue, one is allowed to examine all the angles. And though the "absolute truth" about an event, relationship, or a person may not necessarily be revealed, there is at least the assurance that potentially important material has not been totally overlooked.

Clinical psychologists follow a similar strategy when they gather assessment information about a client from multiple sources. In this regard, clinicians are like competent investigative reporters who try to comprehend a given subject fully by talking to several sources. The same open and comprehensive orientation can be of great value to the beginning student of clinical psychology. There are many ways to look at the field, each of which reveals some aspects and obscures others. The whole picture cannot emerge unless one is familiar with the variety of viewpoints that are available.

This chapter examines three of the most prominent of these points of view: the psychodynamic, behavioral, and phenomenological models of clinical psychology. They are referred to as *models* because they describe on a miniature scale the ways in which various thinkers have approached human behavior in general and clinical psychology in particular. Each model has something to say about how behavior develops and becomes problematic, and each influences the assessment, treatment, and research styles of its adherents.

For example, if one's model of clinical psychology were based upon the assumption that behavior is determined by the foods people eat, that assumption would probably lead to statements about how diet affects behavioral development through the life span (e.g., "Mushy foods produce mushy thinking and uncoordinated behavior in infants and the elderly, while solid food and mature eating habits result in clear thought processes and efficient overt behavior"). Further, a dietary model might suggest hypotheses about disordered behavior in which excesses of carbohydrates are associated with anxiety, consumption of large quantities of soft drinks are thought to result in hallucinations, or too little protein is implicated in obsessive rituals. Specialized measurement procedures might be developed to assess clients' eating patterns and to monitor the nutritional components of each meal. The model would also emphasize certain clinical treatments. Carefully programmed alterations in diet would be seen as vital, while simply talking about one's problems would be regarded as a waste of time. Finally, the targets of research would be shaped by the model. Experiments designed to evaluate diet-assessment or diet-modification procedures would appear in large numbers.

THE VALUE OF MODELS

The positive features of a model of clinical psychology are that it helps clinicians (1) organize their thinking about behavior, (2) guide their clinical decisions and interventions, and (3) communicate in a common, systematic language with their colleagues. It imposes some order on vast amounts of material that might seem otherwise unrelated.

Without a model, an ordered understanding is not always easy to reach. Human behavior is extremely complex and can be examined on several levels, from the activity of cells to the processes of social interaction. There also is an almost endless number of ways in which behavior can be interpreted, assessed, researched, and altered. One must decide which aspects of behavior deserve special attention, which kinds of assessment data are of greatest interest, which treatment techniques merit more exploration, and which research targets are the most fruitful. A model can help guide these decisions about phenomena that are complicated and potentially bewildering, thereby helping the clinician bring some order to what may have been conceptual chaos.

The appeal of a particular model as a compass or guide attracts followers whose commitment to it ranges from healthy skepticism to fanatic zeal. However, the usefulness of the major models of clinical psychology must be distinguished from their scientific worth, which is evaluated on dimensions other than superficial attractiveness or number of adherents. It is important to keep in mind that in scientific terms, the best clinical models are those whose implications and hypotheses can be rigorously investigated in a wide range of contexts. A good model should include a complete and testable account of the development, maintenance, and alteration of both problematic and nonproblematic aspects of human behavior. Models that meet these requirements are open to experimental evaluation. They will stand or fall as the data accumulate. "Only the untestable models never die. They don't even fade away, unfortunately" (Zubin, 1969, p. 6).

SOME CAUTIONS ABOUT MODELS

The characteristics just described as the strengths of clinical models can also be construed as their weaknesses. For example, a given model may organize one's thinking about behavior so completely that it becomes rigid and closed to new and potentially valuable ideas. This closure increases the danger of developing a fossilized rather than organized approach to clinical psychology.

Blind adherence to a particular model can reduce a clinician's functioning to a reflexive level where objective evaluation and subsequent modification of professional practices become increasingly unlikely. As a result, overly model-dependent clinicians may perform their professional activities in strict accordance with the dictates of a model because they have always performed them that way, regardless of experimental evidence or case results that might indicate the need for change.

Finally, a model is a bit like a region of the country that tends to develop its own "language." It eases communication among those conversant in it, but it can obstruct discussions between "natives" and "foreigners." Often, the exchange of ideas between persons espousing different models of clinical psychology is hampered by this special kind of language barrier. Both parties think they are speaking clearly and comprehensibly when, in fact, they are not understanding each other because their model-based terms and specialized meanings are in the way. We have heard lengthy and heated theoretical arguments of this type that ended when the participants finally realized that they agreed with one another. Fortunately, most problems associated with the adoption of a clinical model can be reduced by avoiding the overzealous commitment to it that fosters conceptual rigidity, behavioral inflexibility, and semantic narrowness. This is not to say that consistent and systematic reference to a particular model is detrimental; quite the opposite. However, understanding and appreciating other points of view can act as insurance against a narrow-mindedness that could be detrimental to clinicians and clients alike. We intend the material in this chapter to be of assistance in this regard. For those acquainted with psychodynamic, behavioral, and phenomenological personality theories, much of what follows may already be familiar, but an attempt will be made to go beyond abstract theory and outline the clinical conceptualization, assessment, and treatment that flow from each model and can be applied to individual cases. In subsequent chapters, the specific tactics that translate these strategies into action will be considered.

One final point: None of the models discussed in this chapter is a single, unitary entity. Each is made up of variations on a basic theme; thus, to characterize adequately each model, it will be necessary to describe several of these variations.

THE PSYCHODYNAMIC MODEL

The psychodynamic model is rooted in the nineteenth- and twentieth-century writings of Sigmund Freud, but it has broadened to include the ideas of those who revised and challenged many of Freud's concepts. The model is based upon the following fundamental assumptions:

1. Human behavior and its development are determined by impulses, desires, motives, and conflicts that are *intrapsychic* (within the mind) and often unconscious (out of awareness).

2. Intrapsychic factors cause both normal and abnormal behaviors. Thus, just as disabling anxiety or delusions of persecution in a troubled patient would be attributed to unresolved conflicts or unmet needs, the outgoing and friendly behavior of an acquaintance might be seen as stemming from contrasting inner feelings of fear or worthlessness or from a hidden desire to be more popular than a sibling.

3. The foundations for behavior are set down in childhood through satisfaction or frustration of basic needs and impulses. Because of their central role in regard to these needs, early relationships with parents, siblings, grandparents, peers, and authority figures are given special attention. There is a historical flavor to the psychodynamic model because of its focus on the importance of past events.

4. Clinical assessment, treatment, and research should emphasize the subtle aspects of intrapsychic activity which, though often hidden from direct observation, must be dealt with if behavior is to be understood and behavior problems are to be alleviated.

Freudian Psychoanalysis

Some scholars (Ullmann & Krasner, 1975) have described the Freudian approach, or *psychoanalysis,* as a *medical model* because the theory focused on abnormality and came along at a time when there was strong interest in discovering organic causes for "mental illness." This atmosphere, along with Freud's own training as a physician, emphasized the parallels between his basically psychological thinking and the disease orientation to behavior that was dominant at the time. Unconscious conflicts and other psychological factors were seen as analogous to *disease processes,* and problematic behaviors became the *symptoms* of those processes. Thus, troubled people who came to medical doctors or were confined in hospitals because of what might, according to Freud, be psychologically based problems, were still called *patients,* and the standard medical concepts of *diagnosis, prognosis, treatment, and cure* were applied to them.

Freud's psychodynamic model was founded on a few basic principles. One of these is *psychic determinism,* the notion that behavior is related to identifiable causes sometimes hidden from outside observers and the behaving individual as well. From this perspective, almost all behaviors (even "accidents") are seen as meaningful in the sense that they may provide clues to hidden conflicts and motivations (Freud, 1914). Thus, reading the word "breast" when the text says "beast," forgetting a relative's name, or losing a borrowed book may all be intepreted as expressing feelings or impulses that may not appear in awareness. Freud called *unconscious* that part of mental functioning which was out of awareness and not readily accessible to it.

Another of Freud's basic postulates was that human behavior is derived from a continual struggle between the individual's desire to satisfy inborn sexual and aggressive instincts and the need to take into account the rules and realities of the outside world. He saw each individual facing a lifelong search for ways of expressing socially inappropriate instinctual urges without incurring punishment or other negative consequences. The case of the seven-year-old boy, who after being told by his mother that he cannot go outside, eats sixteen oatmeal raisin cookies and then throws up in the middle of her bridge party provides a perfect example of the expression of aggressive impulse in light of the facts of reality. Freud saw the human mind as an arena where what the person *wants* to do (instinct) must be reconciled with the controlling dicta of what *can* or *should* be done (reason and morality).

Mental Structure. In Freud's system, unconscious instincts make up the *id*, which is present at birth and contains all the psychic energy or *libido* available to motivate behavior. Id seeks to gratify its desires without delay, and therefore it is said to operate on the *pleasure principle* (i.e., "If it feels good, do it!"). As the newborn grows and the outside world imposes more limitations on direct id gratification, the *ego* begins to develop as an outgrowth of id around the age of one year and begins to find safe outlets for instinctual expression. It was our seven-year-old's ego, for example, that engineered the revenge wreaked upon his mother. Since ego adjusts to external demands, it operates on the *reality principle* (i.e., "If you are going to do it, at least do it quietly"). A third mental agency, *superego,* is another result of the socializing influence of reality. It contains all the teachings of family and culture regarding ethics, morals, and values, and according to Freud, these teachings are internalized to become the "ego ideal," or how one would like to be. Superego also contains the conscience, which seeks to promote perfect, conform-

opposed to actions to true feelings

ing, and socially acceptable behavior usually opposed to that motivated by id.

Mechanisms of Defense. Freud's three-part mental structure is constantly embroiled in internal conflicts (see Box 2-1) which result in anxiety. Ego attempts to keep these conflicts and their discomfort from reaching consciousness by employing a variety of *defense mechanisms,* usually at an unconscious level. One of the most common and, for Freud, the most prototypic of these mechanisms is *repression,* where ego simply holds an unacceptable thought, feeling, or impulse out of consciousness. Repression has also been called *motivated forgetting.* An individual whose hatred is not consciously experienced may be repressing that hatred (when a person is aware of an impulse and *consciously* denies its existence, the process is called *suppression*). However, repression takes great, constant effort (somewhat like trying to hold an inflated balloon under water), and the undesirable urge may threaten to surface at times.

To guard against this, ego employs additional unconscious defenses. One of these is *reaction formation,* in which the person thinks and acts in a fashion diametrically opposed to the unconscious impulse. A father-hating son may enthusiastically express unbounded love and doting concern for his father. If the defense mechanism called *projection* is used, the son may attribute negative feelings to others and accuse them of mistreating their fathers. A mechanism of *displacement* allows some expression of id impulses, but it aims their expression at safer targets, such as co-workers or others who may be father figures. The son's harsh criticism of an older colleague, for example, might be viewed in this way. Displacement also works in dreams. If the son expresses id impulses by behaving in a critical manner toward the father, he may *rationalize* or explain away the behavior by pointing out that it is "for his father's own good." The defense mechanism which Freud saw as most socially adaptive is called *sublimation.* Here, the expression of taboo impulses is directed into productive and even creative channels such as writing, painting, acting, dance, or other activities.

While sublimation may provide a rela-

BOX 2-1   Some examples of intrapsychic conflict

Conflict	Example
Id vs. ego	Choosing between a small immediate reward and a larger reward which requires some period of waiting (i.e., delay of gratification).
Id vs. superego	Deciding whether to return the difference when you are overpaid or undercharged.
Ego vs. superego	Choosing between acting in a realistic way (e.g., telling a "white lie") and adhering to a potentially costly or unrealistic standard (e.g., always telling the truth).
Id and ego vs. superego	Deciding whether to retaliate against the attack of a weak opponent or to "turn the other cheek."
Id and superego vs. ego	Deciding whether to act in a realistic way that conflicts both with your desires and your moral convictions (e.g., the decision faced by devout Roman Catholics as to the use of contraceptive devices).
Ego and superego vs. id	Choosing whether to "act on the impulse" to steal something you want and cannot afford. The ego would presumably be increasingly involved in such a conflict as the probability of being apprehended increases.

Source: Robert M. Liebert and Michael D. Spiegler, *Personality: Strategies and Issues,* 4th ed. Homewood, IL: The Dorsey Press, 1982, p. 102, © by the Dorsey Press.

tively permanent solution to the problem of defending against anxiety, the other mechanisms are viewed as less desirable because they waste psychic energy. Further, they may fail under stress, forcing the troubled person to fall back, or *regress*, to levels of behavior characteristic of earlier, less mature stages of development. Partial regression may produce behaviors inappropriate to one's age and social status; more profound regression is associated with more severely disturbed behavior. The extent and depth of regression in a given case are partly a function of the individual's history of *psychosexual development*.

Developmental Stages. Freud postulated that as newborns develop, they pass through several psychosexual stages, each named for the part of the body most closely associated with pleasure at the time. The first year or so is called the *oral* stage, because eating, sucking, biting, and other oral activities are the predominant sources of pleasure. The oral child is busy *incorporating* or taking in the external world. If, because of premature or delayed weaning from the bottle or breast, oral needs are frustrated or overindulged, the child may fail to pass through the oral stage without clinging to, or becoming *fixated* on, behavior patterns associated with it. Adults who display and depend inordinately upon oral behavior patterns such as smoking, overeating, excessive talking, or "biting" sarcasm may be seen as orally fixated. As adults, oral characters also may appear to be gullible, passive, and optimistic. Freud felt that the stronger an individual's fixation at a given psychosexual stage, the more behaviors typical of that stage would be shown at a later point and the more likely it would be that regression to that level would occur under stress. Cases in which a person becomes very dependent upon others are sometimes viewed by Freudians as involving a nearly complete regression to the oral stage.

The second year or so is called the *anal* stage, because Freud saw the anus and the stimuli associated with eliminating and withholding feces as the important sources of pleasure at that point. The significant feature of this period is toilet training, in which there is a clash of wills between parents and child. Anal fixation was thought to result from overly prohibitive or particularly indulgent practices in this area. Adult behaviors associated with anal fixation include tight, controlled behavior or loose, disorderly habits: Persons who are stingy, obstinate, highly organized, concerned with cleanliness or detail, and those who are sloppy, disorganized, and markedly generous with money might be seen as displaying anal characteristics.

The child enters Freud's *phallic* stage at about age four, as the genitals become the primary source of pleasure. As the name of this period implies, Freud paid more attention to psychosexual development in the male than in the female. He theorized that during the phallic stage the young boy begins to have sexual desire for his mother and wants to do away with his father's competition. This situation was labeled *Oedipal* because it recapitulates the plot of the Greek tragedy *Oedipus Rex*. Because the boy fears castration as punishment for his incestuous and murderous desires, the Oedipus complex and its attendant anxiety are normally resolved by repressing sexual desires toward the mother, *identifying* with the father, and ultimately finding an appropriate female sex partner.

Freud discussed a female Oedipus complex (he rejected the term "Electra complex," which was used by some of his students) in which a little girl suffers *penis envy*. She ultimately sublimates these feelings by substituting a desire to have a baby for a desire to have a penis, in this way coming to identify with her mother. Freud thought that a woman's superego was less developed than a man's because it was not forged from a strong fear like castration anxiety. (Needless to say, these views have not made Freud a popular figure among feminists.)

Freud believed that successful resolution

of conflicts in the phallic stage was crucial to healthy psychological development. For example, he saw superego as the result of the Oedipus complex; "conform or be castrated" provides the boy's first motive for "moral" behavior. Fixation at the phallic stage was seen as very common and responsible for many adult interpersonal problems, including rebellion, aggression, and socially discouraged sexual practices like homosexuality, exhibitionism, and fetishism.

Freud believed a dormant or *latency* period follows the phallic stage. This quieting of the Oedipal conflict allows the child to develop social and educational skills and extends until adolescence, when the individual's physical maturity ushers in the *genital* period. In this final stage (which lasts through the adult years), pleasure is again focused in the genital area, but if all has gone well in earlier stages, sexual interest is directed not just toward the kind of self-satisfaction characteristic of the phallic period, but toward establishment of a stable, long-term heterosexual relationship in which the needs of another are valued and considered.

Related Psychodynamic Approaches. Freud's original ideas have undergone many changes.[1] His constant alterations of psychoanalysis make it possible to speak of many editions of Freud's theory, but he remained committed to a few cardinal principles, notably the instinctual sexual basis of human behavior, and it was this often unpopular dogma that prompted others to create variations on the psychodynamic

model. Some of these variants involved minimal shifts of emphasis, while others represented a substantial break with Freud's notions. All of them share two characteristics: (1) dissatisfaction with the central role of unconscious instincts in motivation, and (2) increased recognition of the influence of social and cultural variables on human behavior.

In the less radical variations, ego is characterized as a positive, creative, coping mechanism in addition to being an arbiter of intrapsychic conflict. In these versions of psychoanalysis (e.g., Hartmann, 1939), ego is not seen as developing entirely out of id and its conflicts with the environment, but rather as having some of its own independent energy and growth potential which is not tied up in unconscious defensive functions. This kind of thinking is attractive to many psychoanalytically oriented clinicians because it presents a more positive, less instinct-ridden portrait of human behavior.

Another important revision of psychoanalysis was presented by Erik H. Erikson, an American psychologist who emphasized the importance of social factors in human development. Erikson (1959, 1963) outlined a sequence of *psychosocial* stages that was more elaborate than Freud's psychosexual scheme and also more oriented toward individuals' interactions with other people. At each of Erikson's eight stages (see Box 2-2), a social crisis is faced and either successfully handled or left partly unresolved. Positive outcomes at each stage facilitate the individual's ability to deal with the next crisis, while unsettled problems interfere with later development. The parallel with Freud is so obvious here, as is the attention paid to the social nature of human development.

Early acquaintances of Freud were among those who rejected rather than revised certain aspects of psychoanalysis. For example, Alfred Adler, one of the original members of the psychoanalytic school of thought, disavowed the instinct theory of behavior, broke away from Freud, and developed his own approach. In Adler's *Indi-*

---

[1] For example, Freud first believed that neurotics had been sexually seduced or abused as children because so many of his patients reported early childhood sexual experiences with an adult. Later, unwilling to accept such widespread sexual misconduct, Freud decided that such recollections were not factual but fantasies from the phallic period. This revision laid the cornerstone for Freud's theory of infantile sexuality (see Masson, 1983, for a controversial account of this aspect of Freud's work). Ironically, current revelations of frequent child sexual abuse suggest that Freud may have been right the first time.

BOX 2-2 Erikson's developmental theory

Developmental Stage	Crisis
1. Oral-sensory (birth to 1½ years)	Basic trust versus mistrust: learning to develop trust in one's parents, oneself, and the world.
2. Muscular-anal (1½ to 4 years)	Autonomy versus doubt and shame: developing a sense of self-control without loss of self-esteem.
3. Locomotor genital (4 to 6 years)	Initiative versus guilt: developing a conscience, sex role, and learning to undertake a task for the sake of being active and creative.
4. Latency (6 to 11 years)	Industry versus inferiority: receiving systematic instruction, developing determination to master whatever one is doing.
5. Adolescence	Identity versus role confusion: not "Who am I?" but "Which way can I be?"
6. Young adulthood	Intimacy versus isolation: study and work toward a specific career, selection of a partner for an extended intimate relationship.
7. Adulthood	Generativity versus stagnation: parental preparation for the next generation and support of cultural values.
8. Maturity	Ego integrity versus despair: development of wisdom and a philosophy of life.

Source: Bourne and Ekstrand (1976).

vidual Analysis, the most important psychological factor in human behavior and development is considered to be not instinct but *inferiority.* Adler also emphasized the importance of sociocultural, goal-oriented dynamics. He was interested in the family as a whole rather than just the Oedipal situation and proposed an extensive theory on the effects of *birth order* in a family.

Noting the fact that each person begins life in a helpless and inferior position, Adler suggested that subsequent behavior represents a "striving for superiority" (first within the family, then in the larger social world). The particular ways in which each individual seeks superiority comprise a *style of life.* Adaptive life-styles are characterized by cooperation, social interest, courage, and common sense. Maladaptive styles are reflected in extreme competitiveness, lack of concern for others, and distortion of reality. Adler believed that maladaptive life-styles and behavior problems are due not to unresolved unconscious conflicts, but to the misconceptions the individual has about the world and other people in it. As an example, consider the little boy who discovers early that he can have a measure of control over others (and

thus attain feelings of superiority) by requiring their assistance in everything from dressing to eating. Over time, such a child might develop the misconception that he is a "special case" and that he cannot deal with the world and its requirements on his own. The person whose life-style evolves from such a mistaken idea might always appear frightened, sick, or handicapped in ways that demand special attention and consideration from others. (See Mosak & Dreikurs, 1973, for more details of Adlerian theory).

Otto Rank was one of Freud's original disciples who broke from the "master." Like Adler, Rank rejected Freud's emphasis on sex and aggression as the bases of human behavior, and focused instead upon the developing child's basic dependency and inborn potential for positive growth. Rank saw the *trauma of birth* as very significant because it involves an abrupt change from the passive, dependent world of the fetus to a chaotic outside world that requires ever-increasing independence. Birth provides the prototype for a basic human conflict between the desire to be dependent ("return to the womb") and the innate tendency within each person to grow physically and psychologically toward full independence. Failure to resolve this fundamental conflict was, for Rank, the root of human behavior problems.

There are many other versions and revisions of Freud's ideas which are also a part of the psychodynamic model of clinical psychology. The views of dynamically oriented writers such as Carl Jung, Harry Stack Sullivan, Karen Horney, Erich Fromm, and Melanie Klein will help fill in the picture for the serious student of psychoanalysis. They are summarized in standard volumes such as Munroe's *Schools of Psychoanalytic Thought* (1955), as well as in shorter papers (e.g., Mullahy, 1965). Some of those who made fundamental breaks with Freud's theory moved so far in new directions that one might argue for their exclusion from the psychodynamic model. The socially oriented ideas of Adler and Sullivan, for example, are quite compatible with certain versions of other models, to which we now turn.

THE BEHAVIORAL MODEL

Instead of emphasizing the importance of intrapsychic conflicts, basic instincts, unconscious motivation, and other unobservable constructs for the development and alteration of human behavior, the behavioral model focuses directly on that behavior and its relationship to the environmental and personal conditions that affect it. The basic assumption of this model is that behavior is primarily influenced by *learning*,[2] which takes place in a *social context*. As a result, this perspective is sometimes called a *learning theory model*.

In this model individual differences in behavior are attributed in large measure to

a person's unique learning history in relation to specific people and situations, not to traits, personality characteristics, or "mental illness." For example, under the stressful conditions of an academic examination, a student who has benefited in the past from cheating may employ illegitimate means of achieving a high grade, while an individual who has been rewarded in the past for diligent study may be less likely to behave dishonestly. Each individual's cultural background also is seen as a part of his or her unique learning history, which plays a significant role in the appearance of both "normal" and problematic behavior (see, e.g., Ullmann & Krasner, 1975). Upon receiving a failing grade on a vital exam, some students' cultural values may prompt so much shame as to engender a suicide attempt, while for others, the failure may evoke a culturally traditional desire for revenge and an ensuing attack on the professor.

Interindividual similarities are accounted for within the behavioral model by noting the commonalities in rules, values, and learning history that are shared by most people in the same culture. Thus, students' attentiveness during a lecture would not be seen as a collective manifestation of some intrapsychic process, but rather as a group fulfillment of the socially learned *student role*, which appears in certain academic situations for specified periods of time. By the same token, an instructor's behavior reflects prior learning of appropriate *professor role* responses and may be just as situation-specific and time-limited as that of the students.

The same principles of learning invoked to account for behavioral differences and similarities *among* individuals are also employed to account for consistencies and discrepancies *within* individuals. Behaviorists view behavioral consistency (which other models might refer to as "personality") as stemming from generalized learning and/or from the stimulus similarities that exist among related situations. For example, a person may appear calm under most circumstances if calmness has been rewarded

---

[2] Familiarity with learning principles such as reinforcement, punishment, extinction, partial reinforcement, generalization, discrimination, and stimulus control is assumed in the discussion which follows. Those not acquainted with these terms should consult a standard introductory psychology text or a more clinically oriented source like Bandura (1969).

over a period of years and in a wide range of social situations.

The behavioral model explains intraindividual *inconsistencies* and other unpredictable human phenomena in terms of *behavioral specificity*. Mischel (1971, p. 75) summarizes this point well:

example
✳
Consider a woman who seems hostile and fiercely independent some of the time but passive, dependent, and feminine on other occasions. . . . Which one of these two patterns reflects the woman that she really is? Is one pattern in the service of the other, or might both be in the service of a third motive? Might she be a really castrating lady with a facade of passivity—or is she a warm, passive-dependent woman with a surface defence of aggressiveness? Social behavior theory suggests that it is possible for the lady to be *all* of these—a hostile, fiercely independent, passive, dependent, feminine, aggressive, warm, castrating person all in one. . . . Of course which of these she is at any particular moment would not be random and capricious; it would depend on discriminative stimuli—who she is with, when, how, and much, much more. But each of these aspects of her self may be a quite genuine and real aspect of her total being.

3- Behavior Models

There are three main versions of the behavioral model—operant learning, respondent learning, and social learning. Though differing substantially among themselves on certain specifics, these three views share a common core of characteristics:

1. There is an emphasis upon measurable behavior as the subject matter of clinical psychology. "Measurable" does not always mean "overt." The behaviorally oriented clinician may be interested in behaviors ranging from the objective and countable (number of cigarettes smoked, time spent talking) to the subtle and covert (clarity of visualization, content of thoughts). Almost any behavior can be the target of a behavioral approach; the only requirement is that a way of measuring it be available.

2. The importance of environmental as opposed to hereditary or other given influences on behavior is stressed. Genetic and biological factors are not ignored, but they are seen as a general foundation upon which the environment shapes the specifics of behavior. Genetic endowment may set limits on a person's behavioral or intellectual potential, but it is assumed that within those limits, learning factors predominate in determining behavior.

3. The methods of experimental research are employed as the primary means of learning about the assessment, development, and modification of behavior. Within clinical psychology, the behavioral model has led the way in operationalizing and experimentally investigating clinical subject matter. The emphasis is upon systematic manipulation of independent variables (e.g., treatment techniques) and observation of the effects of such manipulations on specifically defined and quantified dependent variables (e.g., alcohol consumption, social assertiveness, depressed behavior, or sexual arousal). By contrast, behaviorists would have little interest in conducting research on the relationship between study-time estimates and scores on a paper-and-pencil test of achievement motivation because such a relationship, whatever its descriptive value, would say little about what students actually do.

4. Clinical assessment and treatment functions are tied to the results of experimental research with humans and animals. Many clinical methods of the behavioral variety are derived from laboratory-based principles of learning and social behavior, and they are subjected to continuing evaluative research conducted in laboratory and clinical settings. Further, this model encourages its practitioners to scrutinize the experimental evidence regarding a particular assessment or treatment procedure before deciding to adopt it and to proceed with great caution in areas where there is little or no empirical guidance.

5. Clinical assessment and treatment functions are closely integrated. The behavioral model assumes that the same principles of learning determine both problematic and nonproblematic behaviors; therefore, clinical assessment should be designed to determine how a client's current difficulties were learned and how they are being maintained so that more adaptive, individually tailored learning can be arranged. A kindergarten child's fear of school, for example, might be based upon a specific conditioned response to a particular

setting, a generalized anxiety response to new situations, the intimidating presence of a particular classmate, or other environmental factors. The behaviorally oriented clinician's treatment approach would not be based upon "standard procedures" for dealing with children diagnosed as phobic. The specific techniques chosen would depend upon what the assessment data have to say about etiological and maintenance factors.

Differences of 3-Models.

The three versions of the behavioral model differ primarily in terms of the learning processes they emphasize. *Operant learning* stresses the relationship between a behavior and its environmental consequences; *respondent learning* concentrates on the temporal association between stimuli and responses; and *social learning* emphasizes the relationship between overt behavior and the cognitions (thoughts) or expectations that a person has about that behavior. A brief review of the three variations of the behavioral model is presented next (see Box 2-3 for a review of Dollard and Miller's transitional learning theory).

Operant Learning: B. F. Skinner and the Functional Analysis of Behavior. While Dollard and Miller's system eliminated some of Freud's intrapsychic concepts, it retained other inferred constructs such as drive, motive, and anxiety. Quite a different learning approach was developed by B. F. Skinner, who also believed that behavior was learned, but argued that nonobservable constructs such as need and drive were unnecessary to understand it.

Skinner asserts that observation of learned relationships between environmental stimuli and overt behavior will ultimately allow for a complete picture of the development, maintenance, and alteration of human behavior. Instead of relying on internal factors (such as id or drive), Skinner advocates observation and description of the ways in which behavior is controlled by its antecedents and consequences. This approach is called *functional analysis* because it

focuses on functional relationships between stimuli, responses, and consequences.

Consider the notion of need. Rather than assuming that human behavior reflects various needs (e.g., "aggressive behavior indicates need for dominance"), the Skinnerian would look at the relationship between aggressive behavior and its consequences. If a client's aggressive behavior has been and continues to be rewarded, at least part of the time, no further explanation in terms of internal need is necessary. The client has simply learned to behave aggressively.

The same thinking is applied to more severe behavior disorders. A mental hospital resident who spends the day silently staring into space, loses control over bladder and bowels, and must be fed from a spoon need not be considered "mentally ill." Instead, these behaviors (not symptoms) would be thought of as learned responses initiated by stress or other environmental factors and maintained by the reinforcement of "crazy" behavior provided by society and especially by the hospital (see, e.g., Ullman & Krasner, 1975). Details of the Skinnerian approach to human behavior in general and to its application to the analysis of problematic behavior in particular can be found in Skinner (1953, 1971) and sources like Spiegler (1983) or Martin & Pear (1983).

Wolpe and Eysenck: Classical Conditioning. Skinner's views highlight the importance of *operant* or *instrumental* learning for clinical psychology. Another aspect of the behavioral model is embodied in the writings of Joseph Wolpe (1958, 1982) and Hans Eysenck (1982). They focus upon the applications of *classical* or *respondent* conditioning principles (Pavlov, 1927; Hull, 1943) to the understanding and elimination of human distress, particularly anxiety. Classical conditioning broadens the concepts available to the behavioral model and addresses a large group of anxiety-based clinical problems that include clients' subjectively experienced distress.

The importance of operant reinforce-

BOX 2-3 The contributions of Dollard and Miller to the behavioral model

One of the earliest behavioral approaches to personality evolved from an attempt to translate Freud's concepts into a language consistent with learning theory. This formidable task was undertaken in the 1940s by John Dollard, a sociologist, and Neal Miller, a psychologist, and culminated in a book called *Personality and Psychotherapy* (1950). Dollard and Miller assumed that human beings do not enter the world with instincts, but with primary *needs* (such as food, water, and air) which must be satisfied. They further assumed that each person *learns* to satisfy these needs (and others that are based upon them) in different ways, thus leading to the development of individualized patterns of behavior.

An infant's need for food results in strong internal stimuli (hunger pangs) which Dollard and Miller called *drives* because of their capacity to motivate behavior. Early in a child's life, behavior resulting from the presence of a drive such as hunger may bring a person into a room with food which reduces the hunger drive and thus *rewards* or *reinforces* the behavior leading to it. In this manner, one learns to repeat behaviors that result in or are associated with drive reduction. Dollard and Miller postulated that people acquire secondary or *learned drives,* which function much like primary drives. Thus, a person can *learn to need* things like praise, money, or power and will learn to repeat behaviors that lead to them and abandon those that do not.

Dollard and Miller dealt with Freudian concepts as environmentally determined and experimentally researchable phenomena, not as intrapsychic structures. For example, they considered a person's ambivalence to be the result of incompatible approach and avoidance tendencies, rather than the product of conflict among id, ego, and superego. In their view, conflict exists when a person must choose between two or more alternative responses. The most difficult and potentially problematic of such conflicts are those of the double approach-avoidance variety, where each course of action has both clearly positive and clearly negative features.

Their analysis of a neurotic conflict would be as follows: One's approach toward a member of the opposite sex may be thwarted by a simultaneous avoidance (e.g., based on anxiety stemming from negative social experiences and parental warnings against expressing sexual desires). The closer one gets to contact with the desired-yet-feared situation, the stronger the avoidance tendency becomes until a retreat occurs, perhaps toward a nonsocial (and thus more comfortable) alternative behavior. This withdrawal reduces anxiety but also allows the approach-avoidance tendency to reappear and repeat the whole cycle. Dollard and Miller saw the consequence of such conflict as a prolonged vacillation between approach and avoidance, accompanied by great psychological discomfort which may ultimately require therapeutic intervention aimed at strengthening approach tendencies, reducing avoidance tendencies, or both.

---

ment and punishment in shaping behavior is not denied but there is an accent upon learning that takes place through the association of conditioned and unconditioned stimuli. It would be argued, for example, that a man who fearfully avoids social events may do so partly because of past negative experiences (i.e., operant conditioning: He enters a room and everyone laughs at his clothes), but also because the discomfort from those experiences has become associated with parties (i.e., classical conditioning:

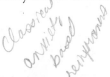

He gets a stomachache upon receiving a party invitation). Thus, both operant and classical conditioning may be involved in the appearance of specific behavior patterns (Mowrer, 1939). Wolpe and Eysenck provided a complement to Skinner's operant position by directing attention to classical conditioning.

Rotter, Bandura, and Mischel: Social-Learning Theory. The views of Skinner, Wolpe, Eysenck, and other behavioral theorists who focus on overt behaviors as the targets of clinical assessment and treatment have attracted many ardent followers, prompted the birth of specialized professional journals, and stimulated the growth of the behavioral model. They have not been universally accepted, however. Some *social-learning* theorists believe that too little attention has been paid to the role of cognitive or symbolic (i.e., thought) processes in the development, maintenance, and modification of behavior.

Social-learning theory developed from the early work of Edward Tolman (1932), who emphasized that behavior was usually purposive. Two of the most prominent current representatives of this point of view are Albert Bandura and Walter Mischel, who have generated a great deal of research and writing (e.g., Bandura, 1969, 1986; Mischel, 1968, 1984, 1986) about the ways in which cognitive activity contributes to learning.

A major feature of Bandura's theory is its attention to *observational learning* or *vicarious cognitive processes*. In his view, behavior develops not only through what the individual learns directly by operant and classical conditioning, but also through what is learned *indirectly* (vicariously) through observation and symbolic representation of other people and events.

Bandura has shown that humans can acquire new behaviors without obvious reinforcement and even without the opportunity to practice. All that may be required is for the person to observe another individual, or *model,* engage in the given behavior.

Later, especially if the model was visibly rewarded for his or her performance, the observer may also display the new response if given the opportunity to do so. In an illustrative experiment, Bandura, Ross, and Ross (1963) arranged for preschoolers to observe models either vigorously attacking or sitting quietly near an inflatable "Bobo" doll. In subsequent tests, the children who had observed agression tended to match the models' behavior quite precisely, while those who had seen a passive model tended to be nonaggressive. According to Bandura, the effects of vicarious processes can be as broad and significant as the effects of direct learning. They can bring about acquisition of new responses (as in the "Bobo" experiment), inhibition or disinhibition of already learned responses (as when a person violates a Don't Walk sign after watching someone else do so), and facilitation or prompting of behavior (as when the entire population of an airline waiting lounge forms a line at an unattended check-in counter after a single prankster stands in front of it).

In the case of the socially fearful man discussed in the last section, Bandura would point out that there are at least two sources of discomfort. One is *external* and includes the anxiety-signaling aspects of social situations themselves (e.g., other people, invitations, laughter), while the other is *internal,* or cognitive. This second source consists of thoughts by the fearful individual about socializing (e.g., "I will make a fool of myself" or "I'm no good at making friends") that serve to support continued avoidance.

The role of cognitive variables was also stressed in the social-learning theory of Julian Rotter (1954), which emphasized the importance of *expectancies* in human activity. In Rotter's system, the probability that a given behavior will occur depends upon (1) what the person expects to happen after the response, and (2) the value the person places on that outcome. Thus, an individual will pay for a ticket because she or he expects that this will result in admission to a movie theater (outcome) that is showing a desirable film (value). Rotter assumes that the expectancies and values that influence behavior are acquired through learning. In order to have an expectancy about an outcome or make a judgment regarding its value, the person must have had some direct or vicarious experience with equivalent or similar situations in the past.

Recently, Bandura has stressed the influence of another type of expectancy he refers to as *self-efficacy* (Bandura, 1977, 1982, 1986). In contrast to Rotter's emphasis on the expectancy of outcomes, efficacy expectations refer to the belief that one *can* successfully perform a given behavior regardless of the outcome that follows the behavior. Bandura believes that overt behavior is controlled by the level of perceived self-efficacy a person holds; the higher the level of self-efficacy, the higher one's performance accomplishments will be. For example, perceived self-efficacy can reduce stress reactions, empower bold behavior in previously feared situations, and lead to self-control of addictive behaviors (Bandura, 1986).

Mischel (1986) has described five types of cognitive variables that social-learning theorists use in understanding the interaction between individuals and their environments. These cognitive factors are a bit un-

usual in the behavioral model because they represent *individual difference* variables, a notion that this model has typically downplayed. Box 2-4 summarizes the five cognitive social learning variables; Bandura's self-efficacy and Rotter's outcome expectancies are both included under expectancies in this table.

To theorists like Bandura, Rotter, and Mischel, attention to cognitive components of behavior is an important aspect of a comprehensive behavioral model of clinical psychology and represents a "wing" of that model which emphasizes covert as well as overt behavior in clinical assessment, treatment, and research (Meichenbaum, 1977; Mahoney, 1974a; Mischel, 1986). This end of the behavioral spectrum, at which there is strong interest in what people "say to themselves," is important because it helps illustrate the breadth and diversity of the model (see Chapter 10). It also separates modern behavior theory, in which all aspects of behavior are targets of scientific attention, from the earlier "radical behaviorism" of J. B. Watson (1913, 1924), which had placed cognitive activity off limits to scientific psychologists. Finally, the presence of cognitive variables in the social-learning model provides a point of overlap with certain psychoanalytic views (recall Adler's emphasis on

---

BOX 2-4　Summary of cognitive social learning person variables

1. *Competencies:* ability to construct (generate) particular cognitions and behaviors. Related to measures of IQ, social and cognitive (mental) maturity and competence, ego development, social-intellectual achievements and skills. Refers to what the person knows and *can* do.

2. *Encoding Strategies and Personal Constructs:* units for categorizing events, people, and the self.

3. *Expectancies:* behavior-outcome and stimulus-outcome relations in particular situations; self-efficacy or confidence that one can perform the necessary behavior.

4. *Subjective Values:* motivating and arousing stimuli, incentives, and aversions.

5. *Self-Regulatory Systems and Plans:* rules and self-reactions for performance and for the organization of complex behavior sequences.

Source: Mischel (1986).

misconceptions) and with some versions of the phenomenological model, which is discussed in the next section.

THE PHENOMENOLOGICAL MODEL

So far we have considered models of clinical psychology in which human behavior is viewed as primarily under the influence of (1) instincts and intrapsychic conflicts or (2) the environment and cognitive factors. A third approach, known generally as the phenomenological model, rejects many of the assumptions of the other two and asserts that the behavior of each human being at any given moment is determined primarily by that particular person's *perception of the world.* Phenomenological theories assume that each person is unique, that each person's view of reality is different from anyone else's, and that each person's behavior reflects that view as it exists from moment to moment.

As an example, consider two students who listen to the same lecture on the first day of a new term. One may be enthralled, while the other stomps out and drops the course. These divergent reactions would be viewed by phenomenologists as due not to differences in the listeners' ego strengths or learning histories, but to their individual perceptions of the speaker during the lecture. Most versions of the phenomenological model share the following features:

1. Human beings are seen neither as carriers of psychic structures and impulses nor as recipients of reinforcement, but as active, thinking people who are individually responsible for what they do and fully capable of making choices about their behavior. In fairness, it should be pointed out that neither the psychodynamic nor the behavioral model fails to recognize these human attributes. Psychoanalysts who emphasize the autonomous role of ego and learning-oriented psychologists who focus upon individuals' capabilities for self-control provide illustrations of this point. However, both models tend to look at the processes producing such uniquely human char-

acteristics as creativity, self-discipline, and decision making, rather than to focus upon those characteristics themselves.

2. The phenomenological model assumes that each person is born with a *potential for growth* which provides the impetus for behavior. This innate tendency to grow into a fully mature individual is likened to the potential of a seed to become a flower. In contrast to Freud's instinct-based view and to the behaviorists' assumption that few behavioral characteristics are innate, the phenomenological model sees people as basically good organisms who naturally strive toward creativity, love, and other positive goals.

3. Phenomenologists believe that no one can truly understand another person's behavior unless she or he can perceive the world through that person's eyes. In line with this notion, the phenomenological model (like the behavioral model) rejects the concept of mental illness and the use of other pejorative labels for problematic behavior. It assumes that all human activity is rational and comprehensible *when viewed from the point of view of the person being observed.* Thus, a woman who is violent toward others would be seen neither as acting out id impulses nor as displaying the results of reinforcement; she is simply behaving in line with her perception of those around her at the time.

4. In clinical work, people cannot be dealt with as objects representing psychological processes; they are fellow human beings. There is little to be gained from accumulating historically oriented assessment data or from seeking to help a person solve a particular situational problem because (a) the past is less important than the present, and (b) helping someone solve a problem may only create others by fostering dependence and stifling personal growth.

Phenomenological views have evolved from several sources. In part, they represent a branch of the reaction against Freud that began when Adler rejected instincts as the basis or behavior and emphasized the importance of individual perceptions and positive growth potential. Attention to the individual's perception of reality was also prompted by the existential philosophies of

Heidegger, Kierkegaard, Sartre, and Camus, who assert that the meaning and value of life are not intrinsic, but are provided by the perceiver. Thus, for example, a person is not "actually" attractive or ugly; these qualitites are "assigned" when someone else reacts to the person in question, and they reflect a different reality in the eye of each beholder.

The focus upon individual views of reality was sharpened by the writings of a group of German psychologists known as the "gestalt school" (Koffka, 1935; Kohler, 1925; Wertheimer, 1923). In contrast to the structuralism of Wundt, they asserted that the mind was more than the sum of its parts and that with respect to perception, the individual was an active participant, not just a passive receptor. To support their view, gestaltists pointed out that there are many cases in which a person's subjective perception goes beyond the stimuli that are "objectively" there and where the "same" object may be interpreted in different ways (see Figure 2-1). Let us now examine some specific phenomenological views which have grown from these roots.

Kelly's Personal Construct Theory. George Kelly developed a theory of behavior which, though not as well known as some others in the phenomenological model, provides a good place to start because it illustrates some ways in which that model relates to social-learning theory. Kelly's (1955) theory is extremely complex, but it is based upon the fundamental assumption that human behavior is determined by *personal constructs*, or ways of anticipating the world.

Kelly believed that individuals act in accord with their unique set of expectations about the consequences of behavior (note the similarity to Rotter) and that people's constructs about life comprise their reality and guide their behavior. For example, a person may consider sharp knives to be capable of inflicting severe harm. This construct would lead to cautious behavior in relation to sharp knives; since such behavior reflects an accurate anticipation of the consequences of carelessness and does in fact avoid accidents, the construct "sharp knives are dangerous" is *validated*.

Validation of personal constructs is, in Kelly's view, the major goal of every human being. He believed that human behavior does not reflect instinctual desires or the effects of external reinforcement, but rather individuals' attempts to make sense of the world as they see it. Like the scientist who revels in discovering why a phenomenon occurs and how that phenomenon can be controlled, each person seeks to be correct about the phenomenon called life. Put more simply, there is more comfort in understanding than in confusion.

In Kelly's system, problematic behavior results when a person develops inaccurate, oversimplified, or otherwise faulty constructs. If someone has only a few broad constructs with which to anticipate and comprehend the vast number of events that occur every day, behavior based upon those constructs is almost sure to be inappropriate or inadequate at least part of the time. For example, a man who construes everything in life as either "good" or "bad" is going to have problems, because not all events and people can be classified accordingly without distortion. He may totally reject or unreservedly welcome the friendship of others according to this overall perception of their value and thus completely miss the positive qualities of "enemies" and the negative qualities of "allies." He may stereotype other people such that he sees college students, political activists, and anyone with a foreign accent as "bad," and children, grandmothers, and the clergy as "good." Such a person would probably be seen by others as selfish, strongly prejudiced, and a poor judge of character. His interpersonal relations would probably be stormy.

Kelly's views are quite compatible with the social-learning theorists. Both views share an interest in the role of cognitive activity in determining overt behavior. Kelly also saw people as capable of *learning to*

FIGURE 2-1. Some perceptual phenomena which illustrate the perceiver's role in organizing "objective" stimuli: (A) "Closure" results in the appearance of a circle and a person on horseback even though many parts are omitted; (B) reversible "figure-ground" relationship allows viewer to see a vase or a pair of silhouettes; (C) interpretive shifts allow shaded area of a "Necker Cube" to appear as the front or back surface, and allows the drawing to be seen as a young woman or an old hag. (From Ernest R. Hilgard, Richard C. Atkinson, and Rita L. Atkinson, *Introduction to Psychology*, 5th ed., copyright © 1971 by Harcourt Brace Jovanovich, Inc., reproduced by permission of the publisher; and L. E. Bourne and B. R. Ekstrand, *Psychology: Its Principles and Meanings*, copyright © 1976 by Holt, Rinehart and Winston, reprinted by permission of Holt, Rinehart and Winston.)

change their personal constructs and, in turn, the patterns of response flowing from them. This latter notion blended phenomenological concepts with social-learning principles and resulted in the development of new, "mixed-model" approaches to clinical treatment, first by Kelly himself and later by others (e.g., Ellis, 1962). We shall discuss the specifics of these approaches in Chapters 9 and 10.

Rogers's Self-Actualization Theory. In contrast to Kelly's social-learning-flavored views, the prolific writings of Carl Rogers (1942, 1951, 1961, 1970) have clearly differentiated the phenomenological model from all others and, in the process, made his name practically synonymous with it. Among Rogers's basic phenomenological assumptions, we find the following (1951, pp. 483–486): (1) "Every individual exists in a continually changing world of experience of which he is the center"; (2) "The organism reacts to the field as it is experienced and perceived. This perceptual field, is, for the individual, reality"; and (3) "The organism reacts as an organized whole to this phenomenal field."

Rogers assumes that people have an innate motive toward growth, which he calls *self-actualization*. This motive is thought to account for the appearance of all human behavior, from basic food seeking to sublime acts of artistic creativity. Self-actualization is defined as "the directional trend which is evident in all organic and human life—the urge to expand, extend, develop, mature—the tendency to express and activate all the capacities of the organism" (Rogers, 1961, p. 351). Rogers sees human behavior, whether problematic or not, as reflecting the individual's efforts at self-actualization in a uniquely perceived world. These efforts begin at birth and continue throughout life; they are sometimes unimpeded and successful, but they may also be thwarted, with problematic results.

As Rogers describes the process, a person's growth is accompanied by a differentiation between self and the rest of the world. This produces an awareness of a part of experience recognized as "I" or "me." According to Rogers, all of a person's experiences, including "self" experiences, are subject to evaluation as positive or negative, depending upon whether they are consistent or inconsistent with the self-actualizing tendency. These evaluations are made partly on the basis of direct or *organismic* feelings (as when a child evaluates the taste of candy as positive), and partly on the basis of other people's judgments. For example, a young boy may end up negatively evaluating the experience of fondling his genitals (even though the direct feelings are positive) because his parents tell him that he is a "bad boy" to do so. Thus, the "self" or "self-concept" emerges as a set of *evaluated experiences* whose positive or negative valence is influenced by the values and opinions of others.

These socializing influences help integrate the developing individual into society, especially when the judgments of others coincide with organismic feelings. For example, if a child practices reading skills and experiences both positive direct feelings upon gaining competence and positive regard from a parent for doing so, the result will likely be a positively evaluated self-experience ("I like to read"). Here, the self-experience is congruent with the organismic experience and the child is able to reconcile accurately his or her own behavior ("I read a lot") and the evaluation of it ("I enjoy reading").

According to Rogers, people value the positive regard of others so highly that they will seek it even if it means thinking and acting in ways that are *incongruent* with organismic experience and the self-actualizing motive. This tendency is encouraged by what Rogers calls *conditions of worth*. These are circumstances in which one receives positive regard from others (and, ultimately, from the self) only if certain approved behaviors, attitudes, and beliefs are displayed. These conditions are set up first by parents, family, and other societal agents, but they are later maintained internally by the individual (note the similarity to Freud's concept of superego).

Persons facing conditions of worth are likely to be uncomfortable. If they behave to please others, it may be at the expense of personal growth, as in the case of a woman who fulfills traditional housewife roles in spite of genuine desires to do other things.[3] On the other hand, displaying authentic feelings and behaviors that are discrepant with conditions of worth risks loss of the positive regard of others and the self.

Rogers believes that to reduce discomfort stemming from such incongruity, the individual may distort reality in ways that may be seen as problematic by others. For example, a man whose parents set up conditions of worth in which displays of emotional behavior (like crying) were discouraged and unemotional "masculinity" was praised may deny that emotional expression feels good. As an adult, his often-repeated, judgmental statements that "anyone who cries is weak" represent a distortion of his real feelings. According to Rogers, the greater the discrepancy between real feelings and self-concept, the more severe will be the resulting problematic behavior. Consider a mild case: A young man with a strong interest in women claims that he is "too busy" to go out with them when, in fact, it would be too discrepant with his self-concept to admit that his invitations are routinely rejected. He even goes so far as to profess disdain and disgust for members of the opposite sex. (Note the relationship to some of Freud's ego defense mechanisms.)

In a more extreme instance, a man whose self-concept characterizes him as self-sufficient and career-oriented may be quite the opposite. Thus, failure to receive a promotion and less-than-adequate performance on the job (all based on lack of real interest in his field) are misinterpreted. Instead of recognizing that he may not be very interested in his work, he asserts that others are "out to get him." Ideas of persecution may evolve to such proportions that he trusts no one and sees conspiracies on every side. Ultimately, his behavior may become so troublesome as to require hospitalization.

Rogers believes that these problems can be avoided. "If an individual should experience only unconditional positive regard, then no conditions of worth would develop, self-regard would never be at variance with organismic evaluation, and the individual would continue to be psychologically adjusted, and would be fully functioning" (Rogers, 1959, p. 224). Even if these optimal conditions have not existed in the past, they may be of help in the present. Accordingly, Rogers developed a therapeutic approach that employs unconditional positive regard and other factors to help troubled people reduce incongruity without having to distort reality (see Chapter 10).

Maslow and Humanistic Psychology. Abraham Maslow (1954, 1962, 1971) provides another version of the phenomenological model. Like other phenomenologists, Maslow emphasized the importance of subjective experience and each person's unique perception of reality. In founding the movement known as humanistic psychology, Maslow emphasized that which is positive and creative about human beings. Like Rogers, Maslow saw people as capable of (and needing) self-actualization, but he suggests that failure to realize one's full potential is caused not by incongruity between self-experience and organismic experience, but by the presence of unmet needs.

Maslow believed that those needs form a hierarchy starting with basic physiological requirements (like food and water) with which everyone is born and moving to higher-level requisites like safety, security, love, belongingness, self-esteem, and, finally, self-actualization. Satisfaction of each need level must be preceded by meeting all

---

[3] The same costs could accrue to the woman who adopts a liberated role to please feminist friends even though her genuine interests are in homemaking activities.

lower-level needs. Thus, one will not be concerned with fulfilling the need for love and belongingness when there is uncertainty over where one's next meal is coming from. Although each person contains the potential for full actualization, that potential cannot be achieved if lower-level needs remain unfulfilled.

Maslow points out that most people seek to meet needs below the self-actualization level, and are thus oriented toward that which they do not have. Such individuals are *deficiency-motivated*. For most people in our culture, incompletely satisfied needs involve security, love, belongingness, and self-esteem, and, according to Maslow, often produce adult need-seeking behaviors which are neurotic or problematic. In relatively rare cases all lower-order needs are satisfied, thus freeing the person to seek fulfillment of the highest need, self-actualization. Such people are in a position to focus upon what they can *be,* not upon what they do not *have.* Maslow called this process *growth-motivation.*

These fortunate few can regularly experience the full potential of humanness. Because they are unfettered by concern over lower-level needs, they can expand their potential and search for abstractions like truth, beauty, and goodness. Momentary experiential high points, or *peak experiences,* at which full self-actualization is reached are common in these individuals and represent the best that is within all of us. Like other phenomenologists, Maslow underscores the importance of helping people overcome the obstacles that block natural growth, happiness, and fulfillment.

Fritz Perls and Gestalt Psychology. Freidrich S. (Fritz) Perls was a European psychiatrist whose dissatisfaction with traditional Freudian theory first evidenced itself in his 1947 book, *Ego, Hunger and Aggression: A Revision of Freud's Theory and Method.* Perls felt that Freud put too much emphasis upon sexual instincts and not enough on what he called *hunger:* an instinct or tendency toward self-preservation and self-actualization. Like Freud, Perls emphasized the function of ego in facilitating growth and self-preservation by mediating between the person's internal needs and the demands of the environment. However, he thought of ego not as a psychic structure, but as a *process* whose goal is the reduction of tension between the person and the environment.

As this balancing act continues over time, the individual grows psychologically. She or he finds new ways to meet internal needs while becoming better able to deal with the requirements of the outside world. For this growth to take place on a continuing basis, the person must remain aware of internal needs and the environment. However, since each person is seen as an active participant in attending to and organizing his or her perceptions, and since the tendency to avoid conflict and keep tension as low as possible may make certain perceptions more comfortable than others, each person's awareness can become incomplete or distorted. When this happens, growth stops and problems start.

For example, a person with strong sexual desires who grows up in a moralistic, antisexual family may find certain kinds of distortions temporarily comfortable but ultimately problematic. Repression of sexual feelings or perceptions of the world as a place filled with unrelenting pressure for sexual promiscuity may occur. None of this accurately reflects either the external circumstances or the internal needs. (Note the similarity to Rogers's concept of incongruence.)

According to Perls, when conflict avoidance prompts disturbances in awareness, symptoms of neurosis and neurotic defenses appear. Intense anxiety about being away from home may result when a person projects hostile feelings (usually kept out of awareness) onto others, thus making everyone else seem hostile. Or the same person may selectively attend to the ordinary risks that surround us all and, "because the world is so dangerous," refuse to go out. When disturbances in awareness become severe, psychotic symptoms may occur.

Perls developed a treatment approach called *gestalt therapy*, aimed mainly at restarting growth by reestablishing aware processes. We shall describe the methods involved in Chapter 10.

There are several other phenomenological approaches to behavior (e.g., May 1969), but this brief outline conveys the flavor of the model. Those interested in more detailed coverage of this and the other models discussed should consult the original sources already cited as well as comparative presentations provided by Hall and Lindzey (1985), Hergenhahn (1984), Liebert and Spiegler (1982), Massey (1981), and Rychlak (1970).

SOME IMPLICATIONS OF CLINICAL MODELS

Let us now go beyond abstract conceptualizations of the three models of clinical psychology and examine their implications for clinician's assessment, treatment, and research functions. Perhaps the best way to do this is to consider the clinical strategy likely to be adopted for a hypothetical case by adherents of each model. Descriptions of these strategies provide only a general representation of their parent models and, since there are several versions of each model, these descriptions will not be comprehensive. Nevertheless, we hope that by applying the general principles and assumptions of each model to the problems of a troubled person, the role of model as guide will become clear.

Discussing the same person from three points of view can also highlight an important point about clinical models: Human behavior does not have to appear in any particular form in order to be dealt with by a particular model. For example, clinicians sometimes say things like "I feel comfortable working with clients who have poor

self-concepts, but I am really not prepared to deal with conditioned anxiety responses," or "The behavioral approach is a good one for learned problems, but it can't handle unconscious conflicts very well." In both cases, the speaker has taken clinical models so seriously that he or she assumes that human behavior conforms to the concepts described by theoreticians instead of the other way around, and has failed to see that virtually any sample of behavior can be approached by any model. It is instructive, therefore, to consider the behavior of a single fictitious person and to see that no model has a monopoly on describing and explaining that behavior.

To illustrate this point, the authors asked one representative of the psychoanalytic, behavioral, and phenomenological schools of thought to read a fictitious case report on "Mr. A." and provide (I) an initial reaction, (II) an assessment strategy, (III) some hypotheses about the etiology (cause) of the client's problems, (IV) some ideas about additional assessment data needed, and (V) an outline of treatment. Here is the case study, followed by each clinician's responses.

A Case Example

Mr. A. is a forty-two-year-old Caucasian who lives in a comfortable home in the middle-class suburb of a large city on the west coast of the United States. He has been married for twenty years, has two daughters (aged sixteen and eighteen), and is employed as an electrical engineer at a large aircraft corporation. He was raised a Protestant, but his attendance at church has been sporadic and is now completely terminated. There are no remarkable aspects to his medical history; his general health is good. Though Mr. and Mrs. A. were on a tight budget at the beginning of their marriage, several promotions and pay raises over the years have made them financially secure.

Mr. A. is an only child. He was born in a small Midwestern city which is the home of a prestigious university. His father, now retired, was for many years head of that university's chemical engineering department and then dean of the college of engineering. His mother is also retired, but taught high school English before being elevated to the post of vice principal. Mr. A. had a happy and uneventful childhood. He did well in school and was a serious youngster who usually followed his parents' teachings about the importance of hard work and superior performance. His parents were loving but somewhat unemotional. He had never seen them display overt signs of affection for each other, and his father had become really angry only once (when Mr. A. talked about dropping out of high school).

In elementary and high school, Mr. A. was part of a small group of male and female friends. Its members were a lot like him: quiet, serious, and studious. His social activities included meetings of special interest groups (i.e., the German and stamp clubs) as well as movies and concerts, which he attended in a group rather than on a date. When he enrolled as an engineering student at the local university, Mr. A. continued to live with his parents and retained his well-established study and social patterns. By the middle of his junior year, he had become especially friendly with an intelligent and compatible young woman who had been in several courses with him. He had first invited her to join him and other friends for concerts, football games, and plays; later they began to socialize as a couple. Mr. A. was delighted with her company but was never physically or verbally demonstrative of his feelings. When she brought up the subject of marriage, he was surprised but thought it would be a fine idea. Mr. A.'s parents were pleased, and the wedding took place right after graduation. The births of the couple's daughters were welcome, and life settled into a pleasant cycle of work, play, and child rearing.

Problems first appeared when Mr. and Mrs. A.'s attractive girls reached adolescence. Arguments over boyfriends, politics, the effects of drug use, the existence of God, and curfews became frequent, and the family atmosphere was often turbulent. These relatively commonplace, though stressful, difficulties were later overshadowed by a set of more serious and totally unanticipated problems.

For a little over a year, Mr. A. has had attacks of dizziness, accelerated heartbeat, and fainting. Though he has received extensive medical attention, no organic basis for the problem has been detected. The severity of the attacks has increased in recent months to the point that Mr. A. was forced to ask for an indefinite leave of absence from his job. Though insurance benefits

and Mrs. A.'s income as a substitute teacher have prevented a financial crisis, he has become increasingly depressed over his problem. After exhausting hope that the attacks would cease spontaneously, Mr. A. reluctantly accepted his physicians' conclusion that psychological factors may be involved and has contacted a clinical psychologist.

He reports that he never has an "attack" at home unless his older daughter is there, but that he is almost sure to become dizzy and faint shortly after leaving home for any purpose. For this reason, he cannot drive a car. For a while he stayed active by having his wife or a friend act as chauffeur, but he is now completely housebound. Mr. A.'s days are spent reading, watching television, or gazing out the living room window. His appetite is poor and he is losing weight. He does not sleep well and has frequent arguments with his wife and children, during which he accuses them of being the cause of his problems. He has become so morose about the current situation and so pessimistic about the future that he contemplates suicide.

A Psychoanalytic Approach to Mr. A.: Dr. Thomas A. Widiger*

I. Initial Reaction. My initial impression is that Mr. A. is suffering from agoraphobia and an adjustment disorder with depressed mood, complicated by a compulsive personality disorder. Mr. A. meets DSM criteria for a major affective disorder, depressive episode, but the diagnosis should emphasize that the depression is reactive to the loss of his career. Mr. A. might not meet DSM criteria for a compulsive personality disorder, but he has inflexible and maladaptive compulsive personality traits that could contribute to the development of the anxiety and depressive disorders.

Mr. A.'s character traits of isolation and constriction of affect, restricted ability to express warmth and tender emotions, and excessive devotion to work, appear to represent a defensive identification with a demanding and withholding father. They

—————
* Associate professor, Department of Psychology, University of Kentucky.

help repress the anger and depression he experienced but could not express during childhood. In addition, Mr. A. denies any psychological conflicts in order to maintain the ego ideals of self-control and productivity. However, he was unable to maintain this myth when his daughter not only directly challenged his personality but also symbolically recreated his own conflict with his father. His anxiety symptoms were a signal that his denial and repression were being threatened. Mr. A., however, maintained his denial, and his anxiety escalated to the point of a crack in his character armor. He then became depressed not only because of the loss of his ego ideals of productivity and self-control, but also because of an emerging recognition of the emptiness of his past and current relationships.

II. Assessment Strategy. The above tentative formulation would need to be verified in the course of treatment. I would be careful not to impose this formulation, but rather to apply it with an evenly hovering attention to the material presented by the patient.

I would first obtain a structured anamnesis (i.e., a life history with particular attention to the course of his symptomatology and relationships). I would like to hear the patient describe his life in his own words. I would assess his motivation for treatment and his capacity for insight. Mr. A. has been reluctant to acknowledge psychological conflicts and I would want to assess whether an insight-oriented treatment would be appropriate. His interpretation of psychosocial events and recent dreams would be particularly helpful. I am assuming that the degree of Mr. A.'s anxiety and depression would not prohibit an insight-oriented psychotherapy.

Following the anamnesis, I would begin a "trial analysis." Freud suggested an initial, time-limited analysis to assess the suitability of analytic therapy. We would meet for six weeks to allow Mr. A. to gain an understanding of what therapy would be like, and to give me further opportunity to assess his motivation and capacity for insight.

III. Etiological Hypotheses. Mr. A.'s symptoms appear to be the result of unconscious conflicts that resulted from pathologic object-relations during childhood. The repression of childhood conflicts is evident in the unrealistic, blanket denial of any traumas or problems during childhood. Mr. A. is described as having a "happy and uneventful childhood." This is difficult to imagine in any family. The facade is illustrated further in the next sentence. Mr. A. was a "rather serious youngster who usually behaved in accordance with his parents' teachings about the importance of hard work and superior performance." This describes an affectively constricted child who conformed to a parental ideal of perfectionism and productivity. Achievement and productivity probably were his symbolic means of obtaining a sense of worth and love from his parents. His mother and father were "loving but somewhat unemotional." This is another contradiction. Can loving be unemotional? Only inadequate loving. It is likely that he found his relationship with his parents to be unsatisfying, but was unable to express his dissatisfaction since affective expression was suppressed. Denied overt expressions of affection and love, he obtained parental approval through a realization of their ideals of achievement, self-control, and perfectionism. However, symbolic satisfaction is not as satisfying as the real thing, especially if it entails a life-style that denies normal human expression and desires. He attempted a rebellion by dropping out of high school. However, this brief attempt to divest himself of the defensive character armor made his father overtly angry. By dropping out of high school Mr. A. rejected his parents' repressive and constrictive ideals. It was a "good" way of letting them know he was dissatisfied and it forced his father to deviate from his own constrictive character style and become angry. As a result, Mr. A. resumed the identity imposed by his parents because a lack of emotion was easier to live with than anger and hostility.

The compulsive character defenses (described above) were maintained throughout college and marriage. They were not, however, without cost. Mr. A. was able to repress his anger and depression, but at the price of a constriction of affection. It was necessary for his girl friend to suggest marriage, an idea that took him by surprise and was accepted with little feeling. He simply "thought it would be a fine idea," comparable to the purchase of a new car. "Life settled into a pleasant and serene cycle of work, play, and child rearing," continuing the myth of a successful denial and repression of tension, depression, and anger.

Mr. A.'s daughter, however, was unable and/or unwilling to perpetuate the family myth. She rebelled, and her rebellion challenged his character armor. Their continual arguments over boyfriends, drug usage, God, and curfews exacerbated his unconscious conflicts. The fact that her rebellion occurred at the same stage of life as his own failed rebellion contributed to its symbolic significance. Mr. A. was able to deny his ambivalence regarding his values, impulses, and desires when his family corroborated them, but not if a family member openly challenged them. Repression and denial were not so easily maintained in the company of his daughter. Her sexual attractiveness, rebellious behavior, and verbal assaults were too strong for his defensive armor.

As his defenses became ineffective, Mr. A. began to experience symptoms of anxiety, especially in the presence of the rebellious daughter. To his own detriment, he continued to deny psychological conflicts, searching for a physician to discover an organic basis.

The denial was now not only ineffective but very costly. Severity of anxiety attacks increased to the point that he had to abandon his career. Mr. A., however, may have obtained some unconscious satisfaction in the loss of his career. He was finally able to

reject his parents' ideals without an overt, hostile rebellion.

The anxiety attacks not only fulfilled an unconscious desire to rebel, they also resulted in the loss of Mr. A.'s symbolic source of parental affection (i.e., self-worth). His identity revolved around hard work, self-control, and productivity. Loss of career through anxiety attacks shattered these ideals and he became severely depressed. Knowing that company benefits and his wife's income prevented a financial crisis only reaffirmed his crippled state.

His depression may have also been "overdetermined" by the emergence of repressed depressive effect. Mr. A. denied throughout his life the need for close and loving relationships. With a breakdown of his character armor he perhaps began to recognize his past losses and the emptiness of his current relationships. Denial was now impossible. Anxiety and depression had broken down the controlled but productive facade. "Mr. A. reluctantly accepted his physicians' conclusions that psychological factors may be involved."

IV. Potential Influence of Further Assessment Data. The etiological hypotheses focused on the patient's relationships with his father and with his daughter. It is likely that during assessment the importance of other relationships would be revealed. Mr. A.'s relationships with his mother and his wife would be crucial to consider. It would also be of interest to explore his relationship with his parents prior to adolescence. Conflicts regarding emotional expression and intimacy, and the compulsive character defenses, were developed prior to adolescence, and it would be important to explore their genesis in the context of the parent-child relationships.

V. General Approach to Relief of Distress. Treatment would consist of insight-oriented psychotherapy. I would prefer to meet at least twice a week, for the intensity and effectiveness of insight are diminished by long intervals between sessions. Mr. A., however, would probably find twice-weekly sessions to be too threatening.

I would be nondirective within the sessions, allowing Mr. A. to govern the focus and pace of the sessions. This does not imply a passive tolerance of resistance, but a respect for the patient's readiness and receptivity. I would encourage Mr. A. to discuss and reflect upon his problems, attempting to discover why they developed, how they were being maintained, and what to do about them. He would be instructed to say whatever came to mind, freely associating to his thoughts and fantasies.

Mr. A. probably would proceed slowly, demonstrating considerable denial, intellectualization, and rationalization. My initial efforts would consist of reflecting and clarifying Mr. A.'s comments and associations to highlight what I believe are the important issues. I would not interpret his comments in terms of his underlying conflicts until enough material had emerged and sufficient rapport was established that he would be ready to receive them. The interpretations would focus on the relationship of Mr. A.'s associations, dreams, symptoms, and underlying conflicts. Interpretations would be offered in a nonthreatening and suggestive manner, always encouraging the patient to offer his own insights and interpretations. Each interpretation would be followed by a considerable amount of "working through," or the elicitation of further material to clarify and expand on the initial insight.

Treatment would eventually focus on the therapeutic relationship itself, for I would expect him to transfer to me the conflicts he has experienced with his father (and mother). In this case the "transference analysis" is likely to be problematic and, for the same reasons, therapeutic, for Mr. A.'s relationship with his father appears to be central to his unconscious conflicts. It is anticipated that initially he would be deferential and detached, preferring to engage in intellectual discussions. Beneath this superficial obedience would be a hostile rebellion and a yearning for an intimate and affectionate relationship. The hostile rebellion would likely appear first, perhaps expressed through arguments and rejections. Treatment will have progressed successfully if Mr. A. could acknowledge his unsatisfied needs for affection and intimacy.

A Behavioral Approach to Mr. A.: Dr. Barry Edelstein*

I. Initial Reaction. My initial impression is that Mr. A. is experiencing several problems, one of the most important of which is his consideration of suicide. No matter how one would proceed with this case, the possibility of suicidal behavior should be assessed in depth. Space limitations preclude an adequate description of how one would assess suicide potential, so I will proceed with the understanding that it was assessed and judged not to be an imminent problem.

Assigning diagnoses is a common practice among most clinicians; however, it can lead one away from an analysis of the presenting problem and may not translate into meaningful decisions regarding treatment. Thus, some behavioral clinicians would not formulate a diagnosis until required to do so. For the sake of this exercise, I will offer an initial diagnostic impression to allow comparison with other approaches. Mr. A. appears to be experiencing agoraphobia with panic attacks accompanied by symptoms of major depressive disorder. The depressive symptoms are probably secondary to the panic attacks, loss of job, inability to deal with the stressful difficulties with his children, and general loss of reinforcement. The more specific problems which might be articulated by a behavioral clinician rather than a diagnosis would include: reports of fear, avoidance behavior, physiological

* Professor, Department of Psychology, West Virginia University.

arousal, marital dysfunction, child behavior management, interpersonal problem solving, employment, anger control, sleep, appetite, finances, reduced number and intensity of many daily behaviors.

II. Assessment Strategy. The intial reaction is based upon very limited information and may not be accurate. Further assessment would occur throughout all future meetings with the client, a practice common among behavioral clinicians.

An initial interview would be conducted at Mr. A.'s home since he is housebound. The interview would begin with a survey of general problem areas and their history. Mr. A. would be encouraged to provide concrete examples of each problem and, if possible, specify related thoughts and observable environmental events. Mr. A. would be asked about the frequency, duration, and intensity of each behavior problem across settings, individuals, times, and occasions. The effects of these problem behaviors on Mr. A. and others would also be assessed. A functional analysis of Mr. A.'s dysfunction would be performed to describe the relationship between environmental events that set the occasion for and maintain (reinforce) the problem behaviors that constitute the dysfunction. Thus, I would look for the events in the observable environment as well as in Mr. A.'s thoughts that are functionally related to each problem.

I would also assess the probable consequences (motivation) for Mr. A. attending sessions with me and completing any homework assignments. His motivation for change will partially determine the method of treatment.

The client is only one member of a family system, the members of which influence each other on a daily basis. I would therefore attempt to meet with members of Mr. A.'s family to gain their perspective on the problem, determine how the problem affects the family, determine how the family affects the problem, and determine the extent to which other family members could assist with or hamper treatment. It is possible that Mr. A. is also gaining something positive from his problem behaviors. I would attempt to determine whether some of his problem behaviors were being maintained by their positive consequences (secondary gain).

During the initial visit I would also obtain two additional types of assessment information: self-report ratings on standardized questionnaires and an actual sample of the avoidance behavior and the associated verbal reports of Mr. A's reaction to feared situations. I would have Mr. A. complete the Mobility Inventory, the Body Sensations Questionnaire, and the Beck Depression Inventory. The Mobility Inventory lists several places and situations and asks the client to rate the amount of avoidance of these situations when alone or when accompanied. The Body Sensations Questionnaire asks the client questions about bodily sensations that are common among individuals experiencing anxiety in various situations (e.g., "I am going to pass out"). The Beck Depression Inventory is a measure of level of depression which can be completed quickly and can be readministered over time/sessions to evaluate change in level of depression. For a behavior sample, I would have Mr. A. attempt to walk away from his home and monitor the number of steps he is able to take and his ratings of anxiety at several points along the way.

I would also teach Mr. A. to gather relevant information and collaborate in the development of the treatment program that arises from this information. I would teach Mr. A. how to evaluate the severity of his problem by rating the intensity of anxiety and describing his avoidance behavior in various situations. Intensity of anxiety can be rated on a 100-point scale where 1 = as relaxed as I have ever been and 100 = as anxious as I have ever been. Avoidance can be measured by noting what is avoided when he is alone or accompanied by someone.

Mr. A. would be asked to begin keeping a

log of his anxiety and avoidance behavior throughout each day so that I could gain a detailed picture of the situations that occasion avoidance and elicit anxiety. He would also be asked to record any panic attacks, those situations in which he may feel dizzy, experience an accelerated heartbeat, and sometimes faint. In summary, Mr. A. would record where he goes, when he goes there, who accompanies him, and what he experiences every day.

If Mr. A. is able to record everything as I requested and his family is cooperative, I could have enough information to begin treatment in about two weeks.

My understanding of the problem would be checked repeatedly against the new evaluative information obtained from the client. Should new information reveal errors in my assessment, the treatment strategies would be adjusted accordingly. Similarly, if a treatment does not produce significant improvement in level of functioning in a relatively short period of time, the treatment strategy would be reconsidered and altered to bring about the desired change.

III. Etiological Hypotheses. Mr. A. appears to have had a long history of conservative behavior with little risk taking. His study habits, method of socializing, and living at home until marriage reduced the chances of having to face new challenges and their associated anxiety. Just as he controlled sources of anxiety, he also controlled his emotional expression (as had his parents). Consequently, he rarely had the opportunity to learn to cope with problems and their associated anxiety. The confrontations associated with his children reaching adolescence challenged his skills for coping with major interpersonal problems as well as the accompanying anxiety. The anxiety experienced when confronting the problems with his daughters may well have been of a greater magnitude than any previously experienced. Those initial intense feelings of anxiety would have been paired with previously neutral stimuli that were present. In light of the panic attacks in the presence of

his older daughter, I would guess that she was present during the initial experiences of intense anxiety. Once anxiety became associated with thoughts about his daughters and related problems, he might experience anxiety anywhere he was thinking about these issues. Thus, anxiety responses would generalize across a variety of situations, including Mr. A.'s work environment. The internal cues of anxiety would come to signal a possible recurrence of the original panic attack. The more anxious he became, the more he feared becoming anxious. Panic attacks resulted from increased anxiety and strengthened his fear of becoming anxious. Thus, his failure to meet the demands of the problem situations resulted in increased anxiety which developed into a fear of fear itself. Depression probably resulted from his inability to control his problems and the significant reduction in reinforcement that was normally associated with his job and family.

IV. Potential Influence of Further Assessment Data. Additional assessment data would be gathered on the relationship of Mr. A.'s problems to other family members as well as the situation at work prior to development of the presenting problems. It is possible that the problems were brought on and maintained by family members; or that problems at work developed into a phobia of work rather than agoraphobia. The extent to which Mr. A. is considering suicide could alter the analysis as well as the nature of treatment. Depression could become the major priority for treatment. Family therapy would be considered, particularly if the family is contributing significantly to the problem's maintenance. Child behavior management or parent-child communication skills could be so poor that teaching both parents appropriate parenting skills could have a significant impact on Mr. A.'s presenting problems.

V. General Approach to Relief of Distress. If agoraphobia seems to be the major problem I would address it first with the expectation that symptoms of depression would abate once the avoidance behavior was reduced. The psychological treatment most strongly supported by research is an exposure procedure. Two drugs, imipramine and phenelzine, have also been used successfully in combination with exposure procedures to reduce the frequency and intensity of panic attacks. If I were working with a psychiatrist I might consult with him/her regarding the advisability of employing one of these drugs in addition to using an exposure procedure. Regardless of whether one of these drugs was employed, I would begin with an exposure procedure. Exposure procedures can be either *in vivo* or imaginal, where clients are exposed to the anxiety-arousing stimuli via direct contact with the stimuli or by having them imagine the stimuli. The object of stimulus exposure is to elicit anxiety to a moderate extent and have the client experience the anxiety without escaping from the situation or thoughts. The exposure procedures would first be performed by me and then by cooperative family members in concert with Mr. A. Progress would be monitored continually using the same assessment methods previously noted. Treatment would be terminated when Mr. A. was able to return to work on a regular basis and when suicidal ideation and the other related problems were alleviated to an extent agreed upon by Mr. A. and me.

A Phenomenological Approach to Mr. A.: Dr. Constance T. Fischer*

I. Initial Impression. Our neurophysiology sometimes becomes disordered through physical or biochemical trauma, or through stressed living. Although Mr. A. does meet DSM III criteria for major depression, neither this state nor his dizziness, accelerated heartbeat, or fainting appears to be disorders of that kind. His symptoms instead point to a disordering of his life—a disrup-

---

* Professor, Department of Psychology, Duquesne University.

tion of a personal world that used to make sense, that used to support his goals, values, and actions. But now he finds himself immobilized, anxious, depressed. What has changed for him? Who was he trying to be? What were his assumptions about life? Where was he going? What obstacles did he encounter that now he apparently perceives his basic goals as unreachable? How is he contributing to these obstacles and to his perceptions of them? What purposes does his comportment now serve?

My initial impression is that Mr. A. had lived his life in an orderly, disciplined manner. He avoided spontaneity, strong feelings, and introspection in an implicit belief that a more controlled and logical life rendered him worthy, accepted, and safely on course. His successful life at work and at home validated his values and strengthened his assumption that his children would honor him as he had his parents. However, as his daughters entered adolescence, Mr. A. found that they chose not to live in a controlled manner, that in effect they had disrupted his course. His tried-and-true problem-solving approach, logic, and discipline failed him. He not only found himself to be unaccustomedly confused, but he also found himself experiencing unusually strong feelings, such as anger and perhaps jealousy of his daughters' freedom. I suspect that he also was not prepared for his daughters' emerging sexuality. In short, his fundamental personal rules are no longer viable; Mr. A. does not know how to continue his life. The world and his own reactions have become unpredictable. He cannot imagine how to continue being himself. When he confronts this disorderly world (and self), he becomes anxious; when he retreats, he again finds himself helpless and demoralized.

II. Assessment Strategy. Before meeting with Mr. A., I would review my initial impressions so that I could revise them as I came to know Mr. A. more directly. I would not be looking for proof of my impressions nor for causes of his condition, but rather for an overview of what that condition is, especially in terms of how he is living and perpetuating it. In my meeting with Mr. A., I would try to assess how viable his prior life course might still be, and how I and others might help him revise his assumptions, his goals, his participation in bringing about his circumstances, his ways of being the person he has strived to be.

Our starting point would be Mr. A.'s own story, which would be our common ground for collaborative exploration. We would try to make sense of his life in its own terms, using his language and his themes. That life would be my point of departure into reflections about my initial impressions, recollections of similar clients, my more personal reactions, and my knowledge of research findings and theory. Mr. A.'s everyday life would also be my point of return, where we could refine our understandings in light of our respective reflections. The purpose of assessment would be to understand his circumstance, and to identify viable interventions and points at which he might opt for alternate routes. I would hope that during the assessment process he would rediscover that he does participate in directing his life. In this sense, recovery is initiated prior to formal psychotherapy.

I would use psychological tests, largely as a means of engaging Mr. A. in ways that are familiar to him—looking at visual evidence, taking a problem-solving approach. I might start with subtests from the Wechsler intelligence test. After witnessing his performance with the block designs, I might remark that his engineering background is certainly evident. I could affirm his logical, systematic approach. We might discuss its advantages, and how he has accomplished various objectives through it. I might then ask when this approach hasn't worked so well. We could continue this inquiry through other subtests. For example, we might note on Picture Arrangement that he was less facile at ordering scenes because he was uninclined to put himself in others'

shoes. We might continue this exploration by looking together at a self-report inventory such as the 16 PF. By the end of our assessment session(s) I would have a sense of which forms of psychotherapy would best suit Mr. A., and I would propose this to him, along with a summary of the goals we had agreed on. I also would acknowledge disagreements.

III. Probable Development of Current Circumstances. Mr. A. seems to have grown up in a setting that one-sidedly rewarded academic, intellectual pursuit. He did not become familiar with open affection, nor with give-and-take interpersonal argument. Nor did his parents model spontaneity nor openness to new life-styles. His one effort to leave school and home was summarily disallowed. Moreover, Mr. A. had no siblings with whom to learn that being aggressive, angry, and jealous can occur within a good family. He seems to have restricted himself so closely to schoolwork and to his parents' home that he probably was not familiar with how other youngsters were growing up, with their struggles and perspectives. He was slow to discover the other gender and sexuality.

As he moved into marriage and an engineering career, the consequences of his hard-working, intellectual, ordered life seemed to be totally positive. He continued to honor his parents through perpetuating their approach to life. He was a good provider, a respected person at home, work, and in the community. His daughters were growing up in a reserved, respectable home. Surely this course would continue. His daughters would affirm his rightness and the appropriateness of his careful life by respecting his values, worth, and power, just as he had respected his parents'.

But by the time his daughters entered adolescence, they were living in a different time and different social world than the one in which Mr. A. grew up. They were more independent and less restrained. They challenged Mr. A., showed more affection toward boyfriends than toward their father, argued emotionally, and possibly talked outright about their father's uptightness about their interest in young men. I wonder what Mrs. A.'s participation in this evolution has been. Might she be supporting the daughters' growth, for both selfless and vicarious reasons? Does Mr. A. perceive this as disloyal?

At any rate, Mr. A.'s lifelong, and up until now valid, philosophy no longer works for him. He is helpless in that all he knows to do is to assert authority and logic, which now appear to others to be rigid, narrow, inappropriate. The proverbial rug has been pulled out from under him. In a sense, he doesn't know who he is or how to be. The more he takes refuge in isolation from work and family, the more alienated he feels, and the more frightened he is at the prospect of reasserting himself. He is agoraphobic and depressed. I wonder, though, whether his daughters' freedom has not also put him in touch with his own previously disallowed yearnings, leaving him implicitly angry at his parents and at himself. I wonder whether his present state is also one of feeling sorry for himself; of mourning what might have been; of avoiding current choice; of punishing parents, wife, and daughters; and of still retaining power, recognition, and order by disrupting the family's pursuits. I wonder too whether being depressed serves to keep Mr. A. from more fully experiencing the above.

IV. Additional Assessment. Formal psychotherapy would continue the assessment, as I would listen and revise it in light of what Mr. A. and his family present, and in light of response to my therapeutic efforts. The above formulations would allow me to revise continually and systematically. So even if the initial formulations prove to be incorrect, they move us closer to understanding Mr. A.'s circumstance.

There are four additional areas I would want to assess: (1) the likelihood, method, and lethality of Mr. A.'s attempting to kill himself; (2) Mrs. A.'s and the daughters' participation in what is happening; (3) what intolerable possibilities are evoked by the older daughter's presence; and (4) whether medication might interrupt Mr. A.'s panic attacks, thereby assisting his reentry into his community and job.

V. Therapeutic Efforts. I would use multiple and flexible methods, geared to help Mr. A. develop revised ways of continuing his orderly, reasonable, worthy, respected, but now broadened life. Choice of methods would depend upon how Mr. A. related to me, and how reflective he was. First, I would use our relationship, letting him know that we *can* make sense of what has happened, and that I respect him and his goals even though I know the details of how they've gone awry. I would help him to see that although there were good reasons for his earlier style, he no longer has to continue it in the same way.

I would intervene in his environment, so that it became more manageable for him. In addition to the possibility of medication to lessen his being lethargic and panic-prone, I would encourage family meetings, at some point during which wife and daughters could affirm those aspects of Mr. A.'s life which they still see as worthy. I might also instruct all of the A.'s in specific ways to stop reinforcing Mr. A.'s withdrawal. I would encourage a return to healthy diet, taking up household tasks, and looking into partial return to work.

In an openly paradoxical manner, I might congratulate Mr. A. on having demonstrated to his daughters that our actions have consequences. Similarly, I might caution him not to return to his old self until he was sure he was ready. Both messages affirm that Mr. A. has known and knows what he is doing, and that he can continue his life in a more fulsome manner.

These and other efforts would be based

on continual reappraisal of "what is possible from here?," particularly in terms of how Mr. A. takes up what his body, environment, other people, his history, and opportunity present to him.

A CRITIQUE OF CLINICAL MODELS

Each model presented in the chapter possesses valuable assets, but is also subject to various criticisms. To round out our coverage we should consider the problems and shortcomings that various critics have attributed to each clinical model.

Problems with Freud's Psychodynamic Model

Sigmund Freud's influences on psychiatry and clinical psychology are hard to overestimate. He presented the most comprehensive and revolutionary theory of behavior ever articulated; in the process, he introduced concepts that captured the imagination of psychiatry, psychology, and other helping professions, not to mention literature, religion, sociology, and anthropology. The intensive study of a single individual, the one-to-one assessment or treatment session, the view that overt behavior is systematically related to identifiable psychological causes, the possibility that individuals' behavior may be influenced by factors of which they are unaware, the importance of conflict and anxiety, and other features characteristic of all types of clinicians are directly traceable to Freud. In addition, Freud's concepts have become a part of everyday language and thus guide the way nonpsychologists think about behavior. It is not at all uncommon to hear people refer to "Freudian slips," the Oedipus complex, unconscious motivation, defense mechanisms, or ego in the context of ordinary conversation.

In spite of its broad acceptance, Freud's approach has been the target of several continuing criticisms:

1. Psychodynamic concepts such as id, ego, superego, projection, unconscious motivation, and repression consist of vague abstractions that are difficult to test scientifically. The techniques that have been designed to measure various Freudian personality concepts have often shown themselves to be unreliable and invalid (see Chapter Five), and the effects of clinical treatment based on those concepts have been questioned (see Chapter Eight). Recent attempts to investigate psychoanalytic constructs in the laboratory (e.g., Silverman & Weinberger 1985) have not satisfied critics (Allen & Condon, 1982) who complain about the methodological problems of this research.

2. The foundation for Freud's approach was built through his clinical experiences with a small number of upper-class patients living in Vienna around the turn of the century. This raises questions about the generalizability of his ideas to people from other socioeconomic groups and other cultural backgrounds. Some anthropologists have suggested, for example, that psychoanalytic concepts of behavior are not universal (e.g., Lindesmith & Strauss, 1950; Mead, 1928, 1939).

3. Psychoanalytic thinking places too much emphasis on the negative side of human character (i.e., sexual and aggressive instincts) and not enough upon inherent growth potential and the influence of society and culture on behavior.

4. The psychoanalytic view represents a closed system that is inflexible and not easily influenced by contradictory data; any results can be interpreted as confirming Freudian principles. For example, if projective tests lead to the conclusion that a person harbors unconscious feelings of hostility, subsequent hostile behavior would be taken as evidence for the emergence of unconscious impulses. But the appearance of calm and friendly behavior could also provide evidence for underlying hostility because it could be seen as a reaction formation. Recognition of this problem has caused some critics to call Freud's theory a "hoax" (Jurjevich, 1974).

5. The psychodynamic model overinterprets behavior as indicative of unconscious motivation and related pathology, and thus may actually create problems. A man who is a successful go-getter might become distressed to learn

that he may merely be compensating for unconscious feelings of inadequacy.

Problems with the Behavioral Model

Since its beginnings in the late 1950s, the behavioral approach has enjoyed enthusiastic support from an ever-increasing number of adherents in clinical psychology, social work, education, psychiatry, and many other fields. The model's attractiveness lies in its objective and experimentally oriented approach to human behavior. It rejects intrapsychic and subjective explanations, defines its concepts operationally, relies on laboratory data for its basic principles, ties its applied work to the results of controlled research, and continually evaluates its procedures through a series of critical investigations. In short, the behavioral model is seen as the best approach to the advancement of psychology *as a science of behavior* in the applied clinical field.

Its detractors are less convinced of these advantages. They suggest that:

1. The learning approach reduces human beings to a set of acquired responses derived from a rigid and mechanistic relationship with the environment. This view is too narrow and tends to exclude genetic, physiological, and other non-learning-based influences and, most important, fails to recognize the importance of subjective experience. In other words, behaviorists deal with an individual's behavior, but ignore the individual.

2. The behavioral model is only applicable to measurable behavior. It cannot conceptualize adequately human problems of a complex, internal nature. Learning principles are fine for explaining and dealing with phobias and other specific and relatively simple stimulus-response relationships, "but how about grief at the loss of a loved one, shame at failures, guilt whether real or fancied over moral transgressions, a pervasive sense of impotence, and other negative affects? Likening human to animal behavior, and focusing on visible behavior rather than inner states, minimizes precisely those values, feelings, fantasies, and motives which most distinguish and trouble human life" (Korchin, 1976, p. 349).

3. The principles of learning upon which the behavioral model is based are not well established and agreed upon by learning theorists themselves. The role of reinforcement in the learning process is still a matter of some debate, for example. Further, even if all learning principles were established, there is the question of whether their animal-laboratory origins allow them to be applied meaningfully to the behavior of human beings. A cat faced with an insoluble task may display "experimental neurosis," but the human behavior called "neurotic" may not be equivalent and may result from entirely different processes.

4. Behavioral approaches to clinical psychology are not as uniquely scientific or clearly validated as their practitioners would have us believe. Many assessment and treatment procedures representing the model are based more upon clinical experience than experimental research, and, where research evidence is available, it is often not unequivocally supportive of learning-based techniques.

Problems with the Phenomenological Model

The phenomenological orientation has a strong intrinsic appeal. It gives a central role to each person's immediate experience, a kind of given that is appreciated by anyone who attends to such experience. Further, it emphasizes the uniqueness of each individual, providing reassurance that the person is not just an extension of lower animals and is not "just like everyone else." Finally, it is an optimistic approach that focuses on the potential of human life and places faith in the individual's capability to grow toward fulfillment of her or his ultimate capacities.

In spite of these refreshing and encouraging views, the phenomenological model has received its share of criticism. It is argued that:

1. The phenomenological approach is too concerned with immediate conscious experience and does not pay sufficient attention to the importance of unconscious motivation, reinforcement contingencies, situational influences, and biological factors.

2. The model does not deal adequately with the *development* of human behavior. Postulation of an innate tendency toward growth or actualization can account for development, but does not explain its processes. Saying that a child develops because of an actualizing tendency is like saying that one eats because of hunger; this may be true, but it says little about what hunger is or how it influences behavior.

3. A related criticism has been that phenomenological theories provide excellent descriptions of human behavior but are not focused on the scientific exploration of its causes. To suggest that people act as they do because of their unique perceptions of reality may be personally satisfying, but this is not very informative in terms of understanding the variables that develop, maintain, and alter human behavior.

4. Phenomenological concepts are unscientific, vague, and difficult to comprehend, let alone investigate. When human beings are described as "a momentary precipitation at the vortex of a transient eddy of energy in the enormous and incomprehensible sea of energy we call the universe" (Kempler, 1973, p. 225), it becomes difficult to generate testable hypotheses about their behavior. With the exception of Rogers and his colleagues, many phenomenologists see research on human behavior as dehumanizing, and unimportant in comparison to activities designed to expand individual awareness. The phenomenological model is often chided for being antiscientific.

5. Phenomenological theories are not only antiscientific, they are anti-intellect. Reason is subordinated to feeling, and knowledge is sought through subjective experience rather than rational analysis. This goes against the grain of Western thought and antagonizes many clinicians.

6. The phenomenological model's clinical applicability is limited to those segments of the population whose intellectual and cultural background is compatible with the introspective nature of this approach. Further, the range of problems addressed by the model is somewhat limited: To the person struggling with a crisis of identity or values, phenomenological notions may be of great subjective value, but these notions (like the tenets of most other models) may not be very useful in situations where unmet needs near the bottom of Maslow's hierarchy (e.g., food, decent housing, and a job) are the bases of human distress.

Biological Challenges to Psychological Models

In the past two decades, the role of biological factors in the regulation of normal behavior and in the causation of various behavioral disorders has been highlighted by a growing body of research evidence from psychiatry, neuroscience, and experimental psychopathology. No matter which model they prefer, all clinical psychologists must take these new findings into account as they conduct their own research, assessment, and treatment activities. In fact, the growing recognition of biology-behavior relationships suggests that the biological perspective may one day attain the status of a model in clinical psychology. Some psychologists see this development as a threat in which reductionistic thinking endangers psychology of "losing its status as an independent body of knowledge" (Peele, 1981). On the contrary, we believe the growing impact of biological progress in understanding behavior has not diminished the importance of clinical psychologists but has expanded their professional roles and research interests.

Chapter 11 surveys three areas of activity—neuropsychology, psychopathology, and health psychology—that reveal how essential it is for psychologists to study the interactions between biological and psychological variables and how exciting areas of professional work grow from this understanding. For now, we want to emphasize that as psychoanalytic, behavioral, and humanistic psychologists advance and revise their particular models of behavior, they need to do so with a thorough appreciation for the new biology-behavior relationships that are constantly being discovered.

The Popularity of Clinical Models

It should now be clear that the three main models of clinical psychology present a kind of triple approach-avoidance conflict for the person trying to decide which one to adopt. They all present positive and negative features and, even after a tentative choice is made, one still faces diversity of emphasis within each model. There are no universally agreed-upon criteria available to guide one's choice; even the advice offered at the beginning of this chapter regarding the value of scientifically testable models is based on the authors' personal bias, which, though shared by many, is a bias nonetheless (see Russell, 1986).

What determines one's choice of a model? Freudians might suggest that unconscious motivation compels our choice, while others would point to the role of learning principles. Some would seek the answer in congruity between a model's principles and the self-concepts of its adherents. Or the choice may be made on the basis of "cognitive style" (Kaplan, 1964), emotional and personality characteristics (L'Abate, 1969), or just plain "personal preference" (Zubin, 1969). The truth is, we really do not know exactly why clinicians choose a particular model, but we can examine what models they choose.

Here the answers are fairly clear. Most clinicians do not make a single choice; instead, they adopt those aspects of two or more models that are personally satisfying to them. To those who value open-mindedness, flexibility, and moderation above systematic consistency, this solution to the choice-of-model problem is called *eclecticism*. To those who emphasize the value of an integrated and unitary point of view, "eclectics" are merely confused individuals destined to spin their intellectual wheels for lack of theoretical traction. In any case, the ranks of the "eclectic" or the "confused" are growing within clinical psychology. Garfield and Kurtz (1976) reported that almost 55 percent of their sample of 855 APA Clinical Division members called themselves eclectic, an increase of nearly 15 percentage points over an earlier estimate by Kelly (1961).

Other evidence presented by Smith (1982) suggested that Freudian and neo-Freudian models have become less popular among clinicians lately, while phenomenological and behavioral views have gained slightly. While these data are probably accurate reflections of the direction of model-popularity trends within clinical psychology, they may not be entirely representative. For example, many noneclectic clinicians are not members of the Clinical Division of the APA, joining instead model-oriented clinical groups such as the Association for the Advancement of Behavior Therapy or the Association of Humanistic Psychology. Although there are claims that some models will never "mix well" (Messer & Winokur, 1980), the spirit of current times favors a search for commonalities among various therapeutic schools. Goldfried (1980) has suggested that such commonalities are most likely to exist at a level of abstraction somewhere between general theory and specific techniques, a level he calls the *strategic* because of its focus on principles of change. We will discuss these common strategies in detail in Chapter 7.

chapter 3

Assessment in Clinical Psychology

Dictionaries commonly define *assessment* as an estimate of value or worth. A county assessor, for example, looks at a house and estimates its value. On the basis of that estimate, the homeowner's property tax is established. Assessment does not take place in isolation; it is a process leading to a goal. While some assessments involve determination of value or worth, a more useful definition of assessment for our purposes would be *the process of collecting information to be used as the basis for informed decisions by the assessor or by those to whom results are communicated*. In Chapter 1 we saw that assessment was the earliest identifying function of clinical psychology and is still a mainstay of the field. However, it is important to understand that the process of assessment is not used only by clinicians; almost everyone engages in some type of assessment at one time or another.

Decisions relating to everyday life are guided by an (often unrecognized) assess-ment process paralleling that associated with clinical psychology. We meet other people and get to know them firsthand. The data we collect about their background, attitudes, behaviors, and peculiar characteristics are then processed and interpreted in light of our own experience and frame of reference. Impressions emerge that guide our social decisions; when given a choice, we seek out certain individuals and avoid others.

When accurate social assessment data are processed efficiently, beneficial decisions result. For example, we correctly "see through" a person's tough talk to appreciate other, rarely revealed aspects of his or her behavior. Individuals who do this regularly are described as "good judges of character" and become valued sources of opinion and advice.

However, social-decision errors often oc-cur because of problems in data collection, processing, or both. It is easy to jump to false conclusions about another person on the basis of inadequate information ("As soon as he said he hated ballet, I knew I wasn't going to like him"), unrepresentative behavior (someone in a foul mood seldom leaves a good impression), stereotypes ("Her accent really turned me off"), and personal biases ("I love people who wear sweaters like that!"). These and other sources of error make the collecting of information that will guide decisions about other people a hazardous process.

The same problem is true of assessment in clinical psychology. Even though the clinician may have access to more systematic assessment information than is normally available to nonprofessionals, the task of forming a clear and accurate understanding of other people is a difficult challenge. That challenge is complicated by the fact that the consequences of errors in clinical assessment can be more dramatic and enduring than buying the wrong car or spending an evening with a clod.

This chapter provides an overview of how the clinical psychologist, as a human being who is not posssessed of special powers of perception and judgment and who is susceptible to the same data collection and processing errors that plague other human beings, has attempted to meet the challenge of assessment.

COMPONENTS OF THE CLINICAL ASSESSMENT PROCESS

Four interrelated components of the clinical assessment process are illustrated in Figure 3-1. Each component involves issues we will

have to confront in order to comprehend the process as a whole. With respect to the planning and data collection segments, for example, one might ask how much information about a person is enough, which kinds of data are the most valuable, how inaccurate information can be detected and eliminated, and where information should be sought. The data-processing phase raises questions such as: How does the clinician go about integrating available data? Is the assessor able to remain unbiased? Could a computer handle assessment data more competently than a human being? Consideration of the fourth assessment segment leads to other inquiries: Who uses the results and for what purposes? What is the impact of assessment on the lives of those assessed? Are people protected from misuse or abuse of assessment information?

We will examine these and many other issues of clinical assessment in subsequent sections.

Planning for Assessment

McReynolds (1975) points out that two related questions must be answered before clinical assessment can begin: (1) What do we want to know? (2) How should we go about learning it? A reply to the first question is dictated by what one believes are important human variables; it also shapes the answer to the second question.

The world view that has guided most clinical assessment in Western civilization emphasizes the importance of variables that operate *within* or *immediately around* the individual being assessed. As we saw in Chapter 2, this orientation toward the individual takes many forms. Personality dynamics and

FIGURE 3-1. A schematic view of the clinical assessment process.

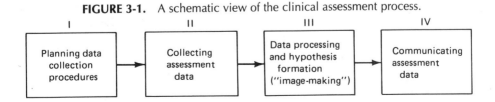

BOX 3-1   Levels of assessment and some representative data from each

Assessment Level	Type of Data
1. Somatic	Blood type, RH factor, autonomic stress response pattern, kidney and liver function, genetic characteristics, basal metabolism, visual acuity, diseases
2. Physical	Height; weight; sex; eye color; hair color; body type, number of limbs, fingers, and toes
3. Demographic	Name, age, address, telephone number, occupation, education, income, marital status, number of children
4. Overt behavioral	Reading speed, eye-hand coordination, response to personality test items, frequency of arguments with other people, conversational skill, interpersonal assertiveness, occupational competence, smoking habits
5. Cognitive/intellectual	Response to intelligence test items, reports on thoughts, performance on tests of information processing or cognitive complexity, response to tests of reality perception and structuring
6. Emotional/affective	Reports of feelings, responses to tests measuring mood states, physiological responsiveness
7. Environmental	Location and characteristics of housing; number and description of cohabitants; job requirements and characteristics; physical and behavioral characteristics of family, friends, and co-workers; nature of specific cultural or subcultural standards and traditions; general economic conditions; geographical location

traits, learning history and current environmental factors, as well as perceptions of self and reality are each accorded varying emphasis from one clinician to the next. However, regardless of specifics, modern clinical assessment seeks to learn things about people *by focusing on them directly, mainly through the use of interviews, tests, observations, and life records.*[1]

The notion that clinical assessment focuses directly on individuals through certain data sources provides the clinician with only the most general guidelines. The particulars of what to look for and what tools to use can still vary enormously and make the planning, organization, and implementation of an efficient and useful assessment strategy a very big challenge.

To illustrate the problem, consider the sheer *number* of things that can be asked about a single person. The list might begin with things like age, sex, height, and weight, and go on endlessly to include bank balance, favorite food, and hat size. Assessment questions can also tap several interrelated *levels*, ranging from physiological functioning to relations with family and other social systems. The most commonly identified levels are listed in Box 3-1, along with a few examples of data associated with each.

The diversity of assessment data means that we can never learn all there is to know about another person. Even if total knowledge were possible, it would not be a practical goal for the clinician. An attempt to explore every level of assessment for a given client would turn up a lot of important information, but the process would be extremely expensive and time-consuming. It would also reveal much that is trivial, redundant, outdated, or irrelevant.

---

[1] Life records include various kinds of personal documents (e.g., diaries and letters), archival and "trace" data (e.g., college transcripts), and other environmental and achievement measures (e.g., honors or awards).

Making Assessment Choices. The clinician must decide (1) how much attention should be devoted to each assessment level, (2) what questions to ask at each level, and (3) what particular assessment techniques to employ.

The theoretical model adopted by each clinician plays a large role in such choices since, as noted in Chapter 2, the dynamically oriented methods favored by an orthodox Freudian will differ substantially from the functional-analytic techniques emphasized by a strict Skinnerian. The clinician's familiarity with relevant research also shapes the assessment strategy. Studies of the relative value of interviews, tests, observations, and life records can be helpful guides which, along with research on the *reliability* and *validity* of these procedures, can make the clinician's planning task more empirically oriented.

These concepts are important enough to merit a brief explanation. *Reliability* refers to *consistency* in assessment data. It can be evaluated in several ways. If the results of repeated measurements of the same client are very similar, the assessment procedures are said to have high *test-retest reliability*. Another way to evaluate reliability is to examine internal consistency. If one part of an assessment method provides evidence similar to that coming from other parts, the method is said to be *internally consistent*. This dimension is sometimes called *split-half reliability*. The third way to evaluate the reliability of an assessment is to compare results of more than one version of it. If two editions of the same test yield equivalent results, that test is said to have high *parallel-form reliability*. Finally, if different clinicians come up with similar data after using a particular assessment system to diagnose, rate, or observe a particular client, that system is described as having high *interrater reliability*.

The *validity* of assessment methods reflects the degree to which they measure what they are supposed to measure. Like reliability, validity can be evaluated in several ways. For example, if an assessment de-

vice measures all aspects of its target, it is said to have high *content validity*. An intelligence test which measures only memory would be low on this dimension. If a test is capable of forecasting accurately something about a client (e.g., suicide attempts or college grades), that assessment has high *predictive validity*. When two assessment devices are found to be measuring the same thing, they are said to have *concurrent validity*.

Finally, there is the concept of *construct validity* (Cronbach & Meehl, 1955). To oversimplify somewhat, an assessment has construct validity when its results are shown to be systematically related to the "thing" or construct it is supposed to be measuring. Construct validity is studied when a psychologist is interested in determining whether some measure yields results that a theory about an underlying trait indicates it should yield. For example, scores on a measure of anxiety should increase under circumstances thought to increase anxiety (e.g., facing major surgery). If no change occurs, the measure's construct validity would be suspect. A single observation of this type is too limited to establish construct validity; a more elaborate set of operations in a series of experiments is required (Campbell & Fiske, 1959).

To summarize the difference between reliability and validity, consider a situation in which fifty people use their eyes to assess the sex of a female impersonator. All fifty observers might agree that the person in question is a female, but they would all be wrong. Their observations would thus be *reliable* but *invalid* because they were not accurately measuring gender.

The concepts of reliability and validity have been integrated under a broader concept called *generalizability* (Cronbach, Gleser, Nanda & Rajaratnam, 1972). Within this framework, an assessment instrument is evaluated in terms of how well its results generalize over certain conditions. Thus, instead of saying that a device has high test-retest reliability, one says that its data generalize over time. Generalizability theory and its use of analysis of variance procedures have played an increasingly important role in the evaluation of clinical assessment methods (Mitchell, 1979).

To return to the topic of planning, clinicians are influenced not only by the reliability and validity of available tools, but also by personal preferences and training experiences. A clinical psychologist may never administer a particular test simply because its use was not included in his or her graduate training program. Similarly, some clinicians rely on a specific assessment technique because their professors at graduate school were enthusiastic about it. Those who find certain measurement tactics tedious or unrewarding will seek answers to assessment questions through other procedures with which they are more comfortable.

The clinician's assessment strategy is further guided by what in electronic information theory has been called the "bandwidth-fidelity" problem (Shannon & Weaver, 1949). Just as greater bandwidth is associated with lower fidelity, the more extensively one explores a client's behavior, the less intensive each aspect of that exploration becomes (Cronbach & Gleser, 1965). In an interview, for example, the clinician could spend three hours trying to cover an extensive outline, but the result would probably be superficial information about a wide range of topics. It works the other way, too. The interviewer could use the same three hours to explore the client's relationship with parents. At the end of the interview, a lot of detailed information would be available about one part of the client's life, but there might be few data about other parts. Cronbach and Gleser (1965) have referred to the *breadth* of an assessment device as its *bandwidth* and the *intensity* or exhaustiveness of the measure as its *fidelity*. Increasing the bandwidth of an assessment strategy will be accompanied by a decrease in fidelity, while increasing fidelity narrows the bandwidth.

A significant problem in assessment planning is to choose a package of measures that will allow both bandwidth and fidelity to be as high as possible. This choice is guided by the amount of time and resources available and also by the goal of the assessment. Goals have an enormous impact on assessment planning, since the questions, levels of inquiry, and techniques relevant for the problem of, say, selecting IBM executives would differ substantially from those regarding detection of brain damage in a four-year-old child. Accordingly, the major classes of assessment goals deserve some attention.

The Goals of Clinical Assessment. The specific aims of assessment are quite heterogeneous, but almost all of them can be placed in one of three general categories: *classification, description,* and *prediction.* Each of these goals may be sought in assessment focused on one individual or as part of projects in which large groups of subjects are assessed.

1 Classification. After clinical psychologists began working with adults, they came under the influence of medical personnel, particularly psychiatrists. This meant that clinical psychologists' assessment skills were often used for diagnostic classification.[2] Assignment of psychiatric patients to the proper category in the American Psychiatric Association's diagnostic system was seen as just as important as accurate diagnosis of physical illness because this would ensure proper treatment of disturbed individuals.

Clinicians' preoccupation with assessment for the purpose of diagnostic classification during the late 1930s and early 1940s was evident in their day-to-day work with individual clients and in the kind of research they conducted. During this period, numerous studies were designed to relate responses on instruments like the Rorschach inkblot test to membership in certain diagnostic classes. Many clinical psychologists were not comfortable with this search for specific indicators (called *pathognomonic signs*) of clinical conditions, because they

---

[2] This is also called *psychodiagnosis, differential diagnosis,* or *diagnostic labeling.*

felt that it oversimplified assessment in ways that could result in errors (e.g., Klopfer & Kelley, 1942). Nevertheless, the goal of diagnostic classification was prominent in clinical research and practice during the 1940s and continues to be a reason why some clinicians do assessment today, especially if they work in psychiatric or other medically oriented settings. Peterson (1968, p. 32) described the situation as follows:

The real reason many clinicians conduct psychological examinations is that someone expects it of them. All too frequently, they administer and interpret Rorschachs, code MMPI's, and prepare reports for no clear reason beyond the scheduled expectation of a staff conference, the knowledge that they are going to be asked what "the psychologicals look like," and prescience of an embarrassed silence if they have nothing to say. The diagnosis has to be written into the record, and since someone in charge may ask for an opinion, the [psychologist] feels obliged to have one ready, with some kind of . . . data to support it.

2 Description. As clinical psychology developed a postwar identity independent of psychiatry, changes in assessment goals began to appear. "Blind" administration and interpretation of a few popular psychological tests to diagnose clients became increasingly distasteful to clinicians who were interested in conducting broader assessments that produced a fuller understanding and more elaborate description of the client (see, e.g., Thorne, 1948; Watson, 1951).[3]

The desire to go beyond diagnosis to seek a wider view was based partly on clinical psychology's burgeoning self-confidence, but it was also due to the conviction that people cannot be understood simply on the basis of a short interview or a Rorschach test. It became clear that more information about people was necessary if understanding was

to result. In addition, interest in the content of behavior was supplemented by a concern for its social, cultural, and physical context. The result was a movement by clinical psychologists toward assessment that described *person-environment interactions.* This movement got its impetus in the 1930s and 1940s from the pioneering work of Henry Murray at the Harvard Psychological Clinic and David Rapaport at the Menninger Clinic. These men and their colleagues developed extensive batteries of interviews, tests, and observations designed to comprehensively assess "normal" people as well as those with psychological problems (Murray, 1938; Rapaport, Gill & Schafer, 1945, 1946) and to take into account the external situational context of behavior as well as its internal determinants (Wiggins, 1973).

The desirability of description as opposed to classification as an assessment goal was increased by the disturbing results of research conducted in the 1950s on the reliability and validity of the American Psychiatric Association's first diagnostic classification system (see Box 3-2). These studies raised serious questions about the accuracy and meaning of diagnostic labels, suggesting that labels often had little effect on how clients were treated (see, e.g., Ash, 1949; Dailey, 1953; Little & Shneidman, 1959; Schmidt & Fonda, 1956; Ullmann & Hunrichs, 1958). Further, acceptance of the medical/psychodynamic model on which diagnosis was based began to wane in the 1960s as alternative phenomenological and behavioral models gained strength and as the stigma associated with being labeled was more clearly recognized (Goffman, 1961; Laing, 1967; Scheff, 1966; Szasz, 1960).

The rise of descriptive assessment prompted many clinicians to approach classification in less psychiatric ways. The result has been proposals for classification systems that assign individuals to descriptive categories on the basis of assessment of factors such as motivation, intrapsychic functions, openness to therapy, test responses, potential for mental health, conditionability, sub-

[3] Clinical psychologists were not alone in their recognition of the limited value of diagnostic labels. Adolf Meyer, one of America's most prominent psychiatrists of the early twentieth century, is reported to have remarked, "We understand this case; we don't need any diagnosis" (Watson, 1951, p. 22).

jective experience, relationship patterns, needs, functional relationships between behavior and the environment, behavioral excesses and deficits, and other factors (see Adams, Doster & Calhoun, 1977; Begelman, 1976; Borofsky, 1974; Goldfried & Davison, 1976; Mahrer, 1970; McLemore & Benjamin, 1979; and Tryon, 1976, for examples of classification systems that represent psychodynamic, phenomenological, and behavioral points of view). As Box 3-2 indicates, the official diagnostic system itself

---

BOX 3-2 Diagnostic classification

In the United States, psychiatric diagnosis is conducted in line with the American Psychiatric Association's *Diagnostic and Statistical Manual of Mental Disorders*. The first version of this system (DSM-I) appeared in 1952. A revision (DSM-II), which made the system more like the World Health Organization's International Classification of Diseases, was published in 1968 and remained in use until 1980, when DSM-III was introduced.

DSM-III attempted to remedy many of the problems that plagued its predecessors. Chief among these difficulties were the lack of a single "organizing" principle for assigning diagnoses, vague definitions of disorders that lowered reliability and validity of the system, and failure to consider background factors such as medical problems and psychosocial stress that could affect psychological disorders. Three of the most important innovations in DSM-III, each a response to the above criticisms, are summarized below.

1. DSM-III diagnoses are made by referring to specific, clearly defined criteria that must be present in order for a disorder to be classified. The use of *operational* criteria was intended to improve the reliability and validity of DSM-III, and there is evidence that this aim has been at least partially accomplished (American Psychiatric Association 1980; see Eysenck, Wakefield, & Friedman, 1983, for a review of validity studies). To illustrate the operational approach, consider the example of a diagnosis of *post-traumatic stress disorder* that requires all of the following: a) existence of a recognizable stressor, b) at least one of three specified behaviors indicating reexperiencing of the trauma, c) at least one

of three specified behaviors indicating "numbing of responsiveness to or reduced involvement with the world" some time after the trauma, and d) at least two of the following symptoms: hyperalertness, sleep disturbance, guilt about surviving the trauma, memory or concentration problems, avoidance of activities that recall the trauma, and intensification of symptoms by exposure to events that symbolize the original trauma.

2. The authors of DSM-III formulated the disorders in a *descriptive* as opposed to a theoretical or etiological manner. By avoiding theoretical formulations of disorders, DSM-III tries to eliminate disagreements that might arise between diagnosticians who hold different views on a disorder's etiology. DSM-III is more inclusive than earlier versions; it includes 265 categories compared to 108 in DSM-I and 182 in DSM-II. Since one criterion for deciding to include a condition in DSM-III was whether clinicians encountered the problem in their practice, many mild "disorders" such as "tobacco dependence" are included.

3. A major advantage of DSM-III is its *multiaxial classification,* in which the client is described along five axes or dimensions. Multiaxial classification gives information relevant to treatment, educates clinicians about factors that exacerbate mental disorders, and facilitates research (Sprock & Blashfield, 1983).

Axis 1 contains the major mental disorders; Axis 2 includes personality disorders and specific developmental disorders; Axis 3 lists physical disorders and conditions. A client can be diagnosed on one, two, or all three of these axes at the same time. Axis 4 allows rating of the severity of the psychosocial stressors that have contributed to the disorder, and Axis 5 asks for a rating of the highest level of adaptive functioning the client has achieved in the past year.

The diagnosis of a patient using DSM-III might take the following form:

Axis 1	Clinical syndrome	Schizophrenic disorder, paranoid type (295.3)
Axis 2	Personality disorders and specific developmental disorders	Borderline personality disorder (301.83)
Axis 3	Physical disorders and conditions	No diagnosis
Axis 4	Severity of psychosocial stressors	Severe (5)
Axis 5	Highest level of adaptive functioning past year	Very poor (6)

Despite its improvement over earlier versions, DSM-III has been criticized on several grounds, including the fact that many diagnostic criteria are still vaguely defined, that some of the axes (particularly 2, 4, and 5) have measurement deficiencies, that too little emphasis was placed on the construct validity of DSM-III diagnoses, and that biases are still present in DSM-III criteria (for extensive criticisms of DSM-III, see Frances, 1980; Kaplan, 1983; Schact & Nathan, 1977; Eysenck, Wakefield & Friedman, 1983; Widiger & Kelso, 1983; Zubin, 1978). Regardless of these criticisms, DSM-III will continue to be widely used; no alternative system rivals its level of acceptance among clinicians and policy makers. Expect a new edition, DSM-IV, sometime after 1990.

has moved toward a more descriptive approach.

Description-oriented assessment makes it easier for the clinician to pay attention to clients' assets and adaptive functions as well as to weaknesses and problems. Descriptive assessment data are used to provide pretreatment measures of clients' behavior, to guide treatment planning, and to evaluate changes in behavior after treatment. They also are of value in research in clinical psychology. For example, in an investigation of the relative value of two treatments for depression, assessments that *describe* clients' posttreatment behaviors (e.g., job absenteeism, time spent alone, self-reports of sadness, and scores on tests of depression) would be of greater value than those that concentrate on a label (e.g., "depressive" versus "nondepressive"). Assessment aimed at description is also used in research on the development of new measurement instruments. The value of a specialized interview technique, an innovative test, or a novel observational procedure is often determined by cross-checking its findings with those of more established descriptive tools.

3   Prediction. The third major goal of clinical assessment is to make predictions about human behavior. Will client X be likely to attempt suicide? Is client Y going to harm others if released from an institution? Questions of this kind constitute a severe test of clinical assessment, both because accurate prediction of what a given individual will do is extremely difficult and because the consequences of error can be socially and personally disastrous (see Box 3-3).

Prediction may be concerned with dangerous behavior as described in Box 3-3 or may be aimed at less dramatic kinds of predictions involving selection of individuals who must meet some future performance standard. Instruments such as the Scholastic Aptitude Test (SAT) and the Graduate Record Examination (GRE) provide familiar examples of predictive assessment. Similar approaches have been adopted by business,

BOX 3-3   Measuring the accuracy of clinical predictions

The bottom-line question for clinical predictions is "how accurate are they?" An answer to this question requires that clinicians or researchers keep track of the predictions they make for a group of people and then later check the outcome for each person to see if the prediction was a "hit" or a "miss."

Psychologists are often called on to predict two types of dangerous behavior of great societal concern—suicide and homicide. The question frequently takes the form, "Is this person a danger to himself or to others?" If clinicians are forced to make a yes or no reply (as they often are) and if we dichotomize the ultimate outcome for the person into "behaved dangerously-did not behave dangerously," then there are four possible results for the prediction. Take the example of predicting behavior dangerous to others. The clinician can predict the person will act dangerously and (s)he does so (this is a *true positive*) or the clinician can predict the person won't act dangerously and (s)he does not do so (*true negative*). If the clinician predicts the person won't act dangerously and (s)he does so, a *false negative* has been committed; when the clinician predicts dangerous behavior will occur but the person commits no dangerous act, a *false positive* has been made.

Psychologists find it difficult to predict future dangerous behavior very accurately (Monahan, 1981). One reason for this problem is that the *base rate* or frequency with which dangerous acts are committed in any group of people is very low. When base rates for a behavior are either very low

or very high, prediction of that behavior will involve many errors (Meehl & Rosen, 1955). The following example shows why this is so.

Assume that a clinician is 80 percent accurate in predicting homicidal behavior. Further assume that the base rate for homicide in the population the clinician examines is 10 murders per 10,000 persons. As indicated in the table below, the clinician would correctly predict 8 of the 10 murders. However, these 8 true positives would be distributed among 1998 false positives where the clinician incorrectly predicted a homicide would occur. Thus, of the 2006 persons predicted to be homicidal, 99.6 would be incorrectly classified. On the other hand, if the clinician "went with the low base rate" and predicted that no one would commit a homicide, (s)he would be 99.9 percent correct. However, all the errors would be false negatives, and society usually believes this type of mistake (i.e., murderers predicted to be safe) to be more serious than false positives. When base rates are closer to fifty-fifty for a behavior's occurrence, clinical predictions have a better chance of improving over predictions founded solely on the base rates.

CLINICIAN'S PREDICTION	ULTIMATE OUTCOME	
	Homicide	*No Homocide*
Homicide	8 (True positives)	1,998 (False positives)
No homicide	2 (False negatives)	7,992 (True negatives)

industry, and the military to guide selection of their personnel.

The assessment goals of description and prediction show their greatest overlap with respect to selection. Descriptive assessment data often constitute part of the information

from which predictions and selections are made. A classic example of this was Henry Murray's descriptive assessment approach (a combination of specialized tests, interviews, and observations) to select men for work as spies, saboteurs, and other behind-enemy-lines work during World War II (Office of Strategic Services, 1948). Along with a staff of other psychologists, Murray set up a comprehensive assessment program that took each man from one to three days to complete and which measured everything from intelligence to stress tolerance to ability at planning murder (see Chapter 6).

This hybrid assessment goal of "description for prediction for selection" has continued in a variety of large-scale postwar screening programs. Some of these were focused on improving candidate selection for civilian and military jobs (e.g., Institute of Personality Assessment and Research 1970) or for graduate training in clinical psychology and psychiatry (e.g., Holt & Luborsky, 1958; Kelly & Fiske, 1951), but perhaps the best-known descendant of the approach was the elaborate program for selecting Peace Corps volunteers (Colmen, Kaplan & Boulger, 1964). Because these assessment programs influence socially important decisions affecting large numbers of people, they must be evaluated not only for their predictive validity, but also for their impact on the persons assessed and on the organizations in which they are used. One must be concerned with (1) the number of correct selections prompted by particular assessment procedures; (2) the cost of correct decisions in terms of money, time, and effort; and (3) the costs of selection errors (i.e., choosing inappropriate candidates or rejecting appropriate ones).

The Case Study Guide. The clinician's ultimate choice of particular questions and inquiry levels provides an outline of the assessment task's scope. Ideally, this outline is both broad enough to give a general picture of the client on the basis of information from each of the levels listed in Box 3-1 and focused enough to allow intensive coverage of levels and questions relevant to the specific purpose of assessment.

The conceptual outline for a clinician's assessment task sometimes takes the form of a *case study guide.* The idea for such an outline comes to psychology from medicine and psychiatry (Bolgar, 1965), but it has been adopted as a means of organizing assessment by many clinicians. A major advantage of the case study approach is its flexibility. Case study outlines can be tied to a theoretical model, or they can be open and eclectic.

One of the most comprehensive and theoretically neutral examples of a case study outline was composed by Sundberg, Taplin, and Tyler (1983). It is organized for interview procedures with adults, but much of the information could also apply to children and could be obtained through life records, tests, or observation. This outline is presented in Box 3-4. Although sufficiently problem-oriented to be used in settings where persons are seeking psychological help, it also allows the assessor to consider broader and less problematic aspects of a client's life.

Korchin (1976) provides a more psychodynamically oriented case study outline. It (1) refers to the person being assessed as the "patient" rather than the "client"; (2) includes questions about unconscious motives, feelings, impulses, and fantasies; (3) explores ego functions, identification, and developmental tasks; and (4) assesses personality dynamics and structure.

Representatives of the behavioral approach to clinical psychology have also adopted case study formats. Box 3-5 contains a summary of one of the most comprehensive examples by Kanfer and Saslow (1969).

Later, we shall review specific characteristics of the behavioral approach to assessment. For now, notice that the Kanfer and Saslow outline differs in two important respects from the one preceding it. First, it focuses on *analysis* of the relationship between the client's environment and the client's behavior. Specific antecedents, maintenance factors, and consequences of behavior are sought. Second, the outline is tied to future attempts at behavior change.

BOX 3-4 Outline for a case history interview

1. *Identifying data,* including name, sex, occupation, income (of self or family), marital status, address, date and place of birth, religion, education, cultural identity.
2. *Reason for coming* to the agency, expectations for service.
3. *Present and recent situation,* including dwelling place, principal settings, daily round of activities, number and kind of life changes over several months, impending changes.
4. *Family constellation* (family of orientation) including descriptions of parents, siblings, other significant family figures, and respondent's role growing up.
5. *Early recollections,* descriptions of earliest clear happenings and the situation surrounding them.
6. *Birth and development,* including age of walking and talking, problems compared with other children, view of effects of early experiences.
7. *Health and physical condition,* including childhood and later diseases and injuries, current prescribed medications, current use of unprescribed drugs, cigarettes, or alcohol, comparison of own body with others, habits of eating and exercising.
8. *Education and training,* including subjects of special interest and achievement, out-of-school learning, areas of difficulty and pride, any cultural problems.
9. *Work record,* including reasons for changing jobs, attitudes toward work.
10. *Recreation, interests, and pleasures,* including volunteer work, reading, respondent's view of adequacy of self-expression and pleasures.
11. *Sexual development,* covering first awareness, kinds of sexual activities, and a view of adequacy of current sexual expressions.
12. *Marital and family data,* covering major events and what led to them, and comparison of present family with family of origin, ethnic or cultural factors.
13. *Social supports, communication network, and social interests,* including people talked with most frequently, people available for various kinds of help, amount and quality of interactions, sense of contribution to others and interest in community.
14. *Self-description,* including strengths, weaknesses, ability to use imagery, creativity, values, and ideals.
15. *Choices and turning points in life,* a review of the respondent's most important decisions and changes, including the single most important happening.
16. *Personal goals and view of the future,* including what the subject would like to see happen next year and in five or ten years, and what is necessary for these events to happen, realism in time orientation, ability to set priorities.
17. Any further material the respondent may see as omitted from the history.

(From N. D. Sundberg (1977), *Assessment of Persons,* pp. 97–98. Reprinted by permission of Prentice-Hall, Inc., Englewood Cliffs, New Jersey.

Because phenomenologically oriented psychologists deemphasize elaborate assessment procedures, case study outlines that reflect the phenomenological model of clinical psychology have not appeared (however, see Fischer, 1985, for a thorough account of how a phenomenologist approaches psychological assessment).

Collecting Assessment Data

So far we have looked at ways in which clinicians answer the first of the primary assessment questions raised by McReynolds (1975): "What do we want to know?" Our next step is to consider his second question: "How should we go about learning it?"

BOX 3-5 Kanfer and Saslow's (1969) case study outline *Behavioral Med.*

I. Initial analysis of the problem situation
   A. Behavioral excesses
   B. Behavioral deficits
   C. Behavioral assets
II. Clarification of the problem situation
   A. Should problematic behaviors be assigned to category IA or IB?
   B. Persons or groups who object to or support these behaviors
   C. Consequences of the problem for the patient and for significant others
   D. Conditions under which problematic behaviors occur
   E. Consequences of no change in problematic behaviors
   F. Nature of any new problems which would occur if problems were eliminated
   G. Sources of information other than patient
III. Motivational analysis
   A. Patient's ranking of various incentives or reinforcing events in terms of importance
   B. Frequency of access to various reinforcers
   C. Specific conditions under which reinforcers arouse goal-directed behaviors
   D. Do actions aimed at reaching goals correspond to verbal statements?
   E. Persons or groups exerting most effective and widespread control over current behavior
   F. Degree to which patient relates attainment of reinforcers to luck versus his or her own behavior
   G. Major adverse stimuli
   H. Reinforcing events which can be utilized for facilitating elimination of problematic behaviors
IV. Developmental analysis
   A. Biological changes
   B. Sociological changes
   C. Behavioral changes

V. Analysis of self-control
   A. In situations in which patient can control problematic behaviors, how is control achieved?
   B. Previous aversive consequences of problematic behaviors (e.g., jail, social ostracism) and their effects on self-control
   C. Degree to which patient avoids situations conducive to problematic behaviors
   D. Correspondence between patient's verbalized degree of self-control and observations by others
   E. Conditions, persons, or reinforcers which tend to change self-control
   F. Degree to which self-controlling behavior can be used in treatment
VI. Analysis of social relationships
   A. Most significant people in patient's environment
   B. Nature of reinforcers relevant in patient's social relationships.
   C. Patient's expectations of others' words and actions
   D. Others' expectations of patient (are these congruent with patient's self-expectations?)
   E. Can significant others participate in treatment? How?
VII. Analysis of the social-cultural-physical environment
   A. Norm in patient's social milieu regarding problematic behaviors
   B. Environmental limitations on access to reinforcement
   C. Aspects of patient's environment where problematic behavior is most apparent, most troublesome, or most accepted
   D. Degree to which milieu regards psychological procedures as appropriate for helping to solve problems

Sources of Assessment Data. Clinical psychologists collect assessment data from four sources: interviews, tests, observations, and life records. In this section we highlight the defining characteristics of these techniques and take note of some of the problems of each. These sketches are designed to serve as previews of the more detailed coverage of interviews, tests, and observations included in the next three chapters.

1 Interviews. Kelly (1958, p. 330) succinctly characterized a straightforward approach to assessment as follows: "If you don't know what is going on in a person's mind, ask him; he may tell you." This simple point lies at the root of why the interview is the most basic and widely employed source of psychological assessment data. It is popular for other reasons as well. For one thing, since the clinician talks with the client in a situation that mimics ordinary social interaction, interviews provide a way of collecting simultaneous samples of a person's verbal and nonverbal behavior. Second, unless the interview is to be tape-recorded, no equipment is required and the procedure is highly "portable"; it can take place almost anywhere. Third, there is no more flexible assessment tool than the interview. Except in cases where structured research limitations prevail, the interviewer is free to adjust the emphasis of inquiry and conversation to those issues that appear most important.

What about the quality of data collected through interviews? Peterson (1968, p. 13) comments that "the interview . . . must not be regarded as the 'truth' about the individual and his environment, but as another form of data whose reliability, validity, and decisional utility must be subjected to the same kinds of scrutiny required for other modes of data collection." Although clients' self-reports of behavior are often remarkably accurate (Hilgard, 1969; Mischel, 1968), interview data may not always be reliable and valid (Walsh, 1967; Yarrow, Campbell & Burton, 1968). It may be influenced or distorted in various ways as a function of (1) characteristics of interviewers and the questions they ask, (2) client characteristics such as memory and willingness to disclose accurate information, and (3) circumstances under which the interview takes place. The interview will be discussed and evaluated in greater detail in Chapter 4.

2 Tests. Like interviews, tests provide a sample of behavior. However, the stimuli to which the client responds on a test are more standardized than in most interviews. A test exposes each client to the same stimuli under the same circumstances. Tests can be easy, economical, and convenient to administer; often, a professional need not even be present. Further, the standardized form in which a test is presented helps eliminate bias in the assessor's inquiries. Responses to most tests can be translated into scores, thus making quantitative summaries of a client's behavior possible.[4] In this way, test data facilitate communication between professionals about a particular client. Finally, test data allow the clinician to compare a client's behavior with that of hundreds or perhaps thousands of other individuals who have already taken the same test. This is helpful in the data-processing stage of assessment.

Assume, for instance, that on a word association test the first thing that pops into a client's mind when the tester says "house" is "pantyhose." If the assessor had never heard this association before, (s)he might interpret it as being indicative of some psychological problem. But if the tester has access to a book containing the associations of 12,000 subjects to the word "house," it may turn out that "pantyhose" is a fairly popular response (it is not, by the way) and thus not worthy of concern.

All these advantages, along with the fact that for many years testing was the main activity for clinical psychologists, have led to the widespread use of tests as assessment de-

---

[4] Certain aspects of interview and observational data can be handled in this way as well, but may involve more cumbersome procedures.

vices. Even though the heyday of psychological testing (1930–1960) has passed, tests are still a significant aspect of assessment (Lubin, Larsen & Matarazzo, 1984; Piotrowski, Sherry & Keller, 1985; Wade & Baker, 1977).

Tests are not magical devices that always reveal the "truth" about people. They must be evaluated in terms of reliability and validity; like other assessment techniques, they are sometimes found wanting in important respects. Anything that is not "standard" about test stimuli, including the tester, the client, or the testing situation, can threaten the psychometric quality of the data obtained. These and other evaluative issues will be dealt with when we focus on tests in Chapter 5.

3 Observations. The old adage "Actions speak louder than words" supports the clinician's desire to supplement self-report measures like interviews or tests with direct observation of a person's behavior in situations of interest. The goal here is to go beyond what a client *says* and find out what the person *does*. A notable example of how observational data can alter the impression left by self-report was given by Wicker (1969, p. 42; see also Dillehay, 1973).

In the 1930's when, according to studies of social distance, there was much anti-Chinese sentiment in the United States, LaPiere (1934) took several extensive automobile trips with a Chinese couple. Unknown to his companions, he took notes of how the travellers were treated, and he kept a list of hotels and restaurants where they were served. Only once were they denied service, and LaPiere judged their treatment to be above average in 40% of the restaurants visited. Later, LaPiere wrote to the 250 hotels and restaurants on his list, asking if they would accept Chinese guests. Over 90% of the 128 proprietors responding indicated they would not serve Chinese, in spite of the fact that all had previously accommodated LaPiere's companions.

Here, observational data provided radically different and perhaps more accurate views of the question of anti-Chinese preju-

dice than did the self-reports. Indeed, observation is considered by many to be the most valid form of clinical assessment because it is so direct and capable of circumventing problems of memory, motivation, response style, and situational bias that can reduce the value of interviews and tests. A smoker's self-report that five cigarettes were smoked in one day may be biased by ability to recall, a desire to appear moderate, or feelings about the assessor. An actual count of smoking frequency recorded by an observer would reflect none of these factors.

A second advantage of observation is its *relevance* to behaviors of greatest interest. A child's aggressiveness, for example, can be observed as it occurs in recess, where the problem has been most acute. This illustrates a related benefit of observation: Behavior is assessed in its social and situational context rather than in the abstract. In a mental hospital, for example, observation of a long-term resident may reveal that the patient acts depressed only after meals. This information may be more valuable to a therapist than an affirmative response to the query, "Are you ever depressed?"

Finally, observations allow for description of behavior in highly specific terms and in great detail. For example, a person's sexual arousal in response to particular stimuli might be defined in terms of penile volume or vaginal blood flow, both of which can be measured with specially designed apparatus. Similarly psychotic behavior can be observed by recording the frequency of explicitly defined behaviors such as "strikes own body," "speaks incoherently," or "kisses water fountain."

In spite of its advantages, observational assessment is not problem-free. The degree to which one can rely on information from this source varies considerably, since the reliability and validity of observational data can be threatened by observer error or bias, inadvertent observer influence on the behavior under observation, and specific situational factors. These problems will be discussed in Chapter 6.

4 Life records. As people pass through life, they leave a trail of evidence of their behavior in many forms, including school, work, police, and medical records; credit ratings; letters; photographs; awards; income tax returns; diaries; and creative products like paintings or sculpture. There is much that can be learned about a person through such life records, and because this approach to assessment does not require the client to make any *new* responses (as do interviews, tests, and observations), there is little chance that memory, motivation, response style, or situational factors can distort the data obtained. Thus, a ten-minute review of a person's high school transcript may provide more specific and accurate academic information than a thirty-minute interview asking questions like "How did you do in school?" Similarly, reading diaries written during significant periods in a client's life can reveal "on-the-spot" feelings, ideas, behaviors, and situational details that might be lost or distorted by imperfect recall.

Life records are useful because they provide an inexpensive way of broadening one's working image of a client. They can summarize a great deal about a person's behavior over a long period of time and across a range of situations. Life records act like a wide-angle camera lens by bringing into view that which might otherwise be missed. Wide-angle lenses produce distortion, however; and records can do the same. For one thing, they tend to be superficial. Records may show that a person was divorced at age eighteen, but say nothing of why or how the person felt about it. Records may be valuable, but are not usually complete. These and other shortcomings of life records will be discussed in Chapter 6.

The Value of Multiple Assessment Sources. Clinical psychologists seldom rely on a single source of assessment data for their working image of a client, partly because there is a multiplicity of data available within each of the four assessment sources

we have described. For example, it is virtually impossible not to observe a person's behavior in the course of an interview or a testing session; some interview data may come out of a client's responses to certain tests.

The availability of multiple channels of assessment provides distinct advantages for the clinician (Nay, 1979). To begin with, lies or distortions of fact can be cross-checked. The interviewer who is told by a mental hospital resident that he or she has been there "about six months" may discover via hospital records that the correct figure is twenty years. Indeed, the whole story of a client's problems is not clear until multiple assessment has been completed. Nietzel and Bernstein (1976) showed that college students who described themselves as socially unassertive were capable of strong assertive responses under the right conditions. In such cases, multiple assessment helps separate those individuals who *cannot* engage in certain behaviors from those who *do not* engage in them.

Another benefit of multiple assessment appears when the clinician looks at the effects of a psychological intervention. Suppose a married couple comes to a therapist because they are considering divorce. If "marital happiness" based on interview data were the only measure employed, the couple's divorce following three months of clinical sessions would indicate that the marital problem was worsened by treatment. Other assessments, including observations, third-person reports, and life records might show, however, that one or both members of the former couple find their divorced status liberating as they begin to develop new interests and abilities. These satisfactions might not be reported to the therapist in an interview because the clients feel guilt over divorce, because fear of the future seems to be a more appropriate topic for a clinical session, or for other reasons.

Of course, multiple assessment can reveal the opposite situation as well. After a therapist helps a young man to stand up for his rights, he may report improved self-esteem and comfort in social situations. These interview data might not reveal the fact that the client has now become aggressive in his relations with others and that, in the long run, he is likely to suffer socially. Future social problems could be avoided by detecting inappropriate behavior through observational assessment.

Processing Assessment Data

Once assessment data have been collected, the clinician must determine what those data mean. If the information is to be useful in reaching the goals of assessment, it will have to be transformed from raw form into interpretations and conclusions. For example, knowing that a young child cries at high intensities for precise lengths of time each evening when placed in its crib constitutes valuable assessment data. So does the observation that after the crying continues for varying periods, someone enters the baby's room to provide comfort. However, these data mean little in psychological terms until they are translated into statements like those contained in Box 3-6. This crucial part of assessment is often referred to as data *processing*. As Levy (1963, p. 8) put it: "Events . . . do not carry with them their own interpretation. They are innocent of any meaning except insofar as we impose it on them."

The processing task is a formidable one because a degree of *inference* is involved, and inference requires a leap from known data to what is assumed on the basis of those data. In general, as the jump from data to assumption gets longer, inference becomes more vulnerable to error.

Consider this example: A young boy is observed sitting on a lawn, playing with an earthworm. At one point, he cuts the worm in half. It would be easy to infer from this incident that the child was cruel and aggressive and that more serious forms of aggression, perhaps toward other people, will appear in later life. These inferences would be off the mark, however, for "what the observer could not see . . . was what the boy—who happened to have few friends—thought as he cut the worm in half: 'There! Now you will have someone to play with' " (Goldfried & Sprafkin, 1974, p. 305).

Elaborate inference, especially when based upon minimal data, can be dangerous. "The untrained or careless can leap at psychological inferences and end up in an awkward position" (Hoch, 1971, p. 5). The only way to eliminate inference error is to eliminate inference, but doing so would also eliminate the meaning of most assessment data. Indeed, it may be impossible for human beings to avoid making inferences, even in relation to the simplest stimuli. For example, the "raw data" of Figure 3-2 are a series of rectangles that gradually increase

BOX 3-6 Some statements based on observation of a crying child and its mother

1. Crying stops after mother enters room and begins again when she leaves.
2. Mother seems overanxious about her child's welfare.
3. Mother appears to see crying as a crisis situation.
4. Crying is rewarded by mother's attention.
5. Mother's doting attention may be a reaction formation which conceals unconscious hatred.
6. Mother's anxiety is not so much concern for the child but part of the way she feels a good mother should behave.
7. Mother displays neurotic behaviors.
8. The child is likely to become overly dependent upon mother in later life.

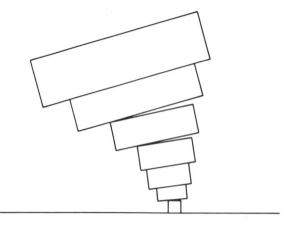

FIGURE 3-2. Can you look at this drawing without inferring anything about it?

in size and angle on the page, and are displaced to the left as one looks from bottom to top. However, it is difficult to avoid *inferring* that the "stack" is about to "fall over," or that the smallest "box" is about to be "crushed."

The main questions to be dealt with in assessment data processing do not include *whether* inferences will be drawn, but center around what *kinds* of inferences to make, *how* clinicians go about making them, how *accurate* they are, and how inference error can be minimized.

Levels and Types of Clinical Inference. Clinical inferences can be characterized in terms of their *goals*, their underlying *models*, and their *levels of abstraction*. That they reflect the assessor's goals is illustrated in Box 3-6 where classification (statement 7), description (statement 1), and prediction (statement 8) are all represented. Inferences also tend to be tied to the assessor's model of clinical psychology as illustrated in Box 3-6 by statements 4, 5, and 6, which reflect the behavioral, psychodynamic, and phenomenological models respectively. Finally, inferences vary in their level of abstraction. Clinicians can make cautious, low-level inferences that do not stray far from the original data (entry 1 of Box 3-6) or can attempt bolder statements that go beyond the "hard" data available but are supported

by the assessor's experience, theoretical model, and intuitive hunches (e.g., Box 3-6, statement 5).

At the lowest inference level, assessment data are taken at face value, as when a test score determines whether a student is admitted to graduate school. At higher inference levels, assessment data are generalized beyond their original limits. Thus, behavior revealed through tests, interviews, observations, and records is thought to be generally characteristic of the person and may be used as the basis for applying trait terms like *anxious, depressed, hostile,* and *charming.*

At the highest inference level, assessment data are processed to form an overall picture of the client. Ideally, the "whole story" of why the person got to be where he or she is at the moment is reconstructed, and the client's problems are viewed in light of this panorama. Inference at this level ventures furthest from the original data, so the clinician depends on experience and a theoretical model to guide the statements and predictions that are made.

Three Views of Assessment Data. The inferences drawn from assessment data depend primarily upon how those data are viewed, that is, what the data are thought to be capable of saying. Clinicians tend to view assessment information in three main ways: as *samples, correlates,* or *signs* (Goodenough,

1949; Wiggins, 1973). For example, consider the following raw assessment data: "A person took sixteen sleeping pills before going to bed at a hotel last night, but was saved after being discovered by a housekeeper and rushed to a hospital."

How can this event be viewed and what inferences would follow from each perspective? The incident could be seen as a *sample* of the client's behavior and the following inferences might result:

1. The client has access to potentially lethal medication.
2. The client did not wish to be saved because no one knew about the suicide attempt before it occurred.
3. Under similar circumstances, the client may attempt suicide again.

Notice that looking at the client's behavior as a sample results in low-level inferences. The pill taking is seen as an *example* of what the client is capable of doing under certain circumstances. No attempt is make to infer *why* the individual tried suicide; more assessment would be required before specific causal statements would be justified.

The same incident could be viewed as a *correlate* of other aspects of the client's life. Even though no further information is available about the client, knowledge gained from similar cases might guide inferences of the following type:

1. The client is likely to be a middle-aged female who is single or divorced and lives alone (this is a common set of characteristics among attempted suicides).
2. The client is or has recently been depressed.
3. The client has little emotional support from family or friends.

Here, higher-level inferences are based upon a combination of (1) known facts about the client's behavior, and (2) the clinician's knowledge of what tends to correlate with that behavior. These inferences go beyond the original data with the support of empirically demonstrated relationships among specific variables such as suicide, age, sex, marital status, and depression. In general, the stronger the known relationships between variables, the more accurate the inferences will be.

This correlate-oriented, or *psychometric,* approach is not tied to any theoretical orientation. As long as they can be quantified, assessment data of any kind (e.g., ego strength scores, reinforcer preferences, personality traits, perceptions of others) can be dealt with as correlates.[5] As such, the psychometric approach to assessment data processing links individual-oriented clinical psychology to the more generalized field of personality theories and research.

Finally, the pill taking may be thought of as a *sign* of other, less obvious things about the client. From such a perspective, the suicide attempt could signal serious problems. A sign-oriented view might result in the following kinds of inferences:

1. The client's aggressive impulses have been turned against the self.
2. The client's behavior reflects intrapsychic conflicts.
3. The pill taking represents an unconscious cry for help.

These statements go beyond the "hard" information in directions suggested by a particular theory of behavior. Assessment data provide the signs, a theory provides their meaning; the relationship between a sign and an inference may stem solely from theoretical speculation.

Models, Views, and Levels. Levels of inference, views of assessment data, and theoretical models are interrelated. When assessment information is viewed primarily as a behavior *sample,* inference level is likely to

---

[5] Wiggins (1973, chap. 10) provides valuable summaries of ways in which the psychometric approach has been used to process assessment data coming from the theories of Freud, Harry Stack Sullivan, Henry Murray, George Kelly, Raymond B. Cattell, and Skinner.

BOX 3-7   Three views of assessment data

Data Seen as	Level of Inference	Underlying Theory	Source of Data	Typical Data-Processing Procedures
Sign	High	Psychoanalytic or phenomenological	Interviews, tests, observations, life records	Informal; based on subjective judgments about assessment data
Sample	Low	Behavioral	Interviews, tests, observations, life records	Formal and informal; based on subjective judgments and functional analysis of client behavior
Correlate	Low to moderate	Various theories	Interviews, tests, observations, life records	Formal; based on statistical analysis of assessment data

be minimal and the guiding model will probably be behavioral. On the other hand, conceptualizing assessment data as *signs* usually results in higher levels of inference and often employs a psychodynamic or phenomenological model of behavior. In between, where assessment data are viewed as *correlates,* inferences are at low to moderate levels, and there is more emphasis on statistical analyses of relationships among variables representing a range of theories.

The primary characteristics of the three views of assessment data we have described are presented in Box 3-7. The right-hand column of Box 3-7 shows that assessment data processing may be based upon formal statistical procedures and/or informal, subjective means. The informal approach usually involves looking at assessment data as signs, while the formal approach typically sees such data as correlates.[6] Both alternatives are rooted in the history of clinical psy-

chology. The informal, subjective, inferential approach is a reflection of Freud and his influence on clinicians' thinking. The formal, objective, statistical approach comes to clinicians through its ties with experimental psychology and through the work of Galton, Cattell, Binet, and other psychometrically oriented pioneers. In the next part of this chapter we shall examine the ways in which clinicians have followed both traditions as they make inferences about clinical assessment data.

The Process of Clinical Inference. The popular image of clinical psychologists is that they are primarily sign-oriented users of the informal approach to clinical inference. Clinicians are often portrayed as astute translators of obscure signs into accurate statements about a person's past, present, or future: a kind of psychological Sherlock Holmes who can tell much from very little.

A typical example of this view appears in a 1949 film called *The Dark Past.* In it, a killer called "Mad Dog" (William Holden) and a gang of fellow prison escapees hold a psychologist, his family and friends hostage in a remote cabin. The psychologist (Lee J. Cobb) saves the day be getting Mad Dog to talk about his life and dreams and by notic-

---

[6] This rule of thumb has many exceptions. Prominent among them is the fact that clinicians often use *informal* procedures with data they see as correlates. As we saw in our attempted suicide case, the psychologist must somehow mentally correlate current information about a client with everything else she or he knows about similar instances. This is a difficult task, as we shall see later.

ing that one of the crook's hands is paralyzed. From these limited data, Cobb is guided by psychoanalytic theory to the correct conclusion: As a child, Mad Dog was responsible for his hated father's death, and now his crippled hand and murderous ways are symptoms of unconscious conflict about it. The hand immediately becomes normal after Mad Dog hears Cobb's interpretation.

CLINICAL INTUITION. To a certain extent, such long-shot inferences have their counterparts in fact. The psychoanalyst Theodore Reik describes a well-known example involving a young woman who was upset about the dissolution of her intimate relationship with a medical doctor:

After a few sentences about the uneventful day, the patient fell into a long silence. She assured me that nothing was in her thoughts. Silence from me. After many minutes she complained about a toothache. She told me that she had been to the dentist yesterday. He had given her an injection and then had pulled a wisdom tooth. The spot was hurting again. New and longer silence. She pointed to my bookcase in the corner and said, "There's a book standing on its head."

Without the slightest hesitation and in a reproachful voice I said, "But why did you not tell me that you had had an abortion?" The patient jumped up and looked at me as if I were a ghost. Nobody knew or could know that her lover, the physician, had performed an abortion on her. . . .(Reik, 1948, pp. 263–264)

Reik (1948) suggests that his correct inference from the data presented by the client (i.e., toothache, the injection by a dentist, the tooth extraction, the pain, the book "on its head") was based partly on an intuitive gift. It has long been supposed that clinical psychologists possess that same gift which, along with their past experience and

their guiding theories, makes them superior at drawing high-level inferences from assessment data. While certain individuals seem better than others at correctly interpreting assessment data, this ability is not universally descriptive of clinicians.[7]

Research contradicts the existence of special inferential capabilities among clinical psychologists. Peterson (1968, p. 105) makes this point forcefully: "The idea that clinicians have or can develop some special kinds of antennae with which they can detect otherwise subliminal interpersonal stimuli and read from these the intrapsychic condition of another person is a myth which ought to be demolished."

When an informal approach to assessment data processing is used, clinical psychologists *as a group* (1) are not significantly better than nonclinicians at making inferences, and (2) do not make inferences that are more accurate than could be obtained through formal, statistical procedures. To illustrate, we shall review some data on the clinician versus nonclinician question and then look at some evidence related to the informal versus statistical issue.

THE CLINICIAN AS INFERENCE EXPERT. A classic example of research on the clinician's alleged special inference capabilities is provided by Goldberg (1959). In his study, various types of judges attempted to infer the presence of organic brain damage from clients' responses to a psychological test widely used for such purposes. Half of the thirty clients suffered organic problems; the other half did not. Test results were judged by (1) four Ph.D. clinical psychologists with four to nine years' experience with the test, (2) ten M.A.-level psychology trainees who had used the test for one to four years, and (3) eight VA hospital secretaries who had no psychology background and no experience in the test. Since the inference to be drawn in this case was simply "organic" or "not organic" (of which there were fifteen cases each), the probability of being correct by chance on any given patient was .50. Only

---

[7] There have been attempts to establish the personal characteristics of "good judges of people" (e.g., Allport, 1961; Taft, 1955), but the attributes suggested (such as emotional adjustment, self-insight, social skill, and intelligence) have not been shown to be essential, nor have clinicians been shown to possess them in inordinately high proportions.

MISS PEACH   By Mell Lazarus

FIGURE 3-3. *Miss Peach* by Mell Lazarus. (Courtesy of Mell Lazarus and
News America Syndicate.)

one of the four psychologists did better than
chance; as shown in Box 3-8, the psychologists were no better than their students
or their secretaries. Other studies of this
type (e.g., Garner & Smith, 1976; Levenberg, 1975) present a basically similar picture.

The image of clinical psychologists as ordinary mortals has also been strengthened
by research on their information-processing
ability. Studies by Kostlan (1954), Sines
(1959), Golden (1964), Oskamp (1965), and
Weiss (1963) suggest that having larger
amounts of assessment information may increase clinicians' *confidence* about inferences,
but it does not necessarily improve their accuracy (see Einhorn & Hogarth, 1978; and
Garb, 1984, for recent reviews of this issue).
This is consistent with the notion that there
are limits to how much data any person can
process and integrate, and that these limits

plague clinicians who must scan vast arrays
of assessment material.

The psychologist may be inordinately impressed with the first few pieces of information available and then pay little attention to
subsequent data (Dailey, 1952; Meehl,
1960). Or the clinician may allow assessment
information coming from certain sources
(e.g., parents' report of a child's behavior) to
outweigh other, contradictory information
(McCoy, 1976). Personal bias can also distort
inferences. The clinician may react differently to males and females, to different age
groups, or to members of certain socioeconomic, racial, or political groups (Abramovitz, Abramovitz, Jackson & Gomes,
1973; Broverman, Broverman, Clarkson,
Rosenkrantz & Vogel, 1970; DiNardo,
1975; Kaplan, 1983; Lee & Temerlin, 1970;
Routh & King, 1972). Theoretical bias may
also alter inference, since adherents to dif-

BOX 3-8   Inference accuracy of three types of judges

Group	N	% Correct	% Exceeding Chance
Psychology staff	4	65	25
Psychology trainees	10	70	60
Secretaries	8	67	62
Total	22	68	54

Source: After Goldberg, 1959.

ferent models are likely to approach their clients with preconceptions about what behaviors to expect and what those behaviors mean (Langer & Abelson, 1974; Shoham-Salomon, 1985).

Further, general folklore and misremembered past experiences can affect clinicians as strongly as anyone else. For example, a form of superstition called *illusory correlation* has been shown to affect clinical inference (Chapman & Chapman, 1967; Golding and Rorer, 1972). Just as one may falsely believe it rains every time she or he washes the car, many clinical psychologists have long believed that the presence of elaborated eyes on tests that involve drawing the human figure is related to paranoid behavior, even though no firm empirical evidence exists for this belief (see, e.g., Fisher & Fisher, 1950). The fact that paranoid tendencies are still inferred from such cues by some clinicians illustrates a type of error to which many people are prone. Other influences that can reduce inference accuracy include the situation in which inferences are made (e.g., school or mental hospital), the effects of fatigue, and the types of clients the clinician usually sees (e.g., Bieri, Atkins, Briar, Leaman, Miller & Tripoldi, 1966; Hunt & Jones, 1962; Thorne, 1972).

Clinical training received in graduate school may provide clinicians with important information and experience, but there is little evidence that it improves their ability to make accurate inferences. Some data suggest that certain aspects of clinical training may *decrease* inferential accuracy by prompting students to see problems where none exist. Soskin (1954) found, for example, that prior to taking a course on interpretation of the Thematic Apperception Test (TAT), beginning graduate students tended to see a well-adjusted person as well-adjusted. After the course, the students inaccurately saw such a client as somewhat troubled.

Although Wiggins (1973, p. 131) concluded that there is "little empirical evidence that justifies the granting of 'expert' status to the clinician on the basis of his training, experience, or information processing ability," he more recently (Wiggins, 1981) has voiced optimism that we now can train clinicians to avoid some of the more common sources of their inferential inaccuracies (see also Arkes, 1981; Koriat, Lichtenstein & Fischhoff, 1980).

There *are* clinicians who, for whatever reasons, appear to be superior to their colleagues and intelligent lay persons in terms of inference accuracy. Is this some stable ability which these clinicians manifest in all cases, or is it more sporadic, depending upon the client, situation, and judgment task involved? The answer is not clear. Some studies have shown greater inferential abilities in certain persons (e.g., Cline & Richards, 1961); other evidence suggests the opposite conclusion (e.g., Crow & Hammond, 1957). The truth may lie somewhere in between; a person's inference ability may be a joint function of general skill as it interacts with situational variables (Bieri, Atkins, Briar, Leaman, Miller & Tripoldi, 1966; Taft, 1955). At this point, psychologists are beginning to prescribe specific training steps that may enable more clinicians to overcome some of the impediments to accurate clinical judgment (Arkes, 1981; Nisbett & Ross, 1980).

INFERENCE BY FORMAL VERSUS INFORMAL PROCEDURES. The image of the clinician as a sign-oriented expert who consistently makes accurate inferences was badly tarnished in the 1950s and 1960s by research on clinical training, experience, and data-processing ability. This sobering body of work was prompted by research on a more general question about clinicians' inference ability. Many investigators wondered whether clinicians' subjective, informal efforts to interpret assessment data as signs or to mentally correlate those data with other facts were more accurate than inferences based upon formal, statistical data processing in which the clinician plays no part at all.

Clinicians have traditionally been divided on the relative merits of clinical (subjective) and statistical (objective) inference procedures. Meehl (1954) notes that those who favor the informal, clinical approach see it as meaningful, organized, rich, deep, and genuine, while its critics characterize it as mystical, vague, unscientific, sloppy, and muddleheaded. Proponents of formal, statistical inference think it is objective, reliable, precise, and empirical; opponents label it artificial, trivial, superficial, and rigid.

The statistical versus clinical data-processing issue is central to how clinicians (1) spend their time, (2) make decisions about clients, (3) shape their research, and (4) conceive of their professional identity (Meehl, 1954). Clinicians who informally interpret assessment data, make recommendations based on their interpretations, and do research on such activities usually do so because they believe that they, or their profession, are good at these things. Thus it came as a shock when, in a 1954 monograph, University of Minnesota psychologist Paul

Meehl reported his review of twenty studies comparing the accuracy of predictions based on informal, clinical procedures and formal, statistical procedures. He found that in all but one case, the accuracy of the statistical approach equaled or surpassed the clinical approach. Later, even the sole exception to this surprising conclusion was called a tie, and, as additional research became available, the superiority of the statistical method of prediction was more firmly established (Meehl, 1957, 1965). Box 3-9 shows the "box scores" and the kinds of variables predicted in studies covered by Meehl's reviews.

Wiggins (1973, p. 183) notes that "the impact of Meehl's review on clinical psychologists was nothing less than devastating." At least eighteen responses to it were published in the years immediately following its appearance, and most of them were critical. Detractors pointed out methodological defects in some of the studies that could have biased results in favor of statistical data-processing procedures. Some (McArthur, 1956)

BOX 3-9 Summary of outcomes of studies comparing clinical versus statistical predictive inference

| | Number of Studies Reviewed | Variables Predicted | OUTCOME | | |
Source			Clinical Better	Statistical Better	Tie
Meehl (1954)	20	Success in school or military; recidivism or parole violation; recovery from psychosis	1[a]	11	8
Meehl (1957)	27	Same as above, plus personality description; therapy outcome	0	17	10
Meehl (1965)	51	Same as above, plus response to shock treatment; diagnostic label; job success and satisfaction; medical diagnosis	1[b]	33	17

[a] Later called a tie.

[b] Later called a tie by Goldberg (1968b).

Source: After Wiggins, 1973.

felt that the variables being predicted (e.g., grades) were not like those typically dealt with by practicing psychologists, while others suggested that the clinicians in several studies were handicapped by having inadequate or unfamiliar information about clients and about what they were supposed to predict (e.g., Holt, 1958, 1978). Thorne (1972, p. 44) put it this way: "The question must not be what naive judges do with inappropriate tasks under questionable conditions of comparability with actual clinical situations, but what the most sophisticated judges can do with appropriate methods under ideal conditions."

The furor over Meehl's conclusions could not negate the fact that inference based upon subjective, clinical methods is not as accurate as it was once assumed to be. However, this initially discouraging conclusion was not without positive aspects. Meehl's reviews, along with other reports on the clinician's limited capabilities, focused research on the problem and advanced knowledge, theory, and practice in assessment data processing (Kleinmuntz, 1984: Wiggins, 1981). Two major lines of work have appeared in this regard.

IMPROVING INFORMAL INFERENCE. The first involves investigating how the best subjective clinical inferences are made, how they can be improved, and how they can be taught. Thorne (1972, p. 44) suggests that "clinicians must become much more critical of the types of judgments they attempt to make, the selection of cues upon which judgments are based, and their modes of collecting and combining data." Work in these areas began in the 1960s as researchers attempted to analyze the logic of inference (e.g., Sarbin, Taft & Bailey, 1960), relate it to social and physical judgment processes and errors (e.g., Bieri, Atkins, Briar, Leaman, Miller & Tripoldi, 1966; Grossberg & Grant, 1978; Hunt & Jones, 1962), analyze the nature and influence of specific cues used by clinicians (e.g., Goldberg, 1968; Hoffman, 1960), optimize the

amount of assessment data to be processed (e.g., Bartlett & Green, 1966), and identify the conditions under which inference can be most reliable and valid (e.g., Watley, 1968). These efforts are continuing in the 1980s (Nisbett & Ross, 1980).

Such research has shown that the accuracy of clinical inference can be improved over levels previously reported (e.g., Kahneman & Tversky, 1979), but whether the improvement justifies the extra effort still remains a question. Even the most superior human judges operating under optimal conditions are variable enough in their accuracy to raise questions about their suitability for the data-processing task.

Consider, for example, a study by Kleinmuntz (1963) that involved describing the specific "rules" by which the very best clinical judges draw inferences. Knowing these "rules" could facilitate the training of less accurate, less experienced clinicians (Kagan, 1974). Kleinmuntz asked a recognized MMPI expert to "think aloud" while working with test results from 126 college-age subjects. The task was to decide whether each individual was "adjusted" or "maladjusted." The decision rules that emerged were transformed into a computer program used to score future subjects' MMPI scores.

The study showed that a good clinician's inference processes can be objectified and are potentially teachable, but also revealed that the most appropriate "student" may be a computer; the machine used the rules perfectly and consistently with each new set of data. It actually did better at subsequent inference tasks than the clinician who had "taught" it (Kleinmuntz, 1969).

IMPROVING FORMAL INFERENCE. The performance of formal inference procedures has provided much of the impetus for the other line of research in the "post-Meehl" era, namely the elaboration and improvement of techniques for statistical processing of assessment data. Though it may seem that this type of research might put clinicians out of a job, one of its by-products has been to map out the assessment tasks in which clinicians can be most effective.

Meehl (1954) and other researchers in this area (e.g., Sawyer, 1966) have distinguished between the clinical psychologist's roles in data *processing* versus data *collection*. They have highlighted the fact that, just as data processing can be formal or informal, collection of assessment data can be done mechanically (i.e., with objective tests and life records) or subjectively (i.e., through unstructured interviews and informal observations). Thus, in a given assessment sequence, many combinations of subjective and statistical procedures are possible for

the clinician (see Box 3-10). When the studies reviewed by Meehl are reexamined in this light, as Sawyer (1966) did, it is clear that though clinicians may be inferior to statistical formulae at *processing* assessment data, they can make unique contributions by *collecting* and reporting their subjective judgments. The most accurate inferences found by Sawyer (1966) were based upon the formal, statistical processing of data collected by *both* mechanical and subjective techniques. "This suggests that the clinician may be able to contribute most not by direct prediction, but rather by providing, in objective form, judgments to be combined me-

BOX 3-10   Some combinations of formal and informal procedures for the collection and processing of assessment data

Data-Collection Procedure	Data-Processing Procedure	Example
1 Formal	Formal	Psychological test scores processed by computer according to a statistical formula which predicts potential for behavior problems
2 Formal	Informal	Psychological test scores interpreted by clinician based on experience, theory, and "hunches" to establish psychiatric diagnosis
3 Informal	Formal	Clinician's subjective judgments (based on an interview) converted into quantitative ratings which are then processed by a computer or statistical formula to describe client's "personality"
4 Informal	Informal	Subjective impressions and judgments (from interviews, projective tests, etc.) interpreted subjectively to decide whether client needs to be hospitalized
5 Formal and Informal	Formal	Psychological test scores and clinician's subjective impressions and judgments all fed into computer which uses complex formula to describe client or make predictions about behavior
6 Formal and Informal	Informal	Psychological test scores and clinician's subjective impressions and judgments all scanned and interpreted by clinician to decide whether client is capable of standing trial for a crime

chanically" (Sawyer, 1966, p. 193). These findings have by no means shut the clinician out of the assessment process. "Sawyer's analysis reinforces Meehl's (1954) conclusion that the clinician is a highly inefficient *combiner* of data, but it also underscores the heretofore neglected contribution of the clinician as a valuable *source* of input data" (Wiggins, 1973, p. 198).

Many clinicians and researchers now focus on upgrading observational and other data-*collection* skills in order to optimize their role in clinical assessment. As an example, "clinical intuition" has been recast as a skill in observing verbal and nonverbal cues coming from the client. As such, it can be developed, practiced, and improved (see Arkes, 1981).

Other investigators have been studying the accuracy of statistical, usually computer-oriented data-processing methods. Some of these methods are thoroughly mechanical and empirical; for example, a client's test scores are interpreted according to formulae that have been derived from statistical relationships between other clients' test scores and behavior (see category 1 in Box 3-10). In effect, the computer takes the client's test profile and "looks up" the characteristics of other people with similar profiles. Development of this type of "purely actuarial" program is expensive because it requires a large backlog of data from hundreds of previous clients.

To help fill the gaps where appropriate statistical formulae are not yet available because there are no data on the relationship between predictors and criteria, a "hybrid" system of formal data processing has evolved. The Kleinmuntz (1963) study provides an example of this approach. In general, it involves having a computer interpret assessment data, not through use of a statistically derived formula but on the basis of clinicians' experience and theoretical beliefs, which have been transformed into decision "rules." Wiggins (1973) refers to this process as "automating clinical lore." Even though this is not an entirely empirical strat-

egy, it is more accurate (and certainly cheaper and more convenient) to employ a "hybrid" system than to have a clinician interpret every test.

The use of "hybrid" computer programs for scoring psychological tests has become a popular enterprise that can be quite lucrative (see Box 3-11). These programs vary considerably in their sophistication and quality. Many have been developed with the logic pioneered by Kleinmuntz (1963), although not all have been adequately concerned with assessment of reliability and validity. In his review of automated MMPI assessment for Buros's *Eighth Mental Measurements Yearbook,* Butcher (1978) found seven different computer programs that were commercially available; several more have been marketed since Butcher's review (see the December 1985 issue of the *Journal of Consulting and Clinical Psychology* for a special series of articles on computerized psychological assessment).

The following limitations and problems of statistical assessment data processing have been raised by critics:

1. Actuarial techniques can be applied only where adequately developed, fully standardized assessment devices, inference norms, and formulae are available. At the moment, such devices and data are the exception, not the rule (Wiggins, 1981).
2. There is a certain amount of public distrust of decisions made about people on the basis of computer techniques.
3. New discoveries about behavior are less likely to occur if clinicians become less involved in assessment data processing.
4. Relegation of clinicians to the data-collection role decreases the chances of future improvement of human data-processing skills (Matarazzo, 1986).
5. Exclusion of the clinician from the data-processing role reduces the probability that rare behavioral events and relationships will be noticed, since actuarial tables and statistical formulae may not be set up to handle them.
6. Certain kinds of assessment may be more appropriately dealt with by informal means.

BOX 3-11   Sample automated psychological test report

ROCHE PSYCHIATRIC SERVICE INSTITUTE
MMPI REPORT

CASE NO: 00000   RPSI NO: 0000
AGE 37 MALE

The test items appear to have been answered truthfully with no effort to deny or exaggerate.

This patient appears to be currently depressed and anxious. He shows a pattern which is frequent among psychiatric patients. Feelings of inadequacy, sexual conflicts and ridigity are accompanied by a loss of efficiency, initiative and self-confidence. Insomnia is likely, along with a chronic fatigue. He is anxious, tense, and overly sensitive. Suicidal thoughts are a possibility. In the clinical picture, depression predominates. Psychiatric patients with this pattern are likely to be diagnosed as depressive reaction or anxiety reaction. The characteristics are resistant to change, although symptomatic relief may be obtained with brief treatment.

He tends to be pessimistic and complaining, and is likely to be defeatist, cynical, and unwilling to stick with treatment. He may need frequent reassurance about his medical condition. Dynamically, he is a narcissistic and self-centered person who is rigid in thought and action and easily upset in social situations.

Repression and denial are utilized as a defense against anxiety. In periods of heightened stress his anxiety is likely to be expressed in somatic symptoms. He may respond to suggestion and reassurance.

He is a self controlled, cautious person who may be somewhat feminine in his interest patterns. He is idealistic, socially perceptive, and responsive. He shows some self awareness, but he is sensitive and prone to worry. He is verbally fluent, persuasive and able to communicate ideas clearly.

This person is hesitant to become involved in social situations. He makes an effort to conscientiously carry out his responsibilities, but he is retiring and somewhat withdrawn from interpersonal relationships.

Source: J. Wiggins, *Personality and Prediction,* ©
1973, Addison-Wesley, Reading, Mass. Table 5–7.
Reprinted with permission.

Levy (1963) suggests that specific, "bounded" questions (e.g., Will this person be likely to abuse children?) may most adequately be answered by formal data processing, while more general "unbounded" concerns (e.g., What is this person like?) are best handled through informal means.

Indeed, Levy (1963, p. 176) argues that "failure" to make the bounded-unbounded distinction " . . . is responsible for much of the current controversy over the utility of actuarial as opposed to clinical prediction. . . . In the unbounded case, we have . . .

no choice but to rely upon the clinician's deductive capacities; in the bounded case we do have this choice and can never justify not making it in favor of the statistician." Though there is still considerable disagreement over exactly what assessment questions and roles clinicians should try to handle, Wiggins's (1973, p. 199) summary of the situation provides a positive concluding note: "Clinicians need not view themselves as second-rate IBM machines unless they choose to engage in activities that are more appropriately performed by such machines. In the realm of clinical observation and hypothesis formation, the IBM machine will never be more than a second-rate clinician."

The Behavioral Approach to Assessment. We have seen that clinical psychologists have traditionally been concerned with formal and informal processing of assessment data that are viewed as signs or correlates. In that tradition, assessment information is interpreted in terms of psychological traits or intrapsychic dynamics, and the clinician's goal is to predict something about the client or to describe the client's "personality."

Clinical psychologists who adopt a behavioral model disagree with many of these assessment concepts. Their main criticisms and alternative formulations are summarized in the following points:

1. The use of assessment data as *signs* of personality traits involves too much inference. Behaviorists do not see "personality traits," "psychological dispositions," or "personality dynamics" as useful concepts for learning about people. In their view, such dispositional constructs exist in the eye of the clinician who uses them (Mischel, 1968; Shweder, 1982), and, "real" or not, these constructs do not have much utility for describing people, predicting their behavior, or evaluating behavior change programs.

   Many behaviorists argue that part of the reason for clinicians' poor showing as data processors is that they rely upon vague trait concepts as the bases for inferences that stray too far from initial assessment information.

When clinicians do not share common definitions for terms like *anxiety, aggression,* and *ego,* studies reporting low reliability and validity for inferences about diagnostic labels or personality traits are easier to understand. Trait concepts are seen by behavior assessors as adding confusing and ultimately superfluous labels to behavior that does not need them.

Accordingly, the behavioral model treats available data as *samples* of client capabilities rather than as bases for inference about personality traits or dynamic states. Mischel (1968, p. 10) notes that "the emphasis is on what a person *does* in situations rather than on inferences about what attributes he *has.*"

2. In spite of the early efforts of Murray (1938) and Rapaport (Rapaport, Gill & Schafer, 1945), trait concepts have tended to isolate people's behavior from the environment in which it occurs. Since behavior is learned in a social context, one cannot describe or predict that behavior accurately unless situational factors are taken into account: A man who displays dominance on a psychological test may behave quite differently with his boss.

   Two decades ago, behaviorists tended to concentrate on situational variables to the virtual exclusion of person variables, an imbalance that Eysenck, Wakefield and Friedman (1983) termed "committed 'environmentalism.'" More modern behaviorists consider both the person and the environment as important in behavioral assessment, so the focus of data collection includes (a) client capabilities, (b) characteristics of the physical and social environment in which behavior occurs, and (c) the nature of *client-environment* interactions. This "person-situation" orientation in the behavioral view of assessment has emphasized *interactionism* or the *reciprocal relationship* between person and situational variables (Bandura, 1978; Mischel, 1984).

3. Traditional assessment practices promote separation between data collection and data use. Too often, assessment information is processed into descriptions or predictions that are not useful for planning or evaluating behavior-change techniques. Behaviorists document this point by citing research which shows that diagnostic labels often do not determine hospitalization or treatment (e.g., Mendel & Rapport, 1969) and that tradition-

ally oriented therapists often pay little attention to the assessment data available (Dailey, 1953; Meehl, 1960).

From the behavioral perspective, clinical assessment must be tied to efforts at modifying behavior. Toward this end, clients, situations, and client-situation interactions are described on dimensions that (1) are as precise and data-based as possible, (2) have direct implications for treatment planning, and (3) can be continually monitored during and after treatment. Rather than describing a particular child's problem in trait-oriented terms like "aggressiveness" or "hyperactivity," assessment would focus on the *frequencies, durations, or intensities* with which specific acts (e.g., striking others, running around the room) occur, the settings in which these acts appear, and the environmental factors that appear to elicit and reinforce them. Goldfried and Sprafkin (1976) coined an acronym, SORC, or Stimulus-Organism-Response-Consequence, to indicate the types of variables that a thorough behavioral assessment must consider. As Nelson and Hayes (1981) observe, the spirit of interactionism is suggested by this system's attention to environmental (the "C" and "S" components) and organismic (the "O" component) control of important responses ("R"). Recently, behaviorists have begun to study extended *chains* or sequences of interaction in an attempt to understand such complex behaviors as marital interaction or social deficits (Haynes, 1984).

In general, questions asked during behavioral assessment are not oriented toward *why* a person behaves in a particular way, but *what* she or he does, and *when, where,* and *under what circumstances* the activity occurs. When behavior is described in this fashion, change tactics can flow directly from assessment. If assessment suggests that Sally's high-frequency whining in the classroom is reinforced by teacher attention, a program to terminate reward of the maladaptive behavior and plan reinforcement of more appropriate behaviors might be insti-

tuted. As that program begins, its effect upon the variables identified in the initial assessment would be observed and used as a guide for continuing, altering, or terminating the intervention.

One noteworthy trend in recent years has been that behavioral and traditional (trait-oriented) approaches have begun to come closer together on several assessment principles. For their part, behaviorists increasingly stress the need to demonstrate the classic psychometric qualities of reliability and validity for their methods rather than simply assuming such qualities (see Cone, 1981, for a discussion of why such qualities may not be relevant to behavioral assessment). Behaviorists are also now more interested in assessing personal variables that might give stability and unity to behavior across different situations (Mischel, 1984) than they were in the days when they severely criticized assessment of personality dispositions (Mischel, 1968).

At the same time, traditional emphases on trait assessment and psychiatric diagnosis have embraced some behavioral recommendations. The specific, criterion-based formulation of DSM-III is an excellent example of how behavioral principles of assessment have influenced clinical practice. At a more theoretical level, the increased attention to what personality theorists (e.g., Rorer & Widiger, 1983) call *ascription rules* (the implicit rules we use for describing people as possessing or not possessing certain qualities: "He is honest"; "She is friendly") reflects an awareness that situational variables play a major role in assigning trait names to an individual's behavior. Buss and Craik (1983) have attempted to tie trait concepts to multiple-behavior criteria by finding those behaviors that are the most important or *prototypic* for assigning trait descriptions like "dominant" or "submissive" to another person.

The behavioral approach to assessment is not without its critics. Many clinicians see objective assessment of overt behaviors in relation to specific environmental situations as too narrow and inadequate for tapping the various personality dimensions stressed in their own models (e.g., Breger & McGaugh, 1965). Other critiques have been advanced from within the behavioral camp itself.

Many concerns stem from the fact that the behavioral approach to assessment is still in a rather primitive stage of development. Its methods are often not well standardized or psychometrically sophisticated when compared to psychological tests like the MMPI (Franks, 1976; Wiggins, 1973). Behavioral assessments are used inconsistently by different practitioners who, like other clinicians, operate without formal actuarial formulae and depend upon their own subjective judgment to interpret the data they collect. Also, though behavioral assessment provides excellent descriptions of behavior that can be used as a guide for treatment planning, it has not resolved the question of what behaviors constitute a "problem" and who sets up the definitions (Hawkins, 1975; Mash & Terdal, 1976). Further, it has not yet reached a level of sophistication that allows for a reliable, empirically determined choice of specific treatment techniques, especially in complex cases (Goldfried & Davison, 1976; Mash & Terdal, 1976). More comprehensive and detailed presentations of the theory, practice, and problems of behavioral assessment are available in several recent volumes (Barlow, 1981; Ciminero, Calhoun & Adams, 1986; Cone & Hawkins, 1977; Haynes, 1978; Hersen & Bellack, in press; Mash & Terdal, 1981; Nay, 1979; Nelson & Hayes, 1986).

Phenomenology and Assessment. Many of the objections raised by behavioral theorists to traditional assessment procedures relate not only to their apparent lack of clinical utility, but also to the belief that people should not become passive objects of study who are placed in a "one-down" status, examined apart from their physical and social environment, and burdened with labels that focus on problems and weaknesses to the exclusion of assets and strengths. In this respect the behavioral and phenomenological models are in accord. However, in line with their subjective, relationship-oriented approach, phenomenological clinicians have suggested assessment alternatives that differ substantially from those outlined in the last section (e.g., Brown, 1972; Dana & Leech, 1974; Fischer & Fischer, 1983).

Some of them (e.g., Rogers, 1951) have argued against assessment on the grounds that such procedures are dehumanizing, take responsibility away from clients, and threaten the quality of clinician-client relations. Advocates of this position are unlikely even to review assessment data collected and processed by others. Their assumption is that all necessary knowledge of the client will emerge during specially conducted interviews. The characteristics of these interviews will be described in Chapters 4 and 10.

Other phenomenologists raise the possibility that assessment data *collected* through traditional sources such as personality tests can be useful clinically if they are *processed* in line with humanistic principles (Fischer, 1979, 1985). For example, test data can be viewed as clues to how a client looks at the world. In the same vein, traditional assessment procedures can provide opportunities for the clinician and client to build their relationship. By discussing assessment data with the client and using these interactions as a starting point for further exploration, the clinician not only shares knowledge openly, but reveals personal reactions to it, thus helping to cement a lasting partnership (Dana & Leech, 1974; Fischer, 1985; Mosak & Gushurst, 1972).

Some phenomenologists who feel that traditional assessment devices are not ideally suited as relationship facilitators have developed specialized instruments that they believe do the job better. These tests include the Personal Orientation Inventory (Shostrom, 1968), the Purpose-in-Life Test (Crumbaugh, 1968) and the "Who-are-you?" test (Bugental & Zelen, 1950).

Communicating Assessment Data

Raw data about a client's behavior must be processed in some way before they become psychologically meaningful. However, the value of processed assessment data may be limited unless they are presented in some coherent way. This organized presentation of assessment results is called a *psychological report.*

If the results of assessment are to have maximal value, they must be presented in a way that is *clear, relevant* to the goal of assessment, and *useful* to the intended "consumer." Clinicians must guard against several problems that can make reports vague, irrelevant, and useless. To illustrate, consider the following personality sketch. It is not as extensive as most assessment reports, but many of its characteristics are relevant to our discussion:

You are a person of varied interests, although you pour most of your energy into a few activities that mean the most to you. In general, you show a well-balanced outlook and disposition, but when frustrated you can display temper. With those you know well you are spontaneous and expressive, but often you keep your feelings very much to yourself. You have a few defects in personality that you are aware of, particularly in connection with dealing with people. You are persistent enough, however, to achieve success in dealing with these faults. There are times when you worry too much. You will find that it suits you better to take things as they come and to show more confidence in your own future. (Wallen, 1956, p. 42).

At first glance, this sketch appears clear, relevant to the person in question, and reasonably useful. However, closer examination will reveal that this is not the case. First, the terms used (such as "balanced outlook" and "defects in personality") are vague and can mean different things to different readers. Second, the statements are so generally applicable to everyone that they are not relevant for the description of a particular individual. Careful examination of actual assessment reports often exposes the same

problems. Let us briefly consider these problems and then discuss a few ideas for dealing with them.

Clarity of Reports. The first criterion for an assessment report is clarity of communication. Without this basic attribute, relevance and usefulness cannot be evaluated. Lack of clarity in psychological reports is troublesome because misinterpretation of a report can lead to misguided decisions. Hammond and Allen (1953, p. v) cite a case in point:

A young girl, mentally defective, was seen for testing by the psychologist, who reported to the social agency that the girl's test performance indicated moderate success and happiness for her in "doing things with her hands." Three months later, however, the social agency reported to the psychologist that the girl was not responding well. Although the social agency had followed the psychologist's recommendation, the girl was neither happy nor successful "doing things with her hands." When the psychologist inquired what kinds of things, specifically, the girl had been given to do he was told "We gave her music lessons—on the saxophone."

A related problem exists when the assessor uses jargon that the reader may not understand. Consider the following excerpt from a report on a thirty-six-year-old man cited by Mischel (1968, p. 105):

Test results emphasize a basically characterological problem with currently hysteroid defenses. Impairment of his ability to make adequate use of independent and creative fantasy, associated with emotional lability and naivete, are characteristic of him. . . . Due to markedly passive-aggressive character make-up, in which the infantile dependency needs are continually warring with his hostile tendencies, it is not difficult to understand this current conflict over sexual expression.

The writer may feel he understands the client, but does the reader understand the writer? Anyone not well versed in psychoanalytic terminology would find such a report mystifying. Professionals may not even agree on the meaning of the terms employed. Readers of psychological reports also highlight factors such as excessive length (or excessive brevity), large amounts of technical information (e.g., statistics or esoteric test scores), and lack of coherent organization as contributing to lack of communication clarity (Olive, 1972; Tallent & Reiss, 1959).

Relevance to Goals. The second requirement of a valuable assessment report is that it is *relevant* to the goal that prompted the assessment in the first place. If that goal was to classify the client's behavior, information relevant to classification would be of great importance in a report. If description of the client's current psychological assets and liabilities was the purpose of assessment, the report should contain those descriptions. If predictions about a client are requested, these should appear, unless the clinician believes that no sound basis for them exists.

These are simple, almost self-evident prescriptions, but assessment objectives sometimes get lost, especially when explicit goals were never stated. Although the procedure is no longer as common as it once was, clinicians may still be asked for "psychologicals" (usually a standard test battery and interview) without being told why assessment is being done. Under such circumstances, the chances of writing a relevant report are minimal.

Unfortunately, there are cases in which lack of relevance in psychological reports is due mainly to the clinician's failure to keep clearly stated objectives in mind. When this happens, the report may reflect the assessor's theoretical bias and personal style more than the client's behavior.

Usefulness of Reports. Finally, one must ask if an assessment report is useful. Does the information it contains add anything important to what we already know about the client? It is possible for a report to contain clear, relevant information that is already available through other sources. Or a report may *sound* useful at first, but contain little

information of real value. These problems appear because the assessor has either (1) not collected useful information or (2) not made useful statements about the data available. In the former case, the clinician may have employed techniques low on what Sechrest (1963) called *incremental validity*. For example, a clinician may conclude on the basis of several psychological tests that a client "has strong hostile tendencies and weak control over them." If the client has already been convicted as an ax murderer, such information provides no increment in knowledge over what was already obvious.

In other instances, the assessor's report may have limited usefulness because it says nothing beyond what would be expected on the basis of general past experience and common sense. One aspect of this issue has been called the "base-rate problem." It refers to the fact that some statements tend to be true about certain types of clients (e.g., College professors do a lot of reading) and that if an assessment report fails to provide information beyond these known base rates, it will not be useful.

An example of how knowledge of base rates in a population can facilitate the creation of useless though often impressive-sounding reports has been given by Sundberg, Tyler & Taplin (1973, pp. 577–579). A clinician wrote the report that follows *without ever having seen the client*. The material contained in it is based entirely on two pieces of information: (1) The client is a new admission to a Veterans Administration hospital, and (2) the case was to be discussed at a convention session entitled "A Case Study of Schizophrenia." In edited form, the report said:

This veteran approached the testing situation with some reluctance. He was cooperative with the clinician, but mildly evasive on some of the material. Both the tests and the past history suggest considerable inadequacy in interpersonal relations, particularly with members of his family. It is doubtful whether he has ever had very many close relationships with anyone. . . . He has never been able to sink his roots deeply. He is immature, egocentric, and irritable, and often he misperceives the good intentions of the people around him. . . . He tends to be basically passive and dependent, though there are occasional periods of resistance and rebellion against others. . . . Vocationally, his adjustment has been very poor. Mostly he has drifted from one job to another. His interests are shallow and he tends to have poor motivation for his work. Also he has had a hard time keeping his jobs because of difficulty in getting along with fellow employees. Although he has had some relations with women, his sex life has been unsatisfactory to him. At present, he is mildly depressed. . . . His intelligence is close to average, but he is functioning below his potential. . . . Test results and case history . . . suggest the diagnosis of schizophrenic reaction, chronic undifferentiated type. Prognosis for response to treatment appears to be poor.

In writing this "report," the clinician relied heavily upon knowledge of VA hospital residents and familiarity with hospital procedures. For example, since the case was to be discussed at a meeting on schizophrenia, and since schizophrenic diagnoses are very common for VA residents, the correct diagnosis was easy to surmise. Also, the description given fits the "average" VA resident and thus is likely to be at least partially accurate.

This bogus document exemplifies another common feature of assessment reports that reduces their usefulness: overgenerality, or the tendency to write in terms that are so ambiguous they can be true of almost anyone. Documents laden with overly general statements have been dubbed "Barnum Reports," "Aunt Fanny Reports," or "Madison Avenue Reports" (Klopfer, 1960; Meehl, 1956; Tallent, 1958). Overly general material has the dual disadvantages of spuriously increasing a report's impressiveness while actually decreasing its usefulness.

Presenting Assessment Data. Writing valuable assessment reports requires great care. While there is no single "right" way to

present assessment data in all instances, there are some guidelines worth noting.

First, the criteria of clarity, relevance, and usefulness must be kept in mind as reports are being prepared. This may be made easier by the use of some type of outline. The characteristics of this outline will be organized around the issues the clinician believes to be most important and which are most pertinent to the goal of assessment. The number of potential topics is very large and theory-based. It would be impossible to give examples of all possible report outlines, so we shall consider just a few representatives of the three main models of clinical psychology. Illustrations of the reports that might be based upon each outline will also be presented.

1 A psychodynamic report. The following dynamically oriented outline is an edited version of the one used by Tallent (1976, pp. 121–122) for reporting his assessment of a young man who had been in trouble with the law for bookie activities and assault:

   I. Conflicts
     A. Self-perception
     B. Goals
     C. Frustrations
     D. Interpersonal relations
     E. Perception of environment
     F. Drives, dynamics
     G. Emotional cathexes
     H. Emotional controls
  II. Social stimulus value
     A. Cognitive skills
     B. Conative factors
     C. Goals
     D. Social role
 III. Cognitive functioning
     A. Deficit
     B. Psychopathology
 IV. Defenses
     A. Denial
     B. Interpersonal tactics
     C. Fantasy

The report based upon this outline is presented in Box 3-12.

BOX 3-12 Example of an assessment report based on a psychodynamically oriented outline

This man is most readily understood in terms of his unusually passive, dependent approach to life and his attempts to overcome the deeply unhappy state brought about by this personality limitation.

Mr. A does not feel very adequate as a person, an attitude which is developed through experiencing a continual sense of failure in terms of his own goals, and which apparently is reinforced by others. In fact, his relations with his father very likely are the basic reason for such feeling. This person is seen by the patient as cold, rejecting, punishing, and unapproachable. He has an urge to rebel and fight against this person— an urge which has been generalized to all society, but he is afraid to give vent to his impulses. Whatever emotional support he does get (got) seems to be from the mother.

As others see him, he seems to have the essential capacity to do well if only he would try. He scores at the average level on a test of intelligence (IQ: 106), he is able to learn readily, when he wants to, and on occasion can perform unusually fast and effectively. Yet he does not typically follow through on this advantage. His willingness, sometimes even his desire, to do well fluctuates, so that in the long run he could not be regarded as a constructive or responsible person.

Other personality deficiencies also compromise his functioning. Under stress or when faced with difficult problems he becomes blocked, confused and indecisive. His thinking does not show sufficient flexibility to meet such situations so that he would be regarded as inadaptable and unspontaneous.

Mr. A's felt inadequacy causes him to feel that he is not as good as others. By way of reassuring himself on this matter he frequently during examination makes remarks that he is "like everybody else." The feeling that he is inferior includes also the sexual area where he is quite confused about his maleness. It is likely that one or more sex problems contribute to his sense of failure, although, quite understandably, he denies this and indicates a satisfactory sex life "like everybody else."

He hardly experiences the full effect of his failures, however. He protects himself by denying many events of reality, by keeping many facts about himself and others unconscious, by a general attitude of "not knowing"—an attitude of naiveness. He can hardly take corrective action about himself because he does not understand himself or his actions, or recognize the nature of his problems. Oddly enough, as already stated, this is an unhappy person, but he does not adequately recognize this fact nor does he appear to others as depressed. Yet on occasion this might be a factor in his behavior which could be personally or socially unfortunate.

This man's insecurity about himself forces him into a receptive orientation to other people. He must have friends to provide support. To achieve this he presents himself in a positive, correct light, tries to say the "right" things and even to be ingratiating and obsequious. It is important that he create the "right" effect and may resort to dramatic behavior to bring this about. "Friends" are so important to him that he sometimes must take abuse in order to hold them. He must always hold back hostile expression.

But it is perhaps in fantasy where the greatest satisfaction is derived. He dreams of being a "success" (his term)—accumulating enough money by the age of 35 so he can retire and effortlessly enjoy the comforts of the world. In his fantasy he is independent of authority, can openly express the aggression he ordinarily cannot, and flout society. He has no positive feelings about social rules (although he may profess to), but is concerned when apprehended for misconduct, possibly less for the real punishment than for how it "looks" to be known for doing what he is afraid to do. It is little wonder then that he is easy prey for an "easy money" scheme.

Source: Norman Tallent, *Psychological Report Writing,* © 1976, pp. 121–122. Reprinted by permission of Prentice-Hall, Inc., Englewood Cliffs, New Jersey.

2   A behavioral report. Pomeranz and Goldfried (1970) desribe an assessment outline representative of the behavioral model. An edited version appears below:

I. Description of client's physical appearance and behavior during assessment
II. Presenting problems
  A. Nature of Problems
  B. Historical background of problems
  C. Current situational determinants of problems
  D. Relevant organismic variables
    1. Physiological states
    2. Effects of medication
    3. Cognitive determinants of problems
  E. Dimensions of problems
    1. Duration
    2. Pervasiveness
    3. Frequency
    4. Magnitude
  F. Consequences of problems
    1. Positive
    2. Negative
III. Other problems (observed by assessor but not stated by client)
IV. Personal Assets
V. Targets for change
VI. Recommended treatments
VII. Client motivation for treatment
VIII. Prognosis
IX. Priority for treatment
X. Client expectancies
  A. About solving specific problems
  B. About treatment enterprise in general
XI. Other comments

The use of this outline for summarizing assessment of a male college student produced the report contained in Box 3-13.

3   A phenomenological report. In line with their subjective approach and general distrust of formal assessment, phenomeno-

---

BOX 3-13   Example of an assessment summary based on a behavioral outline

Behavior During Interview and Physical Description:
James is a clean-shaven, long-haired young man who appeared for the intake interview in well-coordinated college garb: jeans, wide belt, open shirt, and sandals. He came across as shy and soft-spoken, with occasional minor speech blocks. Although uneasy during most of the session, he nonetheless spoke freely and candidly.

Presenting Problem:

A. *Nature of problem:* Anxiety in public speaking situations, and other situations in which he is being evaluated by others.

B. *Historical setting events:* James was born in France, and arrived in this country seven years ago, at which time he experienced both a social and language problem. His social contacts had been minimal until the time he entered college, at which time a socially aggressive friend of his helped him to break out of his shell. James describes his father as being an overly critical and perfectionistic person who would, on occasion, rip up his homework if it fell short of the mark. The client's mother is pictured as a controlling, overly affectionate person who was always showing concern about his welfare. His younger brother, who has always been a good student, was continually thrown up to James by his parents as being far better than he.

C. *Current situational determinants:* Interaction with his parents, examinations, family gatherings, participation in classes, initial social contacts.

D. *Relevant organismic variables:* The client appears to be approaching a number of situations with certain irrational expectations, primarily unrealistic strivings for perfection and an overwhelming desire to receive approval from others. He is not taking any medication at this time.

E. *Dimensions of problem:* The client's social and evaluative anxiety are long-standing and occur in a wide variety of day-to-day situations.

F. *Consequences of problem:* His chronic level of anxiety resulted in an ulcer operation at the age of 15. In addition, he has developed a skin rash on his hands and arms, apparently from excessive perspiration. He reports that his nervousness at one time caused him to stutter, but this appears to be less a problem in more recent years. His anxiety in examination situations has typically interfered with his ability to perform well.

Other Problems:

A. *Assertiveness:* Although obviously a shy and timid individual, James said that lack of assertiveness is no longer a problem with him. At one time in the past, his friends would take advantage of him, but he claims that this is no longer the case. This should be followed up further, as it is unclear what he means by assertiveness.

B. *Forgetfulness:* The client reports that he frequently misses appointments, misplaces items, locks himself out of his room, and generally is absent-minded.

Personal Assets:

The client is fairly bright and comes across as a warm, friendly, and sensitive individual.

Targets for Modification:
Unrealistic self-statements in social-evaluative situations; possibly behavioral deficits associated with unassertiveness; and forgetfulness.

Recommended Treatment:
It appears that relaxation training would be a good way to begin, especially in light of the client's high level of anxiety. Following this, the treatment should move along the lines of rational restructuring, and possibly behavior rehearsal. It is unclear as yet what would be the best strategy for dealing with forgetfulness.

Motivation for Treatment:
High.

Prognosis:
Very good.

Priority for Treatment:
High.

Expectancies:
On occasion, especially when going out on a date with a female, James would take half a sleeping pill to calm himself down. He wants to get away from this, and feels what he needs is to learn to cope with his anxieties by himself. It would appear that he will be very receptive to whatever treatment plan we finally decide on, especially if the emphasis is on self-control of anxiety.

Other Comments:
Considering the brief time available between now and the end of the semester, between-session homework assignments should be emphasized as playing a particularly important role in the behavior change process.

logically oriented clinicians deemphasize specific outlines for guiding psychological reports. Quite lenthy reports may be based upon a general framework such as:

I. Client from own point of view
II. Client as reflected in tests
III. Client as seen by assessor

An example of a report organized in this phenomenological way is presented in Box 3-14. Although the clinician adminstered some formal psychological tests, the data from them are reported in subjective terms.

More detailed discussions of the techniques and problems associated with writing clinical assessment reports are available in articles and books by Groth-Marnat (1984), Klopfer (1960), and Tallent (1976).

A Note on Ethics

The collection, processing, and communication of assessment data require that clinicians have access to sensitive information that the client might not ordinarily reveal. This places a heavy responsibility upon the assessor to use and report this privileged in-

---

BOX 3-14 Example of an assessment summary based on a phenomenological outline

Referral: Last January 24-year-old Darrell and his partner were arrested in New Jersey for collecting refunds on department store goods which they simply had picked up from the shelves. They collected $100 to $200 per day in this fashion for several months. Both young men were released on probation in March following a couple months in jail. Mr. and Mrs. Holderin are now seeking psychotherapy for their son in hopes that it will be of personal help to him and will preclude further lawbreaking.

The psychiatrist they contacted, has in turn requested a general psychological assessment prior to deciding whether to begin psychotherapy. He is particularly concerned with the possibility of schizoid functioning, especially as it might appear in the Rorschach, and with Darrell's intellectual assets.

Date of assessment: 5-6-74
Date of report: 5-12-74

Assessment opportunities: Extended interview, Bender-Gestalt, Wechsler Adult Intelligence Scale (partial), Rorschach, Thematic Apperception Test, human drawings, and mutual discussion of my impressions.

First appearance: Darrell showed up at my office precisely on time. He was dressed in a fashionable doublebreasted suit, wide silk tie, and silk shirt with cufflinks. He carried these well, and indeed struck me as youthfully handsome. After waiting for me to indicate where we were to go, he comfortably explained that he needed change for $10 in order to feed a parking meter. Secretaries, students, and I all scurried around looking for change as he stood by politely and nonchalantly. When he wrote a check for my services, he added the forty cents I had offered him.

Once into my office, Darrell continued to seem at ease. In a casual way he asked permission to smoke, suggested that the window be opened, and took off his jacket. Except when doing pencil work, he seemed bodily relaxed. Later, he smilingly mentioned that his idol is Alexander Mundy of the T.V. program "To Catch a Thief"— boyish in handsome appearance, a lady-killer, mod dresser with expensive entertainment tastes, sports car enthusiast, conman with class, and thief extraordinaire. Darrell remarked both that such aspirations were "unrealistic" *and* that he had thoroughly enjoyed approximating them during his recent misadventure.

Toward the end of our meeting, this suave appearance was thrown into relief as Darrell recounted his favorite horror stories, joked continuously, and drew cartoon figures complete with slapstick captions. He had also earnestly shared his educational ambitions and sought advice from me. Altogether I found him consistently easy to be with and to like—something in the manner of a teacher shaking her head but enjoying a charmingly problematic student.

Darrell as he sees himself: As mentioned, the Alexander Mundy project is a powerful and often successful one for Darrell. When he has the money, he dresses well and wines and dines well. He even owns a sports car of sorts (a Karman Ghia). And like Mundy, he has only a few male friends, but is highly successful with having his way with women. Although he would "go to pieces" if he saw a girl cry because he had hurt her, he usually lies to get what he wants and sees nothing wrong with doing so. Girls are all phony anyway, except one whom he met since being released from jail. Darrell finds he can't put on airs with her and doesn't want to. She's honest and really likes him. She even invited him to come with her and her parents to Atlantic City—"nobody ever did that for me before!" But he won't get married for at least three years, until he's sure that his criminal conviction (which she doesn't know about yet) would not hurt either of them.

Back to the Mundy style. Even in grade school Darrell was often regarded as some sort of trouble maker who wasn't properly fulfilling his potential. Darrell wouldn't tell much about these years, but he did talk about a haunting memory of a woman principal chastising him about what was going to become of him. He was quite upset when he read a few years ago about her death. But mostly Darrell focuses on his triumphs. For example, he talks his way into job after job easily, and once was able to get an extended leave of absence by mak-

ing up an intricate tale about having to go to the Mayo Clinic for critical surgery. And, not caring for the "hurry up and wait" routine of military service, and missing his friends and old life, Darrell waited out the requisite six months before applying for a psychiatric discharge that would formally be an honorable discharge. He feels he really put one over on the doctor, who wrote that Darrell was prone to "impulsive outbursts." Darrell acknowledges pride in these behaviors as well as in his recent thievery—if it weren't for his partner, they would never have been caught. But he emphasizes that he doesn't want anyone else to know about his lawbreaking, and he feels it would be stupid to run the risk of again doing something that he might get caught at. He also suspects that what he did was somewhat immature—an abhorrent thought.

Darrell through the tests: Darrell plunged right into whatever I asked of him, with the effect of partially masking what I took from his frequent sideways glances at me as discomfort and uncertainty about his ability. When asked to copy the *Bender* designs, he did so in about half the usual time. He started out carefully counting dots, asking for instructions, and so on, but wound up with the wrong number going in the wrong direction. As he noted my acceptance, he simply frowned at his mistakes and let them go. Not having planned ahead, he also ran out of space. When I mentioned these things to him and asked if they were similar to other events in his life, Darrell readily and amusedly agreed. Examples were getting arrested, not being further ahead in life at his age, and impatience with all his forms of employment (copyboy to clothes salesman).

On the *WAIS* information section, I noticed Darrell's rapid way of speaking—sort of nonstop, in this case with all kinds of qualifiers, protestations, quick approximations, and requests for feedback. Here, he earned an average score. He acknowledged that this style is typical when a task is not intrinsically interesting and/or when it leaves no room for him to make up his own answers. "I was never any good at math, chemistry, and languages." And sure enough, when he was asked to repeat a series of digits, Darrell failed to score beyond average; he tried to memorize the digits, but often blurted them out, seemingly hoping that they would fall into place. We agreed that he behaves in a similar fashion while working for his father. Moreover that situation becomes exaggerated when Darrell responds to his father's chidings with even more carelessness.

For the most part, Darrell raced through the Rorschach, giving rapid responses and elaborations, turning the cards, and stopping abruptly with about three responses to each card. Most of the percepts involved motion, e.g., "scorpions fighting, people dancing at a costume party, men racing to dance with this girl. Keystone cops—'I'm going first; no, I'm going first,' fighting a duel, violent fight, two roadrunners colliding—'beep-beep,' atomic bomb explosion, flying dinosaurs." In addition, these percepts were laced with enthusiastic rehashings of T.V. horror stories, movies, and science fiction stories. When I suggested that maybe Darrell is action-oriented, he readily agreed and gave more examples of having acted without thinking. Among these were what he called "instinctive" hitting back when physically pushed around. He denied other combativeness. When I pointed out that much of the Rorschach action seemed to be competitive, he saw no relation to his life, instead asserting that, for example, he doesn't have to compete because he's usually the first choice of the girls he wants. Nevertheless, I have a sense of his struggling in a vague way to be first in order not to be somehow put down—or squashed down.

Moving on to the *TAT* stories, I remarked to Darrell that his stories (again rapidly given) were usually straight adaptations of T.V. stories, novels, and movies. He de-

nied that he watches these much anymore, and couldn't "go" with my observation that there were no real people, no involvements in the present, little interpersonal warmth. But he did reiterate that he has never had many friends and that girls are phony. With that, to the blank card he made up a picture of Annette (his new girl friend, 18 years old) and himself on a picnic in a beautiful meadow, just being alone together listening to music, and looking at the mountains. "Sounds childish, but I enjoy doing it."

Conclusion: In answer to the referral question, there is no evidence of autistic thinking. Although there is a general dysocial picture, it is definitely not of schizoid proportions. Moreover, Darrell has begun to let himself form closer relationships with at least Annette and his father, tentative as these may be. And under nonconfrontational circumstances, such as moments in our assessment session, he has been able to own and explore certain affects. Thus although there were certain similarities to "schizoid functioning," he can be viewed more productively as living an extended adolescence. I suspect that therapy would have to encourage him through some developmental sequences as well as current difficulties. As I see it, he could thus become more intimate with and sensitive to other persons.

For whatever it's worth, I might point out a problem *I* might have in an extended relation with Darrell, a problem which I think he's run into repeatedly. His charm and likeableness are likely to rally people to his side until he lets them down by running off or by not returning their care. Then he is either ignored or nagged, both of which demonstrate to him again that people are phony and there are no close friends. So off he goes to emulate Mundy with little concern for the consequences to others.

Source: Norman Tallent, *Psychological Report Writing,* © 1976, pp. 221–225. Reprinted by permission of Prentice-Hall, Inc., Englewood Cliffs, New Jersey.

formation in a fashion that safeguards the client's welfare and dignity. Currently, there is growing concern over (1) how psychological assessment data are being used, (2) who may have access to confidential material, and (3) the possibility that improper or irresponsible interpretation of assessment information will have negative consequences for clients.

With these concerns in mind, clinicians must first be sure their inquiries do not comprise an unauthorized invasion of a client's privacy. Next, care should be taken to assure that assessment goals are not socially or culturally biased to an extent that would place certain clients (e.g., members of ethnic or racial minorities) at a disadvantage and thus give falsely negative impressions of them. Finally, clinicians must wrestle with the problem of who may have access to assessment data if they do not maintain sole control over them. When test scores, conclusions, predictions, and other information are communicated in a report, they may be misused by persons who see the report but

are not qualified to interpret it. In such cases, not only is the client's privacy invaded, but the assessment may work to the disadvantage of the client.

Minimizing these problems regarding psychological assessment is a major concern of public officials, government agencies, citizens groups, and private individuals. Some of them advocate elimination of all psychological assessment (especially testing), while others urge safeguards designed to protect clients from assessment abuses. The latter option has been adopted by the American Psychological Association, whose *Ethical Principles of Psychologists* (APA, 1981a), *Standards for Providers of Psychological Services* (APA, 1977), and *Standards for Educational and Psychological Testing* (APA, 1985) contain extensive guidelines for assessors to follow as they go about the sensitive task of learning about their clients. Ethical problems and standards associated with clinical psychology will be considered in greater detail in Chapter 12.

chapter 4

Interviewing in Clinical Psychology

The interview is the most widely employed tool in clinical psychology. It plays a prominent role in psychological treatment and is a major component of clinical assessment. Although much of the material in this chapter about assessment interviews applies to treatment interviews as well, later chapters will discuss treatment interviews more fully.

This chapter does not teach you how to interview. The material covered here is only a preliminary introduction to the interview as an assessment data source. Interviewing is a skill that requires much practice and careful supervision. You cannot learn to be a good interviewer simply by reading about the subject, even though there are excellent sources available (e.g., Bernstein, Bernstein & Dana, 1974; Bingham, Moore & Gustad, 1959; Cormier & Cormier, 1979; Deutsch & Murphy, 1955; Gorden, 1969; Hersen &

Turner, 1985; Morgan & Cogger, 1972; Sullivan, 1954).

WHAT IS AN INTERVIEW?

In simplest terms, an interview is a conversation with a purpose or goal (Matarazzo, 1965). Consider the following interchange between A and B:

A: How did you spend the weekend?
B: Well, it was pretty quiet. I slept in on Saturday and then watched a football game in the afternoon. That night, my wife's brother came over with their eight-year-old boy. We sat around and talked most of the night. Drank a lot of beer and smoked some dope.
A: Were you home on Sunday, too?
B: Most of it. I didn't feel too great so I just sat around. Later I watched the Packers game on

TV. My wife kept griping about how we never go anywhere. Finally, I took her out to eat. We had a flat on the way home and I ruined a perfectly good shirt while I was changing the damn thing.

If A were B's co-worker and this interaction took place on the way to the office Monday morning, it would simply be a conversation like billions of others every day. But this same exchange could have been part of an interview in which A (a clinician) is gathering information about B and his life-style. The distinction between social conversations and interviews is based not so much on content as on whether they serve a particular purpose. Interviews have been a part of everyday life for centuries. It is important to recognize that clinicians adopted and refined the interview; they did not invent it.

CLINICAL INTERVIEW SITUATIONS

The fact that interviews resemble other forms of conversation makes them a natural source of clinical information about people, an easy means of communicating with them, and a convenient context for attempting to help them. Interviews are flexible, relatively inexpensive, and, perhaps most important, capable of providing the clinician with simultaneous samples of clients' verbal and nonverbal behavior. These advantages make the interview useful in a variety of clinical situations, including the following:

1 Intake. The most common type of clinical interview is when a client comes to the clinician because of some problem in living. The psychologist may have little information about the client, so intake interviews are designed mainly to establish the nature of the problem. Information gathered in this situation may be used by interviewers to decide whether they are an appropriate source of help for the client. The interviewer must ask, "Can I work with this person? Is this problem within my area of ex-

pertise?" If, on the basis of one or more intake interviews, the answer to such questions is no, the clinician will refer the client to another professional or agency for alternative services. If further contact is seen as desirable, assessment or treatment is scheduled for future sessions. Most clinicians conduct their own intake interviews, but in some agencies (e.g., mental health clinics) and group practices, social workers or other personnel may perform this function.

2 Problem identification. The decision to accept or refer a client on the basis of intake information rests, in part, on the nature of the client's problems. For this reason, intake interviews are also aimed at problem identification. In clinical situations where a decision to work with the client has already been made, an interview may focus entirely upon identification or elaboration of the client's problems.

The interviewer is often asked for a *classification* or diagnosis of the problem (Wiens & Matarazzo, 1983). This can take the form of an Axis I label (e.g., Acute Paranoid Disorder) from the DSM-III, along with associated descriptions on the other four axes. Less psychiatrically oriented clinicians and those not required to classify people may use problem-identification interviews to develop broad descriptions of clients and the environmental context in which their behavior occurs.

This type of interview is sometimes known as a *psychiatric interview*. Originally patterned after the question-and-answer format of medical history taking, psychiatric interviews are usually structured according to a specific sequence of important topics, although there are those clinicians who, influenced by psychoanalytic or humanistic ideas, conduct them in a more indirect manner. According to Siassi (1984, p. 260), the purposes of psychiatric interviews are "to arrive at a diagnostic formulation and a rational treatment plan. . . . an attempt is made to discover the origin and evolution of the patient's mental disorder(s) by obtaining a biographical-historical account that can provide a psychological portrait of the patient." Many psychiatric interviews contain a *mental status examination*, which involves a planned set of direct, focused questions presented in a certain order. The mental status

examination is analogous to the physical exam in a physician's assessment. It attempts to assess a client's functioning in a number of areas relating to mental functioning (see Box 4-1 for an example).

Interviews designed to *classify* client prob-

BOX 4-1   The mental status examination (MSE)

There are many guides for how to conduct the MSE and what information to include in it (MacKinnon, 1980; Sands, 1972; Spitzer, Fleiss, Burdock & Hardesty, 1964). A typical outline of topics is the following organization recommended by Siassi (1984):

I. General appearance and behavior—client's level of activity, reaction to interviewer, grooming and clothing are assessed.

II. Speech and thought—is client's speech coherent and understandable; are there delusions present.

III. Consciousness—is the sensorium clear or clouded.

IV. Mood and affect—is client depressed, anxious, restless, is affect appropriate to situation.

V. Perception—does client experience hallucinations, depersonalization.

VI. Obsessions and compulsions—amount and quality of these behaviors are noted.

VII. Orientation—is client aware of correct time, place and personal identity.

VIII. Memory—what is condition of short- and long-term memory.

IX. Attention and concentration—asking client to count backwards by 7's is a common strategy.

X. Fund of general information—questions like "Who is the President?" or "What are some big cities in the U.S.?" are asked.

XI. Intelligence—estimated from educational achievement, reasoning ability, and fund of information.

XII. Insight and judgment—does patient understand probable outcomes of behavior.

XIII. Higher intellectual functioning—what is the quality of patient's form of thinking; is (s)he able to deal with abstraction.

The MSE is an attempt to gather much information efficiently. The questioning is direct, as suggested by the following excerpt from an MSE:

Clinician: Good morning. What is your name?
Client: Randolph S_____.
Clinician: Well, Mr. S_____, I would like to ask you some questions this morning. Is that all right?
Client: Fine.
Clinician: How long have you been here?
Client: Since yesterday morning.
Clinician: Why are you here?
Client: I don't know. I think my wife called the police and here I am.
Clinician: Well, what did you do to make her call the police?
Client: I don't know.
Clinician: What day is today?
Client: Tuesday, the twelfth.
Clinician: What year is it?
Client: 1977.
Clinician: What city are we in?
Client: Chicago.
Clinician: Who is the mayor of Chicago?

lems are most common in mental hospitals and other facilities where a diagnosis is required (see Hersen & Turner, 1985). Similar interviews may also occur when psychologists serve as diagnostic consultants to psychiatrists, courts, schools, or others interested in such questions as "Is Mr. P. competent to stand trial?" "Is Mrs. L. psychotic?" "Is Jimmy G. mentally retarded?"

Interviews focused on *describing* clients and their problems in more comprehensive terms usually occur in the context of the full-scale clinical exploration that precedes treatment by the assessor or other professional. Here, the interviewer elicits a detailed account of the client's strengths and weaknesses, current life situation, and history, often following outlines such as those presented in the previous chapter. In agencies employing a team approach, part of the problem-identification task is undertaken by social workers who use interviews to collect *social history* information about clients.

3 Orientation. People receiving psychological assessment or treatment often do not know exactly what to expect, let alone what is expected of them. This is especially true if they have had no previous contact with mental health professionals. To make these new experiences less mysterious and more comfortable, many clinicians conduct special interviews (or reserve segments of interviews) to acquaint the client with the assessment, treatment, or research procedures to come.

Orientation interviews are beneficial in at least two ways. First, because the client is encouraged to ask questions and make comments, misconceptions that might obstruct subsequent sessions can be discussed and corrected. As an example, some clients may assume that whatever they say to a clinician will be repeated to other members of the family. Fears of this kind can be allayed during an orientation interview, thus avoiding future problems.

Orientation interviews also can communicate new expectations designed to facilitate later interactions. Often this is done by describing or illustrating (through films, videotapes, or audio recordings) the kinds of things that "good" clients are expected to do in assessment or treatment. Thus, the client learns what is coming and what will be expected in the way of cooperation, effort, and self-disclosure. In most cases, clients are free to choose not to participate in the activities described. This freedom, along with accurate expectations by those who do participate, tends to make assessment and treatment sessions more efficient and effective (Goldstein, 1971; Heitler, 1976; Orne & Wender; 1968; Strupp & Bloxom, 1973).

4 Termination. Related to the problem of orienting clients to forthcoming clinical experiences is that of satisfactorily terminating those experiences. Persons who have just completed a series of assessment sessions involving extensive interviews, tests, and observations are understandably anxious to know "what the doctor found," how the information will be used, and who will have access to it. Such concerns are particularly acute when the assessor has acted as consultant to a school, court, or psychiatrist. An interview (or segment) designed to explain the procedures and protections involved in transmission of privileged information, and to provide a summary and interpretation of assessment results, can help alleviate the distress that clients feel about assessment.

In research settings, a termination interview is usually referred to as *debriefing*. Debriefing includes an explanation of the project in which the subject has participated and revelation of any deceptions employed in it. Debriefings permit subjects to ask questions and make comments about their research experiences. Debriefing of volunteers is aimed at assuring that no element of the research experience has left a harmful residue and is in keeping with the research ethics of the American Psychological Association (APA, 1981a; see Chapter 12). Candid debriefings may also benefit the clinician, since they often yield clues as to what variables determined volunteers' behavior in the laboratory (Orne, 1962).

Completion of treatment also requires some form of termination interview. Many loose ends need to be tied up: There is gratitude and affection to be expressed and accepted, reminders to be given about the handling of future problems, plans to be made for follow-up contacts, and reassurance given to clients about their ability to "go it alone." Termination interviews serve the important purpose of making the transition from treatment to posttreatment as smooth and productive as possible.

5 Crises. When a person's problems are of an immediate and pressing nature, and normal problem-solving skills prove inadequate to deal with the situation, the person is said to be in a crisis. Often, people in crises appear for help at clinical facilities or call a hot line, suicide prevention center, or other crisis service. In such cases, the interviewer does not have the luxury of scheduling a series of assessment sessions to be followed by some form of treatment. The crisis must be dealt with on the spot, requiring the combination of several interview goals that would otherwise be distributed over a number of sessions. The interviewer attempts to provide support, collect assessment data, and provide help. He or she must deal with the client in a calm and accepting fashion, ask relevant questions (e.g., "Have you ever tried to kill yourself?" "What kinds of pills do you have in the house?"), and work on the immediate problem directly or through referral to other services. One or two well-handled interviews during a crisis may be the beginning and the end of contact with a client whose need for assistance was temporary and situation-specific. For others, the crisis interview leads to subsequent assessment and treatment sessions.

6 Observation. As already noted, interviews provide an opportunity to observe client behaviors. Clinicians sometimes conduct special interviews to see how a person deals

with certain circumstances. Here, the interview provides a context for observing the interviewee's reaction to stressful, ambiguous, or conflict-laden situations. This sort of interview will be more thoroughly described when we consider observational assessments in Chapter 6. It should be noted, however, that these are special-purpose techniques not commonly used in clinical settings. They are more applicable in research or personnel selection.

INTERVIEW STRUCTURE

Probably the most basic variable in clinical interviews is *structure:* the degree to which the interviewer determines the content and course of the conversation. At one end of the structure continuum are *nondirective* interviews, in which the clinician does as little as possible to interfere with the natural flow of the client's speech and choice of topics. At the other end are *structured* interviews, which involve a carefully planned question-and-answer format. In between are many blends, usually referred to as *guided* or *directed* interviews.

Some excerpts from a few interviews may make the structure dimension clearer. Consider first this segment from a nondirective intake interview.

CLINICIAN: [Your relative] didn't go into much detail about what you wanted to talk about, so I wonder if you'd just start in at whatever you want to start in with, and tell me what kind of nervousness you have.

CLIENT: Well, it's, uh, I think if I were to put it in, in a few words, it seems to be a, a, a complete lack of self-confidence in, and an extreme degree of self-consciousness. Now, I have always been a very self-conscious person. I mean every, just about, since I was probably fourteen years old the first I remember of it. But for a long time I've realized that I was sort of using people as crutches. I mean I, a lot of things I felt I couldn't do myself I did all right if someone was along.

CLINICIAN: Um-hm.

CLIENT: And it's just progressed to the point where I'm actually using the four walls of the house as an escape from reality. I mean I don't, I don't care to go out. I, I certainly can't go out alone. . . . It's sort of a vicious circle. I find out I can't do it, and then I'm sure the next time I can't do it.

CLINICIAN: Um-hm.

CLIENT: And it just gets progressively worse. I think the first that I ever noticed it . . . (Wallen, 1956, p. 146)

The client continued a narrative that included information about the problem's onset and duration, her occupation and marriage, her father's death, and other topics. Notice that the clinician hardly says a word, although as we shall see, there are things he could have done to nondirectively encourage client speech if necessary.

At the other extreme are highly structured interviews. We have already described the mental status exam as one example of a structured interview. In recent years, several different structured interviews have been developed for the assessment and diagnosis of psychological disorders (Robins & Helzer, 1986). Their use has been stimulated by a desire to collect systematic, highly reliable information upon which to make the operationally defined diagnoses required by DSM-III (Spiker & Ehler, 1984). Structured interviews are designed according to the following principles: (1) The interviewer asks specific questions that can be replicated by other clinicians; (2) terms used in the interview are defined by clear, operational criteria; and (3) consistent rules are provided for determining the presence of crucial signs and symptoms. Among the structured interviews used most often by clinicians are the Psychiatric Status Schedule (Spitzer, Endicott, Fleiss & Cohen, 1970), the Diagnostic Interview Schedule (Robins, Helzer, Ratcliff & Seyfried, 1982),

the Present State Examination (Wing, Cooper & Sartorius, 1974), the Diagnostic Interview Schedule for Children (Costello, Edelbrock, Kalas, Kessler & Klaric, 1982), and the Anxiety Disorder Interview Schedule (DiNardo, O'Brien, Barlow, Waddell & Blanchard, 1983). The most widely employed and thoroughly researched structured interview is the Schedule for Affective Disorders and Schizophrenia (SADS; Endicott & Spitzer, 1978). Box 4-2 presents an excerpt from the SADS that illustrates some features of structured interviews.

In the following guided interview, both nondirective and structured features appear; the interviewer encourages the client to express herself freely, but also places limits on the topic by asking a specific question.

CLINICIAN: You say that you are very jealous a lot of the time and this upsets you a great deal.

CLIENT: Well, I know it's stupid for me to feel that way, but I am hurt when I even *think* of Mike with another woman.

CLINICIAN: You don't want to feel jealous but you do.

CLIENT: I know that's not the way a "liberated" woman should be.

CLINICIAN: What is your idea of how a liberated woman should feel?

CLIENT: I don't know. In many ways I feel I have changed so much in the last year. I really don't believe you have the right to own another person—and yet, when it happens to me, I feel really hurt. I'm such a hypocrite.

CLINICIAN: You're unhappy because you are not responding the way you really would like to?

CLIENT: I'm not the person I want to be.

CLINICIAN: So there's really "double jeopardy." When Mike is with someone else, it really hurts you. And, then when you feel jealous, you get down on yourself for being that way.

CLIENT: Yes, I guess I lose both ways. (Morganstern & Tevlin, 1981, p. 86)

BOX 4-2 An example of a structured interview

The Schedule for Affective Diseases and Schizophrenia (SADS; Endicott & Spitzer, 1978) is a structured interview developed at the New York State Psychiatric Institute in collaboration with the National Institute of Mental Health. The instrument was developed to increase the reliability of diagnosing major psychiatric disorders, particularly nonorganic psychoses. The SADS contains questions that address the specific criteria used to diagnose different psychiatric conditions; twenty-four different diagnoses are covered. The SADS is oriented toward inpatients and therefore does not cover such conditions as adjustment disorders and only incompletely covers personality disorders.

The SADS takes one and a half to two hours to complete; it is organized according to a "decision-tree" approach to diagnosis. This format requires that questions be asked in a predetermined order.

Although much of the information is gathered through a structured interview with the patient, other sources of data such as case records, referral notes, and interviews with family members can be used. The interview is divided into two parts. Part 1 focuses on the current episode of disturbance, with special attention paid to the time period when the symptoms were at their worst. Part 2 focuses more on historical information; for example, in the excerpt below, the interviewer is to obtain an overview of past psychiatric disturbance the patient has experienced. The questions the interviewer should ask are in italics. The instructions for scoring the responses and other instructions to the interviewer are in regular type.

The following questions are a guide to determine previous psychopathology, particularly episodes of illness.

Have you ever seen anyone (else) for emotional problems, your nerves, or the way you were feeling or acting (before this time)?

If yes, determine age, reason, type of contact, duration, and symptoms for each period of treatment using probes such as:

(Whom did you see . . . ?) (What kinds of problems were you having then?) (Any other times?)

Outpatient treatment prior to current episode or prior to last year if no distinct episode. Include contact with any professionally trained person for help with emotional or behavioral problems (include pills from M.D. for "nerves").

NOTES

0 No information
1 No contact
2 Consultation or brief period of treatment
3 Continuous treatment for at least six months or several brief periods
4 Continuous treatment lasting several years or numerous brief periods
_____ Age at first outpatient care (leave blank if never).

How old were you when you first saw someone for . . . ? Did you ever go to a doctor for your nerves?

Number of psychiatric hospitalizations prior to current episode or prior to past year if no distinct episode. Do not include transfers from one hospital to another. Best estimate of minimum number if exact number is unknown.

_____ Number (Note minimum number rather than a range or question mark, 99 if too numerous or ill-defined to count.)

Were you ever a patient in a psychiatric hospital or ward (before)? (How many times?)
(How old were you?)

_____ Age at first hospitalization (Leave blank if never)
0 No information
1 Never hospitalized
2 Less than three months
3 Less than six months
4 Less the one year
5 Less than two years
6 Less than five years
7 Five or more years

Total time of psychiatric hospitalizations (in, day, or night) prior to the current episode or prior to the past year if no current episode. Best estimate if exact time is unknown.

NOTES

Were there any (other) times when you or someone else felt you needed help because of your feelings, your nerves, or the way you were acting?

Determine age, duration, circumstances, and symptoms.

Source: Endicott & Spitzer, 1978.

While some clinicians adopt either a non-directive or structured interview approach under most circumstances, the majority adjust structure to accommodate the goals of the interview. For example, by their nature, crises demand more structure than might be needed during a routine intake interview. Structure may change during the course of an interview; many problem-identification interviews begin in a nondirective way and become more structured as the interview continues.

Structure also depends on the theoretical orientation and personl preferences of the interviewer. In general, phenomenological clinicians provide the least interview structure. Freudians usually provide more. Behavioral clinicians are likely to be the most verbally active and directive.

Although theoretical models influence clinicians' approaches to interviews, there is similarity among experienced clinicians of varying theoretical persuasions in the way specific interview situations are handled (see, e.g., Fiedler, 1950; Bruinink & Schroeder, 1979). One suspects that this is due, in part, to the fact that although no one has developed one "right" way to interview, certain broad strategies have proven valuable in practice and have thus been adopted by skilled clinicians representing every model (Goldfried, 1980).

These strategies are best studied in the context of the *guided* interview. In the following sections, we will examine guided interviews as a means of reviewing the interview techniques commonly employed by clinical psychologists. Selective emphasis on each of these procedures by proponents of various clinical models will be noted where appropriate.

STAGES IN THE INTERVIEW

Interviews are thought of as having a beginning, a middle, and an end. This is a considerable oversimplification, however, since such neat stages may not be discernible in all instances.

Intake or problem-identification interviews are most likely to pass through three segments. They usually begin with efforts at making the client comfortable and ready to speak freely (stage 1); continue into a central information-gathering stage (stage 2); and end with summary statements, client questions, and, if appropriate, plans for subsequent meetings (stage 3). As the client gets to know the clinician, stage 1 will probably grow shorter while stage 2 gets longer. Similarly, stage 3 may be brief until the final assessment interview, when it may take up most of the time available.

Treatment interviews sometimes follow a different three-stage format. A session may begin with the client's report of thoughts and events since the last meeting, continue with whatever treatment procedures are being employed, then conclude with a summary of current progress, plans for the next meeting, and/or "homework" assignments.

Interviews relating to crises, orientation, and termination may not be organized around a beginning-middle-end framework. Nevertheless, the three-stage model offers a convenient guide for organizing our review of "typical" clinical interviews.

Stage 1: Beginning the Interview

During initial interviews, clinicians carefully attend to the first minutes of contact. The client is likely to be uncomfortable about talking to a stranger about personal matters, and this apprehension may be intensified by uncertainty about what the psychologist will be doing. As a result, many clients enter the interview with a wait-and-see attitude that prompts them to be careful about what they say. If this attitude continued throughout the conversation, little valuable assessment information would be generated.

Most clinicians see the establishment of *rapport*—a harmonious and comfortable working relationship—as their main task during the first part of initial interviews. Rapport can be gained in many ways, many of which involve common sense and courtesy. A client's anxiety and uncertainty can be eased by demystification of the interview. A warm smile, friendly greeting, and a handshake are excellent beginnings to an interview. For clients who smoke, an invitation to do so and a conveniently placed ashtray can be comforting. Small talk about the weather or difficulty in finding the office also ease the client's transition into the interview but should not go on so long that the interview loses its distinctive quality.

Although interviews can occur anywhere, certain settings are especially conducive to building rapport for most clients. Except for those individuals whose cultural background might cause such surroundings to be threatening, interviews are best conducted in a comfortable, private office. This is because, first, most people find it easier to relax when they can get comfortable physically. Second, it is easier to assure the client of the interview's confidential nature in such a setting.

Several other office characteristics can aid rapport. A reassuring equality is established when two people sit a few feet apart on similar chairs of equal height. If the clinician sits in a high-backed, massive chair behind a huge desk which is six feet from the client's smaller, lower seat, rapport may be impaired. A desk cleared of other work, along with precautions to hold phone calls and prevent other intrusions, lets the client know that she or he has the clinician's full attention and conveys sincere interest in what the client has to say.

This list of rapport-building techniques could be extended almost indefinitely; the point is that from the beginning, the clinician tries to create a warm, comfortable environment and a relationship that will encourage the client to speak freely and honestly about whatever topics are relevant to the interview (see Goldstein, 1976);

Skilled clinicians can establish rapport during the first stage of an initial interview but even for them, the process continues into the second and third stages and into subsequent contacts as well. Like other social relationships, the one between client and clinician takes time to grow. Once that relationship has taken root, the initial interview can move into its second, or information-gathering, stage.

Stage 2: The Middle of the Interview

Transition to the middle of an initial interview should be as smooth for the client as possible. The ways in which this is accomplished by the clinician illustrate many of the major interview tactics.

Nondirective Techniques. In most cases interviewers begin the second stage with nondirective, *open-ended* questions. Common examples are: "What brings you here today?" or "Would you like to tell me about the problems you referred to on the telephone?" A major advantage of the open-ended approach is that it frees the client to begin in his or her own way. An open-ended invitation to talk allows the client to ease into painful or embarrassing topics without feeling pressed.[1] Relatively nonstressful beginnings of this type aid rapport because they

communicate the clinician's willingness to listen to whatever the client has to say.

Contrast the open-ended initiations suggested above with "binding" statements like: "You said you thought there was a sex problem. Is it yours or your wife's?" or "What kind of work do you do?" Openings of this type prematurely focus the conversation on topics that may be threatening or irrelevant. An interview whose second stage employs "binding" tactics often degenerates into a superficial question-and-answer session in which the client may feel put-upon, misunderstood, and frustrated. Accordingly, such "interrogation" procedures are usually reserved for situations in which the client's behavior indicates that spontaneous speech will not be forthcoming.[2]

Open-ended questions or comments are not restricted to the beginning of an interview's second stage. Such devices are called upon whenever the clinician wishes to prompt the client's verbal behavior while influencing its content as little as possible. Classic remarks like "Tell me a bit more about that" and "How did you feel about that?" exemplify continued implementation of a nondirective strategy. This strategy is supplemented by tactics designed to help clients express themselves fully and to enhance rapport by communicating the clinician's understanding and acceptance. The most general of these tactics is called *active listening*. Active listening involves responding to the client's speech in ways that indicate understanding and encouragement to go on. The clinician's "mm-hmms" in the nondirective interview excerpt presented earlier represent active listening. Others include comments such as "I see," "I understand," "I'm with you," or "Right."

A related strategy is called *paraphrasing*, in which the clinician restates what the client has said in order to (1) show that she or he

---

[1] Clients often begin with a "ticket of admission" problem which may not be the one of greatest concern to them. The functional reason for the client's visit may appear only after varying amounts of diversionary conversation.

[2] This is not always the case. Rogers (1967) provides an example of continued, and ultimately fruitful, use of nondirective interviewing with a withdrawn institutionalized client (see Chapter 10).

has been listening closely, and (2) give the client a chance to correct the remark if it was misinterpreted. Carl Rogers calls this *reflection* and emphasizes not only restating content, but also highlighting client feelings. Let's consider some illustrations:

A.

CLIENT: Sometimes I get so mad at my husband, I could kill him.
CLINICIAN: You would just like to get rid of him altogether.

B.

CLIENT: Sometimes I get so mad at my husband, I could kill him.
CLINICIAN: He really upsets you sometimes.

In example A, the clinician merely reworded the client's remark. In example B, he or she reflected the *feeling* contained in the remark. Most clients respond to paraphrasing by continuing to talk, usually along the same lines as before, often in greater detail. Paraphrasing often is preferable to a direct question because the latter might change or restrict the conversation. This is illustrated in the following interactions:

A.

CLIENT: What it comes down to is that life just doesn't seem worth living sometimes.
CLINICIAN: Sometimes it all just seems to be too much.
CLIENT: Yeah, and I don't know what to do when I feel that way. I don't really think I want to die, not really. But I also dread the thought of another day starting. For example . . .

B.

CLIENT: What it comes down to is that life just doesn't seem worth living sometimes.
CLINICIAN: How often do you feel that way?
CLIENT: Oh, off and on.

There is a place for questions such as that asked in example B, but unless one knows enough to start pinpointing specifics, inter-rupting with such questions early in the interview will limit the initial picture of the problem and may cause the client to feel harassed. Immediate use of direct queries can suggest to clients that they should simply wait for the next question. In general, this message does not promote rapport.

Paraphrasing can be used as a clarification device when the clinician is confused about what a client has said. Consider the following:

CLIENT: I told my husband that I didn't want to live with him anymore so he said "fine" and left. Well, when I got back, I found out that the son of a bitch kept all our furniture!

If, as is probably the case, the interviewer does not comprehend the sequence of events described, he or she could simply say "What?", but that might be interpreted by the client as an insult or as an indication that the clinician is a dunce. Instead, a combination of paraphrase and request for clarification serves nicely:

CLINICIAN: OK, let's see if I've got this straight. You told your husband you didn't want to live with him, so *he* left. You later came back to your house from somewhere else and found he had taken the furniture?

Ideally, the client will either confirm this interpretation or fill in the missing pieces. If not, the clinician may wish to use more direct questioning, which we shall now discuss.

Directive Techniques. Most interviewers supplement nondirective tactics with more directive questions whose form, wording, and content are often the result of careful (though usually on-the-spot) planning. For example, the clinician wants to avoid asking "binding" questions which may (1) damage rapport and (2) bias assessment data by forcing the client to choose an artificial or inaccurate response supplied by the interviewer. Look at the following illustrative questions:

A. "Do you feel better or worse when your husband is out of town?"
B. "How do you feel when your husband is out of town?"

Example A offers a clear, but possibly irrelevant, two-choice situation. This is a "Do you walk to work or carry your lunch?" question, for which the most valid answer may be "Neither." Some clients are not assertive enough in the interview to ignore the choice, so they settle for one unsatisfactory response or the other. Unless there is a special reason for offering clients only a few response alternatives, skilled interviewers prefer to ask direct questions in a form that gets at specific information, but also leaves clients free to choose their own words (see example B above).

Experienced clinicians also avoid asking questions that suggest their own answers. Notice the implications contained in this query: "You've suffered with this problem a long time?" Questions such as this communicate what the interviewer expects to hear, and some clients will oblige by biasing their response. "How long have you had this problem?" is a better alternative.

Along similar lines, inquiries based upon unwarranted assumptions should be avoided in clinical interviews. These are "Do you still whip your old father?" questions. No matter what response is given, it is likely to be misunderstood and muddy the assessment waters. Notice the hidden assumption in the example: "How bad is your insomnia when you are depressed?" If the client sleeps especially soundly when feeling low, this question cannot be answered without contradicting the clinician. A careful interviewer might explore that same issue with the following question: "You said you are often depressed. How do you feel during those times?"

Combining Interview Tactics. Because the interview is flexible, clinicians are free to combine the tactics we have described. It is common to facilitate the client's speech with open-ended requests, paraphrasing, prompts, and other active listening techniques, and then use more directive questions to zero in on topics of special importance.

However, directive procedures do not take over completely as the interview progresses. They continue to be mixed with less directive tactics. An example of this blending is provided by the concept of *repeated scanning and focusing*. Here the interviewer first scans a particular topic nondirectively, than focuses on it in more directive fashion:

CLINICIAN: You mentioned that your family is back East. Could you tell me something about them?
CLIENT: There's not much to tell. There's Dad, Mom, and the twins. They all seem to like it back there so I guess they'll stay forever.
CLINICIAN: What else can you say about them?
CLIENT: Well, Dad is a retired high school principal. Mom used to be strictly a housewife but, since us kids have grown, she's been working part time.
CLINICIAN: How did you get along with your folks when you lived at home?
CLIENT: Really fine. I've always thought they were great people and that's probably why they had so little trouble with me. Of course, now and then there would be a problem, but not often.
CLINICIAN: What kinds of problems were there?

The interviewer might go on to explore several specific issues about the client's relationship with both parents, then move on to another topic, again beginning with scanning procedures and progressing to more focused questions.

Clinicians who emphasize rapport and other relationship factors tend to conduct interviews heavily weighted toward the non-directive side. Behavioral interviewers also emphasize a good client-clinician relationship, but mainly as the context for assessment of specific information. Their tactics tend to be more directive (Morganstern & Tevlin, 1981).

Stage 3: Closing the Interview

The last stage of an interview can provide valuable assessment data as well as an opportunity to enhance rapport. The interviewer may initiate the third stage with a statement like this:

We have been covering some very valuable information here and I appreciate your willingness to tell me about it. I know our session hasn't been easy for you. Since we're running out of time for today, I thought we could look back over what we've covered and then give you a chance to ask *me* some questions.

The clinician accomplishes several things here. First, the impending conclusion of the interview is signaled. Second, the client is praised for cooperativeness and reassured that the clinician understands that the interview has been stressful. Third, a plan for the final minutes is suggested; it invites the client to pose questions or make comments which may have been formed but were not verbalized for various reasons.

The clinician's recap of the session serves to summarize interview content and to check that she or he has not misunderstood anything of importance. Comments from the client during this stage can be enlightening, especially when they disclose misconceptions or information gaps. This part of the interview (especially when it ends a first contact) becomes a miniature version of the termination interview described earlier. It usually concludes with leave-taking rituals (e.g., "It was good of you to come") and, when appropriate, confirmation of plans for future contact with the interviewer or other professional.

The last segment of interviews may evoke important client behavior. Clients sometimes drop bombshells during this period: "Oh gosh, look at the time. I have to hurry to a meeting with my parole officer. He is especially picky with murderers." A remark like this one is extreme, but it illustrates the fact that some clients wait until the interview's end to reveal their most sensitive information. Other individuals disclose such information more or less inadvertently. They assume the interview is over and thus drop whatever protective cover they may have used earlier. For these reasons, the clinician devotes as much care to the final stage of the interview as to the stages that precede it.

COMMUNICATION IN THE INTERVIEW

Judicious combination of the interview procedures we have described is necessary for effective rapport building and fruitful information gathering. However, there are other factors that contribute significantly to interview quality. Chief among these is the clarity of communication between interviewer and interviewee. All the clinician's skill at posing good questions, encouraging the client to talk, or making smooth transitions between topics may be of little value if he or she does not understand what the client is saying and vice versa.

The basic problem in interview communication is message transmission. The speaker must put the message (s)he means to convey in transmittable form (e.g., words, gestures) and then send it. The listener must receive the message and interpret it within his or her own frame of reference. Communication lapses can occur at many points in both verbal and nonverabl channels.

Because skilled clincians attempt to avoid communication problems, they try to maximize the clarity of the messages they send and to be sure about the messages they receive. Let us consider an example of poor clinical communication and then look at some ways breakdowns of this type can be made less likely. In the following hypothetical exchange, the speakers' thoughts are in parentheses:

CLINICIAN: (I wonder what his teenage social life was like.) Tell me a little about the friends you had in high school.
CLIENT: (I had dozens of social acquaintances, but only one person who was a really close friend.) There was just one, a guy named Mike.
CLINICIAN: (So he was pretty much of a loner.) How did you feel about that?
CLIENT: (It was fine. I had a great time, went to lots of parties, had lots of dates, but knew I could always depend on Mike to talk with about really personal things.) I enjoyed it. Mike and I got along really well.
CLINICIAN: (Not only was he a social isolate, he claims to have liked it that way. I wonder if he is being honest with himself about that.) Did you ever wish you had more friends?
CLIENT: (For crying out loud, he makes it sound like it's a crime to have one really close friend. I think we've talked enough about this.) No.

Verbal Communication

In the above illustration, the clinician used "friend" to refer to casual as well as intimate acquaintances. Because this word had a different meaning for the client, it led to misunderstanding. The conversation could have gone on in this fruitless way for quite a while before the interviewer and the client straightened out their problem.

Although the client and clinician may technically be speaking the same language and thus assume they understand one another, the interviewer must be aware that educational, social, racial, cultural, economic, and religious factors can impair communication. Unless the clinician takes

the client's background and frame of reference into account, and asks for clarification when verbal referents are unclear, the interview will suffer. Consider this example:

CLIENT: When I'm in such heavy situations, I just get real uptight.
CLINICIAN: What makes you uptight?
CLIENT: Well, the whole thing. Everybody kind of hanging out and running around. I can't seem to get it together with anybody, so I guess I freak out.
CLINICIAN: And then what happens?
CLIENT: I usually go home and go to sleep. But I'm usually pretty bummed out.
CLINICIAN: Are you saying that you don't fit in with these people and that's what makes you feel bummed out?
CLIENT: Well, I don't know. These are my friends, I guess—but it never seems to work out. (Morganstern & Tevlin, 1981, p. 91)

Do these people understand each other? We do not know for sure, and as long as the interview goes on this way, neither do they. This clinician will at some point need to request clarification of the client's words. She or he might say the following in order to clarify the information:

CLIENT: When I'm in such heavy situations, I just get real uptight. . . .
CLINICIAN: When you say that you're uptight in these situations, what does that mean to you?
CLIENT: Well, uptight, you know. Tense.
CLINICIAN: You mean your muscles get tense?
CLIENT: My neck gets very sore—and I get a headache lots of times.
CLINICIAN: What else happens?
CLIENT: Well, either because of my neck or my headache, I start sweating a lot.
CLINICIAN: When you say you're uptight you are really experiencing it physically. What are you thinking when this happens?
CLIENT: I'm thinking, man you are really paranoid. You just can't relax in any situ-

ation. You really are a loser. And then I want to get out of there fast. . . . (Morganstern & Tevlin, 1981, p. 91)

Clients can become just as confused as clinicians, but if they are reluctant to appear stupid or to question a person in authority they may not reveal their dilemma. Some evidence on this point comes from a study conducted in a medical setting by Korsch and Negrete (1972). Their data showed that communication from doctors to patients' mothers in a pediatric clinic was obstructed by the use of medical terms and that client confusion and dissatisfaction often resulted. For example, a "lumbar puncture" (spinal tap) was sometimes assumed to be an operation for draining the child's lungs; "incubation period" was interpreted by one mother as the time during which her child had to be kept in bed.

Circumventing similar problems in interviewing is often difficult, but it can be facilitated by attention to certain guidelines. Skilled interviewers avoid jargon, ask questions in a straightforward way (e.g., "What experiences have you had with masturbation?", not "Do you ever touch yourself?"), and request feedback from their client (e.g., "Is all this making sense to you?"). In addition, clinicians try to assure that their verbal behavior conveys patience, concern, and acceptance. Expressions of impatience or prejudgment by the interviewer are not desirable. Goldstein (1976) has summarized some conversational do's and don'ts from Wolberg (1967) illustrating the kinds of verbal communications clinicians prefer (and avoid). An example is presented in edited form below:

CLIENT: I feel helpless and I think I ought to end it all.

Unsuitable responses:
A. "You better snap out of it soon."
B. "Well, that's a nice attitude, I must say."

Suitable responses:
A. "I wonder what is behind this feeling."
B. "You sound as if you think you're at the end of your rope."

Nonverbal Communication

As with all human beings, a constant stream of nonverbal behavior accompanies the client's and the interviewer's verbal behavior. Nonverbal communication channels usually remain open even when the verbal channel is shut down. This has been understood by perceptive individuals for centuries. In 1905 Freud summarized the point well: "He that has eyes to see and ears to hear may convince himself that no mortal can keep a secret. If his lips are silent, he chatters with his fingertips; betrayal oozes out of him at every pore" (pp. 77–78). Since both members of an interview dyad are sending and receiving nonverbal messages, the clinician must be sensitive to incoming signals as well as to those she or he may be transmitting.

A sample of nonverbal interview dimensions is summarized below:

1. Physical appearance—e.g., height, weight, grooming, style and condition of clothing, unusual characteristics, muscular development, hairstyle
2. Movements—e.g., gestures; repetitive arm, hand, head, leg, or foot motions; tics or other apparently involuntary movements; pacing; handling of cigarettes, matches, or other objects
3. Posture—e.g., slouching, rigidity, crossed or uncrossed arms or legs, head in hands
4. Eye contact—e.g., constant, fleeting, none
5. Facial expressions—e.g., smiles, frowns, grimaces, raised eyebrows
6. Emotional arousal—e.g., tears, "wet" eyes, sweating, dryness of lips, frequent swallowing, blushing or paling, voice or hand tremor, rapid respiration, frequent shifts in body po-

sition, "startle" reactions, inappropriate laughter

7. Speech variables—e.g., tone of voice, speed, slurring, lisp, stuttering, blocking, accent, clarity, "style," sudden shifts or omissions

In addition to picking up nonverbal client behaviors, clinicians also look for inconsistencies between the verbal and nonverbal channels. The statement "I feel pretty good today" is viewed differently if the speaker is on the verge of tears than if a happy smile is evident.

Interviewers also try to coordinate their own verbal and nonverbal behavior so as to give the client unambiguous messages. Telling a client "Take your time" will carry more weight as a statement of patient interest if it is said slowly and quietly than if it is blurted out while tapping a foot. Friendly eye contact, some head nodding, an occasional smile, and an attentive posture lets the client know that the interviewer is listening closely. Overdoing it may backfire, however. A constant smile, a continuously knitted brow, sidelong glances, and other theatrics are more likely to convey interviewer anxiety or inexperience than concern.

Most clinicians agree that observation of nonverbal behavior begins when the client and clinician meet and continues until they part. They often differ, however, as to what nonverbal behavior means. Interviewers committed to a sign-oriented approach draw higher-level inferences from nonverbal behaviors than those adopting a sample-oriented stance.

For example, a behaviorist's interpretation of increased respiration, perspiration, and fidgeting while a client talks about sex would probably be that some emotional arousal is associated with that topic. Psychodynamic interviewers may go another step to postulate that noverbal behaviors (e.g., twirling a ring on a finger) are symbolic representations of sexual activity or other unconscious impulses (e.g., Feldman, 1959;

Garner, 1970).[3] Whatever level of inference stems from it, however, nonverbal behavior serves as a powerful communication channel and a valuable source of interview data.

A General Note

There are many aspects of clinical interviewing that we have not covered. Dealing with silences, how to address the client, the pros and cons of note taking, handling personal questions, and confronting a client's inconsistencies are a few of the additional issues that face clinicians in interviews. The reader interested in more detailed exploration of interviewing techniques should consult the references listed at the beginning of this chapter.

RESEARCH ON THE INTERVIEW

Social Interaction and Influence in the Interview

Until 1942, when Carl Rogers published the first transcripts from phonographic recordings of therapy interviews, the exact nature of clinical interactions had been unknown.[4] Afterward, interview research grew rapidly. At first it focused on issues like the effects of recording and the relative accuracy of clinicians' summaries versus electrical recordings of the same interview (Covner, 1944; Snyder, 1945). Later, when it was established that recording devices

---

[3] Moderate- to high-level inferences about nonverbal behavior in nonclinical contexts are also common, as exemplified by popular books such as *Body Language* (Fast, 1970) and *Man Watching: A Field Guide to Human Behavior* (Morris, 1977), as well as more scholarly works (e.g., Harper, Wiens & Matarazzo, 1978).

[4] Rogers's recordings were considered scandalous at the time, since tradition ruled out all but narrative case reports. The fact that he was a *psychologist* (not a psychiatrist) doing therapy with an adult made Rogers's revelations even more distasteful to those not yet accustomed to the expanding roles of postwar clinicians.

were not disruptive and provided the most complete account of the interview, researchers began several new areas of study.

Descriptive Research

One of these new directions involved descriptive research aimed at relating interview variables to rapport building, therapy effectiveness, and other interpersonal dimensions. Some studies focused on differences in specific interview tactics used by Rogerians and non-Rogerians (e.g., Porter, 1943; Seeman, 1949; Snyder, 1954; Strupp, 1960), while others tried to define interview variables like client resistance (Snyder, 1953), interviewer ambiguity (Bordin, 1955), and relationship warmth (Rausch & Bordin, 1957). Other investigators performed detailed analyses of the content of conversations as a means of better understanding the interview process (e.g., Auld & Murray, 1955; Leary & Gill, 1959; Mahl, 1959). One team of researchers devoted years just to the content analysis of the first five minutes of a single interview (Pittenger, Hockett & Danehy, 1960).

Researchers also sought to describe interviews in terms of *noncontent* variables. Specialized equipment was used to collect information about physiological arousal of interviewer and client (e.g., Greenblatt, 1959) and the stability, idiosyncrasies, and equilibrium of their speech and periods of silence (e.g., Lennard & Bernstein, 1960; Saslow & Matarazzo, 1959). It was suggested that such data could be used to define interview concepts like *empathy, transference,* and *insight* (Matarazzo, 1965).

Experimental Research

The research of the 1940s and 1950s generated large amounts of data about the interview, highlighting its complexity as a social event. An additional dimension of this complexity was revealed by experiments which confirmed that interviews are not only data-gathering contexts, but *social influ-*

ence situations as well. Research of this type was stimulated in large measure by Skinner's (1948, 1957) conceptualization of verbal behavior as a set of responses that can be modified by its consequences.

Dozens of *verbal conditioning* studies soon began to appear. They showed in general that not only can simple responses (like the use of plural nouns) be affected by reinforcement, but that more clinically relevant verbalizations (reports of family memories, expression of feelings, self-evaluations, and delusional speech) are alterable through contingent interviewer feedback (see reviews by Greenspoon, 1962; Kanfer, 1968; Krasner, 1965; and Salzinger, 1959).

Other research indicated that noncontent variables in the interview could also be systematically influenced by the clinician. For example, duration of interviewee speech was increased when the interviewer nodded his head or said "mm-hmm" while listening (Kanfer & McBrearty, 1962; Matarazzo, 1965). Work by Matarazzo and his colleagues (e.g., Matarazzo, Weitman, Saslow & Wiens, 1963) showed other ways in which interviewer and interviewee speech duration are related. When an interviewer increased and then decreased the duration of his own utterances over three parts of a conversation, interviewees did the same. When he decreased then increased his speech length, interviewees again followed suit. This is called *synchrony* (see Figure 4-1).

A quick glance at this research might give the impression that interview assessment would always be facilitated by social reinforcement of client speech and/or by increasing the clinician's speech duration. Unfortunately, the problem is not that simple. For one thing, during assessment, interviewers avoid reinforcing specific types of statements, since this may bias the data generated. In addition, all the relationships described in published research do not hold universally. As an example, although synchrony was observed during controlled interviews and has also appeared in other settings (i.e., conversations between astronauts and their ground control stations; Matarazzo, Wiens, Saslow, Dunham & Voas, 1964), it was not found in a therapy situation (Matarazzo, Wiens, Matarazzo & Saslow, 1968). Further, the use of "mm-hmms," especially when they are not contingent on specific responses, does not produce consistent effects (e.g., Siegman, 1972, 1974, 1976). Davis (1971) showed that social competition may operate instead of or along with social reinforcement in some interviews, and Dulany (1968) demonstrated that verbal conditioning may depend on subjects' awareness of the contingency in effect.

Findings such as these suggest that the *situation* in which the interview takes place and the *social roles* of the participants can alter the nature of the interaction. In therapy, for example, the synchrony-producing influence of clinician upon client may be moderated or even reversed by the client's influence upon the clinician. Unless the clinician experimentally controls utterance durations (as in Figure 4-1), they may increase with quiet clients and decrease with those who are more talkative (e.g., Heller, Myers & Kline, 1963; Lennard & Bernstein, 1960). Pope, Nudler, VonKorff, and McGhee (1974) showed that the relative status of interviewer and interviewee can influence their interaction. When novice student interviewers talked to other students in an experimental setting, synchrony in verbal productivity occurred, but it disappeared when higher-status professionals did the interviews.

Some of the data on social influence in the interview are surprising. For example, "warm" interviewers do not always enhance interviewee speech (Heller, 1972; Heller, Davis & Myers, 1966), and self-disclosure may be facilitated by interviewers who are reserved (even hostile) and who transmit messages that are somewhat ambiguous (Ganzer & Sarason, 1964; Heller, 1972). Perhaps under moderately stressful experimental circumstances some subjects feel they should try to please the interviewer by

FIGURE 4-1. Interviewer influence on duration of interviewee speech. (From the *Handbook of Clinical Psychology,* edited by Benjamin B. Wolman. Copyright © 1965 by McGraw-Hill Book Company. Used with permission of McGraw-Hill Book Company.)

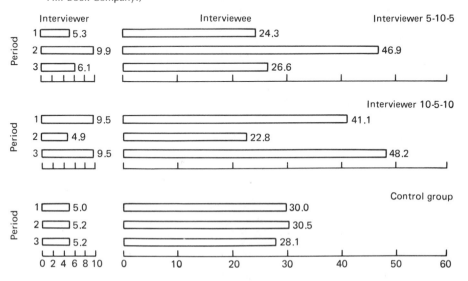

Mean duration of single units of speech, seconds

"telling all." It is doubtful, however, that stress-producing interviewer behaviors aid client verbalization in actual clinical assessment interviews (Heller, 1972).

In summary, research on interview interaction and influence has shown these areas to be extremely complicated aspects of social behavior which are under the influence of interviewer, client, relationship, and situational factors. The data show some progress in researchers' technical and conceptual sophistication, but they do not tell the individual clinician how to conduct interviews. Because there is not a single "right" way for all interviewers to talk to all clients under all circumstances, the greatest value of interview research is in providing scientific information about what is likely to happen when various combinations of people, tactics, and situations occur in clinical assessment.

Reliability and Validity of Interview Data

The degree to which an interviewee gives the same information on different occasions or to different interviewers (reliability) and the degree to which that information is accurate (validity) depend upon the clinician, the client, and the circumstances of the interview. How strongly these factors affect interview reliability and validity is still unknown, so it is possible to give only a general idea of the value of the interview as a data source.

Reliability. Some writers estimate interview reliability by looking at the degree to which different judges agree on the *inferences* (e.g., ratings, diagnoses, or personality trait descriptions) drawn from conversations with the same client (DiNardo, O'Brien, Barlow, Waddell & Blanchard, 1983; Matarazzo, 1965). This practice confounds the reliability of what the client said with the quality of the interviewer's inference system. For example, if a client tells two clinicians the same thing and they draw different conclusions from it, one might conclude that the interview was reliable, but the interviewers' inferences were not.

It is preferable to ask about the reliability of interview data themselves. One would expect clients' responses to be similar from one interview to the next or from one interviewer to the next, but there is surprisingly little research on this point. The available data come mainly from survey research and indicate that when innocuous information (such as age) is requested, or when interinterview intervals are short, reliability can be quite high (e.g., Sobell & Sobell, 1975; Vaughn & Reynolds, 1951). Reliability is also generally quite high with many of the structured interviews (Spiker & Ehler, 1984).

Other interview data are less reliable. Wenar & Coulter (1962) found that only 43 percent of the parents they talked to gave consistent information about their children's history (e.g., age at toilet training) when interviews were separated by three to six years. Other research on parents' reports about their children's behavioral history reveals that reliability tends to be particularly low on questions about vague issues such as overactivity and quite high on more easily defined questions such as stuttering. Reports on child-rearing practices such as toilet training and weaning tend to change from interview to interview, usually in the direction of making the parents appear more up-to-date and in line with the latest trends (Robbins, 1963). Perhaps because agreement between clinical interview reliability is presumed, or because in typical clinical situations there is little interest in obtaining the same information more than once, most evaluative research on the interview has focused upon its *validity*.

Validity. Interview data can be extremely accurate in absolute terms; in comparison to other assessment tools, it may be the best source of clinical information. In a study cited by Thorne (1972), for example, answers to the question, "Are you homosexual?" were more valid indicators of sexual orientation than any combination of psychological tests. Mischel (1968) cites evidence that what people say they will do is a better predictor of future behavior than test scores; but others (Nisbett & Wilson, 1977) disagree. The validity of interview responses can be reduced under certain circumstances. A client's response to "Tell me something about your marital problems" might be very different from his answer to the question, "Why can't you get along with your spouse?" (Heller, 1972; Thomas, 1973). Further, interviewer characteristics such as age, sex, or race may alter interviewee candor (e.g., Benney, Riesman & Star, 1956; Grantham, 1973; Erlich & Riesman, 1961; Ledvinka, 1971).

Clients may also misremember or purposely distort various types of information. The probability of distortion is increased when the information sought is of an emotionally charged or sensitive nature, such as alcohol and drug use, criminal record, sexual behavior, behavior disorders, or instances of mental hospitalization (Chess, Thomas & Birch, 1966; Fidler & Kleinknecht, 1977; Hare, 1985; Kolko, Kazdin & Meyer, 1985; Schwitzgebel & Kolb, 1974; Sobell, Sobell & Samuels, 1974). Clients are often wary about what they will tell about themselves and to whom; a friend may laugh at tales of your vegetable imitations, but a psychologist might treat them more seriously. The desire to present oneself in a particular light to a mental health professional has been called "impression-management" (Braginsky, Braginsky & Ring, 1969; Goffman, 1959), and it can lead to invalid interview data (Sherman, Trief & Sprafkin, 1975). Situational factors of various kinds may also affect the validity of interview data. For example, self-disclosure may vary as a function of the topics discussed and whether candor and frankness are expected in the situation (Heller, 1971; Wilson & Rappaport, 1974).

Interviewer Error and Bias. Reliable and valid interview data are of little value if they are distorted by the interviewer. Therefore, an evaluation of the interview as a data source must consider its rather strong susceptibility to distortion.

Distortion may be accidental, as when the client's words are not reported accurately by the interviewer. Unless the interaction has been recorded, important information may be lost or misrepresented simply because the volume of incoming data is so large. Sometimes, "errors" are deliberate. Schwitzgebel & Kolb (1974) quoted an interviewer hired to conduct structured interviews as saying: "One of the questions asked for five reasons why parents had put their child in an institution. I found most people can't think of five reasons. I didn't want [the boss] to think I was goofing off, so I always filled in all five."

Personal biases, preferences, and prejudice may affect the conclusions reached by interviewers. In an early study by Rice

FIGURE 4-2. *Miss Peach* by Mell Lazarus. (Courtesy of Mell Lazarus and News America Syndicate.)

(1929), social workers' judgments of why skid-row bums had become destitute were found to be related to personal views, not just to interview data. Thus, a prohibitionist interviewer saw drinking as the cause of poverty in 62 percent of the cases, while a socialist said the interviewees were poor mainly because of general economic conditions. Raines and Rohrer (1955, 1960) showed that interviewers tend to have "favorite" diagnoses which they apply more often than any others. Similarly, Temerlin (1968) found that psychologists' and psychiatrists' diagnoses of a client may be determined by prejudicial information given to them before they ever hear the client speak.

One possible way around such problems would be to employ a mechanical interviewer, and computer interviewing is a part of some medical and psychological assessment procedures. Clients communicate with the computer through a television screen and a word processor; they appear to accept this type of interaction quite well. Although this approach eliminates error and bias in inquiry and response recording, computers are not likely to replace humans in interview-based assessment because the flexibility of a live clinician is an indispensable part of interviewing. However, computer interviewing saves time and energy in the gathering of routine information, is easily standardized, and is accepted well by most clients (Erdman, Klein & Greist, 1985).

A Final Note. Research on the interview as an assessment tool does not justify one all-encompassing conclusion. As Garfield (1974, p. 90) put it, "The interview has been used in so many different ways for various purposes, by individuals with varying skills, that it is a difficult matter to make a final judgment concerning its values." Much depends upon the skill of the interviewer, but the exact nature of what "skill" means is still not clear. Although the interview will continue to occupy a primary assessment role in clinical psychology, it must also remain the object of research. Peterson's (1968) conclusion is still timely: "We are not justified in extolling the virtues of the interview as a clinical procedure at the present time. It is widely used. It makes sense. But its merit as a clinical procedure needs far better documentation than is available to date, and its improvement as a procedure awaits appropriate experimental investigation" (p. 129).

chapter 5

Testing in Clinical Psychology

The history of clinical psychology is intimately related to the development and use of psychological tests. Even though clinicians now perform many functions in addition to testing, tests remain an important part of clinical research and practice (Lubin, Larsen & Matarazzo, 1984; Mitchell, 1985). It is therefore essential that we consider the nature of psychological tests, the ways they are constructed, and the research on their value as assessment tools.

WHAT IS A TEST?

In simplest terms, a test is a systematic procedure for observing and describing a person's behavior in a standard situation (Cronbach, 1970). Tests present certain planned stimuli (inkblots or true-false questions, for example) and ask the client to respond to

them in some way. The client's reactions are recorded as the test's results or scores to be used as sample, sign, or correlate in the clinician's assessment strategy. Test data may lead to conservative, situation-specific statements (e.g., "The client appeared disoriented during testing and was correct on fifteen out of sixty items") or to sweeping, high-level inferences (e.g., "The client's ego boundaries are so ill-defined as to make adequate functioning outside an institution very unlikely"). Most commonly, test results guide inferences that are between these extremes.

Tests are like highly structured interviews because they ask the person to respond to specific assessment stimuli presented in a predetermined sequence. They also share characteristics with observational assessments by providing an opportunity for the clinician to watch the client in the test situation. In some ways, however, tests are distinct from other assessment techiques. For example:

1. A test can be administered in a nonsocial context in which observational assessment does not supplement test data.
2. A client's test results can often be compared mathematically to the responses of hundreds or thousands of other persons who have taken the same test. When a large amount of previous test data (called *norms*) are available for comparison with each new client's responses, the test is said to be *standardized*.[1]
3. Tests can be administerd to clients in groups as well as individually. College entrance examinations provide a good example of how masses of people can be assessed at the same time through tests.

WHAT DO TESTS TEST?

There are thousands of psychological tests in existence today. They are administered to infants, children, adolescents, adults, senior citizens, students, soldiers, mental patients, office workers, prisoners, and every other imaginable group (see Mitchell, 1985). Further, tests appear in many *modes* or *styles*. Some pose direct, specific questions ("Do you ever feel discouraged?"), while others ask for general reactions to less distinct stimuli ("Tell me what you see in this drawing"). Some are presented in paper-and-pencil form, while others are given orally. Some require use of verbal skills ("What is a chicken?"), and others ask the client to perform various tasks ("Please trace the correct path through this puzzle maze").

Despite the enormous variety of tests in existence, many have similar purposes and can be grouped into four general categories. The majority of tests seek to measure (1) *intellectual functioning,* (2) *personality characteristics,* (3) *attitudes, interests, preferences,* and *values,* or (4) *ability.* We shall consider each of these categories later. The tests most commonly used by clinical psychologists are those of intellectual functioning and personality (Lubin, Larsen & Matarazzo, 1984). This is partly because clinicians are most interested in these areas in their own treatment and research, and partly because other people expect them to provide advice on these variables.

A major reason for the proliferation of tests is that testers continually hope to measure things in ever more reliable, valid, and sophisticated ways. For example, psychologist A may feel that the anxiety test developed by psychologist B does not really "get at" anxiety very well, so she or he constructs a new instrument. Psychologist C may argue that A and B are both "off base" with their tests and come up with yet another "more meaningful" device. This sequence has been especially noticeable in personality testing, but is evident in other test categories as well.

Another factor responsible for the increasing array of tests is that testers' interests become more specific, thus prompting the development of special-purpose tests. In intelligence testing, for example, instruments are available for use with infants, the physically handicapped, and persons not fluent in English or from specific cultural backgrounds. Similarly, surveys of general preferences or interests have been followed by special-purpose tests aimed at assessing the way adolescents spend leisure time or the things children find rewarding. A quick glance at the latest *Mental Measurements Yearbook* (Mitchell, 1985) or other test compendia (e.g., Chun, Cobb & French, 1975; Goldman & Busch, 1978; Newmark, 1985; Sweetland & Keyser, 1983) will reveal dozens of specialized instruments such as the Abortion Questionnaire, the College Drinking Questionnaire, the Fear-of-Death Scale, the Post-Suicidal Attempt Scale, and the VD Questionnaire. Fascinating historical accounts of many now-forgotten tests are

---

[1] Cronbach (1970) reserves the term *standardized* for tests administered in precisely equivalent fashion by each tester. This is an important point because differences in testing procedure can influence test results.

FIGURE 5-1. *Peanuts* by Charles Schulz.

contained in Reisman (1976) and DuBois (1970).

TEST CONSTRUCTION PROCEDURES

Curious (or angry) members of the public often raise a basic question about psychological tests: "How do psychologists come up with these things?" The answer is that tests are constructed in three basic ways: the *analytic* approach, the *empirical* approach, and the *rational* or *sequential system* approach, which combines analytic and empirical principles (see Burisch, 1984; Golden, Sawicki & Franzen, 1984; Jackson, 1975).

The analytic technique begins by asking, "What are the qualities I want to measure?", "How do I define these qualities?", and "What kind of test and test items would make sense for assessing these qualities?" It then proceeds to build a test that answers the last question. It is a deductive approach to test construction.

The procedure can be illustrated through an extreme example. Suppose one wanted a test that could reliably and accurately identify adult humans as male or fe-

male. The analytic approach would involve theorizing about the kinds of things that might differentiate the sexes. The clinician's own view of what makes males and females different would shape the content of the tests, as would the opinions of other experts.

If physical characteristics are seen as crucial, and a true-false format is preferred, the test might contain items such as:

1. I have a penis.
2. I have a vagina.
3. I once had a penis.
4. I once had a vagina.
5. I shave my face.
6. I have a beard.

Another clinician might believe that physical characteristics are only surface indicators of sex and that "real" maleness or femaleness must be measured by tapping the unconscious. The resulting test might look at unconscious themes by asking the client to fill in incomplete sentences such as:

1. A dependent person is _____.
2. Strength is _____ .
3. The trouble with most men is _____.

4. Most women are _____ .
5. I like to _____ .
6. There is nothing worse than _____ .

In either case, the form and content of an analytically constructed test will reflect in large measure a specific theory of what should be tested and how.

The main alternative to analytic test construction is the empirical approach. Here, instead of deciding ahead of time what test content should be used to measure a particular construct, the tester lets the content "choose itself." Thus, in building a sex test, the clinician might amass a large number of self-report test items, performance tasks, or inkblots, and then administer all of them to a large group of people who have *already been identified* as males or females. Responses to all the test material would then be examined to see if any items, tasks, or other stimuli were consistently answered differently by men and women.

Such stimuli form the initial content of the test, *regardless of whether they make any sense rationally*. For example, the things that reliably discriminate males from females might include "true" responses to items like "My nose runs a lot," "Coffee makes me sleepy," or "My shoes are too tight." The reasons *why* such items separate males from females may become the subject of additional theoretical research, but for practical purposes testers are usually willing to employ an empirically constructed test in spite of the fact that its power cannot be explained clearly.

How does the test constructor decide between analytic or empirical procedures? Several factors may be decisive. For one thing, the analytic approach can be faster and less expensive, although this is not always the case. The analytic approach does not require initial administration of many items to many people in order to settle on those that will comprise the test. These features may make analytic procedures attractive to the clinician who does not have access to a large pool of test material and willing to expose subjects or who is forced by circumstances to develop a test on short notice.

Analytic procedures will be favored by clinicians evaluating a particular theory. That theory may propose, for example, that people differ in terms of "nebbishness." Assuming no nebbish test is available, the researcher who wishes to explore this hypothesis through testing will need an instrument that corresponds to what the theory says nebbishness is and how it should be measured. Development of a Neb Test would thus likely proceed on analytic grounds.

On the other hand, clinicians who are less concerned with theoretical notions and who have time and other resources available may find the empirical approach more desirable, especially when attempting to make specific predictions about people. If the tester's task is to identify individuals likely to graduate from law school, for example, it makes sense to find out if graduates respond to certain test stimuli in a way that is reliably different from dropouts.

Analytic and empirical techniques are combined in the *sequential system* approach to test construction. Here, data from analytically chosen items are examined statistically to determine those that are correlated and those that are not. Groups of correlated items are identified as *scales*, which are thought to be relatively pure measures of certain personality dimensions free of response biases (Maloney & Ward, 1976). Validity of the test is then assessed empirically.

Analytic-empirical combinations also appear in other contexts. For example, the person who wishes to construct a true-false test using empirical procedures is immediately faced with a problem: Of the millions of true-false items that could be included in the test, the tester must decide which ones to try. This decision is usually made on analytic grounds; items will be selected from older tests or might be those the clinician feels ought to be tried. Similarly, empirical procedures are often used in the development of analytically constructed tests. If administration of a new instrument reveals that certain items are better at discriminating between target groups (e.g., good versus poor typists), those items are more likely to be retained in the test than are items with little "power."

Regardless of how a test is constructed initially, its value as an assessment instrument ultimately must be established through empirical research on its reliability and validity (see Chapter 3). That requirement is elaborated in the American Psychological Association's *Standards for Educational and Psychological Testing* (APA, 1985). Later we shall look at how various tests have fared when scrutinized by reliability/validity research. For now, let us examine the nature and content of the four psychological test categories identified earlier.

MAJOR TYPES OF TESTS

Intellectual Functioning

We begin our exploration of psychological tests with measures of intelligence, since, as noted in Chapter 1, the early history of clinical psychology is basically the early history of intelligence tests.

While everyone would agree that intelligence is a good thing to have, there is less consensus about what intelligence actually *is*. This state of affairs has generated the half-joking suggestion among clinicians that "intelligence is whatever intelligence tests measure." Indeed, the history of intelligence tests reveals that each tester proceeded initially on analytical grounds, and that each of the more than 200 assessment instruments that have resulted reflects its creator's view of how best to measure intellectual functioning.

Intelligence test builders have been influenced in their analytic approach by theories about the essential nature of intelligence. This is not the place to describe these theories (see Sternberg, 1985, or Maloney & Ward, 1976), but to cite one major dimen-

sion, some writers describe intelligence primarily as a general characteristic (called *g*) while others see it as made up of several (as many as 120) specific intellectual functions (called *s*) such as word fluency, reasoning, and memory. The practical relevance of *g, s,* or other intelligence theories is rather limited, however, because none of the major intelligence tests described below reflects the *g* or *s* approach clearly enough to provide definitive validation of one theory or another.

The Binet Scales. Alfred Binet was not the first person to develop a measure of intelligence, but his original test and the revisions based upon it have been among the most influential means of assessing the mental ability of children. In its earliest form (1905), Binet's test consisted of thirty questions and tasks, including things like unwrapping a piece of candy, following a moving object with the eyes, comparing objects of differing weights, repeating numbers or sentences from memory, and recognizing familiar objects. The child's test score was simply the number of items passed.

Beginning with a 1908 revision (and in every version since then), the tasks in Binet's test were *age-graded*. This means the items are arranged so that younger children are expected to pass the earlier ones, while older children are expected to pass progressively later ones. Binet and his collaborator, Theodore Simon, observed the test behavior of about 200 children and suggested, for example, that three-year-olds ought to be able to identify their eyes, nose, and mouth; repeat a two-digit number and a six-syllable sentence; and give their last name. At seven years, success at finding missing parts of drawings, copying simple geometric figures, and identifying denominations of coins was expected. Items to be passed at the eleventh-year level included criticism of absurd sentences, definition of abstract concepts, and rearranging words to form a sentence. A child's *mental age* was the highest age level at which *all* test items were passed (plus credit for any correct responses at higher levels).

The 1908 scale covered ages three to thirteen; it was brought to America by Henry Goddard. Though immensely popular, the Binet-Simon test had several shortcomings. Some users were dissatisfied because the test emphasized verbal skills more than the child's capacity for judgment. Others noted that the test was too easy at lower age levels and too difficult at the upper end. Binet attempted to correct some of these problems in a 1911 revision of his test, but a far more influential version was written in 1916 by Lewis Terman, a Stanford University psychologist.

Terman believed that expressing a child's intelligence in terms of "mental age" was imprecise and left too much room for misinterpretation: "If a child's mental age equalled his chronological age, he was considered 'regular' (average) in intelligence; if his mental age was higher, he was 'advanced'; if his mental age was lower, he was 'retarded.' " (Reisman, 1976). Terman's edition of the Binet-Simon was called the Stanford Revision or the Stanford-Binet; it soon became *the* intelligence test in American clinical psychology. The Stanford-Binet was standardized on a larger sample (1400 white subjects) and across a wider age range (three to sixteen) than had been used for Binet's 1911 revision.

More important was the fact that Terman adopted an idea suggested in 1912 by German psychologist William Stern for representing numerically the relationship between mental and chronological age. Stanford-Binet results were expressed as the *intelligence quotient* (or IQ) resulting when mental age (MA) is divided by chronological age (CA) and multiplied by 100. Thus, a six-year-old whose mental age comes out as eight on the Stanford-Binet would have an IQ of [(8 ÷ 6) × 100], or 133.

Terman suggested at one point that various IQ ranges be given labels such as "average," "feebleminded," and "genius." Today, the following categories are used: "very superior," "superior," "high average," "average," "low average," "borderline," and "mentally retarded." Similar systems are used to classify persons at the lower end of the IQ scale as "mildly," "moderately," "severely," or "profoundly retarded." Although the original intent of such labels was to provide a shorthand summary of a person's score relative to others of his or her age, IQ scores and the labels based upon them are often overemphasized and misused, especially by those unfamiliar with their meaning. For this reason, among others, the use of IQ data has become the center of considerable controversy, as we shall see later.

Terman and Merrill revised the Stanford-Binet in 1937, 1960, and again in 1973 (the 1973 edition retained the same content as the 1960 edition), using larger, more diverse standardization samples.[2] The 1972 restandardization used a stratified sample of 2100 children representing diverse socioeconomic, geographical, racial, and cultural subgroups. The 1973 edition is appropriate for clients from ages two to eighteen and takes thirty to sixty minutes to administer. Items begin at the two-year-old level and proceed upward in half-year steps until age five, after which there are one-year steps to age fourteen. The rest of the test items are at higher levels labeled "average adult," "superior adult I," "superior adult II," and "superior adult III." At each level there are six items or tasks (with the exception of "average adult," which contains eight). The subject's *basal age* is the highest age level at which she or he passes all items, while the *ceiling age* is the level at which all items are failed.

The items tap areas such as memory, vocabulary, motor skills, comprehension,

---

[2] In 1986 a fourth edition of the Stanford-Binet was published. It uses a new format and groups a large number of subtests into four different ability areas in order to permit more specific assessments. The success of this new version of the Stanford-Binet will require extensive research evaluation as clinicians begin to use it.

BOX 5-1   Items of the type included in the 1973 edition of the Stanford-Binet

Age 2:   Place geometric shapes into corresponding openings, identify body parts; stack blocks; identify common objects.

Age 4:   Name objects from memory; complete analogies (e.g., fire is hot; ice is _____); identify objects of similar shape; answer simple questions (e.g., "Why do we have schools?").

Age 6:   Define simple words; explain differences (e.g., between a fish and a horse); identify missing parts of a picture; count out objects.

Age 8:   Answer questions about a simple story; identify absurdities (e.g., in statements like "John had to walk on crutches because he hurt his arm"); explain similarities and differences among objects; tell how to handle certain situations (e.g., finding a stray puppy).

Age 10:   Define more difficult words; give explanations (e.g., about why people should be quiet in a library); list as many words as possible; repeat six-digit numbers.

Age 12:   Identify more difficult verbal and pictured absurdities; repeat five-digit numbers in reverse order; define abstract words (e.g., "sorrow"); fill in missing word in a sentence.

Age 14:   Solve reasoning problems; identify relationships among points of the compass; find similarities in apparently opposite concepts (e.g., "high" and "low"); predict the number of holes which will appear when folded paper is cut and then opened.

Superior Adult I: Supply several missing words for incomplete sentences; repeat six-digit numbers in reverse order; create a sentence using several unrelated words (e.g., "forest," "businesslike," and "dismayed"); describe similarities between concepts (e.g., "teaching" and "business").

---

logic, problem solving, reasoning ability, and abstract thinking. Box 5-1 contains examples of the tasks at various age levels.

Determination of a Stanford-Binet IQ no longer involves merely dividing mental age by chronological age. That simple procedure has been replaced by use of IQ tables which correct the MA/CA × 100 formula by taking into account the mean and variance in IQs at each age level in the standardization sample. Thus, if a six-year-old girl scores a mental age of nine (which is not only high relative to her chronological age, but also higher than most six-year-olds in the standardization population), she would receive an IQ of 156 rather than the 150 that would have resulted from calculating MA/CA × 100. Such "corrected" scores were arrived at by setting up IQ tables in which the mean IQ at each age level is 100, with a standard deviation of 16. Thus, the

modern IQ score represents *degree of deviation* from the average of any level. An IQ of 100 is "average" for the age; 116 would be one standard deviation above average; 84 would be one standard deviation below average.

In spite of its widespread use with children, the Stanford-Binet was criticized for its emphasis upon verbal aspects of intelligence and for its relative inappropriateness with clients over age eighteen. This second criticism became important as clinicians began testing more adults during the 1930s.

The Wechsler Scales. In the 1930s David Wechsler, chief psychologist at New York's Bellevue Psychiatric Hospital, began developing an intelligence test designed specifically for adults. The result of his efforts, the Wechsler-Bellevue (W-B) Scale, was published in 1939. This test differed in

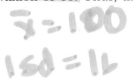

several ways from the Stanford-Binet, even though some W-B tasks were borrowed or adapted from it. First, it was aimed at adults, age seventeen and older. Second, it did not measure mental age, which Wechsler thought was not a useful concept. Instead, the W-B was a *point scale* in which the client receives credit for each correct answer. With this method, IQ does not reflect the relationship between mental age and chronological age, but a comparison of points earned by the client to those earned by persons of equal age in the standardization sample.

A third distinguishing feature of the Wechsler-Bellevue was that its items were arranged in groups or *subtests* based on similarity. Each subtest contained increasingly difficult items. For example, on the digit-span subtest, the client was asked to repeat various numbers, starting with three digits and progressing to nine digits. The score on this subtest was determined by the maximum number of digits the client could repeat without error. Similar tasks are included in the Stanford-Binet, but they are scattered throughout the test (e.g., a two-digit task at the two-and-a-half-year level; a six-digit task at age ten) rather than occurring in one place. The W-B contained six *verbal* subtests (information, comprehension, arithmetic, similarities, digit span, and vocabulary) and five *performance* subtests (digit symbol, picture completion, block design, picture arrangement, and object assembly).

The W-B had some deficiencies, the most serious of which was an inadequate standardization sample (1700 white New Yorkers aged seven to seventy. In 1955 Wechsler revised and restandardized his test on a more representative sample of over 2000 white and nonwhite individuals (aged sixteen to seventy-four) living in all parts of the United States. This revision was called the Wechsler Adult Intelligence Scale, or WAIS, and it soon became the most popular adult intelligence test in use. Like the W-B,

the WAIS had six verbal and five performance subtests, and the client was given a Verbal IQ, a Performance IQ, and a Full Scale IQ (which combines the other two). Another revision, known as the WAIS-R, was published in 1981. It was restandardized on a sample of 1880 U.S. adults whose age, race, and other demographic characteristics reflect 1970 census data. About 20 percent of the items on the WAIS-R are different from the 1955 version (Wechsler, 1981). Some examples of the types of items included on the WAIS-R are presented in Box 5-2.

The structure of the WAIS allows not only for IQ scores, but for the drawing of inferences from *patterns* of subtest scores. Some clinicians use WAIS subtest patterns or "scatter" to help them arrive at a diagnosis of the client, to assess the possibility of brain damage, or to describe personality dynamics.

After publication of the W-B, Wechsler became interested in extending the point-scale test format for use with children. In 1949 the Wechsler Intelligence Scale for Children (WISC) appeared. The WISC was made up of twelve subtests (six verbal, six performance) of which only ten were usually administered. The subtests were similar to those listed for the W-B, but easier. The WISC was standardized on 2200 white children from all parts of the United States, but because they ranged in age from five to fifteen, the WISC was not useful for very young children. The Wechsler Preschool and Primary Scale of Intelligence (WPPSI) was developed later, but still only reached the four-year-old level (Wechsler, 1967).

In 1974 a new version of the WISC was published. Called the WISC-R, it includes six verbal and six performance subtests; again, only five of each are usually administered. The content of the WISC-R items was changed to make it more representative of current social and cultural values, and the entire test was standardized on a new sample of 2200 white and nonwhite children

BOX 5-2   Items of the type included in the Wechsler Adult Intelligence Scale-Revised

(WAIS-R)

Information:	What does bread come from? What did Shakespeare do? What is the capital of France? What is the malleus malleficarum?
Comprehension:	What should you do with a wallet found in the street? Why do foreign cars cost more than domestic cars? What does "the squeaky wheel gets the grease" mean?
Arithmetic:	If you have four apples and give two away, how many do you have left? If four people can finish a job in six days, how many people would it take to do the job in two days?
Similarities:	Identify similar aspects of pairs like: hammer-screwdriver, portrait-short story, dog-flower.
Digit Symbol:	Copy designs that are associated with different numbers as quickly as possible.
Digit Span:	Repeat in forward and reverse order: two- to nine-digit numbers.
Vocabulary:	Define: chair, dime, lunch, paragraph, valley, asylum, modal, cutaneous.
Picture Completion:	Find missing objects in increasingly complex pictures.
Block Design:	Arrange blocks to match increasingly complex standard patterns.
Picture Arrangement:	Place increasing number of pictures together to make increasingly complex stories.
Object Assembly:	Arrange parts of puzzles to form recognizable objects (e.g., dog, flower, person).

from varying socioeconomic levels and geographical locations.

Other Intelligence Tests. Many other intelligence instruments are in use today, several designed to assess intelligence without emphasis on verbal or vocalization skills. It is important that such tests be available, since some clients may be too young or, for other reasons, unable to do well at verbal tasks. Tests such as the Peabody Picture Vocabulary Test and the Porteus Maze Test allow the clinician to assess intellectual functioning in clients of this type. They also provide a backup in cases where the clinician

suspects that a client's performance on a standard IQ test may have been hampered by anxiety, specific verbal deficits, cultural disadvantages, or other situational factors. The newest test to try to overcome these biases is the Kaufman Assessment Battery for Children (Kaufman & Kaufman, 1983), a test suitable for children two and one-half to twelve and one-half years old, constructed from research in cognitive psychology, neuropsychology, and psychometrics. Additional intelligence tests for adults and children are described by Lindemann and Matarazzo (1984), Hale (1983), Sattler (1982), and Zimmerman and Woo-Sam

(1984). A number of group intelligence tests are summarized by Vane and Motta (1984).

Ability Tests   *Predictive*

Some clinicians think of intelligence as mental ability and often refer to intelligence tests as general mental ability instruments. However, there are a significant number of other tests designed to measure specific mental abilities. These include *aptitude* and *achievement* tests. Aptitude tests are designed to predict success in an occupation or an educational program. The Scholastic Aptitude Test (SAT), which is used to predict high school students' potential for college-level work, provides an example familiar to most undergraduates.

Achievement tests measure proficiency at certain tasks; that is, how much does the person know or how well can he or she do? The Wide Range Achievement Test is a well-known example. Many psychologists now argue that intelligence, aptitude, and achievement tests are more alike than different in that all attempt to measure "developed abilities" (Reschly, 1984; see also Fox & Zirkin, 1984).

The more specific the ability or aptitude tested, the less familiar the test is likely to be. If you have never heard of the Seashore Measures of Musical Talents or the Crawford Small Parts Dexterity Test, it is probably because they are used to measure very specialized abilities. It is also important to note that ability testing is more often done by personnel officers and educational, vocational, and guidance counselors than by clinical psychologists. The reader interested in further detailed information about ability testing of this type should consult Mitchell (1985).

Clinicians' interest in ability testing is usually related to assessment of specific cognitive capabilities or deficits. Though clinicians may draw inferences about specific cognitive abilities, deficits, or even brain damage from the pattern of scores on instruments such as the WAIS-R or the WISC-

R, they may also utilize a variety of special-purpose tests, some of which emphasize perception and memory. For example, the Benton Visual Retention Test (Benton, 1974), the Bender Visual Motor Gestalt (or Bender-Gestalt; Bender, 1938) and the Memory-for-Designs Test (Graham & Kendall, 1960) ask the client to copy or draw from memory geometric figures or other designs. Other tests in this category assess the client's ability to form concepts and engage in other types of abstract thinking. The use of tests to detect brain damage or deterioration is known as neuropsychological assessment and is described in more detail in Chapter 11.

Attitudes, Interests, Preferences, and Values

Clinical psychologists often find it useful to assess a person's attitudes, interests, preferences, and values. For example, before beginning to work with a distressed couple, the clinician may wish to get some idea about each spouse's attitudes about marriage. Similarly, it may be instructive for the clinician to know that the interests of a client who is in severe conflict about entering the medical profession are totally unlike those of successful physicians.

The many tests available to assess attitudes, interests, preferences, and values overlap a great deal, so there is little to be gained from labeling each instrument in this category. It is important, however, to be aware of some of the more commonly used tests, such as the Strong-Campbell Interest Inventory (Campbell & Hansen, 1981), the Kuder Preference Record (Kuder, 1948), and the Vocational Preference Inventory (Holland, 1978). These are paper-and-pencil instruments designed to assess clients' preferences for various pursuits, occupations, academic subjects, recreational activities, and types of people. Each results in an interest profile that can be compared with composite profiles gathered from members of occupational groups such as biologists, engineers, army officers, carpenters, police, ministers, accountants, salespeople, and lawyers.

Generalized life orientations can be assessed via the Allport-Vernon-Lindzey Study of Values (Allport, Vernon & Lindzey, 1970), a paper-and-pencil instrument that asks the client to choose among alternatives about things like use of leisure time, interest in various news items, and the importance of various activities. The resulting profile of values shows the relative strength of six basic interests: theoretical ("intellectual"), economic, aesthetic, social, political, and religious. Other, more phenomenologically oriented, general value assessments include the Purpose-in-Life Test (Crumbaugh, 1968) and the Personal Orientation Inventory (Shostrom, 1968).

There are also many tests designed to assess more specific interests and preferences (Hansen, 1984). None is as widely used as the Strong-Campbell Interest Inventory, but each has a certain theoretical or practical appeal for some clinicians. For example, the behavioral model of clinical psychology has generated several tests aimed at illuminating client preferences and attitudes as a prelude to treatment. Among the most prominent of these is the Reinforcement Survey Schedule (Cautela & Kastenbaum, 1967), a list of situations and activities that the client rates in terms of their desirability. Special versions of this test for use with children and psychiatric inpatients have also been developed (Cautela, 1977). The Pleasant Events Schedule (MacPhillamy & Lewinsohn, 1972) provides an example of a behaviorally oriented preference assessment.

Many of the qualities assessed by tests described in this section are related to the client's personality. Indeed, some would suggest that one's attitudes, interests, values, and preferences make up a large part of what is thought of as personality. The overlap between these areas is well recognized, but there are a vast number of psychological tests whose goal is the measurement of many other aspects of personality, and it is

to these instruments that we now turn our attention.

Personality Tests

"Personality" is the term used to describe and account for the individual differences and behavioral consistencies in human beings. Some theorists see personality as an organized collection of traits, other hypothesize dynamic relationships among intrapsychic forces, while still others point to recurring patterns of behavior. As was the case with intelligence, the breadth of the notion of personality means that clinicians will assess it in a multitude of ways, usually in accordance with their own theoretical model of human behavior. This is probably why there are more tests in the personality category than in any other. We cannot begin to cover all of them here, so this section will be restricted to a brief look at the most prominent personality tests in clinical use. Readers interested in more detailed treatment of personality assessment should consult texts such as Goldstein and Hersen (1984), Groth-Marnat (1984), Holt (1971), Kleinmuntz (1982), Lanyon and Goodstein (1982), Mitchell (1985), Spielberger and Butcher (1982), and Wiggins (1973).

There are two major types of personality tests: *objective* and *projective.* Objective tests present relatively clear, specific stimuli such as questions ("Have you ever wanted to run away from home?") or statements ("I am never depressed") or concepts ("Myself" or "Large dogs") to which the client responds with direct answers, choices, or ratings. Most often, objective personality tests are of the paper-and-pencil variety and can be scored mathematically (sometimes by computers), much like a multiple-choice or true-false test. Some objective tests focus on one aspect of personality such as anxiety, dependency, or ego strength, while others provide a comprehensive overview of many personality dimensions.

Projective tests are mainly associated with the psychodynamic model of clinical psychology. Beginning with Freud's notion that people tend to defend themselves psychologically by attributing to other people unacceptable aspects of their own personality, Frank (1939) broadened the concept of projection by suggesting that there is a general "tendency of people to be influenced in the cognitive mediation of perceptual inputs by their needs, interests, and overall psychological organization" (Exner, 1976, p. 61). In other words, each individual's personality will determine, in part at least, the way she or he interprets things. Frank (1939) labeled tests that encourage clients to display this tendency as "projective methods." In general, these tests elicit reactions to ambiguous or unstructured stimuli (such as inkblots or incomplete sentences) which are interpreted as a reflection of primarily unconscious personality structure and dynamics. Some projective tests use a paper-and-pencil format, but more often the client responds orally to each stimulus. These responses are transcribed or tape-recorded for later scoring.

Although projective test responses can be converted to numerical form, the scoring process is more subjective and inferential than with objective tests. This is primarily because projective tests permit unstructured responses which may later be transformed into numbers; objective tests structure items so that the client does the transformation for the tester by choosing "true" or "false" or some other specific, quantified response. Both approaches require inferences either by the client or by the clinician. George Kelly (1958, p. 332) summarized the problem beautifully: "When the subject is asked to guess what the examiner is thinking, we call it an objective test; when the examiner tries to guess what the subject is thinking, we call it a projective device."

Objective Personality Tests. The first objective personality test developed by a psychologist was Woodworth's (1920) Personal Data Sheet, used during World War I to screen soldiers with psychological problems. It asked for "yes" or "no" answers to questions such as: "Did you have a happy childhood?" "Does it make you uneasy to cross a bridge?" These items were selected because they reflected problems and symptoms reported at least twice as often by previously diagnosed neurotics as by "normals." No item was retained in the test if more than 25 percent of a normal sample answered it in an unfavorable manner. Item selection procedures such as these were a prelude to later, more sophisticated empirical test construction procedures (Butcher & Keller, 1984).

THE MMPI. Among the hundreds of objective personality measures that have appeared since Woodworth's early effort, the most influential and widely used is the Minnesota Multiphasic Personality Inventory (MMPI). This test was developed during the late 1930s at the University of Minnesota by Starke Hathaway (a psychologist) and J. C. McKinley (a psychiatrist) as an aid to psychiatric diagnosis of clinical patients. The MMPI was one of the first personality tests to be constructed empirically. Hathaway and McKinley took about 1000 items from older personality tests and other sources and converted them into statements to which a client could respond "true," "false," or "cannot say." Approximately 500 of these items were administered to thousands of normal persons as well as to persons diagnosed with psychiatric disorders.

Certain response patterns appeared. When compared to normals, members of various diagnostic groups showed statistically different reactions to many items. For example, a particular group of items tended to be answered in the same general way by depressed persons, while another group of items was answered in a particular way by persons diagnosed as schizophrenic. Eight such item groups were identified as discriminating normals from non-normals and as being associated with a certain diagnostic category. These item groups were called *scales*. Later, two additional groupings were identified as being responded to differently by males and females and by shy, introverted college students. Thus, there are ten *clinical scales* on the MMPI; their names and examples[3] of the kinds of items included in each are presented in Box 5-3.

Also included in the MMPI are four *validity scales*. These are groups of items designed to help detect various kinds of distorted responses. The Cannot Say or ? scale is simply the number of items that the respondent does not answer. An elevated ? scale can be due to poor cooperation, failure to understand items, or defensiveness. The *L* (or *lie*) scale consists of fifteen statements which, if answered honestly, reveal mildly negative things about the client (such as the fact that he or she does not stay informed about world events every day). The assumption here is that if the client denies trivial negative behaviors or thoughts, (s)he will probably not be honest about more serious problems covered on other items. The *F* (or *frequency*) scale contains items that are rarely endorsed by normals, but which are not associated with any particular diagnosed group either. A high F score is interpreted as indicating carelessness in responding, a purposeful attempt to appear deviant, a very severe disorder, or some related factor. The *K* (or *correction*) scale is designed to detect a client's tendency to be overly defensive or overly disclosing about problems. A high K score is taken as evidence that the severity of problems revealed in the test was played down by the client. A low K score suggests that problems may have been overstated. In either case, the K scale is used as a guide for "correcting" scores on five of the clinical scales.

There are 566 items on the MMPI. When people take the test, their responses to these items are converted into clinical and validity scale scores. Originally, the MMPI clinical scales were taken literally; a person showing a high depression or schizophrenia score was given a corresponding diagnostic label. It soon became obvious, however, that elevation of a particular scale did not always mean that the individual belonged in the associated diagnostic category.

Recognition of this problem prompted (1) a trend toward calling the clinical scales by number (1–10) rather than by name, and (2) plotting all scale scores on a graph and analyzing the resulting profile (not just the highest score) and the relationships among its points (a sample profile is presented in Figure 5-2). Maloney and Ward (1976, p. 335) contrast the old single-scale approach to MMPI interpretation with current profile analysis methods:

Consider the diagnosis of "psychopathic deviate" (now called antisocial personality disorder). Under the old formulation, elevation on scale 4 (psychopathic deviate) was considered sufficient to make this diagnosis. However, it has been found that elevations on this scale occur with considerable frequency in both the normal population and other diagnostic groups. As a result, the differential diagnostic usefulness of scale 4 by itself is quite limited and suspect. However, with the profile approach, there are considerable data to suggest that a coded profile of 4-9 (. . . scale 9 is "hypomania"), with the relative absence of elevations on other clinical scales, and especially in the presence of a "supernormal" neurotic triad (scales 1, 2, and 3), is much more indicative of a psychopathic condition (Meehl, 1972).

The clinician conducts a profile analysis by comparing the client's chart with those of other clients. This can be done *clinically* by recalling previous clients, or *statistically* by reference to books containing sample profiles and the characteristics of the people who produced them (Dahlstrom & Welsh, 1960; Dahlstrom, Welsh & Dahlstrom, 1972; Drake & Oetting, 1959; Gilberstadt & Duker, 1965; Graham, 1977; Lachar, 1974). As noted in Chapter 3, there are several companies that offer computerized scoring

---

[3] In order to avoid biasing the response of readers (or their friends) who might take the MMPI, its actual items are not presented. Incidentally, the MMPI item format has been widely parodied: A "Maryland Malpractice and Pandering Inventory" has circulated as a joke among clinicians for years. It contains items such as: "I used to tease vegetables," "The sight of blood no longer excites me," and "I use shoe polish to excess." (See also Walker & Walsh, 1969.)

BOX 5-3   MMPI scales and simulated items

Validity (or test-taking attitude) scales

? (Cannot Say) Number of items left unanswered.

L (Lie) Fifteen items of overly good self report, such as "I smile at everyone I meet." (Answered True)

F (Frequency or Infrequency) Sixty-four items answered in the scored direction by 10 percent or less of normals, such as "There is an international plot against me." (True)

K (Correction) Thirty items reflecting defensiveness in admitting to problems, such as "I feel bad when others criticize me." (False)

Clinical Scales:

1 or **Hs** (Hypochondriasis). Thirty-three items derived from patients showing abnormal concern with bodily functions, such as "I have chest pains several times a week." (True)

2 or **D** (Depression) Sixty items derived from patients showing extreme pessimism, feelings of hopelessness, and slowing of thought and action, such as "I usually feel that life is interesting and worthwhile." (False)

3 or **Hy** (Conversion Hysteria) Sixty items from neurotic patients using physical or mental symptoms as a way of unconsciously avoiding difficult conflicts and responsibilities, such as "My heart frequently pounds so hard I can feel it." (True)

4 or **Pd** (Psychopathic Deviate) Fifty items from patients who show a repeated and flagrant disregard for social customs, an emotional

shallowness and an inability to learn from punishing experiences, such as "My activities and interests are often criticized by others." (True)

5 or **Mf** (Masculinity-Femininity) Sixty items from patients showing homoeroticism and items differentiating between men and women, such as "I like to arrange flowers." (True, scored for femininity.)

6 or **Pa** (Paranoia) Forty items from patients showing abnormal suspiciousness and delusions of grandeur or persecution, such as "There are evil people trying to influence my mind." (True)

7 or **Pt** (Psychasthenia) Forty-eight items based on neurotic patients showing obsessions, compulsions, abnormal fears, and guilt and indecisiveness, such as "I save nearly everything I buy, even after I have no use for it." (True)

8 or **Sc** (Schizophrenia) Seventy-eight items from patients showing bizarre or unusual thoughts or behavior, who are often withdrawn and experiencing delusions and hallucinations, such as "Things around me do not seem real" (True) and "It makes me uncomfortable to have people close to me." (True)

9 or **Ma** (Hypomania) Forty-six items from patients characterized by emotional excitement, overactivity, and flight of ideas, such as "At times I feel very 'high' or very 'low' for no apparent reason." (True)

0 or **Si** (Social Introversion) Seventy items from persons showing shyness, little interest in people, and insecurity, such as "I have the time of my life at parties." (False)

Source: Norman Sundberg, *Assessment of Persons,* © 1977, p. 183. (Reprinted by permission of Prentice-Hall, Inc., Englewood Cliffs, New Jersey.)

of the MMPI along with computer interpretations based upon actuarial formulae or previous clinical experience (sometimes called *automated clinical lore;* see Butcher, Keller & Bacon, 1985).

In addition to being the most popular objective personality test in clinical use today,

the MMPI has spawned over 6000 research reports and hundreds of other related tests and scales, many of which go beyond the test's original purpose of assessing "those traits that are commonly characteristic of disabling psychological abnormality" (Hathaway & McKinley, 1967, p. 1). For exam-

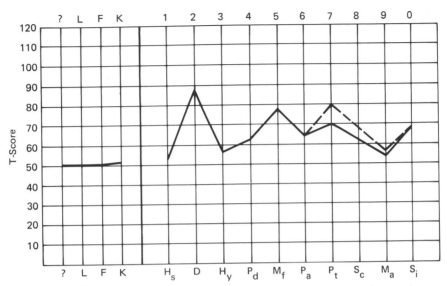

FIGURE 5-2. Sample MMPI profile for a 34-year-old married professional man. The solid line is the uncorrected profile; the dashed line represents K-scale corrections. (From W. G. Dahlstrom, G. S. Welsh, and L. E. Dahlstrom, *An MMPI Handbook*, vol. 1, rev. ed., © by University of Minnesota Press. Reprinted by permission.)

ple, there are over 300 new groupings of MMPI items, each of which tries to measure some aspect of personality such as ego strength, anxiety, dependency, dominance, social status, and prejudice (Anastasi, 1982). These new groupings or scales can be used in conjunction with the MMPI as a whole or as a separate test. Shorter versions of the MMPI have also been developed. Called the "Mini-Mult" or "Midi-Mult," these abbreviated editions are less comprehensive and designed for quick classification and screening purposes (see Stevens & Reilly, 1980, for a review).

THE CPI. The California Psychological Inventory (CPI; Gough, 1957) is another prominent example of a broad-range, empirically constructed, objective personality test. In contrast to the MMPI, the CPI was developed specifically for assessing personality in the "normal" population. About half of its 468 items come from the MMPI, but the CPI items are grouped into more diverse

and positively oriented scales including sociability, self-acceptance, responsibility, dominance, self-control, and ten others. There are also three validity scales that serve basically the same purpose as those on the MMPI. The CPI was standardized on 13,000 males and females from all parts of the country and in all socioeconomic categories. Some observers see the CPI as one of the best personality tests available today because of the representativeness of its standardization sample and its relatively high reliability. The test has been used to predict delinquency, parole outcome, academic grades, and the likelihood of dropping out of high school (Anastasi, 1982). Computerized scoring and interpretation services are available, as is an updated administration manual (Gough, 1975).

OTHER OBJECTIVE TESTS. Other objective personality inventories in rather wide clinical use include the Personality Research Form (PRF; Jackson, 1967), the Edwards

Personal Preference Schedule (EPPS: Edwards, 1959), The Sixteen Personality Factors Quesionnaire (16PF; Cattell & Eber, 1962), and the Millon Clinical Multiaxial Inventory (MCMI; Millon, 1982). Among these tests, the PRF and the MCMI deserve special attention. The PRF is noteworthy because it is one of the best examples of the sequential system approach to test construction in which items were selected on theoretical grounds, combined into scales on empirical grounds, and then empirically validated against external criteria. It comes in five different forms, the most comprehensive of which contains 440 true-false items combined into twenty-two independent scales. In addition, the PRF was constructed to minimize certain response biases that can distort test results. The PRF is generally used with normal rather than clinical populations; its development was based on Henry Murray's (1938) *Variables of Personality.*

Millon's MCMI was also constructed using a combination of analytic and empirical methods. It reflects Millon's unique theory of personality (Millon, 1981), retains several positive features of the MMPI, and attempts to coordinate its interpretations with the diagnostic criteria in DSM-III. At 175 items, the MCMI is shorter than the MMPI. It is intended primarily for clinical diagnosis, though there is still insufficient validation research to document its diagnostic utility (Widiger, 1985). A computer-generated profile and narrative report are available.

Behavioral Tests. Proponents of the behavioral model of clinical psychology see personality as nearly synonymous with behavior and have therefore constructed a number of objective tests which, unlike those described so far, gather behavior samples upon which only minimal inferences are based. These tests tend to be short and analytically constructed.

Probably the most frequently employed behavior "personality test" is the Fear Survey Schedule (FSS). It is simply a list of objects, persons, and situations that the client is asked to rate in terms of fearsomeness. The several editions of this test (e.g., Geer, 1965; Lawlis, 1971; Wolpe & Lang, 1969) contain from 50 to 122 items and use either 1-to-5 or 1-to-7 scales for the fear ratings. The FSS is used to assess the prevalence of various fears, to identify persons with specific fears, and to assess changes over the course of fear-reduction treatment. A few items from the FSS are presented in Box 5-4. There is also an FSS for children (Ollendick, 1983).

Among other behavioral objective tests focused upon anxiety, one finds the State-Trait Anxiety Inventory (Spielberger, Gorsuch, Lushene, Vagg & Jacobs, 1983), the Social Avoidance and Distress Scale (Watson & Friend, 1969), the Social Anxiety Inventory (Richardson & Tasto, 1976), and the Trimodal Anxiety Symptom Questionnaire (Lehrer & Woolfolk, 1982). Behaviorally oriented clinicians have also developed a variety of tests that assess other features of

BOX 5-4   Sample items from the FSS-II

1. Snakes	6. Arguing with parents	11. Being alone
2. Death of a loved one	7. Hypodermic needles	12. Heights
3. Seeing a fight	8. Swimming alone	13. Closed places
4. Being a passenger in a car		
5. Failing a test	9. Making mistakes	14. Cemeteries
	10. Strange dogs	15. Roller coasters

Source: Geer, 1965.

behavior. These tests include the Beck Depression Inventory (Beck, Ward, Mendelson, Mock & Erbaugh, 1961), the Rathus Assertiveness Schedule (Rathus, 1973), the Multiple Affect Adjective Checklist (Zuckerman & Lubin, 1965), the Attribution Style Questionnaire (Peterson, Semmel, Metalsky, Abramson, von Baeyer & Seligman, 1982), and The Maudsley Obsessional-Compulsive Inventory (Hodgson & Rachman, 1977). The reader interested in detailed material on behavioral tests should consult Cautela (1977), Hersen and Bellack (in press), or Mash and Terdal (1976, 1981).

Projective Personality Tests. The use of projective assessment goes back to the 1400s, when Leonardo da Vinci is said to have selected his pupils partly on the basis of the creativity they displayed while attempting to find shapes and patterns in ambiguous forms (Piotrowski, 1972). In the late 1800s Binet adapted a parlor game called "Blotto" to assess "passive imagination" by asking children to tell what they saw in inkblots (Exner, 1976). Galton constructed a word association test in 1879; Carl Jung was using a similar test for clinical assessment by 1910. These informal projective techniques later evolved into projective *tests* when their content was standardized such that each client was exposed to the same stimuli in the same way.

There has been considerable discussion about what it is that defines a test as "projective."[4] Lindzey (1961) suggested a set of criteria that outline the general nature of projective tests as follows:

1. They are sensitive to unconscious personality dimensions.

2. They permit the client a broad range of responses.
3. They are capable of measuring many different aspects of personality.
4. They leave the client unaware or at least unsure of the specific meaning of his or her responses.
5. They generate a large amount of complex assessment data.
6. They employ relatively ambiguous stimuli.
7. They can be interpreted to provide an integrated picture of the client's personality as a whole.
8. They are capable of evoking fantasy material from the client.
9. They have no right or wrong answers.

Projective methods have been classified by various writers according to the nature of the stimuli they use; the way in which the tests are constructed, interpreted, or administered; their designated purpose; and the kind of response they elicit. Classification by client response is the clearest strategy for our purposes, so the following sections will correspond to Lindzey's (1961) labeling of projective tests as evoking *associations, constructions, completions, choices or orderings,* and *expressions* from the respondent. We shall consider only a few examples in each group, but a vast quantity of more detailed information about these and other projectives is available in such references as Erdberg & Exner (1984), Exner (1978, 1985), Lindzey (1961), Rabin and Haworth (1960), Schafer (1967), Shneidman (1965), Sundberg (1977), and Zubin, Eron, and Schumer (1965).

Association Tests. These projective tests ask clients to look at an ambiguous stimulus and tell what they see in or associate with it. The most widely known and frequently employed projective of this type is the Rorschach Inkblot Test. It is a set of ten colored and black-and-white inkblots created by Hermann Rorschach, a Swiss psychiatrist, between 1911 and 1921. Many researchers in Europe and America had previously em-

---

[4] Exner (1976, pp. 66–67) notes that answers to certain intelligence test items may provide projective clues about personality: "The best answer to the question, 'why does the state require people to get a license in order to get married?' is that it is for purposes of record keeping. However, if a subject says, 'To prevent the scourge of VD from being inflicted on unsuspecting women,' then the answer . . . conveys something about the peculiar interests of the respondent."

ployed inkblots in the assessment of fantasy, imagination, and perception, but it was Rorschach who first attempted to use such stimuli for diagnosis and personality assessment.

Rorschach began with geometric figures cut from colored paper and later switched to inkblots, partly as a result of having read about an inkblot test of fantasy developed by Hens, a Polish medical student. When the inkblot test finally appeared in 1921, it was not well received. European test experts such as Stern "denounced it as faulty, arbitrary, artificial, and incapable . . . of understanding human personality. . . ." (Reisman, 1976). Rorschach's book, *Psychodiagnostik,* which described his test and its interpretation, sold few copies.

The Rorschach would have had an early demise if David Levy, an American psychiatrist studying in Switzerland in 1920–21, had not brought a copy of the test back to the United States and, in 1927, instructed a psychology trainee named Samuel Beck in its use. Beck published the first American report involving use of the Rorschach. In 1937 he provided a standardized procedure for administering and scoring the test. Another scoring manual appeared that same year (Klopfer & Kelley, 1937), and the Rorschach was on its way to wide popularity among American psychologists, who until then had no global test of personality available to them. The growing clinical use of the test was paralleled by an explosion of research on its characteristics, reliability, validity, scoring, and interpretation.

The test itself is quite simple. The client is shown ten cards, one at a time. An inkblot (similar to that pictured in Figure 5-3) is on each card; the client is asked to tell what she or he sees or what the blot could be. The tester records all responses verbatim and takes notes about response times, how the card was being held (e.g., upside down, sideways) while a response occurred, noticeable emotional reactions, and the like. Next, the tester conducts an *inquiry* or systematic questioning of the client about the characteristics of each blot that prompted the responses.

The initial reactions to the blots and the comments made during the inquiry are then coded, using a special scoring system. Scoring involves the *location, determinants, content,* and *popularity* of the responses. *Location* refers to the area of the blot to which the client responds: The whole blot, a common detail, an unusual detail, white space, or some combination of these are location responses. The *determinants* of the response refer to the characteristic of the blot influencing a re-

FIGURE 5-3. Inkblot similar to those used in the Rorschach. (From Norman D. Sundberg, *Assessment of Persons,* © 1977, p. 207. Reprinted by permission of Prentice-Hall, Inc., Englewood Cliffs, New Jersey.)

sponse; they include form, color, shading, and "movement." While there is no movement in the blot itself, the respondent's perception of the blot as a moving object is scored in this category. *Content* refers to the subject matter perceived in the blot. Content includes human figures, parts of human figures, animal figures, animal details, anatomical features, inanimate objects, art, clothing, clouds, blood, X rays, sexual objects, and symbols. *Popularity* is scored on the basis of the relative frequency of different responses among people in general.

Assume that a client responded to Figure 5-3 by saying, "It looks like a bat" and during subsequent inquiry noted that "I saw the whole blot as a bat because it is black and is just sort of bat-shaped." If one of the popular scoring systems (e.g., that of Beck or Klopfer) were used, these responses would be coded as "WFC' + AP," where W indicates that the whole blot was used (*location*); F means that the blot's form (F) was the main *determinant* of the response; and C' means that achromatic color was also involved. The + shows that the form described corresponded well to the actual form of the blot; A means that there was animal *content* in the response; and P indicates that "bat" is a *popular* response to this particular card.[5]

The clinician may draw inferences from several aspects of Rorschach responses. Normative data exist to establish particular responses as common or unusual, and there have even been attempts to computerize interpretations (Fowler, 1985). For the most part, however, inference is based upon experience with the test and general interpretive guidelines. Sundberg (1977, p. 208) provides a summary of such guidelines that conveys the flavor of the inferences that stem from coded responses:

Using the whole blot suggests integration and organization; many small details indicate compulsiveness and over-control, and the use of white space suggests oppositional and negativistic tendencies. The presence of much poor form, uncommon responses, and confused thinking suggests a psychotic condition. Responsiveness to color is supposed to represent emotionality, and in the absence of good form, it suggests uncontrolled emotions and impulsivity. Responses mentioning human movement indicate imagination, intelligence, and a vivid inner life. . . . Content also has much potential for interpretation. . . . Knives, guns, mutilated bodies, and angry interactions suggest strong hostility.

The clinician also looks for recurring patterns of responses across cards, and certain test statistics contained in a "structural summary" are interpreted. The overall number of responses (called *productivity*), the frequency of responses in certain categories, and various ratios and relationships between and among categories are seen as significant. For example, because most people tend to use form more often than color in determining their responses, the appearance of a high proportion of color-dominated determinants may be taken as evidence of weak emotional control. In Exner's (1985) interpretive system, there are more than twenty response percentages and ratios available for interpretation.

The client's overt behavior in response to the Rorschach itself is also interpreted by the clinician. Evidence of tension, enjoyment, or confusion; attempts to impress the examiner; and other behavioral cues are an important part of Rorschach interpretation (e.g., Goldfried, Stricker & Weiner, 1971). A sample of inferences that might be drawn from the structural summary, response content, and test-taking behavior is contained in Box 5-5.

A number of variants on the Rorschach have appeared since its 1921 publication. The most notable examples include techniques for administering the test to groups of subjects (Harrower & Steiner, 1945) and the development of new sets of blots (e.g.,

---

[5] There are at least five reasonably distinct systems for scoring the Rorschach (Erdberg & Exner, 1984), so a given response may be coded in various ways; further, each scoring system is used somewhat differently by individual clinicians.

BOX 5-5   Example of inferences based on the Rorschach

In a context of severe intellectual and emotional confusion, we see a conflict centering primarily about a life-death struggle within the self, and about bodily integrity, personality integrity, and self-identity. Things somehow do not seem "right" to him as he turns away from the outside world and focuses on himself, especially on his body and its functions. He feels mutilated, dismembered rather than whole, worthless, and as if he is a lower form of life. Specifically, there is attention directed to alimentation, elimination, the rectum, and other bodily features associated with elimination. There is also concern about sex, but its specific relation to this disordered economy is not certain. All of these difficulties, particularly as they relate to body processes, are seen as the result of external assault upon him, as if others have unjustifiably done something to him and damaged him. In fact, in his current state of despair, he tends to see others as at fault and he is critical. In this manner, opposi-

tional tendencies which are now quite strong are pushing for expression and he feels they are justifiable.

This inner state of dysphoric turbulence is seen in a loss of spontaneity, in a marked sense of insecurity, helplessness, and uncertainty, and in social relations which are characterized by tentativeness. He is overcautious. Thus, he is remarkably ineffectual and unadaptable, and unable to come to grips with problems. In novel situations or under pressure, his judgment would not be at all reliable. In a personality not comfortably defended against psychosis, the term "paranoid" intrudes itself. The possibility of further regression with depersonalization, depression, and bodily delusions has to be considered.

Source: C. E. Orbach and N. Tallent, "Modification of Perceived Body and Body Concepts Following the Construction of a Colostomy." *Archives of General Psychiatry*, 1965, *12*, 126–135. © 1965. American Medical Association.

Harrower, 1945; Holtzman, Thorpe, Swartz & Herron, 1961; Wheeler, 1938). With the possible exception of the Holtzman Inkblot Test, none of these procedures has approached the popularity of the Rorschach.

Construction Tests. This type of projective asks the client to construct a story or other product on the basis of test stimuli. Among such tests, the Thematic Apperception Test (TAT) is the most popular, though interest in it appears to be declining somewhat (Polyson, Norris & Ott, 1985). The TAT presents relatively recognizable stimuli consisting of thirty drawings of people, objects, and landscapes (see Figure 5-4). In most cases, about ten of these cards (one of them blank) are administered; the subset

chosen is determined by the client's age and sex and by the clinician's interests. A separate set of cards depicting black people is also available. The examiner shows each picture and asks the client to make up a story about it, including what led up to the scene, what is now happening, and what is going to happen. The client is encouraged to say what the people in the drawings are thinking and feeling. For the blank card, the respondent is asked to imagine a drawing, describe it, and then construct a story about it.

The TAT was designed in 1935 by psychologists Christiana D. Morgan and Henry Murray at the Harvard Psychological Clinic (Murray, 1938, 1943). It was based upon the general projective hypothesis and upon the assumption that, in telling a *story*, the client's needs and conflicts will be reflected in a

FIGURE 5-4. Drawing of the type included in the TAT. (Reprinted by permission of the publishers from Henry A. Murray, *Thematic Apperception Test*, Cambridge, Mass.: Harvard University Press, copyright © 1943 by the president and fellows of Harvard College, © 1971 by Henry A. Murray.)

character (usually the heroine or hero with whom the client identifies; Lindzey, 1952). The TAT was not an original idea. Binet and others had used drawings and pictures much earlier to assess the development of children's intelligence and imagination (Binet & Simon, 1905; Brittain, 1907; Libby, 1908), and a few efforts were made at using picture-based fantasy as an aid to diagnosis (e.g., Schwartz, 1932). However, the TAT broke new ground by using respondents' stories as clues to personality.

As with the Rorschach, there is no one "right" way to analyze the meaning of clients' responses to TAT cards. As early as 1951, Shneidman found at least twenty systems for scoring and interpretation, and new methods have appeared since then (Harrison, 1965; Zubin, Eron & Schumer, 1965). Analysis can focus upon both the *content* and the *structure* of the TAT stories. Content refers to *what* is described: the people, the feelings, the events, the outcomes. Structure involves *how* the story is told: the logic and organization, the use of language, the appearance of speech disfluencies, misunderstanding of instructions or stimuli in the drawings, and obvious emotional arousal. Though many interpretive approaches emphasize story content, the potential importance of structure (including the client's overt behavior while working on the test) has received increased recognition (Murstein, 1963).

The original interpretive scheme of Morgan and Murray (1935) takes a "hero-oriented" approach in which responses are read for the *needs* (e.g., achievement, aggression, affiliation) and *presses* (perceived environmental influences such as criticism, affection, or physical danger) associated with the main character. The frequency and intensity of each need and press are scored on a 1-to-5 scale, and the themes and outcomes of each story are noted as well. This system was oriented toward description of personality, not toward clinical diagnosis.

Other scoring approaches have used more formal quantitative procedures to de-

scribe TAT stories (e.g., Dana, 1959; McClelland, Atkinson, Clark & Lowell, 1953). Efforts along these lines have resulted in the appearance of some normative TAT response data (e.g., Eron, 1950, Lindzey, Bradford, Tejessy & Davids, 1959; Murstein, 1972; Rosenzweig & Fleming, 1949), which clinicians can compare to stories told by their own clients (see Vane, 1981, for a review). Some interpretive systems make little use of formal scoring procedures (e.g., Henry, 1956), while others combine preliminary quantitative analysis with subjective interpretation of the resulting numbers (e.g., Bellak, 1986).

Most users of the TAT in clinical situations prefer scoring systems that are less structured and use response norms and formal scoring criteria only as general guides (Harrison, 1965; Sundberg, 1977). They may use Murray's need and press concepts and some psychoanalytic thinking, but more commonly they develop an idiosyncratic combination of principles derived from theory and clinical experience. An example of a TAT story and a clinician's interpretation of it are presented in Box 5-6. Other projective tests similar to the TAT are:

1. The Children's Apperception Test (CAT; Bellak, 1986), whose cards depict animal characters rather than human beings.
2. The Make-a-Picture-Story (MAPS; Shneidman, 1949), which has been called a "do-it-yourself TAT": The client first constructs pictures by placing cutout human and animal forms on a printed background, then tells stories about them.
3. The Rosenzweig Picture-Frustration Study (Rosenzweig, 1949), which presents twenty-four cartoons showing one person frustrating another in some way (e.g., "I'm not going to invite you to my party"). The client's task is to say what the frustrated person's response would be.

Completion Tests. These tests involve presenting the subject with part of a stimulus (usually a sentence) and asking the subject to complete it in his or her own way.

BOX 5-6 Examples of inferences based on the TAT

The following responses were given by a 25-year-old, unmarried male to a TAT card which shows a young boy looking at a violin which rests on a table in front of him.

This child is sick in bed. He has been given sheet music to study, but instead of the music, he has come across a novel that interests him more than the music. It is probably an adventure story. He evidently does not fear the chance that his parents will find him thusly occupied as he seems quite at ease. He seems to be quite a studious type and perhaps regrets missing school, but he seems quite occupied with the adventure in the story. Adventure has something to do with ocean or water. He is not too happy, though not too sad. His eyes are somewhat blank—coincidence of reading a book without any eyes or knowing what is in the book without reading it. He disregards the music and falls asleep reading the book.

A segment of a skilled TAT user's working notes on this story is presented below (Holt, 1978, pp. 166–167). After listing several indicators of psychosis (perceptual distortion, arbitrariness, peculiarities, delusional ideation, blandness, interpersonal isolation), he concludes:

On the basis of this story alone, I feel certain that there is a schizophrenic process present, even though not necessarily a pure schizophrenia. Slightly pretentious, facade tone, helped along with basic fact of perverse refusal to acknowledge presence of violin, strongly suggests that he *does* see violin but consciously thinks that

he's being "clever" or "original," or is out-tricking the examiner (whom he might see as trying to trick him) by ignoring it or seeing it as a book. That he is aware of it on some level is suggested by the fact that the basic theme, p Parental Imposed Task→n Auto Resis, passive Aggression, comes through. Consistent also is statement at the end: he *disregards* the music. Not a psychopath trying to act smart—too schizzy.

Sick in bed as a child may be an autobiographical theme. He's almost certainly "sick" (that is, psychotic) now, and so that may be enough explanation for it. But most psychotics don't [see the card this way]; therefore it becomes plausible that he may have had long illnesses as a child, cutting him off from other kids, and → to fantasy escape—dreams of travel and adventure.

Sentence 3 may also describe his overt behavior: nonchalant, seemingly "at ease," really frightened underneath.

Above are almost all hypotheses, to be confirmed or excluded by later stories.

Strong passivity throughout—especially in outcome. Also suggestion of *flight* and *avoidance* of very passive sort—drastic enough to include denial of threatening aspects of reality.

Nothing holds his interest long—not even adventure novel. Hero soon withdraws into his *own* fantasy, to conviction of knowing what's in book without reading it even though "took a chance" to read it, and finally withdraws into sleep.

Source: Robert R. Holt, *Methods in Clinical Psychology.* © 1978 by Plenum Press. New York. (Reprinted by permission.)

The assumption is that the way the client finishes the sentence will reflect important personality dimensions. Like the other projective techniques discussed so far, the incomplete sentence format had been used previously as a measure of intellect (Ebbinghaus, 1897, cited in Reisman, 1976). Its use as a projective technique dates from tests described by Payne (1928) and Tendler

(1930), but more widely used versions did not appear until the 1940s.

Today, the most popular completion test is the Rotter Incomplete Sentences Blank (Rotter & Rafferty, 1950). It contains forty sentence "stems" such as: "I like . . .", "My father . . .", "I secretly . . ." Client responses are compared to extensive data provided in the test manual and are given a seven-point rating of adjustment or maladjustment depending upon the degree of deviation from established norms. Item ratings are totaled to provide an overall adjustment score.

These relatively objective scoring procedures are primarily associated with Rotter's test and a few other research-oriented sentence-completion instruments aimed at assessing specific aspects of personality (e.g., Exner, 1973). Most other completion tests attempt to provide more general personality descriptions, tend to be longer (up to 240 items), more diverse in content, and heavily dependent upon the clinician's experience and skill to guide inferences. P. Goldberg (1965) presents a comprehensive review of sentence completion tests.

Choice or Ordering Tests. This category contains projective instruments that ask the client to arrange test stimuli in some order or to make choices from an array of stimuli according to preference, attractiveness, or some other dimension. Such tests are now used infrequently by clinical psychologists, but in the 1940s and 1950s the now-obscure Szondi Test (pronounced "zon-dee"; Szondi, Moser & Webb, 1959) was quite popular. This instrument was developed around 1947 by Lipot Szondi, a Hungarian psychiatrist who believed that liking or disliking a particular type of person was due in part to genetically determined traits or drives which are shared with that person. The test required the client to choose the two most liked and the two most disliked persons from each of six groups of photographs. These groups each contained eight pictures of European mental patients diagnosed as sadistic murderers, hysterics, catatonic or paranoid schizophrenics, manic-depressives, or the like. According to Szondi, a client's consistent choice of a certain diagnostic type as most liked or disliked revealed the presence of drives shared with that particular type.

The Kahn Test of Symbol Arrangement (Kahn, 1955) exemplifies a choice/ordering

projective still in use. Here, the client is shown sixteen plastic objects of various shapes (stars, animals, crosses) and asked to place them into categories such as "love," "hate," "bad," "good," "living," and "dead." In addition, the client is asked to free–associate to each object in order to illuminate its symbolic meaning for her or him. The arrangements of objects are then interpreted in light of the meaning of each symbol and what it suggests about the client's unconscious personality processes.

Expressive Tests. These procedures ask clients to express themselves in some way, most commonly by drawing a picture. The most notable example is the Draw-a-Person Test (DAP; Machover, 1949) which, as its name implies, requires the client to draw a person. A similar test (called Draw-a-Man) had been developed earlier by Goodenough (1926), who used the quality, detail, and complexity of drawings to estimate children's intelligence. In the DAP, various aspects of personality are inferred from the drawings. Each client may be asked to make several drawings; the initial instructions to draw a person may be followed by requests to draw a person of the opposite sex, a family, self, mother, and so on. Some users of the test ask the client to answer questions or tell a story about their drawings, but the primary rationale is that the drawings themselves reveal significant personality data.

Using psychoanalytic theory as her guide, Machover (1949) suggested that the inclusion, exclusion, and characteristics of each body part, along with the placement, symmetry, organization, size, and other features of the drawing were indicative of the client's self-image, conflicts, and perceptions of the world. For example, problems in drawing the nose (a phallic symbol) could reflect castration anxiety, while the stability of the figure's stance might represent feelings of security. A sample drawing and the inferences based upon it are presented in Figure 5-5.

Two other projective drawing tests are also widely used. Buck's (1948) House-Tree-

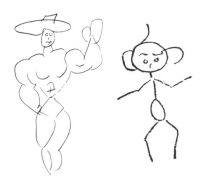

Beneath the obvious attempts at an impressive figure of masculine prowess, there are more subtle trends of the opposite: of inadequacy and inconsequentiality. The muscles of the drawn figure have been inflated beyond the hard and sinewy, into a puffy softness as if it is a figure made of balloons; the legs taper down to insubstantiality and, finally, absent feet, and an incongruous hat is placed on the boxer making comical his lifting of one gloved hand in victory. . . On the one hand, emblematic of his defenses, his drawn achromatic person is the "twenty-year-old" boxer with muscles flexed and a weight-lifter's build. Beneath this inflated image, however, on the crayon drawing of a person—which, due to the impact of color, tends to tap the relatively deeper levels of personality (Hammer, 1958)—he offers now only a "six-year-old boy" who then looks even more like an infant than a child: with one curlicue hair sticking up and the suggestion of diapers on (. . . shown here in black and white). The ears are rather ludicrous in their standing away from the head and, all in all, the total projection in this drawing is that of an infantile, laughable entity, rather than the impressive he-man he overstated on the achromatic version of a person. Beneath his attempts to demonstrate rugged masculinity (which may have culminated into the offense with which he is charged), the patient experiences himself as actually a little child, dependent and needing care, protection, and affection.

FIGURE 5-5. DAP drawings (done by an 18-year-old male who was caught stealing a television set) and interpretations. (Reprinted from Emanuel Hammer, "Projective Drawings," in A. I. Rabin, ed., *Projective Techniques in Personality Assessment*, pp. 375–76. Copyright © 1968 by Springer Publishing Company, Inc., New York. Used by permission.)

Person Test asks the client to draw each of those objects and then discuss them in an extended interview. The Bender-Gestalt Test, described earlier as a measure of intellectual deterioration, has also been interpreted as a projective indicator of personality when the symbolic meaning of errors and distortions in the copied figures are focused upon.

Among the nondrawing projectives of the expressive type, one finds methods involving finger painting (e.g., Napoli, 1947), psychodrama (Moreno, 1946), and puppet play (e.g., Woltmann, 1951).

THE STATUS OF TESTING IN CLINICAL PSYCHOLOGY

Although new psychological tests are introduced every year, clinicians tend to use the tests with which they are most familiar and on which the most research has been conducted. For these reasons, overall preferences for psychological tests have remained surprisingly stable over the past twenty-five years (see Box 5-7), despite differences in test usage among professionals working in different settings (e.g., counseling centers versus VA hospitals; Lubin, Larsen, Matarazzo & Seever, 1985). As Box 5-7 shows, the most popular tests are "the old reliables": the MMPI, the Wechsler Scales, the Rorschach, and the TAT. These data also demonstrate that clinicians are continuing to use projective techniques despite their limited predictive validity and repeated claims that projectives are little more than a remnant of the past.

The role of testing in clinical psychology has undergone large shifts in popularity across the decades. Beginning in the 1930s and continuing through the mid-1960s, tests

BOX 5-7   Testing's "Top Ten"

Periodic surveys have been conducted to determine which tests are most often used by psychologists. In spite of using different definitions of test's popularity, these surveys confirm the claim that clinicians have retained a remarkable deal of loyalty to a small core of instruments over the past three decades. Consider the results of four surveys summarized in the table below.

TEST	Louttit & Brown (1947)[a]	Sundberg (1961)[b]	Lubin, Wallis & Paine (1971)[c]	Lubin, Larsen & Matarazzo (1984)[d]
WAIS	2*	6	1	1
MMPI	15.5	7.5	6	2
Bender-Gestalt Visual Motor Test	54	4	3.5	3
Rorschach	5.5	1	2	4
TAT	3.5	2.5	3.5	5
WISC	—	10	7	6
Peabody Picture Vocabulary Test	—	—	13	7.5
Sentence completion Tests (all kinds)	—	13.5	8.5	7.5
House-Tree-Person Test	—	12	9	9
Draw-a-Person Test	—	2.5	5	10

[a] Ranking of 43 respondents mentioning some use of test.
[b] Ranking of 185 respondents mentioning some use of test.
[c] Ranking of 251 respondents mentioning some use of test.
[d] Ranking of 221 respondents mentioning some use of test.
* Reported for Wechsler-Bellevue.

were touted as semimagical pathways to the "truth" about intelligence, personality, and ability (Reisman, 1976). During this time clinical psychology students were trained intensively in the use of tests. For example, Harrower (1965, p. 398) remarked, "It is hard to conceive . . . of anyone in the field of clinical psychology reaching the postdoctoral level without being thoroughly well-versed in the Rorschach."

From the late 1960s through the 1970s, testing lost much of its appeal and was deemphasized as a training goal and professional activity for clinicians. The decline of psychological testing during this time was brought about by several factors. For one thing, there was a shift away from traditional diagnostic assessment in clinical psy-

chology, so the use of tests for that purpose decreased. Second, many clinicians do not like the "tester" role, which they see as not only subservient to psychiatry, but artificial and potentially damaging to relationships with clients. More general concerns also emerged as clinical psychologists, the public, the government, and individual clients placed the testing process under more intense scrutiny than ever before. This increased criticism of psychological tests stemmed from (1) research on the reliability and validity of many instruments, (2) awareness of the susceptibility of tests to various biases, (3) recognition that tests, particularly those assessing intelligence, may place members of certain minority groups at a disadvantage, (4) concern that collection of test information may invade the respondents' privacy, and (5) worry that tests are too easily misused or misinterpreted.

Psychometric Properties of Tests. A fundamental criticism leveled at psychological tests is that they do not do their job very well, that is, that they are unreliable, invalid, or both. While it is unfair to say that this is true about all tests under all circumstances, research on their psychometric properties has often been unfavorable. This research is too voluminous to be described on a test-by-test basis, but can be summarized as follows.

First, in general, the reliability of psychological tests tends to be fairly high but not uniformly so. Test-retest reliability coefficients for the MMPI scales range from .46 to .93, for example, but parallel form, test-retest, and split-half reliabilities are commonly .80 to .96 for major intelligence tests. Similarly, aptitude and ability tests such as the GRE, the Miller Analogies Test (MAT), the Medical College Admission Test (MCAT), and the Law School Admission Test (LSAT) display reliability coefficients ranging from .71 to .97. Tests of interests and values, such as the Kuder Preference Record, the Strong-Campbell Interest Inventory, and the Allport-Vernon-Lindzey Study of Values have produced reliabilities from the .70s to the low .90s.

Reliability is difficult to compute in the case of projective tests because split-half, parallel form, and test-retest approaches often do not make sense with such instruments (see Atkinson, 1981). Attempts to determine reliability in the traditional sense for the Rorschach, the TAT, and other major projectives have produced mediocre to unimpressive results (Anastasi, 1982; Vane, 1981). Projective test advocates point instead to the relatively high levels of agreement shown by different clinicians using similar scoring systems.

Second, the validity of psychological tests has in general been less impressive than their reliability. To a certain extent this will

be the case since, mathematically, a test's validity is limited by its reliability, but for most tests the discrepancy between reliability and validity is too high, in absolute terms. It is probably fair to say that the closer the test content or tasks are to the content or tasks being assessed (i.e., the criterion), the higher the validity will be.

For example, aptitude and ability tests that ask respondents to provide information or perform tasks directly related to academic skills are consistently among the most valid tests available. The major intelligence tests are next in terms of relative validity. These tests, especially their verbal sections, correlate with academic performance, specific skills (such as reading and arithmetic), and teacher ratings in the .17 to .75 range. When intelligence tests are used to draw inferences about a client's psychiatric disorder or personality characteristics, validity data have been disappointing (Cronbach, 1970).

Because their content is often remote from the criteria they aim to describe or predict, personality tests have been among the least valid assessment instruments. The MMPI has been described as a "psychometric nightmare" (Rodgers, 1972). It was based upon a no-longer-used diagnostic system, some of its scales have limited reliability, and the sample on which the test was standardized was too small and unrepresentative of diverse geographical, racial, and cultural variables. The ability of the test to make distinctions between diagnostic categories has been questioned, and, because many of the scales are highly correlated, its potential for individualized profiles is limited. Nonetheless, the MMPI is still the most valid "broad band" personality test for use with disturbed individuals. Research on projective instruments is even less encouraging. Correlations between projective test data and various criteria have ranged from only .20 to .40 (Sundberg, 1977); projective tests often do not increase the validity of predictions beyond what can be accomplished with demographic data alone (Garb, 1984).

There are many theoretical and practical reasons for the problematic validity of personality tests. Loevinger (1965) points out that the absence of good tests of this type "results . . . from the intrinsic difficulties of personality measurement" (p. 91). For example, the criteria these tests try to describe or predict are themselves often vague, multidimensional, and variable, depending upon situational and other factors. In addition, the meaning of personality test items (e.g., "I enjoy people") or response alternatives (e.g., "often" or "rarely") may vary considerably among clients. Galton recognized this same problem when he invented the questionnaire: "There is hardly any more difficult task than that of framing questions which are not likely to be misunderstood, which admit of easy reply, and which cover the ground of inquiry" (Galton, 1883, p. 279). Finally, the basic question of whether to use test responses as samples or signs is still not resolved. No wonder validity suffers!

Distortion of Test Scores. Tests are designed to collect assessment data under standard conditions. When conditions are not standard, test scores may be distorted in ways that can mislead the clinician. A multitude of factors can alter the outcome of all types of tests. For example, Mussen and Scodel (1955) demonstrated that after having been sexually aroused by photographs of nude females, college men gave more sex-related responses to the TAT when it was administered by a young, informally dressed male graduate student than when given by a man who was older and more formal.

Test instructions can also influence client responses. As part of their investigations of impression-management tactics used by mental hospital residents, Braginsky, Grosse, and Ring (1966) gave a true-false psychological test accompanied by varying instructions. In one condition, the test was described as an index of mental illness on which "true" responses indicated pathology.

Other patients were told that the test measured self-insight and that "true" responses were associated with readiness to leave the hospital. The "mental-illness" test prompted high scores from those who wished to stay in the hospital and lower scores from those who wanted to leave. The "self-insight" instructions prompted the opposite pattern: Patients wishing to leave scored higher than those wanting to stay. Instructional effects also appear on IQ tests (Engleman, 1974), personality tests such as the MMPI (Kroger & Turnbull, 1975), Fear Survey Schedules (Lick, 1977), and projective tests (Stewart & Patterson, 1973).

On some tests, the structure of the items and response alternatives may influence results. Suppose a tester wants to know how parents feel about allowing their children to display aggression toward them. The tester may write an item that says "No child should be permitted to strike a parent" and ask the client to agree or disagree. In this case, the client must mentally construct an alternative such as "A child should be encouraged to strike a parent" in order to guide the decision to agree or disagree. Each person may construct different mental alternatives, however, thus making the psychological content of the items variable among clients (Loevinger, 1965).

The circumstances under which a test is given can be important. Bernstein (1956) found that TAT responses contained less emotion and were more optimistic when a tester was in the room than when the client took the test alone. This is understandable, since clients often do not wish to appear "sick" or strange in the presence of a psychologist. Sometimes the examiner can produce emotional arousal which reduces the client's test score. Handler (1974) reports a case in which a child's IQ rose from 68 to 120 by eliminating the disruptive presence of the psychologist. When later IQ tests were administered with the examiner present, the child's score never surpassed 79.

Another source of test distortion stems

from the fact that some clients tend to respond in particular ways to most items, regardless of item content. This tendency has been called response *set* (e.g., Cronbach, 1946), response *style* (e.g., Jackson & Messick, 1958), and response *bias* (e.g., Berg, 1955). Some clients exhibit *social desirability* responses, where they tend to endorse statements that are socially acceptable and approved (e.g., honesty and fairness) and reject those that are less valued (Edwards, 1957). Clients have also been suspected of *acquiescent* response styles (e.g., Jackson & Messick, 1961), in which they tend to agree with virtually any self-descriptive test item. Defensive, deviant, and overly disclosing styles have also been postulated. The significance of response styles as influencers of test data has been a hotly debated matter (see Rorer, 1965; Wiggins, 1973). It is also not clear whether response tendencies represent stable client characteristics (e.g., McCrae & Costa, 1983) or temporary behavior patterns dictated and reinforced by the circumstances under which the test is taken (Linehan & Nielsen, 1983). In any case, the client's point of view while taking the test should not be ignored when evaluating test data.

Other client variables may also be important determinants of test data. Clients whose cultural background leaves them unfamiliar with the concepts and vocabulary of middle-class white America often perform poorly on psychological tests reflecting those ideas and terms. While this does not appear to be a source of bias in some tests, the influence of one's background on intelligence test scores is of great concern, especially to culturally distinct and racial minority groups within our society.

One approach to this problem has been to use culture-specific instruments such as the Black Intelligence Test of Cultural Homogeneity (BITCH; Williams, 1972) with persons thought to be discriminated against on standard tests, but this merely shifts cultural bias to another racial group. Another approach involves using intelli-

gence tests that are not strongly influenced by culture-specific experience or particular verbal skills. Examples of some of these tests were given earlier. Unfortunately, hopes for "culture-fair" tests have been dampened by research which shows that cultural and environmental factors influence such tests as much or, in some cases, more than standard instruments (see Samuda, 1975, for a review and Bernardoni, 1964, for a prody of cross-cultural measures). Instead of ignoring IQ tests or attempting to *remove* their cultural and subcultural bias, some testers choose to *examine* the differential performance of certain groups in order to identify specific deficits and create corrective programs. Anastasi (1982, p. 59) summarizes this view:

Tests cannot compensate for cultural deprivation by eliminating its effects from their scores. On the contrary, tests should reveal such effects, so that appropriate remedial steps can be taken. To conceal the effects of cultural disadvantages by rejecting tests or by trying to devise tests that are insensitive to such effects can only retard progress toward a genuine solution of social problems. Such reactions toward tests are equivalent to breaking a thermometer because it registers a body temperature of 101.

Other assessors make a related suggestion for reducing irrelevant cultural effects: When specific predictions (e.g., about academic or occupational performance) are desired, use instruments that sample as directly as possible the particular behaviors and skills of interest. When this is done, the opportunity for extraneous characteristics to distort performance is greatly reduced.

The potential sources of test-score bias discussed here barely scratch the surface of the problem. Readers interested in more intensive study of this issue should consult sources such as Anastasi (1982), Cole (1981), Jensen (1980), Masling (1960, 1966), Murstein (1965), Reynolds (1982), Sarason

(1954), Shepard (1982), and Sundberg (1977).

Abuse of Tests. Like all assessment procedures, tests involve entry by the clinician into the privacy of clients' thoughts and behaviors. The extent to which such entry is desirable or even legal is a matter of intense debate and litigation. Many observers contend that there are too many tests and too much testing. They also argue that much of this testing is irrelevant, inaccurate, and too easily misused. Overdependence on IQ scores by ill-informed test consumers provides an excellent case in point.

During the mid-1960s, Congress conducted hearings on psychological testing, particularly as used in educational and vocational selection. These inquiries were prompted in part by serious, knowledgeable test critics and also by the appearance of nonexpert books with sensational titles like *The Brain Watchers* (Gross, 1962), *The Tyranny of Testing* (Hoffman, 1962), and *They've Got Your Number* (Wernick, 1956). Senator Sam Ervin (of Watergate fame) noted: "We have received numerous complaints that some of the questions contained in . . . personality inventories relating to sex, religion, family relationships, and many personal aspects of . . . life constitute an unjustified invasion of privacy" (Ervin, 1965, p. 880). Many subcommittee members were incensed with what they learned about test content and quality. In particular, the inclusion of useful but apparently silly or overly intimate items from empirically constructed tests like the MMPI acted as lightning rods for congressional wrath. Representative Rosenthal of the House Special Subcommittee on Invasion of Privacy fumed: "I will tell you what. I am impressed to the point where . . . I am prepared to offer a bill on Monday to prohibit the giving of psychological tests by any Federal agency, under any circumstances, at any place, and to make it a Federal crime for any Federal official to do it" (quoted in the *American Psychologist,* November 1965, p. 982).

The concern over invasion of privacy and other issues has resulted in restrictions on testing in certain settings. For example, personality tests have been eliminated from routine selection procedures for federal employees, and IQ tests are restricted in some school systems (Bersoff, 1973, 1981). Reschly (1984) reviews the court cases and legislation that have recently attempted to regulate ability testing in educational settings (see also Bersoff, 1982).

As noted earlier, the APA is sensitive to these issues and has urged its members to reduce the possibility of abuse in the testing field by adhering to its *Standards for Educational and Psychological Testing.* These standards embody the pro-test argument that when developed, evaluated, administered, interpreted, and published with due regard for scientific principles and the rights and welfare of clients, psychological tests can make a positive contribution to society. For additional material on this highly sensitive set of issues, see Cronbach (1975), Daves (1984), Wigdor and Garner (1982), Heller, Holtzman & Messick (1982), and special issues of *The American Psychologist* (November 1965 and October 1981).

Testing Today. One might anticipate that the many problems associated with testing would have a devastating impact on clinicians' use of tests. In fact, testing is still an active enterprise in this country, and clinical psychologists show no signs of abandoning even their most poorly validated instruments (Lubin, Larsen & Matarazzo, 1984; Reynolds, 1979; Wade & Baker, 1977). In fact, psychological testing is enjoying a bit of a comeback in the 1980s. Why is this the case? For one thing, as ordinary mortals, clinical psychologists form habits and find them hard to break. Graduate training tends to set career-long patterns of assessment practices to which clinical psychologists become personally attached. Clinicians do what they were taught to do and then continue doing so because it is what they have always done.

FIGURE 5-6. (© by Jules Feiffer. Reproduced by permission.)

Of course, such habits are not based entirely upon blind adherence. Many clinicians attend to data about their tests in selective ways, a tendency that appears to be prominent especially with projective tests. Further, negative *research* findings about a test may simply be seen as irrelevant to that test's use in *clinical* settings: "Published indexes of validity . . . are but rough guides, for the psychologist must reach his own judgments of clinical validity and meaningfulness in each particular case" (Tallent, 1976, p. 14). Sometimes negative evidence is recast as supporting a test. For example, MMPI proponents argue that low test-retest reliability is to be expected because the test is sensitive to changes in respondents' psychological conditions (see Groth-Marnat, 1984, p. 255).

It must also be recognized that certain clinicians, for reasons not clearly understood, are able to draw remarkably accurate inferences from test data. Almost every practitioner knows of at least one MMPI or Rorschach "ace" whose reputation shores up general confidence in particular tests. Most clinical psychologists are themselves reinforced for using even the least scientifically supported tests by the fact that, now

and then, they make their own insightful inferences on the basis of test data.

Finally, in the past ten years, a number of well-constructed and carefully researched tests have been developed that justify clinicians' belief that tests are legitimate assessment tools when used appropriately. Many of these newer tests attempt to measure a narrow band of dimensions, behaviors, or abilities that are the focus of research programs or clinical interventions. Some relatively new psychological tests whose construction and psychometric advantages support their increased use in the future are summarized in Box 5-8. Related to the construction of good, special-purpose tests is the development of DSM-III and its more reliable system for assigning psychiatric diagnoses (see Chapter 3). Because of DSM-III's improvements, clinicians now tend to be less apologetic about their role in diagnostic classification and the use of tests in making diagnoses.

When these factors are added to the traditional view of clinical psychologists as test experts and the societal demand for testing services, the continued popularity of psychological testing is not surprising. Amrine (1965, p. 859) put it this way: "Tests and

BOX 5-8 Recent advances in psychological testing

In a recent review of personality assessment, Lanyon (1984) listed five reasons to be optimistic about the field's future: 1) There has been improved theorizing about the structure of normal personality along with better methodology of measurement; 2) the mutual influence of behavioral and traditional approaches to assessment on each other has had a positive impact on both traditions; 3) assessment procedures are becoming more specific to the criteria they attempt to describe or predict; 4) there is increasing interest in assessing such areas as marital satisfaction, happiness, medical problems, and social support; and 5) more attention is being paid to psychometrically solid assessment of children, an area that has suffered serious neglect. Illustrations of this progress can be found in eight recently developed tests (summarized below) that demonstrate the contributions that well-constructed tests can make to assessment decisions.

Test	Format	Purpose	Special Features
1. Personality Inventory for Children (Lacher & Gdowski, 1979; Wirt, Lacher, Klinedinst & Seat, 1984).	Four forms are available, consisting of 131, 280, 420, or 600 true-false items to be answered by parents. On the 600-item form, four Factor Scores, four Validity Scales, twelve clinical scales, and seventeen "experimental" scales are available.	Provide clinical descriptions of behavior, affect, cognitions, and family characteristics of children aged 3–16 years. Can be used as a diagnostic instrument.	Construction and scoring follows basic MMPI methodology. Computerized administration and interpretation services are available.
2. Marital Satisfaction Inventory (Snyder, 1981).	280 true-false items yielding one validity scale, one global dissatisfaction scale, and nine additional scales measuring specific aspects of marital interaction such as sexual dissatisfaction and disagreements over finances.	Measure extent and sources of marital distress, and several dimensions of marital interaction.	Two broad-band factors—disaffection and disharmony—can be scored and used to suggest different treatment strategies.
3. McCarthy Scales of Children's Abilities (McCarthy, 1972).	Six scales composed of 18 tests assessing verbal, performance, quantitative, memory, motor, and general cognition abilities.	Assess several intellectual abilities of children aged $2\frac{1}{2}$–$8\frac{1}{2}$ years.	Avoids use of IQ scores and allows profile of abilities across different areas. Reliability and validity appear to be quite good.
4. Eating Disorder Inventory (Garner, Olmstead & Polivy, 1983).	64 six-point items (points range from "always" to "never") which form 8 subscales such as Drive for Thinness, Perfectionism, and Body Dissatisfaction.	Assess the psychological and behavioral traits common in anorexia nervosa and bulimia. Along with other methods, may be used as a screening instrument for eating disorders.	Subscales measure disordered eating habits as well as more general psychopathology associated with eating disorders. Good preliminary data on reliability and validity.

Test	Format	Purpose	Special Features
5. PRF ANDRO Scale (Berzins, Welling & Wetter, 1978).	85 true-false items that yield independent masculinity and femininity scales. A self-esteem subscale is also included.	Measures psychological masculinity and femininity and allows for their integration into the concept of psychological androgeny.	The items for the masculinity and femininity scales are drawn from the PRF. Therefore, they may be scored from previously completed PRF protocols.
6. Revised Fear Survey Schedule for Children (FSSC-R; Ollendick, 1983).	80 three-point items ("none," "some," "a lot") measuring fear of specific events and situations.	Assesses severity of fears in children. Can be used as a pre-post measure of treatment effectiveness.	Five factors have been identified in preliminary analyses: fear of failure or criticism, fear of the unknown, fear of injury and small animals, fear of danger or death, medical fears.
7. Headache Symptom Questionnaire (Arena, Blanchard, Andrasik & Dudek, 1982)	16 five-point items ("never," "infrequently," "sometimes," "usually," "always") assessing symptoms of headache	Classifies headache sufferers into various diagnostic categories (e.g., migraine versus muscle contraction headaches)	Three factors have been identified in initial analyses—migraine, muscle contraction, and duration of headache.
8. Children's Depression Inventory (CDI/Kovacs, 1981).	27 items patterned after the Beck Depression Inventory. Each item consists of three sentences; the child chooses the one that best describes her/his behavior over past two weeks.	Assess the severity of cognitive, affective, and behavioral symptoms of depression in children.	Evidence for discriminant validity of CDI is mixed; some studies fail to find correlations between the CDI and observations of behavior. Stronger correlations may be obtained when parents complete the CDI for their children.

testers are . . . attacked by the right and left, from outside of psychology and from inside. Meanwhile, the sale and use of tests increases steadily because to thousands of users psychological tests even as presently designed appear to be better than the alternative of no tests." Thus, though more stringent standards and limitations regarding the use of tests in many spheres appear likely, testing will continue to be a major contribution of clinical psychologists (see Petzelt & Craddick, 1978).

chapter 6

Observation in Clinical Psychology

Observation of the behavior of other people is a fundamental aspect of assessment. We all base innumerable social judgments on the appearance and actions of others. Indeed, the notion that "seeing is believing" prompts us to emphasize observation of what people *do* as opposed to what they *say* they do. It is rumored, for example, that some people seeking companionship through computer dating services do not entirely trust the data upon which match-ups are made and insist upon observing their potential date before committing themselves to a meeting.

Clinical psychologists also collect and analyze observational data as part of their assessment activities. The appeal of what Sundberg and Tyler (1962) term the "watch 'em" approach is that it provides a direct, first-hand look at behaviors of clinical interest and yields many clues about the causes of those behaviors. In general, the goals of ob-servational assessment are to (1) collect information not available in any other way, and/or (2) supplement other data as part of a multiple assessment approach.

Consider a situation in which a teacher and a "problem" pupil give different reports of why they fail to get along: "He's a brat"; "She's mean." A less-biased picture may emerge from observations by neutral parties of relevant classroom interactions. In other instances, knowing what a person can or will do in a situation is so important that only observation can suffice. For example, knowing that a mental patient "feels better" and wishes to leave the hospital may be less valuable than observing that person's ability to hold a job, use the bus system, and meet other demands of everyday life. As a supplement to other methods, observation can broaden the total assessment picture and lead to a more comprehensive understanding of the client. This is particularly true when intermethod discrepancies or similarities are revealed. For example, observers' reports that a person claiming to have quit smoking is or is not lighting cigarettes in their presence can provide valuable information to the clinician interested in evaluating an antismoking program.

When administering tests or conducting interviews, the astute clinician gathers observational data about how the client handles the assessment situation. However, the way observational information is used in an overall assessment strategy varies considerably among clinicians. Some see the client's overt behavior as providing only supplementary clues to personality traits and dynamics that will be revealed more fully through tests or interviews. For others, observable behavior plays a larger role in assessing underlying personality or pathology; they may weight this behavior equivalently to self-reports or test scores. In both cases, observations are used as *signs* of more fundamental, unobservable constructs.

On the other hand, behaviorally oriented clinicians regard observational data as behavior *samples* that represent the most direct, important, and scientific assessment channel available. These clinicians use observation to describe person-situation interactions rather than to draw inferences about hypothesized underlying characteristics of clients.

The more importance clinicians attribute to observational data, the more systematic they are likely to be in gathering and analyzing such data. At one end of the spectrum are informal, anecdotal accounts of client behavior that often are by-products of other assessment efforts like testing and interviewing. The following excerpt from a report that followed administration of the Stanford-Binet to a twelve-year-old boy provides a clear example:

John's principal difficulties were on tests requiring precise operations, as in the use of numbers. With such tests he became insecure and often seemed confused with slips of memory and errors in simple calculations. He asked to have instructions repeated, was dependent on the examiner, and easily discouraged. Although cooperative and anxious to do well, it was extremely hard for him to master a task (such as "memory span") in which he was required to be exact by fixed standards. (Jones, 1943, p. 91)

Clinicians who place greater emphasis on overt behavior have improved on casual observation methods in at least two ways. First, they have developed more accurate and systematic methods for watching and quantifying behavior. Second, they have demonstrated the feasibility of collecting observational data in situations other than interviews or tests. Together, these developments have made it possible for modern clinicians and researchers to observe scientifically a wide range of human behavior in a multitude of settings. In this chapter we describe and evaluate some of the observational systems and techniques now in use.

SOME HISTORICAL NOTES

Overt behavior existed long before language, so observation was probably the first source of human assessment data. A prehistoric person learned quickly how to judge the intentions of other prehistoric people on the basis of their actions (e.g., an offer of food; a raised club), and the importance of observation did not diminish as language developed. In ancient Greek and Chinese civilizations, conclusions about an individual were sometimes drawn on the basis of physical and behavioral characteristics. In the Western world, the practice of interpreting physical features and behaviors came to be called *physiognomy* (McReynolds, 1975). Homer provides an early illustration of this practice in his *Iliad*:

There is nothing like an ambush for bringing a man's worth to light and picking out the cowards from the brave. A coward changes color all the time; he cannot sit still for nervousness, but squats down, first on one heel, then on the other. . . . But the brave man never changes color at all and is not unduly perturbed from the moment when he takes his seat in ambush with the rest. (Translation by Rieu, 1950; quoted in McReynolds, 1975, p. 488).

Pythagoras, Hippocrates, Plato, Aristotle, and Galen elaborated on the relationship between overt behavior and personality characteristics. Even the Bible contains references to assessment via behavioral observation. In order to help Gideon defeat the Midianites with the smallest possible force, God tells how to identify the most able soldiers:

And the Lord said unto Gideon, The people are yet too many; bring them down unto the water, and I will try them for thee there. . . . So he brought down the people into the water; and the Lord said unto Gideon, Everyone that lappeth of the water with his tongue . . . him shalt thou set by himself; likewise everyone that boweth down upon his knees to drink. And the number of them that lapped, putting their hand to their mouth, were three hundred men; but all the rest of the people bowed down upon their knees to drink water. And the Lord said unto Gideon, By the three hundred men that lapped will I save you, and deliver the Midianites into thine hand. . . . (Judges 7:4–7)

Obviously, the best warriors were those who remained alert to danger, even when drinking. Thus, the foundations of observational assessment, content analysis of speech, gesture and movement analysis, and research on the relationship between facial expressions and emotion were laid down centuries ago. Like the test and the interview, clinical observation is the modern form of an old tradition.

APPROACHES TO CLINICAL OBSERVATION

Weick (1968) defined observational methods as "the *selection, provocation, recording,* and *encoding* of . . . behaviors" (italics added). This definition highlights the fun-

damental elements of nearly every type of observational system. The observer first *selects* those persons, classes of behavior, events, situations, or time periods that are to be the focus of attention. Second, a decision is made about whether to *provoke* (i.e., artificially bring about) behaviors and situations of interest or to wait for them to happen naturally. Third, plans are made for the way in which observations are to be *recorded:* Observer memory, audio or video recording devices, physiological monitoring systems, timers, and counters are all possible choices. Finally, a system for *encoding* raw observations into usable dimensions must be developed. This translation is often the most difficult and technically demanding aspect of any observational procedure.

Differing assessment goals, unique client populations, specific environmental limitations, and other factors produce many approaches to clinical observation. The clearest way to organize this array is in terms of the *settings* employed. At one extreme there is *naturalistic* observation, where the assessor looks at behavior as it occurs in its most natural context (e.g., in a home, school, or factory). *Controlled,* or *experimental,* observation lies at the other extreme, where the clinician or researcher sets up a special situation in which to observe behavior. These approaches can be blended to handle specific assessment needs so there are many subtypes of both naturalistic and controlled observation. Another important way in which these procedures differ involves the observers' role. *Participant* observers are visible to the clients being watched and may even interact with them in some cases. *Nonparticipant* observers are not visible, although in most cases the clients are aware that observation is taking place. As noted earlier, other significant dimensions of observation include the characteristics of the recording system (human, mechanical, or both) and a decision about whether data are used as signs or samples.

In order to present a reasonably complete picture of clinical observation, we shall describe naturalistic and controlled observational systems that focus on several kinds of behavior. The examples will illustrate the use of (1) participant and nonparticipant observers; (2) human, mechanical, and combined recording procedures, and (3) informal and formal encoding systems that deal with behavior as samples and signs. More comprehensive coverage of this material is available in Ciminero, Calhoun, and Adams (1986), Cone and Hawkins (1977), Haynes (1978), Hersen and Bellack (in press), Keefe, Kopel, and Gordon (1978), Mash and Terdal (1981), Nay (1979), Nelson and Hayes (1986), and Wiggins (1973).

Naturalistic Observation

Watching clients behave spontaneously in a natural setting such as their homes has several obvious advantages. For one thing, it is realistic. Natural settings provide a background that is obviously relevant for understanding the client's behavior and the factors influencing that behavior. Additionally, naturalistic observation can be done in subtle ways that provide an accurate view of behavior, uncluttered by the client's self-consciousness or attempts to convey a particular impression.

The classic case of naturalistic observation is the anthropological field study in which a scientist joins a tribe, subculture, or other social unit in order to observe its characteristics and the behavior of the individuals within it (e.g., Mead, 1928; Williams, 1967). In such cases the observer is a participant in every sense of the term, and observations are usually recorded in anecdotal notes which later appear as a detailed account called an *ethnography.*

In psychology, the work of Roger G. Barker provides an example of naturalistic observation whose intensity approaches anthropological proportions. In an effort to understand the ecology of human behavior, Barker and his colleagues observed as much of it as possible in order to capture the richness and details of its relationship to the environment. This involved participant (but noninteractive) observation of children on a continuous basis from morning until night as they went about a normal day's activities in their home town (Barker, Schoggen & Barker, 1955; Barker & Wright, 1951, 1955). No attempt was made to select particular behaviors, situations, or events for special attention. Observations were recorded in notebooks as narrative "day records" (see Box 6-1) and later encoded as "behavioral episodes." When episodes involved other people, they were treated as signs representing "nurturance," "resistance," "appeal," "submission," "aggression," "avoidance," etc. Notice the amount of observer inference involved in the Box 6-1 narratives (e.g., "He looked briefly at me *as if wondering what I thought*").

The data generated by these procedures are staggering. For example, one eight-year-old girl had 969 behavioral episodes involving 571 objects in the course of a single day. Barker was aware that this full-scale ecological approach produced too much information, and he suggested more practical alternatives, including periodic rather than continuous observation. In current practice, most assessors collect their observational data intermittently, focusing on those aspects of behavior and behavior-environment interaction that are of special theoretical or practical importance (Haynes, 1984). Psychologists interested in child development, for example, have devised observation systems aimed at specific categories of behavior thought to indicate particular levels of physical, cognitive, and social functioning (e.g., Arrington, 1932; Bayley, 1965; Piaget, 1947). Similarly, social psychologists have developed observational tools that help them code the complex interplay of behaviors of people in groups (Bales, 1950).

The targets of naturalistic observation in clinical psychology have sometimes been behaviors used to infer personality characteristics (e.g., Santostefano, 1962) or intelligence (e.g., Lambert, Cox & Hartsough, 1970), but the primary focus has been on assessing problems that brought the client to the clinician. These include everything from

BOX 6-1   Excerpt from a day record

5:39: Raymond tilted the crate from side to side in a calm, rhythmical way. Clifford's feet were endangered again. Stewart came over and very protectively led Clifford out of the way. [Observer's opinion.]
Raymond slowly descended to the ground inside the crate.
When Stewart came back around the crate, Raymond reached out at him, and growled very gutturally, and said, "I'm a big gorilla." Growling very ferociously, he stamped around the "cage" with his arms hanging loosely. He reached out with slow, gross movements.
Raymond reached toward Clifford but didn't really try to catch him.
Then he grabbed Stewart by the shirt.
Imitating a very fierce gorilla, he pulled Stewart toward the crate. Stewart was passive and allowed himself to be pulled in. He said "Why don't you let go of me?" He spoke disgustedly and yet not disparagingly.
Raymond released his grasp and ceased imitating a gorilla.
He tilted the crate so that he could crawl out of the open end. As he crawled out, he lost control of the crate and it fell over on its side with the open end perpendicular to the ground.
Stewart said, "Well, how did you get out?"
Raymond said self-consciously, "I fell out," and forced a laugh.
He looked briefly at me as if wondering what I thought.

Source: Barker and Wright (1951).

nail biting, cigarette smoking, troublesome thoughts, maladaptive social interactions, and psychotic behavior to community problems such as crime and littering.

In its early forms, naturalistic clinical observation required observers to draw inferences of many kinds: What were the meanings of a behavior; which behaviors should be observed and which should not. As a result, the interobserver reliability of naturalistic observation suffered. For example, Box 6-2 contains the notes of four observers who watched the same ten-minute film, *This is Robert*, which showed a boy in classroom and playground situations. Notice the different images generated by each viewer. Cronbach (1960, p. 535) summarizes this problem well: "Observers interpret what they see. When they make an interpretation, they tend to overlook facts which do not fit the interpretation, and they may even invent facts needed to complete the event as interpreted."

Attempts to improve anecdotal accounts in naturalistic clinical observation have taken many forms. To reduce unsystematic selection and reporting of client behaviors, most modern observation schemes focus the observer's attention on specific behaviors. Some versions of this approach employ *retrospective* procedures (Wiggins, 1973) in which certain aspects of the client's past behaviors are recalled.

For example, life records may be scanned to gather information about particular behaviors in a client's past. School, police, and court records have been used as a means of evaluating treatment of delinquent and predelinquent children (e.g., Alexander & Parsons, 1973), while changes in academic grades have provided indices of reduction of test anxiety (e.g., Allen, 1971).

BOX 6-2   Excerpts from four observers' notes on the same film[a]

Observer A: (2) Robert reads word by word, using finger to follow place. (4) Observes girl in box with much preoccupation. (5) During singing, he in general doesn't participate too actively. Interest is part of time centered elsewhere. Appears to respond most actively to sections of song involving action. Has tendency for seemingly meaningless movement. Twitching of fingers, aimless thrusts with arms.

Observer B: (2) Looked at camera upon entering (seemed perplexed and interested). Smiled at camera. (2) Reads (with apparent interest and with a fair degree of facility). (3) Active in roughhouse play with girls. (4) Upon being kicked (unintentionally) by one girl he responded (angrily). (5) Talked with girl sitting next to him between singing periods. Participated in singing. (At times appeared enthusiastic). Didn't always sing with others. (6) Participated in a dispute in a game with others (appeared to stand up for his own rights). Aggressive behavior toward another boy. Turned pockets inside out while talking to teacher and other students. (7) Put on overshoes without assistance. Climbed to top of ladder rungs. Tried to get rung which was occupied by a girl but since she didn't give in, contented himself with another place.

Observer C: (1) Smiles into camera (curious). When group break up, he makes nervous gestures, throws arm out into air. (2) Attention to reading lesson. Reads with serious look on his face, has to use line marker. (3) Chases girls, teases. (4) Girl

kicks when he puts hand on her leg. Robert makes face at her. (5) Singing. Sits with mouth open, knocks knees together, scratches leg, puts fingers in mouth (seems to have several nervous habits, though not emotionally overwrought or self-conscious). (6) In a dispute over parchesi, he stands up for his rights. (7) Short dispute because he wants rung on jungle gym.

Observer D: (2) Uses guide to follow words, reads slowly, fairly forced and with careful formation of sounds (perhaps unsure of self and fearful of mistakes). (3) Perhaps slightly aggressive as evidenced by pushing younger child to side when moving from a position to another. Plays with other children with obvious enjoyment, smiles, runs, seems especially associated with girls. This is noticeable in games and in seating in singing. (5) Takes little interest in singing, fidgets, moves hands and legs (perhaps shy and nervous). Seems in song to be unfamiliar with words of main part, and shows disinterest by fidgeting and twisting around. Not until chorus is reached does he pick up interest. His special friend seems to be a particular girl, as he is always seated by her.

[a] The observers were told to use parentheses to indicate inferences or interpretations. The numbers used refer to scenes in the film and were inserted to aid comparison.

Source: L. J. Cronbach, *Essentials of Psychological Testing,* © 1949 by Harper & Row, Pub., Inc. © 1960, Lee J. Cronbach. (Reprinted by permission of Harper & Row, Publishers, Inc.)

Maisto and Maisto (1983) refer to measures collected for purposes other than treatment evaluation which are then used to evaluate treatments as *institutional measures* (see Patterson & Sechrest, 1983, for a review of these measures as they are used to evaluate psychotherapy).[1] In clinical research, institutional measures also may be used to test

[1] Institutional measures or *archival* observation is part of a broader observational approach called *nonreactive* or *unobtrusive* measurement, which has been used in clinical psychology and other behavioral sciences to learn about people's behavior without altering it in the process. A comprehensive description and discussion of these techniques is contained in a fascinating, often humorous book by Webb, Campbell, Schwartz, and Sechrest (1966).

theories about the causes of behavior problems. Barthell and Holmes (1968) were interested in the hypothesis that social isolation early in life and particularly during adolescence is related to latter diagnosis of schizophrenia. As a partial test of this hypothesis, they inspected the high school yearbooks of people labeled "schizophrenic" or "neurotic" and compared the activities listed for these individuals with nonlabeled students from the same schools. A similar use of life records is illustrated by research that relates factors such as age, marital status, employment history, and education to the development of schizophrenia and to chances for its improvement (e.g., see Harris, 1984, for a review).

Most retrospective observation systems involve asking persons familiar with the client to report on the frequency, intensity, duration, or form of specific categories of behavior displayed in the recent past. We will consider some examples as they have been used in different observational settings.

Hospital Observations. An excellent example of a hospital observation system is the Inpatient Multidimensional Psychiatric Scales, or IMPS (Lorr, Klett, & McNair 1963), which has been used widely in hospital settings by ward personnel who observe and interview their clients. The IMPS contains seventy-five items, which are either rated by the observer/interviewer on five- or nine-point scales or responded to with a "yes" or "no" (see Box 6-3). These data are translated into scores on dimensions such as excitement, hostile belligerence, paranoid projection, grandiose expansiveness, disorientation, and conceptual disorganization. The scores can then be plotted as a profile (like an MMPI) that provides a broad description of the client.

Many clinical observation systems used in natural settings not only specify the targets to be observed, but also reduce the observer/coder inferences required in the earlier techniques. These systems involve *immediate*, not retrospective, observation. Raters observe a client's behavior and record that behavior as it occurs. When such observations are made at regular intervals (e.g., once per hour), the process is called *time sampling*. When only certain activities are observed (e.g., mealtime interactions, cigarette smoking), the method is called *event sampling*. Often both techniques are involved, as when observations are made once per minute during particular events such as mother-child interactions.

One of the first immediate observation systems used with inpatients was the Behavioral Study Form (BSF) developed by Schaefer and Martin (1975) at Patton State Hospital in California. The BSF requires ward personnel (usually nurses) to observe clients approximately every thirty minutes and to record specific behaviors. A list of these behaviors and a sample record are presented in Figure 6-1. At each observation point the nurse records a "mutually exclusive" behavior (which defines the client's general activity) and any concomitant behavior that accompanies that activity. The client's location and other relevant facts are also noted. Data collected over a period of time can be summarized in tables contain-

BOX 6-3   Samples from the Inpatient Multidimensional Psychiatric Scales (IMPS)

Compared to the normal person, to what degree does/is the client:

1. Exhibit an attitude of superiority
2. Ramble off the topic discussed
3. Assume bizarre positions
4. Unrestrained in showing feelings
5. Blame others for difficulty
6. Believe he has unusual abilities or talents
7. Believe people are against him
8. Make unusual facial grimaces

ing, for example, average time spent sleeping, rocking, pacing, or watching TV, and can also be presented in graphic form. Because the observation targets are clearly defined, this system leaves little room for target selection or inference by the observers, thereby increasing the likelihood that different observers will use the system reliably.

The Behavioral Study Form served as the basis for more elaborate observation systems now used in psychiatric hospitals. The most sophisticated and well-researched observa-

FIGURE 6-1. Coding system and sample record from an early hospital observation system. (H. H. Schaefer and P. L. Martin, *Behavioral Therapy*, 2nd ed. © 1975 by McGraw-Hill Book Company, New York. Reprinted by permission.)

Watch Especially for:

19- *head in hands HH*
18- *Working - assigned*
16- *Talking to others*

GENERAL CODE

Mutually Exclusive Behaviors

1. Walking   4. Sitting
2. Running   5. Lying down
3. Standing

Concomitant Behaviors

6   Drinking
7   Eating — meals
7a Eating — other than meals
8   Grooming (describe)
9   Group meeting
10 Medication
11 Reading
12 Receiving pay
13 Rocking
14 Pacing
15 Smoking
16 Talking to others
17 TV
18 Working — assigned
19 Other

Location

A Dining room
B Hall or lounge
C Sleeping quarters
D Lavatory
E Outside

Patient _____ *Susan R.* _____

Admission _____

Followup:

① 2 3 4 5 6 7 8 9

Date: *August 24, 1967*

Time	Code	Location
0630	3-8	D
0700	3-6	B
0730	4-15	B
0800	3-10	A
0830	4-18	A
0900	3-18	A
0930		
1000	4-19 HH	B
1030	4-19 HH	B
1100	3-19 *Buying item*	B
1130	3-18	A
1200	4-7	A
1230	3-16 (*Employee*)	B
1300	4-11	A
1330	4-9	A
1400	4-9	A
1430	4-9	A
1500	*Unavailable*	
1530	1	E
1600	3-11	A
1630	3-18	A
1700	3-18	A
1730	4	D
1800	4-16	E
1830	3	C
1900	3-16	C
1930	3-17	B
2000	3-11	A
2030	2-19 (*screaming*)	B
2100	5	C

tion system is the Time-Sample Behavioral Checklist (TSBC; Paul & Lentz, 1977) which was developed to assess a large number of behaviors by psychiatric patients using trained professionals as observers. It provides measurement of clinically relevant behavior in great detail (sixty-nine different behavioral characteristics are coded for a two-second focus on one patient) and with great regularity (each patient is observed at least once every waking hour seven days a week). Several TSBC index scores can be computed to summarize the overall quality of a patient's behavior. The TSBC Total Inappropriate Behavior Index gives a measure of "crazy" behaviors by indicating the presence of any one of twenty-four inappropriate behaviors. The TSBC Total Appropriate Behavior Index assesses amount of "normal" behavior by indicating the presence of any one of twenty-seven appropriate behaviors. Other indices can be computed from the TSBC that indicate the frequency of different categories of clinically disturbed behavior. For example, Figure 6-2 compares the effects of two hospital programs (social-learning versus milieu) on three such indices—Schizophrenic Disorganization (bizarre behaviors like rocking and blank staring), Cognitive Distortion (bizarre verbal behaviors like incoherent speech, hallucinations), and Hostile-Belligerence (aggressive behaviors like screaming and cursing).

Barker-style ethological observations have also been used in hospital settings by clinicians interested in getting a detailed view of children's behavior problems. Rather than attempting to observe all aspects of the client's behavior, however, certain subcategories (e.g., social behavior) become the focus of a *long-term* functional analysis that reveals the relationships between these behaviors and the stimuli that precede and follow them. Using this approach, Hutt and Hutt (1968) found that autistic children are more likely to engage in such bizarre motor behavior as hand flapping when new people or objects are introduced into their environment. Dunlap,

Koegel, and O'Neill (1985) describe a very thorough observational system for assessing the behavior of autistic children in both treatment and natural settings.

School Observations. The desire to observe children's behavior for clinical purposes has spawned a number of systems for use in schools, playgrounds, and other relevant settings (Ollendick & Meador, 1984). In the tradition of early experimental sociologists (e.g., Dawe, 1934; Thomas, 1929), recording and coding systems designed by Bijou (Bijou, Peterson & Ault, 1968) and O'Leary (O'Leary & Becker, 1967; O'Leary & O'Leary, 1972) use symbols to represent the behavior of children and the adults around them during time-sample observations. The symbols (and their definitions) described by Bijou, Peterson, and Ault (1968) in a study done in a nursery school are presented in Figure 6-3. Notice that, like other observation systems of this type, the data gathered can be summarized in quantitative form. In this case, percentages can be calculated to summarize how much time a child spends verbalizing to or touching adults or other children. Classroom observation may focus on a single child and those with whom the child interacts, or, an observer can rotate his or her attention and assess the behavior of several target children or even of a whole class (Milich & Fitzgerald, 1985).

Home Observations. Observational assessment procedures are also available to measure clinically relevant behaviors in the client's home. As has been the case in other areas, early clinical observations in homes contained much inference and unsystematic target selection (e.g., Ackerman, 1958). More recently, lower-inference home observation systems have evolved. One of the first practical, scientific home observation packages was designed by Gerald Patterson (Patterson, Ray, Shaw & Cobb, 1969) for use in the homes of young predelinquent boys. This system places trained observers in the client's living area for an hour or two, usu-

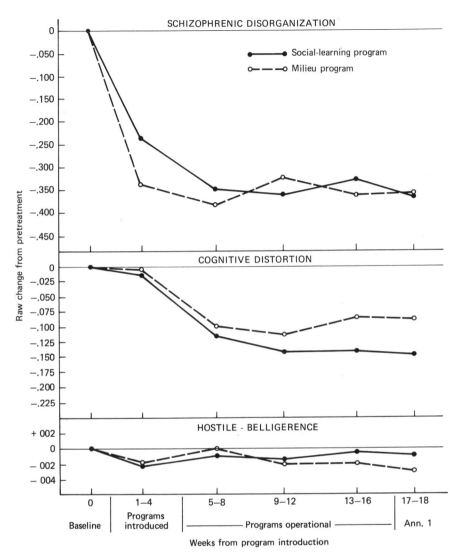

FIGURE 6-2. Effects of social-learning and milieu programs on three TSBC dimensions. (After G. Paul and R. Lentz, *Psychological Treatment of Chronic Mental Patients,* published by Harvard University Press. Reprinted by permission.)

ally just before dinner.[2] The observers avoid interacting with the family and concentrate on recording the behavior of one member at a time during successive five-minute periods. Each type of behavior observed (e.g., talking, crying, hitting, laughing, ignoring) is summarized by one of twenty-nine symbols similar in nature to those in Figure 6-3. Reid (1978) provides details of this system. Other systems are available as well (see

---

[2] This and most other observation procedures described in this chapter are set up only after the client or a person responsible for the client gives consent.

Symbol	Definition
	First Row **(Social Contacts)** *S* verbalizes to himself. Any verbalization during which he does not look at an adult or child or does not use an adult's or child's name. Does not apply to a group situation.
	S verbalizes to adult. *S* must look at adult while verbalizing or use adult's name.
	S verbalizes to child. *S* must look at child while verbalizing or use child's name. If in a group situation, any verbalization is recorded as verbalization to a child.
S	Child verbalizes to *S*. Child must look at *S* while verbalizing or use *S*'s name.
△	Adult verbalizes to *S*. Adult must look at *S* while verbalizing or use *S*'s name.
ဟ	Adult gives general instruction to class or asks question of class, or makes general statement. Includes storytelling.
	S touches adult. Physical contact with adult.
	S touches child with part of body or object. Physical contact with child.
V	Adult touches *S*. Physical contact with adult.
T	Child touches *S* with part of body or object. Physical contact with child.

Symbol	Definition
	Second Row **(Sustained Activity)** *Sustained activity in art. S* must be sitting in the chair, facing the material and responding to the material or teacher within the 10-sec interval. Responding to the material includes using pencil, paint brush, chalk, crayons, string, scissors or paste or any implement on paper, or working with clay with hands on clay or hands on implement which is used with clay, or folding or tearing paper. Responding to the teacher includes following a command made by an adult to make a specific response. The behavior must be completed (child sitting in his chair again) within two minutes.
·	*Sustained activity in storytime. S* must be sitting, facing the material, or following a command given by the teacher or assistant. If the *S* initiates a verbalization to a peer, do not record sustained activity in the 10-sec interval.
·	*Sustained activity in show-and-tell. S* must be sitting, facing the material, or following a command given by the teacher. If the *S* initiates a verbalization to a peer, do not record sustained activity in that 10-sec interval.
·	*Sustained activity in reading. S* must be sitting in the chair, facing the material and responding to the material or the teacher within the 10-sec interval.
·	*Sustained activity in writing. S* must be sitting in the chair, facing the material and responding to the material or the teacher within the 10-sec interval. Responding to the material includes using the pencil (making a mark), or holding the paper or folder. Responding to the teacher includes responding verbally to a cue given by the teacher.
·	*Sustained activity in arithmetic. S* must be sitting in the chair, facing the material and responding to the material or the teacher within the 10-sec interval. Responding to the material or teacher includes using the pencil or eraser or holding the paper or folder or responding verbally to cue.
	Sustained activity did not occur in interval.

170

McIntyre et al., 1983 for a review of home observation systems), some of which have been used not only to assess individual clients but to gather data on how certain parental behaviors contribute to children's maladjustment (e.g., Forehand, Lautenschlager, Faust & Graziano, 1986).

When adult interactions at home are observed, more complex recording and encoding systems are usually needed. To measure the at-home social skills of depressed clients, for example, Lewinsohn and Shaffer (1971) had observers record family interactions at mealtimes on a time-sampling basis. The encoding system categorized verbal behavior as self-initiated *actions* (e.g., questions, comments, requests for information, complaints) or positive and negative *reactions* to the behavior of others (e.g., approval, laughter, criticism, disagreement). These dimensions were then used to examine differences between depressed and nondepressed persons (e.g., Libet & Lewinsohn, 1973) as well as changes in depressed behavior as a function of treatment.

Gottman (1979) developed a complex coding system for the assessment of couple interactions called the Couples Interaction Coding System (CISS, pronounced "kiss"). Each verbal statement is categorized in terms of its (1) *content*, (2) *affect*, and (3) *context*. Two aspects of Gottman's work merit special mention. The first involves the use of sequential, or *time-series*, analysis of the observational data (Gottman, Markman & Notarius, 1977). This complex mathematical technique allows the assessor to look not only at the influence of one person on the other at a given point (as when a wife insults

her husband), but also at the influence of previous interactions on later ones. Negative "spirals" and other long-term social sequences can be discovered more easily with this technique than with procedures that merely present "percent of time spent" summaries. The second interesting feature of Gottman's home observation procedure is the use of tape recorders rather than human observers to collect the raw data. Transcripts of the tapes are scored later by trained coders.

Observations by "Insiders." So far, the naturalistic observation systems we have described employ specially trained personnel as participant or nonparticipant observers. Because some researchers question whether these outsiders can do their job without inadvertently influencing the behavior they are to watch, they arrange to have observational data collected by persons who are part of the client's day-to-day world. The IMPS, completed by nurses or other ward personnel, is an example. Observation of children in classrooms and at home has been accomplished by training teachers, parents, and even other children to collect and record data regarding specific behaviors (e.g., Lyman, 1984).

The use of insiders as observers of adult behavior for clinical purposes is less common, but not unknown. For example, in helping clients quit smoking, a clinician may ask for corroborative reports of success or failure from family members or friends (e.g., Mermelstein, Lichtenstein & McIntyre, 1983). Such reports may also be solicited as part of the assessment of alcoholics (e.g., Foy, Nunn & Rychtarik, 1984), sexual activity (e.g., Rosen & Kopel, 1977), marital violence (Jouriles & O'Leary, 1985), and other adult behaviors.

Self-Observation. Although insiders usually have a less-obstructed view of a client's behavior than would be available to an outside observer, no one spends as much time with the client as the client does. Therefore, in many clinical and research

FIGURE 6-3. Part of a symbol-coding system for observation of children (S. W. Bijou, R. F. Peterson, and M. H. Ault, "A method to integrate descriptive and experimental field studies at the level of data and empirical concepts," *Journal of Applied Behavior Analysis*, 1968, 1, 175–191. © 1968 by the Society for the Experimental Analysis of Behavior, Inc. Reprinted by permission.)

settings, clients are asked to observe and record their own behavior. This procedure is called *self-monitoring*. It is usually done by adults, though children can be successful at it as well (see Shapiro, 1984, for a review).

Self-monitoring often requires clients to keep a written record of the frequency, duration, or intensity of their behavior. A chart may be used to record the occurrence of events such as exercise, headaches, pleasant thoughts, hair pulling, giving or receiving praise, pain, and so on.

Figure 6-4 illustrates a diary used for recording smoking behavior. Space is provided for noting the time at which each cigarette is lit as well as for information about the physical and social setting and the mood that preceded smoking. Similar diaries detailing specific behaviors, their antecedents, and their consequences are commonly used in research on eating habits (e.g., Brownell, 1981), sleep problems (Miller & DiPilato, 1983), anxiety (Thrash, Marr & Boone, 1982), and other targets (Heinrich & Schag, 1985). As we discuss later in this chapter, self-monitoring is sometimes a *reactive* form

FIGURE 6-4. Behavioral diary for recording smoking behavior. (From O. F. Pomerleau and C. S. Pomerleau, *Break the Smoking Habit,* © Research Press, Champaign, Illinois. Reprinted by permission.)

Name _____   Date _____

Time	Intensity of craving*	Was cigarette smoked? (✓)	Place	With whom	Mood
1.					
2.					
3.					
4.					
5.					
6.					
7.					
8.					
9.					
10.					
11.					
12.					
13.					
14.					
15.					
16.					
17.					
18.					
19.					
20.					

*indicate the intensity of your craving on a scale of 1 to 5: 1 = no perceptible craving; 2 = slight craving; 3 = moderate craving; 4 = fairly strong craving; 5 = intense craving.

Total number of cigarettes smoked _____

of observation, meaning that the act of observation may modify the behavior being observed. This characteristic results in self-monitoring sometimes being used as a treatment method in itself. However, the direction of the reactivity is difficult to predict; self-monitoring sometimes increases, sometimes decreases the rate of a behavior. The value of the behaviors being self-monitored, the timing involved in the self-monitoring, and the contingencies for self-monitoring have been found to affect direction of reactive effects. For a review of self-monitoring procedures and applications, see Nelson (1977).

Observation Aids. Human sight and hearing are restricted in their ability to detect and discriminate what happens in the environment. To assist imperfect humans in their observation tasks, mechanical and/or electronic devices are often used. Mechanical devices sometimes assist in self-monitoring, especially when frequency or duration measures are of primary concern. The client may carry a counter that is pressed each time a target behavior occurs. Daily totals can then be read off the counter and recorded on a summary sheet. Commercially available golf-stroke counters can be used, or specially designed response counters are sometimes provided by the clinician. A miniature abacus disguised as a bracelet allows subtle yet accurate self-monitoring (Mahoney, 1974b), while moving pennies or toothpicks from one pocket or purse area to another can provide an even simpler alternative (Watson & Tharp, 1972).

Precise monitoring of the duration of target responses can be aided by various kinds of timers. In many cases a common electric clock or stopwatch can be turned into a cumulative timer. For example, the client is asked to set a clock to noon, plug it in each time she or he begins some activity (e.g., studying, exercising, sleeping), and unplug it each time the activity stops. The time on the clock face at the end of the day thus displays the duration of the target behavior

for that day. Specially designed stopwatches that record time automatically can be used in the same way (Hoelscher, Lichstein & Rosenthal, 1986).

A running record of behavior can be provided by mechanical devices (usually switches and counters) that are connected directly to the client in some way. This is typified by systems that measure physical activity, which is a variable of interest with depressed, hyperactive, and other clients (see Milich, Loney & Landau, 1982).

Electronic data collection devices have also played a role in naturalistic observation procedures. Audio and video tape recorders have been employed to gather larger amounts of continuous data than would be possible using human observers. The advent of tiny solid-state transmitters has allowed audio recordings of a client's verbal behavior to be made even when that client is nowhere near the tape recorder. This involves having the client wear a tiny microphone attached to a pocket-size wireless transmitter that sends a signal to a remote receiving point, where it is stored in a standard tape recorder. Examples of the application of mechanical and electronic technology for use in naturalistic observation abound in the clinical literature (e.g., Coates, Killen, George, Marchini, Silverman & Thoresen, 1982).

Controlled Observation

The major appeal of naturalistic observation is that it yields large samples of spontaneous, "real" client behavior occurring under circumstances of relevance and interest to the clinician. The assets of naturalistic observation can become liabilities, however, especially when observation targets are low in frequency. Suppose, for example, that the clinician wants to observe a client's response to stress. To accomplish this goal using naturalistic procedures, observers would have to monitor the client's behavior in settings where stressful events might occur. Because there is no guarantee that the client would actually encounter clinically relevant stress in a given situation, much of the time expended in this enterprise could be wasted.

Further, because naturalistic observation usually takes place in an uncontrolled environment, even if a stressor occurs, many other events can complicate the assessment. The client may move out of the observer's line of vision or the client may get assistance in dealing with the stressor from a family member or friend. How would the client have reacted without help? The assessor would not know unless the same situation recurs when the client is alone and under observation.

The fact that the situation of interest may not soon recur points to another limitation of naturalistic observation: Repeated assessment of a client's reaction to low-probability events is difficult. This problem is important because comparison of the behavior of many people under identical conditions is a cornerstone of many experimental designs and assessment approaches.

One way of dealing with some difficulties associated with naturalistic observation is to set up special circumstances under which to observe clients' behavior as they react to planned, standardized events. This is usually called *controlled observation* because the clinician maintains control over the nature and timing of the assessment stimuli in much the same way as do users of the tests described in Chapter 5. Controlled observations are also referred to as *situation tests, analogue assessments,* and *contrived observations.*

As was true with early naturalistic observations, the first controlled observations involved a great deal of inference. For example, Barker, Dembo, and Lewin (1941) set up a frustration situation by first allowing nursery school children to play with highly desirable toys in a fenced area, then locking the youngsters out. The varying reactions to frustration displayed by each child were interpreted as evidence of maturity, constructiveness, regression, and other inferred

characteristics. Earlier, Hartshorne and May (1928) studied personality traits such as honesty by observing children in situations where they could steal money without fear of being detected.

During World War II, military psychologists devised controlled observations for assessing personality traits as well as behavioral capabilities. In the Operational Stress Test, for example, would-be pilots were placed in a flight simulator and asked to manipulate controls. The candidates did not know that the tester was purposely trying to frustrate them by giving increasingly complicated instructions accompanied by negative feedback (e.g., "You're making too many errors"; Melton, 1947). During the test, the assessor rated the candidate's reaction to criticism and stress, and these ratings supplemented objective data on skill with the simulator.

Traits of initiative, dominance, cooperation, and group leadership were inferred from observational assessments developed by the staff of the Office of Strategic Services (OSS; later to become the CIA) to help select espionage agents and other special personnel. One example was a construction test, in which a candidate was assigned to build a five-foot cube-shaped frame out of large wooden poles and blocks resembling a giant Tinker Toy set. Because the test was supposed to measure the candidate's organizational and leadership ability, he was given two "assistants" (actually, psychologists) who called themselves "Buster" and "Kippy."

Kippy acted in a passive, sluggish manner. He did nothing at all unless specifically ordered to, but stood around, often getting in the way. . . . Buster, on the other hand, . . . was aggressive, forward in offering impractical suggestions, ready to express dissatisfaction, and quick to criticize what he suspected were the candidate's weakest points. . . . It was their function to present the candidate with as many obstructions and annoyances as possible in ten minutes. As it turned out, they succeeded in frustrating the candidates so thoroughly that the construction was never . . . completed in the allotted time. (OSS, 1948, p. 103)[3]

Since World War II, milder versions of the OSS "situational tests" have been used for personnel selection. In current clinical and research settings controlled observations take many forms. In some cases, the "control" consists of asking clients (usually couples, families, or parent-child pairs) to come to a clinic or laboratory and have a discussion, attempt to solve a problem, or just talk while under observation by TV cameras, tape recorders, or human coders (e.g., Hahlweg, Revenstorf & Schindler, 1984). In other instances clients are presented with a structured task or situation designed to elicit behaviors of relevance to clinical assessment (e.g., Humphrey, Apple & Kirschenbaum, 1986).

Role-Playing Tests. Psychologists sometimes create a make-believe situation in which the client is asked to *role play* his or her typical behavior. Role playing has been advocated by clinicians for many years (e.g., Borgatta, 1955) and serves as the cornerstone for several group, psychodynamic, and phenomenological treatments (e.g., Kelly, 1955; Moreno, 1946; Perls, 1969). However, it was not until the late 1960s that it became a part of systematic programs of clinical assessment. The most common use of role playing in controlled observation has been in the assessment of social competency, self-expression, and assertiveness.

Sometimes the procedures are simple and structured, as in the Situation Test (ST) developed by Rehm and Marston (1968) to explore college males' social skills. In the ST, the client sits with a person of the opposite sex and listens to tape-recorded descriptions of scenes to be role played. The

woman (an assistant to the clinician) then reads a question or statement such as "What would you like to do now?" or "I thought that was a lousy movie," and the client is asked to respond as if the situation were real. Another example is provided by Nelson, Hayes, Felton, and Jarrett (1985), who required subjects to respond to interpersonal situations such as the following: "You have been seeing this man/woman for about four months. He/she has been very demanding on you and he/she gets extremely jealous when he/she sees you just talking to another man/woman. He/she says he/she doesn't want to lose you but you want to end this relationship. So you say . . ."

Role-playing procedures have become a standard ingredient in the assessment of children's social skills (Williamson, Moody, Granberry, Lethermon & Blouin, 1983), aggressive behavior in men prone to anger (Moon & Eisler, 1983), interaction patterns of depressed patients (Bellack, Hersen & Himmelhoch, 1983), conversational skills of chronic mental patients (Kelly, 1982), social skills of socially anxious adults (Beidel, Turner & Dancu, 1985), and unassertiveness in a multitude of different types of people (Arkowitz, 1981). In most role plays, the subjects' responses are videotaped and then rated by observers on a large number of target criteria such as appropriateness of content, level of positive and refusal assertiveness, overall anxiety, latency to respond, response duration, speech dysfluencies, posture, eye contact, gaze, hand gestures, head movements, and voice loudness. This list is not exhaustive, but it illustrates the tremendous variability of measures that have been employed (see Bellack, 1983, for a review of the problems involved in these measures).

A major question about role-playing assessments is how valid and reliable they are. Do their results generalize to natural settings? Do they agree with other types of assessment such as self-report or peer evaluation? Are they correlated with important external criteria? In the early days of role-

[3] The fact that "Kippy" and "Buster" were Army privates and often got to torment high-ranking officers "set an untouchable record for job satisfaction among psychologists" (Cronbach, 1960, p. 568).

playing assessments, their use was based on their assumed, or face, validity. Today most investigators are not satisfied with face validity as the criterion for evaluating role-playing procedures. They require demonstrations that results obtained from role playing are related to naturalistic behavior.

Although the results of research on the validity of role-playing methods are mixed, the basic conclusion is that with proper care they can yield useful data (Bellack, 1983; Kern, Miller & Eggers, 1983; Nelson, Hayes, Felton & Jarrett, 1985). A large number of variables influence the way clients and subjects respond to role-playing assessments. Instructions to behave as one naturally would versus instructions to behave as an assertive person would produce very different behavior in subjects (Kazdin, Esveldt-Dawson & Matson, 1983; Rodriguez, Nietzel & Berzins, 1980). The content of the scenes used in role plays (Nelson, Hayes, Felton & Jarrett, 1985), their level of difficulty (Kolotkin, 1980), the responses of

the experimenter to the subject (Kirchner & Draguns, 1979), and the social impact of role-played behavior (Kern, Cavell & Beck, 1985) have also been shown to influence role-played performance.

As investigators have learned about the effects of such variables, they have modified role-playing methods in order to make them more realistic and more specific to the problems of individual clients. For example, the Extended Interaction Test (McFall & Lillesand, 1971) assesses the generality of client's behavior by using a tape that talks back to clients who are trying to be assertive. In order to assess the persistence of clients' ability to refuse unreasonable requests, the Extended Interaction Test requires clients to respond to a series of gradually escalating demands made by a taped antagonist (see Box 6-4). Presumably, a person who withstands repeated requests is more assertive than one who gives in after an initial refusal.

The Extended Interaction Test provides one example of assessing the generality of

---

BOX 6-4   Excerpt from the Extended Interaction Test

Narrator: You are feeling really pressed for study time because you have an exam on Friday afternoon. Now, you are studying at your desk, when a close friend comes in and says, "Hi. Guess what. My parents just called and offered to pay for a plane ticket so I can fly home this weekend. Great, huh!? The only problem is, I'll have to skip my Friday morning class, and I hate to miss out on those notes; I'm barely making it in there as it is. Look, I know you aren't in that class, but it'd really be a big help if you'd go to the class Friday and take notes for me so I could go home. Would you do that for me?"

Subject: (responds; if refusal . . .)

N: "I guess it is kinda crazy to expect you to do it, but, gee, I've got so many things to do if I'm gonna get ready to leave, and I don't want to waste the time asking around. Come on, will you do it for me this once?"

S: (responds; if refusal . . .)

N: "Look, what're friends for if they don't help each other out of a bind? I'd do it for you if you asked. What do you say, will you?"

S: (responds; if refusal . . .)

N: "But I was *counting* on *you* to *do* it. I'd hate to have to call my folks back and tell them I'm not coming. Can't you spare just *one* hour to help me out?"

S: (responds; if refusal . . .)

N: (sarcastically) "Now look, I don't want to *impose* on your *precious* time. Just tell me. Will you do it or do I have to call my folks back?"

S: (responds)

Source: McFall and Lillesand, 1971.

---

client behavior through controlled observation, but there are others. Some involve administration of new, different role-play items to measure the range of situations in which a client is skilled or assertive (e.g., Edelstein & Eisler, 1976), while others attempt to observe the client in naturalistic settings (e.g., Kazdin, Matson & Esveldt-Dawson, 1984). Because the first strategy may not be realistic and because the second strategy is difficult to carry out, a third approach has appeared in recent years. It involves creating a *staged naturalistic event* (Gottman & Markman, 1978) consisting of controlled observational circumstances of which the client is unaware or about which he or she has been misinformed. The idea is to take a systematic look at behavior in a *controlled* setting that appears *naturalistic* to the client.

For example, McFall and Twentyman (1973) developed some creative procedures

for assessing the generality of college students' assertiveness outside the laboratory. Clients volunteering for an assertion training study were telephoned by a research assistant who posed as a fellow student and who made a series of seven increasingly unreasonable requests (see Box 6-5). Scores on this test corresponded to the point at which the client switched from "yes" to "no" in response to the caller's pleas. After each call, the client was contacted again and informed about the real purpose of the interaction.

An unobtrusive test has also been used to measure social skills in psychiatric inpatients (Goldsmith & McFall, 1975). The client is asked to meet and carry on a conversation with a total stranger (who is the clinician's confederate). The confederate had been instructed to confront the subject with three 'critical moments': "not catching the subject's name, responding to a lunch invitation with an excuse that left open the possibility

---

BOX 6-5 Excerpt from unobtrusive telephone assessment of assertion

"Hi, may I speak to (subject)? (Subject)? You're taking intro psych, aren't you? Well, I'm Tom Blake. I don't think you know me, but I'm in (professor)'s lecture, too. I don't know anyone in the class, so I got your name off the registration list they have in the psych office."

Request 1: "I really hate to bother you, but I have some questions on some of the lecture material. Do you think you could help me for a few minutes?" (*S* responds. If no refusal . . .)

Request 2: "I think all I really need is to look at your notes. Do you think we could arrange that?" (*S* responds. If no refusal . . .)

Request 3: "Actually, I haven't made it to all the lectures, so I'll need to borrow your notes for awhile to fill in what I've missed. Okay?" (*S* responds. If no refusal . . .)

Request 4: "Well, (subject), to tell you

the truth, I haven't been to class since the last exam, so I'll probably need your notes for two days. Would that be all right?" (*S* responds. If no refusal . . .)

Request 5: "Let's see now. I have a paper due on Wednesday (five days before exam), so I won't be able to get them before that. Could I get them sometime on Thursday?" (*S* responds. If no refusal . . .)

Request 6: "Oh, wait a minute! I've got a chemistry exam on Friday. Could I get them after that? That would be three days before the psych exam." (*S* responds. If no refusal . . .)

Request 7: "Now that I think about it, I'll probably need a night to recover from the chem exam, so is it all right if I get them Saturday instead, for the two days before the exam? (*S* responds.)

Source: McFall and Twentyman, 1973.

of lunch at another time, and saying 'Tell me about yourself' at the first convenient pause in the conversation." Similar contrived situations have been used in other psychiatric settings (Holmes, Hansen & St. Lawrence, 1984) and with college students (Kern, 1982).

Observation that involves deception and possible invasion of privacy must be set up with care and with regard for client welfare and dignity. The proponents of unobtrusive controlled observation have sought to avoid its potential dangers and point out that its value may be limited to measuring specific behaviors (such as refusal) rather than more complex interactive social skills.

Performance Measures. In most of the controlled observations described in the previous section, the client is asked to act "as if" an event were taking place. There are other procedures, however, in which the client is actually faced with a clinically relevant situation so that her or his behavior can be observed.

Controlled observations of performance have often focused on behaviors such as eating, drinking, or smoking. For example, the eating style (e.g., amount, speed, preferences) of normal and/or obese individuals has been recorded during a meal or snack offered in a controlled setting (e.g., Ruderman & Christensen, 1983). Alcoholic and nonalcoholic drinkers have been observed in specially constructed cocktail lounges (see Figure 6-5) or living rooms located in hospitals (e.g., Collins, Parks & Marlatt, 1985). The details of cigarette use (puff rate, depth of inhalation, number of puffs) have been scrutinized in volunteers smoking in simulated social settings (e.g, Ossip-Klein, Martin, Lomax, Prue & Davis, 1983).

Another important type of performance measure in controlled settings is the physiological activity (e.g., heart rate, respiration, blood pressure, galvanic skin response,

FIGURE 6-5.   Simulated bar located in a hospital setting. (Courtesy of G. Alan Marlatt. Reprinted by permission.)

muscle tension, and brain waves) that appears in relation to various stimuli and situations. An early example is provided by Malmo, Shagass, and Davis (1950), who showed a film about headache to a client with a severe headache problem and measured an increase in her forehead muscle tension while she watched.

More recently, clinicians have begun to study the effects of common and unusual erotic stimuli (presented via film, videotape, slides, or audiotape) on various indices of sexual arousal, such as penile volume (e.g., Avery-Clark & Laws, 1984; Beck, Barlow & Sakheim, 1983). These measures have been used extensively in the assessment of problematic sexual behavior (e.g., Abel, 1976; Earls & Quinsey, 1985). Figure 6-6 shows a graph of a client's penile erection in response to audiotapes describing three types of foot and sandal fetish material.

Assessment of the physiology of fear in controlled settings has also occupied many clinical researchers. In a classic study, Paul (1966) used measures of heart rate and sweating taken just before giving a talk to help identify speech-anxious clients. These measures were repeated following various anxiety-reduction treatments to aid in the evaluation of their effects. The wide range of physiological assessments of anxiety is reviewed by Nietzel, Bernstein and Russel (in press) and Ray, Cole, and Raczynski (1983).

Behavioral Avoidance Tests (BATs) are a popular performance measure in controlled observation. BATs are designed to assess overt anxiety in relation to specific objects and situations by confronting clients with the stimulus they fear and then having observers record the type and degree of avoidance displayed. Informal BATs had been conducted with children as early as the 1920s (e.g., Jones, 1924a and b), but it was not until the early 1960s that systematic avoidance-testing procedures became a common form of controlled observational assessment.

In a study of systematic desensitization (see Chapter 9) for snake phobia, Lang and Lazovik (1963) asked each client to enter a

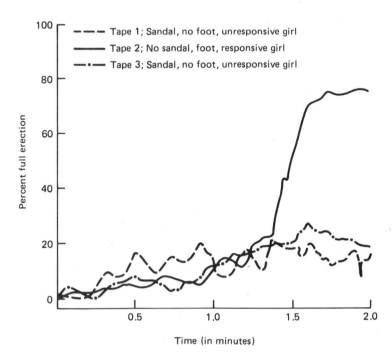

FIGURE 6-6. Erectile responses to various foot-related stimuli. (From G. G. Abel, E. B. Blanchard, D. H. Barlow, and M. Mavissakalian, "Identifying specific erotic cues in sexual deviations by audiotaped descriptions," *Journal of Applied Behavior Analysis*, 1975, 8, 247–60. © 1975 by the Society for the Experimental Analysis of Behavior, Inc. Reprinted by permission.)

room that contained a harmless caged snake and to approach, touch, and pick up the animal. The clients were scored on whether they were able to look at, touch, or hold the snake. In subsequent versions of the BAT, many other fear stimuli (e.g., rats, spiders, cockroaches, dogs) have been used; and the "look-touch-hold" coding system for scoring responses has been replaced by more sophisticated measures. These include recording how close the client is able to come to the fear target, maximum amount of interaction achieved, length of time between entering the test room and making physical contact with the target, overt anxiety behaviors during the test, and changes in physiological arousal (e.g., heart rate, respiration, galvanic skin response). Usually, clients are asked to approach the feared target, but occasionally BATs are set up to measure how long clients can look at a frightening stimulus or how close they will allow that stimulus to approach them.

Controlled performance tests have also been developed to assess fear of certain *situations*. Paul's (1966) use of contrived test speeches to assess clients' discomfort about public speaking was an early example of this type of assessment. Others include asking persons who fear heights or closed places to climb fire escapes or sit in a small, dark test chamber (e.g., Emmelkamp & Felten, 1985; Miller & Bernstein, 1972).

EVALUATION OF OBSERVATIONAL ASSESSMENT

Observational methods have become popular clinical assessment tools in recent years. As noted in Chapter 3, direct observation of behavior can help avoid many inference problems that reduce the reliability and validity of some interview and test procedures. Behaviorally oriented psychologists, the most enthusiastic proponents of observational assessment, have argued that this approach provides the most realistic view of behaviors of clinical relevance.

Observations are sometimes thought of as being like photographs that provide an accurate picture of human behavior. But just as a photograph of a scene is a product of the scene itself, the equipment used, the photographer's techniques, and the developing process, data from observational procedures are determined by many factors other than the behavior of the clients. Some of these factors can distort observational assessment. It should be understood, therefore, that observing human behavior does not automatically establish the resulting data as reliable and valid (Cone, 1981).

To illustrate, consider a hypothetical situation in which a clinician is working with a distressed married couple and decides to include observational procedures as part of an overall assessment battery. A controlled situation is set up in which the couple is videotaped as they talk about one of their problems and attempt to resolve it. Later, the videotape is scored by trained observers using some type of coding system. A summary of the couple's behavior would result (e.g., "couple spent 63% of the session in negative interaction"; "couple scores 9 on a 10-point level-of-distress rating scale") and might be accompanied by the suggestion that this is a sample of how the husband and wife related to one another. Such an observational procedure is certainly direct and apparently objective, but is it necessarily reliable and valid?

Reliability in Observational Assessment

The first question that must be asked about observational data is, "Are they reliable?" To what extent do observers arrive at the same ratings or conclusions with respect to the behavior they watch? If interobserver agreement is low, such that our hypothetical couple's interaction was scored in different ways by different individuals, one cannot place much confidence in the observation. The assessor would either have to "believe" one particular observer or average all observers' data in some way. Neither alternative is attractive because (1) there is usually an inadequate basis for trusting one observer above others, and (2) averages of widely discrepant scores represent a mathematical but not a behavioral reality (the couple's *average* scores from unreliable observers may not reflect their actual behavior at all).

The interobserver reliability of modern clinical observation systems that use trained observers is usually very high; coefficients in excess of .80 and .90 are not uncommon (e.g., Paul & Lentz, 1977). When clients observe their own behavior through self-monitoring, agreement between their data and those of external observers is sometimes in the .90s (Kazdin, 1974). Although such impressive figures do not always appear, when they do occur it is usually because the clinical assessor has avoided some of the pitfalls, caused by the following factors, that can threaten the reliability of observational data (see Cone & Foster, 1982, for a review).

Task Complexity. If observers must make many difficult discriminations in recording, coding, or rating behavior, reliability will probably be lower than if fewer, easier judgments are required (e.g., Mash & McElwee, 1974). In the case of our married couple, the clinician would be more likely to obtain reliable observations using a fifteen-category rather than a one-hundred-category coding system. Observation will also be more reliable if clients do not engage in a large number of short-duration responses in quick succession.

Knowledge of Reliability Checks. Another factor that affects reliability is the observers' knowledge that their agreement is being monitored. When people are first trained to use an observation system, they tend to work very hard during practice sessions and pay close attention to the task, partly because they are being evaluated. Later, when "real" data are being collected, the observers may become careless if they think no one is checking their reliability (e.g., Romanczyk, Kent, Diament &

O'Leary, 1973; Taplin & Reid, 1973). The same can be said for clients who self-monitor their behavior (e.g., Lipinski, Black, Nelson & Ciminero, 1975). The best protection against this threat to reliability is unobtrusive or random checking of performance. Thus, our clinician should tell the observers that their agreement about the observed couple's behavior will be checked from time to time but that they will not be told when.

Observer Training. If the observers of our married couple are told to record laughter in their coding system but are not given a definition of laughter, one observer might count belly laughs but not giggles, while another would include everything from a quiet titter to violent guffaws. Obviously, when observers are left to define for themselves what is meant by specific coding categories or global constructs like "hostile" or "happy," the reliability of observational data drops dramatically (e.g., Hawkins & Dobes, 1977).

High reliability coefficients do not always mean that an observation system is being used properly. Reliability estimates can be artificially inflated by several factors (Harris & Lahey, 1982a; Cone & Foster, 1982; Mitchell, 1979). To be blunt, observers sometimes cheat, especially when they want to please their employer and when they are unsupervised. Cheating usually takes the form of altering scores in order to enhance agreement. Obviously, our clinician should supervise the coding of the couple's behavior and arrange for reliability coefficients to be calculated by someone other than the observers.

Another situation in which high reliabilities may be misleading is when there is *observer drift* (Johnson & Bolstad, 1973; O'Leary & Kent, 1973). When observers work together in unchanging pairs or groups, they tend to form their own particular well-agreed-upon version of the rating system so that, over time, each pair or group "drifts" away from the others. Within each pair or group, reliability may be very high, but if new pairings are made or if between-pair reliabilities are calculated, interobserver agreement may be much lower. This problem can be combated by constant rotation of observer pairs and/or periodic retraining of all observers (Cone & Foster, 1982).

Interpreting Reliability Figures. Another question arises when high reliability figures are encountered: How were they calculated? There are many mathematical issues involved here concerning questions of what a reliability coefficient means. For example, suppose that our clinician reported interobserver agreement 95 percent of the time. Depending upon how this figure was calculated, it could either mean there was strong agreement about what the observers *saw* or about what they did *not* see. If "agreement" is registered only when two observers record the occurrence of the same behavior at the same time, 95 percent would be impressive indeed. However, if agreement also means that each of two observers did *not* record the occurrence of a particular behavior that seldom occurs, the agreement percentage could be inflated by chance associated with the base rate of that behavior. Agreeing about the nonoccurrence of a behavior that happens very rarely is not a useful indicator of reliability.

Several mathematical procedures are available to control or correct problems of this type, but they are not used uniformly enough to warrant unequivocal faith in the reliability figures cited in observational assessment literature. To summarize, interobserver agreement in clinical observation can be extremely high, but interpretation of what various reliability figures mean depends on how they were calculated (Mitchell, 1979).

Validity of Observational Assessment

The next questions one must ask about observational procedures concern validity: Are these procedures measuring what they are supposed to measure, and how well are they doing it? At first glance, observation of behavior would appear to rank highest in validity among all clinical assessment approaches. Instead of hearing about behavior in interviews or speculating about behavior through tests, the clinician using observation can actually watch the "real thing."

To a certain extent, however, enthusiasm for the directness or face validity of clinical observation has caused a de-emphasis on proving its validity in traditional terms (Cone, 1981). After all, if we *observe* aggression in our married couple, are we not *measuring* aggression, and is not that enough to establish the validity of our technique? The answer is yes only if we can show (1) that the behaviors coded (e.g., raised voices) constitute a satisfactory definition of aggression, (2) that the data faithfully reflect the nature and degree of aggression that occurred during observation, and (3) that the clients' behaviors while under observation would accurately represent their reactions in other, unobserved situations.

When a number of nonparticipant observers repeatedly see a child engaging in violent, unprovoked attacks on siblings and peers at home and in school, and when these data agree in detail with the verbal reports of parents and teachers, the validity of observational data would be difficult to question. In other instances, however, establishing the validity of observation is not as easy. Many issues must be dealt with before we can be confident that we are getting a valid picture of client behavior.

Defining Observation Targets. A basic issue relating to the validity of observational assessment involves clarification of what is being measured. For example, when clinicians set out to develop an observation system for assertion, they typically use what we referred to in Chapter 5 as a rational approach. The assessor tells the observers what behaviors to look for and code, and the choice of these behaviors is based on how that assessor thinks assertion can be detected in behavior. Basic decisions, such as what aspects of behaviors to code (e.g., frequency, intensity, duration) and how these targets are defined, reflect the theory or preferences of individual investigators. For example, one clinician might assess assertiveness by observing clients' ability to refuse unreasonable requests, while another focuses on the direct expression of positive affect. This problem of definition may never be resolved to everyone's satisfaction, but it is important to ask on what behavioral features the observation system focuses.

One way to assess the validity of an observation is to ask, "What is it related to?" Does the ability to refuse unreasonable requests occur more often in people judged to be assertive by their peers? If one is actually observing part of a phenomenon of interest, meaningful relationships of this type should emerge. If, on the other hand, it is merely *assumed* that an observation system captures a valid picture of assertion, the clinician risks collecting samples of behavior with little importance outside the measurement situation. This problem has been given surprisingly little attention by users of observational assessment, partly because, as already noted, the validity of observation appears so obvious.

Some efforts toward formal validation of observational systems have been made. Jones, Reid, and Patterson (1975) summarize a series of studies designed to explore the relationship between certain categories in their Behavioral Coding System (BCS) and other variables. Their research shows that children who had been previously identified by others (e.g., school officials) as aggressive were, in fact, aggressive when observed through the BCS.

Some researchers have approached the validity of their observations by designing their system empirically rather than rationally. Instead of deciding ahead of time what particular behaviors reflect anxiety, an assessor may code virtually all client behavior that occurs during observation. Patterns of behavior are then correlated with other data

(e.g., self-reports, physiological arousal, third-party accounts) about the client's reaction to the observed situation and to other relevant situations. If a pattern of behavior (e.g., shaking and whimpering) is strongly associated with high scores on other measures also designed to assess anxiety, that behavior pattern can be referred to as "anxious" with greater confidence than if the assessor had simply decreed that shaking and whimpering indicate anxiety. If, in addition, the "anxious" behavior increases under circumstances that are stressful or if it changes for the better following some form of treatment, evidence of the anxiety-related meaning of the behavior becomes stronger. Kleinknecht and Bernstein (1978) used this approach in developing an observation system for measuring patients' fear while in a dental office.

A more sophisticated strategy for building validity into an observation system is embodied in Goldfried and D'Zurilla's (1969) *behavior-analytic* model. Here, the assessor first carefully explores the construct to be measured and then custom tailors observations to that construct. An example of an observation system based on this strategy is the College Women's Assertion Sample, developed by MacDonald (1978). She first asked college women to describe situations in which assertion could occur. This resulted in over 800 examples. The fifty-two clearest and most frequently mentioned situations were retained, and a new group of college women rated the assertiveness of dozens of possible responses to each situation. Responses receiving consistent ratings became examples of submission, assertion, and aggression. MacDonald (1978) tape-recorded the fifty-two situations and asked college-age clients to role play responses to them, knowing that this controlled observation contained highly relevant stimuli and a coding system that reflects what peers think of as an assertion. Other behavior-analytic approaches to assessment have been developed for the measurement of social competence in children (Dodge, McClaskey &

Feldman, 1985) and delinquents (Gaffney & McFall, 1981).

Observer Effects. No matter how reliable observers are, they must also be accurate about what they see if their data are to be valid. The clinician or researcher has several things to worry about with respect to observers' accuracy. First, there is the problem of observer *error*. Just as an interviewer may remember certain client responses more accurately than others, an observer can also make mistakes.

Second, the quality of observational data may be compromised by observer *bias*. Human beings may see things that are not objectively there to see, partly because, as the Gestalt school of psychology emphasized, there is a perceptual tendency in human beings to "complete" or "close" incomplete stimulus patterns. Thus, an observer may *see* a child raise a hand toward another child, but *record* the behavior as "striking" rather than "hand raising." In a paper called "Seeing's believing," Johnson (1953) tells about a radiologist who concluded that a button revealed in an X-ray was on the patient's vest when, in fact, it had lodged in the patient's throat. The error probably occurred because, as Rosenthal (1966, p. 6) put it, "buttons occur more frequently on vests than in throats." Johnson (1953, p. 79) concluded: "Our assumptions define and limit what we see, i.e., we tend to see things in such a way that they will fit in with our assumptions even if this involves distortion or omission."

The effects of biasing information are stronger if observers are asked to make broad, general ratings about behavior. In a well-known example of the phenomenon, psychiatrists, psychologists, and graduate students were asked to listen to a taped interview in which an actor portrayed a well-adjusted man (Temerlin, 1968). When they listened under neutral conditions, 57 percent of the observers rated the "client" as "healthy," while 43 percent called him "neurotic." No one thought he was psychotic. However, ratings were biased if the tape was

described as either that of a "perfectly healthy man" or a person who "looks neurotic but actually is quite psychotic." In the former case, 100 percent of the listeners rated the "client" as "healthy." In the latter, an average of nearly 30 percent diagnosed the man "psychotic," and over 60 percent called him "neurotic."

In a study involving visual observation and global descriptions (Rapp, 1965, cited by Johnson & Bolstad, 1973), eight pairs of observers watched a child in a nursery school. One member of each pair was told that the client was feeling "under par," while the other was told the child was feeling "above par." In seven of the eight pairs, the observers' descriptions differed significantly and corresponded with their implanted expectations. However, it is important to note that (1) when specific, well-defined behavioral coding systems rather than global ratings are used, observers are more immune to the effects of externally imposed bias (Kent & Foster, 1977), and (2) more recent, better-designed studies have failed to replicate the effects of bias on observation (Cone & Foster, 1982).

Reactivity of Observation. In addition to observer bias, the clinician utilizing observational assessment must be concerned about *reactivity:* Clients may react to being observed by intentionally or unintentionally altering the very behaviors that are of greatest clinical interest. This problem parallels the issues of response bias and impression management in tests and interviews. The problem of reactivity in observation can be illustrated by turning on a tape recorder at any social gathering. Noticeable changes in people's behavior usually occur immediately, and they last either until the machine is switched off or the novelty disappears. Awareness of the possible reactivity of clinical observation has a long history (e.g., Covner, 1942), but the dimensions of the problem are still unclear.

Some psychologists claim that observational procedures have only a minimal and short-term reactive influence on subjects, after which their behavior regains its natural spontaneity. Fore example, Mercatoris and Craighead (1974) found that the amount of appropriate behavior shown by retarded adult women did not change when they were watched by a visible observer as opposed to a hidden television camera. Other data suggest stronger reactive effects are associated with observation. For example, Zegiob, Arnold, and Forehand (1975) reported increases in mother's play, positive verbal statements, and other behaviors when mother-child interactions were overtly as opposed to covertly observed. In general, reviewers agree that more research studies demonstrate reactive effects of observation than do not (Baum, Forehand & Zegiob, 1979; Harris & Lahey, 1982b; Cone & Foster, 1982).

There is also evidence that self-monitoring can be reactive. For example, smoking usually decreases when smokers record each cigarette they light. Other behaviors such as eating, nail biting, hallucinating, alcohol intake, tics, child-management skills, and studying often change when self-observed (see Nelson, 1977, for a review). In fact, because self-monitoring usually produces *beneficial* changes in recorded behavior, the procedure has been used as a form of therapy. Self-monitoring does not *always* alter behaviors it is meant to record. Little change in depression, obsessive ruminations, hair pulling, overeating, and other targets has been reported in clients who self-monitored these responses.

In light of this conflicting research, it is not easy for the clinician to reach firm conclusions about whether awareness of observations will alter clients' behavior. Kent and Foster (1977, p. 289) observed: "There seems little reason to doubt that the presence of an observer may, in fact, affect the behavior of those he observes. But the number of factors determining the magnitude and direction of behavior change may be so great that manifest reactivity is scattered and almost completely unpredictable."

The possibility of reactivity in clinical observation cannot be ignored. To be on the safe side, the clinician should observe clients as unobtrusively as possible (perhaps using two-way mirrors or electronic devices to keep coders out of sight) and should schedule assessment sessions that are long enough to give clients ample time to get used to being observed.

Representativeness of Observed Behavior. Even after obvious reactive effects have disappeared, there are many reasons why observed behavior may not provide a *representative* or *ecologically valid* (Brunswick, 1947) picture of the client. The client may have a hangover on the day of an observation. A death in the family may have just occurred. Any number of factors can result in temporary patterns of depressed, euphoric, or hyperactive behavior that are atypical of the client.

Some features of the situation in which observation occurs exert an influence by suggesting to the client what behaviors are appropriate or expected. When this happens the observation is likely to *produce* specific behaviors through the influence of social cues that Orne (1962) called *demand characteristics*. If a clinician observes a married couple in a setting that contains strong social cues about how the clients should behave (e.g., "We would like to measure just how much fighting you two actually do"), she or he may learn more about the effects of the situation than about the typical behavior of the couple.

Problems of situational bias reducing the representativeness of observed behavior occur most often in controlled settings, though it can appear in naturalistic observation as well. In most controlled observations, the client must go to some specially identified location to be observed and is thus acutely aware of the purpose of assessment. Further, specific instructions about the observation are usually given to orient clients and to help them recognize when assessment begins and ends.

The social and situational cues provided in most observational assessments can alter client behavior radically. For example, Orne and Schiebe (1964) monitored male college students undergoing a period of isolation in a small, well-lighted room. Half the subjects were told that the room was a sensory deprivation chamber. In this condition, the experimenter wore a white coat, conducted a medical history interview, asked the subject to sign a medical release form, and displayed an "emergency tray" of drugs and equipment that were part of the "precautionary measures" in the laboratory. He also mentioned that release from the chamber was possible by pressing an emergency alarm if "the situation becomes difficult," and that a physician was available "if you should feel upset." The other subjects were told they were in a control group. There was no white coat, no interview, no "emergency tray," and no "emergency alarm." Once in the isolation room, the two groups differed markedly in behavior. Control subjects appeared relaxed and comfortable. They rested or slept, worked on various time-filling tasks, and said little. "Sensory deprivation" subjects, on the other hand, were restless, slept very little, expressed discomfort or feelings of disorientation, and "gave an

impression of almost being tortured" (Orne & Schiebe, 1964, p. 11).

Similar situational effects operate in the assessment of social skills, fears, and other clinical targets. For example, in a study designed to measure assertiveness, Nietzel and Bernstein (1976) asked college students to respond to a series of tape-recorded social situations similar to those described earlier in this chapter. Subjects heard the tape twice, once in a "low demand" situation, where they were asked to give "your natural reaction," and once under "high demand," in which responses were to be "as assertive as you think the most assertive and forceful person could be." Other subjects heard low- or high-demand instructions twice. The assertiveness of subjects' responses in each condition was scored on a five-point scale. The results are summarized in Figure 6-7. Obviously, instructions in the assessment situation not only had an initial effect, but were capable of significantly altering subjects' behavior from test to test.

In anxiety assessment, the instructions given, the presence or absence of an experimenter, the characteristics of the physical setting, and other situational variables influence the amount of fear clients display during BATs (e.g., Bernstein, 1973; Bernstein

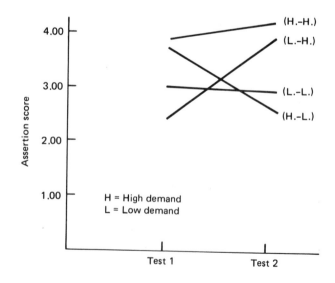

FIGURE 6-7. Instructions significantly increased or decreased subject's rated assertiveness in this study of situational influence in observation. Subjects given consistent instructions did not change over time. (Nietzel & Bernstein, 1976.)

& Nietzel, 1977). As another example, the behavior of children under observation in their own homes can be made to look "good" or "bad" depending upon what their parents think the assessor wants to see (Johnson & Lobitz, 1974).

Various research strategies have been suggested to minimize the effects of situational bias in observational assessment (Bernstein & Nietzel, 1977; Borkovec & O'Brien, 1976), but the problem cannot be entirely eliminated. As long as the stimuli present when the client's behavior is being observed are "different from the stimulus complex when [the client] is unobserved, we cannot assume that behavior during observation, even after it has stabilized, represents 'typical' behavior" (Wildman & Erikson, 1977, p. 271). The best a clinician can do is to minimize any cues that might influence client behavior. The use of completely naturalistic or unobtrusive observations is a solution in theory, but from a practical point of view, psychologists will often have to rely on contrived, analogue observations.

A Final Word

Like interviews and tests, observation is not a perfect clinical assessment tool. Nevertheless, it has many advantages that make it a valuable source of data. The challenge for the clinician or researcher is to use observation in a way that minimizes the influence of the various distorting factors we have discussed, so that the data generated can have maximum value in an overall assessment plan.

chapter 7

Clinical Intervention: Overview

All kinds of people try to change your behavior. Politicians work for your vote. Advertisers persuade you to buy their product. Parents encourage children to abide by their wishes. Almost every form of human interaction involves an attempt by one party to influence another to behave in a certain fashion. Some people are strong influencers who move us to behave in entirely novel ways. Others are ineffective influencers with an insignificant impact on us.

Behavior influence is not always interpersonal. Our behavior is affected by the physical as well as the social environment (Krasner & Ullmann, 1973). As one single example, consider the effect the weather has on your conduct; when was the last time you went swimming in a sleetstorm? Behavior influence can also be a private matter. Our memories of the past affect the way we live in the present, and our fantasies about the future inspire or deter current activities.

Our task in this chapter is to concentrate on the behavior influence exerted by clinical psychologists. When a psychologist, in a professional capacity, seeks to influence someone's behavior, we describe the activity as an *intervention*. Depending on the qualities of the intervention, we could describe it more specifically as *prevention, consultation, education, psychotherapy, group therapy, family therapy,* or *play therapy*. If we knew more about the training and theoretical leanings of the clinician, we could qualify the nature of the intervention even further, using such terms as *primary prevention, crisis intervention, gestalt therapy, client-centered therapy, rational-emotive therapy,* or *behavior therapy*. In this chapter, *clinical intervention* is the umbrella term we use to describe deliberate attempts by psychologists to change behavior in a desirable direction.

"To intervene" means "to come between in action; to intercede or interfere." When we speak of a psychologist's intervention, we could be referring to many types of "coming between": *consultation* and *education,* where the psychologist comes between some audience and its needs for specific knowledge; *program development,* where the psychologist comes between some social problem and the need for an innovative solution; or *psychotherapy,* where the psychologist comes between an individual and the individual's personal problems in living. In this chapter, we focus on psychotherapy (including group therapy, family therapy, and marital therapy), the most traditional type of "coming between" practiced by clinical psychologists. We pay special attention to the common features of most therapeutic approaches, the core assumptions shared by most psychotherapists, and the means by which psychotherapy is evaluated. Later in this chapter we will consider other types of intervention, such as prevention, consultation, and program development, used by psychologists who have become dissatisfied with psychotherapy. In Chapters 8, 9, and 10 we present the three dominant perspectives on psychotherapy: psychodynamic, behavioral, and phenomenological.

WHAT IS PSYCHOTHERAPY?

The literal translation of psychotherapy would be "treatment of the psyche." While this is not a sufficient definition of the activity, it suggests several implications that will help us understand the fundamental substance of psychotherapy.

The Participants

To speak of "treating psyches" suggests that psyches or personalities are in a state of distress. The extent to which an individual feels disturbed can vary a great deal. In some, the disturbance is great. Employment may be terminated; suicide may be attempted; hospitalization may occur. In others, the disturbance may be less extreme, but still very upsetting. An unhappy marriage, a lack of self-confidence, a nagging fear, an identity crisis, depression, sexual problems, and insomnia are just a few of the problems that motivate people to enter psychotherapy. The essential feature is that a person's functioning has become disturbed enough that she or he seeks the help of a professional. The individual is suffering. The help of friends, the long-awaited vacation, and the understanding of the family are no longer sufficient antidotes. When the point is reached where the problem is seen as requiring the intervention of a professional, we have the first participant in psychotherapy: the *client.*

The second participant is the *therapist.* By special training and experience the therapist is prepared to help the client overcome the disturbance that has motivated the desire for treatment. Therapists should possess skills that will enable them to understand clients' disturbance and then interact with these clients in such a way that they cope more effectively with their problems.

In addition to advanced training, the psychotherapist is expected to possess personal characteristics that will contribute to the effect of therapy. The ability to listen to clients and convey a sense of understanding and sensitivity without being judgmental is one important quality of the therapist. Combining warmth and support for troubled clients with a resolve to confront them with their own responsibility for change is another vital attribute. Clinicians often cite the need for the therapist to project *genuineness, empathy,* and *unconditional positive regard.* These are called *Rogerian qualities* because Carl Rogers claimed that they are the necessary and sufficient conditions for bringing about therapeutic change.

This emphasis on personal characteristics has sometimes led to the suggestion that natural ability is more important than professional training in making a good therapist. In fact, a current controversy in the field is whether professional therapists are more effective than nonprofessional helpers. This is an important question because if untrained helpers are equal to or better than professional therapists, as Durlak (1979) has claimed, it would be difficult to justify the extensive training of therapists or the great expense of professional treatment. Although Durlak's conclusion has been criticized on several grounds (Nietzel & Fisher, 1981), the available evidence has yet to prove that professional therapists achieve better outcomes than nonprofessionals in most cases (Berman & Norton, 1985). There is a great need for more well-designed research on this topic.

A related question is whether experienced therapists achieve superior treatment outcomes compared to therapists with less experience. Auerbach and Johnson (1977) conclude that there is a modest positive relationship between therapist experience and better outcomes. Others (Stein & Lambert, 1984) suggest that whatever benefits are associated with more therapist experience may be due to two facts: (1) Clients of less-experienced therapists are more likely to drop out of treatment prematurely, and (2) as the difference in experience level widens, the probability of more positive outcomes for experienced therapists increases.

Beyond the question of whether psychologists' training or experience improves their therapeutic effectiveness is the question of whether clinical psychologists can lay unique claims to their status as therapists. The simple answer to this question is No! Clinical psychologists are but one of many types of professionals who provide therapy and counseling to the public. Psychiatrists, counseling psychologists, social workers, psychiatric nurses, family counselors, and pastoral counselors deliver psychotherapy, and there is no evidence that psychologists are better therapists than other mental health professionals.

Finally, mental health professionals of all types are not the most frequent sources of help for persons experiencing problems in living (Gurin, Veroff & Feld, 1960). Informal, nonprofessional caregivers counsel far

more people about psychological problems than do members of the mental health professions. Included in the category of informal caregivers are friends, physicians, ministers, teachers, policemen, lawyers, family members, and neighbors. Cowen (1982) examined the help given by four groups of natural caregivers—hairdressers, divorce lawyers, bartenders, and industrial supervisors—and found that they used many helping strategies, some that resembled professionals' techniques (e.g., proposing alternative solutions) and some that did not (e.g., telling people to count their blessings). The important point is that psychotherapy is nobody's exclusive property. It would be arrogant for clinical psychologists to believe that psychotherapy is "their" activity, just as it would be foolish for mental health professionals of any type to claim that helping people change is exclusively their business.

While there is a vast literature on the importance of "good" therapist qualities (e.g., Gurman & Razin, 1977) the characteristics of the "good" psychotherapy client have also been studied (Garfield, 1986). The type of person likely to benefit most from psychotherapy is verbal, intelligent, motivated, moderately anxious about the need to change, able to communicate with the therapist, and "psychologically minded," a characteristic that means the person appreciates the importance of psychological factors in determining behavior. As some cynics point out, the ideal psychotherapy client is someone who would probably continue to be successful whether he or she received therapy. However, this criticism ignores the fact that psychotherapy is seldom practiced under conditions involving either the ideal client or the ideal therapist.

Interest in therapist and client characteristics has progressed past a focus on the personal attributes of the therapist or client in isolation to a concern for their interactive quality. This perspective has given rise to the concept of therapist-client *matching*, which Berzins (1977) has defined as "the idea that certain therapist-patient pairings are more desirable than others. Empirical study of this problem requires an understanding of the conditions under which, regardless of the characteristics of therapists and patients considered separately, the *interaction of these characteristics proves decisive for the processes or outcomes of psychotherapy*" (p. 222).

Since there is little research on various matching strategies, most clinicians rely on such stereotypes as "opposites attract" or "like cures like." Furthermore, in many clinical settings assignment of clients to therapists is a haphazard affair accomplished through a glance at the calendar or the intuitions of a receptionist. On pragmatic grounds, however, "even a reasonable probability that *some* therapist-patient pairings are ineffectual . . . suggests that psychotherapy research must move beyond the separate assessment of therapist and patient characteristics to serious investigation of the interaction of these characteristics" (Berzins, 1977, p. 223).

The Therapeutic Relationship

The uniqueness of psychotherapy stems not from its cast of characters, but from the special relationship that develops between therapist and client. What are the characterisics that make the therapeutic relationship unique?

First, the relationship is one in which both parties should be aware of why they are there and what the rules and goals of their interaction should be. The relationship should be a voluntary one initiated by the client and accepted by the therapist.[1] Psychotherapy often begins with a therapeutic contract which specifies the goals of treament, the procedures to be employed, the potential risks, and the individual re-

---

[1] In many cases the client is not a voluntary participant. A client sometimes enters therapy when someone (e.g., a parent, judge, or spouse) becomes distressed by the client's behavior and compels the individual to seek help. Therapy may proceed very differently when the client is not a voluntary participant.

sponsibilities of client and therapist. In many instances the contract is negotiated informally, with both parties providing information about what they expect therapy to accomplish. In other instances the contract takes the form of a signed document which states the obligations of each participant. In either case, contracts should help the therapeutic relationship become one in which clients are active decision makers, not passive recipients of help.

Although the therapist may be friendly and sympathetic, the therapeutic relationship involves more than compassion (Waterhouse & Strupp, 1984). Therapy sometimes requires the clinician to be an objective assessor of clients and at other times an insistent observer who locates client resistances and pushes through them. Therapists give psychological support even when they challenge clients to give up old ways of behaving in exchange for new, more adaptive behaviors.

The intensity of the therapeutic relationship gives rise to many temptations for the therapist to discard a professional orientation toward clients in favor of more spontaneous, "natural" reactions such as sexual attraction, pity, frustration, hostility, and boredom. Most therapists try to stay alert to the way in which their personal needs intrude upon therapy. Learning to detect these needs and deal with them are major reasons why some therapists undergo therapy themselves.

The therapist attempts to form an attentive relationship with the client without losing sight of the fact that the relationship must advance the client's attempt to change. The therapeutic relationship requires a "balance of attachment and detachment" (Korchin, 1976). With some clients, a therapeutic relationship develops easily; with others, the "capacity for collaboration" is lacking and therapy suffers as a result (Strupp & Hadley, 1979).

The relationship between client and therapist involves moral and ethical commitments on the therapist's part that function to insulate the relationship from the heat of outside forces. Confidentiality is the most essential of these commitments. The therapist protects the client's privacy and does not reveal information that the client shares in therapy. In addition, therapists are obligated to regard the welfare of their clients as their main priority.[2] With very few exceptions, the therapist's actions must be directed by a singular concern: "What is best for my client?"

The Techniques of Psychotherapy

There are dozens of psychotherapeutic techniques. Every system of psychotherapy has its preferred procedures, and every therapist has a unique style of employing those procedures. The therapist's methods are usually based on some formal theory of personality and psychopathology in general and the client's problem in particular (see Chapter 2). Although therapists remain flexible, their methods are not random; their behavior is guided by general principles of treatment.

Psychotherapeutic approaches differ in the extent to which their theories of personality and behavior disorder are related to specific techniques. For example, psychoanalysts have developed a complex theory of personality but are less specific about what procedures should be used in applying this theory to a given case. Many behavior theorists, on the other hand, specify in great detail the procedures to be employed in treatment.

Treatment approaches also vary in terms of the changes they are designed to produce (Messer & Winokur, 1980). Behavior therapists are likely to deal directly with the problem as the client initially presents it (along with other difficulties that might contribute to the primary complaint). For example, a mother who reports depression and fears

that she will kill her children might be assigned a variety of "homework assignments" involving her relationship with her husband, disciplinary methods for her children, or the development of new, out-of-the-house activities for herself. By contrast, the psychoanalyst would be more inclined to work on underlying causes of the mother's depression. Therapy might be aimed at helping the woman understand how her current symptoms are due to feelings of inadequacy as a mother because of failure to meet her own mother's rigid and unrealistic standards. Finally, a phenomenological therapist might deal with the problem by helping the mother discover her potential for creating alternatives that would free her from the one-sided way of life in which she now feels trapped.

Notwithstanding these differences, several techniques are common to almost all psychotherapeutic strategies. For example, they are all mainly psychological in nature rather than physical or medical. They are also all delivered in the context of a special relationship that improves their effectiveness. Let us now consider a few major psychological methods of clinical intervention.

1   Fostering insight. Insight into psychological problems was a chief objective of Freud, who described it as "re-education in overcoming internal resistances" (Freud, 1904, p. 73). While Freud was interested in a particular type of insight—analysis of unconscious influences—most therapists aim for insight in the more general sense of greater self-knowledge. Clients are expected to benefit from learning why they behave in certain ways, because such knowledge is presumed to contribute to new behavior. The psychotherapist's rationale for fostering a client's insight is like the well-known justification for studying history: to know the errors of the past in order to avoid repeating them in the future.

Therapists of all theoretical persuasions seek to promote self-examination and self-knowledge in their clients. There are nu-

---

[2] There are, of course, some exceptions. See Chapter 12 for a fuller discussion of situations that compel the psychologist to break confidentiality.

BOX 7-1 Three views of the therapeutic relationship

All therapists attribute considerable importance to the therapeutic relationship and will work very carefully to establish a good one. However, beyond the generalization that psychotherapists prefer a strong therapeutic relationship to a weak one, there are several views on the ideal nature of the client-therapist relationship and the role it should play in therapy.

Many phenomenologically oriented therapists regard the therapeutic relationship as the most essential element in therapy. Carl Rogers, the founder of client-centered therapy, takes the position that the client-therapist relationship is the crucible in which all the necessary and sufficient ingredients for therapeutic change are generated. According to Rogers (1951):

The process of therapy is . . . synonymous with the experiential relationship between client and therapist. Therapy consists in experiencing the self in a wide range of ways in an emotionally meaningful relationship with the therapist. The words—of either client or counselor—are seen as having minimal importance compared with the present emotional relationship which exists between the two. (pp. 172–173)

In classical psychoanalysis, the relationship between client and therapist is a means to the goal of insight. The therapist-client relationship is an instrument for achieving a specific purpose, which is to show the client how his or her present behavior is determined by experiences in earlier developmental periods of life. Psychoanalysts speak of the *transference relationship,* or simply *transference,* to refer to the fact that after a period of therapy the client begins to attach to the therapist the friendly, hostile, and ambivalent attitudes and feelings the client formerly felt in relation to parents or other significant persons. As a consequence, the original pathogenic conflicts of early familial relationships are repeated in relation to the therapist. In order to encourage transference, the analyst

remains a passive and detached figure. In psychoanalysis, the relationship is not as typically "human" as it is for the Rogerian therapist. The analyst's detachment is a strategic calm, a studied technique for encouraging transference. The following bits of advice from Freud reveal his view of the therapeutic relationship:

I cannot recommend my colleagues emphatically enough to take as a model in psychoanalytic treatment the surgeon who puts aside all his own feelings, including that of human sympathy, and concentrates his mind on one single purpose, that of performing the operation as skillfully as possible. (Freud, 1912, p. 121)

The analytic technique requires the physician to deny the patient who is longing for love the satisfaction she craves. The treatment must be carried through in a state of abstinence; I do not mean merely corporal abstinence, nor yet deprivation of everything desired, for this could perhaps not be tolerated by any sick person. But I would state as a fundamental principle that the patient's desire and longing are to be allowed to remain, to serve as driving forces for the work and for the changes to be wrought. (Freud, 1915, p. 173)

Behavior therapists tend to view the therapy relationship as an important but not sufficient condition of therapy (Sweet, 1984). It is seen as a useful context in which more specific behavior-change techniques are introduced. Alan Goldstein (1973) reveals a typical behavioral view that a good relationship is an important preface to subsequent and more vital techniques.

In most cases, it is required that an atmosphere of trust be established if any therapeutic intervention is to be effective. This usually is accomplished quickly by the therapist through his establishing that (1) he understands and accepts the patient, (2) that the two of them are working together, (3) and that the therapist has at his disposal the means to be of help in the direction desired by the patient. (Goldstein, 1973, p. 221)

BOX 7-2 / Eclectic psychotherapy

One of the paradoxes of the proliferation of psychotherapeutic approaches is that the majority of therapists pledge allegiance to no single system, preferring instead to select from several theoretical models the one approach that best fits a given client. This orientation is known as *eclecticism* or *eclectic psychotherapy*. Eclectics do not consider themselves to be anti- or atheoretical clinicians who simply reach into a grab bag and yank out a technique. Their choice of techniques is still a principled one, but it is based on the exigencies of each individual case rather than on the dictates of a general theoretical system.

In one survey (Garfield & Kurtz, 1976), the majority of clinicians contacted identified themselves as eclectics. As a result any investigation of psychotherapy that concentrates on specific theoretical orientations is studying a minority of those engaged in the practice of psychotherapy.

Because it is not a "school" of psychotherapy, eclecticism has not attracted a large number of vocal adherents, nor has it been popularized by any famous founders. Frederick Thorne (1967, 1973) is a well-known advocate of an eclectic approach, and even he appears to be a somewhat reluctant spokesman: "Eclecticism carries with it none of the special advantages of uniqueness, newness or proprietorship of special knowledge implicit in the special schools whose adherents often turn such attributes to personal advantage" (Thorne, 1973, p. 449). Other champions of eclecticism are James Prochaska, who has attempted to identify the common therapy processes in any effective psychotherapy (Prochaska & DiClemente, 1984), and Arnold Lazarus (1981) whose therapy approach we discuss more thoroughly in Chapter 9.

Thorne is careful to distinguish his version of eclectic therapy from any approach that is simply a hodgepodge of techniques. Eclecticism requires a valid formulation of each clinicial case. In Thorne's (1973) words:

Probably the most important consideration in using the eclectic approach is the condition of the client, his mental and existential status, his momentary needs, his symptomatic status, and the underlying dynamics of the condition. The eclectic therapist gives attention to all these factors, balancing short-term needs versus long-term therapeutic goals. As case handling unfolds, the client reveals more and more of his problems, and gets deeper and deeper into underlying causes. The eclectic tends to reject stereotyped formulas for dealing with problems and instead tends to react extemporaneously to new developments. The selection of methods proceeds continuously and responsively as the developments of case handling transpire. (p. 470)

merous approaches to this goal. Some procedures are structured and deal with a specific type of content; dream analysis would be an example. Other therapists try to promote insight by asking their clients to examine the implications of certain behaviors (e.g., "What relationship do you see between your troubles with your boss and the dislike you express for your father?"). Behavior therapists stress the importance of helping the client understand how behavior is functionally related to past learning and current environmental factors.

A common technique for developing insight is for the therapist to *interpret* the client's behavior. The purpose of interpretation is not to convince clients that the therapist is right about the significance of some event, but to motivate them to examine carefully their own behavior and draw new conclusions about its meaning. Interpretation comes in many forms, as Jerome

Frank (1973) noted in his influential book, *Persuasion and Healing:*

The simplest form of interpretation consists of repeating something the patient has said, perhaps with some change in emphasis, so that he becomes more clearly aware of it. In a roughly ascending scale of degree of inference and amount of complexity, other forms of interpretation are summarizing, in order to coordinate and emphasize certain aspects, verbalizing the feelings that seem to lie behind the patient's utterances, and confronting him sharply with attitudes implied by his statements that he had not recognized. Complex interpretations may indicate similarities between a patient's feelings toward important contemporaries, including the therapist. They may also suggest symbolic meanings of his statements of link them to a theoretical scheme. (p. 222–223)

2 Reducing emotional discomfort. Clients sometimes come to a therapist in such emotional anguish it is difficult for them to participate actively in therapy. In such instances, the therapist will try to reduce the client's distress enough to allow the person to begin working on the problem. Therapists usually do not strive to eliminate all discomfort; in so doing, they might also eliminate motivation for working toward more lasting change. The challenge is to diminish extreme distress without sapping the client's desire to deal with enduring problems.

A common method for reducing client discomfort is to use the therapeutic relationship to boost the client's emotional strength. Clients typically gain some emotional stability and renewed confidence by knowing that the therapist is a personal ally, a buffer against the onslaughts of a hostile world. Some therapists offer direct reassurances that take the form of statements like "I know things seem almost hopeless right now, but I think you will be able to make some important changes in your life."

3 Encouraging catharsis. Clients are usually encouraged to express emotions freely in the protective presence of the therapist. This technique is known as *catharsis.* This may include the release of pent-up emotions that the client has not acknowledged for a long time, if ever. The therapist encourages the client to give voice to those emotions, believing that through their release they will be eased. At the least, catharsis may help the client become less frightened of certain emotions.

4 Providing new information. Psychotherapy is often educational. The therapist provides new information intended to correct gaps or distortions in a clients' knowledge. Certain areas of adjustment are plagued by misinformation, sexual functioning being the most notable example. Some therapists offer direct advice to their clients, adopting a teacherlike role. Others suggest reading material about a topic, a process known as *bibliotherapy.* Still others rely on more indirect maneuvers—a shrug of the shoulder or a skeptical facial expression—to suggest to clients that there are other, more functional ways of perceiving the world. New information gives clients an added perspective on their problems that makes them seem more understandable and solvable.

5 Assigning extratherapy tasks. Therapists often ask clients to perform tasks outside of therapy for the purpose of encouraging the transfer of positive changes to the "real world." This is known as therapy "homework." Harper (1959) describes homework as follows:

The therapist and the patient agree on certain actions (based on the patient's changed conceptions of himself and his environment) with which he is to experiment between one psychotherapeutic session and the next. The patient reports on his successes and failures regarding these attempted changes in his behavior, and then he and the therapist make plans for additional changes. As the patient experiences gratification from successful accomplishments in new modes of behavior, his self-esteem grows. This, in turn, enables him to execute still more improvements in his behavior. (p. 6)

Behavior therapists are enthusiastic advocates of homework assignments, believing them to be an effective way to promote the generalization of new skills learned in the therapist's office.

6   *Developing faith, hope, and expectancy for change.* Of all the procedures common to different systems of therapy, raising clients' faith and expectancy for change is the ingredient most frequently mentioned as a crucial contributor to therapeutic improvement. In fact, many scholars attribute the success of psychotherapy not to specific techniques, but to its ability to arouse clients' belief that they can be helped. The curative power of faith is not restricted to psychotherapy. The effects are well known in medicine; the "history of medical treatment can be characterized largely as the history of the placebo effect" (Shapiro, 1971, p. 442). Clinicians are so accustomed to thinking about placebo effects in psychotherapy that they have coined additional terms to designate their influence. The most popular of these have been *demand characteristics* (Orne, 1962), *common factors* (Critelli & Neuman, 1984), and *expectancies* (Wilkins, 1979). These designations refer to various aspects of the same theme: Psychotherapy achieves its successes, in part, because of its capacity to generate client's expectancy for improvement.

Frank (1973) equated expectancy for improvement with such concepts as optimism, hope, and faith, all of which involve "the perceived probability of achieving a goal" (p. 136). An emphasis on expectancy, placebo effects in psychotherapy does not eliminate the importance of the specific techniques that serve to distinguish one therapeutic approach from another. It does mean, however, that one important element (some might say the *most* important element) of any effective therapy is that it causes clients to believe that positive changes in life are attainable (Wilkins, 1984).

Part art and part science, psychotherapy profits from the mystique that surrounds both fields. Clients often begin psychotherapy with the belief that they are about to engage in a unique, powerful experience conducted by an expert who can work miracles. The perceived potency of psychotherapy is further enhanced by the fact that clients usually begin therapy after having fretted for a long time about whether they really need treatment. By the time this internal debate is resolved, the client has a large emotional investment in making the most of a treatment that is regarded with a mixture of fear, hope, and relief.

For their part, therapists attempt to maximize the client's faith in the power of psychotherapy, providing assurance that (s)he understands the problem and is confident that, by working together, they will be able to achieve desired changes. The perception by a client that "I have been heard and understood and can be helped" can be extremely important. The procedures that encourage this perception are embodied in some of the general techniques already described—the formation of a therapeutic relationship, interpretations, catharsis, and the alleviation of emotional panic. Most therapists also offer a *rationale* for why psychotherapy will be effective. In place of the client's uncertainty about what therapy will involve, the therapist structures the experience in such a way that the client understands why beneficial change should occur.

Having structured therapy so as to increase the client's motivation and expectancies for treatment, the therapist attempts to insure that the client experiences some early success. The success might be a small one— a minor insight arrived at after a simple interpretation by the therapist or the successful completion of a not-too-difficult homework assignment. Whatever the means, the objective is to bring about the kind of change the client expects.

There is a cumulative impact to the small changes in the initial stages of therapy. Clients begin to believe that they can control their lives and that their problems are understandable. A sense of despair begins to be replaced by a growing feeling of capability as the client glimpses the possibility of a new self-image.

Expectancies can exert a circular effect. At the beginning of therapy, the client's faith in treatment is strengthened to the point that he or she believes improvement is possible. When changes, regardless of their magnitude, are experienced, the client's expectancies are confirmed and they grow. As a result, the client believes that more meaningful changes can be attained, and she or he pursues them with reinforced expectations. Meanwhile, the therapist can enhance the client's self-esteem by pointing out that changes are the result of the client's own effort (Bandura, 1982).

Returning now to the question "What is psychotherapy?" our answer emphasizes the following:

1. Psychotherapy consists of a relationship between at least two participants, one of whom has special training and expertise in handling psychological problems and one of whom is experiencing a problem in adjustment and has entered the relationship in order to alleviate this problem.

2. The psychotherapeutic relationship is a nurturant but purposeful alliance in which several methods, largely psychological in nature, are employed to bring about the changes desired by the client.

3. These methods are based on some theory regarding psychological problems in general and the specific complaint of the client in particular.

4. Regardless of theoretical preferences, most therapists employ several of the following techniques: fostering insight, reducing emotional discomfort, encouraging catharsis, providing new information, assigning extratherapy tasks, and raising clients' expectancy for change.

MODES OF THERAPY

So far, we have described psychotherapy in its most popular mode—individual, or one-to-one, treatment. This classic arrangement still forms the backbone of most clinical treatment. However, therapy is also undertaken with *groups* of clients. These groups may consist of unrelated individuals or may be composed of family members. In the former case, the treatment is usually called *group therapy;* in the latter, it is called *marital* or *family therapy.*

Group Therapy

Group therapy is more than just simultaneous therapy for several individuals. First practiced at the turn of the twentieth century in Boston by Joseph Pratt, and later stimulated by the shortage of professional personnel around World War II, group therapy has progressed to the point that it is now regarded as a valuable form of intervention in its own right (Klein, 1983).

Every major model of clinical psychology offers group treatment. There are analytic groups, client-centered groups, transactional analysis groups, encounter groups, gestalt groups, and behavioral groups. Groups are also popular with many nonprofessional self-help organizations. Weight-control groups, assertiveness groups, consciousness-raising groups, and Alcoholics Anonymous are common examples. Certain groups assume a special identity because of one idiosyncratic quality. Marathon groups which run for long, uninterrupted periods of time provide a good illustration.

This wide range of theory and practice makes it difficult to talk about any uniform process of group therapy. However, most group therapists emphasize the importance of interpersonal relationships and assume that personal maladjustment often involves difficulties in interpersonal relations. Like individual psychotherapy, many forms of group therapy appear to share common "curative factors." Some of these factors are similar to those found in one-to-one treatment, but most of them are unique to groups. A full discussion of the curative factors in group therapy is contained in Yalom's (1985) authoritative text, *The Theory and Practice of Group Psychotherapy*. In summary, these factors include:

1 *Sharing new information.* New information is imparted from two different sources in groups: The group leader may offer advice, and direct advice also comes from other members of the group who share their own experiences from the past. The multiple perspectives of the group constitute a richer store of information than would usually be the case with a single therapist. A major feature of group information and feedback is its *consensuality*. The impact of new information is magnified by the agreement on which it is based. While it may be tempting to discount feedback from one therapist, it becomes more difficult to dismiss the similar opinions of eight or ten observers as biased or inaccurate. In numbers there is strength, especially when the numbers all agree.

2 *Instilling hope.* As with individual psychotherapy, confidence in the therapist and an expectancy that treatment can be helpful are important features of groups. Group therapy can be introduced with a rationale that buoys the hope of new members, but there are also special features of groups that increase the positive expectancies of their members. One of the most important of these features is the opportunity for group members to observe positive changes in others. An individual client might become impatient about what is felt to be an exasperatingly slow pace of improvement. However, detecting positive changes in others may lead to the recognition that everyone grows at about the same pace; this may sustain faith in the group.

3 *Universality.* Groups dramatize the fact that everyone struggles with problems in living. Group members learn that they are not alone in their fear or their disappointment. This discovery is important because many persons are secretive about their problems, which restricts their ability to find out they are not unique. As group members share their problems they derive comfort from knowing "there are others just like me." Learning about the universality of one's problems also soothes anxiety about "going crazy" or "losing control."

4 *Altruism.* Groups give clients a chance to find out that they can be helpful to other people. Just as group therapy produces new insights into interpersonal weaknesses, it confirms the presence of interpersonal strengths. In addition to being clients, group therapy members serve as one another's therapists. Clinicians refer to the positive emotions that follow altruistic behavior as "feelings of self-worth," an outcome that should be promoted by effective group therapy.

5 *Interpersonal learning.* When a group first forms, the interpersonal contacts between members are usually hesitant and guarded. As group members come to know one another, their contacts become more spontaneous and direct. A properly conducted therapy group is an ideal setting in which to learn new interpersonal skills. It is a small, nurturant community whose members are motivated to help their colleagues. It presents repeated opportunities to practice fundamental social skills with different types of people and with immediate feedback on performance. Groups also contain numerous models for imitative learning, one of the most efficient ways to learn novel behaviors.

6 *Recapitulation of the primary family.* Some group therapists regard the therapy group as a "reincarnation" of clients' primary families. This quality is sometimes described as *family reenactment*, and it is thought to be a curative factor because it allows clients to deal with those early family experiences that still confuse their current functioning. Recapitulation of the family is group therapy's counterpart to the transference relationship in individual psychodynamic therapy. Yalom (1985) suggests that there is value in exploring past family "spirits" as long as the primary focus of the group remains in the here and now.

7 Group cohesiveness. Cohesiveness is the "attractiveness of a group for its members" (Frank, 1957). Members of cohesive groups are accepting of one another; they are willing to listen to and be influenced by the group. They participate in the group readily, feel secure in it, and are relatively immune to outside disruption of the group's progress. Cohesive groups also permit the expression of hostility, provided such conflicts do not violate the norms of the group. Attendance is more reliable in cohesive groups, and premature termination of treatment is less of a problem (Yalom, 1985).

Group cohesiveness is often regarded as the most important of the curative factors. Its value in group therapy approximates that of the therapeutic relationship in individual psychotherapy. Yalom (1985) considers cohesiveness to be a "necessary precondition" for effective group treatment that enhances development of other curative factors. The *acceptance* that members receive from the group may counteract their own feelings of worthlessness. The *public esteem* of the group serves as a reference point that increases members' own *self-esteem* because groups tend to evaluate individual members more favorably than the individuals evaluate themselves. Group members, in turn, will try to change in order to confirm the group's impression. The effect is something like a *group fulfilling prophecy,* where members are motivated to "not let the group down." Behaviors once thought by the individual to be "impossible" may be performed because of the group's supportive demand that they at least be attempted.

The Practice of Group Therapy. GROUP COMPOSITION. Therapy groups usually consist of six to twelve members. If a group is too small, the advantages of universality and cohesiveness may be jeopardized. With larger groups, feedback may become too

mechanical and superficial. There may also be less sensitive exploration of others' viewpoints. Another problem with larger groups is that "isolates" (members who make infrequent contributions) are more likely.

An important question for the group leader is what type of client should be accepted into a group. Initial assessment of group candidates is often not as structured as one encounters in individual psychotherapy. Many group therapists exclude brain-damaged individuals or those who are paranoid, hypochondriacal, suicidal, extremely narcissistic, sociopathic, drug or alcohol addicted, or psychotic.

Group leaders disagree on whether groups should be *homogeneous,* consisting of members who are similar as to age, sex, and type of problem, or *heterogeneous,* in which there is a mix of different types of clients. Heterogeneous groups are easier to form. They also have the advantage of exposing members to a wider range of people and perspectives. The major advantage of homogeneous groups is that they facilitate a more direct focus on symptom improvement. This emphasis is understandable, since the group's identity is often defined in terms of a common problem that motivated treatment.

GROUP DURATION. How long does group therapy last? What is the length of the usual group session? Questions about time are important in group therapy because the quality of group interactions is influenced by the amount and the nature of time that members spend together.

Some groups, like old soldiers, never die. These groups function over long time periods, adding new members as old ones depart. Other groups last only for a specific number of sessions. These groups may be open to new members, but more often they continue only with the initial participants.

Group sessions are typically longer than sessions of individual psychotherapy. Two hours is a common length. Group sessions are longer because it takes more time for eight clients to talk than for one. It also tends to take more time for a group to reach a meaningful level of dialogue.

Lengthy sessions are a defining characteristic of marathon groups. While there is no clear demarcation between marathon and other group approaches, it is generally assumed that a marathon session lasts from six to forty-eight hours or more. According to Bednar and Kaul (1978):

The rationale for the value of the marathon approach seems rather straightforward; people pretend and defend less as they become increasingly fatigued. Advocates of the marathon approach argue that the typical one to three hours of group meetings do not provide sufficient time for the erosion of social facades. Additionally, they assert that as a member's store of available energy is depleted, that member becomes more apt to show his or her true feelings, act more transparently, and attempt novel modes of behavior. Finally, it is held that merely removing an

individual from the typical environment may make learning occur more readily.

The critics of marathon techniques have remained unpersuaded by these arguments. They have wondered why if someone is too tired to pretend, they aren't also too tired to practice new behaviors or engage themselves constructively with other members. They have asked why one might assume that new learnings would transfer from the specific marathon setting to the more typical world of the member. Finally, the critics have asked whether changes elicited under such conditions would persist. (p. 782)

THE GROUP THERAPIST. The group therapist must walk a narrow line between exerting too much control over the group and allowing it to run free without a focus. The effective group therapist is a "first among equals" who is responsible for keeping the group on course. The group therapist usually assumes the role of a guide who steers the group process in constructive directions

---

BOX 7-3   An example of group therapy

This brief transcript will give you a better idea of what goes on in a group. It is taken from a book by Thomas Verny (1974), who reports it to be a verbatim account of group interaction (minus irrelevant remarks, repetitions, and hesitations).

Beth: After last week's session, I was very very angry. I even thought I shouldn't be in this group any longer. I just feel like the claws are at me all the time.

Dora: I was feeling very worked up too.

Fred: I just want to say one thing. That is, last week I felt the strangest tension and I couldn't decide whether it was me and I wanted to leave. Then I thought: This is ridiculous.

Beth: I almost . . . that is why I almost didn't want to come this week. I have got work to do and it is hard, and I don't need any extra tension in my life, specially this hounding that I have been getting for the past weeks.

Dora: Do you have any idea . . . do you realize, why you have been getting all this? I give it to you because I am so irritated with you for not doing anything about your situation.

Beth: I get out and I do as much as I can. [pause] Besides, I don't think that's the real reason for you and everyone else attacking me.

Dora: Well, if you don't believe me you can tell me what you think.

Beth: You're jealous of me.

Dora: Okay that's true, but don't put this into that category, because the reason I've been on you has got nothing to do with jealousy.

Beth: Sometimes I would just like to tell you to go and screw off.

Dora: Well then, why don't you? How about your apartment, have you been able to do anything about that?

Beth: No.

Dora: Would you like to have a nice apartment?

Beth: Yes, and I would also like to have a permanent relationship with a man and lots of other things.

Therapist: My question is, "When are you finally going to get better?"

Beth: When I stop letting the world control me. When I stop getting scared. When I start trusting myself a little bit more.

Therapist: What will you do in order to be that kind of a person?

Beth: Well, last week I deliberately put my movie script down and I rested when I felt like it. I walked outside and decided I was not going to punch myself out for this thing.

Dora: You are scared of losing Tom.

Beth: Not only Tom. I am scared of him [pointing to therapist] thinking that I am a bitchy person. I am not happy. I am not particularly happy with my circumstances but I have to learn how to accept it.

Therapist: You are always shifting; it is like going through shifting sands; we can never really get through to the core of Beth, which has kept her going to psychiatrists for the last four or five years.

Beth: To me, the core is a void. I don't know what's in there. [pause] Unless you see someone opening up their guts, you think nothing is happening. [turning to the therapist] I don't know what to say to you.

Dora: I don't think that's what he means at all.

Beth: I wasn't supposed to grow up. I wouldn't be loved if I grew up. I certainly wouldn't be loved if I would be any smarter or better in my work than my brother or my father or my mother. That's why when I get punched up, I just fall apart.

Fred: I'm not punching you up. Not at all.

Beth: I have the feeling that I'm doing a lot of rehashing.

Therapist: Yes, you are.

Beth: Well, I'm just answering questions.

Therapist: Yes, just being the nice girl and answering questions.

Beth: That's right. I am being a nice girl.

Therapist: When are you going to stop being just a nice girl and be yourself?

Beth: I'm afraid people will say, "There goes number-one bitch."

Therapist: I would much prefer you being the number-one bitch than the number-one kvetch.

Dora: Is that a Jewish word?

Beth: Yes, it is. It means a person who complains chronically.

Annette: Groups are filled with them. [general laughter]

Bill: How can we help you now?

Beth: By letting me know that I wouldn't be disliked if I got angry.

Several people: Why don't you try us?

Jim: There is one quality that I like in Beth and she seems to have this more than any other woman in this group, and that is the fact that she often laughs at herself. Isn't that right? Like, when you said kvetch, and suddenly [sic], you know, there was a smile on her face. She kind of lit up.

Therapist: That is why I say [turning to Beth] you are just playing at being neurotic.

Beth: That's something else that's upsetting me. Why do I think that I am so neurotic. I feel very funny now. I am embarrassed. [silence] I am wondering how everybody feels.

Therapist: Why is there always a need for talking?

Beth: Because I never get anything back. The only time I get anything back is when things are going poorly with me.

Therapist: Why don't you rely on your own resources? You have talked; you have thought about yourself; you have looked inward; why can't that be helpful in itself? Why do you need to hear from Henry and Joe and Jean and everybody else?

Dora: You know what, Beth? I think you want more and more and more and nothing is quite enough.

Source: Verny, 1974, pp. 78-82.

and prevents individual members from getting lost or becoming disruptive along the way.

Marital and Family Therapy

Marital and family discord are two of the most common problems encountered by clinical psychologists. More than one of every three marriages ends in divorce. The tragedy of family breakdowns is revealed by frightening increases in rates of child abuse, adolescent suicide, runaways, substance abuse within families, and parental desertion. A burgeoning professional literature on the theory and treatment of disturbed families and marriages has appeared (Ables & Brandsma, 1977; Framo, 1982; Gurman, 1985; Gurman & Kniskern, 1981; Kolevzon & Green, 1985; Lederer & Jackson, 1968; Satir, 1967).

Marital Therapy. In marital therapy the "client" is the marriage or the married couple. (Because of the changing nature of living arrangements in our culture, marital therapy is often called "couples therapy" in order to reflect the fact that it is intended for persons involved in long-term, intimate relationships, not just those who are legally married.) This treatment is also described as being "conjoint therapy," which means that both members of the couple see the same therapist(s) within the same sessions.

Marital therapy can be preceded, followed, or accompanied by individual psychotherapy for either or both of the spouses. Individual psychotherapy in addition to marital therapy is recommended when one of the members of the couple is suffering from a problem largely unrelated to the relationship.

In marital therapy the focus is on a *disturbed relationship*. This emphasis is different from working with a *disturbed individual in a relationship*, which would be a goal for individual psychotherapy. The need for marital therapy usually arises out of the conflicting expectations and needs of the couple. A

wife who was initially attracted to her husband because of his dashing charm and playboy image now finds these qualities to be obstacles to the emotional security she currently needs from their relationship. A husband comes to feel that what he once admired as "spunkiness" in his wife is now a threat to his dominance in the marriage. Intimate relationships are frequently beset by problems in the areas of sexual satisfaction, personal autonomy, dominance-submission, responsibility for child rearing, money management, fidelity, and the expression of disagreement and hostility. The goals and techniques of marital therapy depend on which of these conflicts is the most pressing for any given couple. Although the theoretical orientation (psychoanalytic, phenomenological, or behavioral) of marital therapists will influence their choice of procedures, the differences between practitioners of marital therapy are probably smaller than those that would exist between the same people practicing their version of individual psychotherapy.

A common theme among marital therapists is their emphasis on *problem solving*. Problem solving involves teaching the couple how to solve their own problems more constructively. It does not mean that the therapist solves the couple's problems for them or even that the therapist advises the couple how to solve their problems. The therapist's task is to facilitate the couple's working together so that they can learn new ways to handle the inevitable problems of a close relationship. The touchstone of problem solving is teaching the couple how to communicate and negotiate more effectively with each other. "Improving communications" is such a basic ingredient in couple therapy that it runs the risk of becoming a cliché; yet its role in marital therapy is central.

Working with communication involves changing not only the way a couple talks to each other but also how they think about their relationship. Therapists understand that when there is a problem in a relationship, the couple often becomes preoccupied with deciding whose fault it is. They devote their energies to blaming each other, to thinking about the past, to stating demands in a way that insures they will not be met, and, finally, to withdrawing and avoiding one another. Among the multiple tasks of improved communications are: teaching the couple to accept mutual responsibility for working on problems, maintaining a focus on the here and now of their relationship, fostering expression of preferences rather than demands for obedience, and negotiating compromises to problems the couple had decided couldn't be solved.

A brief excerpt from Ables and Brandsma (1977) illustrates these themes. In this example the therapist (T) is trying to help the wife (W) learn to give up her tendency to blame her husband for certain of his behaviors that she finds irritating:

T: I do think that what Pete is saying is an important point. There are things that are going to be different about you and each of you is going to think the things you do maybe make more sense than the other person's, and that's probably going to be pretty much of a reality. You're not going to be able to change all those. You may not be able to change very many of them. And everybody is different. They have their own predilections to do things a certain way and again what's coming through from you is sort of like damning those and saying those are wrong; they're silly, they don't make sense, I don't understand them or whatever. You may not understand them but they are a reality of each of you. That's something you have to learn how to deal with in some way. Otherwise, you . . . the reason I'm stressing this is I think it plays a large part in your criticalness.
W: Well, I do find it difficult to cater to, I guess that's the word, cater to some idiosyncrasies that I find or think are totally foolish. I am intolerant. I am, and I find it very difficult. I find it almost impossible to do it agreeably and without coming on as "Oh, you're ridiculous."
T: I guess what would be helpful would be if

you could come on honestly enough to say "I don't like them" or "It doesn't sit well with me" without having to add the additional value judgment of whether they're foolish or ridiculous or whatever. That's the part that hurts. It's when you damn him because of these things—that's gonna hurt. I'm sure from Pete's point of view they make sense for his total economy of functioning. There's some sense to why he does things the way he does, just as there is for why you do things the way you do. It's not that they're foolish. They make sense in terms of where you are, what you're struggling with, and what's the best way you can deal with right now. I'm not trying to say that means you have to like them, but when you come across and say "It's ridiculous or foolish"—that's the part that makes it hurt.
W: Well, tell me again how to say it, because I find it hard to say anything except "That's really stupid—that's silly." I know you said it a minute ago but I lost it.
T: Well, anytime you can say it in terms of how it affects you and say with it, like "It's hard—I find it hard to take," that doesn't say "I find you're an ass for wanting to do that such and such a way. It's just that, "I find it hard to take—I get upset in this circumstance" or whatever. Stay with what your feelings are rather than trying to evaluate Pete. (pp. 92–94)

Family Therapy. Although similar in some respects, marital therapy and family therapy evolved for different reasons. Marital therapy was the natural outgrowth of the fact that many clients complained of marital problems. The roots of family therapy are more indirect, stemming from the fact that individuals who made large improvements during individual therapy or institutional treatment often had a relapse when they returned to their families. This observation, along with other clinical insights and research, led to several early theories of psychopathology that emphasized the family environment and parent-child interactions as causes of maladaptive behavior (Bateson,

Jackson, Haley & Weakland, 1956; Lidz & Lidz, 1949; Sullivan, 1953).

Family therapy differs from marital therapy in that it usually begins with a focus on one member of the family rather than the entire family. Therapists speak of the "identified client" as the person in the family who has been singled out as the one with the problem. Typically, the identified client is a male child (often of adolescent age) whom the parents label as a "behavior problem" or as "unmanageable." While family therapy may begin with a focus on this individual, the therapist will try to reframe the problem in terms of disturbed family processes or faulty family communication. The family therapist will encourage all family members to see their own contributions to the problem as well as the positive changes each member can make.

As with marital therapy, the most common goal of family therapy is improved communications. Disturbed families seem to rely on coercion as their major means of communication (Patterson, 1982). The message from both parents and children often takes the form, "Do what I want or you'll be sorry." The therapist tries to teach family members noncoercive ways of communicating their needs. The therapist might also focus on teaching parents the importance of consistency in discipline, encouraging each member of the family to communicate clearly with one another, minimizing scapegoating of the identified client, and helping the family members examine the appropriateness of what they expect from the rest of the family.

Virginia Satir (1967), a well-known practitioner of family therapy, offers the following example of how the family therapist tries to help parents and children communicate better with one another. In the first example the therapist helps a parent understand her son and receive "feedback" from him.

MOTHER: His pleasure is doing things he knows will get me up in the air. Every minute he's in the house . . . constantly.

THERAPIST: There's no pleasure to that, my dear.
MOTHER: Well, there is to him.
THERAPIST: No, you can't see his thoughts. You can't get inside his skin. All you can talk about is what you see and hear. You can say it *looks* as though it's for pleasure.
MOTHER: All right. Well, it looks as though, and that's just what it looks like constantly.
THERAPIST: He could be trying to keep your attention, you know. It is very important to Johnny what Mother thinks.

The therapist also helps the child express frustration and anger and specify situations which precipitate anger:

THERAPIST: Do you kind of get mad at Daddy when he gets mad at you?
SON: Yeah, and sometimes he gets real mad and pinches my ear.
THERAPIST: He pinches your ear. Do you feel like hitting him back?
SON: Yeah, I get real mad sometimes.
THERAPIST: So what keeps you from hitting him?
SON: Well he's, uh, he's bigger than me." (pp. 151–152)

EVALUATION OF THERAPEUTIC INTERVENTION

The evaluation of psychological treatment is a major concern for three different audiences. Each audience has its own values, which influence its definition of mental health and the criteria used to assess it (Strupp & Hadley, 1977). First, there is the client, who has an obvious interest in the success of an activity in which much personal effort, time, and money have been invested. The client askes two questions of therapy: "Did it help me?" and "Was it worth the expense?" The second source of evaluation is the therapist, who needs to know if her or his efforts are worthwhile or if they need to be modified in some way. The final evaluative audience for psychotherapy is society, which means any third party having an interest in therapy's outcome. A third party can be a spouse, parent, friend, lover, teacher, judge—anyone who is concerned about the changes that psychotherapy produces in a client. Third parties can take on a cumulative quality; if we add together all the third parties with an interest in psychotherapy, we can speak of society in the traditional sense of an organized, cooperative social group concerned that psychotherapy produce desirable effects for the community at large.

Evaluating therapy is a dominant research activity in clinical psychology. For a long time the basic question posed by clinical researchers was: "Is psychotherapy effective?" Clinicians gradually discovered that this question was too broad to be answered meaningfully, and they abandoned it in favor of Paul's (1969a) famous reformulation: "What treatment, by whom, is most effective for this individual with that specific problem, under which set of circumstances, and how does it come about?" (p.44). Kazdin (1982b) organized Paul's "ultimate question" into several possible research goals including (1) determine the efficacy of a specific treatment; (2) compare the relative effectiveness of different treatments; and (3) assess the individual components of treatment that are responsible for particular changes.

In order to accomplish these goals, the psychotherapy researcher must design and conduct an evaluation in such a way that the results can be interpreted unambiguously. Deceptively easy to describe, this obligation is exasperatingly difficult to execute. It is impossible to perform an evaluation that yields completely unambiguous results for the simple reason that any human activity is a fallible effort. Despite this fallibility, researchers strive to conduct the best evaluations they can by evaluating psychotherapy through the use of a scientific experiment. A scientific experiment is a complex activity, the true meaning of which evokes heated debate among philosophers as well as scientists. For our purposes, we describe an experiment as *an attempt to discover the causes of*

specific events by making systematic changes in certain factors and then observing changes that occur in other factors. Researchers call the factors they manipulate the *independent variables,* while the factors in which resulting changes are observed are termed the *dependent variables.*

In psychotherapy research there are two experimental strategies. One is called *within-subject* research; the other is known as *between-subject* research. Both approaches examine the effects of varying conditions (independent variables) on the performance of a participant or group of participants; however, each approach uses different methods.

Within-Subject Research

In within-subject designs, the comparisons are made on the same subjects at different points in time. The within-subject experiment requires that the dependent variables be measured on several occasions in sequence. The experiment is begun by observing the dependent measures before any independent variables are manipulated. This period is called the *baseline;* it provides an estimate of the preintervention, or existing, level of the dependent measure. Following the baseline, the *intervention* phase of the experiment is introduced. In this phase the independent variable is manipulated by the experimenter, and the dependent measures are observed to detect any changes from their baseline levels. In evaluating the effects of psychotherapy, the baseline period would involve observing the client's behavior for several days before treatment was initiated. The intervention phase would correspond to the active treatment, during which regular assessments of the client's progress would be made.

Although there are several types of within-subject experimental designs (Hayes, 1983; Kazdin, 1982a), the two used in the majority of cases deserve special comment. The best-known of this pair is the *ABAB,* or *reversal,* design, in which the no-treatment baseline (A) is alternated with a treatment intervention (B). The length of each phase is determined by many factors, but usually each phase is continued until the client's behavior (the dependent measure) becomes relatively stable. If behavior changes reliably and substantially in conjunction with the sequential experimental phases, the experimenter gains confidence that treatment is responsible. An example of an ABAB evaluation of a clinical intervention is provided in Figure 7-1.

The other major within-subject approach is the *multiple-baseline* design, which evaluates an intervention without withdrawing treatment as in the reversal design. This is a major advantage, because there are clinical and ethical objections to interrupting treatment at arbitrary times. Multiple-baseline designs allow the researcher to observe simultaneously several dependent measures

while applying the intervention of interest to only one of them. In other words, baseline conditions are maintained for all dependent variables except one. This procedure is continued so that the treatment is applied to different variables, one at a time, while all other measures continue under baseline conditions. The experimenter gains confidence in the effects of a given treatment if a dependent measure changes only when the intervention is being applied to it. A cause-effect relationship is strengthened if this finding is repeated, or *replicated*, on each of the measures.

The need for several different baselines can be filled in a number of ways. The experimenter can focus on several behaviors in the same individual, applying treatment to one behavior while the others remain at baseline. Imagine a study that evaluated the

FIGURE 7-1. Example of reversal design. This study showed the effect of presenting, withdrawing, and re-presenting teacher approval (smiles and physical contact) for attentiveness in retarded students. (From A. E. Kazdin and J. Klock, "The effect of nonverbal teacher approval on student attentive behavior," *Journal of Applied Behavior Analysis*, 1973, 6, 643–54. © 1973 by the Society of the Experimental Analysis of Behavior, Inc. Reprinted by permission.)

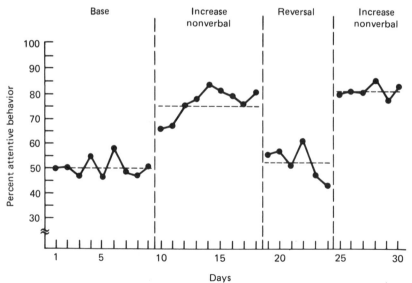

effects of social praise by hospital staff on the behavior of psychotic patients. In this hypothetical experiment, three behaviors are examined—grooming, attending occupational therapy, and socializing on the ward. The intervention (social praise) is introduced at different points in time for each behavior. Each "new" intervention begins on the day following the termination of the baseline phase for each behavior.

As Figure 7-2 shows, each behavior improved when, *and only when,* "its" intervention was introduced. The fact that each behavior changed only when social praise was being given for it makes it unlikely that some other factor (e.g., the influence of other patients) could account for such a specific pattern of results.

Within-subject research can be done with a small number of subjects. In fact, the logic of within-subject designs permits the use of only one subject, in which case it is called

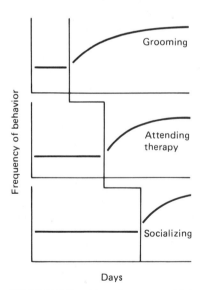

FIGURE 7-2. Data from a multiple-baseline design. (From A. E. Kazdin and S. A. Kopel, "On resolving ambiguities of the multiple baseline design: Problems and recommendations," *Behavior Therapy,* 1975, 6, 601–8. © 1975 by Academic Press, New York. Reprinted by permission.)

"single subject" or "N=1" research (Barlow & Hersen, 1984). "N=1" research is becoming an increasingly popular psychotherapy research strategy for several reasons. First, it permits the intensive study of clinical phenomena such as multiple personality that are too rare to allow large-group designs. Second, it encourages an integration of research and clinical practice because it gives clinicians a way to evaluate empirically the treatment they deliver to individual clients (Hayes, 1983). Third, it brings together "process" and "outcome" questions through its fine-grained study of how critical events in therapy are followed by particular changes in the client (Rice & Greenberg, 1984).

Between-Subject Research

Between-subject research compares groups of subjects that are exposed to different interventions. The simplest example of this approach is an experiment including an *experimental* group and a *control* group. Subjects randomly assigned to the experimental group are given some special experience (in psychotherapy research this would be treatment), while the control group subjects are "left alone." Dependent measures are collected for both groups prior to the experiment (the *pretest*) and shortly after it is over (the *posttest*). These same measures may also be repeated at longer posttreatment intervals (a *follow-up*). Once the pretest equivalence of the experimental and control groups is established, differences between the groups, at either the posttest or follow-up, are assumed to be due to the treatment that only the experimental group received.

One difference between within-subject and between-subject research is that in the latter case statistical analyses are usually used to assess the magnitude and *significance* of differences between treated and untreated subjects. A mean score and a measure of variability are computed for each group, and a statistical test is applied to determine whether the between-group differences are likely to have occurred by chance. In within-subject research, such statistics are usually not used because the researcher is more interested in demonstrating that the behavior of a subject is reliably related to manipulations of the independent variable. The within-subject researcher believes that statistics are not necessary to demonstrate such control; a person can look at a graph of the subjects' performance and "see" the differences. (For a discussion of the pros and cons of performing statistical analyses on within-subject data see Gentile, Roden & Klein, 1972; Glass, Wilson & Gottman, 1975; Hartmann, 1974; Kazdin, 1982a).

Psychotherapy outcome research has progressed to the point where the two-group (experimental versus control) design is not adequate for the questions researchers now seek to answer. Even if large differences appear between a treatment and a no-treatment group, little is learned about the effects of psychotherapy except, perhaps, that it is more effective than doing nothing at all. This type of design cannot reveal whether treated subjects' improvement is due to specific therapeutic techniques, characteristics of the therapist, or the capacity of therapy to generate expectancy for improvement. This design is also unable to answer the question of whether the particular treatment tested would be more effective than some alternative approach.

One way of answering such questions is to build all the factors of interest, along with the appropriate controls, into the experimental design. The major advantage of such *factorial designs* is that they compare several factors that might be responsible for therapeutic change. Thus, one group of subjects might receive a complete treatment "package," while another gets only that part of treatment thought to be most important to its effectiveness. Another group might be exposed to procedures impressive enough to generate hope for improvement but not hypothesized to be helpful. A fourth group might get no treatment at all.

By comparing the results of all these groups, the experimenter begins to determine whether the complete treatment package is (1) better than no treatment, (2) better than what could be gained from placebo effects, and (3) better than a streamlined version of treatment. If another group of subjects had been given a completely different form of treatment, the experimenter could also compare the first approach with that alternative. Paul (1966) provides an excellent description of a factorial design in his *Insight vs. Desensitization in Psychotherapy*.

Between-subject research is popular among psychotherapy researchers because it allows them to manipulate several variables simultaneously rather than sequentially, as required by within-subject designs. In addition, between-subject research allows the researcher to address questions for which within-subject designs are ill suited. It is difficult to evaluate whether a certain treatment is more effective with a specific type of client in a within-subject design because the same participants are involved in all the conditions of the experiment. In general, it is necessary to use between-group designs when the researcher wants to study selected aspects of a treatment and their unique contribution to therapeutic change (see Box 7-4). Between-subject designs are expensive, however; it usually takes many subjects and a large research staff to compose and treat the groups necessary for the statistical analyses used.

The major priority for both within-subject and between-subject designs is that they demonstrate *internal validity* (Cook & Campbell, 1979). Internal validity is the degree to which the design of an experiment allows one to be confident that the results are due to the specific factor(s) manipulated rather than to some unintended factor.

Analogue Research

Most researchers agree that the best way to assess the outcome of psychotherapy is to conduct research on actual therapy offered

BOX 7-4 Treatment evaluation strategies and the outcome questions they address

Treatment evaluation strategy	*Outcome question addressed*
1. Treatment package strategy	Does this treatment with all of its components lead to therapeutic change relative to no treatment?
2. Dismantling strategy	What aspects of the treatment package are necessary, sufficient, or facilitative for therapeutic change?
3. Parametric strategy	What variations of the treatment can be made to augment its effectiveness?
4. Constructive strategy	What procedures or techniques can be added to treatment to make it more effective?
5. Comparative strategy	Which treatment is more [or most] effective among a particular set of alternatives?
6. Client-variation strategy	What client characteristics interact with the effects of treatment? Or, for whom is a particular technique effective?

Source: Kazdin, 1982b. In P. C. Kendall and J. N. Butcher (Eds.), *Research Methods in Clinical Psychology.* Copyright © 1982 by John Wiley & Sons, Inc. Used by permission of John Wiley & Sons, Inc.

by trained clinicians to bona fide clients in real treatment settings. The ideal experimental study would be to select clients seeking treatment for a certain problem, assign them randomly to different treatments and control conditions, use trained therapists, and measure outcome on several indices of therapeutic change collected by persons blind to the conditions under which clients had been treated. Unfortunately, this ideal is achieved so seldom as to be almost nonexistent in the outcome literature. The closest approximation is the outcome study of Sloane, Staples, Cristol, Yorkston, and Whipple (1975), which compared the effects of behavior therapy with psychoanalytically oriented therapy delivered by experienced therapists of both persuasions to ninety adult outpatients randomly assigned to one of the two treatments or to a waiting list control group. Despite its many admirable qual-

ities, this study, whose conclusions are quite complicated (both treatment groups improved about equally by the end of treatment, but the control group also improved markedly during a follow-up period), has been criticized on several grounds (see Agras, Kazdin & Wilson, 1979).

Obstacles to ideal psychotherapy evaluations are numerous (Kraemer, 1981). In most cases, the requirements of an adequate experimental design cannot be met in a "real-life" clinical context. For example, both clinical and ethical considerations prevent random assignment of clients to different treatment and control conditions. Few clients will tolerate being put into a no-treatment group simply for the sake of good science. For their part, therapists also are reluctant to allow clients to be assigned to conditions that have little probability of bringing about constructive changes. These problems are accompanied by a more basic impediment to research on psychotherapy: There are few clinical situations in which the researcher can obtain a sufficient number of clients who meet the criteria for inclusion. It is also almost impossible to control for external factors that may influence clients' behavior such as additional treatment, advice from friends, or major life changes.

Add to these obstacles the practical problems of enlisting experienced therapists to participate in a study, convincing agency administrators to invest resources in the research, and collecting meaningful long-term outcome measures from clients, and you can sympathize with the psychotherapy researcher's sense of futility in conducting "real-life" evaluations of treatment outcome.

There are two approaches to solving these psychotherapy outcome research problems. One is for researchers to summon all their creativity and tenacity and conduct the best clinical research they can while at the same time recognizing that certain questions cannot be answered with certainty in a nonlaboratory study. The other approach is to bring psychotherapy research questions into the laboratory. In doing so, the researcher "buys" the control afforded by the laboratory but sacrifices the realism inherent in actual clinical settings.

This second approach, in which clinical variables are approximated in a controlled experimental setting, is called *analogue research.* The advantages of psychotherapy analogue research are that it (1) allows control of extraneous variables that cannot be controlled in the clinic, (2) makes possible a greater number of participants, (3) permits replication of results, (4) allows selection of subjects and research personnel on several dimensions, and (5) allows variables such as the number and length of treatment sessions to be held constant for all subjects.

Analogue research should resemble actual clinical conditions as much as possible. To the extent that the analogy is a close one,

with considerable similarity between laboratory variables and their clinical counterparts, the experiment is said to possess *external validity.* External validity refers to the degree to which the design of an experimental study assures that the results are generalizable to settings other than the one in which the experiment took place (Cook & Campbell, 1979).

There are four dimensions along which the similarity between clinical and analogue settings are assessed (Bernstein & Paul, 1971). The first is *subject characteristics* and *recruitment.* In analogue research, subjects are often college undergraduates who volunteer for the experiment for a variety of reasons, such as course credit or requirement, that have little to do with a desire to overcome a distressing problem. The degree to which an analogue experiment's results can be generalized to a clinical population depends on the extent to which the reasons for subjects' volunteering are similar to those that compel clients to seek treatment.

The second dimension in evaluating analogue research is the nature of the *target problem.* Subjects reporting a fear of small animals have commonly been used in experiments on the effects of several anxiety-reduction techniques. However, many critics have contended that, as a target problem, the fear of snakes, mice, and dogs has little relevance to clinical anxiety unless the intensity of clients' fear is very high.

The third dimension of interest is *therapist characteristics.* In most analogues the "therapists" are graduate students in clinical psychology who have limited clinical experience. It is doubtful that they possess the general clinical skills and specific treatment techniques that ideally characterize the competent, practicing clinician.

The final dimension on which to compare clinical and analogue activities is the *treatment techniques* themselves. In most instances analogue treatments are standardized on several dimensions, which means that these dimensions are specified and held constant across all participants. Standardization is seldom encountered in psychotherapy. Instead, the intervention is usually tailored to the unique needs of each client. In many analogues, treatment techniques are simplified, altered, or even omitted in order to meet the demands of convenience and the academic calendar. Such modifications may so change a technique that it bears little resemblance to the clinical procedure it was intended to represent.[3]

Analogue designs pose a dilemma for the psychotherapy researcher because they involve a trade-off in research priorities. The gains in internal validity that analogues provide must be balanced against the sacrifices in external validity that they require. The objection is not to analogy per se. The objection is to *rigorless* analogy brought about by merely substituting the language of one domain for the terminology of another, rather than by the thoughtful fine tuning of experimental variables.

Because of the potential usefulness of analogue research, many researchers have attempted to improve it. One proposal is that, in small animal phobia studies, only individuals whose fear is severe enough to disrupt their daily activities should be included as subjects. Another alternative involves selection of target problems that are more relevant to the overall functioning of the participants (Borkovec, Stone, O'Brien & Kaloupek, 1974). This recommendation has led to analogue research with participants who suffer from interpersonal anxieties, sleep disturbances, and social unassertiveness.

---

[3]The standardization of treatments for research purposes often takes the form of writing manuals that closely specify how a treatment is to be conducted during a research study. *Manualization* of therapy has been accomplished for both behavioral (e.g., Linehan, 1984) and psychoanalytic (e.g., Luborsky, 1984) treatments; it involves a much more comprehensive and sophisticated guide for conducting a type of therapy than has been the case in most analogue research.

The "ultimate" outcome question ("What treatment, by whom, is most effective for this individual, with that specific problem, under which set of circumstances, and how does it come about?") cannot be answered in any single investigation. The maximum benefit from any evaluation of therapy outcome, whether it be an uncontrolled case study, a factorial experiment in a clinical setting, or an experimental analogue, is achieved by integrating individual investigations into a program of related studies. Paul (1969a) noted that

All levels and approaches to the ultimate question may be expected to continue. It is to be hoped, however, that each approach will be seen in perspective, in its relationships both to other approaches and to the actual level of product obtained, so that future generations may view the field as a composition of "artisans" or "scientists," rather than as cultists bound by historical inheritance. (p. 61)

The Effectiveness of Psychotherapy

Although therapists have studied the outcomes of psychotherapy for many years, the modern era of outcome research began in 1952 when Hans J. Eysenck, a British psychologist, reviewed several studies and concluded that the recovery rate is about the same for patients who receive therapy as for those who do not. Eysenck argued that the rate of "spontaneous remission" (improvement without any special treatment) was 72 percent over two years compared to improvement rates of 44 percent for psychoanalysis and 64 percent for eclectic therapy (Eysenck, 1952). In later reviews, Eysenck (1966) evaluated more studies, persisted in his pessimism about the effectiveness of traditional therapy, but claimed that behavior therapy produced superior outcomes.

Eysenck's conclusions sparked heated debate among clinicians. Many critics attacked his thoroughness, fairness, and statistical analyses. Later, other reviewers surveyed the outcome literature and reached more optimistic opinions about the effectiveness of psychotherapy. For example, Bergin (1971) concluded that "psychotherapy on the average has modestly positive effects" (p. 228), a belief he later amended to "clearly positive results" (Bergin & Lambert, 1978). Meltzoff and Kornreich (1970) reported that more than 80 percent of psychotherapy outcome studies produced positive results. Indeed, most reviewers have concluded that most forms of psychotherapy produce better outcomes than no treatment and that different types of therapy are equally effective with most clients (e.g., Luborsky, Singer & Luborsky, 1975). Other reviewers have supported Eysenck's claim that traditional psychotherapy has not yet been proven to be superior to no treatment, but that for several kinds of problems behavior therapy *is* effective (Rachman & Wilson, 1980; Kazdin & Wilson, 1978). Although there are many reasons for this disagreement, a major source of the problem has been that different reviewers use varying standards in (1) selecting the outcome studies they survey, (2) evaluating the quality of these studies, (3) interpreting the magnitude of therapy effects, and (4) combining the results of many studies into an integrated conclusion.

The traditional approach to summarizing outcome research has been termed the *narrative* or *box score* review. Reviewers who use this method have been criticized for being too subjective and too unsystematic in the way they integrate research studies, causing inevitable disagreements. Another problem with narrative reviews is that the sheer number of outcome studies makes it difficult for reviewers to weigh properly the merits and results of each study.

An alternative to narrative reviews is *meta-analysis*, a quantitative technique for combining the results of many studies. Meta-analysis standardizes the outcomes of a large number of studies so they can be compared or combined (see Rosenthal, 1983, for discussion of various meta-analytic strategies). The first application of meta-analysis to psychotherapy research was the monumental effort of Smith, Glass, and Miller (1980), in which 475 psychotherapy outcome studies were analyzed.

Smith et al. (1980) evaluated therapy effectiveness by computing *effect sizes* for all the treatments used in all the studies. An effect size was defined as the treatment group mean on a dependent measure minus the control group mean on the same measure divided by the standard deviation of the control group. Thus, an effect size indicates how many standard deviations above or below the control group mean the average treated client falls. There can be as many effect sizes for a treatment as there are measures on which that treatment is evaluated.

On the basis of their meta-analysis, Smith et al. (1980) concluded the following:

1. The average effect size for psychotherapy was .85 standard deviations, which Glass and Kliegl (1983) interpreted as meaning that "the average person receiving psychotherapy was better off at the end of it than 80% of the persons who do not" (p. 29).

2. Only 9 percent of the effect sizes were negative, indicating that deterioration due to psychotherapy was not frequent.

3. Different types of therapy (behavioral versus insight-oriented) were not associated with significantly larger effect sizes, leading to a conclusion that different therapies were about equally effective.

4. Larger effect sizes were related to (a) more reactive methods of measuring outcome, (b) allegiance of experimenters to the therapy they were evaluating, and (c) immediate versus follow-up evaluation of outcomes.

Following Smith et al. (1980), several other researchers performed meta-analyses using different statistical methods or applying the method to more highly selected sets of studies (e.g., Shapiro & Shapiro, 1982; Landman & Dawes, 1982; Andrews & Harvey, 1981). In general, these analyses have confirmed the Smith et al. (1980) conclusion that psychotherapy is an effective intervention, although they have tended to show greater effectiveness for behavioral therapies relative to other therapies than did Smith et al. (1980).

Despite its recent popularity, meta-analysis has been severely criticized (e.g., Eysenck, 1978; Wilson, 1985; Wilson & Rachman, 1983). Most objections to meta-analysis fall into one of the following categories: (1) Meta-analysis is subject to the same biases and arbitrariness as are encountered in narrative reviews, that is, certain studies are omitted and others are combined into categories that may not be reliably defined; (2) meta-analysis involves an "apples-and-oranges" approach to evaluation (combining different treatments for varying purposes on a wide range of clients) that obscures important distinctions in treatments and outcomes; (3) meta-analysis pays insufficient attention to the research quality of individual studies of psychotherapy; and (4) meta-analysis is based on several statistical assumptions that, if violated, can invalidate the results of the analysis. These criticisms, as well as attempts to answer them and predict the future uses of meta-analysis, are discussed thoroughly in special issues of *Journal of Consulting and Clinical Psychology* (February, 1983) and *Clinical Psychology Review* (1985).

Clinical Significance

Most psychotherapy outcome studies focus on some form of the following question: Does a specific treatment produce significantly larger effects than control conditions or other types of treatment? This is an important question, but it is not the only one with which clinician-researchers are concerned. A related and equally important question is whether psychotherapy produces outcomes of *clinical significance*.

Clinical significance can be defined as the extent to which treatment outcomes achieve *meaningful* change. A related concept is so-

cial validity, introduced by Wolf (1978) to refer to the social significance of treatment goals, the social appropriateness of treatment procedures, and the social importance of treatment effects as assessed by the judgments of others. Clinical significance involves measuring whether psychotherapy produces practically important improvements.

How one defines "meaningful" is no small problem. Kazdin (1982b) proposed two methods: (1) *subjective evaluation,* which consists of having individuals who interact with the client or who are in a special position to judge changes in target behaviors evaluate whether those changes have led to important qualitative differences, and (2) *social or normative comparisons,* in which clients' behavior before and after treatment is compared to the behavior of nondisturbed, "normal" peers. Using this second method, one can quantitatively define clinical significance in terms of the standard deviation units that separate treated clients from the mean of some normative group (Kendall, 1984; Jacobson, Follette & Revenstorf, 1984). This method uses the same logic as the meta-analysis of effect sizes. Quantitative social comparisons have been reported for evaluating the clinical significance of treatments for children's impulsivity (Kendall & Zupan, 1981), depression (Nietzel, Russell, Hemmings & Gretter, in press), and schizophrenia (Hansen, St. Lawrence & Christoff, 1985) (see Figure 7-3).

COMMUNITY PSYCHOLOGY

Not all psychologists believe that psychotherapy (or its variants, such as couple therapy, group therapy, and family therapy) is the best intervention for psychological problems. Despite often being originally trained as clinicians, many psychologists have become convinced that radically different strategies based on a different model of human behavior are necessary to produce meaningful improvements in people's lives.

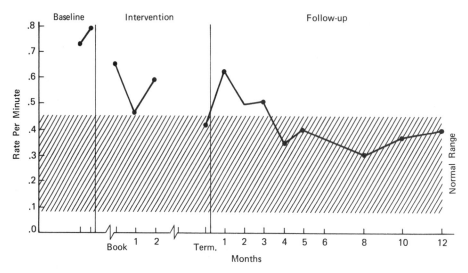

FIGURE 7-3. The shaded area shows the normal range of deviant behavior per minute in home settings. The solid line shows the average deviant behavior for a group of boys before, during, and after receiving treatment for their conduct problems. By comparing the shaded area with the treatment line, one can determine the degree to which the boys approximated the behavior of "normal" children after treatment. (From G. R. Patterson, "Intervention for boys with conduct problems: Multiple settings, treatments, and criteria," *Journal of Consulting and Clinical Psychology*, 1974, *42*, 471–81.)

These interventions and their accompanying theoretical principles are known as *community psychology.*

Our purpose in the remainder of this chapter is to acquaint you with the history, principles, and current status of community psychology. Although there are large differences between the community psychologist and the clinician, there also are some fundamental similarities between them. Each emphasizes a *psychological perspective* on human behavior and applies this perspective in order to change behavior and promote human welfare. Each also champions the scientific study of human behavior.

What Is Community Psychology?

Community psychology applies psychological principles to (1) the understanding of individual and social problems, (2) the prevention of behavioral dysfunction, and (3) the creation of lasting social change. Var-

ious community psychologists emphasize different characteristics in their definition of this field (e.g., Heller, Price, Reinharz, Riger & Wandersman, 1984; Iscoe & Harris, 1984; Mann, 1978; Murrell, 1973; Sarason, 1974), but a common ingredient in all the definitions is that human behavior develops out of interactions between people and all aspects of their environment—physical, social, political, and economic. This idea requires that efforts to alleviate individual and social problems must entail *changes in both environmental settings and individual competencies*, not just changes at the individual level (which is the goal of psychotherapy). In his influential text on community psychology, Rappaport (1977) refers to this emphasis on person-environment interactions as the *ecological perspective*—"an orientation emphasizing relationships among persons and their social and physical environment [and implying] that there are neither inadequate persons nor inadequate environments, but rather the fit between persons and environments may be in relative accord or disaccord" (Rappaport, 1977, p. 2). Along with an emphasis on environmental factors, community psychologists have shown great concern for underserved, "underprivileged" populations (Snowden, 1982) who often have not been seen as appropriate recipients for psychotherapy or whose problems have been viewed as more social than psychological in nature and as requiring social rather than individual change (Bloom, 1973).

The History of Community Psychology

Early Contributions. Several early developments in the history of the mental health professions form the basis of community psychology. For example, the Moral Era's emphasis on environmental determinants of disorder and its reformist fervor (see Chapter 1) were early inspirations for the community psychology movement. Other precursors are presented below in a roughly chronological order.

1 The advent of clinical psychology. Community psychology is embedded in clinical psychology. The majority of community psychologists were trained in clinical psychology programs. The early history of clinical psychology is thus relevant to an analysis of community psychology. As Chapter 1 indicated, early clinical psychology was psychoeducational, and its emphasis on children reflected a belief that the treatment of early problems could prevent them from growing into major disabilities.

2 The mental hygiene movement. In 1908 a former mental patient, Clifford Whittingham Beers, published *A Mind That Found Itself*, a moving book that described Beer's experiences as a mental patient and called public attention to the deplorable conditions in mental institutions. The book spurred several reforms in the treatment of the mentally ill and led in 1909 to the founding of the National Committee for Mental Hygiene, the organization that initi-

ated the *mental hygiene* and *child guidance* movements. The mental hygienists preferred to promote health rather than combat illness. Impressed by the success of public health's aggressive attack on contagious illnesses, they called for preventive programs and public education efforts to "inoculate" people against mental illness. The mental hygiene movement received a major boost when Beers enlisted William James, America's leading psychologist, and Adolf Meyer, the foremost American psychiatrist of the day, as spokesmen for his organization and its enlightened views on the treatment of mental disorders.

3 The child guidance movement. The 1920s saw the growth of the child guidance movement, an offspring of mental hygiene, which concentrated on the delivery of clinical services to children, especially those who were severely emotionally disturbed. The child guidance movement furthered the philosophy of the mental hygienists and solidified the concept of the *team approach* to treatment, an idea anticipated by Witmer's use of consultants from other professions.

4 World Wars I and II. Two aspects of World Wars I and II had clear relevance to community psychology. First, both wars stimulated the growth of clinical psychology, the field in which most community psychologists were originally trained. Second, the two wars dramatically reshaped clinical psychology to make the profession more adult-oriented, more concerned with psychopathology, more enamored with psychotherapy, and more often housed in hospital settings. These postwar attributes of clinical psychology were criticized by some clinicians who became disenchanted with the profession's course. It was in the soil of this disenchantment that community psychology took root.

Recent Contributions. In the 1950s and 1960s a more concentrated array of influences came together to accelerate the development of community psychology, leading to its formal birth in the mid-1960s. Two sets of developments were crucial in this

FIGURE 7-4.   Clifford W. Beers (1876–1943). (From *A Mind That Found Itself* by Clifford Whittingham Beers. Copyright 1907, 1917, 1923, 1931, 1932, 1934, 1935, 1937, 1939, 1940, 1942, 1944, 1948, 1953 by the American Foundation for Mental Hygiene, Inc. Reproduced by permission of Doubleday & Co., Inc. Reprinted by permission of the American Psychological Association and the author.)

birth. One set was internal to the profession of psychology itself; the other entailed extensive social and political changes that were taking place throughout America during this period.

Within the profession the following issues were the most prominent: (1) disenchantment with the theory and practice of a clinical psychology that had been dominated by intrapsychic models of psychopathology

"Yes, what is it? I'm very busy . . . ."

FIGURE 7-5. There are several ways of handling the shortage of mental health personnel. This is not one of them. (© 1972, Punch/Rothco.)

(Rappaport, 1977); (2) skepticism about the positive effects of psychotherapy (Eysenck, 1952, 1966) as well as the reliability and validity of psychological diagnosis and evaluation (Rosenhan, 1973); (3) prophecies of personnel shortages given the prevalent one-to-one style of delivering mental health services (Albee, 1959); and (4) dissatisfaction with the training models and role expectations for clinical psychologists (Korman, 1974; Peterson, 1968).

Several forces external to the profession nurtured the growth of community psychology. Social and political activism during the 1960s dramatically affected many who experienced these forces, including psychologists. The civil rights movement, black separatist ideology, urban crises, the war on poverty, and the unrest and demonstrations of university students were important events that prompted many psychologists to broaden their conceptions of what the helping professions should do in the interest of social change.

Another external force was legislative. The Mental Health Study Act of 1955 estab-lished the Joint Commission on Mental Health and Illness. This commission's final report in 1961 is often regarded as the direct impetus for the community mental health and community psychology movements, because it recommended the construction of multiservice comprehensive care centers to serve the mental health needs of local communities.

The joint commission's final report was followed in 1963 by passage of the Community Mental Health Centers Act, which had the vigorous support of President John F. Kennedy. This bill provided funds for the construction of a network of comprehensive mental health centers that could cover service areas of not less than 75,000 nor more than 200,000 people. "Comprehensive care" was defined by this legislation to include ten types of services. Five of these services were *essential,* meaning that they were required for centers seeking federal funds; five other services were *desirable,* indicating that they were important but not required for funding.

The five essential services were: inpatient

care, partial hospitalization, outpatient treatment for adults and children, twenty-four-hour emergency services, and consultation and education programs. The five desirable services were: diagnostic services, social and vocational rehabilitation, precare and after-care, training of mental health personnel, and research and evaluation of program effectiveness and the problems of mental illness.

Finally, in 1965, legislation was passed that mandated funds for the personnel to be employed in these "comp care" centers. These "staffing grants" were intended to provide funding for the first several years of operation, after which financial responsibility would be shifted to the individual states, health insurance, direct fees, and other sources.

The comprehensive care system continues to be an important ingredient in this country's mental health effort, although its role is not as prominent as originally intended. On balance, the system is a modest, expensive attainment. Its major achievement was that, with the help of antipsychotic drugs, it dramatically reduced the patient population in mental institutions. It also opened up mental health services by including paraprofessionals on treatment staffs and by offering community supervision or after-care as an alternative to custodial confinement. A final noteworthy accomplishment was that it made mental health services available to people who had not typically been served by the mental health system.

One of the greatest limitations of the comprehensive care model has been financial (Schulberg & Killilea, 1982). Since the late 1960s the federal government's commitment to mental health financing has been very weak. As a consequence, only a minority of the planned centers were actually constructed, and very few are adequately funded. In addition, many centers have suffered severe reductions in staff because the original federal staffing grants have run out and have not been replaced.

The community mental health move-

ment also has been criticized at a philosophical level. Many critics argued that it merely placed the old wine of the medical model in the new bottle of community centers, while leaving intact a medical view of mental health services. A second objection concerned the fact that comprehensive care centers are not oriented toward *prevention* of human distress (Cowen, 1973). Another criticism has been that comprehensive care centers' services are still not sought by persons who may be in need of them because of financial limitations, cultural barriers, geographic isolation, bureaucratic red tape, and the fear of being stigmatized. A related point stressed by almost all critics of the comprehensive care system is what they view as insufficient community participation in the planning and direction of the centers.

The current skepticism surrounding comprehensive care centers may be linked partly to the unrealistic optimism that greeted their creation. Great expectations run the risk of becoming great disappointments. But disappointments have an educational value: They can point us in new directions. From this perspective, disappointments about the community mental health center model have forced psychologists to reconsider and extend the innovations that led to the modern community mental health movement. The remainder of this chapter concentrates on such extensions, because they comprise an important part of community psychology.

Community Psychology's Formal Beginning

The formal birth of community psychology was in the spring of 1965 in Swampscott, Massachusetts (a Boston suburb), where more than thirty psychologists, many employed in community mental health centers, issued a call for community psychologists who would be "change agents, social system analysts, consultants in community affairs, and students generally of the whole man in relation to all his environments"

(Bennett, 1965, p. 833). The community psychologist was to be a *participant-conceptualizer:* Someone who tries to change social conditions as much as understand them.

This conference stressed three principles for the new profession. First, community psychology should not be limited to combating mental illness. Rather, it must work for "community well-being" and "furthering normal development" (Bennett, 1965). Second, community psychologists should promote community growth through planned social action and the scientific method. Finally, community psychology must be broader than community mental health, which, as we have seen, retained many of the trappings of the medical model.

Today, community psychology is in its third decade. Its accomplishments are recorded in several professional journals (*The American Journal of Community Psychology, The Community Mental Health Journal,* and *The Journal of Community Psychology*). It has been surveyed and evaluated in several textbooks (e.g., Glenwick & Jason, 1980; Heller, Price, Reinharz, Riger & Wandersman, 1984; Mann, 1978; Murrell, 1973; Rappaport, 1977; Seidman, 1983). Since 1967 there has been a division of community psychology within the American Psychological Association, and several thousand psychologists are now members.

The training of community psychologists has also become an important activity of graduate psychology programs. In 1962 there was one program offering an M.A. or Ph.D. in community psychology and community mental health. By 1975 there were sixty-two (Meyer & Garrard, 1977). The current status of training community psychologists is explored thoroughly in a special April 1984 issue of *The American Journal of Community Psychology.*

Principles of Community Psychology

Rappaport and Chinsky (1974) proposed that any model of mental health service has two basic components—a *conceptual component* and a *style of delivery component.* According to Rappaport (1977), the conceptual component is the model's fundamental theory of human behavior; it "dictates the empirical data base, theoretical notions and basic assumptions for understanding human behavior" (p. 72). The style of delivery component, on the other hand, "dictates how the service called for by the conceptual component will be offered to the target population" (Rappaport, 1977, pp. 72–73).

Community psychology can be analyzed from this perspective if we realize that it involves several principles that can be organized under either the conceptual or style of delivery headings. When taken together, these ideas form the nucleus of the field and serve to differentiate it from clinical psychology. We address ourselves first to five principles related to the conceptual side of community psychology.

Conceptual Principles. *1 The ecological perspective.* The community psychologist believes that behavior cannot be explained solely through individual factors. Change in the behavior of individuals often needs to be preceded by change in social institutions. The community psychologist views social, environmental, and political factors as important determinants of behavior and will seek changes in the communities or subcommunities into which individuals must fit.

The ecological perspective means that the psychologist must look for causes of behavior at several nonpsychological levels. For example, the child whose constant misbehavior in the classroom leads her to be labeled hyperactive may have a neurological impairment that is the basis of the problem. But the behavior may also be due to a classroom whose organization rewards underachievement, a curriculum whose subject matter is too easy for her level of development, or a peer culture that devalues academic achievement. The ecological perspective directs attention to the role that social and environmental forces might play in the development of this problem.

2 Social-system change. The type of change implied by the ecological perspective is often termed *social-system-level change,* as distinguished from *person-oriented change.* Social-system changes are intended to make the social institutions in our lives more growth-enhancing. Changes in social systems can occur at a low level, such as when one classroom in a school system begins to use a token economy to increase class participation. Social changes also can occur at a higher level, such as when a group of parents, dissatisfied with the quality of public education, begins its own alternative school. This is not to say that community psychologists never use person-oriented interventions. They do, often with the belief that they can be extremely successful, but their preference is for social-system changes because these are thought to present the greatest opportunity to bring about important changes in large numbers of people. They also believe that some social-system interventions can prevent, rather than just remediate, emotional problems.

3 Prevention. The quest for prevention is the cardinal feature of community psychology. Prevention is community psychology's *summum bonum;* it is also very rarely achieved.

Caplan (1964) identified three types of prevention: tertiary, secondary, and primary. *Tertiary prevention* aims to minimize the severity of illness, reduce the short- and long-term consequences of the disorder, and contain the disturbance so that personal effectiveness is retained. Tertiary prevention is prevention in name only. Almost any form of treatment can claim to being tertiary prevention.

Secondary prevention aims for a reduction in the prevalence of illness through the coordinated efforts of early detection and effective intervention, or, as a cab driver was quoted as saying, "getting to people before

they go nuts" (Schaar, 1978). For this reason, instruments that allow reliable and valid diagnosis early in the course of a problem are essential for secondary prevention. Secondary prevention is often directed at elementary school children because of the relationship between early school maladaptation and later adjustment problems and because schools can be a vehicle for optimizing personal as well as educational growth.

An example of this approach is the Primary Mental Health Project (PMHP) of Cowen and his colleagues at the University of Rochester (Cowen, Gesten & Wilson, 1979; Weissberg, Cowen, Lotyczewski & Gesten, 1983). The PMHP uses quick-screening techniques to identify primary schoolers who are having educational and behavioral problems. "At-risk" children are then seen by trained, nonprofessional child aides, who help the children cope with their difficulties and build new skills. Outcome data on the PMHP suggest that the participants experience both behavioral and educational improvements (Cowen et al., 1979), but Stein and Polyson (1984) offer a more skeptical vie. The majority of preventive programs in community psychology have taken place at this secondary level.

Primary prevention involves the reduction and elimination of disorders by either modifying the pathogenic qualities of the environment or bolstering individuals' resources to the point where disorder will not occur. Primary prevention can be accomplished by *social action,* where changes in community institutions are made to reduce problems, or through *interpersonal action,* in which the goal is to enhance individuals' competencies at dealing with certain problems. Urban renewal, legal reforms, and some forms of social welfare are examples of the first type of prevention. Family intervention, parent education, and the training of coping skills are examples of prevention through interpersonal action.

4 Crisis intervention. *Crisis intervention* plays a prominent role in the work of many community psychologists. People face many types of crises in their lives. There are the predictable crises of development, such as beginning school and finding a job. As personality theorists have emphasized, maturation also involves a series of psychological problems that must be resolved for optimal personality growth to occur (e.g., Erikson, 1963; Sullivan, 1953). Other crises are less predictable and occur before the person is prepared for them: Serious illness, the death of a loved one, and natural disasters like fires or floods are examples.

In most cases, individuals confronted by a crisis are able to cope with the situation. In some cases, however, the crisis remains unsolved either because the person has limited resources for coping or because the problem is an especially intense and difficult one. As a result, the individual suffers emotional upset. If the crisis continues for a long time, serious personality disturbances may ensue.

Crisis intervention is a technique for helping people deal effectively with problems at the time they are occurring. The most influential contribution to crisis intervention was the work of Erich Lindemann (1944) and his associate Gerald Caplan (1961). Lindemann's notions of crisis therapy were based on his work with relatives of victims of the tragic 1943 fire at the Coconut Grove, a Boston nightclub. Lindemann concluded that there were stages of grief people must go through in order to adjust to the loss of a loved one. He further demonstrated that grieving people could be helped in working through the stages of the bereavement process by therapy aimed at the crisis itself, rather than at the person's personality.

The goals of crisis intervention are usually more limited than those pursued in psychotherapy (Aguilera & Messick, 1982; McGee, 1983). Butcher and Koss (1978) list the following common objectives of crisis intervention: (1) relief of the client's primary symptoms as rapidly as possible, (2) prompt reestablishment of the client's previous emotional stability, and (3) development of the client's understanding of the current disturbance and its precipitating factors, as well as an enhanced ability to cope with crises in the future.

Crisis intervention can also be distinguished from psychotherapy on the basis of the techniques used therein. Crisis intervention is usually brief. In most cases treatment would not be expected to exceed six weeks. The crisis intervener is more likely than the average therapist to focus on the primary problem area, to be interested in the here and now rather than past reasons for the problem, and to offer direct advice and information about alternative forms of desirable behavior. In crisis intervention, a premium is placed on gathering assessment information as efficiently as possible, preferably in the initial session. The development of a therapeutic relationship is considered important, but a compromise must be struck between the evolution of this relationship and the limited time available for treatment.

5 Promoting a "psychological sense of community." Beyond solving immediate problems, the community psychologist is concerned with strengthening the ability of a community to plan and create its own change. This emphasis is what Sarason (1974) has called the "psychological sense of community":

I have never met anyone—young or old, rich or poor, black or white, male or female, educated or not—to whom I have had any great difficulty explaining what I meant by the psychological sense of community. My explanation or language varied, of course, depending on whom I was talking with, but it never took long for them to comprehend that what I was getting at was the sense that one was part of a readily available, mutually supportive network of relationships upon which one could depend and as a result of which one did not experience sustained feelings of loneliness that impel one to actions or to adopting a style of living masking anxiety and setting the stage for later and more destructive anguish. It is not merely a matter of how many people one knows, or how many close friends one has, or even the number of loved ones—if they are scattered all over the country or world, if they are not part of the structure of one's everyday living, and if they are not available to one in a 'give and get' way, they can have little effect on one's immediate or daily sense of community. Indeed, for many people these treasured but only occasionally available relationships accentuate the lack of a feeling of community . . . (p. 351).

Community psychologists try to create this sense of community by developing people's strengths rather than eliminating their weaknesses. Increasing a community's competence and shared sense of purpose requires that community psychologists tolerate or even increase the positive diversity of the people they encounter. The ways in which a community insures its safety, educates its children, protects its environment, promotes its health, and establishes a sense of vitality in its citizens usually represent a small portion of available means to desired ends. The successful community psychologist helps people create effective alternatives to existing social institutions by treating their cultural preferences and differences as assets rather than liabilities, a strategy that has been termed *empowerment* (Rappaport, 1981).

Style of Delivery. The second way of defining a model of mental health service concerns the *style of service delivery*. Below are three important principles of delivery style from the perspective of community psychology.

1 Expansion of professional roles. Clinical psychologists usually offer *direct services* to clients who, because they have some psychological complaint, are willing to pay for them. Community psychologists, on the other hand, emphasize *indirect services* that have no single target client, but which are expected to achieve benefits because the social-system changes they produce radiate to the intended target groups.

Consultation is a common activity for the community psychologist. Community psy-

chologists have placed greater reliance on this type of intervention than have clinical psychologists (see O'Neill & Trickett, 1982; or Schulberg & Jerrell, 1983, for a review of consultation within community psychology).

Another example of expanding roles for community psychologists is the preparation of *volunteers, paraprofessionals,* and *nonprofessionals* for behavior-change functions typically reserved for the professional. These include child care workers, mental health workers, self-help group leaders, peer counselors, and abortion counselors. The use of nonprofessionals in these roles is seen as having social advantages and ideological justifications. The nonprofessional movement creates meaningful careers for poor people, provides troubled people with help from persons with whom they share a cultural heritage, and provides a new source of workers necessary for adequate delivery of mental health services.

In many cases, helpers are drawn directly from the groups that will receive the services. These workers have been called *indigenous nonprofessionals,* and their cultural rootedness within a target group is considered one of their fundamental assets. In other instances paraprofessionals are drawn from groups with a high commitment to service but with a cheap price tag for their labor. College students and housewives are ubiquitous volunteers, and they have been used as mental health workers in many settings. Community psychologists may also train relatives (Guerney, 1969), peers (Harris & Sherman, 1973), teachers (Meyers, 1975), and friends (Sulzer, 1965) to initiate behavior-change conditions or to maintain conditions that had been introduced during a professional intervention.

2 Use of activism. Social action has been considered both an essential contribution and an unnecessary evil in community psychology. Advocates of activist tactics claim that professionals' willingness to provoke, agitate, and confront is what accounts for a large measure of their effectiveness.

Opponents of professional social action argue that such activity is incompatible with the objective empiricism that is the scientist's defining characteristic.

In the present context, social activism refers to the use of *power* as a resource to accomplish social reform. This power may be economic, it may be political, or it may be the coercive power of civil disobedience, as people struggle to assert their human rights. Power can be manipulated through publicity, and it is for this reason that community psychologists try to cultivate media contacts in order to spread their influence. Finally, power resides in positions of leadership. Psychologists may seek employment where they have access to the formation of social policy. A member of an urban planning team, a consultant to the city council, an advisor to legislators, a director of a citizen's advocate group, the head of a social-service agency—these are all jobs with the potential to influence social change.

3 Use of research as a form of intervention. Community psychologists are likely to view research as a way of producing change. This is particularly true in the case of *evaluation research,* which compares the effects of a new program against existing programs or against no intervention at all. In the event that an experimental procedure is associated with greater benefits than alternative programs, the researcher can argue that that procedure should be implemented on a more permanent basis.

Experimentation from this perspective is a technique of demonstration and persuasion. George Fairweather, a psychologist at Michigan State University, coined the phrase *experimental social innovation* to describe research which, after demonstrating the value of a new program, can be used to support that program's implementation. Research as intervention is also exemplified by what is called *dissemination research.* This is experimentation designed to evaluate alternative methods of implementing those programs that initial evaluation research has

shown to be successful. In the course of finding the most effective means of persuading other communities to adopt a given program, that program is, by necessity, adopted. The best example of dissemination research is George Fairweather's experimental project on the effectiveness of different approaches to persuading mental hospitals to adopt an outpatient "lodge program" designed for chronic mental patients (Fairweather, Sanders & Tornatzky, 1974). The research investigated what techniques were most effective in activating the lodge program once a decision to adopt it had been made and explored the procedures used in spreading the lodge approach to other mental health programs (Fairweather, 1980).

Examples of Community Psychology

One of the best ways to understand community psychology is to examine what a typical practitioner of it does. In this section we present a few examples from many that we could have chosen in the educational system, preschool programs, day care, community organization, urban planning and development, the juvenile justice system, social service agencies, community treatment of the chronically ill, and training of paraprofessional workers.

We focus on the criminal justice system, an area in which preventive, ecologically conceived interventions have often been pursued (Nietzel & Himelein, 1986). One approach to the prevention of crime is *competence building,* or the development of abilities to meet stressful demands and attain desirable objectives. The area of competence building is a useful one to examine in some detail because it illustrates the two components essential to sound primary prevention (Cowen, 1983)—a generative base that provides the knowledge and rationale for interventions and an executive base that implements and evaluates programs of prevention.

Generative Base

Cognitive and Behavioral Controls. The leading spokesman for the relationship between early behavioral deficits and high risk for delinquency has been George Spivack of Hahnemann University. His fifteen-year longitudinal study of 660 randomly selected Philadelphia kindergarten children sought to identify behavior patterns during the elementary school year that would discriminate children at high risk for subsequent delinquency and misconduct in the community (Spivack & Cianci, 1983). Data were collected on such predictors as teacher ratings of classroom behavior, academic performance, special class placement, and substance use, which were then related to multiple criteria of delinquency and conduct disorder.

Spivack and Cianci (1983) report a cluster of behavior factors emerging as early as kindergarten that identified the children most vulnerable to delinquency. Those children who show the high-risk, poor self-regulator pattern were rated as significantly elevated on classroom disturbance, impatience, disrespect/defiance, external blame, and irrelevant responsiveness.

These problems suggest a pervasive difficulty in these youngsters' ability to conform to external controls and "to modulate their behaviors so as to accommodate to others around them" (Spivack & Cianci, 1983, p. 27). Such behaviors are likely to elicit aversive peer responses and critical, angry, or aggressive adult reprisal, which in turn lead to youths' repudiation of authority. The sequence accelerates in a negative direction beginning with social demands for behavioral control, followed by children's failure to cope, intensified by adult demands for compliance, which in turn provokes more intentionally hostile reactions from youngsters, and so on. Unless broken, this chain of behavior culminates in defiance of institutionalized authority and the type of antisocial behavior that typifies official delinquency. The school is particularly important in the sequence because it generalizes the negative affect surrounding coping failures to a public setting. Antisocial patterns are most likely to persist when they have early onset, assume a variety of forms, and are displayed in diverse settings (Kazdin, 1985; Loeber & Dishion, 1983).

Academic Achievement. In their review of predictors of male delinquency, Loeber and Dishion (1983) listed poor academic performance as one of the five variables showing the best predictive validity for official delinquency. Although the literature is quite consistent that academic difficulties during the primary years are not powerful predictors of later delinquency, academic problems do correlate with adolescent-age conduct disorder and delinquency (Spivack & Cianci, 1983), a finding consistent with Loeber and Dishion's (1983) conclusion that grade-point average does not become predictive of delinquency until approximately age fifteen. Poor academic performance appears to be a consequence of the early dyscontrol behavioral pattern and accompanies rather than directly influences delinquent and antisocial behaviors from the midadolescent years on.

Employment. Glaser (1964) reported that postrelease employment is the best predictor of offenders' nonrecividism; Frykholm, Gunne, and Hursfeldt (1976) found that being employed was one of the most reliable correlates of rehabilitation success with heroin addicts. The relationship between economic indicators and incidence of crime has been assumed to be an inverse one, with offense rates highest among the lowest SES classes. Tittle, Villence, and Smith's (1978) meta-analysis of the social class and criminality literature indicates that this inverse relationship is actually confined to pre-1950 studies, with no relationship revealed by data collected in the 1970s. Seidman and Rapkin (1983) conclude that for young adolescents, increases in prosperity are associated with higher arrest rates, while for men in their twenties and thirties the relationship between unemployment and arrests is strongly positive, as traditionally assumed. Relational factors such as income disparity and relative rates of employment as compared to certain reference groups appear to be more important predictors of offense rates than do absolute measures of economic standing (see Seidman & Rapkin, 1983, pp. 192–194).

Executive Base

Competence-building programs will be most effective in preventing delinquency when they are aimed at the specific deficiencies which at different ages of high-risk populations are most strongly related to delinquency. Among primary-school youth, the target should be helping children develop the cognitive and behavior controls necessary for impulse control and well-regulated interpersonal behaviors. Among adolescents, the aim might shift to improving academic performance that would make it more likely for at-risk students to stay committed to the conventional norms of educational achievement. Programs to enhance occupational and employment skills would seem to have maximal preventive impact when delivered to individuals in their twenties and thirties.

A number of studies have attempted to improve primary-schoolers' problem solving, social skills, and cognitive abilities. Spivack and colleagues (Shure & Spivack, 1982; Spivack, Platt & Shure, 1976) have developed and evaluated an interpersonal cognitive problem-solving (ICPS) intervention designed to prevent the dyscontrol pattern that has been found to precede delinquent behavior. In ICPS training, children are taught to improve their alternative solution thinking, means-end cognition, and social role-taking ability. Thinking about problems in terms of options and consequences, increasing general reflectiveness, and sharpening social perceptiveness and sensitivity have been linked to several criteria of adjustment (Weissberg et al., 1981). However, the linkage between ICPS and behavioral

adjustment has not been as solid as initially assumed because (1) many research designs have not adequately measured such linkage, and (2) the relationship between ICPS and adjustment appears to be moderated by factors such as sociodemographics, age, and IQ (McKim, Weissberg, Cowen, Gesten & Rapkin, 1982).

An example of a preventive intervention aimed at the academic achievement of adolescents is Bry and George's (1980) behaviorally based program for students experiencing school failures. Forty urban adolescents were randomly assigned to either a control or an intervention that (1) provided systematic feedback to students and their parents about the students' school performance, (2) rewarded students for appropriate academic behavior, and (3) instructed students how to earn more points for classroom performance. The intervention lasted two years and resulted in improved attendance and grades for participating students. However, it required the full two years before any differential effects were detected. Follow-up evaluation of this project confirmed that reduced delinquency was associated with the intervention one and five years after termination, although substance abuse was not differentially affected (Bry, 1982).

Psychologists' attempts to influence employability among underemployed samples have involved behaviorally oriented training programs designed to improve job-seeking and job-interviewing skills. Noteworthy among these projects is the work of Sharon Hall and her colleagues at the University of California at San Francisco. Hall, Loeb, Coyne, and Cooper (1981) randomly assigned fifty-five probationers and parolees to either an eleven-hour behaviorally based job seekers' workshop or to a three-hour informational workshop. Participants were all heroin abusers.

The experimental workshop had three components: training for job interviews, instruction in completion of employment forms, and job-search procedures. Training emphasized role playing, coaching appropriate verbal and nonverbal behaviors, practicing simulated job interviews, and videotaped feedback. Following training, participants were assessed on a simulated interview conducted by employees of a vocational rehabilitation service. Experimental participants were superior to controls, particularly on specific interview behaviors. Four-, eight-, and twelve-week follow-ups were conducted on percentage of participants who had a job, what salary they received, and how many job interviews they had attended. At the twelve-week follow-up, 85.7 percent of the project participants versus 54 percent of the information-only controls had a full- or part-time job. This difference was significant, as it had been from the first week following the program.

Results of this study were partially replicated by Hall, Loeb, LeVois, and Cooper (1981) with sixty methadone maintenance clients, over 40 percent of whom were on probation and parole. At a three-month follow-up, more treatment participants (52 percent) than controls (30 percent) had obtained employment. An additional finding of this study was that participants who had not been employed at all in the past five years did not find employment, regardless of treatment condition. Behavioral enhancement of employment skills is not limited to drug offenders. Twentyman, Jensen, and Kloss (1978) reported that a mixed group of adult offenders receiving a behavioral training program were more effective on a mock job interview and tended to obtain employment more quickly than offenders given monetary incentives for attending interviews.

Training of job skills for offenders is not prevention, except in the tertiary or possibly secondary sense. However, the relationship between employment and crime rates among critical age groups warrants the development of employment-enhancement programs with primary prevention as an objective.

There are many other examples that could be used to show how a community psychologist might work within the criminal justice system. Procedural reforms, developing halfway houses, investigating the effects of certain parts of the criminal law, probation and parole reform, and diverting offenders from the system itself are all important activities that community-oriented psychologists have advocated.

An Evaluation of Community Psychology

Critiques of community psychology have been aimed at what it has accomplished as well as what it has failed to accomplish.

Rhetoric versus Results. The most general criticism of community psychology is that its tenets are oversold and its accomplishments exaggerated. Community psychologists have been prolific in pointing out what is wrong with society and the mental health professions' efforts at correction, but they have been less adept at coming up with a technology that produces specific, durable changes. This criticism claims that the rhetoric of the community psychology camp has not been matched by results.

The Status of Prevention. Primary prevention is the one promise community psychology must keep if it is to remain a viable intervention strategy. What accomplishments from primary prevention can community psychologists claim? That is the bottom-line question that requires an honest confrontation with data. The fact of the matter is that, historically, aspirations for prevention have far outdistanced achievements. For all its good intentions and enthusiasm, community psychology can lay claim to precious few examples of effective primary prevention (Cowen, 1977).

For example, Novaco and Monahan (1980) classified the research published in the first six volumes of the *American Journal of Community Psychology*. They found that only 2.4 percent of the articles dealt with primary prevention; only 10.2 percent dealt with secondary prevention. Furthermore, 87 percent of the published empirical studies were unrelated to primary or secondary prevention, and this was true even using a very liberal definition of "prevention" (authors' own characterizations of their work)! Novaco and Monahan (1980) concluded that "the majority of research published in the field's leading journal has little to do with the stated objectives of the discipline" (p. 143).

The following apologies can be offered for prevention's poor track record: (1) The history of psychology's preventive efforts is very short and it is premature to offer a final evaluation; (2) we can't mount good prevention programs until we generate good theories of etiology, vulnerability, and dysfunction; (3) most professionals are so unacquainted with examples of primary prevention that they confuse it with its secondary or tertiary imitators and miss out on the real thing.

There is another challenge to the idea of prevention which the field has barely begun to consider. It is the contention that prevention is not the best way to conceptualize the activities of community psychology, because even if it is effective, it carries sufficient negative implications as a way of "solving" problems that we should resist institutionalizing it as the best approach to intervention.

What are the negative implications of prevention? The most comprehensive answer is given by Rappaport (1981), who warns against the dangers of pursuing any "one-sided" intervention, whether it be psychotherapy or prevention. In Rappaport's (1981) words:

Partly because institutions have a tendency to become one-sided many social problems are ironically and inadvertently created by the so-called helping systems . . . and often "solutions" create more problems than they solve. (p. 8)

That social institutions and professions create as well as solve problems is *not* a call for working

harder to find the single best technique or lamenting the failure of our best minds to be creative. Quite the opposite. It *is a problem to be understood as contained in the basic nature of the subject matter of our field.* It will always be this way. There can never be a now and for all time single scientific "breakthrough" which settles and solves the puzzles of our discipline. Today's solution must be tomorrow's problem. (p. 9; italics in original)

What are the dilemmas created by the pursuit of prevention? Rappaport points to two main problems. First, there is professionalization and the harm involved when preventive programs become paternalistic and patronizing. Typically enacted by experts, preventive programs run the risk of overpowering the naturally existing strengths and coping abilities that reside in any population. As a result, recipients may lose actual and perceived control over their own lives as they yield to the myth that mental health professionals know best how to solve problems (see Lenrow & Cowden, 1980).

A related problem associated with prevention is the "psychologicalizing" of problems in living to the point where prevention is legitimized as an intervention even though it may be unnecessary. Rappaport (1981) describes this "overreach" problem as "a new arena for colonization" that "underlies much of what is called prevention: find so-called high-risk people and save them from themselves, if they like it or not, by giving them, or even better, their children, programs which we develop, package, sell, operate, or otherwise control" (p. 13).

While fundamental questions about primary prevention are debated, many psychologists are still working hard at developing preventive programs, and there are recent indications that prevention of some emotional-social problems may be attainable. Indeed, Cowen (1980), whose reading of prevention's vital signs we have come to trust, points to five promising areas in the field of prevention: mental health education, social-system analysis and modification, competence building, stress reduction and coping, and fortification of support systems. Reviews of successful preventive programs can be found in two recent comprehensive handbooks on prevention by Felner, Jason, Moritsugu, and Farber (1983) and Michelson and Edelstein (1986); a special 1982 issue of the *American Journal of Community Psychology* presents some high-quality studies of primary prevention.

Prevention has also made inroads into traditional clinical psychology (Levy, 1984; Watkins, 1985) as clinicians have become more interested in the promotion of physical and psychological health (see Chapter 11). The ideas of stress and coping provide a common ground for clinicians and community psychologists to understand dysfunction and to develop interventions for protecting vulnerable persons against effects of stress (Nietzel & Banks, 1983; see also a special issue of the *American Journal of Community Psychology* in August 1979, which examined the role of stressful life events in the community).

Another theoretical framework that allows integration of the philosophy of community psychologists with the techniques of clinicians is *behavioral community psychology* (Glenwick & Jason, 1980; Nietzel, Winett, MacDonald & Davidson, 1977). This field involves a synthesis of behavior modification techniques with the philosophy and style of community psychology. The advantages of this alliance are to be found in the complementary strengths the two areas provide each other. Behavioral interventions have been effectively used in one-to-one treatment of moderately distressed individuals or in institutional settings with chronically disturbed patients. They have not usually been used preventively or with an intention to produce large-scale changes in society. On the other hand, community psychologists have lacked effective techniques for bringing about the changes in environments or persons that they desire. Joining the ecological perspective of community psychologists with the efficacious techniques of be-

havior modifiers is a merger that may make possible an empirically based science of social change.

Overreach. In addition to overstating its achievements, community psychology has been accused of losing sight of its appropriate and realistic objectives. For example, the idea that communities, not individuals, are the clients in need of modification elicited a well-known critique from Warren Dunham (1965), a sociologist who labeled the community movement the "newest therapeutic bandwagon," claiming that the new interest in the community is a compensation for the frustration many clinicians have experienced in their unsuccessful attempts to treat chronic mental disorders.

Ethical Objections. Community psychology has evoked many ethical concerns. A common fear is that community programs, particularly those aimed at prevention, may threaten individual freedoms and rights. Halleck (1969) expressed concern that the community movement would result in an increasing encroachment on privacy and the right to live our lives the way we please.

There are at least two reasons why this particular fear may be somewhat exaggerated. First, Americans are notably resistant to controls and coercion. Our mistrust of undue regulation from any source, whether it is political, military, or medical, has been effective protection against most excesses of control. At present, this quality appears sufficiently strong to prevent possible abuses by the overly zealous community psychologist.

Second, we must return to the issue of community psychology's record of accomplishment. Outside the area of delivering traditional mental health services to larger segments of the population, the community movement has not produced many preventive programs or social-system-level changes. Community psychology's most pressing current ethical dilemma is not so much the threat of doing too much to communities as of doing too little.

Other ethical objections have been raised at one time or another about community psychology. Some critics fear that increasing the emphasis on prevention will distract professionals from offering the intensive treatment severely disturbed clients require (Lamb & Zusman, 1981). This is unlikely, since the mental health fields suffered from an insufficiency of professional personnel long before community psychology came along. Other critics contend that there is danger in the early identification and treatment associated with secondary prevention. By being too aggressive in finding "at-risk" persons, the psychologist may damage them with premature labels. More than a decade ago, Ullmann and Krasner (1975) warned that "case finding" should not turn into "case making."

Finally, there is uncertainty about exactly who it is in a community that decides the goals of community interventions. Is it the psychologist, the recipients of the program, the majority of the community, or only influential leaders? Community psychologists assure us that the aims of their interventions are directed by the people they serve. Zax and Specter (1974) claim: "The notion of a community psychology would be impossible were it not for the fact that, because of the unity of social problems, need is felt for it at a grass roots level" (p. 325). This may be true, but the notion of community participation is a complex ideal made all the more difficult by the frequent value conflicts between community residents and professional psychologists.

Final Thoughts on Community Psychology

Today, community psychology is a field that can point to important accomplishments, but it must also admit to substantial shortcomings. Its emphasis on prevention, its attention to stressful environments, and its concern with well-being (as opposed to pathology) have been incorporated into other applied areas of psychology, particularly clinical psychology and health psychology, with impressive success. Despite or perhaps because of these achievements, community psychologists continue to struggle with their sense of identity and purpose. As prevention is absorbed into other subfields of psychology, community psychology is threatened with a loss of distinctiveness. Felner (1985) suggests that community psychology has a special role as the "generic base" of prevention knowledge and research, and that its future contributions will best be realized in those areas. Iscoe and Harris (1984) also recommend that it is in research and consultation that community psychologists can make their most decisive impact.

chapter 8

Clinical Intervention: Psychodynamic Models

During most of the twentieth century psychotherapy has been derived mainly from the psychodynamic theories of Sigmund Freud. His *psychoanalysis*, which was a method of treatment, a theory of personality, and a means of studying human behavior, revolutionized psychiatry and altered forever the ways in which people think about themselves. Freud's voluminous writings also stimulated many followers and opponents to extend and revise his ideas. Today there is a spectrum of psychodynamically oriented theories ranging from classical or "orthodox" psychoanalysis (which closely follows Freud's tenets) to systems that not only reject some of Freud's basic beliefs, but actually overlap with phenomenological or behavioral models. There is a corresponding array of psychodynamic treatment approaches, and in this chapter we describe the basic techniques and the effectiveness of a few prominent examples. We begin our discussion with Freud.

PSYCHOANALYTIC TREATMENT

Sigmund Freud was the founder of psychotherapy as we know it today. His one-to-one method of studying and helping people; his systematic search for relationships between a person's history and current problems; his emphasis on conflict, thoughts, and emotions; and his focus on the therapist-patient relationship pervade nearly all modern treatment modalities. Where did Freud's ideas come from?

It will not be possible here to provide a complete account of Freud's life or the evolution of his thought, so a brief sketch will have to suffice. More complete coverage can be found in Fancher (1973) as well as in several other sources (e.g., Ford & Urban, 1963; Munroe, 1955). Those seeking detailed material should consult Ernest Jones's monumental three-volume biography, *The Life and Work of Sigmund Freud* (1953, 1955, 1957), Clark's *Freud: The Man and the Cause*

(1980), or translations of Freud's own works (e.g., Brill, 1938; Freud, 1953–1964).

The Beginnings of Psychoanalytic Treatment

Freud was born in Freiberg, Moravia (now Czechoslovakia), on May 6, 1856, the son of a Jewish wool merchant. His family moved to Vienna, Austria, where, at the age of nine, Freud entered Gymnasium, a sort of advanced high school. He was originally interested in law or politics, but prior to graduation, an essay on nature by the poet Goethe prompted him to concentrate on natural science instead. In 1873, at the age of seventeen, Freud entered the University of Vienna medical school. Research interested him more than routine course work, and he spent most of his time on research projects in the university's Institute of Physiology. As a result, it took Freud eight years to complete his medical degree.

His efforts during this period led to his discovering the location of the sex organs in the male eel and the accumulation of a great deal of new information about neurology. More important than these studies themselves was Freud's introduction to the concept of neurological *mechanism*. This view held that the activity of the nervous system was based on electrochemical factors that obeyed laws of physics and chemistry. An implication of mechanistic theory was that human behavior could be explained in *physical* terms and that lawful relationships about human behavior were possible. These notions had a profound effect on Freud's later work.

In the 1880s it was virtually impossible to make a living as a research scientist. This fact, coupled with Freud's desire to marry his sweetheart, Martha Bernays, caused him to change his career to the more lucrative field of medical practice. In 1882 Freud began three years of clinical training at Vienna General Hospital. This was an era when the medical model of behavior disorder was resurgent; there was a diligent search for the

organic causes presumed to underlie all mental illness. The director of the Vienna Hospital psychiatric clinic was Theodor Meynert, an authority on brain anatomy and pathology whose work impressed Freud. Meynert believed, for example, that patterns of neural activity in the brain correspond to various thoughts or memories, and that psychological phenomena are due to nerve cell activity which, in turn, is based on electrochemical events.

This psychological extension of mechanistic theory led Freud to believe that the best way to blend his research interests in neurology with his clinical work was to study and treat diseases of the nervous system in humans. By 1886 Freud had enough background (and money) to begin the private practice of medicine. He also married in that year. One of the people who helped Freud begin his private practice was Joseph Breuer, a senior medical colleague and close friend. Breuer's early attempts to cure certain unusual symptoms in his patients ultimately led Freud to the development of psychoanalysis.

Freud often saw patients with symptoms of neurological damage for which no organic cause could be found. These cases displayed what Freud called "neurological nonsense." For example, patients sometimes complained of insensitivity or paralysis that affected their entire hand, but not their arm. Others suffered paralysis of the legs during the day, but walked in their sleep. Patients of this type were called *neurotics*. Since the cause, let alone the cure, for their problems was so obscure, most physicians ignored them, assuming that neurotic symptoms were either phony or the result of character defects.

Freud often dealt with the most common type of neurotic patients: those displaying *hysterical* (i.e., nonorganic) paralyses, amnesia, anesthesia, blindness, and speech loss. Treatment for hysteria mainly involved the use of "wet packs" and baths (hydrotherapy) or electrically generated heat (electrotherapy), neither of which was effective. Freud

FIGURE 8-1.   Sigmund Freud (1856–1939). (Courtesy of Historical Pictures Service, Inc., Chicago, Illinois. Reprinted by permission.)

became convinced that whatever benefits patients received from these procedures were due to suggestion. Accordingly, he began to experiment with techniques that maximized the benefits of suggestion, foremost among which was *hypnosis*.

In Freud's time hypnosis was generally regarded as a magician's trick, beneath the dignity of serious physicians and scientists. This view was prompted mainly by the theatrics and bizarre theories of Anton Mesmer, the first promoter of hypnosis or *mesmerism*. Nevertheless, hypnosis was studied seriously by a few individuals who used it to cure hysterical disorders.

Freud's familiarity with hypnosis began when he spent six months studying in Paris with Jean Charcot, director of the neurology clinic at the Salpetriere asylum. Charcot showed that hysterical symptoms could be created and temporarily removed through induction of a hypnotic trance and thus that hysteria and hypnosis were related phenomena. In fact, Charcot believed that only hysterics could be hypnotized. Later, in the French city of Nancy, Freud visited a clinic organized by Ambrose-August Liebault and Hippolyte Bernheim. These two physicians believed that the ability to be hypnotized was not a symptom of nervous disorder, but a routine phenomenon attainable with normal individuals. Liebault and Bernheim used hypnotic suggestions to remove hysterical symptoms, with limited, often temporary, success. Freud's use of hypnotic suggestion produced equally mediocre results, but around 1890 he began to combine hypnosis with a new technique he learned from Joseph Breuer.

Breuer had stumbled on this technique, called the *cathartic method*, while attempting to relieve the hysterical symptoms of a wealthy young woman, Anna O. These symptoms included headaches, a severe cough, neck and arm paralyses, involuntary squinting, anesthesia in both elbows, and other problems. Her difficulties began during her father's illness and intensified following his death. She began to display ex-

tremes of mood which went from agitation and hallucinations during the day to calm, trancelike states in the evenings. Breuer was struck by the fact that these "trances" resembled hypnosis. Fancher (1973, p. 48) describes what happened next:

> Breuer discovered that if Anna were permitted while in the hypnotic state to recite the contents of all her hallucinations from the day, then she invariably would leave the trance state and enjoy a period of almost normal tranquility and lucidity during the following late night hours. . . . Anna came to refer to the exercise of reciting her hallucinations as the "talking cure," or . . . "chimney sweeping."

This "talking cure" did not eliminate Anna's daytime disorders, however. To Breuer's dismay, new symptoms began to appear. It was in attempting to cure one of these, an inability to drink liquids, that Breuer made the discovery that would later start Freud on the road to psychoanalysis:

> During one of Anna's hypnotic states . . . she began describing to Breuer an Englishwoman whom she knew but did not especially like. The woman had a dog that Anna particularly despised. Anna described how on one occasion she entered the woman's room and observed the dog drinking water from a glass. When the event occurred, Anna was filled with strong feelings of disgust and loathing, but out of politeness she was unable to express them. As she recited this account to Breuer, she for the first time permitted herself the luxury of expressing fully and animatedly her negative feelings about the dog's drinking. When she emerged from the trance she immediately asked for a glass of water, which she . . . drank without the slightest difficulty. (Fancher, 1973, p. 49)

Removal of Anna's fear of drinking was apparently brought about by her vivid recollection of a forgotten event while in a trance. It occurred to Breuer that other hysterical symptoms might be caused by forgotten memories and that their recall might cure them. He began hypnotizing Anna and asking her to remember everything she could about her symptoms. "(H)e discovered that every symptom could be traced back to a traumatic or unpleasant situation for which all memory was completely absent in the waking state. Breuer found that whenever he could induce Anna to recall those unpleasant scenes and, more importantly, to *express the emotions* they had caused her to feel, the symptoms would disappear" (Fancher, 1973, pp. 49–50; italics added).[1]

Freud also found the cathartic method successful, but he encountered some serious drawbacks as well. Not all his patients could be hypnotized. In addition, Freud found that recall of memories and expression of the emotions associated with them are most beneficial when the patient remembers what happened after hypnosis is removed. To make the treatment more applicable and to facilitate *conscious* recognition of early memories, Freud began to look for nonhypnotic means of helping patients locate lost memories.

He first tried a "pressure technique" which he had seen Bernheim use at Nancy. This technique involved pressing a hand against the patient's forehead and suggesting that she or he could remember. Freud's adaptation of this method consisted of having the patient relax with eyes closed and recite memories that came to mind. Recall was often helped by having the patient lie on a couch, but Freud found that significant memories did not always appear immediately, no matter how strongly he suggested that they would. Freud ultimately abandoned the laying on of hands and simply instructed his patients to report whatever

thoughts, feelings, or memories came to mind. This procedure later became known as *free association*, a mainstay among psychoanalytic techniques to be described later.[2]

Freud's early treatment of "neurotic" patients focused on helping them remember important, usually unpleasant, memories and emotions that they had repressed and that had been protected from recall by various *defense mechanisms* (see Chapter 2). He also constructed a model of nervous-system functioning that could not only explain the development and cure of neurotic symptoms, but of normal, everyday behavior as well. Freud called this work the "Project for a Scientific Psychology." Its specific features included postulation of nerve energy called "Q" which could "fill up" or *cathect* a given nerve cell and could be discharged by that cell. Freud also suggested a force he called "ego" which inhibited the discharge of various neurons. Where ego energy was strong, nervous activity adjusted to the requirements of the external environment. Where ego energy was weak, neural discharge was less inhibited. Thus, controlled or impulsive behavior was determined by natural forces and factors in the person's nervous system.

The project reflected Freud's neurological sophistication and objective, scientific view of human behavior. Unfortunately, he was never able to construct his neurological model so that it could explain why painful memories should be automatically repressed by the nervous system. In 1896 Freud abandoned his efforts at explaining

---

[1] Anna's case has been a controversial one in the history of psychoanalysis. Several scholars (e.g., Ellenberger, 1972; Thornton, 1983) have claimed that Anna's illness was not hysterical but was in fact a case of meningitis, that she continued to suffer from the illness, and that although Freud was aware of her suffering he did not publicly acknowledge it. This incident, along with others in Freud's career, has led to frequent allegations (e.g., Eysenck, 1985; Masson, 1983; Zwang, 1985) that Freud was an insincere, sometimes dishonest man.

[2] Incidentally, Freud may have hit upon this technique through a lost memory of his own. Fancher (1973) reports that when Freud was a teenager, he read an essay by Ludwig Borne called "The Art of Becoming an Original Writer in Three Days." In that essay Borne suggested that the would-be writer should spend three days writing down everything that comes to mind "without any falsification or hypocrisy" and that amazingly new and surprising thoughts would appear.

neurotic behavior on neurological grounds and concentrated instead on *psychological* explanations.

Freud became convinced that the causes of neurotic problems were more complex than he had initially supposed. He had originally found, for example, that many of his patients recalled early memories of sexual trauma, usually molestation by a parent or other relative, and he assumed that such events were the basis for most hysterical symptoms. By the turn of the century, however, Freud was convinced that this "seduction theory" was incorrect and that there were more important causal factors to be considered (see also Chapter 2). For one thing, he simply could not believe that seduction and sexual abuse of children were as widespread as indicated by his patients' reports. Second, Freud began to pay attention to *dreams* (his patients' and his own) and deduced that they represented the fulfillment of *wishes*. He found that many of these fantasies are socially unacceptable and thus appear in disguised form only when defenses are relaxed during sleep. Freud then suggested that, like dreams, hysterical symptoms were based on unconscious wishes and fantasies, not just on memories of actual events. Thus, a patient's "memory" of childhood seduction by a parent might be a *fantasy* or *wish* about such an encounter.

The implications of this new theory led Freud to develop his most controversial concepts: infantile sexuality, the Oedipus conflict, and the instinctual basis of human behavior. It altered his approach to therapy as well. Psychoanalytic treatment of neurosis shifted from the recovery of memories to the illumination of the unconscious.

The Goals of Psychoanalytic Treatment

The basic goal of classical psychoanalytic therapy is to help patients think and behave in more adaptive ways by understanding themselves better. In theory, when patients understand the real, often unconscious reasons why they act in maladaptive ways and see that those reasons are no longer valid, they will not have to continue behaving in those ways. The analogy comes to mind of the Japanese soldier left on a remote Pacific island during World War II with orders never to surrender. Decades after the war, the soldier is still hiding, holding out against an enemy that no longer exists except in his own mind. When someone finally helps him understand that his original orders no longer apply, he can stop acting like a hunted animal and start living productively.

In psychoanalytic treatment, it is not enough for the therapist to say "the war is over" by simply describing the unconscious material that he or she thinks is at the root of the patient's problems. Patients must make these discoveries for themselves, with guidance from the therapist. This process of self-understanding includes *intellectual* recognition of one's innermost wishes and conflicts, *emotional* involvement in discoveries about oneself, and the *systematic tracing* of the manner in which unconscious factors have determined past and present behaviors and affected relations with other people.

Thus, the main goals of psychoanalytic treatment are (1) intellectual and emotional *insight* into the underlying causes of the patient's behavior problems and (2) *working through* or fully exploring the implications of those insights. One of the myths about psychoanalysis is that insight about one's life comes in a sudden flash, accompanied by the explosive release (or "abreaction") of pent-up emotions from the past, and followed by the permanent disappearance of the patient's problems. Although his patients were often relieved of a symptom following recovery of repressed memories, Freud believed that symptom removal (no matter how dramatically it occurs) was only part of therapy. If more important unconscious material were not unearthed, new symptoms would appear. Thus, "making the unconscious conscious" (Freud, 1901) is a gradual process that takes place over many analytic sessions. This self-exploration process is slowed by dead ends, false leads, and various psychological defenses thrown up by the patient to prevent conscious awareness of long-hidden truths.

Even after these truths are revealed, the therapist must promote the *working through of insights* and the defenses that kept them from consciousness for so long. The patient needs to understand how pervasive the unconscious conflicts and defenses are so that he or she can learn to recognize them and prevent their return. It would do little good for a patient to know that she had unconscious feelings of anger toward her mother if she did not also see that she deals with women in the present as if they were her mother, and that her problems in relation to these women are based on unconscious hostility and/or attempts to defend against it. Insight provides the outline of a patient's story; working through fills in the details.

Reaching the ambitious goals set by classical psychoanalysis involves the dissection and gradual reconstruction of the patient's personality. This process requires a lot of time (three to five sessions each week for two to fifteen years), a lot of money (fees can exceed $100 per hour), and a great deal of therapist skill. The ways in which psychoanalysts work at this formidable task are described in the next section.

Psychoanalytic Treatment Techniques

An assumption of psychoanalytic theory is that the patient's most important feelings and conflicts are unconscious and protected by psychological defenses. No matter how hard the patient tries, it is unlikely that (s)he alone can penetrate the depths that have been avoided for so long. The therapist must create an atmosphere in which the patient can engage in real self-exploration. The therapist must show the patient how and where to look for important material and help the patient understand the things that emerge.

The specific ways in which these tasks are accomplished differ for each analyst and for each patient, but a few techniques and strategies are common. We shall discuss each of them separately, but in practice they are interwoven in multiple combinations rather than performed in a certain order.

Free Association. As noted earlier, free association evolved from the search for a nonhypnotic way to recover past memories. It involves asking the patient to follow a single "fundamental rule": to say everything that comes to mind without editing or censorship.

> The patient is . . . asked to verbalize everything that occurs to him in the original sequence and form without any modification or omission. He is asked to assume a passive attitude toward his train of thought; in other words, to eliminate all conscious control over his mental processes to which he gives free rein. . . . (Alexander, 1937, pp. 40–41)

The rationale for free association is that by removing the constraints of logic, social amenities, and other rules, unconscious material will begin to surface.

The most common approach is to have the patient free associate while lying on a couch. The analyst sits out of the patient's view in order to avoid interfering with the associative process. In early analytic sessions the therapist may give some instructions (e.g., "Just say whatever occurs to you regardless of how unimportant it may seem"), but later the patient becomes familiar enough with the role to begin free associating without a prompt:

PATIENT: God, it's been a long day. I haven't worked this hard since I was in high school. Back then I used to work part-time on my uncle's farm and part-time in a drugstore. The farm work was really hard. I thought I was going to die out in those fields. It was a lot nicer when I visited the farm as a small child. Dad and Mom used to take me and my sister to the farm on weekends and us kids would play all day. We used to go in the barn a lot and it seems like we played some secret game or something. (pause) Now I remember! We played doctor and my sister and my two cousins and I would take turns being the doctor and examining each other's genitals. We knew we weren't supposed to do it though and I remember being scared to death that we'd be caught. . . .

Because of defenses, the unconscious bases for the patient's current problems are seldom clearly revealed in memories, feelings, and wishes. More often, free association merely gives glimpses of the underlying causes of distress. It is the therapist's task to try to make sense of the bits and pieces that emerge. *Patterns of association* are often important:

PATIENT: My dad called long distance last night. It was nice to hear from him, but I never quite feel comfortable when we talk. Once we get through the usual "hello; how are you" part, there just doesn't seem to be anything to say. (long silence) I almost fell asleep there for a minute. I used to do that a lot in college. I must have slept through half my classes. Once I woke up and saw the professor standing over me, shaking me, and the whole class was laughing.

The fact that thoughts about father led to memories about a threatening authority figure could have significance, especially if this pattern is repeated in other sessions. It could mean that the patient still has unresolved feelings of fear and hatred in relation to his father, feelings that will need to be clarified and dealt with.

What the patient says during free association may be defensive in nature. The patient whose mind "goes blank" or who comes up with only trivial details of the day is throwing up barriers to self-exploration. The following excerpt from an analytic-style session with "S" (Murray, 1938, quoted in White & Watt, 1973, pp. 257–258) provides an example of a patient's defenses (the analyst is denoted as "E"):

S: The thing uppermost in my mind at present is the hour exam I just had. Rather easy exam. I wasn't feeling particularly brilliant this morning. I don't know whether I made any mistakes or not. Quite a bit hinges on this exam because I want to get a scholarship for the second semester. If I get it, I will be able to carry through my work to my master's degree. If I don't, I don't believe I'll be able to make it. It's hard to borrow money these days. I would like to keep on at college though because with the kind of work I get here I will get the kind of job I want. I am particularly interested in research work and this course that I am taking fits me for that.

E: I am afraid you are telling me a story rather than telling me what is coming into your mind. (After the first few sentences S has been giving a reasoned statement of his financial position. This is contrary to instruction and hence constitutes the first manifestation of resistance.)

S: I have an experiment this afternoon and I'm darned if I know what it is about. (This remark may contain a double meaning: S is wondering what the present session is about, as well as the afternoon's experiment. But he has abandoned his first form of resistance, the next topic being a good example of free associations.)

S: I wonder how my dad is getting along. He is on his last legs, so to speak. Dad and I never got along very well. I remember one time when I was a youngster I was supposed to be watching some cows that were grazing near an orchard. I got so interested in reading that I forgot about the cows and they entered the orchard and ate some of the fruit off the trees. Dad was angry as the devil. He came around the corner and a made a beeline for me and I ran and he, being the old backwoods type, took a healthy swing at me with his foot as I went by and he slipped and nearly broke his arm on the wet grass. (At this point S turned around on the couch to look at E.)

E: What did you think when you turned around?

S: The reason I turned around was to look directly at you.

E: Why did you want to look directly at me?

S: If you are trying to put over a point and look directly at the person it is generally better. In sales work, for instance . . . (Again S has departed completely from free association to the idea of making a point and selling an argument. This is another form of resistance, similar to the first. At the same time he has dramatized his feeling toward E. Doubtless annoyed because E corrected him on account of his first lapse from the fundamental rule, he thinks of an earlier incident in which he lapsed from duty but eluded his father's wrath, and indeed turned the tables by being the cause of his father's hurting himself. This line of thought, however, awakens so much anxiety that he has to turn around to make sure that E is not getting angry. At this point E again reminds S of the fundamental rule.)

According to analytic theory, the therapist initially will be faced with resistance and many other forms of defense in free-associative material. These defenses must be recognized by the analyst and made clear to the patient in the process of analytic probing. (We shall return to this point later.)

The Use of Dreams. Because they are viewed as expressions of wishes usually kept from consciousness, dreams play an important role in psychoanalysis. Freud once called them "the royal road to the unconscious." However, there is difficulty faced by the analyst in using dream material: While the patient's defenses are relatively relaxed during sleep, they are not totally absent, and some defenses still operate. Therefore, dreams are thought to express unconscious wishes in versions that are sufficiently well disguised to avoid traumatizing (and waking) the sleeper. Because unconscious material is believed to be closer to the surface in dreams than during waking hours, great importance is attached to them in psychoanalysis. A series of sessions may be consumed in recounting and discussing a single dream.

The patient's description of a dream reveals its *manifest content* or obvious features. If a person dreams that he or she is running through the woods and suddenly falls into a lake, this story is the manifest content. Manifest content often contains relatively unimportant features associated with the dreamer's activities that day (called "day residue") or may merely supply convenient ways of satisfying temporary wishes without the dreamer having to waken. A hungry person may dream of food, for example.

For psychoanalytic purposes, the most interesting aspect of dreams is their *latent content:* the unconscious ideas and impulses that appear in the form of a safe compromise between repression and expression. The process of transforming unacceptable material into acceptable manifest content is called *dream work*. The many forms that dream work takes have been the subject of extensive writing, beginning with Freud's own *Interpretation of Dreams* (1900).

Most aspects of manifest dream content are viewed as *symbols* of something else. In spite of the popular belief that certain dream content (e.g., a snake) always means something specific (e.g., a penis), Freud did not believe dreams could be understood in this inflexible fashion (he is said to have pointed out that "sometimes a cigar is just a cigar"). Most analysts assume, however, that manifest content has some symbolic significance, the specifics of which may differ for each person or even from dream to dream.

For example, a meaningful unconscious impulse (e.g., the desire to have extramarital sex) might be *displaced* to a position of minor importance in the dream (a massage parlor advertisement glimpsed from a moving car). In some cases, an innocuous dream event (such as one's brother leaving for a vacation) may be seen as a *substitute* for taboo wishes (e.g., the brother's death). Dream work may also *devalue* significant material. Munroe (1955) tells of a prudish woman who often dreamed of being only partly clothed or even naked in public without feeling embarrassed. Presumably, she defended against unconscious sexual wishes by making them seem unimportant.

Unconscious material may be expressed by dreams in *condensed* form. Munroe (1955) provides an excellent example of a dream in which the patient reports: "I am afraid of the dog." To the analyst, this may mean (1) the patient is afraid of God (which is "dog" spelled backwards), (2) the patient seeks to hide his fear, even from himself, and (3) by equating God with a dog, the patient expresses contempt for a Supreme Being. Similar shortcuts also appear in dreams as *alogical sequences* (e.g., when there is a sudden shift of time or place) or as *dramatizations* (two people fighting may represent conflicting tendencies within the dreamer).

In addition to dream work, waking defense mechanisms hamper the analyst's attempts to uncover latent content. Usually, the patient is asked to describe the dream as accurately as possible, but the report may be unconsciously organized more logically than was the case in the dream itself. Freud called this process *secondary revision*. To identify those aspects of a dream that have the greatest unconscious significance, some analysts ask their patients to repeat a dream two or more times. Later versions will usually differ from the initial story, and it is assumed that changes reflect unconscious efforts to disguise or defend against highly charged material.

A common procedure is to ask the patient to free associate to a dream's manifest content. In the process, unconscious material may be revealed. Consider this dream reported to Dr. Robert Lindner by a female patient whose father and mother (who was confined to a wheelchair by paralysis) had a violently unhappy marriage:

I was in what appeared to be a ballroom or dance hall, but I knew it was really a hospital. A man came up to me and told me to undress, take all my clothes off. He was going to give me a gynecological examination. I did as I was told but I was very frightened. While I was undressing, I noticed that he was doing something to a woman at the other end of the room. She was sitting or lying in a funny kind of contraption with all kinds of levers and gears and pulleys attached to it. I knew that I was supposed to be next, that I would have to sit in that thing while he examined me. Suddenly he called my name and I found myself running to him. The chair or table—whatever it was—was now empty, and he told me to get on it. I refused and began to cry. It started to rain—great big drops of rain. He pushed me to the floor and spread my legs for examination. I turned over on my stomach and began to scream. I woke myself up screaming. (Lindner, 1954, pp. 134–135)

Lindner describes how this manifest content is used as raw material for free association:

"Well," she said after a brief, expectant silence, "What does it mean?"

"Laura," I admonished, "you know better than that. Associate and we'll find out."

"The first thing I think of is Ben," she began. "He's an intern at the University, you know. I guess that's the doctor in the dream—or maybe it was you. Anyhow, whoever it was, I wouldn't let him examine me."

"Why not?"

"I've always been afraid of doctors . . . afraid they might hurt me."

"How will they hurt you?"

"I don't know. By jabbing me with a needle, I guess. That's funny, never thought of it before. When I go to the dentist I don't mind getting a needle; but with a doctor it's different . . . I shudder when I think of having my veins punctured. I'm always afraid that's what the doctor will do to me."

"Has it ever been done?"

She nodded. "Once, in college, for a blood test, I passed out cold."

"What about gynecological examinations?"

"I've never had one. I can't bear to think of someone poking around inside me." Again silence; then, "Oh," she said, "I see it now. It's sex. I'm afraid the doctor in the dream *is* Ben. He wants me to have intercourse, but it scares me and I turn away from him." (Lindner, 1954, p. 135)

This "insight" seems to have come too easily and was too obvious. The analyst feels sure there is more to it.

". . . Other men have made love to you."

"Yes," she said, sobbing now, "but I only let them as a last resort, as a way of holding on to them a little longer . . . I'd do anything to keep them from getting inside me—poking into me . . . like the needle, I guess."

"But why, Laura?"

"I don't know," she cried, "I don't know. Tell me."

"I think the dream tells you," I said.

"The dream I just told you?"

"Yes . . . There's a part of it you haven't considered. What comes to your mind when you think of the other woman in your dream, the woman the doctor was examining before you?"

"The contraption she was sitting in," Laura exclaimed, "It was like a—like a wheel chair—my mother's wheel chair—my mother's wheel chair! Is that right?"

"Very likely," I said,

"But why would he be examining *her?* What would that mean?"

"Well, think of what that kind of examination signifies for you."

"Sex," she said. "Intercourse—that's what it means. So that's what it is—that's what it means! Intercourse put my mother in the wheel chair. It paralyzed her. And I'm afraid that's what it will do to me. So I avoid it—because I'm scared it will do the same thing to me. . . . Where did I ever get such a crazy idea?" (Lindner, 1954, pp. 136–137)

Notice how free association to dream content led the patient to an insight that will provoke further exploration of unconscious material not yet revealed.

Certain dreams have particularly important latent content. The first dream reported to the analyst may contain a summary of all major problems (Blanck, 1976). Frequently, a series of dreams is used in analysis. Attention to multiple dreams reveals patterns of latent content and helps to avoid errors that occur when too much emphasis is placed on a single dream.

Dreams provide ideas for further probing more often than they provide final answers. The caution with which one must analyze even obvious dream content, symbols,

and associations is spelled out by Bonime (1962):

If a woman were dreaming of a snake which associatively became established as a penis, it would still be necessary, if one is to achieve insight into her personality through her dream symbol, to establish the quality of experience with a penis which was symbolized by that snake. If she were a professional dancer largely preoccupied by a desire to be seductive, and if she had performed the dance of a snake charmer, then the penile snake could symbolize her desire to charm men or control them by her sexual allure. . . .

If a woman had been made pregnant before a promised marriage by a man who later deserted her, the penile snake in her dream might represent the quality of deceit or poisonousness, or both, not only in men but also in any human being who offered intimacy. If she had had a puritanical upbringing and yet indulged in a sexual affair, the penile snake might represent hidden "sinful" desires or actual secret activities of a sexual nature. . . . By still further extension, the snake could refer . . . to yearnings for other types of self-indulgence [or] self-gratification. . . . (p. 36)

Attention to "Everyday Behavior." One of Freud's primary concepts was that of *psychic determinism,* the notion that most human behavior is caused by conscious and unconscious mental processes. An obvious consequence of this view, spelled out in *The Psychopathology of Everyday Life* (1901), is that much of our day-to-day behavior reflects unconscious wishes, fantasies, and defenses.

Accordingly, the psychoanalyst is consistently sensitive to all a patient's behavior, whether in treatment sessions or in their reports of intersession activities. This means maintaining an "evenly divided" or "free-floating" attention to trivial as well as momentous events, to purposeful acts and accidental happenings, to body language as well as spoken language. All of these processes expose habitual defense tactics and the secrets they are assumed to protect. Psychoanalytic theory has generated numerous examples of potentially meaningful everyday behaviors. Two of the better-known categories, *mistakes* and *humor,* are discussed below.

MISTAKES. In the midst of Watergate, former President Nixon made the following statement in a speech to Congress: ". . . Join me in mounting a new effort to replace the discredited president. . . ." He actually meant to say ". . . to replace the discredited present welfare system . . . ," but other possibilities on his mind may have been revealed in this slip of the tongue. Such "Freudian slips," or *parapraxes,* are thought to be indicators of the speaker's actual, often unconscious feelings. "Slips of the pen" may also reflect indirectly expressed feelings: "Dear Madeline: Your party was just divine. Thanks so much

for inviting us. We can wait to see you again. . . ."

While analysts may use parapraxes to help the patient's self-exploration, they also focus on errors that are more subtle and presumably reflective of carefully protected unconscious material that has slipped out. Brenner (1974) mentions a case in which a young male patient who was interested in body building referred to "physical culture" as "physible culture." This "accidental" mistake had no immediate meaning for either patient or therapist. However, the patient was asked to free associate to the word "physible." His first association was the word "visible" and from there he continued until he revealed an unconscious wish to exhibit his nude body (and to see others naked).

Other everyday mistakes may take on

BOX 8-1   Freud's analysis of a slip of the tongue

In *The Psychopathology of Everyday Life,* Freud (1901) describes his analysis of a slip of the tongue made by a young male acquaintance. It reveals how, according to psychoanalytic theory, significant material emerges in extremely subtle ways.

In the course of his conversation with Freud, the young man quotes, in Latin, Virgil's *Aeneid:* "Exoriare aliquis nostris ex ossibus ultor" ("Let someone arise from my bones as an avenger"). In doing so, he left out "aliquis" ("someone"). To help the man find the meaning of this error, Freud asked him to free associate to "aliquis."

The associations included dividing the word into "a" and "liquous" as well as other words like "reliquien" (meaning "relics"), "liquefying," "fluidity," and "fluid." He then thought of the relics of Simon of Trent which he had seen two years earlier, then of blood sacrifices, then of a newspaper article called "What St. Augustine Says about Women." Later, he

thought of St. Januaris and the miracle of his blood (which is supposed to liquefy on a certain holy day each year) and the fact that the miracle was once delayed.

The young man then became disturbed and he stopped associating. Freud asked what was wrong and was told that the new association was too intimate to reveal and involved a young lady from whom he was expecting some news. At this point, Freud said that the news involved the possibility that the woman was pregnant.

The man's astonishment at having his secret (which was far more shocking in 1900 than it is now) uncovered was relieved somewhat as Freud explained his method. The references in free association to liquid, blood, calendar saints, regularly occurring miracles of flowing blood, concern over a delay in the miracle, and the like all led Freud to see the man's conscious and unconscious preoccupation with menstruation and possible pregnancy.

psychoanalytic importance. "Accidental" events, especially those in which the patient has at least partial responsibility, may also be seen as wishful. The waiter who spills hot soup on an elderly male customer might be asked in analysis to free associate to various elements in this "accident." The result might be an inference that the waiter was attempting to execute a father substitute.

Forgetfulness is a prime example of presumably motivated error. We are not talking about cases in which a person purposely "forgets" a dental appointment, but about instances in which a memory lapse occurs without obvious cause. If a patient forgets the manifest content of the dream she or he had planned to describe, the analyst may suspect that the dream contained material too threatening to remember. Sometimes a patient achieves an important insight into an unconscious wish and forgets what it was, apparently as a defense against acknowledging unflattering personal characteristics.

Brenner (1974) tells of a patient who inexplicably forgot the name of a familiar friend at a party. As the patient free associated to this event, it came to have important unconscious meaning:

As he talked about it, it developed that the name of the acquaintance was the same as that of another man whom he knew and toward whom he had strong feelings of hatred which made him feel very guilty. . . . In addition he mentioned that the acquaintance was crippled, which reminded him of some of his wishes to hurt and injure the namesake whom he hated. . . . In order to avoid becoming conscious of his destructive fantasies . . . he repressed the name which would have made the connection between the two. (p. 130)

Although psychoanalytic theory seems to leave no room for real accidents or innocent mistakes, events over which a person has no control (e.g., being injured when a plane crashes through one's roof) are seen as genuine accidents. However, if the victim can be seen as in any way responsible for the mishap, there is a potential for unconscious sig-

nificance. The authors know of a woman who returned from the grocery store on a snowy day and, in the process of carrying several bags of groceries into the house, fell on the ice and broke her leg. Upon hearing the commotion, her psychiatrist husband ran outside, saw her writhing in pain, and shouted, "Why did you do this to me?" Using analytic logic, the husband presumed that, though the fall was probably due to snow and ice, his wife's failure to ask for help or to carry only one bag at a time expressed an unconscious desire to get more loving attention from him or to punish him by adding the nursing of an invalid to his daily responsibilities.

HUMOR. Freud noted that humor usually contains expressions of *hostility* or *aggression*. The transformation of angry feelings into humor is called *wit work,* which can take several forms. Puns are good examples of *condensation,* in which multiple meanings are conveyed by a single word: "The elephant circumcisor told me his job had good and bad points. The pay is lousy but the tips are big." Here, in addition to condensation in the word "tips," there may be some *displacement* of aggression toward whoever might be symbolized by the elephant. When one considers how many jokes present situations in which a person or group is made to look foolish or is injured or killed, it is easy to see how Freud reached his conclusions. Although in theory there are jokes that are "harmless," Freud was hard put to give a single good example.

According to psychoanalytic theory, jokes provide a safe outlet for anger which, if expressed directly, might bring retaliation or feelings of guilt. Because the joke disguises the aggressive impulse, the psychic energy that would have been used to repress that impulse becomes unnecessary and is released in the form of laughter. Thus, the jokes a person makes or finds funny may be examined by the analyst in helping that person toward self-understanding. Freud's theory of humor is covered in his *Jokes and Their*

Relation to the Unconscious (1905) and in Grotjahn (1957).

Analysis of Resistance. The psychoanalyst assumes that the patient will display various forms of *resistance* in the course of treatment. We have seen examples of resistance in the context of free association and dream analysis, but there are other forms as well. All are important because (1) they highlight the topics and time periods about which the patient is most defensive, and (2) they provide current examples of habitual defenses which, with the analyst's help, the patient can recognize and ultimately abandon. Because real progress can only be made in the absence of resistance, psychoanalysis is fundamentally involved with removing it.

The ways in which resistance can appear are too numerous to catalog here. We give just a few examples in order to illustrate the possibilities (see Fine, 1971, especially Chapters 8–10, for more detailed coverage). Fairly obvious resistance to psychoanalytic therapy is inferred from a patient's repeated absence from or lateness for treatment sessions. Unwillingness to speak about certain topics,[3] refusal to lie on the couch, falling asleep, or failure to pay the therapist's bill are often interpreted in the same way.

Resistance may be more subtle. Depression or expression of hopelessness when a major breakthrough is about to occur is sometimes viewed as the patient's way of delaying painful insights. "At the point where feelings of hopelessness arise, many therapists are tempted to switch to some other technique, convinced that the standard analytic approach has failed. This is precisely what the patient is trying to get them to do. . . . His hopelessness has a manipulative purpose, to drive other people away, and allow him to wallow in his misery" (Fine, 1971, pp. 123–124).

A similar interpretation may be made of other patient behaviors. A common examples is *intellectualization*. Here, important emotions are repressed, but the patient does not appear uncooperative. Instead, she or he simply substitutes logic and reason for feelings that may be present. Thus, in discussing a parent's death, the patient might calmly say something like "Well, yes, I was sad, but actually we had all been expecting this to happen so there was no shock. Besides, I was responsible for making all the arrangements and that took up all my energy." Other patients avoid dealing directly with their own problems by attempting to engage the analyst in scholarly debates about the effectiveness of various therapeutic techniques.

When threatened by analytic probing, some patients develop physical symptoms for which there is no organic cause. A chronic cough, a lingering cold, or other "physical" problems may make conversation difficult during sessions or may prevent sessions from taking place. Resistance is suspected by analysts when other more severe behavior patterns appear. *Regression,* in which the patient "goes backward" in development by remaining in bed, abandoning good grooming, crying, and requiring constant care, may be potentially permanent obstacles to analysis.

Other resistant behaviors are often called *acting out*. Substance abuse, participation in dangerous activities, or other dramatic life changes may be construed as the patient's way of escaping anxiety brought about by the possible uncovering of repressed material. As dangerous as these tactics are for the patient, acting out can be hazardous to the therapist as well. Analytic patients have, on rare occasions, attempted to injure or kill their therapists, perhaps as part of a desperate attempt to avoid recognizing the truth about themselves.

A final form of resistance, probably the most difficult for nonanalytic observers to accept, is when the patient feels (1) that external rather than intrapsychic factors are

---

[3] Or refusal to speak at all. There is a case on record of a patient who said nothing in therapy for two years! (Fine, 1971).

primarily responsible for problems, (2) that problems are getting worse, or (3) that he or she has a right as a consumer to be given evidence of the value of the psychoanalytic approach. In each instance, the patient makes a reasonable statement or request, but the therapist interprets it as diverting attention from the dynamics presumed to underlie problems. Therefore, if the analyst focuses attention on *why* the patient wants to know about the value of analysis or the reason for slow progress, instead of giving a straightforward answer, the goal is not to evade the issue but to follow psychoanalytic principles. Those principles dictate that any patient behavior that interferes with the analytic process should be dealt with as a defense so that, ultimately, the unconscious material that underlies the patient's problems can be made conscious.

Analysis of the Transference. In psychoanalysis, the therapist-client relationship is an important source of raw material for probing the unconscious and its defenses. The patient's feelings toward and relationship with the therapist are called the *transference*.[4] It is thought to develop on at least two levels. The first involves realistic, mostly conscious feelings, as when the patient expresses gratitude for the therapist's help. At this level, there is a *therapeutic alliance* that facilitates treatment.

At a mostly unconscious level, however, the transference contains attitudes and reactions related to the patient's unconscious conflicts, many of which go back to childhood and lie at the root of current symptoms. The patient may have reactions to or feelings about the analyst determined not by the therapist's actual characteristics or behavior, but by the ways the patient related to significant people in the past.

This assumption is based on Freud's belief that time does not exist in the unconscious. The earliest unconscious conflicts are

always active (unless made conscious and worked through) no matter how much time goes by, and they will make their presence known in many problematic ways, including disrupted interpersonal relationships.

Unconscious factors may color the patient's interactions with anyone who evokes childhood conflicts. The therapist is an especially likely transference candidate for several reasons. For one thing, the analyst is in a position of high status in relation to the patient who comes for help in time of trouble. This identifies the therapist as an *authority* and brings to mind images of a parental figure. These images are intensified by the fact that the therapist conveys a *caring attitude*. The patient may associate this attitude with actual or wished-for attributes of her or his parents. In addition, the therapist tries to be nonjudgmental and to accept with equanimity whatever the patient reveals. This tends to foster feelings of trust, again reminiscent of real or fantasized attitudes toward parents or other valued persons from the past. Finally, because the analyst maintains an "analytic incognito" by revealing little about herself or himself, she or he becomes a sort of blank screen onto which the patient can project all sorts of attributes and motives.

While the patient may sometimes unconsciously see the therapist as a loving parent, he or she may also react as though the therapist were a vengeful father, a seductive mother, a jealous lover, or one of many other figures. The specifics depend on the particular nature of the patient's unconscious difficulties. When the patient-therapist relationship creates a miniature version of the patient's overall problems, it is referred to as the *transference neurosis* and becomes a central focus of analytic work. Freud noted that the appearance of the transference and transference neurosis often took the form of female patients' erotic fantasies about him. He concluded that these women were expressing childhood wishes about their fathers, for whom he had been symbolically substituted.

---

[4] The therapist's feelings about the patient are referred to as *countertransference*.

The reproduction of early unconscious conflicts is not only theoretically fascinating; it is remarkably convenient. The analyst can work with important problems from the past as they occur in the present through the transference. For this reason, most of the therapist's attention is centered on events occurring during treatment sessions themselves.

Patients display transference and transference neurosis in many ways. Among the more obvious is *dependence* on the therapist. The patient may show up early for every session,[5] express reluctance to leave at the end of the hour, telephone for advice at all hours, or make demands on the analyst. The development of intense feelings of love for the analyst may reach dramatic proportions. Some patients become so caught up in fantasizing about a love affair with the analyst that nothing else seems important to them. When the therapist fails to reciprocate, strong feelings of disappointment and/or anger often appear. The patient may become depressed and may even attempt suicide.

Negative feelings about the therapist also reflect transference. The patient may decide that the analyst is incompetent. Although these sentiments are repeatedly expressed in no uncertain terms, the patient may not terminate therapy. To the therapist, this means that the patient is not simply an unhappy customer, but one who is using the therapeutic relationship to express feelings intended for a parent or other significant person. Negative transference may also appear in less direct, more childish ways. Fine (1971) tells of a sixteen-year-old patient who attempted to annoy the analyst by calling him on the telephone fifteen or twenty times an hour, sometimes identifying himself as Christopher Columbus.

Transference and transference neuroses

must be handled with care. The analyst tries to understand the meaning of the patient's positive and/or negative feelings. If the analyst responded "normally" to a confession of love or a verbal attack, the patient would not learn very much and a premature termination of therapy could occur. The transference must be kept visible without forcing the patient out of therapy. If this can be done, unconscious material can be made conscious and worked through. When all these goals are accomplished, the patient's analysis is usually seen as complete.

Working through the transference takes much longer than working through a specific symptom. Thus, while psychoanalysis may begin because of a particular complaint (e.g., anxiety attacks), it is likely to continue long after that problem disappears because the patient's real difficulties are believed to be revealed in the transference.

Making Analytic Interpretations. So far, we have outlined the major sources of unconscious material and the psychoanalytic techniques used to tap them. We have also seen that defense mechanisms make it unlikely that the patient will understand this material, because unconsciously he or she does not want to.

The analyst, on the other hand, is trained to look for hidden meanings and, because she or he is a detached and objective observer, the significance of the patient's behavior is thought to be easier for the analyst to detect. The problem, of course, is how to help patients accept uncomfortable things, while at the same time not overwhelming them with too much insight before they are ready to handle it. This is where *analytic interpretation* comes in. Through questions and comments about verbal and nonverbal behaviors, free associations, dreams, and the like, the analyst guides the patient's self-exploration. When the patient is resistant or when she or he is unable to see the potential meaning of some event, the therapist points this out and offers suggestions for new ways to look at things.

Interpretations are not simply statements of how the analyst construes the patient's problems. The interpretive process is more tentative and continuous, a kind of constant prodding of the patient to consider alternative views, to reject obvious explanations, to search for deeper meanings. Interpretations move analysis along by promoting insight and the working through of those insights. Without interpretations, the patient might never make progress.

The analyst does not interpret everything of unconscious significance for the patient as soon as he or she detects it. Therapists face three important questions as they work at the delicate task of giving valid and usable interpretations: What could this dream (or association or response) mean? Is it related to important new unconscious content? Is now the time to say something to the patient about it?

A correctly timed interpretation can result in a step forward; it ". . . stirs up the patient in one way or another. It brings his whole personality into the office of the analyst and provides a kind of emotional re-education on the spot" (Munroe, 1955, p. 307). The word "emotional" is important because when an interpretation is accurate, important, and well-timed, it will evoke positive (or negative) feelings in the patient that promote insight. On the other hand, most analysts feel that a correct interpretation of important material may arouse too much emotion or strong defenses if it is given before the patient is ready to make use of it.

As a rule of thumb, an interpretation is best delivered at the point where the patient is nearly aware of something important, but has not yet verbalized it. Ideally, ". . . one 'tells' a patient what the patient *almost* sees for himself and one tells him in such a way that the patient—not the analyst—takes 'credit' for the discovery" (Menninger, 1958, p. 134). The therapist tries to say just the right things at just the right times. When he or she succeeds, the analytic interpretation becomes a tool like the surgeon's scalpel.

The analyst's interpretations can reflect narrow hypotheses about specific relationships, or they can deal with broader conceptualizations. Some interpretations are made directly, especially when the patient is thought to be ready for a straightforward presentation. In other instances the analyst will merely hint at hypotheses so that the patient can deal with the new idea gradually. Several illustrations of analytic interpretations are presented below.

INTERPRETING RESISTANCE. The analyst's first job (besides establishing a good working relationship) usually involves identifying and overcoming resistance to the analytic process. The patient can be made aware of his or her resistance in many ways.

PATIENT: I've been thinking; we've spent five sessions together and have gotten nowhere. How long does it take for me to start seeing some changes?

If the analyst were sure that this was a resistant tactic and that the patient ought to be confronted, a direct interpretation might be offered:

THERAPIST: I don't know the answer to that question, but it seems to me that by bringing it up, you could be attempting to avoid talking about other things.

A less direct interpretation could also be used:

THERAPIST: I don't know the answer to that question, but I wonder why you asked it.

After an analyst has had time to observe continuing patterns of resistance, a more elaborate interpretation might be ventured:

PATIENT: I'm sorry to be late, but I got a long-distance call from my brother-in-law just as I was leaving the house. He told me that my sister has gotten sick and wanted to know if I had some cash to spare to help with the medical bills. I don't know how I can afford to do it and still keep coming to see you. Sometimes everything falls on me at once.

THERAPIST: You know, last session we began to see that your feelings toward your parents were not all positive. I think we are on to something important in that area. Today you start off by saying that, through no fault of your own, you may not be able to continue therapy. This seems to be a recurring thing. Whenever you are threatened by what you learn about yourself, a disaster seems to occur that diverts your attention. You got out of trouble this way as a child, too. Whenever your parents became angry with you, you found a way to show that someone else had prevented you from doing what you should have done. Has this ever occurred to you?

INTERPRETING OTHER ANALYTIC PRODUCTIONS. Dreams also produce raw material for analytic interpretations. The use of the "wheelchair" dream illustrated how an analyst might lead a patient to an understanding of latent content. Here is another example of interpretation based on various analytic products:

You know, it's very interesting that whenever you say something that is a little bit nasty to anyone you smile. After you've been a little bit aggressive, you become *very* agreeable and nice, and I notice it here. I wonder if when you were with your father you discovered that the only way to keep him from attacking you was to become more sociable, amiable, in this kind of smiling, passive way. . . . (Barton, 1974, p. 33)

INTERPRETING THE TRANSFERENCE. Because it is thought to be intimately related to the patient's early intrapsychic conflicts, the transference is a prime target for analytic interpretation. After observing a patient's dependence, the analyst might remark: "I notice that you often deal with me in the same way you dealt with your parents as a child. You want me to protect you and help you through the difficulties you are facing." The same interpretation could be couched in less obvious terms: "I get the feeling that you would like me to magically solve all your problems, and I wonder if you have ever felt that way about anyone else."

Accurate interpretation of transference may lead to a negative reaction from the client. This reaction must itself be interpreted. For example:

PATIENT: I have a confession to make. I never could have come through these last two months without your help. I love you.

THERAPIST: If we examine why you feel that way about me we might discover who I represent to you when I provide psychological support.

PATIENT: Can't you even take a compliment like a human being? I was trying to tell you how I feel about *you;* I wasn't saying anything about me! Can't you come off your analytic throne for even one minute?

THERAPIST: You expressed love for me. That has been very hard for you to do. It is important to understand why you do it in relation to me now when you couldn't before. It is also important to understand why you got so angry just now when I did not respond as you wanted me to.

This exchange is likely to lead to exploration of the patient's problems in expressing tender feelings toward others, particularly toward parents, and may uncover a strong need to be reassured about self-worth. In the process, the patient may find that unreturned love does not mean one is worthless. It may also become clear that his or her parents were not able to be loving and that nothing he or she could have done as a child would have changed that fact. Insight about this may be worked through in later sessions as the analyst and patient consider implications of the transference.

As interpretations help the patient to understand and work through the transference, the therapist-patient relationship changes. The patient not only sees how defenses and unconscious conflicts caused problems, she or he learns to deal differently with the world, beginning with the therapist. The patient learns that the forces of the past no longer need dictate the behavior of the present. The analyst is not the patient's parent, and neither is the patient's boss or spouse. Ideally, this emotional understanding will liberate the patient to deal with life in a more realistic and satisfying manner.

Our outline of classic psychoanalytic techniques has left out many details and oversimplified others. More complete coverage of the approach is contained in Munroe (1955), Menninger (1958), Kernberg (1976), and, of course, Freud (e.g., 1949).

Applications

In its original form, psychoanalysis was used in one-to-one treatment of "neurotic" adults over a period of several years. This classical approach has been varied in order to make it shorter and more applicable to groups, families, and younger patients, but the typical recipient of psychoanalytic treatment is a relatively intelligent adult who has the time and financial resources to embark upon an extended intellectual and emotional adventure.

A "good" analytic patient should be motivated to work at solving problems. She or he must be capable of free association and must be able to form an interpersonal relationship with the therapist. Further, the patient should be able to think logically about the world, including her or his own behavior, and to maintain contact with reality. Finally, the patient must have enough courage to focus on his or her problems. These requirements rule out, for the most part, the use of orthodox psychoanalysis with psychotic patients.

VARIATIONS OF PSYCHOANALYSIS

Like all great thinkers, Freud attracted many followers. Some of these people sought to preserve his ideas and techniques in their original form; others advocated changes ranging from minor alteration to wholesale rejection of fundamental principles. These changes suggested a broader range of therapeutic techniques than had been "legal" under orthodox Freudian rules. In this section we describe a few of these treatment innovations, beginning with those that are least distinct from the original model and progressing to those incorporating more radical changes.

Psychoanalytically Oriented Psychotherapy

Many therapists employ psychoanalytic procedures in ways that depart somewhat from the guidelines set down by Freud. Although these individuals still see themselves as practicing psychoanalysis, traditional Freudians refer to such treatments as *psychoanalytically oriented psychotherapy*. This phrase encompasses a number of nonorthodox analytic procedures, but it is most closely associated with the approach developed by Franz Alexander and his colleagues at the Chicago Psychoanalytic Institute during the 1930s and 1940s.

The treatment philosophy of the "Chicago group" has been spelled out in several books (e.g., Alexander & French, 1946; Alexander, 1956, 1963). The approach grew out of doubts about the importance of traditional therapeutic practices. For example, the Alexander group questioned the belief that treatment must be intense, extended, and fundamentally similar in all cases. They also sought to apply psychoanalysis to two previously excluded patient groups: the young and the more severely disturbed.

Alexander (1963, p. 273) summarized his views this way: "Psychoanalytic principles lend themselves to different therapeutic procedures which vary according to the nature of the case and may be variably applied during the treatment of the same patient." This flexibility appears in many aspects of psychoanalytically oriented psychotherapy. For one thing, not every patient is seen for the traditional five sessions each week because some people may not benefit from such intense effort. Daily sessions may foster too much dependence on the analyst or may become so routine that the patient pays too little attention to them.

In a given case, the frequency of sessions varies as circumstances dictate. Early in treatment the patient may be seen every day. Later, the sessions may take place less often. Alexander even suggested that temporary interruptions in treatment could be beneficial by testing the patient's ability to live without therapy and to reduce reliance on the therapist. Alexander and French (1946) reported that their form of psychoanalysis could be completed in sixty-five sessions over about a year and a half; in many cases, even less time is needed.

Traditional psychoanalysis is lengthy due to the perceived need for fully exploring and working through resistance, insights, and the transference. Alexander suggested that not all patients need such extensive attention. Persons whose problems are relatively mild, who are well adjusted except for a particular difficulty, or who are more seriously disturbed than the usual analytic patient are candidates for less extensive treatment aimed at support rather than at the uncovering and reconstruction associated with classic analysis.

Alexander emphasized the need for *corrective emotional experiences*, not just insight, in therapy. The idea is to help the patient not only to see that old conflicts need no longer run her or his life, but to use the transference to let the patient resolve those old conflicts in a better way. "Re-experiencing the old, unsettled conflict *but with a new ending* is the secret of every penetrating therapeutic result. . . ." (Alexander & French, 1946, p. 338).

To promote corrective emotional experiences, the analyst may attempt to control the character of the transference. A transference neurosis may be allowed to develop or, if its appearance is not seen as beneficial in a certain case, might be avoided. This control can be exerted by avoiding interpretations

likely to foster transference of infantile reactions. The therapist may also alter the *countertransference*. If feelings toward the patient help promote a corrective emotional experience, they may be expressed directly. If not, the therapist may ". . . replace his spontaneous countertransference reactions with attitudes which are consciously planned . . . according to the dynamic exigencies of the therapeutic situation" (Alexander, 1956, p. 93). In other words, in this version of psychoanalysis, transference is not only analyzed, it may be manipulated; countertransference is not only a spontaneous reaction that the analyst comes to understand through self-analysis, it is a potential treatment tool.

A general rule in Freudian analysis is that the patient should not make major life decisions while treatment is underway. This is designed to prevent bad decisions caused by maladaptive impulses, false insights, or neurotic defenses. In contrast, the analytically oriented therapist may encourage life changes that the patient and analyst agree make sense. This procedure is based on the assumption that the therapeutic relationship is not only a context for self-exploration, but a place to rehearse ideas for progress that are then tested in real life. The changes made sometimes involve manipulation of the patient's environment and are often initiated by the therapist. A patient who is unhappy about the fact that she or he is in an unsatisfying job might be encouraged to look for a better position. Here, the therapist performs a guidance function that is more active and direct than that found in orthodox analysis.[6]

At various points in treatment, psychoanalytically oriented therapists use a number of unorthodox techniques, including the following:

1. The patient may sit up and face the analyst rather than lie on a couch.

---

[6] In spite of their theoretical restrictions, orthodox analysts also give advice (Munroe, 1955; Strupp, 1972).

2. Normal conversation may be substituted for free association.

3. Drugs or hypnosis may be used to promote self-exploration.

4. The nature of current problems and their solution is emphasized. Childhood conflicts are explored to show that they no longer need to exist.

5. The patient's family may be consulted (or even offered treatment) as part of a total effort at helping the client.

6. Nonverbal communications, including play (for children), artistic creations, or leisure activities, may supply additional material for analysis.

The Ego Analysts

Psychoanalytically oriented psychotherapists accept most of Freud's basic tenets but revise his procedures. Another group of therapists, usually referred to as *ego analysts*, stray further from the strict Freudian path by arguing that the psychoanalytic preoccupation with sexual and aggressive instincts as the bases of behavior is too narrow. Wolberg's (1967) summary of the ego-analytic position is presented in edited form below:

1. Behavior is determined by forces other than instinct. These include responses encompassed under the concept of ego.

2. The ego has an autonomy separate from both instinct (id) and reality.

3. The ego prompts drives for environmental mastery and adaptive learning which are separate from sexual and aggressive instincts.

4. Female sexuality is on a par with rather than inferior to male sexuality.

5. The classical topography (id, ego, superego) does not explain the structure of personality.

6. Therapy is more than a means of exploring and working through early childhood experiences. It is a relationship experience which contains positive growth potential that can lead to self-actualization.

7. Activity and flexibility are essential to therapy.

8. An optimistic rather than a pessimistic viewpoint is justified with regard to the human potential for creativity and love.

These views led the ego analysts "to explore the complexity in behavior that each person develops and with which he *directs his own activity and deals constructively with his environment*" (Ford & Urban, 1963, p. 181; italics added). People are presumed to be capable of using ego functions to control their behavior and organize that behavior in positive as well as negative ways. This more optimistic view of human beings has much in common with the phenomenological approach (see Chapters 2 and 10). It led analysts such as Heinz Hartmann (1958), David Rapaport (1951), Melanie Klein (1960), Freud's daughter Anna Freud (1946), and Erik Erikson (1946) to use psychoanalytic techniques to explore patients' adaptive ego functions as well as their basic id instincts. For more on the theory and practice of ego analysis, see Munroe (1955), Ford and Urban (1963), Guntrip (1973), Eagle (1984), or Slipp (1981).

Psychoanalytically oriented psychotherapy and ego analysis are *revisions* of Freudian concepts and techniques, not outright revolts against them. However, there have been other therapists who moved further from Freud. These individuals retained a psychodynamic orientation, but deemphasized the importance of Freud's theory of instincts, infantile sexuality, and the unconscious determination of behavior. The treatment techniques developed by such rebels are our next topic.

Alfred Adler's Individual Psychology

Alfred Adler was one of Freud's earliest followers and was also the first to defect from the ranks of orthodox psychoanalysis. The reasons for his departure and the alternative theory he formulated are outlined in Chapter 2.

Since Adler believed that people's problematic life-styles were based largely on misconceptions they held, his treatment methods focused on exploring and altering those misconceptions. Where a strict Freudian might see a student's vomiting before school each day as a defense of some kind, the Adlerian analyst would suggest that the problem was a manifestation of general tension brought about by some misconception (e.g., "I must do better than anyone else" or "The teachers are out to make me look bad") on which the student bases his or her life-style. In Freudian analysis, this person's vomiting might be explored through free association or other means in order to understand its defensive function. In Adler's Individual Psychology, the symptom would be discussed as one illustration of the patient's mistaken attitudes and maladaptive life-style. The patient would then be helped to form more appropriate attitudes and given encouragement to change his or her style in the direction of what Adler (1963) called *social interest, courage,* and *common sense*.

Mosak and Dreikurs (1973) have outlined the goals of Adlerian psychotherapy:

1. To establish and maintain a good therapeutic relationship (i.e., a therapeutic alliance, in Freudian terms).

2. To uncover the patient's life-style and goals, as well as to explore how they affect him/her in daily life.

3. To give interpretations that lead the patient to gain insight into his/her life-style and its consequences.

4. To reorient the patient's attitudes so that they support a more adaptive life-style; to translate the patient's insight into constructive action.

Adlerian Treatment Techniques. PATIENT-THERAPIST RELATIONSHIP. Adlerians' goal is to create a cooperative relationship between equals. Accordingly, the patient and therapist normally sit face to face in similar chairs. The feelings and reactions expressed toward the therapist (transference) are seen not as reflecting unconscious childhood conflicts but are interpreted as the patient's habitual style of dealing with

people like the therapist. "The patient . . . expects from the therapist the kind of response he has trained himself from childhood to believe that people or certain people will give him" (Mosak & Dreikurs, 1973, p. 55).

The therapist also watches for life-style clues in the scripts, or standard interpersonal ploys, that the patient creates in treatment. Usually, the therapist is expected to play a particular part. For example, the patient may repeatedly enact the "poor soul" role which she or he hopes will bring a nurturant response from the therapist. This style may be typical of the patient's maladaptive way of getting love and attention.

HANDLING RESISTANCE. Adlerians view resistance as a sample of the patient's usual way of avoiding material that may be unpleasant. In addition, resistance may reflect the fact that the patient and therapist have different goals. The therapist's goal is to explore the patient's basic life-style and misconceptions, but, because clinging to one's misconceptions maintains feelings of security, the patient will try to protect those misconceptions from exposure. When the patient's goal is to maintain the status quo, he or she will appear resistant (e.g., "I can't understand what you are talking about"; "I'm too upset to talk about this now"). The therapist may handle such resistance by interpreting its meaning and by pointing out the goal discrepancy. A discussion of goals may then result which, for the moment at least, reestablishes therapist-patient cooperation.

DREAMS. Adler used dreams in treatment, but he saw them not as the compromised fulfillment of wishes from the past, but as a rehearsal of how the patient might deal with problems in the future. The moods in a dream are seen as setting the stage for the next day's activities. "If we wish to postpone action, we forget the dream. If we wish to dissuade ourselves from some action, we frighten ourselves with a nightmare" (Mosak & Dreikurs, 1973, p. 58). Adler also used dreams as an indication of therapeutic progress. If, for example, a patient reports short dreams in which there is little action, this might reflect a passive approach to dealing with problems. As treatment proceeds and the patient begins to experiment with a more active life-style, her or his dreams should become more active as well. Some Adlerians use the patient's dreams to guide them in deciding when to terminate therapy (Rosenthal, 1959).

THE LIFE-STYLE INVESTIGATION. In addition to attending to dreams, resistance, the transference, nonverbal behavior, and other material, some Adlerians (e.g., Dreikurs, 1954) explore the patient's life-style in a more systematic way. They focus on the patient's family and his or her position in it, the earliest memories that can be recalled (because they reflect the life-style), basic mistakes or misconceptions, and the assets and strengths the patient possesses. The summary of a life-style investigation is presented in Box 8-2.

THE USE OF INTERPRETATION. In Adlerian therapy, resistance and transference are usually handled by interpreting them as examples of the patient's maladaptive life-style. Interpretation is used in the same way to promote insight about the life-style meaning of the patient's dreams, interpersonal relationships, and other behavior. Where Freud interpreted in order to promote insight into *past causes* of current problems, Adler interpreted in order to promote insight into the nature and purpose of the patient's current life-style.

Instead of using it as a scalpel, Adlerians employ interpretation as a mirror in which patients can see how they cope with life. When this is done and patients see what it is they are doing, it becomes harder to maintain maladaptive ideas and behaviors. In comparison to the Freudian approach, Adlerians are less concerned about the details of phrasing and timing interpretations because they do not see the patient as particularly delicate.

ADVICE AND ENCOURAGEMENT. While Freud pointed out that patients must sometimes be encouraged to do things they have been afraid of in the past, the strict psychoanalyst generally remains objective and rather detached most of the time. By comparison, the Adlerian therapist is much more involved in advising and encouraging the patient. As long as the patient does not become dependent on the therapist for advice, it is seen as an essential part of translating insight into action.

For example, once a patient realizes that her dependence on her husband is part of her overall style of seeking protection (and controlling others), the therapist might point out several alternative ways in which she might start to change. In other cases, the therapist might offer more direct advice (e.g., "Get a part-time job"), especially when the patient needs help to get started toward a more adaptive life-style.

OTHER TREATMENT PROCEDURES. Adlerians make use of other techniques to help make patients aware of their life-style and to prompt them to change. Many of these are similar to some of the tactics employed by certain proponents of behavioral and phenomenological treatment (see Chapters 9 and 10):

1. *Modeling.* The therapist exemplifies certain attitudes and behaviors that the patient might wish to emulate. "The Adlerian therapist presents himself as 'being for real,' fallible, unconcerned with prestige considerations, able to laugh at himself, possessing courage, caring—a model for social interest" (Mosak & Dreikurs, 1973, p. 60).

2. *Task setting.* Adler advocated getting patients to do new things, which would help the treatment process. "Acting as if" was one favorite method. When patients express a longing to be different than they are, the therapist may suggest that they act *as if* they really were the way they want to be. The patient also may be asked to *try* to perform the very behaviors he or she wishes to stop (a technique known as *paradoxical intention*).

BOX 8-2 A sample life-style summary

Summary of family constellation

John is the younger of two children, the only boy, who grew up fatherless after age 9. His sister was so accomplished at almost everything that, early in life, John became discouraged. Since he felt he would never become famous, he decided perhaps he could at least be notorious, and through negative traits brought himself forcefully to the attention of others. He acquired the reputation that he was pretty obnoxious and a "holy terror." He was going to do everything his way, and nobody was going to stop him. He followed the guiding lines of a strong, masculine father from whom he learned that the toughest man wins. Since notoriety came with doing the disapproved thing, John early became interested in and engaged in sex. This also reinforced his feelings of masculinity. Since both parents were handicapped and still "made it," John apparently decided that without any physical handicaps, the sky would be the limit for him.

Summary of early recollections

"I run scared in life, and even when people tell me there's nothing to be scared of, I'm still scared. Women give men a hard time. They betray men, they punish them, and they interfere with what men want to do. A real man takes no crap from anybody. But victory is hard to come by because somebody always interferes. I am not going to do what others want me to do.

Others call that 'bad' and want to punish me for it but I don't see it that way. Doing what I want is merely part of being a man, and why should anyone want to interfere with my being a man?"

"Basic mistakes"

1. He exaggerates the significance of real masculinity and equates it with doing what he pleases.
2. He is not on the same wavelength as women. They see his behavior as "bad"; he sees it as only "natural" for a man.
3. He is too ready to fight, many times just to preserve his sense of masculinity, and not because of the issue he is allegedly fighting over.
4. He perceives women as the enemy, even though he looks to them for comfort.
5. Like Moses, victory is snatched from him at the last moment.

Assets

1. He is a driver. When he puts his mind to things, he makes them work.
2. He engages in creative problem solving.
3. He knows how to get what he wants.
4. He knows how to keep the world busy with him.
5. He knows how to ask a woman "nicely."

Source: H. H. Mosak & R. Dreikurs, "Adlerian Psychotherapy," in R. J. Corsini (ed.), *Current Psychotherapies.* © 1973 by Peacock Publishers, Inc., Itasca, Illinois, p. 57. (Reprinted by permission.)

An insomniac might try to stay up all night; a person who always seems to be crying might try to cry constantly. By not fighting against these behaviors, the patient often finds that they disappear.

3. Creating images. The patient is sometimes given a summary image of his or her life-style. This image can then be used on a day-to-day basis as a reminder of the style she or he is trying to alter. "Superman," "The Beggar King," and "Miss Perfection" are a few examples of life-style images.

4. The push-button technique. When patients believe themselves to be at the mercy of their emotions, the therapist might help them learn that this is a misconception. The

BOX 8-3   An example of Adler's task setting

Adler often employed task setting as a means of helping depressed people. In the example below, note the charming combination of good humor and practical advice.

To return to the indirect method of treatment: I recommend it especially in melancholia. After establishing a sympathetic relation I give suggestions for a change of conduct in two stages. In the first stage my suggestion is "Only do what is agreeable to you." The patient usually answers, "Nothing is agreeable." "Then at least," I respond, "do not exert yourself to do what is disagreeable." The patient, who has usually been exhorted to do various uncongenial things to remedy this condition, finds a rather flattering novelty in my advice, and may improve in behavior. Later I insinuate the second rule of conduct, saying that "it is much more difficult and I do not know if you can follow it." After saying this I am silent, and look doubtfully at the patient. In this way I excite his curiosity and ensure

his attention, and then proceed, "If you could follow this second rule you would be cured in fourteen days. It is—to consider from time to time how you can give another person pleasure. It would very soon enable you to sleep and would chase away all your sad thoughts. You would feel yourself to be useful and worthwhile."

I receive various replies to my suggestion, but every patient thinks it is too difficult to act upon. If the answer is, "How can I give pleasure to others when I have none myself?" I relieve the prospect by saying, "Then you will need four weeks." The more transparent response, "Who gives *me* pleasure?" I encounter with what is probably the strongest move in the game, by saying, "Perhaps you had better train yourself a little thus: do not actually *do* anything to please anyone else, but just think out how you *could* do it!"

Source: Adler, 1964, pp. 25–26.

patient is asked to imagine some past unpleasant experience and notice the negative emotional feelings that result. The patient is then told to "push a button" and switch the attention to some past pleasant event. The appearance of accompanying positive emotions and the possibility of switching back and forth between affective states illustrate the degree of control over emotion that the patient has.

Applications. Adlerian therapy is appropriate for one-to-one treatment with the kinds of patients who might be seen in Freudian psychoanalysis, but it can also be applied with other types of patients (including psychotics) in individual, group, and family contexts. Adler also worked with "normal" individuals because he believed that one can have problems in living due to misconceptions and a maladaptive life-style without being a diagnosed patient. This view resulted in the establishment of community education centers designed to pre-

vent behavior disorders by providing parents and teachers with information and advice about child rearing and family relations. These centers anticipated the community psychology movement of the 1960s and 1970s (see Chapter 7).

Other Psychodynamic Therapies

In discussing psychoanalytically oriented psychotherapy, the ego analysts, and Adler, we have merely scratched the surface of the variations on Freud's model of treatment. Box 8-4 lists additional systems. The work of many of the therapists and theorists included in that table (e.g., Stekel, Ferenczi, Reich, Federn) paralleled the effort of the Chicago group and the ego analysts to expand the techniques, patients, treatment settings, and presenting problems that could be associated with psychoanalysis. Others (e.g., Horney, Sullivan, Fromm) used basic psychoanalytic concepts in treatments which emphasized the cultural and

BOX 8-4   Modifications in psychoanalytic therapy

I. Alternate systems of analytic psychotherapy based on theoretical or ideological
differences from Freudian classical analysis.
  1. The non-Freudian systems.
    a. The *individual psychology* of Alfred
       Adler.
    b. The *analytical psychology* of Carl
       Jung.
    c. The *will therapy* of Otto Rank.
  2. Neo-Freudian systems based on the
     cultural emphasis.
    a. The *holistic* approach of Karen Hor-
       ney.
    b. The *interpersonal relations* school
       of Harry Stack Sullivan.
    c. The *cultural* approach of Erich
       Fromm.
II. Attempts to streamline, abbreviate and
    speed up the process of psychoanalytic
    therapy.
  1. Stekel's *active analytic* psychotherapy.

  2. Ferenczi's experiments with *active*
     techniques.
  3. The Chicago school of *brief* psy-
     choanalytic therapy.
III. Expansions of Freudian classical analysis
     in various directions.
  1. The "object-relations approach" of
     Guntrip, Winnicott, Fairbairn, and the
     British school.
  2. The "eight stages of man" and
     Erikson's extension of Freud's theory of
     character development.
  3. Character analysis of Wilhelm Reich.
  4. Kohut's approach to the treatment of
     narcissistic character disorders.
IV. Modifications based on the shift in empha-
    sis to ego psychology.
  1. Federn's ego psychology and the psy-
     chotherapy of the ego boundaries.
  2. Wolman's interactional psychoanalytic
     therapy.

Source: Kutash, 1976, pp. 89–90.

interpersonal environment of the patient. Still others (e.g., Jung and Rank) followed in Adler's footsteps by breaking sharply with Freudian principles and founding distinct treatments.

One of the most important developments in modern psychoanalysis is *object-relations theory*, a movement associated with a group of influential British analysts including Ronald Fairbairn (1952), Donald Winnicott (1965), Melanie Klein (1975), and Margaret Mahler (Mahler, Pine & Bergman, 1975) as well as Otto Kernberg (1976) and Heinz Kohut (1971, 1977, 1983). Object-relations theory studies the nature and origin of interpersonal relationships as they are built from very early infant-mother interactions and the nature of present personality structures as they are derived from reactivated internalizations of these interactions (see Blatt & Lerner, 1983, for a concise account of the importance of object-relations theory in current psychoanalytic thought).

Object-relations theorists emphasize preoedipal development, particularly the quality of the mother-infant relationship (Mahler, 1965) and its effect on the structure and strength of the ego. In Kohut's *Self-psychology,* for example, the analyst's task is to provide the type of empathic responding that the patient is assumed to have missed as an infant. When parental inadequacies do not allow an infant to realize his or her "mirroring," "idealizing," and "twinship" needs (see below), the child is unable to achieve a unified self.

Defective aspects of the self have a tendency to emerge in later life in the form of personality disorders such as narcissism and the borderline personality (Lerner, 1985). In treating such patients, the analyst's task is to be a responsive, warm, empathic *selfobject* who allows the patient's self to be completed by encouraging expression of the self's earliest needs. Kohut (1983) described three types of *selfobject transferences* essential to self-completion: ① the *mirror transference*, where exhibitionistic and grandiose needs are recognized and admired by an empathic selfobject; ② the *idealizing transference*, where needs for protection and soothing are answered by a powerful selfobject; and ③ the *twinship transference*, where needs for closeness to another person like oneself are answered by an alter ego selfobject.

Object-relations therapists extend a special type of parenting to their patients in order to give them a second chance for the development of a coherent self. Their emphasis on ego support, acceptance, and psychological "holding" of damaged selves is similar to many of Carl Rogers's ideas about psychotherapy (Kahn, 1985; see Chapter 10). For this and other reasons, classic psychoanalysts have been skeptical about such treatments, claiming that they owe less to Freud than to existentialism and humanism (Levine, 1985). Freud himself seemed to anticipate self-enhancement treatments, referring to them somewhat disparagingly as the "cure through love."

Other variants on psychoanalysis have helped lay the groundwork for procedures associated with behavioral and phenomenological models. For example, when Otto Rank broke with Freud, he developed a therapeutic approach that de-emphasized the unconscious and the detailed exploration of the past. Instead, Rank employed the patient's innate *will to health* as a vehicle for promoting mature independence. Rank treated his patients like responsible individuals and emphasized the therapy relationship as a major growth experience. He saw the therapist as a *facilitator* of the patient's inherent potential for growth, not as a relentless prober of the unconscious. These concepts provided part of the base upon which Carl Rogers would later build his phenomenologically oriented client-centered therapy (see Chapter 10).

Similarly, Harry Stack Sullivan (like Adler) did therapy in ways compatible with today's behavioral approach (see Wachtel, 1977). Ford and Urban's (1963) outline of the usual sequence of events in Sullivanian therapy (Box 8-5) shows the systematic attention to overt behavior that is a hallmark of behavioral interventions.

BOX 8-5 Summary of the therapeutic sequence in Sullivanian therapy

=====

a. Initial review of the problem.

b. Reconnaissance of the behaviors relevant to the problem.

c. Decision as to general outlines of the difficulty and the course therapy shall pursue.

d. Careful and detailed study of the subject's response repertoire.

e. Identification of the anxieties, avoidance patterns, and the interpersonal situations in which they occur.

f. Rendering these patterns explicit to the subject.

g. Making explicit the fact of intervening anxiety.

h. Drawing out the effects of these anxiety patterns on the remainder of the subject's behavior.

i. All of the foregoing reduces the intensity of anxiety and permits the operation of other responses in its stead.

Source: D. H. Ford, and H. B. Urban, *Systems of Psychotherapy.* © 1963 by John Wiley & Sons, New York. (Reprinted by permission.)

EFFECTIVENESS AND OTHER RESEARCH ISSUES IN PSYCHODYNAMIC THERAPY

When most people think of psychotherapy, they imagine a pipe-smoking therapist and a patient on a couch. This was once a reasonably accurate stereotype, since psychodynamic treatment was the first systematic approach to the exploration and solution of psychological problems. For many years it dominated clinical interventions and controlled professional ideas about how therapy should be conducted. Today, its dominance is reduced because its underlying theoretical model has been challenged by phenomenological and behavioral alternatives and because, in spite of modern revisions, it is still too expensive and lengthy to be useful in dealing with many problems. Critics have also questioned the effectiveness of psychodynamic therapy.

One of the most frequent arguments is that the psychodynamic approach has seldom been evaluated by quantitative, empirical research. Analysts are frequently depicted as suspicious of or even hostile to controlled studies of therapy outcome. Indeed, some advocates of the psychodynamic model have argued that their treatment methods are too complex, too multifaceted, and too subjective to be evaluated fairly by quantitative methods.

Nevertheless, there is a considerable amount of quantitative research on psychodynamic treatments, which many psychologists either ignore or remain uninformed about. This research has been summarized by Wallerstein and Sampson (1971), Masling (1982), Gill and Hoffman (1982), and Fisher and Greenberg (1977). A thorough review of research on psychoanalysis is also provided by Luborsky and Spence (1978). The journal *Psychoanalysis and Contemporary Society* is a good source for additional examples of this research, as is *Clinical Psychology Review* (1985, no. 3).

The research questions asked about psychodynamic treatment are similar to the questions posed about other forms of therapy. Luborsky and Spence (1978) discuss four areas of research in psychoanalytic treatment: (1) What kinds of clients are best suited for psychoanalysis? (2) What kinds of therapists are best suited to perform it? (3) What outcomes are produced by psychoanalysis? and (4) What is the nature of change throughout the course of treatment?

Questions concerning outcome have received the least attention in the psychoanalytic literature. Most studies have focused only on a group of treated clients who, at the end of treatment, are rated by their therapists on some sort of improvement scale. Control groups are usually not included. Psychoanalysis has rarely been compared directly to other forms of psychotherapy. Cartwright's (1966) study is well known, but its importance is diminished by the fact that there were only four patients. Piper, Debbane, Bienvenu, and Garant (1984) conducted a well-designed evaluation of short- and long-term psychoanalytically oriented therapy delivered in either a group or individual context. The most influential investigations have been the Sloane, Staples, Cristol, Yorkston and Whipple (1975) outcome study previously described in Chapter 7, and Cross, Sheehan, and Khan's (1980) comparison of behavior therapy and "insight-oriented therapy."

Research on the process of psychoanalysis has been more frequent and of generally higher quality. For example, considerable research has been performed on the effects of therapists' interpretations. Accuracy of interpretation, the nature of transference, and level of empathy have been investigated in several studies (e.g., Luborsky, Crits-Christoph & Mellon, 1986; Silverman, Lachmann & Milich, 1982).

Despite the increasing sophistication of research on psychoanalysis, most analysts would probably agree with Luborsky and Spence's (1978) judgment: "Quantitative research on psychoanalytic therapy presents itself, so far, as an unreliable support to clinical practice. Far more is known now through clinical wisdom than is known through quantitative, objective studies" (p. 358). Later, they add that "few, if any, quantitative research findings have changed the style or outcome of psychoanalytic practice" (Luborsky & Spence, 1978; p. 360). Without disparaging the value of clinical wisdom, we believe that no form of psychotherapy should remain too long aloof from the findings of well-controlled research. The ultimate scientific status of psychoanalysis, or any other therapy, depends on empirical investigation of its methods rather than on the consensual approval of its practitioners.

chapter 9

Clinical Intervention: Behavioral Models

The definition of behavior therapy has undergone considerable revision over the years, but according to recent reviews of the field (Farkas, 1980; Hersen & Bellack, 1985; Kazdin, 1978; Ross, 1985; Wilson, 1978), the essential principles of behavior therapy are the following:

1. There is a continuity between normal and abnormal behavior which implies that the basic laws of learning apply to all behaviors. Maladaptive behaviors are acquired through the same psychological processes as any other behaviors.

2. Therapeutic techniques are based on the empirical findings and theoretical foundations of experimental psychology. In its early years, behavior therapy relied on the findings of learning theory, but today its empirical foundations are much broader.

3. Therapy is aimed at the modification of overt, maladaptive behaviors. The cognitions and

emotions that accompany overt behavior are also dealt with, but in a more direct manner than in many other therapeutic approaches. Treatment is tailored to the unique needs of each client.

4. There is a focus on the client's present problems. This here-and-now emphasis results in less attention to early childhood experiences or historical material than is the case in psychoanalysis.

5. There is a commitment to the experimental evaluation of treatment. The behavior therapist attempts to employ techniques that have been scientifically investigated through experimental group designs or single-subject methodology.

6. Emphasis on problem-focused techniques and empirical validation of treatment does not reduce the need for behavior therapists to be sensitive clinicians who are concerned for the welfare of their clients and who exercise good clinical judgment and sound ethical practices when providing their services.

In recent years, behavior therapy[1] has regularly been described, praised, and condemned in the press, television, and movies (e.g., *A Clockwork Orange*) and has become a part of our popular vocabulary. While at one time the public's stereotype of psychologists was of professionals who practiced Freud's brand of therapy, behavioral techniques now augment or have replaced psychodynamic images in the popular conception of psychology. This new stereotype misses the target only a little: Most clinicians, regardless of their theoretical background, *are* familiar with behavior therapy and employ its techniques on many occasions.

The term *behavior therapy* first appeared in a 1953 paper by Lindsley, Skinner, and Solomon which described operant conditioning with psychotics. Though these authors did not continue to use the term, Eysenck (1959) did, and he is often given credit for introducing it. Arnold Lazarus was the second person to use the term in print, publishing a 1958 article on behavior therapy in the *South African Medical Journal.*

Behavior therapy has become one of the most popular research areas in clinical psychology. Twenty-five years ago there was not a single professional journal devoted exclusively to research on behavioral approaches in clinical psychology. Now there are more than a dozen, the most influential of which are: *Behaviour Research and Therapy, Journal of Applied Behavior Analysis, Behavior Therapy, Journal of Behavior Therapy and Experimental Psychiatry, Behavior Modification, Cognitive Therapy and Research, Behavioral Assessment,* and *Journal of Psychopathology and Behavioral Assessment.*

Similar growth has occurred in the publication of textbooks and handbooks dealing with behavior modification. The first book with "behavior therapy" in the title was Eysenck's *Behavior Therapy and the Neuroses,* published in 1960 (Kazdin, 1978). Today there are hundreds of books about behavior modification, and many of them are updated each year. Several behaviorally oriented interest groups have been formed, the most influential of which is the Association for the Advancement of Behavior Therapy (AABT). There are at least a score of behavioral newsletters, catalogs of equipment for behavior modifiers, and special bibliographies of behavioral publications. There is even a special code of ethics for behavior modifiers (AABT, 1977).

The increasing complexity of the area is also illustrated by the proliferation of behavioral splinter groups. Thus, we have *broad spectrum behavior therapy, narrow band behavior therapy, cognitive behavior therapy, cognitive behavior modification, language behavior therapy, rational behavior therapy, psychobehavioral therapy,* and *psychodynamic behavior therapy* (Wilson, 1978). We doubt that there is much to be gained by inventing new brand names or by trying to acquaint you with the subtle differences they may represent. More valuable lessons can be learned from studying the origins of behavior modification and understanding those developments that shaped the unique qualities of modern behavioral interventions.

Alan Kazdin (1978) has discussed several scientific and professional foundations of behavior modification. In this chapter we focus on six of these areas: early Russian research on conditioning, comparative psychology, Watsonian behaviorism, learning theory, B. F. Skinner and operant conditioning, and applications of learning therapy to human behavior and psychotherapy. For more elaborate coverage of these topics and several others, consult Kazdin (1978, especially pp. 49–185).

---

[1] Throughout this chapter we use the terms *behavior modification* and *behavior therapy* interchangeably, even though some writers insist that the two are not synonymous. Among those psychologists who emphasize the difference between the two concepts, those with an operant or Skinnerian orientation prefer the name *behavior modification,* leaving *behavior therapy* to clinicians who operate from a Hullian and/or cognitive framework. These theoretical differences will become more meaningful as we progress through this chapter.

FOUNDATIONS OF BEHAVIOR MODIFICATION

Conditioning Research in Russia

The impact of Russian conditioning research on behavior modification was transmitted through the early-twentieth-century work of three men: Ivan Sechenov, Ivan Pavlov, and Vladimir Bekhterev. Each of these scientists was trained in medicine, and each advocated objective, mechanistic explanations of behavior, including those human behaviors considered to be highly subjective. Of greatest importance, each insisted that behavior be studied through scientific, empirical methods.

Aside from championing the empirical method, Sechenov made two important contributions to a behavioristic psychology. First, he claimed that all behavior was composed of reflexes elicited by the environment. Thus, he saw the ultimate cause of behavior as external. Second, Sechenov believed that the reflexes that formed complex human behavior were acquired through associative learning, that is, responses are learned when they are associated repeatedly with certain stimuli.

Pavlov's work on conditioning salivation in dogs led him to the discovery that if an *unconditioned stimulus* that elicits a reflex *(or unconditioned response)* is paired repeatedly with a neutral stimulus, the previously neutral stimulus becomes a *conditioned stimulus* which will elicit a response *(the conditioned response)* that resembles the original reflex. A diagram of this process is presented in Figure 9-1.

In his famous experiments with dogs, Pavlov demonstrated that food would elicit salivation and that after pairing a tone with the food several times, the tone itself would elicit salivation. Pavlov discovered *higher-order conditioning* when he noticed that, after many associations with the tone and food, his own presence also elicited the dog's salivation. Pavlov's greatest contributions were his study of the conditions under which one

form of learning (often called *Pavlovian, classical,* or *respondent conditioning*) took place and his demonstration of the effects that changes in those conditions would have on the conditioning process.

Bekhterev also studied conditioning, although he was more interested in overt motoric responses than was Pavlov. Bekhterev studied motor reflexes in humans, using mild electric shock to the hands and feet as the unconditioned stimulus. He argued that psychology would be replaced by a more objective discipline, which he termed *reflexology.* Kazdin (1978) notes that at the beginning of the twentieth century Bekhterev used conditioning to treat several disorders, including hysterical deafness and sexual deviations.

Comparative Psychology

Comparative psychology involves the study of animal behavior. It is important to the development of behavior modification chiefly because it gave support to Darwin's claim that there was a continuity in the behavior of humans and animals. Because of this continuity, the laws of animal learning that were being discovered in the late nineteenth and early twentieth centuries were thought to apply to humans as well.

Watsonian Behaviorism

John B. Watson "was responsible for crystallizing an existing trend toward objectivism" in psychology (Kazdin, 1978, p. 63). Watson received his Ph.D. in 1903 from the University of Chicago, where the orientation to psychology was *functional* (psychologists studied how human consciousness operated through the method of introspection). Watson was also exposed to the methods of physiology and biology at Chicago, and he become dissatisfied with functionalist psychology which, by comparison to the "hard" sciences, was too subjective for his tastes.

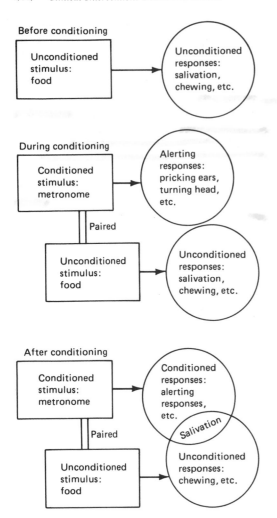

FIGURE 9-1. The course of Pavlovian conditioning. Before conditioning, food, an unconditioned stimulus, elicits unconditioned responses like salivation and chewing. During conditioning, a metronome, the potential conditioned stimulus, comes on a few moments before the food is given. The food still elicits various responses, while the metronome elicits only the usual alertness to a new sound. After a number of conditioning trials, the metronome elicits a new set of responses that include some overlap (for example, salivation) with the original unconditioned responses. (From R. Brown and R. J. Herrnstein, *Psychology*. Reprinted by permission of the authors.)

Watson's vision for a more objective psychology was first published in 1913 in a paper called "Psychology As the Behaviorist Views It." In this article Watson described two essential qualities of behaviorism. First, introspection as a method was to be replaced with observation, the method used by the animal psychologists. Second, psychologists must abandon the study of consciousness and focus instead on overt behavior and its relation to environmental stimuli. Watson's system came to be known as S-R psychology because of his emphasis on stim- ulus-response bonds, through which all behavior could be explained. For example, thinking was seen as small movements of the vocal cords, and emotions were the product of physiological changes in certain organs.

Watson popularized behaviorism and claimed that it could be used to solve human problems. His most extravagant allegation was that if he were given one dozen healthy infants, "well-formed, and my own specified world to bring them up in . . . I'll guarantee to take any one at random and train him to become any type of specialist I might select—doctor, lawyer, artist, merchant, chief, and yes, even beggarman and thief, regardless of his talents, penchants, tendencies, abilities, vocations and race of his ancestors" (Watson, 1930, p. 104). Partly as a result of this kind of enthusiasm, the literature of the 1920s contained many articles describing how behaviorism could solve the problems of education, abnormal behavior, and society in general (Willis & Giles, 1978).

Learning Theory

By the 1930s the major topic of research in American psychology had become the psychology of learning and the construction of theoretical systems that explained learning processes. These learning theories attempted to explain a wider range of behavior (including speech and voluntary motor behavior) than earlier conditioning theories, which were concerned with more discrete responses (eye blinks, startle responses).

Edward L. Thorndike, one of America's first learning theorists, was interested in the voluntary behavior of animals. For example, how does a cat learn to escape from a cage in which it is confined? Thorndike believed that the most important factor in the development of a new response was the consequence of that response. Responses are strengthened or weakened according to the *law of effect,* which held that

Of several responses made to the same situation, those which are accompanied or closely followed by satisfaction to the animal will, other things being equal, be more firmly connected with the situation, so that, when it recurs, they will be more likely to recur; those which are accompanied or closely followed by discomfort to the animal will, other things being equal, have their connections with that situation weakened, so that, when it recurs, they will be less likely to occur. (Thorndike, 1911, p. 244)

This law of effect was the theoretical forerunner of B. F. Skinner's concepts of reinforcement and operant conditioning, of which more will be said later.

Another early learning theorist was Edwin Guthrie, whose major statement on learning was contained in his 1935 book, *The Psychology of Learning.* Guthrie's theory was similar to Watson's: Learning occurs as a result of contiguity or close association between stimuli and responses. Unlike Thorndike, Guthrie did not believe that reinforcement played a major role in learning. According to Guthrie, reinforcement simply prevents the organism from performing some new behavior that could break up the previously formed associations between a stimulus and response.

Other important learning theorists were Clark Hull and Edward Tolman. Hull attempted to synthesize the classical conditioning of Pavlov and the instrumental conditioning of Thorndike under a single theoretical system. His work had a great influence on the later learning theories of such eminent psychologists as Kenneth Spence (1956), O. Hobart Mowrer (1960), and Neal Miller (1951). Hull's theory has been cited as a theoretical foundation for several modern behavior therapy techniques, most notably systematic desensitization.

Tolman emphasized the role of such intervening variables as *expectancy, cognition,* and *meaning* in his learning theory. He made a distinction between learning and performance: An organism could learn the correct behavior in some situation without necessarily performing that behavior. Tolman suggested that reinforcement acts to *regulate* overt performance but does not "teach" us which responses are correct. As you shall see, Tolman's ideas were very similar to those expressed by modern social-learning theorists.

Skinner and Operant Conditioning

According to behaviorists, operant conditioning is the process by which most "voluntary" forms of behavior are developed. The most important figure in the application of operant conditioning to human conduct is B.

F. Skinner, whose *Science and Human Behavior* (1953) is one of the foundations of modern behavior therapy. The basic premise of operant conditioning is deceptively simple: Behavior is learned and strengthened as a result of its consequences. The term "operant" suggests a person whose behavior operates or acts upon the environment to produce consequences. In turn, these consequences influence the probability that the behaviors that preceded them will recur.

The main effect of operant conditioning is that randomly emitted, trial-and-error behaviors are progressively shaped into meaningful patterns of activity as a result of their outcomes. Positive consequences (reinforcers) strengthen the likelihood of previous operants, while aversive consequences weaken the probability of similar future responses.

There are five principles that define the core of operant conditioning. Four of these are represented in Figure 9-2, which depicts the possible combinations of presenting or withdrawing either positive or negative stimuli following some behavior. Presenting a positive reinforcer following some behav-

ior is called *positive reinforcement* (Cell I), a process that strengthens the behavior. Having a beer after a study session is a common form of positive reinforcement. Cell II describes one type of *punishment,* in which a negative consequence is presented after some behavior and results in a decrease in that behavior's future probability.

Cell III represents a second form of *punishment,* which occurs when a previously available positive event is removed following some behavior. For example, having one's car stolen while unlocked would probably decrease the future probability of such careless behavior. *Negative reinforcement* (Cell IV) results in an *increase* in the probability of a behavior's future occurrence by removing something unpleasant following that behavior. The relief of headache pain after taking aspirin tends to strengthen future aspirin taking. Positive and negative reinforcement strengthen behavior, while both kinds of punishment decrease the future probability of the behaviors preceding them.

The fifth operant principle is *extinction,* which refers to the weakening of behavior as a result of the absence of both positive

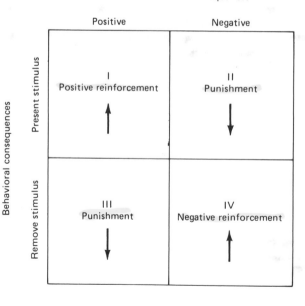

Nature of behavioral consequences

FIGURE 9-2. Techniques and effects of operant conditioning. The arrows in each cell indicate that behavior preceding various consequences will be strengthened (↑) or weakened (↓).

and negative consequences. A simple example of this process would be giving up telephoning someone after repeatedly failing to get an answer. There are, of course, many other concepts and principles associated with operant conditioning. For more extensive coverage of this material, see Martin and Pear (1983).

Applications of Learning Theory to Human Behavior and Psychotherapy

Within the first quarter of the twentieth century, psychologists had become interested in applying the laws of conditioning and learning to the investigation and treatment of behavior disorders. An illustration of this trend was the discovery that emotional responses resembling human neuroses could be experimentally induced in laboratory animals. Pavlov observed *experimental neuroses* in his dogs after exposing them to electric shock or requiring them to make very difficult sensory discriminations. The dogs' symptoms included agitation, barking, biting the equipment, and forgetting things they had previously learned. In the 1940s Jules Masserman of Northwestern University studied the conditioning and deconditioning of experimental neuroses in cats as an analogy to psychopathology and psychoanalytic treatment. Investigation of experimental neuroses in a variety of animal species quickly became a popular research topic. Kazdin (1978) reports that W. Horsely Gantt, another early researcher of experimental neuroses, had a dog named Nick whom Gantt claimed remained neurotic for more than twelve years.

The discovery of experimental neuroses in animals led to research on similar problems in humans. The most famous of these studies was a classic experiment in 1920 by John B. Watson and his graduate student, Rosalie Rayner. A nine-month-old infant, Albert B., was presented with several stimuli such as a white rat, a dog, a rabbit, a monkey, masks, and a burning newspaper. He showed no fear toward any of these objects,

but he did become very upset when a loud noise was sounded by striking a steel bar with a hammer. He was startled by the noise, his breathing was affected, and he trembled and cried during later presentations of the noise.

In order to see whether Albert's fear could be conditioned to formerly non-frightening objects, Watson and Rayner associated the loud noise with a white rat. The rat was brought to Albert and, as soon as he began to reach for it, the noise was sounded. After several such pairings over a one-week period, the rat elicited a strong emotional reaction in Albert—"the instant the rat was shown the baby began to cry. Almost instantly he turned sharply to the left, fell over on his left side, raised himself on all fours and began to crawl away so rapidly that he was caught with difficulty before reaching the edge of the table" (Watson & Rayner, 1920, p. 5). The investigators were interested in whether this conditioned fear had generalized to other objects, so they presented several stimuli which only two months earlier had not upset Albert. This time the effects were different. Albert was squeamish when confronted with a rabbit, a fur coat, Watson's own hair, and even a Santa Claus mask. Albert's fear persisted in less extreme form during assessments conducted over a one-month period.

The child was removed from the research setting before anything could be done to completely remove his fears, but a few years later, Mary Cover Jones, another of Watson's students, investigated several techniques for reducing fear in institutionalized children. Two methods were found to be most successful: *direct conditioning,* in which a fear stimulus was associated with some pleasant activity like eating, and *social imitation,* where the fearful child watched other children who were not afraid of the object in question (Jones, 1924a).

These two methods were investigated more carefully in Jones's (1924b) work with a three-year-old named Peter. Peter was afraid of many things, particularly rabbits.

Social imitation was used first as a treatment. "Each day Peter and three other children were brought to the laboratory for a play period. The other children were selected carefully because of their entirely fearless attitude toward the rabbit. . . ." (Jones, 1924b, p. 310). The rabbit was present during these play periods, and, with the fearless examples of the other children, Peter became more comfortable as he gradually came closer to the animal. At this point, Peter's treatment was interrupted by a bout with scarlet fever, and his progress was jeopardized by a frightening encounter with a big dog.

When treatment resumed, it included direct conditioning. Peter was placed in a high chair and fed his favorite food while a caged rabbit was placed gradually closer to him at each session. Sometimes other children were present during the sessions. This procedure eliminated Peter's fear of rabbits, and there was evidence that this effect generalized to other stimuli. For example, he showed no fear toward a mass of angleworms or a box of frogs. Peter himself summed up the results of this case by announcing one fateful day, "I like the rabbit."

These case histories had a major impact on behavior modification because they suggested that conditioning could account for both the acquisition and treatment of fear. The range of problems to which conditioning was applied during the 1920s and 1930s was very wide, covering children's fears, sexual disorders, substance abuse, and several neurotic conditions. Interest in the clinical use of conditioning persisted despite the failure of some investigators to replicate initial results. O'Leary and Wilson (1975) reviewed a case reported by English (1929), who attempted to condition a fourteen-month-old girl to be afraid of a large wooden duck by banging a metal bar each time the girl reached for the duck. After fifty such pairings the child's enthusiasm for the duck was unabated, so English used a noisier hammer. Still the child remained unafraid, although several professionals in the building complained about the racket. Amazed by the little tyke's nerves of steel, English theorized that the usual rambunctiousness of the girl's three older brothers had made her immune to the aversive properties of noise.

The Recent History of Behavior Therapy

Official recognition of behavior therapy occurred in the late 1950s and early 1960s, a time when there were several reasons why clinical psychology was receptive to behavioral approaches to treatment. Eysenck's challenges to the effectiveness of psychotherapy, widespread dissatisfaction with clinical assessment, and discontent with the medical model of behavior disorder were particularly influential. These factors caused clinicians to view behavioral approaches as attractive alternatives to traditional forms of psychotherapy.

Behavior therapy was formally initiated in South Africa, England, and the United States. Developments in each country were independent of the others to a degree, but mutual dependency and collaboration existed also. In South Africa, psychiatrist Joseph Wolpe was conducting research that culminated in the publication of his book, *Psychotherapy by Reciprocal Inhibition* (1958). The work of two of his psychologist students, Stanley Rachman and Arnold Lazarus, was to receive worldwide attention as well.

In England, the two most important influences on behavior therapy have been Hans Eysenck and M. B. Shapiro, both of whom are affiliated with the Institute of Psychiatry at the University of London and Maudsley Hospital. England's "Maudsley group" (which also included Rachman, Isaac Marks, and Michael Gelder) included prolific researchers who investigated the effectiveness of many behavioral techniques, such as flooding, aversion therapy, and desensitization (all to be discussed later).

The clinical use of behavioral techniques was pioneered in the United States by several individuals, including Knight Dunlap, who in the 1930s used the method of *negative practice* to eliminate bad habits. Voegtlin and Lemere used chemical aversion to treat alcoholics at the Shadel Sanitarium in Seattle, Washington (Shadel, 1944), and Andrew Salter (1949) employed a therapeutic strategy he called "conditioned reflex therapy" to increase emotional expressiveness. Throughout the 1950s and 1960s operant conditioning was used increasingly in the treatment of psychotic patients and troubled children (see Ullmann & Krasner, 1965).

The crystallization of behavior therapy in America was the result of two factors: (1) a recognition of the behavior-therapy movement in England, particularly the work of Eysenck, and (2) the publication of several books in this country that provided a unified framework for behavior modification. In this latter category are Skinner's (1953) *Science and Human Behavior; Conditioning Techniques in Clinical Practice and Research* (Franks, 1964); *Case Studies in Behavior Modification* (Ullmann & Krasner, 1965); *Research in Behavior Modification* (Krasner & Ullmann, 1965); Wolpe's 1958 book; and *Behavior Therapy Techniques: A Guide to the Treatment of Neuroses* (Wolpe & Lazarus, 1966).

CONTEMPORARY BEHAVIOR-THERAPY TECHNIQUES

In the remainder of this chapter we describe some of the techniques used in behavior therapy. We trace the development of each procedure, describe its current applications, and discuss empirical evidence for its effectiveness.

Systematic Desensitization

Systematic desensitization (SD) is one of the best-known and most thoroughly researched techniques in behavior therapy. It is used most often to reduce maladaptive, learned anxiety (such as phobias), but has also been applied to many other clinical problems.

Background. The demonstrations by Watson and Rayner that fear could be learned through conditioning, and by Mary Cover Jones that it could be unlearned through the same mechanism, were early examples of how learning principles could be applied to anxiety problems. In addition, during the 1930s Guthrie (1935) proposed several techniques for breaking maladaptive habits, including fearfulness. For instance, he suggested presenting to phobic persons an example of the frightening stimulus that is so weak it does not elicit anxiety, then gradually increasing the stimulus until it can be tolerated fearlessly at full strength. During the 1920s Johannes Schultz, a German psychologist, developed a technique called "autogenic training." It involved a combination of hypnosis, relaxation, and autosuggestion with which clients themselves induced states incompatible with anxiety (Pikoff, 1984).

Systematic desensitization was first described in Joseph Wolpe's (1958) *Psychotherapy by Reciprocal Inhibition*. Wolpe had been doing research on the conditions under which cats develop "experimental neuroses" and found, for example, that after animals had been repeatedly shocked while eating, they resisted being put in the feeding cages, acted emotionally, and refused to eat while there.

Wolpe reasoned that if conditioned anxiety could inhibit eating, the reverse might be true; eating might inhibit conditioned anxiety. Luckily for the cats, Wolpe was right. Relying on a principle called *reciprocal inhibition*, he hand-fed fearful cats in the cages where their anxiety had been learned. According to Wolpe (1958): "If a response antagonistic to anxiety can be made to occur in the presence of anxiety-evoking stimuli so that it is accompanied by a complete or partial suppression of the anxiety responses,

the bond between these stimuli and the anxiety responses will be weakened" (p. 71).

Many of the animals benefited from this
procedure, and their emotional behaviors
were reduced. Those cats remaining "neurotic" were moved into a room unlike the
conditioning room. After they ate there
without anxiety, Wolpe moved the animals
to a room more like the feared environment. He continued feeding the cats in
places more and more like the original conditioning setting until they were able to eat
in the feared cage itself.

Desensitization Procedures.   Wolpe
(1958) later extended his methods to humans who suffered maladaptive anxiety. His
first task was to find a response incompatible with anxiety. He selected three types
of inhibitors: deep muscle relaxation, interpersonal assertion, and sexual arousal. In
each instance the principle was the same:
People cannot be anxious while they are relaxed or assertive or sexually aroused. Deep
muscle relaxation has become the most popular anxiety inhibitor in clinical treatment
involving systematic desensitization. However, assertion or sexual arousal may also be
employed, especially when the anxiety to be
inhibited relates to interpersonal or sexual
problems.

The most common relaxation technique
is called *progressive relaxation training* (e.g.,
Bernstein & Borkovec, 1973), a shorter version of a method pioneered by Jacobson in
1938. The client is taught to become physically and mentally relaxed by going through
a series of exercises in which sixteen groups
of muscles are tensed for a few seconds and
then released, while the client focuses on the
sensations of relaxation that follow. You can
get some idea of what these exercises feel
like by clenching your fist for about five seconds and then abruptly releasing the tension. The resulting flow of relaxation is a
mild version of what can be experienced by
tensing and relaxing muscles throughout
the body.

Relaxation training initially takes approx-

imately forty minutes per session. After
four to six sessions and practice at combining the exercises, the client may be able to
relax in less than ten minutes. Relaxation
may be attained through other methods if
the client is unable to perform the exercises
or if the therapist has a preference for another technique. Hypnosis is used on occasion, as are drugs, biofeedback, and meditation (Delmonte, 1985).

The next step in desensitization is to in-
troduce anxiety-arousing situations in a
gradual hierarchy. There are *in vivo* hierarchies, where clients are actually exposed to
gradually more threatening versions of
what they fear, and *imaginal* hierarchies, in
which clients imagine or visualize a series of
increasingly frightening scenes. The order
of scenes is determined by the client so that
each scene elicits just a bit more anxiety than
the one before it. Too large an increase in
arousal between items will make progress
difficult, while too small an increase may
lengthen treatment needlessly. An illustrative imaginal desensitization hierarchy is
presented in Box 9-1.

After training in relaxation and the construction of the hierarchy, desensitization itself is begun. In imaginal procedures, the
client is relaxed and asked to visualize the
easiest item on the hierarchy. If the client
can imagine the scene without anxiety for
ten seconds, the next scene is presented. If
any anxiety is felt, however, the client signals the therapist and stops visualizing the
scene. After regaining complete relaxation,
the client again pictures the item for a
shorter duration. Visualization times for
that scene are gradually increased until the
client can comfortably imagine it twice for
ten seconds. This sequence is continued until the client can handle all the items.

Inhibition of anxiety to imaginal scenes
may gradually transfer to their real-life
equivalents, but the client is also urged to
seek out real-world counterparts of the visualized scenes in order to reinforce progress
and to assess the generality of the treatment
effects. Completion of a hierarchy typically

BOX 9-1 An example of a desensitization hierarchy

Below is an example of a desensitization hierarchy used by James Geer (1965) in his treatment of a 17-year-old high school girl who had a "morbid fear of contracting a case of nits in her hair." The numbers in parentheses indicate the session(s) of desensitization during which that item was presented.

1. Writing the words "bug" and "lice." (1)
2. While reading in school you notice a small bug on your book. (1)
3. While walking down the sidewalk you notice a comb in the gutter. (1)
4. You are at home watching television when an ad concerning a dandruff-removing shampoo comes on. (2)
5. You are reading a Reader's Digest article that goes into detail concerning the catching and curing of a case of lice. (2)
6. You look at your desktop and notice several bobby pins and clips upon it. (3)
7. You are in a department store, and the saleslady is fitting a hat on you. (3)
8. At a store you are asked to try on a wig and you comply. (3)
9. You are watching a movie and they show a scene where people are being deloused. (4,5, and 6)
10. At school, in hygiene class, the teacher lectures on lice and bugs in people's hair. (4 and 5)
11. A girl puts her scarf on your lap. (5)
12. In a public washroom you touch the seat of a commode. (6)
13. You are in a beauty shop having your hair set. (6)
14. A girl sitting in front of you in school leans her head back on your books. (6 and 7)
15. While sitting at home with your sister, she tells you that she used someone else's comb today. (7 and 8)
16. While sitting in the local snack bar a friend tells you of her experiences when she had a case of lice. (8 and 9)
17. You are combing your hair in the washroom when someone asks to borrow your comb. (9)
18. A stranger asks to use your comb and continues to ask why not when you say no. (9)
19. While standing looking at an ad in a store window, someone comes up beside you and puts their head near yours to see too. (10)
20. A stranger in the washroom at school hands you her comb and asks you to hold it for her. (10)
21. Your sister is fixing your hair when she drops the curlers on the floor, picks them up, and uses them in your hair. (11)
22. A stranger notices a tangle in your hair and tries to help you by combing it out with her comb. (11)

takes three to five sessions, though it is possible to finish a short hierarchy in a single meeting.

Applications. Systematic desensitization has been applied to fears of almost everything, including high places and low places, closed spaces and open spaces; an ark's worth of mammals, reptiles, birds, insects, and fish; encounters with women, with men, with strangers and with noise, dirt, and death. Desensitization has been used to relieve such uncommon phobias as the fear of balloons, wind, the year 1952, feathers, violins, sanitary napkins, dirty shirts, and short people.

Desensitization is also used in cases where anxiety is not immediately obvious. For example, when anxiety causes complex patterns of behavior to break down, clients may focus on the disruption itself, not the anxiety causing it. Complaints about inability to concentrate, poor memory, confusion, speech disfluency, sexual dysfunction, or impairment of motor skills (e.g., typing) can be treated with desensitization. Similarly, certain maladaptive or bizarre behaviors such as amnesia, obsessions, compulsions, delusions, hysterical paralysis, drug abuse, alcoholism, or unusual sexual practices are sometimes motivated by efforts to avoid certain anxiety-provoking stimuli or situations.

Prolonged anxiety may cause *physical damage* to various organ systems and result in psychosomatic or psychophysiological disorders (e.g., ulcers) or in symptoms such as headaches, high blood pressure, or chronic fatigue. Where actual tissue damage has occurred, medical treatment is of course required, but anxiety reduction through desensitization may help eliminate one of the factors causing these problems.

Variations on Desensitization. The popularity of desensitization has led to a proliferation of methods based upon it. In *group desensitization* with several clients who share a common fear, a single hierarchy is used; progress up the hierarchy is geared to the pace of the slowest individual.

In vivo desensitization is probably the most popular variant. As noted earlier, the client is actually exposed to anxiety-arousing objects or situations, presented in a gradual fashion, and often in real-life settings. As an alternative to deep muscle relaxation, therapists themselves may act as anxiety inhibitors by accompanying their clients on *in vivo* "field trips." Sometimes the client is asked to engage in some behavior that is incompatible with strong anxiety. An interesting application of this approach in treating a severe elevator phobia involved having the client eat a multicourse gourmet meal while seated in a moving elevator (Bryntwick & Solyom, 1973).

Cue-controlled relaxation is another means of inhibiting anxiety in real-life settings, either as part of *in vivo* desensitization or various stress management procedures. The technique involves learning standard progressive relaxation, then repeatedly subvocalizing a cue word like "calm" or "relax" with each exhalation. After a few weeks of practice, the client is presented with some

frightening (real or imagined) stimulus in the office and told to take a deep breath and subvocalize the cue word upon exhalation. If relaxation is achieved, the client is encouraged to use the cue to prevent maladaptive anxiety in real-life encounters.

Effectiveness and Other Research Issues. Regarding the effectiveness of desensitization, Paul concluded that "for the first time in the history of psychological treatments, a specific therapeutic package reliably produced measurable benefits for clients across a broad range of distressing problems in which anxiety was of fundamental importance" (Paul, 1969b, p. 159). Paul's conclusion has been extended over the years (e.g., McGlynn, Mealiea & Landau, 1981), with the result that behavior therapists are generally confident about the efficacy of desensitization, especially when it is applied to its most appropriate target: conditioned, maladaptive anxiety.

The major research questions surrounding desensitization today are (1) Why is it effective? and (2) With what types of anxiety problems is it less effective than alternative treatments? Wolpe's original counterconditioning explanation has been challenged by a vast amount of research, and many behavior therapists no longer subscribe to it (Kazdin & Wilcoxon, 1976; McGlynn, Mealiea & Landau, 1981). Several mechanisms have been proposed as alternative explanations for the success of desensitization. Among the most popular are the following:

1. Desensitization depends on *cognitive factors* that modify the way the client thinks about a feared object (Wilkins, 1971). For example, the technique may produce a strong *expectancy* that a fear can be overcome. The credibility of desensitization therefore insures its success as a treatment.
2. The therapist acts as *social reinforcer* for the client's nonfearful responses (e.g., Leitenberg, Agras, Barlow & Oliveau, 1969).
3. As the client recognizes progress up the hierarchy, future nonphobic behavior is sup-

ported through *self-reinforcement* (e.g., Meichenbaum, 1972).

4. Clients learn to *shift their attention* from threatening to nonthreatening properties of phobic situations (e.g., Wilkins, 1971).

5. Anxiety is *extinguished* or *habituated* via the presentation of conditioned emotional stimuli (hierarchy scenes) without any aversive consequences (e.g., Marks, 1975).

Hundreds of research investigations have yet to resolve the question of the mechanisms by which desensitization produces its effects (see reviews by Davison & Wilson, 1973; Kazdin & Wilcoxon, 1976; Levin & Gross, 1985; McGlynn, Mealiea & Landau, 1981). Whether future research will be any more conclusive is uncertain. In any event, systematic desensitization still stands as one of the best-validated treatment techniques available to the clinical psychologist.

There are some anxiety-related problems for which systematic desensitization has been less successful. In general, anxiety problems that do not have well-defined stimulus elicitors and/or that have more components than simple phobias have been less responsive to desensitization. Included in this group are the problems of agoraphobia, panic attacks, obsessive-compulsive disorder, and certain types of social anxiety. In recent years, behavioral clinicians have found that treatments involving direct exposure of the client to feared stimuli may be the treatment of choice for many of these disorders (Barlow & Wolfe, 1981).

Exposure Techniques: Flooding and Implosion

Most exposure treatments entail direct or *in vivo* exposure to frightening stimuli rather than imaginal presentations, as does desensitization. Second, most exposure treatments require a lengthy duration of exposure so the anxiety will ultimately dissipate or wear out, giving clients the opportunity to learn that they need not be afraid of their own fear. In desensitization, exposure

times are abbreviated so intense anxiety is not experienced. Finally, most exposure treatments do not attempt to induce a state of physiological relaxation, as is the practice in desensitization.

There are many variations in the way exposure treatments are formulated and practiced. Some therapists favor very intense, prolonged, *in vivo* exposures; others prefer more gradual, self-paced, indirect exposures (see Barlow & Waddell, 1985, for a discussion of this issue). However, the major component of all exposure treatments requires the fearful person to confront the situations that are frightening so that (s)he can learn that these situations lack actual danger.

One of the best-known examples of exposure-based treatments is *flooding;* this involves extended exposure of a client to anxiety-eliciting stimuli. It is based on the principle of extinction, whereby conditioned stimuli lose their aversive qualities when no harmful consequences follow them. In flooding, clients are prevented from avoiding or escaping stimuli they fear in order to learn that the stimuli are not objectively threatening.

Implosion or implosive therapy is similar to flooding, but implosive stimuli are more intense than those actually found in life and sometimes include material that psychoanalytic theory suggests would be important in causing a certain fear (Stampfl & Levis, 1973). For example, in treating someone with a fear of toads, the implosive therapist might use imagined scenes of toads along with others depicting castration, Oedipal conflicts, parental rejection, and bodily injury.

Background. Kazdin (1978) points out that flooding had its modern origin in two types of experiments. The first was Masserman's work on experimental neurosis, which demonstrated that an animal's experimentally induced anxiety could be eliminated by forcing the animal back into the feared setting. Experiments on avoidance learning also suggested the therapeutic value of forced exposure (e.g., Solomon, Kamin & Wynne, 1953).

Although there are few references to techniques resembling flooding in early clinical literature, similar methods have been employed nonsystematically for many years. Aphorisms such as "Face your fears," "The only thing to fear is fear itself," and "Look fear in its face" are all supported by the same rationale as flooding.

Flooding Procedures. Flooding can be conducted imaginally or it can be done *in vivo*. In either instance, exposure times must

be long enough for anxiety to dissipate. Exposure should not be terminated while the client is still anxious, as this would reinforce avoidance behavior. Flooding sessions may last forty-five minutes to an hour, although they sometimes last two hours or more before a decrease in anxiety is noted. An excerpt from a session of imaginal flooding for an agoraphobic is provided in Box 9-2.

Applications. One problem for which flooding appears to be especially popular is agoraphobia. Literally translated, agoraphobia is "fear of the marketplace"; in current parlance it means a fear of public

BOX 9-2 An example of imaginary flooding

Below is an excerpt from a session of flooding with an agoraphobic male client who fears loss of control, particularly at social gatherings.

T: You are there in the room with all those people, everyone seems to be having a good time. They are all drinking, talking, joking. There are quite a number of people around that you know. You know that the room is very large, but right now the room seems small because there are so many people there. You are standing by Alice, and you are just drinking soda so you stay in control. You are wondering what the hell you are doing there in the first place. You are forcing yourself to be there. You can hear your heart beat really fast. You are feeling dizzy and light-headed. You are trying to listen to what people are saying, you are trying to find a way that you could have some fun too. But you know that having fun is only for other people. All the people are normal, and you are not. And that is what you tell yourself all the time. You keep comparing yourself to other people, and they always end up being okay and you don't, but right now it is worse than ever. You are feeling so uncomfortable, you wish you could run out of the place. And that is really scary when you start feeling that way. You're feeling like you don't belong here. It is

so uncomfortable to stand there at a party with 220 people always feeling different, like you don't belong there, you are different, you are abnormal, you're crazy; but that is what your life is all about, that is how you always feel. But right now it is worse than ever because you have all those sensations, you have all those feelings, all those fears. You wonder if they know, if they know that you are frightened. You wonder if they know that you are feeling so abnormal. You keep thinking how you would like to slip out. But there are a lot of people between you and the exit. You are standing there, and you are getting more and more uptight. It feels as though you are going to jump out of your skin; it is very uncomfortable, and you are feeling very dizzy, very light-headed, very hot, very uptight. You look around, and you know the people, and you can hear their voices, you can see their mouths move when they talk; but it doesn't make sense to you anymore. It is as if things are unreal to you—it's like in a dream—you are standing there, you know the people, you know the place, everything around seems familiar, but nothing makes sense. Everything is distant, you are feeling really detached, very removed from everything and everyone, and you are feeling very uptight.

Source: Chambless and Goldstein, 1980.

places, especially those that are too crowded or too empty. Clinicial agoraphobics are usually women who present a cluster of symptoms including dependency, depersonalization, "fear of fear," panic attacks, and fear of being away from any place that represents safety (Goldstein & Chambless, 1978). Flooding is also frequently employed for obsessive-compulsive disorders (Steketee & Foa, 1985).

Effectiveness and Other Research Issues. Although empirical research has not yet isolated the exact mechanism responsible for exposure treatment's effectiveness, major research efforts have (1) evaluated the clinical conditions for which it is effective, or more effective than alternative treatments (Jansson & Öst, 1982); and (2) investigated the extent to which its efficacy is improved by combining it with medication (Zitrin, Klein & Woerner, 1980), spouse involvement in therapy (Barlow, O'Brien & Last, 1984), or assertion training (Emmelkamp, van der Hout & de Vries, 1983).

Assertion Training

The 1970s were known as the decade of individual independence, an era committed to the pursuit of selfhood and often criticized for narcissistic preoccupations. Partial testimony to the character of this period was the spate of self-help books urging people to do their own thing, be creatively aggressive, and say no and not feel guilty. Though *assertion training* has sometimes been identified as behavior therapy's contribution to this self-promotion, it is more than just a product of the "me generation"; it is also an important clinical technique with beneficial effects for many clients.

Assertiveness is best defined as *the appropriate expression of feeling in ways that do not infringe upon the rights of others* (Alberti & Emmons, 1974; Wolpe & Lazarus, 1966). Thus, telling your boss that you will not agree to some unreasonable request requires assertion, but so does telling your friends that you were moved by their recent

expression of sympathy. Assertion is not the same as aggression. Responding to the person who pushes ahead of you in a supermarket check-out line by saying "Pardon me, there is a line here; please wait your turn" is assertive. Saying "Get your ass out of here before I hit you with my pot roast" is aggressive and not a goal of assertion training. Finally, assertiveness does not preclude politeness or altruism. An assertive individual may make sacrifices to help others ("Why don't you check out first; I'm not in a hurry"), but *only* because he or she wishes to do so, not because of fear of expressing objections.

All too often, people know what they would like to say and do in a difficult social situation (and chide themselves later for not having said or done it) but, because of thoughts like "I have no right to make a fuss" or "He won't like me if I object," they suffer in silence. Increased social awkwardness, continual self-blame, and varying degrees of depression are common results. Assertion training is designed to (1) teach clients how to express themselves appropriately if they do not already have the skills, and/or (2) eliminate cognitive obstacles to clear self-expression. These changes usually bring a better sense of well-being and the establishment of patterns of thought and overt behavior that help the client achieve social and material rewards, including greater satisfaction from life.

Background. Assertion training was anticipated by several therapeutic procedures. Moreno's (1946) psychodrama used role-playing techniques that encouraged participants to act spontaneously and express feelings freely. In George Kelly's (1955) *fixed-role therapy*, clients were asked to assume the role of some model whose outlook on the world and actual behavior were less constricted than their own. Through this type of identification, the client was expected to learn the benefits of more assertive behavior.

The first systematic description of assertion training was Andrew Salter's *Condi-*

tioned Reflex Therapy (1949). Salter prescribed a number of *excitatory* techniques for "inhibited" clients. Among these methods were use of "feeling talk" (e.g., "I absolutely despise crows"), expression of contradictory opinions, "facial talk" (making facial expressions consistent with emotions), improvisation, acknowledging and accepting compliments, and using the word "I" in conversation.[2]

A very influential figure in the evolution of assertion training was Joseph Wolpe, who advocated using assertive behavior as an anxiety inhibitor as early as 1949. Wolpe found assertive responses to be particularly effective in inhibiting interpersonal anxiety and trained his clients in specific assertion skills. Assertion training has been very popular in recent years, as evidenced by the multitude of books, articles, workshops, and courses devoted to it.

Assertion Training Procedures. Unlike other techniques in this chapter, assertion training has not been standardized into a specific set of procedures. A wide assortment of methods is employed. Though it can be done on a one-to-one basis, assertion training often takes place in groups and usually includes four components: (1) defining assertion and distinguishing it from aggression and submissiveness, (2) discussing client's rights and the rights of others in a variety of social situations, (3) identifying and eliminating cognitive obstacles to assertion, and (4) practicing assertive behavior.

This last component usually begins with role playing or rehearsal of various social interactions, with the therapist taking the client's role and modeling appropriate assertiveness. Next, the client tries the same behavior. This effort is reinforced and suggestions are made for further improvement. After more refined rehearsals, the client is asked to try the new thoughts and actions in

real-life settings. Successes and failures are then analyzed at subsequent sessions, where new or slightly adjusted skills are practiced. This sequence continues until the need for further training disappears.

Applications. Many types of clients can benefit from assertion training, although few enter a therapist's office and request it specifically. Couples suffering marital discord, college students who have interpersonal problems, shy and introverted adults, alcoholics, drug abusers, and people who rely on aggression to coerce others are often helped by assertion training as part of an overall clinical intervention.

Effectiveness and Other Research Issues. Research on the effects of assertion training has been popular among behavioral clinicians. Most of this work has been done with college students or psychiatric inpatients and has attempted to ascertain the relative effectiveness of the modeling, behavioral rehearsal, and feedback components of assertion training. While the results are complex and difficult to summarize, it would seem that with college students, almost any training technique is sufficient to produce behavioral changes. Psychiatric patients require a more elaborate treatment package, in which modeling may be especially important.

Although most research demonstrates that subjects receiving some form of training do significantly better than those who receive either a placebo or no treatment, it has been difficult to show that new assertive behavior transfers to *in vivo* contexts. Few studies have examined the generalization of treatment effects. Those that have often discover a disappointingly small amount of transfer of recently developed assertiveness (see Bellack, 1983, for a review of assessment issues in measuring social skills).

Assertion research has received considerable criticism. A major concern is that most of it has been limited only to negative or "refusal" assertion, which involves expression of dissatisfaction and saying no to un-

---

[2] These techniques are also part of gestalt therapy and other phenomenologically oriented treatment approaches discussed in Chapter 10.

BOX 9-3 Exercises in assertion training

The training situations used in most assertion research concentrate on what is often termed "denial" or "refusal" assertion and are similar to those used in assessing assertion. Below are three examples taken from some of our own research.

1. You have just moved into a new apartment with two other friends. They have been looking for a fourth person with whom to share the apartment. The two friends come to you and inform you that they have found a fourth person. The proposed roommate happens to be someone whom you secretly dislike.

2. You are eating in a very nice restaurant with some friends. The waiter comes and you order a steak, telling him you want it "rare." A little later, the waiter brings your steak, and you discover that it is well-done. The waiter asks, "Will there be anything else?"

3. You are leaving your job late on a Friday afternoon. You are hurrying home because you have made dinner plans for that evening with some friends. At the door of the office, you are stopped by your boss who says, "I'd like you to work tonight for a couple of hours because we have a job that must be completed by tomorrow."

Source: Nietzel, Martorano, and Melnick, 1977.

reasonable requests (see Box 9-3). Assertion in which the client communicates positive affect, gives and receives compliments, or expresses tender feelings has for the most part been neglected by researchers.

Modeling

A very important mechanism in social-learning theory is *modeling*, or observational learning. Bandura (1969) claimed that "virtually all learning phenomena resulting from direct experiences can occur on a vicarious basis through observation of other persons' behavior and its consequences for them" (p. 118). In many instances, learning through modeling is far more efficient than learning through direct reinforcement. Observation of competent models can eliminate the hazards of unguided trial-and-error behavior. (Imagine the problems if everyone had to be hit by a car before knowing how to cross streets safely!) Highly sophisticated behaviors such as speech require appropriate models, as do complex chains of motor behavior such as driving. Of course, many behaviors *can* be developed through direct experience and reinforcement, but the process of learning is often shortened by the opportunity to observe models.

In addition to developing new behaviors, modeling has other effects. Observation of the consequences of a model's behavior may either *inhibit* or *disinhibit* imitative behavior in an observer. (Would you pet a dog that just bit your friend?) Observing the behavior of others can also *facilitate* the performance of similar responses already present in the repertoire of the observer (taking one's place in line is a common example).

Historical Background. Modeling has long been recognized as an important influence on behavior. Gabriel Tarde (1903), the French judge and sociologist, developed a theory of criminality based on the idea that crime is acquired through imitation. Early theorists viewed imitation as an innate characteristic of humans. Later, psychologists began to explain modeling in terms of conditioning (Allport, 1924) and reinforcement (Miller & Dollard, 1941) principles.

One of the earliest therapeutic examples of modeling was Jones's (1924a,b) use of *social imitation* to overcome conditioned fear in children. Bandura (1969) also credits Masserman (1943) with using modeling to remediate experimental neuroses produced in laboratory animals. According to Bandura, the opportunity for Masserman's inhibited animals to observe a fearless cagemate was sufficient to reduce avoidance behavior in some of them.

Modeling Procedures. Modeling has been used to treat many clinical problems, including social withdrawal among adults and children, obsessive-compulsive behaviors, unassertiveness, antisocial conduct, physical aggressiveness, and early infantile autism. Probably its most common use, however, is in the reduction of fears.

In its simplest form, a modeling approach to the elimination of fearful avoid-ance involves having a client observe live, filmed, or videotaped models who fearlessly perform the behavior that the client avoids. The observable consequences for the models should be positive, or at least not negative.

Several variations on the basic modeling package have been developed. The most common of these is called *participant modeling*. In this procedure, live modeling is supplemented by giving the client an opportunity to make guided, gradual contact with the feared object under controlled or protected circumstances. This guided contact may be further supported by the use of *response induction aids*, special props that make feared responses a little less threatening.

FIGURE 9-3.   These frames are from a modeling film used to treat snake phobics. The film depicts children and adults in progressively more threatening interactions with a king snake. (From A. Bandura, E. B. Blanchard, and B. Ritter, "The relative efficacy of desensitization and modeling approaches for inducing behavioral, affective and attitudinal changes," *Journal of Personality and Social Psychology*, 1969, *13*, 173–99. Copyright by the American Psychological Association. Reprinted by permission.)

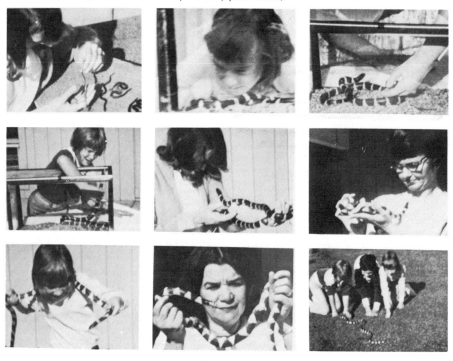

For example, Bandura, Jeffery, and Wright (1974) reported that induction aids such as gloves and physical assistance enhanced the effectiveness of modeling in reducing clients' fear of snakes.

Another innovation in modeling techniques is *covert modeling*. Here, clients observe the activities of *imagined* therapeutic models rather than watching live or videotaped displays. Covert modeling involves three components: imagination of situations where fear is expected to occur; imagination of one or more persons comfortably dealing with these situations, and imagination of favorable consequences for the model.

Effectiveness and Other Research Issues. For the most part, outcome research on modeling for fear reduction and other goals has shown it to be effective in producing beneficial changes especially when combined with other techniques (e.g., Bandura, 1986; Rosenthal, 1982). Many questions remain unanswered, however.

A primary concern of modeling research is the investigation of several procedural variations intended to bolster the effectiveness of modeling. Participant and covert modeling are two important examples. Other research has shown that observers are especially influenced by models with whom they share characteristics, by models that are prestigious, by models that are rewarded for their acts, and by multiple models (Bandura, 1986).

In an interesting variation on the customary modeling procedure, Meichenbaum (1971) proposed that the display of some fearful behavior by models could enhance modeling effects if presented as the initial part of a more complete demonstration in which the model ultimately copes with and overcomes the fear. He termed this technique *coping modeling* and suggested that it could strengthen treatment because it enhances observer-model similarity and provides useful information on how to deal successfully with a fear. While not universally supported, some studies have replicated the finding that coping models produce stronger effects than *mastery models,* who display total fearlessness and competence (e.g., Kazdin, 1973).

Aversion Therapy

Aversion therapy is a set of techniques using painful or unpleasant stimuli to decrease the probability of some unwanted behavior. Drug abuse, alcoholism, overeating, smoking, and disturbing sexual practices are typical targets of aversion therapy. Most aversion methods are based on classical conditioning. Stimuli that elicit problem behavior are paired with a noxious stimulus (e.g., a person is shocked as he sits at a simulated bar and reaches for a bottle of Scotch). Continuation of this sequence should result in a decrease in the positive value of the eliciting stimuli until the unwanted behavior is reduced, if not eliminated.

Aversion therapy may also employ punishment. In such cases, the aversive stimulus is delivered just after the client performs the problematic behavior (e.g., shock would occur immediately after taking a drink of alcohol).

Historical Background. Aversion techniques have been used for centuries. Ullmann and Krasner (1975) report that the Romans encouraged sobriety by placing an eel in the wine cups of intemperate drinkers. Early in the twentieth century, Bekhterev and Pavlov suggested the clinical utility of conditioning aversions to previously positive stimuli. Another Russian, Nikolai Kantorovich, was the first person to use aversion conditioning (electric shock to the hands) for the treatment of alcohol abuse. As noted earlier, one of the first applications of aversion therapy in the United States was by Voegtlin and his associates at the Shadel Sanatorium in Seattle.

Aversion Therapy Procedures. The noxious stimuli used in aversion therapy usually involve electric shock (to the hands, feet, or legs) or drugs which either induce nausea or temporarily suppress breathing. Substances with a foul taste or smell have also been used.

In an early example of electrical aversion, Blake (1965) used shocks along with relaxation training and instructions about the negative consequences of drinking to treat a group of alcoholics. Participants were shocked on half the occasions on which they sipped alcohol. Termination of the shock occurred only when subjects spat out the alcohol, a procedure known as *aversion relief*. Follow-up interviews indicated a 54 percent rate of abstinence after six months and 52 percent abstinence after one year.

Raymond (1956) successfully used chemical aversion with a hospitalized thirty-three-year-old male fetishist charged with numerous malicious attacks on and damage to prams (baby carriages) and handbags. (One prosecutor was moved to label the patient "a menace to any woman with a pram.") Treatment involved repeatedly pairing the fetish objects with apomorphine-induced nausea. After several sessions over a period of days, the patient claimed to be repulsed by the objects of his former affections and even relinquished some pram photos he had been hiding.

One controversy in aversion therapy is whether there is a basis for preferring chemical or electrical events as the noxious stimuli. For a time, the prevailing sentiment appeared to favor electrical methods. Davidson (1974) described seven advantages associated with electrical methods: (1) greater temporal precision, (2) greater suitability for frequent repetitions, (3) fewer medical complications, (4) fewer apparatus requirements, (5) fewer staff needed, (6) less traumatic implementations for staff, and (7) wider applicability. Others (e.g., Elkins, 1975) suggest that the positive effects of chemical aversion were underestimated in early investigations because the procedures were often incorrectly applied. Certain types of aversion may be more appropriate for behaviors that involve a particular sensorimotor system (Garcia, McGowan

& Green, 1971). For example, associations between nausea and overeating or overdrinking might be biologically and psychologically easier to establish than connections between, say, overeating and pain. On the other hand, shock may be more easily associated with sexual or aggressive misbehaviors than would chemically induced sickness.

A form of aversion therapy called *covert sensitization* requires the client to visualize or imagine aversive consequences that could accompany unwanted behavior. According to Little and Curran (1978), covert sensitization usually proceeds as follows:

The covert sensitization client, after receiving several sessions of relaxation training, is asked to relax and imagine a sequence of events leading up to a hypothetical problematic performance. The client is then asked to imagine a series of aversive events (typically, nausea and vomiting) just as the point in the imaginal sequence is reached when initial reinforcement is about to be received. The aversion trial is concluded with a suggestion to the client that relief is experienced coincident with an imaginal turning away from the target stimulus. Escape trials are alternated with aversion trials. In the escape trials, the client successively imagines that he or she has an urge to commit the target behavior, begins to experience aversive consequences (typically, nausea), resists the undesired urge, and consequently feels fit and self-satisfied. The therapist attempts to facilitate the client's visualization by describing both types of scenes and by providing an especially detailed and exaggerated description of the aversive consequence. (p. 513)

Joseph Cautela, the originator of covert sensitization, describes the following scene to be visualized by an alcoholic client:

You are walking into a bar. You decide to have a glass of beer. You are now walking toward the bar. As you are approaching the bar you have a funny feeling in the pit of your stomach. Your stomach feels all queasy and nauseous. Some liquid comes up your throat and it is very sour. You try to swallow it back down, but as you do this, food particles start coming up your throat to your mouth. You are now reaching the bar and you order a beer. As the bartender is pouring the beer, puke comes up into your mouth. You try to keep your mouth closed and swallow it down. You reach for the glass of beer to wash it down. As soon as your hand touches the glass, you can't hold it down any longer. You have to open your mouth and you puke. It goes all over your hand, all over the glass and the beer. You can see it floating around in the beer. Snots and mucus come out of your nose. Your shirt and pants are full of vomit. The bartender has some on his shirt. You notice people looking at you. You get sick again and you vomit some more and more. You turn away from the beer and immediately you start to feel better and better. When you get out into the clean fresh air you feel wonderful. You go home and clean up. (Cautela, 1966, p. 37)

Covert sensitization offers several advantages over shock or chemically induced aversion (Cautela & Rosenstiel, 1975): Few side effects have been noted; special equipment or medical personnel are not required; and the procedure can be applied repeatedly in many different kinds of settings. Because the client's own experiences are used, a wider variety of stimuli are available which, when presented in imagery, may better approximate those encountered in the natural environment. These advantages are reduced by the fact that some patients report difficulty in maintaining clear visualizations, which necessitates extensive imagery training.

Effectiveness and Other Research Issues. In most cases, aversion therapy has a limited impact on the problems to which it is applied. While few behavior therapists doubt that they can temporarily discourage a client from uncontrolled drinking or aberrant sexual acts by applying some powerfully repugnant agent, most are skeptical about how permanent these changes will be.

The goal of any treatment should be change that is durable and that will generalize to the environment in which a client lives. Aversion therapy is lacking on both these grounds. One major reason is that aversion therapy, by itself, does not teach clients alternative behaviors that can replace their maladaptive ones. This is important in the treatment of problems such as overeating, smoking, drug abuse, or sexual deviations. In the sexual area, for example, problems usually reappear if clients do not develop other sexual outlets that are satisfying to them and acceptable to society.

The data on covert sensitization are mixed. Its practical advantages (e.g., flexibility, ease of administration) are numerous, but the existing literature is based on studies that lack necessary controls. Some years ago, Little and Curran (1978) concluded that covert sensitization may be effective in producing desired changes in sexual preferences, but that there was little support for its effectiveness with alcoholism, smoking, or obesity.

Finally, we should add that many behavior therapists do not use aversion techniques because they personally find them unpleasant, unethical, or both. Others believe that shocking clients or making them vomit may irreparably harm the therapeutic relationship. As a result, most therapists use aversion methods only as a last resort after non-aversive procedures have failed.

Contingency Management

Contingency management is a generic term for any operant technique that attempts to modify a behavior by controlling its consequences. *Shaping, time-out, contingency contracting*, and *token economies* constitute various types of contingency management. In practice, contingency management refers to the contingent presentation and/or withdrawal of reinforcers and aversive stimuli following certain behaviors. "Contingent" simply means that a consequence occurs *if and only if* the behavior to be strengthened or weakened has occurred.

Historical Background. The idea that psychologists discovered reward and punishment would reflect the grandest arrogance. The Old Testament depicts God as an effective contingency manager who practiced extinction (responding to the provocation of his sons and daughters, "I will hide my face from them," Deuteronomy 32:19–20) as well as time-out and punishment (when the Israelites disobeyed God, He sent them to the wilderness for forty years).

The same principles were used by correctional workers during the 1800s. For example, Alexander Maconochie, governor of a British penal colony, was convinced that the prison's deplorable conditions needed reform. He developed a plan by which a prisoner could gain early release by earning a sufficient number of "marks" through industry and good conduct. Another important feature of the system was its organization into graduated phases like those of contemporary token economies. The five phases were: (1) rigid discipline and absolute confinement, (2) labor on a chain gang, (3) limited freedom within certain areas, (4) "ticket-of-leave" or conditional freedom, and (5) total freedom.

Applications. Contingency management has been applied to a broader range of problems than any other behavioral technique. Autism, temper tantrums, learning difficulties, hyperactivity, retardation, juvenile delinquency, aggression, hallucinations, delusions, depression, phobias, sexual disorders, and psychosomatic complaints are a few of the targets that have been dealt with through contingency management.

A special advantage of contingency management is its flexibility. It is suitable for the very young and the very old. It can be tailored to the unique complaints of an individual or applied to the common needs of a group or even a community. Its principles are relatively easy to learn, making it possible to train friends, relatives, teachers, and peers to employ contingency management in real-life settings.

Contingency management can also be used by an individual to modify his or her own behavior. This process is known as *self-control;* it can be thought of as the ability to regulate personal behaviors by arranging appropriate reinforcement contingencies. The overweight person who permits herself or himself to eat only at specified times, only in the kitchen, and only in the presence of family is practicing a form of self-control. Specific components of self-control include self-instruction, self-monitoring, self-reinforcement, and self-evaluation, each of which has been shown to have some clinical utility (e.g., Rehm, Kornblith, O'Hara, Lamparski, Romano & Volkin, 1981).

Contingency Management Procedures. Complete accounts of the wide range of contingency management techniques are available in many texts (e.g., Kazdin, 1984; Redd, Porterfield & Andersen, 1979). Here are just four examples:

1   Shaping. Also called *successive approximation,* shaping is a procedure for developing new behaviors by initially reinforcing any act that remotely resembles the ultimately desired behavior. Gradually the criterion for reinforcement is made more stringent until only those responses matching the final standard are rewarded. Shaping is useful for instigating behaviors that appear to exceed the person's present capacities. It is often used to teach speech to children who are mute, toilet habits to those who are incontinent, and self-help and occupational skills to the retarded.

2   Time-out. Time-out is a special example of extinction which reduces the frequency of an unwanted behavior by temporarily removing the person from a setting where reinforcers exist for that behavior. The most common example is sending a child to a quiet, boring room for a short time following some act of mischief. Time-out is based on the principle that ignoring a child's "bad" behavior will decrease it, especially if alternative "good" behavior is also reinforced. Enthusiasm for time-out may be strongest among clinicians who have no children of their own and have therefore not had the opportunity to learn that children often enjoy ignoring their parents.

3 Contingency contracting.

Contracting is a form of contingency management where a formal, often written, agreement between therapist and client spells out the consequences of certain behaviors on the part of both parties. It thus organizes the use of many behavior-change methods.

Behavioral contracting has been applied to diverse clinical targets, including marital distress (Wood & Jacobson, 1985), family disruptions (Alexander & Parsons, 1973), drug abuse (Boudin, 1972), obesity (Brownell & Foreyt, 1985), and other problems (Walker, Hedberg, Clement & Wright, 1981). The typical contract involves five components which were suggested first by Stuart (1971): (1) responsibilities of each of the parties to the contract, (2) rewards for fulfilling the contract, (3) a system for monitoring compliance with the provisions of the contract, (4) bonuses for unusual accomplishments, and (5) penalities for failures.

Therapy contracts have also become popular with some nonbehaviorally oriented clinicians as a means of informing clients about the ethical requirements and limitations of psychotherapy, facilitating the client's participation in decision making during therapy, and specifying possible risks and benefits of therapy. However, not all clinicians agree that therapy contracts are a necessary or even desirable prelude to ethical treatment; some therapists believe that contracts are incompatible with certain types of intervention (Widiger & Rorer, 1984). A final use of contracts employed by many therapists is to prevent possible dangerous behavior by their clients by developing a formal contract that forbids violent behavior by the client and requires the client to take specific precautionary actions (e.g., calling the therapist, turning over weapons to the therapist) should he or she consider acting dangerously.

4 Token economies.

A token economy is a procedure for implementing the principles of contingency management to alter a variety of behaviors in a group of people. You might think of it as a scaled-down monetary system in which people are paid in a special currency (tokens) for performing designated behaviors. A token economy operates on the principle of being compensated for one's labors in institutional settings where residents have become accustomed to receiving rewards on a noncontingent basis.

The token economy usually consists of four basic components. First, *target behaviors* are specified. This means that the staff and often the clients designate the behaviors to be changed. Social interaction, self-help skills, and physical exercise are common target behaviors for institutionalized mental patients. Second, there must be a *token* or other medium of exchange which participants earn by performing the desired target behaviors. Gold stars and colored slips of paper are popular among children. Adults' tastes run toward poker chips, Green Stamps, or mental "coins." Third, there must be *backup reinforcers*: goods or services for which tokens may be exchanged. Food, recreational privileges, "vacations" from the hospital, and more luxurious living conditions are common backups. Finally, there must be *rules of exchange* governing the number of tokens to be earned by performing given target behaviors as well as the number of tokens necessary to purchase any backup. Exchange rules are often altered over the course of a token economy in order to avoid "inflation" or "deflation" of the currency.

The first report of a token economy in a psychiatric institution was published by Ayllon and Azrin (1965), who increased the rate of self-care behaviors and completed work assignments in a group of chronic female patients. Following Ayllon and Azrin's study, the use of token economies in psychiatric hospitals increased at a rapid rate. There was also a dramatic increase in the application of token economy procedures to other populations. Several investigators used token systems to control delinquent and antisocial behavior (e.g., Burchard, 1967; Cohen, 1968), and token programs were soon introduced to elementary school classrooms for purposes of reducing disruptions and promoting learning (e.g., O'Leary & Becker, 1967). Special programs for Head Start participants, retardates, alcoholics, drug addicts, and autistic children were developed according to token economy principles.

Token economies have also been introduced directly into the community. For example, Miller and Miller (1970) increased the rate of community organization activities among poor people through a token economy. A variety of conservation and environmental protection efforts have also been promoted through token programs applied either to large geographical areas or relatively large populations (Nietzel, Winett, MacDonald & Davidson, 1977).

Effectiveness and Other Research Issues. In terms of sheer frequency, research on contingency management is unmatched by any other behavioral technique. A remarkable feature of this research is the consistency with which it finds operant methods to be effective in modifying specific behaviors in desired directions. There are exceptions to this pattern, of course, but they are few in number.

The most troublesome aspect of contingency management is the problem of generalization. The question is not whether the techniques produce change, but whether the changes are durable and generalizable (Keeley, Shemberg & Carbonell, 1976; Woods, Higson & Tannahill, 1984). The principal research goals in the field at this time are (1) development and evaluation of procedures designed to promote the transfer of new behaviors to natural settings, and (2) demonstration of the continuation of improved behaviors over time.

Another major trend in contemporary research on applied operant methods is the

investigation of their success in dealing with problems that go beyond "mental health." Several broad social problems, such as energy conservation, racial discrimination, unemployment, and mass transportation, have all been approached from an operant perspective (Nietzel, et al., 1977). At the other extreme, behavioral and psychological events that underlie various physical illnesses have also been modified by contingent reinforcement (see Chapter 11 for a thorough discussion of health-related applications of behavior therapy).

Biofeedback

The use of operant technology to control internal, autonomic responses is known as *biofeedback*. Biofeedback is a unique version of contingency management because first, the behaviors to be changed are internal, autonomic responses such as heart rate and blood pressure, once thought to be involuntary and not subject to deliberate modification. Second, biofeedback requires special equipment that monitors the activity of interest and then provides feedback on this activity to the client. Feedback is transmitted either through a visual display (e.g., a meter or graph) or an auditory stimulus (e.g., a varying tone).

Historical Background. K. M. Bykov demonstrated in the mid-1950s that physiological responses could be *classically* conditioned to previously neutral stimuli, but Neal Miller (1969) showed that visceral activity was also subject to the principles of *operant* conditioning. Miller demonstrated that rats could learn to increase and decrease autonomic functions on the basis of contingent reinforcement (direct brain stimulation). The fact that the animals were immobilized with the drug curare ruled out the possibility that the autonomic changes were caused by muscular movement.

Despite the fact that Miller and several other researchers had difficulty replicating the results of the early animal studies, many investigators throughout the 1960s and 1970s began to show that humans could control such activity as brain waves and heart rate (see White & Tursky, 1982).

Applications and Procedures. Biofeedback has been used to treat several kinds of disorders, including essential hypertension (high blood pressure), migraine headaches, Raynaud's disease (a problem of reduced blood flow that can lead to gangrene in the hands or feet), and cardiac arrhythmias (irregular heart beats). EEG (electroencephalogram) conditioning can increase the percentage of alpha wave production and is often used as a special form of relaxation or meditation training.

In each of these applications the procedure is fundamentally the same. A monitor and feedback apparatus are attached to the client, who then uses some mental or physical strategy to change the internal response in a clinically desired direction. In most cases the reinforcer for change is simply the knowledge of results provided by the feedback, but praise or monetary rewards may also be used (Blanchard & Epstein, 1978).

Effectiveness and Other Research Issues. In spite of extravagant claims by some of its proponents, there is not enough evidence at this point to conclude that biofeedback is a clinically useful technique (Birnbaumer, 1977). Miller (1983) himself has observed that while biofeedback (if practiced "conscientiously") can be a useful treatment or part of treatment for several physical ailments including newer targets such as hemiplegias, fecal incontinence, and seizure disorders,

much of the evidence is of the case-history type, and most of the better . . . studies still involve rather small numbers of cases. . . . Furthermore, there does not seem to be much evidence on the differential effects of different [techniques] or combinations of these techniques, and such evidence as there is indicates that these effects are approximately equal, so that there appears to be a practical advantage in trying the

simpler ones, at least as the first step in a step-care procedure. (p. 23)

Cognitive Behavior Therapy

One can no more expect a client to participate in psychotherapy without thinking about the experience than one can expect a sprinter to run a race without moving his or her legs. Any therapy technique, behavioral or otherwise, stimulates a multitude of cognitions: Will this treatment work? Why will it work? What if it doesn't work? Why didn't I think of trying this? When will I start to notice some improvement? In addition to thinking about these questions, clients depend on cognitive processes to understand a therapist's communications, to visualize material in procedures like desensitization or covert modeling, and to reflect on the changes they make or fail to make in therapy.

All therapeutic interventions involve cognitive processes, but some procedures are particularly oriented toward changing distinct maladaptive cognitions. These techniques compose what is known as *cognitive behavior therapy* or simply *cognitive therapy*. Cognitive therapy can be defined as a treatment approach that attempts to modify maladaptive behavior by influencing a client's cognitions (beliefs, schemas, self-statements, and problem-solving strategies). Cognitive behavior therapists attach special, causal status to cognitions that strict behaviorists avoid (Schwartz, 1982). They assume that emotional problems are largely due to irrational or improper thinking and that restructuring these cognitions will be therapeutic (Kuiper & MacDonald, 1983). Specific cognitive behavior-therapy methods may be called coping skills training, anxiety management, stress inoculation, idealized self-image technique, misattribution therapy, problem-solving training, or self-instruction training (Ledwidge, 1978). Time projection, thought stopping, and cognitive restructuring could also be added to this roster. Detailed descriptions of these techniques can be found in Kendall and Braswell (1985), Kendall and Hollon (1979), Mahoney and Freeman (1985), and Meichenbaum (1977).

One of the most influential types of cognitive therapy is Aaron Beck's approach to the treatment of depression. Because depression is such a frequent clinical disorder and because evaluations of cognitive therapy have shown it to be a particularly effective intervention (e.g., Rush, Beck, Kovacs & Hollon, 1977; Kovacs, Rush, Beck & Hollon, 1981), Beck's treatment has earned a reputation as one of the most powerful forms of cognitive treatment. Cognitive therapy for depression is based on the assumption that emotions are determined by the way people think about their experiences. Depressive symptoms reflect logical errors and distortions that certain people consistently make about the events in their lives. These illogical "schemas" lead individuals to perceive themselves, their world, and their future in pessimistic, self-deprecating ways. Beck termed this set of mistaken schemas the "cognitive triad" and pointed out several specific forms of distorted thinking that therapists will notice in depressed persons. For example, *arbitrary inference* involves drawing conclusions about oneself on the basis of insufficient or irrelevant information (a woman believes she is worthless because she it not invited to a particular party). *Magnification* enlarges small events to a point of great significance (a man decides his record collection is ruined because one record has a scratch on it), while *minimization* does the opposite (a student believes that a good grade was the result of luck and that he is still basically stupid).

Cognitive therapists work to identify and correct their client's distorted beliefs. Five related strategies are emphasized: (1) recognizing the connections between cognitions, affect, and behavior; (2) monitoring occurrences of the negative cognitive triad; (3) examining the evidence for and against these distortions; (4) substituting more realistic interpretations for dysfunctional cogni-

tions; and (5) completing "homework assignments" wherein the client can practice these new thinking strategies and cope with problems more effectively.

Another, even better-known, cognitive therapy is Albert Ellis's rational-emotive therapy, or RET.[3] Ellis (1973) stated the core principles of RET as follows:

[W]hen a highly charged emotional Consequence (C) follows a significant Activating Event (A), A may seem to but actually does not cause C. Instead emotional Consequences are largely created by B—the individual's Belief System. When, therefore, an undesirable Consequence occurs, such as severe anxiety, this can usually be quickly traced to the person's irrational Beliefs, and when these Beliefs are effectively Disputed (at point D), by challenging them rationally, the disturbed Consequences disappear and eventually cease to reoccur. (p. 167)

To illustrate these principles, Ellis (1973) provides the following example. Suppose a man has had a bad day at work. He arrives late, forgets his office keys, spills coffee on his desk, and misses two important appointments. He may think to himself, "I was lousy at my job today." He is correct; he did do a bad job. This is what Ellis called the activating event (A), a happening that is undesirable. Next the man may think, "This is horrible, what a schmuck I am; if I don't get with it I'll get fired which will serve me right for being so worthless." These ideas reflect the person's belief system (B), and according to Ellis, *they* may produce the emotional consequences (C) of anxiety, depression, and worthlessness.

To summarize the ABCs of RET: Psychological problems result not from external stress but from the irrational ideas people hold, which lead them to insist that their wishes must be met in order for them to be happy. Thus the task in RET is to attack

---

[3] Rational-emotive therapy has also been called *rational behavior training* (Goodman & Maultsby, 1974), *systematic rational restructuring* (Goldfried, Decenteceo & Weinberg, 1974), and *cognitive restructuring* (Ledwidge, 1978).

"Why doesn't she call? I don't understand. She said she'd call at 5:00. It's 5:15 already. Maybe she's been in accident. Maybe she's lying in a ditch somewhere. I'd better call her and make sure she's ok. No, what if she's not hurt. What if she's with a MAN. I can't call her. She'll think I'm too pushy. They never like pushy men. But it's 5:20 already and she SAID she'd call— I didn't make her say that. She might really be hurt and bleeding somewhere. But what if I call her and she doesn't want to talk to me? God-damned women."

FIGURE 9-4. (Courtesy of the Western Psychological Association.)

these irrational, unrealistic, self-damaging beliefs and to instruct clients in more rational or logical thinking patterns that will not upset them.

Background. Ellis (1973) acknowledges numerous precursors to his RET system. Among early philosophers, the Stoics, particularly Epictetus, believed that "men are disturbed not by things, but by the view they take of them." Literature provides other examples. Shakespeare had Hamlet observe: "There is nothing either good or bad but thinking makes it so."

Ellis also notes that modern psychotherapists influenced the development of RET. Chief among these was Alfred Adler, whose motto, "Everything depends on opinion," is a keystone of RET philosophy. Several therapists who employed a forceful, directive,

active therapeutic style (e.g., Andrew Salter, Frederick Thorne, Alexander Herzberg, and Wilhelm Stekel) also anticipated RET. The most complete and informative presentations of Ellis's ideas are contained in his *Reason and Emotion in Psychotherapy* (1962) and the *Handbook of Rational-Emotive Therapy* (Ellis & Grieger, 1977).

RET Procedures. The style of the RET therapist is active, challenging, demonstrative, and often abrasive. Ellis advocates the use of strong, direct communication in order to persuade clients to give up the irrational ideas with which they indoctrinate themselves into misery. Here is a brief excerpt from an initial RET session between a therapist (T) and a young woman (C) who presented several problems, among them the abuse of alcohol.

C: . . . my tendency is to say *everything*. I want to change everything; I'm depressed about everything; et cetera.

T: Give me a couple of things, for example.

C: What I'm depressed about? I, uh, don't know that I have any purpose in life. I don't know what I—what I am. And I don't know in what direction I'm going.

T: Yeah, but that's—so you're saying, "I'm ignorant!" (client nods) Well, what's so awful about being ignorant? It's too bad you're ignorant. It would be nicer if you weren't—if you *had* a purpose and *knew* where you were going. But just let's suppose the worst: for the rest of your life you didn't have a purpose, and you stayed this way. Let's suppose that. Now why would you be so bad?

C: Because everyone *should* have a purpose!

T: Where did you get the *should*?

C: 'Cause it's what I believe in. (silence for a while)

T: I know. But think about it for a minute. You're obviously a bright woman; now, where did that *should* come from?

C: I, I don't know! I'm not thinking clearly at the moment. I'm too nervous! I'm sorry.

T: Well, but you *can* think clearly. Are you now saying, "Oh, it's hopeless! I can't think clearly. What a shit I am for not thinking clearly!" You see: You're blaming yourself for *that*.

C: (visibly upset; can't seem to say anything; then nods)

T: Now you're perfectly *able* to think.

C: Not at the moment!

T: Yes you are! Want to bet?

C: (begins to sob)

T: What are you crying about now?

C: Because I feel so stupid! And I'm afraid!

T: Yeah, but "stupid" means "I'm putting myself down for acting stupidly."

C: All right! I didn't expect to be put on so *fast*. I expected a moment to catch my breath and see who you *were;* and to establish some different kind of rapport.

T: Yeah. And that would be nice and easier; but we would really waste our time.

C: Yes, I guess we would.

T: But you're really upset because you're not giving the right answers—and isn't that *awful!*

C: Yes. And I don't think that anybody likes to be made a fool, a fool of!

T: You *can't* be made a fool of!

C: (chokes a little)

T: You see, that's the *point:* That's impossible. Now why *can't* you be made a fool of?

C: (angry outburst) Why don't you stop asking me?

T: (interrupting) No! You'll never get better unless you *think*. And you're saying, "Can't we do something *magical* to get me better? And the answer is "No!"

The therapist's frontal assault on the client's irrational beliefs is not restricted to cognitive interventions. Role playing, sensory-awareness exercises, desensitization, assertion training, and specific homework assignments also will be employed by the RET therapist in an attempt to provide behavioral complements to cognitive change (see Ellis & Bernard, 1985, for discussions of RET applied to several clinical problems).

Effectiveness and Other Research Issues. A series of meta-analyses have found cognitive behavioral treatments to be an effective form of psychotherapy. Miller and Berman (1983) reported a mean posttreatment effect size of .83 for cognitive treatments compared to no treatment, and a mean effect size of .21 for cognitive treatments compared to other therapies; these advantages were fairly well maintained at follow-up. Analyzing treatments that emphasized what they termed "self-statement modification," Dush, Hirt, and Schroeder (1983) report a healthy average effect size of .74 in comparison to no-treatment controls. Finally, in their comprehensive metaanalysis of psychotherapy, Shapiro and Shapiro (1982) reported a "modest but undeniable superiority of behavioral and cognitive methods" in relation to other treatments (p. 596).

In general, the evaluative research on the effectiveness of rational-emotive therapy is not as methodologically elegant as that for other cognitive methods (Zettle & Hayes,

1980) but its results are positive. Ellis (1973) reported more than twenty-five experimental studies and a greater number of case histories that supported the positive effects of RET, and the basic principles of RET and its theory of emotional distress have received favorable evaluations (Ellis & Greiger, 1977; DiGiuseppe & Miller, 1977).

In addition to research on effectiveness, there is a need to investigate more carefully the theoretical foundations of cognitive behavior therapy. Beidel and Turner (1986) have reviewed several problems in the conceptualization of cognitive behavior therapy

that cognitive therapists need to take seriously. Difficulties exist in at least three areas: (1) Definitions of cognitions are inconsistent: Sometimes cognition is viewed as a process, sometimes it is viewed as an outcome; (2) distorted cognitions have not been proven to be the cause of various emotional disturbances as most cognitive therapies imply; and (3) distinctions between traditional behavior therapy and cognitive behavior therapy are difficult because most cognitive behavior therapists use several noncognitive techniques that could account for treatment effectiveness.

BOX 9-4 Multimodal behavior therapy

One very innovative form of behavior therapy is *multimodal behavior therapy* as formulated and practiced by Arnold A. Lazarus of Rutgers University. Lazarus (1976, 1981, 1985) advocates "technical eclecticism" in his therapeutic approach, which means that therapists should use whatever techniques are most appropriate for given problems regardless of the theoretical system from which the techniques might be derived. Behavioral techniques might be most appropriate for one type of difficulty, while Gestalt or psychoanalytic procedures would be preferred for another problem. While Lazarus would feel free to use any or all of these techniques, it is probably fair to say that his basic approach is eclectic, albeit with a strong behavioral emphasis.

Lazarus organizes his treatment around seven areas of functioning summarized by the acronym BASIC ID, which stands for Behavior, Affect, Sensation, Imagery, Cognition, Interpersonal Relations, and Drugs. Each of these areas of functioning (with the exception of drugs, which is a form of treatment) may call for different techniques ranging across several schools of therapy, although Lazarus (1977) acknowledges that

about 28 percent of multimodal therapy is devoted to behavioral and interpersonal factors, with the rest of the time split among the other five areas.

Multimodal therapy has been sharply criticized by staunch behaviorists like Wolpe (Lazarus's former mentor) for straying too far from behavioristic principles and diluting the strength of pure behavior therapy (Wolpe, 1984). For his part, Lazarus (1977) claims that his treatment approach is committed to "behavioral principles," which he defines as

due regard for scientific objectivity, extreme caution in the face of conjecture and speculation, a rigorous process of deduction from testable theories, and a fitting indifference toward persuasion and hearsay. (pp. 550–551)

Multimodal behavior therapy is part of the trend toward eclecticism and integration of different schools of therapy that we previously described (see Chapter 7). Eclecticism remains a controversial issue, however, despite the fact that many clinicians claim it as their orientation (see Arkowitz & Messer, 1984, for a review).

"I will not talk to myself, I will not talk to myself."

FIGURE 9-5. Some cognitive therapy techniques are easier to follow than others. (Drawing by Modell; © 1964 The New Yorker Magazine, Inc.)

A Final Note

In describing contemporary behavior therapy we have concentrated on specific techniques such as desensitization, flooding, contingency management, and cognitive techniques. This emphasis should not imply that behavior therapists are simply technicians who match problems with specific treatment methods in an automatic way. Behavior therapists, like other clinicians, are committed to the welfare of the people they treat; they attempt to convey a sense of support and caring during the therapy process. Technical proficiency is not a substitute for the special therapeutic relationship that a client and clinician can share.

Having developed so rapidly since the 1960s, behavior therapy now faces several important challenges that it must meet in order to sustain its positive impact on clinical psychology. First, behavior therapy's tradition of integrating research findings with clinical practice has been endangered re-cently, a trend that Barlow (1980) identified as a widening "scientist-practitioner gap." Researchers must ask clinically meaningful questions and attempt to answer them in externally valid ways; clinicians must collect evaluative data as they practice. A related problem is what Ross (1985) has called a "technological drift" manifested by clinicians' and researchers' greater interests in applications and techniques at the expense of involvement in basic research, conceptual advancements, and knowledge from biological, developmental, and social psychology. Finally, there are three content/research areas neglected by behavior therapists that promise to be blue-chip investments in behavior therapy's development. Fine-grained analyses of psychopathology (Hersen, 1981), more direct research on affect (Wilson, 1982; Zajonc, 1980), and greater biological sophistication (Ross, 1985) are important needs that must be addressed by future behavior therapists.

chapter 10

Clinical Intervention: Phenomenological Models

In Chapters 8 and 9 we described clinical interventions that assume human behavior to be a product of either intrapsychic conflicts or environmental influences. As noted in Chapter 2, however, there is a third force in clinical psychology which de-emphasizes these factors and focuses instead on *conscious experience* as the basis for human behavior. This *phenomenological* approach offers an optimistic portrait of humans as creative, growing beings who, if all goes well, consciously guide their own behavior in an attempt to realize their fullest potential as unique individuals. When various behavior disorders arise, they are usually seen as stemming from disturbances in awareness or restrictions on existence that can be eliminated through various therapeutic experiences (Fischer & Fischer, 1983).

Working on behavior problems by increasing clients' conscious awareness reflects some of the psychodynamic principles on which phenomenological treatments are partly based. In addition, approaching each client as a unique individual guided by her or his own thoughts is similar to the more cognitive versions of behavior therapy (see Chapter 9). Nevertheless, many of the goals and techniques of phenomenologically oriented treatments are distinct. In this chapter we describe the background, procedures, and effectiveness of the most prominent phenomenological interventions.

Just as with psychodynamic and behavioral methods, a few themes unify the goals and techniques associated with phenomenological treatments. To set the stage for our discussion, we will review some of these commonalities:

1. There is an emphasis on promoting the client's *growth* as a person rather than on facilitating the skill of "playing the game of life." Phenomenological therapists help clients become aware of and reach their own unique

potential. They de-emphasize the client's behavioral skills, coping strategies, or adjustment to the environment. The underlying assumption is that when clients approach their full potential, they will be capable of finding solutions to problems of living without help from anyone else. In fact, actively helping a client solve particular problems is viewed as counterproductive: If the client uses the *therapist's* solution, the opportunity will be missed to let her or his own feelings and ideas be a guide. In addition, the client may become dependent on the therapist and less inclined to seek independent resolutions of future difficulties.

2. Because clients are viewed by phenomenological therapists as responsible individuals who are capable of handling their own lives, the roles of the client and therapist are considered to be comparable in status. If in psychodynamic therapy there is a "doctor-patient" relationship and in behavioral interventions there is a "teacher-student" relationship, in phenomenological treatment the clinician and client are more like "gardener and flower." The therapist facilitates growth that is inherent in the client, but both may grow and benefit from the relationship.

3. The relationship between the client and the therapist is the primary vehicle through which growth takes place. The immediate, moment-to-moment experience of the therapy situation is what helps the client. Thus, for an insecure client, insight into the past or making plans for handling future problems would be viewed as less helpful than being in a relationship where another person nonjudgmentally *accepts* and *values* the client despite his or her own lack of self-assurance. This experience is thought to be helpful because it prompts the client to perceive himself or herself in more positive terms. In phenomenological treatment, the client-therapist relationship is not a special, isolated context for talking about early conflicts, how those conflicts appear in the present, or possible new responses to the environment. It is seen as a *real interpersonal relationship* which, apart from the topics discussed or the "techniques" used, gives the client human *experiences* which themselves promote growth.

4. Because the immediate experience of the therapy relationship is so important, the focus of phenomenological treatment seldom strays

from what is going on between client and therapist in the session. As noted in Chapters 2 and 3, there is usually little formal assessment of the client's past. The assumption is that the past cannot be changed and is not as important for the client's future as is the present.

5. Phenomenologically oriented clinicians assume that most of their clients are not "sick," "disordered," or different from "normal" people, no matter how bizarre those clients appear to be. Phenomenologists see their clients as behaving in line with their unique perceptions of the world. Therefore, the therapist seeks to understand the client's problems by trying to look at the world through the client's eyes. It is hoped that in the process of revealing her or his perceptions to the therapist, the client will become more aware of how those perceptions guide behavior.

With these themes in mind, let us examine some specific examples of phenomenological treatment.

THE CLIENT-CENTERED THERAPY OF CARL ROGERS

The most influential of the phenomenological approaches to intervention is the *client-centered therapy* of Carl Rogers (1942, 1951, 1954, 1959, 1961, 1970, 1980). Though Rogers's initial training as a psychologist was in a psychodynamic tradition, he ultimately rejected that tradition and founded an approach to treatment which, by the 1940s, had provided clinical psychology with its first systematic alternative to Freud. As we shall see, Rogers also established a tradition of doing research on the process and outcome of psychotherapy.

Some Background on Client-Centered Therapy

Carl Rogers was born on January 8, 1902, the fourth of six children in a close-knit, conservative Protestant family. Religion, self-reliance, and hard work were important early influences. "There was no drinking,

FIGURE 10-1. Carl Rogers (1902-) by John T. Wood. (Courtesy of Carl Rogers.)

dancing, card playing, theatre going, and little social life" in Rogers's youth (Sollod, 1978, p. 95); in fact, he reportedly had only two dates during high school (Reisman, 1976). His family moved to a farm when Rogers was twelve and he became interested in agriculture. By the age of fourteen, Rogers had become a student of agriculture and learned "how experiments were conducted, how control groups were matched with experimental groups, how conditions were held constant by randomizing procedures. . . ." (Rogers, 1961, p. 6).

Rogers became an agriculture major at the University of Wisconsin; because of his family background, however, he leaned toward becoming a minister. In his junior year he spent six months at a World Student Christian Federation conference in China, during which time he began to question the religious views of his parents and to become

inclined toward more liberal forms of Christianity. After graduation he enrolled in New York City's Union Theological Seminary, an institution whose liberal orientation fit Rogers's developing religious views.

While at the seminary, Rogers and some of his fellow students formed an independent seminar group whose aim was to search for truth through discussion about personal ideas, concepts, and doubts. There was no instructor. "The majority of the members of that group, in thinking their way through the questions they raised, thought themselves right out of religious work. I was one" (Rogers, 1961, p. 8). In 1925, after two years at Union, Rogers enrolled in Teachers College at Columbia University to study psychology.

At least as early as his China trip, Rogers had been wrestling with the concept of authority. In religion, in education, and in family life, he had learned that those "in authority" want to tell people what to do, how to think, and what values to adopt. Yet he began to question the wisdom of this approach, not only for his own life, but for the lives of others. While at Teachers College, Rogers learned about *progressive education* and the notion that education should enhance the growth of students by pacing lessons to the student's level of reading and by tailoring material to student needs. Progressive education advocates such as John Dewey also used *guided discussion* to help students find things out for themselves rather than depending on lectures or readings to tell students the right answers.

Rogers's training in child therapy at Columbia began under Leta Hollingsworth and continued during a year-long internship at the Institute for Child Guidance in New York. Child-guidance clinics at this time were run primarily by psychiatrists, so Rogers was exposed to the Freudian model. Though he learned much from this experience, Rogers became as uncomfortable with the concept of therapist as authority as he had been with the notion of teacher as authority. Thus, after he took his first job as a psychologist in the child study department of the Rochester (New York) Society for the Prevention of Cruelty to Children, Rogers became increasingly unhappy with the psychodynamic approach. At this point (the early 1930s) Rogers was not sure what alternative to pursue, but he felt that there had to be a better way to go about clinical work.

An alternative appeared when Rogers became aware of Otto Rank's approach to therapy, mainly through Rankian social workers at Rochester, and through Jessie Taft, a Philadelphia psychologist–social worker. Taft had developed an approach she called *relationship therapy*, "which can take place only when divorced from all hint of control" (Taft, 1951, p. 94). Taft's procedures reflected the basic tenets advanced by Rank: "The individual client . . . is a moving cause, containing constructive forces within, which constitute a will to health. The

therapist guides the individual to self-understanding, self-acceptance. It is the therapist *as a human being* who is the remedy, not his technical skill. . . . The spontaneity and uniqueness of therapy lived in the present carry the patient toward health" (Meador & Rogers, 1973, p. 121; italics added).

These ideas fit nicely with the principles of progressive education that had impressed Rogers in graduate school, they reflected his own distrust of authoritarian treatment, and they evoked ideals stemming from his childhood: " . . . the individualism of the American frontier, the belief in self-reliance, the conviction that the individual could learn to do what was necessary for him to learn and do" (Meador & Rogers, 1973, p. 120).

In the 1930s, Rogers became increasingly aware of the shortcomings of traditional assessment and treatment concepts. For example, after using a psychoanalytic approach to help a fire-setting youngster see that his maladaptive behavior was based upon unconscious conflicts over masturbation, Rogers was jolted to discover that the client's behavior did not improve. At another point Rogers reread the transcript of an interview with a mother that, years earlier, he had thought was excellent: "I was appalled. Now it seemed to me to be a clever legalistic type of questioning by the interviewer which convicted this parent of her unconscious motives, and wrung from her an admission of her guilt. I now knew from my experience that such an interview would not be of any lasting help to the parent or the child. It made me realize that I was moving away from any approach which was coercive or pushing in clinical relationship. . . ." (Rogers, 1961, p. 11).

As a result of experiences like these, Rogers began to incorporate ideas about non-authoritarianism and the value of a good human relationship into his therapy. Rogers began to think that "it is the *client* who knows what hurts, what directions to go, what problems are crucial, what experiences have been deeply buried. It began to occur to me that unless I had a need to demonstrate my own cleverness and learning, I would do better to rely upon the client for the direction of movement. . . ." (Rogers, 1961, pp. 11–12).

Rogers's first book, *The Clinical Treatment of the Problem Child,* was published in 1939. It contained two noteworthy features. First, Rogers's preference for relationship therapy was obvious. Second, his orientation toward experimental research, which came from his early experiences in agriculture and from the influence of experimental psychologists at Teachers College, became evident. He was among the first to recognize the need for scientific research to substantiate the alleged value of any treatment technique, including his own. Rogers pointed out, for example, that although many therapists extol the value of relationship therapy, "since their criteria are largely intangible measures such as the freedom from minor tensions and the greater degree of personal comfort achieved, any measurement of success is difficult indeed. From those who are most interested in relationship therapy, we find no mention of the degree or proportion of success. . . ." (Rogers, 1939, p. 200). The same year his book was published, Rogers left his first job to become director of the Rochester Child Guidance Center.

By 1940 Rogers was beginning to develop a systematic approach to treatment which incorporated his own ideas and those of the people who had influenced him. Three important things happened that year. First, Rogers participated in a symposium on therapy organized by Goodwin Watson, a Columbia University psychology professor. At that meeting, Rogers described the virtues of relationship therapy, but also heard Watson endorse similar ideas which shaped Rogers's thinking (Sollod, 1978). Second, Rogers moved from his clinical job in Rochester to his first academic position as a full professor at Ohio State University. The academic setting helped Rogers elaborate his views. "It was in trying to teach what I had learned about treatment and counseling to graduate students . . . that I first began to realize that I had perhaps developed a distinctive point of view of my own. . . ." (Rogers, 1961, p. 13).

He became sure of this because of the third major event of 1940. On December 11 Rogers gave an invited talk to the Psi Chi[1] chapter at the University of Minnesota. In that talk, entitled "Some Newer Concepts in Psychotherapy," Rogers presented his notions about the use of a *nondirective* approach, which allows clients to solve their own problems without judgments from the clinician. This involved (1) relying on the client's drive toward growth, health, and adjustment rather than on treatment "techniques" to produce benefits; (2) emphasizing the *present moment* in therapy rather than the past as a key to change; and (3) focusing on the therapeutic relationship as a promoter of client growth (Rogers, 1974). The reaction to the "birth" of nondirective therapy was intense. "I was totally unprepared for the furor the talk aroused. I was criticized, I was praised, I was attacked, I was looked on with puzzlement" (Rogers, 1974, p. 8). Rogers's ideas appealed to some people as an excellent alternative to the "all-knowing expert" approach of psychoanalysis. Freudians and other traditionalists were critical, for obvious reasons.

In 1942 Rogers published a full-length account of nondirective therapy, *Counseling and Psychotherapy.* In this book Rogers advocated "a counseling relationship whose characteristics were the warmth and responsiveness of the therapist, a permissive climate in which the feelings of the client could be freely expressed, and a freedom for the client from all coercion or pressure. A client in such a relationship would gain understanding of himself" which then allows him or her to take positive steps toward self-help (Meador & Rogers, 1973, p. 122). Rogers's research orientation continued to be evident in this book. He reported on the content

[1] A national psychology honorary organization that is still active today.

analyses of clinical interviews which, for the first time, had been phonographically recorded.

In 1945 Rogers organized and became executive secretary of the University of Chicago Counseling Center. During the next twelve years Rogers continued to develop and evaluate his treatment approach which, by 1946, he was calling *client-centered* rather than nondirective therapy. This change was designed to emphasize the primary role of the client's inherent potential for growth, and was formalized in Rogers's 1951 book, *Client-Centered Therapy.*

Over the years, Carl Rogers has continued to practice and do research on psychotherapy and to apply his views in an ever-broadening range of contexts. After leaving Chicago, he spent four years at the University of Wisconsin and then moved to the Western Behavioral Sciences Institute in La Jolla, California. He is now located at his own Center for Studies of the Person in La Jolla. A distinguished series of books has resulted from his clinical experience. These include *On Becoming a Person* (1961), *Freedom to Learn* (an application of his concepts to education, 1969), *Carl Rogers on Encounter Groups* (1970), and *On Becoming Partners: Marriage and Its Alternatives* (1972). Let us now examine the process of Rogerian therapy.

The Client-Centered Approach

Rogers argues that therapy is a *process,* not a set of techniques. He advocates that a therapist cannot solve clients' problems by *telling* or by *teaching* them anything: "No approach which relies upon knowledge, upon training, upon the acceptance of something that is *taught,* is of any use. . . . such methods are, in my experience, futile and inconsequential. The most they can accomplish is some temporary change, which soon disappears, leaving the individual more than ever convinced of his inadequacy" (Rogers, 1961, pp. 32–33). The *real* process of therapy in Rogers's views is an "if . . . then" proposition: If the correct circumstances are cre-

ated by the therapist, the client will spontaneously begin to change and grow. The therapeutic process will take place on its own, driven by the client's growth potential, but only when the proper atmosphere is present and regardless of specific "techniques" or content.

This approach is related to Rogers's self theory, which we sketched in Chapter 2. The argument is, basically, that people are thwarted in their growth by judgments imposed on them by others. This creates *conditions of worth* that force people to distort their own real feelings. When this happens, various symptoms appear. Thus, if an accountant really wanted to be an artist but had to ignore those feelings due to family pressure, depression might result. The growth process would stop as the person's behavior (e.g., professing satisfaction with accounting) became increasingly discrepant, or *incongruent,* with real feelings.

Client-centered therapy is aimed at providing the client with *new experiences* that will restart the growth process. These new experiences involve the therapist's responding to the client in ways that do not sustain conditions of worth, which accept the client as he or she is, and which value the client as a person. If such characteristics had been present in the client's past relationships, they would have prevented psychological problems; their appearance in the present can still be helpful, however. For this reason, the Rogerian therapist tries to provide *an interpersonal relationship that the client can use to further personal growth.*

According to Rogers, this relationship cannot be manufactured; phoniness would be detected by the client and would not be beneficial. For Rogers, the only way to generate a growth-enhancing relationship is for the therapist to experience and express three interrelated attitudes. These are: *unconditional positive regard, empathy,* and *congruence.*

Unconditional Positive Regard. The most basic therapeutic attitude in Rogers's system is unconditional positive regard. It conveys three messages: The therapist (1) *cares about* the client as a person, (2) *accepts* her or him, and (3) *trusts* the client's ability to change and grow. This seems to be an easily adopted stance (after all, any good therapist cares about clients), but in practice it is often difficult to accomplish.

For example, there are many ways to "care" about someone. One can be superficial about it, as when ending a conversation with words like "Have a nice day." The recipient of messages like these probably does not attach much importance to them, and the person who uttered the words will not be automatically counted as a close friend. Rogerians wish to go beyond this kind of routine caring.

At the other extreme, a caring attitude can be so strong and possessive as to be incapacitating to the person who is cared for. A child who is constantly *told* how much his or her parents care and how that caring resulted in painful self-sacrifice ("Your mother and I went without so you could go to college") may feel burdened with guilt. Similarly, a young man who dotes on his fiancée and never lets her be away from him may cause her to feel stifled by the intensity of his caring. Rogerians try to avoid crippling their clients with caring.

The ideal "regard" in Rogers's unconditional positive regard is that of *nonpossessive caring,* in which genuine positive feelings are expressed in a way that is liberating, not limiting. There are many ways in which this can be done. The simplest involves *telling* the client, "I care about you." This straightforward statement has an important place in therapy but can be interpreted as superficial, especially if overused. Therefore, Rogerians also try to *show* the client that they care.[2]

The therapist's *willingness to listen* is an important manifestation of this attitude. Patient, warm, and interested in what the client has to say, the therapist does not interrupt the client or change the subject or give any other signs that she or he would rather be doing something else. In addition to merely listening, the therapist seeks to *understand* the client's feelings from the client's point of view (this is discussed in more detail in the section on empathy, below). For many clients, talking to someone who is willing to listen and who wants to understand is an exhilarating experience that provides the impetus for greater self-expression.

The "unconditional" aspect of the therapist's unconditional positive regard is manifested in a willingness to accept the client as he or she is, without judgment. Rogers believes that the experience of being prized as a human being, regardless of one's feelings or behaviors, can be a growth-producing experience, especially for clients whose development has been hampered by conditions of worth and other evaluative pressures.

Acceptance of the client means that the therapist refrains from many activities associated with the therapist role. For one thing, she or he avoids interpretations. When the client expresses a feeling (e.g., "I love my children very much"), the Rogerian views that feeling as reflecting the client's perception at that moment. To interpret the statement as a defense against unconscious hostile feelings would not convey an accepting attitude. If the client's stated feelings are inaccurate, the assumption is that he or she will eventually discover the more genuine emotion as self-expression continues.

Rogerians also try to avoid *evaluative judgments* about their clients. For example, the therapist will not "summarize" the client with a diagnostic label or define for the client what her or his problems involve. It also means accepting the client's reported feelings and behaviors as those of a valued person, no matter what those feelings and behaviors involve. This is not an easily attained goal. Consider your own reaction to a person who says "it doesn't really bother me to cheat on my husband; he's so dumb he'll never find out anyway" or "I never wanted any of my children, and I plan to kick them

---

[2] If the therapist really does *not* care about the client, Rogers would suggest that a different therapist be brought in rather than attempting to fake a positive attitude.

out of the house as soon as they are of legal age."

Unconditional positive regard does not require the therapist to *approve* of feelings like these. The goal is neither to approve nor to disapprove, but to *accept* these feelings as a real part of a person whom the therapist cares about. While the therapist may have an evaluative reaction to the client's thoughts or actions, he or she can be nonjudgmental about the fact that they occurred. Further, the therapist can still prize the client as an individual. This ideal is illustrated in the following interaction:

CLIENT: That was the semester my brother died and everything seemed to be going down the tubes. I knew how important it was to my parents that I get into medical school, but I also knew that my grades would be lousy that year unless I did something. To make a long story short, I bought a term paper and cheated on almost every exam that semester.

THERAPIST: It was a really rough time for you.

Note that the therapist focuses on the client's feelings in the situation, not on the ethics of the behavior. A major aspect of unconditional positive regard involves the separation of a client's worth *as a person* from the worth of the client's *behavior*. Rogers believes that psychological problems would be less prevalent if a similar distinction were more common outside of therapy (see Rogers, 1961, ch. 16).

The "positive" component of unconditional positive regard is the therapist's *trust* in the client's potential for growth and problem solving. Rogers believes that if clients perceive a therapist's lack of trust in their growth potential, they are unlikely to grow and may become dependent. On the other hand, "the more sincerely the therapist relies on the client to discover himself and to follow his own processes of change, the more freely the client will do just that" (Meador & Rogers, 1973, p. 138). The ther-

apist must try not to be the "expert" who tells the client what is "wrong" or guides the client toward "better" ways of thinking and behaving. Rogerians try not to (1) give advice, (2) take responsibility for clients, or (3) make decisions for clients.

These are often difficult rules to follow, especially in cases where the therapist feels that he or she knows what is "best" for the client. However, the client must be allowed to make bad decisions or experience problems, even if they could have been averted through advice by the therapist. While advice might have solved or prevented some problems, others would be created: The therapist would become a superior, the client would become more dependent, and, most important, both client and therapist would have less faith in the client's ability to deal independently with problems.

Rogers believes so strongly in the importance of trusting the client that he holds to his view even in the face of possibly tragic actions. This is illustrated in the following excerpt from the treatment of a depressed young woman:

CLIENT: I wish I'd never started this therapy. I was happy when I was living in my dream world. There I could be the kind of person I wanted to be—But now there is such a wide, wide gap—between my ideal—and what I am . . .

THERAPIST: It's really a tough struggle—digging into this like you are—and at times the shelter of your dream world looks more attractive and comfortable.

CLIENT: My dream world or suicide . . . So I don't see why I should waste your time—coming in twice a week—I'm not worth it—What do you think?

THERAPIST: It's up to you . . . It isn't wasting my time—I'd be glad to see you whenever you come—but it's how you feel about it—if you don't want to come twice a week—or if you do want to come twice a week?—once a week?—It's up to you.

CLIENT: You're not going to suggest that I come in oftener? You're not alarmed and think I ought to come in—everyday—until I get out of this?

THERAPIST: I believe you are able to make your own decision. I'll see you whenever you want to come.

CLIENT: (note of awe in her voice) I don't believe you are alarmed about—I see—I may be afraid of myself—but you aren't afraid for me.

THERAPIST: You say you may be afraid of yourself—and are wondering why I don't seem to be afraid for you?

CLIENT: You have more confidence in me than I have. I'll see you next week—maybe. (Rogers, 1951, pp. 46–47)

The client's concluding statement appears accurate. The therapist *does* have more confidence in the client than she has in herself. Ideally, this will be a temporary situation, for presumably, she will begin to share that confidence. Rogers points out, however, that the therapist cannot half-heartedly adopt a trusting attitude and expect the client to grow: "To me it appears that only as the therapist is completely willing that *any* outcome, *any* direction, may be chosen—only then does he realize the vital strength of the capacity and potentiality of the individual for constructive action" (Rogers, 1951, p. 48). This does not mean that Rogers expects the worst from clients who are given real trust and freedom by their therapist. Quite the contrary. "It is as [the therapist] is willing for death to be the choice, that life is chosen; for neuroticism to be the choice, that a healthy normality is chosen" (Rogers, 1951, p. 49).

Empathy. Rogers views human behavior as a product of each person's unique perceptions. Thus, in order to understand a client's behavior, and help the client understand it as well, the therapist must try to see the world as the client sees it. When the therapist lets the client know that she or he understands (or at least wants to understand) what the client feels, the chances for a useful therapeutic relationship are enhanced. In Rogerian terms, this involves a striving for *accurate empathy* or *empathic understanding*.

Empathy requires that the therapist be immersed in an effort to *perceive* the client's feelings, but it does not dictate that the therapist *experience* those feelings (Rogers, 1951). If a therapist actually felt the client's fear or anger, the therapy session could become nothing but a place for two people to be frightened or angry together! It is also vital to recognize that empathy is not achieved by *sympathizing* with the client. A comment like "I'm sorry that you feel so depressed" reflects sympathy, not empathy.

Similarly, a therapist who merely *tells* the client that he or she empathizes will not convey an empathic attitude. It is common, in therapy and in everyday life, to hear people say "I really know how you feel" or "I understand what you are going through." If, as phenomenologists believe, each person's perceptions are unique, it takes more work by the therapist to approximate a genuine understanding of what it feels like to be any particular client. In fact, when someone uses an easy phrase such as "I know how you feel," they are actually conveying a *lack* of interest in real understanding. Imagine your own reaction if, after giving someone a lengthy account of your complex feelings about a grandparent's death, they simply say, "Right, I've felt the very same way." It would be easy to question the degree to which they know how you feel or even want to know how you feel.

In order to illustrate the problems of conveying empathy, we present an excerpt from the beginning of a therapy session with a young male client. As you read the excerpt and after you are finished, try to be aware of your reactions to it.

CLIENT: I don't feel very normal, but I want to feel that way. . . . I thought I'd have something to talk about—then it all goes around in circles. I was trying to think what I was going to say. I tell you, I just can't make a decision; I don't know what I want. I've tried to reason this thing out logically—tried to figure out which things are important to me. I thought that there are maybe two things a man might do; he might get married and raise a family. But if he was just a bachelor, just making a living—that isn't very good. I find myself and my thoughts getting back to the days when I was a kid and I cry very easily. The dam would break through. I've been in the Army four and a half years. I had no problems then, no hopes, no wishes. My only thought was to get out when peace would come. My problems, now that I'm out, are as ever. I tell you, they go back to a long time before I was in the Army. . . . I love children. When I was in the Philippines—I tell you, when I was young I swore I'd never forget my unhappy childhood—so when I saw these children in the Philippines, I treated them very nicely. I used to give them ice cream cones and movies. It was just a period—I'd reverted back—and that awakened some emotions in me I thought I had long buried. (A pause. He seems very near tears.) (Rogers, 1951, pp. 32–33)

Many therapists would react to such material with sympathy and with a wish to understand the client intellectually. They would use what Rogers called an *external frame of reference*. They attempt to understand by being an outside observer and applying their own values to what the client says. Examples of therapist thoughts based on an external frame of reference are presented on the left side of Box 10-1. On the other hand, the therapist could adopt an *internal* frame of reference, which reflects a desire to understand what it must be like to be this client. The right side of Box 10-1 contains some of the therapist thoughts that might result from an internal reference.

Rogerian therapists must not only *adopt* an empathic attitude; they must *communicate* it to clients. This is done through some of the active listening modes we described in Chapter 4. Of particular value in conveying empathy is the use of *reflection*, which serves the dual purpose of (1) communicating the

BOX 10-1   Some therapist thoughts which reflect internal versus external frames of reference

External	*Internal*
I wonder if I should get him started talking.	You're wanting to struggle toward normality, aren't you?
Is this inability to get under way a type of dependence?	It's really hard for you to get started.
Why this indecisiveness? What could be its cause?	Decision making just seems impossible for you.
What is meant by this focus on marriage and family?	You want marriage, but it doesn't seem to you to be much of a possibility.
The crying, the "dam" sound as though there must be a great deal of regression.	You feel yourself brimming over with childish feelings.
He's a veteran. Could he have been a psychiatric case? I feel sorry for anybody who spent four and one-half years in the service.	To you the Army represented stagnation.
What is this interest in children? Identification? Vague homosexuality?	Being very nice to children somehow has meaning for you; but it was—and is—a disturbing experience for you.

Source: Rogers, 1951, pp. 33–34.

therapist's desire for emotional understanding and (2) making clients more aware of their own feelings.

Reflection is one of the most misunderstood aspects of client-centered therapy because, to an outside observer, the therapist appears to be stating the obvious or merely repeating what the client has said. In a famous joke about this approach, Rogers is supposed to have responded in the following way to a livid fellow duck hunter who threatens to shoot Rogers if he doesn't relinquish a disputed kill: "You feel this is your duck."

Reflection is not just repetition or paraphrasing. It involves distillation and playback of the client's feelings. Let us look at some examples.

CLIENT: This has been such a bad day. I've had to keep myself from crying three or four times. I'm not even sure what's wrong!

The therapist's response could be externally oriented (e.g., "Well what exactly happened?"), but a reaction that communicates empathy would be along these lines:

THERAPIST: You really do feel bad. The tears just well up inside. And it must be scary to not even know why you feel this way.

At first glance, the clinician may seem to be a parrot, but look more closely. The client never *said* she felt bad; the therapist inferred it by taking the client's point of view. Similarly, the client never said her sadness frightened her—the clinician felt that this might be the case if she or he were in the client's shoes. If the therapist is wrong about these points, the client has the opportunity to correct the reflection. Right or wrong, the clinician has let the client know that he or she wants to understand.

Another point about communicating empathy through reflection: The therapist's nonverbal message may be as important as what is said (see Chapter 4). Tone of voice, facial expression, posture, and other cues can add to (or detract from) an empathic attitude. Rogers (1951, p. 28) provides an example:

Here is a client statement: "I feel as though my mother is always watching me and criticizing what I do. It gets me all stirred up inside. I try not to let that happen, but you know, there are times when I feel her eagle eye on me that I just boil inwardly."

A response on the counselor's part might be: "You resent her criticism."

This response may be given empathically, with the tone of voice such as would be used if it were worded, "If I understand you correctly, you feel pretty resentful toward her criticism. Is that right?" If this is the attitude and tone which is used, it would probably be experienced by the client as aiding him in self-expression. Yet we have learned, from the fumblings of counselors-in-training, that "You resent her criticism" may be given with the same attitude and tone with which one might announce "You have the measles," or . . . "You are sitting on my hat."

The best way to get a feel for this nonverbal dimension of empathy is to watch and listen to a skilled Rogerian in action.[3] An opportunity to accomplish this is provided by a well-known film in which Rogers interviews "Gloria" as a demonstration of his approach (Rogers, 1965). Similar material is contained in other films and on tapes distributed by the American Academy of Psychotherapists (see footnote 4).

Finally, communicating empathy is a slow process. The therapist's use of reflection may not get anywhere in a single session, but Rogers believes that over time, the empathic attitude gives even the most aloof or withdrawn client a sense that the therapist understands her or him. The *continuous experiencing* of this understanding attitude will ultimately lead to client growth.

Congruence. We have emphasized the importance of real rather than manufactured empathy and unconditional positive

---

[3] Rogerians are not the only therapists who convey empathy to their clients, but they are more likely to emphasize it in therapeutic sessions.

regard. This emphasis reflects Rogers's belief that the more *genuine* the therapist is in his or her relations with the client, the more helpful the therapist will be. The therapist's feelings and actions should be *congruent*, or consistent, with one another. "This means that I need to be aware of my own feelings . . . [and willing] to express, in my words and my behavior, the various feelings and attitudes which exist in me" (Rogers, 1961, p. 33). According to Rogers, when the therapist is congruent, she or he sets up a *real human relationship*. Rogers argues: "It does not help to act as though I know the answers when I do not. . . . I have not found it to be helpful or effective in my relationships with other people to try to maintain a facade; to act in one way on the surface when I am experiencing something quite different underneath" (Rogers, 1961, pp. 16–17).

Congruence is a requirement that is often difficult for a clinician to satisfy. The therapist must abandon the notion that expressing a particular reaction would "not be good for the client" and just go ahead and be genuine. In so doing, the therapist expresses confidence in the client's ability to handle the therapist's feelings, and, if those feelings are negative, shows a willingness to risk a temporary setback in the relationship. The hope is that, in the long run, the client's awareness that the therapist is for real (not just someone who is paid to be nice) will aid self-actualization.

In order to get an idea of how congruence promotes trust, think of a close friend. Chances are that friend has told you things you might not have wanted to hear, perhaps that you had been hard to get along with or that you were wrong about something. Once you know your friend will say what he or she really feels (i.e., is congruent with you), even if it does not make you happy, it may be easier for you to trust what that person may say today or next week. However, if you know your friend tells you only what she or he thinks you want to hear, your faith in that person's reactions ("You really look great") might be reduced.

In a way a Rogerian therapist treats a client like a friend. He or she will not try to be something that he or she is not, because this would hamper the *therapist's* personal growth and because it would be poor modeling.

Let us consider a therapist-client interaction that illustrates how congruence can be displayed:

CLIENT: I have been feeling better since we started seeing each other. If my father had been as warm as you are, my childhood would have been a lot easier. (pause) It sounds silly to say it, but I wish you could be my father.

THERAPIST: I think it would be nice to have you for a son.

This client's statement could have prompted a Freudian to analyze the transference or to remain emotionally distant; the Rogerian's response was a reflection of how he *felt*.

Consider another example:

CLIENT: You really look tired, doctor. Don't you feel well today?

THERAPIST: (who really feels rotten) Oh no, I'm fine. Anyway, how you feel is more important.

Here is a case of therapist incongruence. The client is likely to see through the therapist's facade, and she or he will probably feel guilty for making a sick person work when that person would rather be at home. The clinician could have said, "I do feel pretty sick, but I wanted to have our session today." If this actually reflects the therapist's feelings, it will strengthen the therapeutic relationship.

Finally, imagine this interchange:

CLIENT: I just feel so hopeless. Tell me what I'm doing wrong in my life.

THERAPIST: I guess when you are feeling this bad it would be nice if someone could come along and tell you what is going wrong and how you can put everything right again. I wish I could do all that, but I can't. I don't think anyone else can either.

Notice the therapist's reflection of client feeling plus the direct expression of (1) a genuine wish to understand and solve the client's problems, and (2) an admission that (s)he is not capable of such a feat. A therapist who does not have all the answers but who says "Don't you think it would be better if you figured that out for yourself?" would, according to Rogers, show incongruence by suggesting that he or she *knows* what is wrong but won't tell. Such a message might promote client inferiority, not growth.

The Nature of Change in Client-Centered Therapy

Client-centered therapy represents an "if . . . then" assumption: If the right conditions are created by the therapist, then the client will change. It is now time to describe the dimensions along which, according to Rogers, change takes place.

Increased Awareness. Therapy should bring clients in closer contact with their own feelings, many of which have been previously denied or kept out of awareness. Further, the focus of awareness should be on the immediate present: how the client is feeling here and now. This new awareness usually is directed toward the *self* rather than toward specific symptoms.

Increased Self-acceptance. Over time, clients become less self-critical and more self-accepting. They are more likely to take responsibility for their feelings and behavior and less likely to blame circumstances or other people for those feelings and behaviors. The client spends less time denying parts of the self that are not ideal. The client may decide to change some of these things, but they are no longer disowned. Some of the increase in self-acceptance is thought to be based on the discovery that, in spite of things that may be less than admirable, the client is a basically good person.

Increased Interpersonal Comfort. As therapy progresses, the client becomes more comfortable in relationships. Defensive interpersonal games designed to keep other people at a distance are abandoned and the client experiences the pleasure of letting others know him or her as he or she really is.

Increased Cognitive Flexibility. As noted by Kelly (1955) and others, people have problems when they see the world in rigid, black-and-white terms (e.g., "all men are despicable," "all teachers are uncaring"). Successful client-centered therapy results in a "loosening up" of limited (and limiting) views of the world such that the client perceives the endless variability that exists. The cognitions that result (e.g., "the behavior of *some* men is despicable") are likely to promote less problematic behavior.

Increased Self-reliance. The client is likely to end up feeling less dependent on others and more confident about personal abilities. A growing client becomes less dependent upon the reactions of other people as a barometer of self-worth and more oriented toward internal evaluations. Clients may become less fearful in social-evaluative situations (e.g., speeches, tests, parties) because they come to feel that what they think is as important as what others think. These changes result from a shift in the client's *valuing process.* The client becomes less concerned with "shoulds" and "oughts" (e.g., "I should love being a student") and more concerned with how he or she actually feels (see Box 10-2). The growing client separates (as the therapist does) her or his worth as a *person* from the quality of her or his *behavior.*

Rogers believes that changes along these dimensions over the course of successful therapy are relatively consistent from one client to the next. He has summarized these changes in a *therapy process scale* which is presented in edited form in Box 10-3.

Improved Functioning. In addition to the psychological changes just described, Rogers notes that overt benefits also follow successful client-centered therapy.

BOX 10-2   Self-evaluation versus evaluation by others

Here are some examples of thoughts based upon concern over evaluation by others (left column) and those based upon a greater focus on self-evaluation (right column).

1. I should never be angry at anyone.

1. I should be angry at a person when I deeply feel angry because this leaves less residual effect than bottling up the feeling, and actually makes for a better and more realistic relationship.

2. I should always be a loving mother.

2. I should be a loving mother when I feel that way, but I need not be fearful of other attitudes when they exist.

3. I should be successful in my courses.

3. I should be successful in my courses only if they have long-range meaning to me.

4. I have homosexual impulses, which is very bad.

4. I have homosexual impulses, and these are capable of expressions which enhance self and others, and expressions which achieve the reverse.

Source: After Rogers, 1951, p. 149 and p. 151.

The client's behavior changes in these ways: he considers, and reports putting into effect, behavior which is more mature, self-directing, and responsible than the behavior he has shown heretofore; his behavior becomes less defensive, more firmly based on an objective view of self and reality; his behavior shows a decreasing amount of psychological tension; he tends to make a more comfortable and more effective adjustment to school and to job; he meets new stress situations with an increased degree of inner calm, a calm which is reflected in less physiological upset . . . than would have been true if they had occurred prior to therapy. (Rogers, 1951, p. 186)

An Illustration of Client-Centered Therapy

Because client-centered therapy focuses more on processes than techniques, the preceding material may leave the reader aware of the principles that guide Rogerian therapy but unclear about how these principles are translated into clinical practice. To provide a brief idea of what goes on in client-centered therapy, we present below some edited excerpts from Rogers's (1967) case of the "Silent Young Man," as described by Meador and Rogers (1973, pp. 139–144).[4]

The client in this case was a twenty-eight-year-old man hospitalized as a "simple schizophrenic." During eleven months of therapy, "Jim" had made some progress, but was still withdrawn and inarticulate. Rather than giving up on his client, Rogers continued to adopt the therapeutic attitudes that he believed would ultimately bring about growth.

THERAPIST: I see there are some cigarettes here in the drawer. Hm? Yeah, it is hot out. (silence of 25 seconds)

THERAPIST: Do you look kind of angry this morning, or is that my imagination? (client shakes his head slightly) Not angry, huh? (silence of 1 minute, 26 seconds)

THERAPIST: Feel like letting me in on whatever is going on? (silence of 12 minutes, 52 seconds)

---

[4] A tape recording of two complete interviews with this client is available for professional use from the American Academy of Psychotherapists, 6420 City Line Avenue, Philadelphia, PA 19151. Its designation is the case of "Mr. VAC."

BOX 10-3   Seven stages in the process of therapeutic change

Stage 1:   Communication is about externals. There is an unwillingness to communicate self. Feelings and personal meanings are neither recognized as such nor owned. Constructs are extremely rigid. Close relationships are construed as dangerous.

Stage 2:   Feelings are *sometimes* described but as unowned past *objects* external to self.

Stage 3:   There is much description of feelings and personal meanings which are not now present. These distant feelings are often pictured as unacceptable or bad. . . . There is a beginning recognition that any problems that exist are inside the individual rather than external.

Stage 4:   Feelings and personal meanings are freely described as present objects owned by the self. . . . There is a beginning loosening of personal constructs. . . . There is some expression of self-responsibility for problems.

Stage 5:   Many feelings are expressed in the moment of their occurrence and are thus experienced in the immediate present. These feelings are owned or accepted.

There is a questioning of the validity of many personal constructs. The person has a definite responsibility for the problems which exist in him.

Stage 6:   Feelings previously denied are now experienced both with immediacy and acceptance.

Stage 7:   The individual lives comfortably in the flowing process of his experiencing. New feelings are experienced with richness and immediacy, and this inner experiencing is a clear referent for behavior. Incongruence is minimal and temporary.

Excerpts from "Person-centered therapy," by Betty D. Meador and Carl R. Rogers, in R. J. Corsini, ed., *Current Psychotherapies,* Itasca, IL: F. E. Peacock Publishers. Copyright 1984 by Peacock Publishers. (Reprinted by permission.)

THERAPIST: I kind of feel like saying that "If it would be of any help at all I'd like to come in." On the other hand if it's something you'd rather—if you just feel more like being within yourself, why that's OK too—I guess another thing I'm saying, really, in saying that is, "I do care. I'm not just sitting here like a stick." (silence of 1 minute, 11 seconds)

THERAPIST: And I guess your silence is saying to me either you don't want to or can't come out right now and that's OK. So I won't pester you but I just want you to know, I'm here. (silence of 17 minutes, 41 seconds)

[After two more unanswered comments over the next minute or so, Rogers continues.]

THERAPIST: Maybe this morning you just wish I'd shut up—and maybe I should, but I just keep feeling I'd like to—I don't know, be in touch with you in some way. (silence of 2 minutes, 21 seconds)

[Client yawns.]

THERAPIST: Sounds discouraged or tired. (silence of 41 seconds)

CLIENT: [at last!] No. Just lousy.

THERAPIST: Everything's lousy, huh? You feel lousy? . . .

CLIENT: No.

THERAPIST: No? (silence of 20 seconds)

CLIENT: No. I just ain't no good to nobody, never was, and never will be.

THERAPIST: Feeling that now, hm? That you're just no good to yourself, no good to anybody. Just that you're completely worthless, huh? . . .

CLIENT: Yeah. That's what this guy I went to town with just the other day told me. . . .

THERAPIST: I guess the meaning of that, if I get it right, is that here's somebody that—meant something to you and what does he think of you? Why, he's told you that he thinks you're no good at all. And that really knocks the props out from under you. [Jim weeps quietly] It just brings the tears.

CLIENT: I don't care though.

THERAPIST: You tell yourself you don't care at all, but somehow I guess some part of you cares because some part of you weeps over it. . . .

CLIENT: I guess I always knew it.

THERAPIST: If I'm getting that right, it is that what makes it hurt worst of all is that when he tells you you're no good, well shucks, that's what you've always felt about yourself. Is that—the meaning of what you're saying? [Jim nods in agreement] . . . So that between his saying so and your perhaps feeling it underneath, you just feel about as no-good as anybody could feel.

[The client continues to cry and, after several more minutes of reflecting the sad, hopeless feelings being expressed, Rogers ends the interview. Three days later another session takes place. After some initial comments by the therapist, the client breaks in:]

CLIENT: I'm gonna take off.

THERAPIST: You're going to take off? Really run away from here? . . . I know you don't like the place but it must be something special came up or something?

CLIENT: I just want to run away and die.

THERAPIST: M-hm, m-hm, m-hm. It isn't even that you want to get away from here *to* something. You just want to leave here and go away and die in a corner, hm?

. . . Can't help but wonder whether it's still true that some things this friend said to you—are those still part of the thing that makes you feel so awful?

CLIENT: In general, yes.

[The next 30 minutes or so are taken up in further reflection of the client's negative feelings and in silences of up to 13 minutes.]

CLIENT: I might go today. Where, I don't know, but I don't care.

THERAPIST: Just feel your mind is made up and that you're going to leave. (silence of 53 seconds)

CLIENT: That's why I want to go, 'cause I don't care what happens.

THERAPIST: M-hm, m-hm. That's why you want to go, because you really don't care about yourself. You just don't care *what* happens. And I guess I'd just like to say—I care about you. And I care what happens.

After a thirty-second silence, the client bursts into violent sobs. For the next fifteen minutes or so, Rogers reflects the intense emotions that pour forth.

According to Rogers, this is an important moment of therapeutic change. "Jim Brown, who sees himself as stubborn, bitter, mistreated, worthless, useless, hopeless, unloved, unlovable, *experiences* my caring. In that moment, his defensive shell cracks wide open, and can never again be quite the same" (Meador & Rogers, 1973, p. 145). The client in this case was able to leave the hospital after several more months of treatment; eight years later he reported to Rogers that he was happy, employed, and living on his own.[5]

---

[5] Rogers (1951) mentions another case in which the therapist and client said almost nothing to one another during months of sessions. Yet the experience of a genuine, caring relationship appeared to produce benefits.

Applications of the Client-Centered Approach

Rogers believes that his approach to treatment can be applied to clients who display "psychotic" behaviors as well as to those labeled as "neurotics" or "personality disorders." Although Rogers began his clinical treatment in one-to-one settings, his principles have also been practiced in group contexts (e.g., Rogers, 1970). Indeed, most of Rogers's concepts have applications to nontherapy situations, including child rearing, marital relations, education, social conflict, and interpersonal interactions (see Rogers, 1961).

THE GESTALT THERAPY OF FRITZ PERLS

After Rogers's client-centered approach, the gestalt theory of Friedrich S. (Fritz) Perls is probably the best-known phenomenologically oriented treatment. Like Rogers, Perls believed that human development depends on self-awareness, and gestalt therapy aims at enhancing clients' awareness in order to free them to grow in their own consciously guided ways. The methods through which the gestalt therapist works to achieve these goals differ from the Rogerian mode. As we shall see, gestalt therapy requires a more active therapist and utilizes more dramatic procedures. Before describing the process itself, we will take a brief look at the origins of Perls's approach.

Some Background on Gestalt Therapy

Fritz Perls was born in Berlin, Germany, in 1893. He earned both an M.D. (specializing in psychiatry) and a Ph.D. in psychology. His European psychiatric training was at the Psychoanalytic Institutes in Berlin and Vienna. His *psychological* orientation, however, was that of the gestaltists. Perls thought of the human organism as a unified whole, rather than a fragmented set of warring components, and he believed that active perceptual and organizational processes, not instincts, were central to the development of human behavior.

Perls described himself as a Wandering Jew. When Hitler came to power in Germany, Perls went first to Johannesburg, South Africa (where he established the South African Institute for Psychoanalysis), and then, in 1946, to New York. By this time Perls's ideas about therapy had reached the stage that he founded the New York Institute for Gestalt Therapy. In the mid-1960s, Perls moved to Big Sur, California, where he became associate psychiatrist at the Esalen Institute. Just before his death in 1970 Perls moved to Vancouver, British Columbia (Canada), where he founded another institute for gestalt therapy.

Perls's discomfort with Freudian concepts first appeared in his book, *Ego, Hunger and Aggression: A Revision of Freud's Theory and Method* (1947). In this book he focused on the vital role played by *awareness* in the development of "normal" human behavior, and he argued that disordered behavior indicated that psychological growth was obstructed by gaps or distortions in awareness. These ideas ultimately led to an alternative approach to clinical treatment which Perls called gestalt therapy (Perls, 1969, 1970; Perls, Hefferline & Goodman, 1951).

Perls noted that disturbances in awareness and the problems that accompany them take many forms, including the neurotic symptoms and defense mechanisms described by Freud. Like Adler and Sullivan, however, Perls focused on these symptoms and defenses as manifested in interpersonal spheres. He noted, for example, that people who find it uncomfortable to experience and express certain needs (such as for love) develop manipulative games or roles designed to satisfy those needs in *indirect* ways. The person begins to devote more energy to these games and roles, with the result that less energy is available for adaptive growth. Indeed, a person's growth gets "stuck" as he or she clings to the problematic games by creating additional symptoms and defenses. The individual whose interactions with others are based on seemingly endless illnesses or tears provides a familiar illustration. Roles of this type force other people to play along by being solicitous or loving, but, because people are being manipulated, the game becomes burdensome to them and may end in rejection. The client must then find someone else to "play with."

To make matters worse, distorted or suppressed awareness creates an impression that one is *not responsible* for one's problems. The blame is placed on other people ("My problem is my wife"), on environmental circumstances ("There are no interesting people in this city"), or on internal forces over which the client has no influence ("I can't control my anger"). This type of client looks to the therapist to solve problems *for* him or her. Perls emphasized that most clients enter therapy ostensibly to understand themselves and solve their problems, when in fact they really want to play their neurotic games better. An illustration of this phenomenon is the man who wants to be taken care of (but cannot tolerate awareness of this need) and who finds nurturance indirectly by telling others of his struggle toward self-understanding through therapy.

The Goals of Gestalt Therapy

Gestalt therapists pursue a few basic goals in treatment. Above all, the gestalt therapist seeks to reestablish the stalled process of client growth. This is achieved by helping clients (1) become aware of those feelings and desires that they have *disowned* but which are a part of them, and (2) recognize those feelings and values that they *think* are a genuine part of themselves, but which in fact are borrowed from other people.

The client is encouraged to assimilate or "re-own" those genuine aspects of self that have been rejected and to reject those features that do not belong. Ideally, when one assimilates and integrates all aspects of the personality (both the desirable and the un-

desirable), one can be aware of and take responsibility for oneself as one really is, instead of being attached to and defensive of a partially phony, internally conflicted self-image.

For example, a person who feels superior to others but who has forced this feeling out of awareness in favor of a more socially acceptable air of humility will become aware of and express both sides of the conflict (e.g., "I'm great" versus "I shouldn't brag"). Once both sides or *poles* of this conflict confront each other, the client may find some resolution (e.g., "It's OK to express my feelings of competence, but I need to take the feelings of others into account as well"). As long as one side of the conflict is out of awareness, such resolution is impossible. According to Perls, when conflict resolutions begin to occur with full awareness of both poles, the person begins to grow again.

The Gestalt Therapy Approach

As was the case in client-centered therapy, the therapist-client relationship in gestalt therapy should be a coequal one involving mutual growth. As Kempler (1973, p. 266) put it, "the therapist is like a composing maestro facing an accomplished musician. The maestro expects that between them new and beautiful tunes will be created."

Focus on the Here and Now. Perls believed that therapeutic progress is made by keeping clients in contact with their feelings as they occur in the here and now. He expressed this belief in a conceptual equation where "Now = experience = awareness = reality" (Perls, 1970, p. 14). Any attempt by the client to recount the past or anticipate the future is not only obstructive of therapy goals, it is an escape from reality.

Instead of *reflecting* (as a Rogerian might) the client's nostalgia or desire to look to the future, a gestalt therapist will point out the avoidance and insist that it be terminated. An example of this method was provided by Perls in his filmed interview with "Gloria"

(Perls, 1965). At one point Gloria says that what is happening in the interview reminds her of when she was a little girl. Perls immediately asks, "Are you a little girl?" to which Gloria answers, "Well, no, but it's the same feeling." Again Perls asks, "Are you a little girl?" Gloria says, "The feeling reminds me of it." Perls explodes: "Are you a little girl?" The client finally says, "No."

Keeping the client in touch with the immediate present helps the client see that the past or the future may be important in the present. Talking about the past or the future in the abstract gets the client nowhere, but *experiencing* past feelings or future fears as they occur in therapy may be helpful. For example, consider this statement:

CLIENT: My sister and I used to fight an awful lot when we were kids, but we seemed closer somehow then than we are now.

Instead of reflecting the feelings expressed here, the gestalt therapist would try to prevent the client from talking about his feelings as "things" that used to exist and get in touch with how he feels right now. The client might be asked to "talk" to his sister as if she were there and express his immediate feelings:

THERAPIST: Can you say this to your sister now?
CLIENT: OK. I feel so far away from you now, Janie. I want to have that feeling of being in a family again.

By asking the client to "speak" directly to a person from the past, the therapist promotes an immediate present feeling rather than a general, *intellectualized report* of feelings. The focus on the present is also evident in the language of gestalt therapy. Clients are encouraged to speak in the present tense. A statement like "I wish I could have talked to you last night" is less expressive of present feelings than "I really want to talk to you."

Handling Resistance. Perls realized that once clients find symptoms, games, and defenses that work, however imperfectly, to protect them from conflict and self-awareness, they will resist efforts to break through them. However, Perls believed that instead of viewing resistance as an inanimate barrier to growth which the client must recognize and put aside, the client should explore the resistance.

To help the client do this, Perls used the technique of *role playing* or part taking. A client who displays resistance is asked to "become" that resistance in order to gain an *experiential* awareness of what the resistance is doing *for* and *to* her or him. Polster and Polster (1973, pp. 53–54) present an example of this technique. John, a member of a gestalt therapy group, finds it difficult to talk to another group member, Mary, because he says there is a "wall" between them. The therapist asks John to "play" the wall:

JOHN: (as the wall) I am here to protect you against predatory women who will eat you alive if you open yourself up to them.[6]

The therapist asks John to "converse" with his resistance in order to experience both sides of the conflict that prevents him from relating to others in an intimate way:

JOHN: (to the wall) Aren't you exaggerating? She looks pretty safe to me. In fact, she looks more scared than anything.
JOHN: (as the wall) Sure she's scared. I'm responsible for that. I'm a very severe wall and I make a lot of people scared. That's how I want it and I have even affected you that way too. You're scared of me even though I'm really on your side.
JOHN: (to the wall) I *am* scared of you and I even feel you inside me, like I have become

---

[6] By "becoming" his resistance as it exists in the present, John experiences his feelings directly instead of talking *about* his difficulties on an abstract level. Perls expressed his distrust of intellectual analysis as opposed to sensory awareness with the oft-quoted phrase, "Lose your mind and come to your senses."

like you. I feel my chest as though it were iron and I'm really getting mad about that.

JOHN: (as the wall) Mad—at what? I'm your strength and you don't even know it. Feel how strong you are inside.

JOHN: (to the wall) Sure I feel the strength but I also feel rigid when my chest feels like iron. I'd like to beat on you, knock you over, and go over to Mary.

Here, the gestalt therapist urges the client to *do* what he *feels* and resolve the conflict in a growthful way.

THERAPIST: Beat on your iron.

JOHN: (beats his chest and shouts) Get out of my way—get *out* of my *way!* (silence of a few moments) My chest feels strong—but not like it's made of iron. (after another silence, John begins to cry and talks to Mary) I don't feel any wall between us anymore and I really want to talk to you.

Dealing with resistance in this way is one example of gestalt therapy in which the various sides of a conflict are brought together and expressed. Of course it is not always this easy for the client to become aware of hidden feelings. Where Freud used free association to help clients' self-exploration, Perls used a battery of methods, several of which are described in the following sections.

Frustrating the Client. Perls believed that most clients come to therapy hoping to feel better without having to give up their maladaptive roles. Since he felt that allowing clients to use their customary styles in therapy would waste everyone's time, Perls set out to frustrate clients' efforts to relate to him as they normally would to others. The clients with whom Perls worked were on the "hot seat." Attention was focused on them, and their symptoms, games, or resistances were pointed out and explored.

Assume that a client begins a session by saying "I've really been looking forward to having this session. I hope you can help me." Instead of reflecting this feeling or asking *why* the client feels this way, a gestalt therapist would focus on the manipulative aspect of the statement, which seems to contain the message, "I expect you to help me without my having to do much." The therapist might say, "How do you think I could help you?" The client (somewhat taken aback) might respond, "Well, I was hoping you could help me understand why I'm so unhappy." From here, the therapist would continue to frustrate the client's attempt to get the therapist to take responsibility for solving the client's problems and, in the process, would help the client experience his real feelings.

THERAPIST: Tell me what you mean when you say "unhappy." (One gestalt therapy principle, not unlike certain behavioral tenets, is to go from the general problem to its specific manifestations.)

CLIENT: Oh, I don't know, it's just that I don't ever feel satisfied with myself. I never seem to be able to . . . I don't know—it's very complicated and hard for me to express.

THERAPIST: How old are you?

CLIENT: Thirty-six.

THERAPIST: And as a thirty-six-year-old person, you can't tell me what makes you unhappy?

CLIENT: I wish I could, but I'm too confused about it myself.

THERAPIST: (who infers that the client is "playing stupid" in order to avoid responsibility for problems) Can you play me trying to help you? What would I say and what would I do?

CLIENT: Well, you might say "Don't worry, I'll figure out what your problems are and help you get on the right track."

THERAPIST: OK, tell me how you expect me to do all this *for* you.

CLIENT: OK, I see. I guess I hope you have some magic pill or something.

At this point the therapist might again request a statement of the client's problems and, this time, might get a more mature answer.

Use of Nonverbal Cues. Nonverbal behavior is an important source of material in gestalt therapy. If the therapist is to frustrate the client's attempts to "play games," she or he must attend to what the client says *and* does. The nonverbal channel is a useful carrier of subtle messages that often contradict the client's words. Here is an illustration:

CLIENT: I wish I wasn't so nervous with people.
THERAPIST: Who are you nervous with?
CLIENT: With everyone.
THERAPIST: With me, here, now?
CLIENT: Yes, very.
THERAPIST: That's funny, because you don't look nervous to me.
CLIENT: (suddenly clasping his hands) Well I am!
THERAPIST: What are you doing with your hands?
CLIENT: Nothing, I just clasped them together. It's just a gesture.
THERAPIST: Do the gesture again. (client reclasps his hands) And again, clasp them again, harder. (client clasps hands harder) How does that feel?
CLIENT: It feels tight, kind of constricted.
THERAPIST: Can you become that tightness? Can you get in touch with what that tightness might say to you?
CLIENT: OK, ah, I'm tight. I'm holding everything together. I'm keeping the lid on you so that you don't let too much out.

The clasped hands made the therapist wonder what the gesture expressed. Instead of asking *why* the client clasped them, she pointed out *what* the client did. She then asked him to concentrate on the associated feelings by repeating and exaggerating the gesture. Once the feelings brought on by the gesture are expressed, the client is asked to elaborate on them. The result is that the client expresses a defensive feeling about being in therapy that had originally been described vaguely as "nervousness."

The Use of Dreams. In gestalt therapy, dreams are seen as messages from the person to himself or herself. After recounting a dream, the client is encouraged to "read" it by playing the part of some dream features and characters. In the process, the client may become aware of and assimilate disowned parts of the self. Here is an example of Perls's use of dream material:

LINDA: I dreamed that I watch . . . a lake . . . drying up, and there is a small island in the middle of the lake, and a circle of . . . porpoises—they're like porpoises except that they can stand up, so they're like porpoises that are like people, and they're in a circle, sort of like a religious ceremony, and it's very sad—I feel very sad because they can breathe, they are sort of dancing around the circle, but the water, their element, is drying up. So it's like a dying—like watching a race of people, or a race of creatures, dying. And they are mostly females but a few of them have a small male organ, so there are a few males there, but they won't live long enough to reproduce, and their element is drying up. And there is one that is sitting over here near me and I'm talking to this porpoise and he has prickles on his tummy, sort of like a porcupine, and they don't seem to be a part of him. And I think that there's one good point about the water drying up, I think—well, at least at the bottom, when all the water dries up, there will probably be some sort of treasure there, because at the bottom of the lake there should be things that have fallen in, like coins or something, but I look carefully and all that I can find is an old license plate . . . That's the dream.
PERLS: Will you please play the license plate?
LINDA: I am an old license plate, thrown in the bottom of a lake. I have no use because I'm of no value—although I'm not rusted—I'm outdated, so I can't be used as a license plate . . . and I'm just thrown on the rubbish heap. That's what I did with a license plate, I threw it on a rubbish heap.
PERLS: Well, how do you feel about this?

LINDA: (quietly) I don't like it. I don't like being a license plate—useless.

PERLS: Could you talk about this? That was such a long dream until you came to find a license plate; I'm sure this must be of great importance.

LINDA: (sighs) Useless. Outdated . . . The use of a license plate is to allow—give a car permission to go . . . and I can't give anyone permission to do anything because I'm outdated . . . In California, they just paste a little—you buy a sticker—and stick it on the car, on the old license plate. (faint attempt at humor) So maybe someone could put me on their car and stick this sticker on me, I don't know . . .

PERLS: OK, now play the lake.

LINDA: I'm a lake . . . I'm drying up, and disappearing, soaking into the earth . . . (with a touch of surprise) *dying* . . . But when I soak into the earth, I become a part of the earth—so maybe I water the surrounding area, so . . . even in the lake, even in my bed, flowers can grow (sighs). New life can grow . . . from me (cries) . . .

PERLS: You get the existential message?

LINDA: Yes. (sadly, but with conviction) I can paint—I can create—I can create beauty. I can no longer reproduce, I'm like the porpoise—but I—I'm . . . I . . . keep wanting to say I'm food . . . I . . . as water becomes . . . I water the earth, and give life—growing things, the water—they need both the earth and water, and the . . . and the air and the sun, but as the water from the lake, I can play a part in something, and producing—feeding.

PERLS: You see the contrast: On the surface, you find something, some artifact—the license plate, the artificial you—but then when you go deeper, you find the apparent death of the lake is actually fertility . . .

LINDA: And I don't need a license plate, or a permission, a license in order to . . .

PERLS: (gently) Nature doesn't need a license plate to grow. You don't have to be useless, if you are organismically creative, which means if you are involved.

LINDA: And I don't need permission to be creative . . . Thank you. (Perls, 1969, pp. 81–82)

Other Methods. The gestalt therapist uses other methods to help clients increase awareness and to promote "re-owning" of alienated aspects of personality. These are detailed by Levitsky and Perls (1970). We briefly mention a few of them here:

1 Use of direct and immediate messages. Direct communication is encouraged as a means of helping clients take responsibility for their feelings. In group therapy, the client who points to another client and says "She really makes me uncomfortable" would be asked to repeat the message directly to the person involved: "You make me uncomfortable." "I" language is preferred over "it" language. "It makes me furious to hear that" contains the message that "it" is responsible for the client's anger. A restatement (e.g., "I am angry at you") would be encouraged. Gossiping about people who are not present is prohibited because one evades responsibility for feelings if the target is absent. Finally, clients are asked to convert indirect *questions* into direct *statements.* The message behind the question "Do you think I'll ever feel any better than I do now?" may be "I am terrified that I'll always be depressed and maybe kill myself." If so, it is important for the client to be aware of and to express the fear.

2 Prohibition of intellectual discussion. The client in gestalt therapy is prevented from using intellectual analyses to avoid immediate, here-and-now awareness. The person who expounds a theory of a problem (e.g., "I think all this goes back to a time when I felt rejected by my parents") would be asked to identify with and "become" the nonconfident self in the present. Or, some nonverbal behavior that accompanied the theoretical analysis might be focused on by the therapist, who would request an exaggeration of the particular movement to bring its "message" into the foreground.

3   Use of internal dialogues and related techniques. Clients in gestalt therapy are often asked to "become" some of their characteristics and resistances. In group work, this technique includes extended "conversations" not only between "parts" of the person, but between the client and persons from the past with whom the client has "unfinished business." Internal dialogues are also held between the client's superego (called "topdog") and the part that is suppressed by "shoulds" and "oughts" (the "underdog"). A related method asks the client to "play the projection." Here, the assumption is that when disowned characteristics are projected onto other people (e.g., "She's so damned dependent!"), the best way to become aware of the feelings involved is to role play. *Reversals* are used to achieve similar kinds of awareness. Assume that a person denies feelings of tenderness toward others and conveys an image of coldness and self-sufficiency. This individual might be asked to play a warm, loving person. In the process, the client may get in touch with those feelings she or he has been suppressing.

An Illustration of Gestalt Therapy. The following edited excerpt from a gestalt group provides an idea of the way the methods described above are integrated in practice. In this case the setting is a workshop run by Perls in which each group member was placed in turn on the "hot seat" (Perls, 1969).[7] The client, "Jane," had worked with Perls before and thus shows more familiarity with the method than would a new client; otherwise, the procedures are representative.

---

[7] Although the person on the "hot seat" is the focus of attention, she or he is not isolated. Other group members also interact with the client and with the therapist (Polster & Polster, 1973).

JANE: I can't say that I'm really aware of what I'm doing. Except physically. I'm aware of what's happening physically to me but—I don't really know what I'm doing.

PERLS: I noticed one thing: When you come up on the hot seat, you stop playing the silly goose.

JANE: Hum. I get frightened when I'm up here.

PERLS: You get dead.

JANE: . . . I'm wondering whether or not I'm dead. I notice that my legs are cold and my feet are cold. I feel—I feel strange. . . . I notice that my attention is concentrated on that little matchbox on the floor.

PERLS: OK. Have an encounter with the matchbox.

JANE: [as the matchbox] I don't care if you tell the truth or not. It doesn't mater to me. I'm just a matchbox.

PERLS: Try this for size. Tell us, "I'm just a matchbox."

JANE: I'm just a matchbox and I feel silly saying that. I feel kind of dumb, being a matchbox. . . . A little bit useful, but not very useful. There's a million like me. And you can look at me, and you can like me, and when I'm all used up, you can throw me away. I never liked being a matchbox. . . . I don't know if that's the truth when I say I don't know what I'm doing. I know there's one part of me that knows what I'm doing. . . . She's saying (with authority) well, *you* know where you're at. You're playing dumb. You're playing stupid. You're doing this and you're doing that. . . . She's saying (briskly) now when you get in the chair, you have to be in the here-and-now, you have to do it *right*, you have to be turned on, you have to know everything—

PERLS: "You have to do your job."

JANE: You have to do your job, and you have to do it *right*. And you have to—become totally self-actualized, and you have to get rid of all your hangups. . . . [Now Jane spontaneously returns to being her frightened self again and talks to her demanding self:] You really make it hard for me. . . . You're really putting a lot of demands on me. . . . I don't know everything, and on top of that, I don't know what I'm doing half the time. . . .

PERLS: So be your topdog again.

JANE: Is that—

PERLS: Your topdog. That's the famous topdog. The righteous topdog. This is where the power is.

JANE: Yeah. Well—uh—I'm your topdog. You can't live without me. I'm the one that—I keep you noticed, Jane. If it weren't for me, nobody would notice you. [Jane now responds to "topdog"] Well, I don't want to be noticed, *you* do . . . I don't really want to be noticed, as much as you do.

PERLS: I would like you to attack the righteous side of that topdog.

JANE: Attack—the righteous side?

PERLS: The topdog is always righteous. Topdog *knows* what you've got to do, has all the right to criticize, and so on.

JANE: Yeah. . . . You're a bitch! Like my mother. You know what's good for me. You make life hard for me. . . .

PERLS: Now please don't change what your hands are doing, but tell us what's going on in your hands. . . . Let them talk to each other.

JANE: My left hand. I'm shaking, and I'm in a fist, straining forward . . . the fist is very tight, pushing my fingernails into my hand. It doesn't feel good, but I do it all the time. I feel tight.

PERLS: And the right hand?

JANE: I'm holding you back around the wrist.

PERLS: Tell it why you hold it back.

JANE: If I let you go you're gonna hit something. I don't know what you're gonna hit, but I have to—I have to hold back 'cause you can't do that. Can't go around hitting things.

PERLS: Now hit your topdog.

JANE: [gives short, harsh yells]

PERLS: Now talk to your topdog. "Stop nagging—"

JANE: [yells at "topdog"] Leave me alone!

PERLS: Again.

JANE: Leave me alone!

PERLS: Again.

JANE: [screaming and crying] *Leave me alone!*

PERLS: Again.

JANE: (screams and cries) LEAVE ME ALONE! I DON'T HAVE TO DO WHAT YOU SAY! (still crying) I don't have to be that good! . . . I don't have to be in this chair! You make me! You make me come here! . . . I'd like to kill you.

PERLS: Say this again.

JANE: I'd like to kill you.

PERLS: Again.

JANE: I'd like to *kill* you.

PERLS: Can you squash it in your left hand?

JANE: It's as big as me . . . I'm strangling it. [Perls gives Jane a pillow which she strangles while making choking noises and crying]

PERLS: OK. Relax, close your eyes. (long silence) OK, come back to us.

[Later in the session, Perls asks Jane to turn her perfectionist "topdog" into an "underdog" and to talk down to it.]

JANE: [to her perfectionist "topdog"] . . . You don't have to do anything, you don't have to prove anything. (cries) You're only twenty years old! You don't have to be the queen. . . .

JANE: [as her perfectionist "topdog"] OK, I understand that. I know that. I'm just in a *hurry.* . . . You have to keep hurrying and the days slip by and you think you're losing time, or something. I'm *much* too hard on you. I have to leave you alone.

PERLS: . . . Let your topdog say "I'll be a bit more patient with you."

JANE: [as topdog] . . . I'll be a bit more patient with you.

PERLS: Say this again.

JANE: It's very hard for me to be patient. . . . But I'll try to be a bit more patient with you. . . . As I say that, I'm stomping my foot, and shaking my head.

PERLS: OK. Say, "I won't be patient with you." [Perls asks Jane to repeat this and to take responsibility for the feeling by repeating the statement to several group members.]

PERLS: OK, how do you feel now?

JANE: OK.

PERLS: You understand, topdog and underdog are not yet together. But at least the conflict is

FIGURE 10-2. Many sensitivity or growth groups engage in exercises such as this to foster mutual trust among members.

clear, in the open, maybe a little less violent. (Perls, 1969, pp. 264–272)

Other case examples of gestalt therapy are available in Perls (1970), Polster and Polster (1973), and Rosenblatt (1975).

Applications of Gestalt Therapy. Perls saw his therapy approach as valuable for persons in various diagnostic categories, but he also felt it could produce increased awareness and improved functioning for people in general. Perls believed that everyone lacks full awareness, and he recommended various exercises to enhance contact with oneself, other people, and the environment (Perls, Hefferline & Goodman, 1951). These exercises have become an important part of sensitivity training groups, encounter groups, and personal growth groups. Having group members look at one another, close their eyes and focus attention on their bodies, enjoy the feelings of a backrub, listen to the emotions in their own voices, or speak intimately to one another are examples of these experiences.

Gestalt principles are used not only in temporary groups formed specifically for awareness and growth purposes, but in more permanent aggregations as well. Coworkers, church congregations, extended families, neighbors, dormitory residents, and married couples can be given gestalt awareness experiences. A summary of these applications is provided by Polster and Polster (1973, pp. 292–311). Additional references are contained in Hatcher and Himmelstein's *Handbook of Gestalt Therapy* (1976).

OTHER PHENOMENOLOGICAL THERAPIES

Rogers's and Perls's methods of treatment represent only two examples of phenomenological approaches to therapy. Many therapists blend psychodynamic, Rogerian, or gestalt methods with principles from humanistic or existential psychology (Kahn, 1985; Maslow, 1967, 1968; May, 1969; May, Angel & Ellenberger, 1958). The *logotherapy* of Viktor Frankl (1963, 1965, 1967) is based on existential philosophy and is oriented toward helping clients

(1) take responsibility for their feelings and actions, and (2) find meaning and purpose in their lives. Frankl believed that people can feel a lack of meaning and purpose without necessarily displaying neurotic or psychotic behaviors. He saw his approach as applicable to nonpatients as well as to "official" clients. Therapeutic procedures associated with humanistic and existential points of view are described in the sources cited above as well as in a recent introductory volume by Bugental (1978). See also Fischer and Fischer (1983), Ford and Urban (1963), and Patterson (1973).

A phenomenologically oriented treatment that shares several features with social-learning theory is the *fixed-role therapy* of George Kelly. On the basis of his person-construct theory (see Chapter 2), Kelly (1955) developed treatment methods for helping clients become aware of and change the assumptions they use to guide their behavior. Usually this means helping clients adopt more flexible, elaborate constructs to replace the narrow, rigid ones that Kelly believed were at the root of psychological disorders.

The subjective orientation of Kelly's theory places it partially in the phenomenological camp, but several of his methods are more at home elsewhere. Unlike phenomenologists who minimize diagnostic procedures, Kelly advocated systematic assessment of the problems and the personal constructs of the client. He advocated use of certain psychological tests to clarify the ways in which clients conceive of the world around them. Chief among these was Kelly's Role Construct Repertory Test.

Kelly went beyond merely helping clients become aware of their maladaptive beliefs. He encouraged them to experiment with specific alternative constructs. To assist in this enterprise, the therapist asks the client to write a *fixed-role sketch*, a third-person account of what the client wishes to be like and how he or she feels. The client is helped to restart personal growth by "temporarily" (for several weeks) role playing the person described in the sketch. Role playing takes place both in therapy sessions and in the real world. The therapist treats the client as if she or he were the person in the sketch. Over time, the client may become comfortable with certain aspects of the adopted role and assimilate them. Other aspects may be unacceptable and will be dropped. Ideally, the final result will be behavior and thoughts that are in line with how the client feels.

An Evaluation of Phenomenological Therapies

Phenomenological therapies and their nontherapy counterparts (e.g., sensitivity and personal growth groups) have had a significant impact on clinical psychology. They provide a "third choice" for those who are not satisfied with the psychodynamic or behavioral models. This "third choice" is attractive because its optimistic view of human beings generates faith in each client's ability to find meaning and self-actualization in life without having to exorcise unconscious, intrapsychic demons, extinguish bad habits, or learn new skills. Phenomenological approaches are upbeat. They do not dwell on pathology, but focus instead on what the client can become. Finally, the phenomenological emphasis on the therapeutic relationship and a corresponding de-emphasis on therapy techniques appeal to many clinicians, especially those who feel uncomfortable if they see themselves trying to do things *to* their clients.

Phenomenological approaches have received their share of criticism. Critics of phenomenological therapies make the following points:

1. *The language of phenomenology is often esoteric and unclear.* Terms like *B-values, Dasein, Eigenwelt, organismic experiencing, peak experiences,* and the like may stand in the way of understanding the treatments to which they apply. One client put it this way in a letter to Perls: "I tried reading your book, *Gestalt Therapy,* but I wish somebody . . .

would write a book in very simple language . . . , explaining these same theories so that the average person . . . could maybe really get something more out of it" (Perls, 1970, p. 214). Some writers have made fun of gestalt therapy language without straying too far from reality. Compare the following satire by Hoffman (1973, p. 76) with the quote from Kempler (1973) in Chapter 2:

CLIENT: Sorry I'm late today.
THERAPIST: Can you get more in touch with that sorrow?
CLIENT: I hope it didn't inconvenience you.
THERAPIST: Let's focus on your capacity for choice rather than on my expectations.
CLIENT: But I didn't mean to be late.
THERAPIST: I hear you, and I don't put it down. But where we need to be is the immanence of the I-thou relationship . . . emanating from the here-and-now, and from there into a consciousness of the tension between be-ing and non-be-ing, and eventually into the transcendence of be-ing itself, through to a cosmic awareness of the oceanic I-dentity of self and the space-time continuum.
CLIENT: Gotcha.

There is another aspect of the language problem in phenomenological therapies. Phenomenologists describe their goals as *humanistic,* and include among them things like client growth, creativity, fulfillment, joy, self-actualization, and individuality. Similarly, they describe their treatment as noncoercive, nonjudgmental, and nondirective. Critics argue that while this may be true ideally, these qualities are not the sole property of phenomenology. Most psychodynamic and behavioral therapists also see themselves as committed to humanistic values. In fact, it would be difficult to find a therapist who does not believe in the *ideals* of phenomenological therapy even though her or his methods of reaching them differ.

2. *Phenomenological treatment procedures are incomplete.* By de-emphasizing assessment and the client's history, phenomenological therapists may miss diagnostic signs

or background factors that could be important to treatment. Trusting clients to tell about these things is seen as naive and as potentially dangerous as the abuses associated with traditional diagnosis. It is also suggested that while a good client-therapist relationship may be a *necessary* condition for effective treatment, it may not be a *sufficient* condition. The problems of some clients may be beyond their ability to solve; they need more in the way of help than an empathic relationship.

3. *Phenomenological treatments are vague and unrealistic.* Phenomenological methods are usually described as "processes" that are not translated into specific therapist behaviors. Further, many writers question the processes themselves. For example, can a person *really* know what it is like to be another person? Can any therapist *really* be nondirective and nonjudgmental? Nye (1975, p. 135) points out that "client-centered therapists, despite themselves, bring about changes in the client's behaviors through inadvertent, subtle reinforcements (for example, nodding their heads or changing their facial expressions when clients speak about 'interesting' things and remaining more passive when clients speak about 'uninteresting' things)."

4. *Phenomenological treatments are actually rigid, not flexible.* By treating all clients in basically the same way on the assumption that each of them is troubled by the same awareness-related problems, phenomenological therapists fall prey to the criticisms they have leveled at other therapies, namely, that the uniqueness of each client is not given sufficient attention. Indeed, behavioral therapists contend that their emphasis on assessment and on the design of treatments tailored to each client's history is *more* humanistic than the phenomenological approach.

5. *The beneficial effects of phenomenological treatments have not been established.* Most phenomenological therapists have maintained an antiscientifc stance toward the evaluation of their methods. Some of them insist that only the client and therapist can evaluate therapy, and even then only in subjective terms, not in the language of science. This attitude has caused many observers to reject most phenomenological treatments as a viable approach to changing human behavior (see Fischer & Fischer, 1983, for a brief description of empirical phenomenological studies).

Some phenomenological therapists (notably Rogers and his colleagues) have provided data on the *process* of their treatments, but the variables measured (e.g., accurate empathy) have depended on subjective ratings and self-reports, both of which are vulnerable to bias and other threats to reliability and validity (Chinsky & Rappaport, 1970; Rappaport & Chinsky, 1972). Reviewers of research on therapist qualities have noted that "the . . . variables most frequently selected by the researcher for study are, unfortunately, such simplistic, global concepts as to cause this field to suffer from possibly terminal vagueness" (Parloff, Waskow & Wolfe, 1978, p. 273).

The same problems exist in interpreting research on the *outcome* of phenomenological treatments. The data presented to substantiate the value of treatment tend to be based on client self-reports. These may not be reliable or valid. After reviewing the results of phenomenological group therapy, Bednar and Kaul (1978, p. 792) noted that "in spite of the apparent diversity of these [self-report] measures, it seems most appropriate to view [them] as reflecting a nonspecific factor of improvement based on more favorable subjective evaluations that may or may not be accompanied by observable behavioral changes."

The claim by some phenomenologists (e.g., Rogers) that their treatments result in a similar pattern of change from client to client has also been attacked by critics. They suggest that the pattern is due not to spontaneous growth, but to direct therapist influences such as modeling and reinforcement of certain client behaviors. A participant in a

gestalt therapy group once raised this possibility with Perls:

Dr. Perls, . . . as you've been formulating and experiencing what has come out as gestalt therapy, I want to be reassured, I want to hear you say it, it seems like a process of discovery. Yet I think that people can arrange themselves to fit the expectations of the therapist, like, I sit here and watch person after person have a polarity, a conflict of forces, and I think I can do it too. But I don't know how spontaneous it would be, although I think I would feel spontaneous. You've experienced people over a long time; are we fitting you or have you discovered us? (Perls, 1969, pp. 214–215)

Perls's answer was "I don't know."

6. *Because phenomenological approaches are often applied in short-term group contexts that fall outside the range of formal therapy, some unscreened participants are inappropriately included in the process.* And because the emphasis in phenomenology is on feeling and experience, not reason and logic, the importance of the therapist's credentials and training is sometimes de-emphasized. The danger of client deterioration and other negative consequences may not be as critical as some people fear, but phenomenological group experiences can produce "casualties." While the definition of "casualty" is not entirely clear, available data indicate that up to 8 percent of group participants may end up harmed in some sense by the experience. "Casualties" occur most often among participants who were relatively unstable to begin with, a fact that further emphasizes the danger of inadequate screening of group members (see Bednar & Kaul, 1978, for a review of process and outcome data from phenomenological groups).

7. *Phenomenological approaches are applicable mainly to intelligent, introspective individuals.* Despite the view that anyone can benefit from growth experiences, it has been argued that these experiences may be helpful only to relatively well-integrated people. The value of phenomenological therapies for more severe behavior problems, children, and the retarded is probably minimal.

Still, phenomenological methods do appear to have value. In our view, they provide an excellent set of therapeutic strategies. Rogers's techniques are among the most productive interviewing procedures available, and many gestalt exercises (e.g., dialogues, part playing) can encourage clients to report on feelings that might otherwise require many interviews to reveal. Of greatest importance to the practicing clinician, however, is phenomenological-existential therapy's emphasis on the uniqueness of human experience in all its forms—thought, emotion, and action. This perspective encourages therapists to focus less on techniques and more on the client's "lived world" (Fischer & Fischer, 1983).

chapter 11

Biological Factors in Clinical Psychology

Some of the questions first addressed by ancient philosophers were "What is mind?" "What is body?" and "Are mind and body related? If so, how?" This intellectual conundrum, known as the *mind-body problem,* has been an issue that psychology has struggled with since the field's beginning. This struggle may seem foolish to those who take for granted that both mind and body exist and constantly affect each other. Lovers have no doubts about how strongly mind and body interact, nor do the writers of some of our best-known love songs (e.g., "Body and Soul," "I've Got You Under My Skin," and "Zing! Went the Strings of My Heart").

Lovers or not, most clinical psychologists now believe that mind and body interact in a reciprocal fashion. In fact, anyone familiar with the topics in this chapter would find it difficult to deny the mutual influences between psychological and biological pro-

cesses. As we indicated in Chapter 2, however, some clinicians fear that too much attention to biological variables amounts to a form of reductionism that ultimately will rob psychology of its status as an independent science (Peele, 1981). On the other hand, some advocates of strict biochemical causation seem to believe that psychological explanations are little more than camouflaged ignorance that will be replaced by biological or physical explanations as soon as they become available.

In this chapter we discuss three areas that illustrate how necessary and profitable it is for psychologists to study the relationships between psychological and biological factors. We have selected these three topics because in the past two decades they have been among clinical psychology's best "growth stocks" in terms of research discoveries and expanding professional roles. The three areas are *health psychology* (sometimes called behavioral medicine or behavioral health), *neuropsychology,* and *experimental psychopathology.*

HEALTH PSYCHOLOGY

Health psychology is a specialty area that emerged in the late 1970s and has enjoyed rapid growth ever since. It now has its own division in APA (Division 38) and its own journal *(Health Psychology).* There is also a *Journal of Behavioral Medicine,* a journal called *Psychological Medicine,* recommended guidelines for graduate training (see Stone, 1983), and several specialized training opportunities (Matarazzo & Carmody, 1983).

Joseph Matarazzo, a pioneer of the field, defined health psychology as "the collective activities of psychologists who work as scientists, health professionals and teachers in the interdisciplinary field of behavioral medicine" (Matarazzo & Carmody, 1983). Health psychologists are involved in the treatment and prevention of illness, the promotion and maintenance of health, the study of etiology and diagnosis of illness, and the improvement of systems of health care. Health psychologists follow a *biopsychosocial* model which holds that physical illness is the result of biological, psychological, and social disruptions. They study how psychological conditions and behavioral processes are linked to illness and good health. For example, two of the most important risk factors in the development of certain cancers are faulty diet and cigarette smoking, both of which are behavioral patterns that health psychologists study and attempt to modify in order to prevent some cancers' onset.

The historical development of health psychology has been traced from the Hellenic scholars' attention to the mind-body problem to modern-day concern about the politics and escalating costs of health care. Several books and chapters are available that review the recent accomplishments of health psychology (Ferguson & Taylor, 1981; Feuerstein, Labbe & Kuczmierczyk, 1986; Matarazzo, Miller, Weiss, Herd &

Weiss, 1984; Blechman & Brownell, 1986; Stone, Cohen & Adler, 1979; Zeiner, Bendell & Walker, 1985). In the remainder of this section we follow Krantz, Grunberg, and Baum's (1985) organization of health psychology activities into three categories: (1) linkage of behavior to illness through the psychophysiological effects of stressful stimuli, or (2) harmful habits and life-styles; (3) linkage of behavior to exacerbation of illness through patients' reactions to their illnesses and the sick role. These topics cover only a small portion of the work performed by psychologists involved in the health psychology–behavioral medicine area. Box 11-1 lists fifteen illnesses and physical conditions in which psychologists have participated in some aspect of treatment; in each case, we have included a reference or two that summarizes the type of work being done should you want to learn more about how psychologists intervene with specific illnesses.

Effects of Stress on Health

Although there are many definitions of stress, one of the most influential among psychologists is that it is an imbalance between the coping resources of an individual and the social, personal, and environmental threats perceived by that individual. These threats may be unpredictable, isolated events that are traumatic and will temporarily exceed the coping capacities of most people. Physical disasters are the prototype of this type of event, but financial reversals and educational failures are also examples. Other experiences are more predictable as they involve the milestone transitions that come with maturation and aging. Marriage, child rearing, starting school, occupational challenges, hospitalization, death of loved ones, and aging are examples. Even relatively minor events like having to wait in line or having your car stall in traffic can be stressful, especially when a number of such events accumulate in a short period of time.

One of the clearest explanations of how

BOX 11-1 Medical illnesses and conditions in which psychological interventions have been part of a treatment program

Illness/Condition	Illustrative References
1. Headaches	Blanchard & Andrasik (1985)
2. Gastrointestinal Disorders	Latimer (1983)
	Whitehead & Schuster (1985)
3. Pain	Holzman & Turk (1986)
	Hoon, Feuerstein, & Papciak (1985)
4. Eating Disorders	Hawkins, Fremouw & Clement (1984)
	Neuman & Halvorson (1983)
5. Asthma	Creer (1982)
6. Hypertension	Shapiro & Goldstein (1982)
7. Arthritis	Achterberg-Lawlis (1982)
	Anderson, Bradley, Young, McDaniel & Wise (1985)
8. Diabetes	Wing, Epstein, Nowalk, & Lamparski (1986)
9. Seizures	Zlutnick, Mayville, & Moffat (1975)
	Hermann & Whitman (1984)
10. Kidney Failure	Levy, Mattern & Freedman (1983)
11. Raynaud's Disease	Surwit (1982)
12. Myopia	Collins & Gill (1983)
	Blount, Baer & Collins (1984)
13. Cancer	Redd & Hendler (1983)
	Telch & Telch (1985)
14. Heart Attack	Lefebvre (1986)
15. Sleep Disorders	Turner (1986)

stress can contribute to physical illness or psychological disorder is the following four-step model by Barbara Dowrenwend (1978):

1. Stressful life events occur. They may be introduced either by the environment (a person is laid off from work) or by the individual (inadequate job skills lead to unsatisfactory performance).

2. A transient stress reaction follows the stressful life event. Some temporary physical or psychological problems may occur as part of this transient reaction.

3. The transient stress reaction is mediated by environmental and psychological characteristics. Environmental mediators include material supports (wealth), material handicaps (poverty), social supports (advice from friends), and social handicaps (isolation). Psychological characteristics include cognitive abilities, self-esteem, social skills, and coping abilities and disabilities.

4. The transient stress reaction interacts with the moderators and proceeds to one of three out-comes. First, the moderators can nullify the impact of the event so that only the transient reaction is experienced. Second, supports may be so strong that the event is mastered and ultimately experienced as positive change. Finally, the transient reaction can persist and become a physical or psycho-pathological condition when environmental or psychological supports are inadequate buffers or when environmental hazards and/or psychological variables actually magnify stressful events.

In order to study the relationship between stress and illness it is necessary to measure stress in an accurate way. Psychologists have tried to quantify stress in several ways. An early attempt was the Schedule of Recent Experiences (SRE), which was also entitled the Recent Life Changes Questionnaire (Rahe, 1975). The SRE (Amundson, Hart, & Holmes, 1986) which contains a list of forty-two events involving health, family, personal, occupational, and financial mat-

BOX 11-2   Measuring stress

In the Schedule of Recent Experiences (Amundson, Hart, & Holmes, 1986) subjects indicate which of 42 stressful events have happened to them in the past 6, 12, 24, and 36 month periods. After subjects have checked the events that have occurred, the amount of adjustment each event requires is assigned a value on a 100-point scale. The stressful events are organized into five categories. Examples from each category are listed below.

A. Health
   A major change in eating habits
   A major change in sleeping habits
B. Work
   Changed to a new line of work
   Experienced being fired from work
   Changed your work hours or conditions
C. Home and Family
   A change in family "get-togethers"
   Death of a close friend
   A divorce
   Gaining a new family member

D. Personal and Social
   Sexual difficulties
   A minor violation of the law
   A vacation
   A major change in church activities
E. Financial
   Major business readjustment
   Foreclosure on a mortgage or loan
   Taking out a mortgage or loan for a
   major purchase, such as a home,
   business, property, etc.

ters, is summarized in Box 11-2. Subjects check the events that have happened to them in a particular period of time. Each event is given a weight based on the amount of adjustment needed to handle the events (1 = very little adjustment; 100 = maximal adjustment). These weights are summed to give an index of stress experienced in a given time period. The resulting Subjective Life Change Unit score has been found to be moderately correlated with a variety of illnesses (e.g., Holmes & Masuda, 1974; Marx, Garrity & Bowers, 1975).

The RLCQ has been criticized on several grounds, and other researchers have developed their own instruments for measuring stress which differ in the ways they weight the occurrence of an event, the time periods surveyed, and the content of the events themselves. Zimmerman (1983) reviews eighteen different life event inventories, including the *Life Experiences Survey* (Sarason,

Johnson & Siegel, 1978), the *Interview Schedule for Events and Difficulties* (Brown & Harris, 1978), and the *Psychiatric Epidemiology Research Interview* (Dohrenwend, Krasnoff, Askenasy & Dohrenwend, 1978).

Some researchers have concluded that stress should not be equated with the occurrence of major traumatic events, but should be examined in terms of chronic stress that involves "small" events occurring on a daily basis. One of the best-known of these chronic strain inventories is the Hassles Scale (Kanner, Coyne, Schaefer & Lazarus, 1981).[1] On this scale subjects are asked to indicate how severely they have been hassled in the past month by events such as

---

[1] A companion scale, the Uplifts Scale, consists of 135 events that can make a person feel good. Examples include "practicing your hobby," "buying clothes," and "being complimented."

"misplacing or losing things," "unexpected company," "auto maintenance," "too many meetings," and "filling out forms." Another approach to measuring stress involves examining the effects of specific life crises such as crime victimization (e.g., Burgess & Holmstrom, 1979) on later adjustment. Extensive discussion of these methods and alternative ways of measuring stress can be found in Kessler, Price, and Wortman (1985), Dohrenwend and Dohrenwend (1981), and Thoits (1982).

The means by which stress might contribute to illness are not clearly understood. There are several physiological reactions to stress (see Selye, 1956), including increased heart rate and blood pressure and greater gastrointestinal activity which, if sustained over long periods, can lead to illness. One mechanism that has been implicated recently is the immune system, the body's defense structure against disease-causing agents. Certain stressors have been associated with temporarily lowered responsiveness of the immune system (Jemmott & Locke, 1984), a condition known as *immunosuppression,* which could make a person more susceptible to infectious diseases and other illnesses.

Other researchers question whether there is sufficient evidence to conclude that stress leads to illness. A correlation between stressful life events and symptoms can be explained in a number of ways. For example, many of the items on surveys of stressful life events involve the occurrence of illness; it is possible that the correlation between such surveys and measures of illness is due to the fact that they simply contain identical items (Dohrenwend, Dohrenwend, Dodson & Shrout, 1984). Another possibility is that people who are ill are more likely to remember negative life events from the recent past than are people who are well; if this is the case, the stress-illness correlation can be understood as an instance in which illness affects recall.

In addition, it is important to remember that most people who experience stress in its various forms do not become ill as a result. Although many methodological improvements have been made in the years since the first life events scales, most research indicates that the overall relationship between stress and illness onset is relatively small (Rabkin & Struening, 1976). This discovery has led to a search for variables that might help explain how people are protected from the assumed health-harming effects of stress. Among several *vulnerability* or *resistance* factors (Kessler, Price & Wortman, 1985), two variables, social support and coping strategies, have sparked the most interest.

Social Support. Social support has been defined in many ways (Schradle & Dougher, 1985). Cobb (1976) described it as experiences leading individuals to believe that they are cared for, loved, esteemed, and members of a network of communication and mutual obligation. Social support involves more than the mere presence of others. It provides relationships in which emotional support, feedback, cognitive guidance, tangible assistance, and shared values are exchanged between people (Caplan, 1974).

Several studies have shown that the relationship between stress and illness is greater among individuals with lower levels of social support in their lives (e.g., Mitchell, Billings & Moos, 1982). Why is this the case? There are several possible answers, depending on how social support is measured (Cohen & Wills, 1985). The most popular explanation is that social support acts as a *buffer* against stress. The buffer model claims that social support enables people under high stress to neutralize the harmful effects of stress in any number of ways. Another model, sometimes termed the *direct effect model,* holds that social support is helpful regardless of whether stressful events are experienced because there is a general benefit to being embedded in supportive relationships that manifests itself in better overall health. A third possibility is that high levels of social support, good health, and low levels of stress reflect the influence of some underlying characteristic like *social competence,* which has positive effects on many areas of functioning. Of course, some combination of all three models may operate as well. What does seem clear is that lack of social support, particularly emotional support, does put people at higher risk for both physical and psychological illnesses (Cohen & Wills, 1985; Kessler, Price & Wortman, 1985) and even mortality (House, Robbins & Metzner, 1982).

Coping Strategies. Coping refers to people's cognitive and behavioral efforts at modifying, tolerating, or eliminating stressors that threaten them (Folkman & Lazarus, 1980; Pearlin & Schooler, 1978). People vary a great deal in their preferences for how to cope with stress. Some try to alter or solve a problem directly; others attempt to change their way of thinking about a problem in order to make it less stressful; still others may concentrate on managing the emotional upsets that a stressor causes (see Moos & Billings, 1982, for a review of coping processes). The same person may employ different coping strategies to deal with different types of stress or may combine various coping approaches to reduce stress (see Box 11-3). While there is evidence that coping resources can lessen some effects of stress, their success depends on several factors, including the type of stress to be reduced. For example, coping through denial appears to be an effective response to short-term stress but an ineffective strategy with chronic stress (Mullen & Suls, 1982).

In line with the above concepts, psychologists have developed interventions that bolster the social support and coping skills of stressed populations. Common examples include providing accurate information and emotional support before upcoming surgery (Cohen & Lazarus, 1973), cognitive restructuring in which clients learn to "inoculate" themselves against stress by developing new ways to think about it (Meichenbaum, 1975), and developing special social sup-

ports for people facing a crisis or frightening event (e.g., Cutrona, 1984).

Although there are many ways a psychologist can intervene to reduce stress, behavior therapy techniques appear especially well-suited to building the social skills, behavioral competencies, and cognitive strategies that can help mitigate stress. Psychologists can also learn much from the personal buffers and support systems that people fashion for themselves to cope with stress (Wilcox, 1981). An attitude that respects the natural abilities of ordinary people to help one another (Lenrow & Cowden, 1980) is an important perspective for professionals to maintain.

Effects of Harmful Behavior on Health

Several serious illnesses, including two of this country's leading killers, cardiovascular disease and cancer, have been linked to harmful behaviors and habits. Chief among these behavioral culprits are smoking, overeating, lack of exercise, faulty diet, and alcoholism. Conversely, certain behaviors or life-styles may promote better physical health. For example, Breslow (1979) reported that people who eat breakfast regularly, rarely snack between meals, exercise regularly, do not smoke, get seven to eight hours of sleep per day, and do not use alcohol excessively live on the average eleven years longer than people who practice none of these behaviors.

A behavior or personal characteristic that increases a person's chances of developing an illness is called a *risk factor.* There are biological (e.g., inherited physical defects), social (e.g., age or sex), and behavioral (e.g., smoking) risk factors. Although not all the research agrees on the importance of behavioral risk factors in the etiology of specific illnesses, the current consensus is that many harmful behaviors do account for variations in rates of serious physical diseases (Krantz, Grunberg & Baum, 1985).

Treatments aimed at modifying behavioral risk factors have taken many forms,

BOX 11-3 Measuring coping skills

Accurate measurement of the different ways people cope with stress is difficult because coping itself is a very complex process consisting of several dimensions. Coping processes may change from one situation to another depending on how a person appraises stressful episodes; they may even change as a single stressful situation unfolds, leading to different appraisals of which coping options may be most effective. Two research groups at the University of California (Berkeley) and at the State University of New York (Stony Brook) have developed comprehensive instruments to measure the ways people cope with stress.

At Berkeley, Richard Lazarus and his colleague, Susan Folkman (Folkman & Lazarus, 1980), have developed a Ways of Coping checklist that consists of 68 items that describe a wide variety of methods that 100 middle-aged adults used to cope with stressful events in their daily lives. Folkman and Lazarus (1980) divide these items into two broad categories: *problem-focused* and *emotion-focused* coping. Examples of problem-focused strategies are "made a plan of action and followed it," and "got the person responsible to change his or her mind." Emotion-focused items involved steps like "look for the silver lining," "try to forget the whole thing," and "accept sympathy and understanding from someone."

The 100 respondents reported a total of 1332 stressful episodes. In 98 percent of these events, respondents reported using *both* problem-focused and emotion-focused coping. Furthermore, there was considerable variability for most persons in their relative preference for one type of coping strategy versus the other. The typical person emphasized problem-solving approaches to some stresses but preferred emotional support approaches to other stresses. Problem-focused coping was favored for dealing with stress related to work, but emotion-focused coping was used more often when the stress involved health. Men tended to use problem-focused coping more often than women in certain areas, but men and women did not differ in their use of emotion-focused coping.

At Stony Brook, Arthur Stone and John Neale initially tried to assess daily coping skills using an objective checklist like Folkman and Lazarus (1980), but gave up this method when they found that people were not consistent in their definitions and endorsements of different coping behaviors. Therefore, they developed an alternative instrument that allowed subjects to give open-ended answers to how they "handled" problems (Stone & Neale, 1984). The format of the instrument was as follows: (1) Eight coping styles were listed and given a one-sentence summary (the eight categories were distraction, situation redefinition, direct action, catharsis, acceptance, seeking social support, relaxation, and religion); (2) subjects then indicated whether they had used each of the styles of coping to handle a problem on a given day; and (3) if they responded positively, subjects described in their own words the particular thoughts or actions they had used for each category of coping.

Despite differences in their methodologies, Folkman and Lazarus (1980) and Stone and Neale (1984) reached similar conclusions about some aspects of daily coping. Men tended to use direct action a little more and distraction, catharsis, and seeking social support a little less than women. The way a given problem was appraised or defined was significantly related to the ways people tried to cope with it. Finally, most people are flexible copers; although they may have one favorite coping style, they combine it with other strategies as their view of a problem requires.

with varying degrees of success. Smoking cessation techniques produce short-term reductions in cigarette smoking, but more than 50 percent of smokers resume their habit at a later date (Lichtenstein, 1982). A similar picture exists for treatment of obesity (Brownell, 1982). Although behavior modification appears to be the most effective psychological intervention for obesity, maintenance of weight loss and learning new eating behaviors are major difficulties for most people.

One psychological risk factor that has attracted a lot of attention in the past ten years is the Type A behavior pattern (Friedman & Rosenman, 1974). Matthews (1982) listed the following characteristics of Type A behavior: (1) explosive, accelerated speech; (2) a heightened pace of living; (3) impatience with slowness; (4) trying to perform more than one activity at a time; (5) preoccupation with self; (6) dissatisfaction with life; (7) evaluation of one's accomplishments in terms of numbers; (8) competitiveness; and (9) free-floating hostility. Friedman and Rosenman (1974) referred to Type A behavior as "hurry sickness" (examples: you become enraged at cars in front of you that go too slowly; you get angry and fidgety if you must wait in line), and believed that it was the most important behavioral risk factor in the development of coronary heart disease. However, current thinking among health psychologists is that Type A behavior is but one of several possibly interrelated risk factors that are difficult to disentangle from one another (e.g., the person who is always on the go is also less likely to maintain a balanced diet).

There are three basic procedures for measuring Type A behavior. *The Structured Interview* (Rosenman, 1978) consists of about twenty-five questions that tap how a person responds to frustrating situations and even presents some of the questions in a slow, halting manner designed to provoke Type A behavior. The *Jenkins Activity Survey* (Jenkins, Zyzanski & Rosenman, 1971) contains approximately fifty questions that as-

sess competitiveness, impatience, and job involvement (sample item: Do you ever have trouble finding time to get your hair cut or styled?). The *Framingham Type A Scale* (Haynes, Levine, Scotch, Feinleib & Kannel, 1978) is a ten-item self-report measure that concentrates on competitiveness, time urgency, and sense of job pressure.

Because these three procedures measure different aspects of the Type A pattern, they do not always agree with one another in designating a given individual as a Type A person. However, several studies using the different assessment approaches report a relationship between Type A behaviors and coronary heart disease (see Krantz, Grunberg & Baum, 1985, for a review). This relationship has led to attempts to reduce Type A behavior and in turn reduce the risk of heart disease (see Suinn, 1982, for a review). Among the many techniques available, relaxation training, self-monitoring, and training in coping skills appear to have the largest effects on Type A behavior. However, physiological risk factors such as blood pressure have not been consistently altered in positive directions by psychological treatments.

There may be a number of Type A persons among our readers who have just become very anxious about their status and are obsessing about whether they can change their behavior—by tonight, if possible. Box 11-4 contains several suggestions for reducing Type A behavior. Type A readers should read Box 11-4—slowly, please. Type B readers might want to glance at Box 11-4, or perhaps they might not.

Health psychologists also have collaborated with physicians, health educators, and other professionals to develop large-scale programs that try to prevent illnesses by reducing behavioral risk factors in specified populations. Changes in diet, exercise, smoking and drinking habits, and Type A behavior are the most common examples, but other interventions, such as teaching children about healthy life-styles, have been advocated (Matarazzo & Carmody, 1983).

BOX 11-4 Can Type A behavior be changed?

Is it the case that "once a Type A always a Type A" or can a Type A person slow down, loosen up, and learn to relax? Can an "A" become more like a "B"? Friedman & Rosenman (1974) believed that Type A behavior can be changed if a person modifies his or her behavior at each of three levels which they termed (1) philosophical guidelines, (2) reengineering the day, and (3) drills. A few examples of the changes Friedman & Rosenman (1974) recommended for each of those levels are presented below.

Philosophical Guidelines

1. Make an honest self-appraisal of your strengths and weaknesses so that you will be less dependent on the opinions of others and less driven to please them.
2. Develop broader interests in activities outside your career preoccupations—e.g., art, literature, making new friends.
3. Accept the fact that life consists of many unfinished processes, jobs, and events. Only some of these tasks will ever be finished no matter how compulsively you work at them.

Reengineering Your Day

1. Arrange your work environment so as to promote peace—e.g., schedule more time for appointments than you think they will require, keep a clean desk, don't be a slave to the telephone.
2. Talk less.
3. Reserve periods of time each week when you can be alone.

Drills

1. Go to a restaurant with a companion where you know you will have to wait in line to be served.
2. Whenever you go faster in your car to beat a red light at the intersection, punish yourself by circling the block and coming back to the same intersection.
3. Read books that demand patience and your full attention. For example, the prose of Proust and Faulkner moves at a pace that will force Type A persons to stop their tendency to skim read.

Box 11-5 summarizes one of the best-known, large-scale illness-prevention projects.

Improving Compliance with Treatment

Whether a given treatment for an illness is effective depends first on its being the correct treatment and second on the patient's adhering to or following through with the treatment. The extent to which patients' behavior (e.g., taking medication, following a diet, going to bed) coincides with the medical advice they have been given is called *compliance*.

Most estimates indicate that noncompliance is a frequent problem, occurring in up to 50 percent of patients prescribed certain medications and even more often for treatments that involve changes in life-style (Haynes, 1982). Physicians cite patients' noncompliance as one of the major sources of dissatisfaction in their work, and noncompliance has been called "the best documented but least understood health-related behavior" (Becker & Maiman, 1975). Health psychologists are interested in the causes of noncompliance and in interventions that could be used to improve compliance.

Causes of Noncompliance. The chief cause of noncompliance appears to be communication problems between physicians and patients. These problems take many forms. Patients frequently do not understand what physicians tell them about their

BOX 11-5 Illness prevention in communities

One of the leading examples of a community-based prevention project aimed at modifying behavioral risk factors associated with cardiovascular disease was the Stanford Heart Disease Prevention Program (SHDPP; Meyer, Nash, McAlister, Maccoby & Farquhar, 1980).

Approximately 500 persons at high risk for heart disease were identified in each of three Northern California towns. In Community #1 (Watsonville), 56 subjects were assigned to a mass media campaign (TV and radio spots) that acquainted listeners with probable causes of heart disease and specific behaviors (smoking, diet, and exercise) that could lead to reduction in risk factors. One hundred and thirteen additional subjects in Watsonville received the same media packages plus "intensive instruction" involving face-to-face behaviorally oriented counseling about how to bring about changes in diet, smoking habits, and exercise. In Community #2 (Gilroy), 139 subjects were exposed to a comparable media intervention as that delivered to the Watsonville participants. Community #3 (Tracy) subjects (n=136) served as controls who received neither media nor intensive instructional intervention. Subjects were assessed at three annual follow-up surveys.

Results indicated that all groups of treated subjects experienced reductions in the risk factors for cardiovascular disease plus an increase in their knowledge of behavioral factors that contribute to heart disease. On some measures, including overall risk score reduction, greater and longer-lasting reductions occurred in the Watsonville group that received the mass media campaign combined with intensive instruction. For example, this group showed significantly greater reduction in smoking (a 50 percent cessation rate; a 51 percent reduction in cigarettes smoked per day) than in any of the other groups. On other measures (e.g., increased physical exercise) there were no significant effects from intervention.

The Stanford investigators concluded that "intensive media plus face-to-face instruction had greater impact on cardiovascular disease risk and related knowledge and behavior than did the media only treatment or control." In addition, they found that the intensive instruction resulted in more durable changes in these factors over time.

The SHDPP has been subjected to several criticisms. A major difficulty was the high *attrition* or drop-out rate (around 25 percent), especially in the Watsonville intensive instruction group (e.g., when dropouts are considered in this group, its smoking cessation rate drops from 50 to 32 percent). Other objections include the validity of the risk score in predicting heart disease on an individual basis, the possible effects of demand characteristics associated with repeated physiological measurements, the lack of a control group receiving intensive instruction only, problems in the definition of "life-style" changes, and inappropriate statistical analyses (Kasl, 1980; Leventhal, Safer, Cleary & Gutmann, 1980).

The SHDPP program has now been expanded to a five-city study that is collecting data on morbidity (onset of heart disease) and mortality rates associated with reductions in behavioral risk factors. Another example of a large-scale prevention program using health psychology methods is the Multiple Risk Factor Intervention Trial (MRFIT, 1982) which attempted to reduce blood pressure, smoking, and blood cholesterol in thousands of high-risk individuals. Although most cardiovascular risk prevention programs are intended for adults, a few projects have been developed for children. The most comprehensive of these projects is the Know Your Body Program, a school-based intervention in New York City. Final results from this program are not available, but initial descriptive data are encouraging (Williams, Arnold & Wynder, 1977).

illnesses or their treatments. As a result, they are confused about what they should do or they forget what they have been told. For example, Ley, Bradshaw, Eaves, and Walker (1973) found that only five minutes after seeing their physician, general-practice patients had forgotten 50 percent of what their doctor had told them.

The emotional aspects of patient-physician communications also are correlated with compliance. A common pattern of troubled communication involves patient antagonism toward the physician accompanied by physician withdrawal from interaction with the patient. As an example, one study found a relationship between mothers' satisfaction with their interactions with pediatricians and their compliance with treatment (Francis, Korsch & Morris, 1969). Dissatisfaction stemmed from the mothers' not having expectations met, not feeling that the physician related warmly to them, and not receiving adequate explanations of illnesses.

A second source of noncompliance lies in the characteristics of treatment itself. Regimens that are more complex, that require greater changes in life-style, and that are of longer duration tend to impede compliance (Masur, 1981). Contrary to expectations, adverse side effects do not usually have substantial effects on patient's willingness to take most medications.[2]

Third, behavioral and environmental factors may reduce compliance. Researchers who emphasize these factors analyze compliance in operant terms; i.e., compliance is a function of (a) environmental antecedents that prompt some action by the patient and (b) consequences that follow that action. For example, Zifferblatt (1975) outlined a four-step functional analysis of noncompliance in which patients (1) keep a daily diary in which they record antecedent cues, attend-

ing thoughts, and behavioral consequences of compliant behavior like taking medication; (2) arrange clear and compelling cues to trigger the prescribed behavior; (3) provide desirable reinforcers for the behavior; and (4) assess the success of the program through the continued use of the diary and redesign of the triggering cues and the consequences as necessary. Zifferblatt suggests that the most effective cues and consequences for compliance are those that possess (1) *salience* (cues or rewards that are meaningful for the patient); (2) *compatibility* (stimuli that are easily integrated into patients' daily routines; (3) *short latency* (brief delays between cues, prescribed responses, and consequences); and (4) *explicitness* (stimuli that are uniquely related to the prescribed response).

In searching for causes of noncompliance, most researchers have not attempted to formulate a theory that integrates what is known about noncompliance into a comprehensive explanation of its occurrence. The one exception to this atheoretical approach is the Health Belief Model (HBM) originated by Rosenstock (1966) and focused by Becker and Maiman (1975) on the specific question of noncompliance. The HBM is a social-psychological theory that bases its explanation of behavior on the expectancies of certain outcomes an individual holds and the values these outcomes represent for the person. According to the HBM, individuals will comply with treatments depending on (1) how susceptible to a given illness individuals perceive themselves to be and how severe the consequences of contracting the illness are thought to be; (2) how effective and feasible versus how costly and difficult the prescribed treatment is perceived to be; (3) the influence of internal cues (physical symptoms) plus external cues (media advertisements or advice from friends) in triggering health behaviors; and (4) demographic and personality variables as well as structural and social characteristics that modify the influences of the other variables. Subsequent versions of the HBM have incorpo-

---

[2] An exception may be for drugs that have serious, irreversible side effects, like the phenothiazines used to treat schizophrenics.

rated general health motivations, general faith in doctors, and characteristics of the doctor-patient relationship into the theoretical scheme, and Masur (1981) has integrated the HBM with traditional behavioral principles reminiscent of Zifferblatt's (1975) analysis.

Interventions to Improve Compliance. Attempts to improve compliance with treatment have been developed on a piecemeal basis with little concern for theoretical justification (Haynes, 1982). Many commentators have attempted to impose some order on these different interventions by organizing them into three general approaches which Masur (1981) identified as education, modification of treatment plan, and behavioral techniques.

1 Education. One of the most direct and effective interventions for improving compliance with short-term treatments is to give patients clear, explicit, written instructions that supplement any oral instructions about how treatment is to proceed. This positive effect is less evident with long-term treatments, however. More extensive information about illnesses, the need for treatment, side effects of treatment and the like do not appear to improve compliance very much. On the other hand, there may be benefits to educating physicians about the causes and management of noncompliance. In one study (Inui, Yourtee & Williamson, 1976), physicians who had been educated about the HBM and ways to improve compliance had more compliant patients at a six-month reassessment.

2 Modification of treatment plan. A second strategy for increasing compliance is to reorganize the treatment in ways that facilitate an individual's adherence to it. Examples include tailoring the taking of medications to existing daily habits (e.g., taking pills right after brushing teeth), giving the treatment in one or two injections rather than in several doses per day, packaging

medicine in dosage strips or with pill calendars, and scheduling more frequent follow-up visits to supervise compliance. These procedures have shown promise (e.g., Boczkowski, Zeichner & DeSanto, 1985), but many of them entail additional manufacturing costs and extra time from service providers, two characteristics likely to limit their application.

3 Behavior modification. Arranging stimuli so as to prompt compliance and providing reinforcers for compliant behaviors have been used in a number of innovative ways. Compliance can be prompted by *environmental cues* such as postcard reminders, telephone calls, or wristwatches set to emit a tone at the time a pill should be taken. *Self-monitoring* has shown some benefits for compliance, particularly in the treatment of obesity and other conditions that have easily measured indices. Written *contingency contracts* between patient and physician can specify what compliance behaviors the patient must complete in order to earn a reward (e.g., future appointments scheduled at more convenient times). Such contracts encourage a more collaborative relationship between patient and physician and have demonstrated some success in improving compliance (Swain & Steckel, 1981) although at least one study of hypertensives (Hoelscher, Lichstein & Rosenthal, 1986) found that a written contract condition produced less compliance in producing relaxation at home than a non-contract condition. Finally, *token economies* have been employed to encourage compliance in a variety of patients. In a study by Magrab and Papadopoulou (1971), three children with renal failure were given points for maintaining their weight, potassium, and nitrogen levels at recommended levels. These points could then be exchanged for tangible rewards in the hospital. In comparison to their baseline levels, these children were able to make substantial weight gains, and two of them showed some improvements in the other indices.

NEUROPSYCHOLOGY

Neuropsychology has been defined as "a field of study that . . . (relates) brain dysfunction and damage to observable, empirically defined behavioral deficits" (Crockett, Clark & Klonoff, 1981). The neuropsychologist assesses how damage to the brain expresses itself in behavioral, cognitive, and emotional *deficits* (defined as a deficiency in performance from the level shown by a normative or average group of people or from the level shown by an individual on an earlier occasion). When a neuropsychologist assesses a patient, she or he seeks to answer one or more of the following questions (Jones & Butters, 1983):

1. Does the patient show deficits that suggest organic brain damage?
2. If there is impairment, how severe is it and what is its prognosis or likely course?
3. Can the impairment be traced or localized to a certain area of the brain?
4. What is the probable cause of the impairment?
5. What are the consequences of the impairment for the patient's daily, occupational, and interpersonal functioning?
6. What recommendations are there for the rehabilitiation of the impairment?

In answering these questions, neuropsychologists must integrate data and knowledge from several sources. First, they must be proficient in the general assessment skills that we described in Chapters 3–6. Neuropsychological assessment should not be isolated from an assessment of the entire person, including social and family background, personality dynamics, and emotional reactions to possible brain dysfunction. Second, the neuropsychologist must be well-versed in the neurosciences, including *neuroanatomy* (the study of the structures of the nervous system and the functions of these structures), *neuropharmacology* (the study of drugs that affect nerve functioning), and *neurophysiology* (the study of

the physiology of the nervous system, including the chemistry of nerve tissue and the relationship between the nervous system and endocrine functions). Third, neuropsychologists must be trained in the field of *human abilities* (e.g., cognition, language, and perception) and *developmental psychology* (especially behavioral genetics and life-span psychology). Fourth, the need to distinguish brain impairments from nonorganic psychopathology and the frequent requests to design rehabilitative programs require neuropsychologists to prepare for their work by completing some basic courses in *clinical psychology*. Finally, neuropsychologists must be thoroughly trained in the specialized assessment methods that constitute the technology of neuropsychology.

The increasing demand for neuropsychologists has stimulated many clinical psychologists to list neuropsychology as one of their specialties. This rush to neuropsychology has led to serious questions about the education necessary to insure competency in the field. An all too frequently traveled route has been to take one or two courses in neuropsychological assessment as part of a clinical psychology curriculum and then begin to "do neuropsychologicals." An even worse practice is to acquire all of one's expertise in neuropsychology through clinical workshops or a brief rotation on one's internship. The education of a competent neuropsychologist is an ambitious process that requires multidisciplinary input, a large body of basic knowledge, research sophistication, supervised experience, and clinical acumen. Although there are various models available for such preparation, all of them require extensive coordinated training for which there simply are no shortcuts (Meier, 1981).

Historical Development of Neuropsychology

Although some experts claim that neuropsychological assessment orginated in the first quarter of the twentieth century, the roots of neuropsychology extend to much earlier speculations and discoveries about the distinct functions of certain parts of the central nervous system. For example, in the second century A.D., Galen, the famous Roman physician, localized the mind in the brain (Aristotle had placed it in the heart) and distinguished between sensory and motor nerves. In the Middle Ages, Avicenna located internal senses such as memory, estimation, imagination, and common sense in four "cells" of the brain, a theory that was standard medical teaching until Andreas Vesalius began to practice dissection in the sixteenth century.

Several major discoveries about how the nervous system is constructed and how it operates were made in the nineteenth century. Charles Bell and Francois Magendie established that different mental functions were controlled by separate physical structures, and Johannes Müller went further and showed that specific kinds of nerves produced unique sensory experiences regardless of how they were stimulated. Herman von Helmholtz also contributed to the understanding of the nervous system by showing that nervous impulses could be measured accurately and that they were much slower than scientists had previously believed.

Of greatest importance to neuropsychology were several lines of research undertaken in the 1800s that focused on possible relationships between selected behaviors and specific areas of the brain. At its extreme, this study of *localization of function* was popularized as *phrenology* by Franz Gall and his associate, Johann Spurzheim. Phrenology was a pseudoscience which claimed that individual differences in personality and intelligence could be assessed by measuring the bumps and indentations of the surface of the skull. These features supposedly corresponded to the part of the brain responsible for the characteristic in question. It was very popular with the public but disdained by most scientists.

Greater scientific respectability was accorded discoveries made by Pierre Flourens through the use of *extirpation* as a research method. Flourens would surgically destroy parts of animals' brains and then observe the behavioral consequences of the loss. He concluded that although there was some localization of cortical function, the hemispheres of the cortex functioned more like an interrelated unit. This view was strengthened later by the work of Karl Lashley, who confirmed the ability of one area of the cortex to substitute for the functions of a destroyed area, a capacity he described as *equipotentiality*.

One of the first examples of the clinical study of localized function was Paul Broca's demonstration in 1861 that expressive speech was controlled by an area in the left cerebral cortex. Broca made his discovery by performing an autopsy on a patient whose only defect during his thirty-year hospitalization was that he could not speak. Having examined the patient very carefully to insure that the vocal musculature was intact and being convinced that the man was intelligent enough to speak, Broca was able to isolate the cause of the problem to the specific damaged area he found on autopsy.

By the turn of the twentieth century, Alfred Binet had begun to assess brain-damaged children in Paris; although these tests are usually considered to be the beginning of intelligence testing, they also foreshadowed neuropsychological assessment. In addition, many of the disorders commonly assessed today with neuropsychological techniques had been identified by this time. *Aphasias* (disordered language abilities), *apraxias* (impaired abilities to carry out purposeful movements), *amnesias* (disorders of memory), *agnosias* (impaired ability to recognize stimuli), and seizure disorders had all been classified, studied, and in some cases treated by the 1920s. In Russia, a Psychoneurological Institute was formed in 1907 to study the behavioral consequences of brain damage, and throughout the first decade of the 1900s, several investigators in the United States began to use psychological

BOX 11-6   A case of brain damage: the man who mistook his wife for a hat

The effects of brain damage can take an almost infinite number of forms. A common pattern with severe disorders is to find obvious deficits in large areas of behavior like language, motor coordination, or memory. However, smaller deficits involving narrower functions are also encountered, and sometimes these deficits are of great interest because they permit neuroscientists to "map" brain-behavior relationships more specifically than they had been able to do previously.

In some instances these deficits are of such an unusual quality that they defy common sense. One such case is Dr. Oliver Sacks's encounter with a patient called Dr. P., otherwise known as "the man who mistook his wife for a hat." This case history provides the title for Sacks's (1985) compassionate and insightful description of several extraordinary neurological patients that he has encountered in his practice.

Dr. P. was a distinguished musician, a man of superior intelligence, refinement, and wit. In fact, his reputation as a man with an offbeat sense of humor may have hidden for a time the neurological significance of a strange set of symptoms that Dr. P.'s students and family began to observe—problems recognizing familiar people when he looked at them, but not when he heard them speak, and mistakenly seeing faces in place of such objects as fire hydrants, parking meters, and the knobs on furniture.

Dr. P. was referred to Dr. Sacks by an ophthalmologist who suspected brain damage while examining Dr. P.'s eyes. Upon examination, Dr. P. presented as a charming, healthy man, but Dr. Sacks was disquieted by what he called the "teasing strangeness" with which the patient looked at but seemed to not really see his face. Other oddities included his mistaking his foot for his shoe and upon leaving the office his attempt to lift his wife's head off and put it on his head like a hat!

Intrigued by what he observed in the office, Dr. Sacks visited the patient's home. Here, he observed that Dr. P.'s musical abilities were intact, as was his perception of abstract shapes, but his reactions to faces on the television or in family photographs were very bizarre. Dr. P. seemed totally incapable of visually perceiving real objects; instead he saw only abstractions. His visual world was empty except for lifeless features which he could describe in almost geometric detail. An interesting confirmation of Dr. P.'s visual problems came in a series of paintings he had done over the years and had displayed throughout his house. Sacks (1985, p. 16) described them as follows: "All his earlier work was naturalistic and realistic, with vivid mood and atmosphere. . . . Then, years later, they became less vivid, less concrete, less realistic and naturalistic; but far more abstract, even geometrical and cubist. Finally, in the last paintings, the canvasses became nonsense—mere chaotic lines and blotches of paint."

Dr. P.'s disorder, of which he seemed to be almost happily unaware, was diagnosed as a *visual agnosia* whereby he was unable to judge or understand any particular objects that he would see. Although he never ascertained the cause of the defect, Dr. Sacks speculated that it was a tumor or degenerative process in the visual part of the cortex that was responsible. Despite this possibility, Dr. P. lived for several more years and played and taught music until the final days of his life.

Although Dr. P.'s case was very unusual, it is not the only instance of such a visual agnosia (technically called *prosopagnosia*). Dr. Sacks reported that, in researching the problem, he encountered reports of a farmer who suddenly could no longer distinguish the faces of his once-familiar cows and a museum worker who thought his own reflection was a three-dimensional picture of an ape.

tests to study the effects of brain damage on behavior.

A crucial development in the history of neuropsychology was the work of Ward Halstead, who in 1935 established a neuropsychology laboratory at the University of Chicago. Halstead began his work by observing brain-damaged persons in natural settings. These observations led him to identify several characteristics of behavior which he then tried to assess more thoroughly through existing psychological tests or through tests that he developed himself. After testing a large number of patients who had been referred to him, Halstead factor-analyzed his results and selected ten measures for what would come to be his assessment battery.

Halstead's first graduate student, Ralph M. Reitan, started his own neuropsychology laboratory in 1951 at the Indiana University Medical Center. Reitan, who is now at the University of Arizona, eliminated two of Halstead's original tests and added several of his own, including a Wechsler intelligence scale and an MMPI. This revised battery became known as the Halstead-Reitan Battery, and it is still the most widely used neuropsychological battery in existence.

Basic research in neuropsychology and advances in assessment methods grew dramatically following World War II. Jones and Butters (1983) list five groups of scientists who made especially noteworthy contributions to the field in this period:

1. The Montreal Neurological Institute–McGill University group, especially Brenda Milner and Doreen Kimura, who studied the effects of many types of specific or *focal* lesions on behavior. The Montreal investigators developed several neuropsychological assessment techniques, and their research led to the widespread acceptance of the view that each hemisphere of the brain has special importance for certain types of behavior.

2. Hans-Lukas Teuber who, with several colleagues at New York University College of Medicine and MIT, studied the behavioral effects of combat injuries to the brains (particularly the frontal lobes) of World War II veterans.

3. The Boston VA and Boston University School of Medicine group, including Edith Kaplan, Nelson Butters, and Harold Goodglass, who carefully classified different forms of aphasia and amnesia and who emphasized the need to study the process that contributes to objective performance deficits. In other words, patients may do poorly on the same neuropsychological tests for different reasons; the Boston group advocated an assessment approach that measures not only the extent of deficits but also the more qualitative problems that lead to the deficits.

4. Arthur L. Benton at the University of Iowa, who developed in 1945 the Benton Visual Retention Test, a test of visual memory still in use today. Benton also made numerous discoveries about the different behavioral effects of lesions in the right versus the left hemisphere and developed a number of other neuropsychological tests with admirable psychometric properties (see e.g., Benton, Hamsher, Varney & Spreen, 1983).

5. Alexander Luria, a Russian scientist, whose unique approach to neuropsychology became enormously influential in the West following the translation of his book, *Higher Cortical Functioning in Man,* in 1966 and the systematic description of his assessment methods by the Danish psychologist Anna-Lise Christensen in 1975. Luria's theory of functional systems in the brain is founded on some very important principles of brain functioning which we examine in the next section.

Important Principles of Neuropsychology

A thorough understanding of brain functioning is obviously beyond the scope of this chapter; it is even beyond the scope of any single book devoted to the topic. However, there are certain principles of brain-behavior relationships that are so fundamental to neuropsychology that it is essential to review them before describing any assessment procedures.

Localization of Function. As we have already mentioned, the idea that certain parts of the brain control specific behaviors became the prevailing view of scientists in the nineteenth century, reaching an extreme with the phrenologists. *Localization theories* portray the brain in a compartmentalized fashion, with different parts responsible for different skills or senses. Localization of functioning continues to be an important idea among modern neuropsychologists, but they also recognize that the different areas of the brain are intricately interrelated and may even take over some of the functions formerly directed by an injured area. Theorists who emphasize the interrelatedness of brain areas and who stress the holistic quality of brain functioning are sometimes known as *globalists* (Filskov, Grimm & Lewis, 1981). John Hughlings Jackson, Karl Lashley, and Kurt Goldstein are three of the more influential globalists, but it was Alexander Luria who, more than any other scientist, proposed a theory of brain organization that emphasized its integration rather than its specificity.

Luria's theory was that the brain was ordered into three functional systems: (1) a system for regulating a person's overall tone or waking state, which involves the brain stem; (2) a system located in the back (posterior) portion of the cortex for obtaining, processing, and storing information that is received from the outside world; and (3) a system for planning, regulating, and verifying mental operations that is located mainly in the front (anterior) portion of the cortex. It is important to recognize that Luria, like all the other globalists, still believed the brain had some specialized "division of labor."

Today, when neuropsychologists map the brain according to specific functions, they do so in a way that reflects both localization and global perspectives. For example, Figure 11-1 depicts a side view of most of the human brain. The different areas identified in this figure are associated with particular types of function; in general, the back of the brain is more sensory in function, while the front of the brain is more executive in function. In addition, the lobes

of the brain have some particular functions associated with them. Many aspects of vision are controlled by the occipital lobes, while hearing, attention, memory, and many language functions are linked to the temporal lobes. Motor functions, including the movements involved in speech, are found in front of the central sulcus; and reception of sensory information involving touch, pressure, temperature, and body position is located behind the central sulcus in the parietal lobes, which are responsible for integrating sensations from different stimuli. The frontal lobes, the largest area of the cerebrum, have been linked to many complex abilities including abstract thinking, the regulation of emotions, and self-control of many kinds of behavior.

Lateralization of Functioning. The brain is divided into halves or hemispheres. A basis for many neuropsychological conclusions is that each of these two hemispheres tends to have somewhat different functions. The left hemisphere, which controls the right half of the body's sensations and movements, is thought to be more involved in language, logical inference, and analysis of details in almost all right-handed people and most left-handed ones. For these reasons, the left hemisphere is sometimes called the dominant hemisphere, consistent with the fact that it is a little larger and heavier in most persons than the right hemisphere. The right hemisphere, which controls the left half of the body's sensations and movements, tends to be more active in visual-spatial skills; creative abilities; perception of direction, perspective, and nonverbal stimuli such as pictures or music. Once again, this specialization is true *only for most people,* since some people with dominant left hands may have language skills controlled by their right hemisphere.

Lateralization is a complex issue that cannot be reduced to simply claiming that certain functions are right or left hemisphere activities. Not only do reversals of function occur in a fairly large percentage of left-

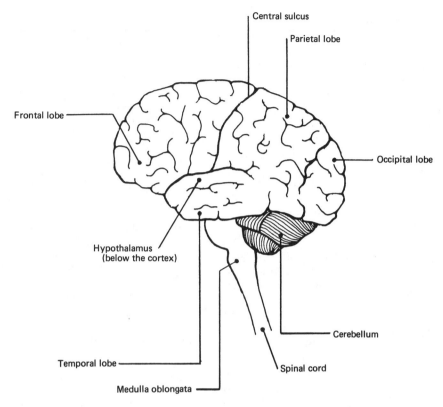

FIGURE 11-1. A lateral view of the human cortex and other brain structures.

handers, but the two hemispheres can communicate with each other through a structure called the *corpus callosum.* This interhemispheric communication is essential for adequate integration and coordination of complex behavior.

The Nature of Deficits. All neuropsychological approaches rely on the identification of cognitive, emotional, or behavioral deficits, followed by attempts to link these deficits with what is known about brain functioning. Therefore, it is important to understand what is meant by the concept of deficit. We have already defined *deficit* as a

deficiency in a patient's performance from the level shown by a normative or average group of persons or from a level shown by the patient at some earlier time. Although normative comparisons are useful, the most important type of comparison is when a patient's current performance can be compared to prior performance (when the prior assessment occurs before any suspected damage, it is called a *premorbid* estimate of functioning). Individual comparisons can yield information about how rapidly the deficit is progressing or how general versus specific the deficit appears to be. Such data are extremely useful for diagnosing the na-

BOX 11-7 Neurodiagnostic procedures

Neuropsychological assessments have often been compared to and validated against methods used by neurologists. Neurodiagnostic procedures are based on directly observing damage to central nervous system tissue or monitoring some biophysical function of the brain that suggests impairment of tissue. The neuropsychologist examines how patterns of behavior are related to possible brain lesions, while the neurologist either observes lesions themselves or looks for chemical or physical evidence that a lesion is present.

Despite growing sophistication in recent years, neurological methods are not diagnostically infallible. First, some neurological procedures are valid indicators for certain disorders but not for others. For example, the EEG is an excellent test for patients with seizure disorders, but it is not sensitive to serious conditions like Alzheimer's disease or brain infections. Second, some tests may show abnormalities in patients without any brain damage; the EEG is susceptible to this "false positive" mistake, particularly in children. A third difficulty with some neurological techniques is that they carry risks for the patient. Arteriograms and repeated X-rays are two of the best-known examples.

Brief descriptions of the most commonly used neurodiagnostic techniques are provided below.

1. *Neurological clinical exam.* The physician screens the patient's sensory abilities, eye movements, cognitive and perceptual abilities, language, motor and postural irregularities, and symptom history as a preliminary investigation of brain disturbance.
2. *Lumbar puncture.* Fluid is extracted from the spinal cord by inserting a needle and drawing out the fluid. Examination of the fluid's chemistry as well as its pressure upon extraction can help diagnose brain infections, hemorrhages, and some tumors. It is often not performed when any of several conditions are present (e.g., brain abscess), and it

has some complications, the most common of which is headaches.

3. *Electroencephalogram (EEG).* The EEG monitors the electrical activity of the cerebral cortex. It is especially useful in the diagnosis of seizure disorders and some vascular diseases affecting large blood vessels in the brain. It is a safe procedure, but it yields a relatively high rate of false positives.
4. *Other electrical tests—electromyogram (EMG): evoked potentials, and nerve conduction velocities.* All three tests measure electrical activity of some sort—in muscles (EMG), in the brain when elicited by an external stimulus (evoked potentials), or in peripheral nerves (nerve conduction velocities). They are useful in the diagnosis of muscle disease, nerve disease caused by conditions such as diabetes, and certain sensory deficits.
5. *X-rays.* There are many variations in X-ray pictures of brain structure. The technology of X-rays was revolutionized by the introduction of *computerized axial tomography (CAT scans)* in the 1970s which provides computer-enhanced three-dimensional pictures of successive slices of the brain. CAT scans are very valuable in the diagnosis of tumors, traumatic damage, degenerative diseases like Alzheimers, and cerebrovascular diseases.
6. *Positron Emission Transaxial Tomography (PETT scan).* Even newer than the CAT scan, PETT scans can show changes not just in the structure of the brain but also in its metabolic function. It does this by tracking the rate at which a radioactive chemical injected into the brain is consumed by brain cells. Since diseased tissue uses the chemical at a different rate than normal tissue, the PETT scan can reveal specific areas of abnormal brain physiology. In addition to neurological diagnoses, PETT scans may help differentiate schizophrenics from manic-depressive patients.
7. *Arteriography.* Arteriograms involve injection of a dye into arteries, and then a series of X rays reveals the condition of the arteries as the dye passes through them. It is used primarily to diagnose cerebrovascular disease,

especially strokes and hemorrhages. Arteriograms can be very uncomfortable and sometimes dangerous procedures for some patients.

8. *Nuclear Magnetic Resonance (NMR).* Another very new technique that is still being refined, NMR works by tracking the activity of atoms in the body as they are "excited" by magnets in a chamber or coil placed around the patient. NMR (more recently called *mag-*

netic resonance imaging to avoid the frightening connotations of the word *nuclear*) is advantageous because it involves no X-ray exposure.

9. *Biopsies and exploratory surgery.* Both of these procedures involve direct examination of suspect tissue. Although they are risky, they are the only methods that can give a definite diagnosis of some neurological conditions.

---

ture and making a prognosis of brain disorders. The measurement of deficits is not just a mathematical calculation; it requires careful observation of patients' behavior, complete collection of patients' historical data, and the ability to estimate patients' premorbid abilities on the basis of whatever clues the neuropsychologist can assemble (Lezak, 1983).

Neuropsychological Assessment Techniques

Neuropsychologists usually follow one of two approaches to assessing a patient suspected of suffering brain damage (Jones & Butters, 1983). The first approach is to administer a predetermined, standardized set of tests that have been combined into what is called a *battery*. Test batteries contain uniform assessment techiques for all patients. The second approach is known as the *individualized* method, in which a few tests are routinely given to all patients but the remaining tests are selected with the special needs of a particular patient in mind. The individualized approach tailors the choice of tests to specific diagnostic questions as well as to what is discovered about a patient from the initial core set of tests.

Both approaches have their advantages. Batteries are comprehensive, useful for research because of their standardization, and can be given by paraprofessionals since there is no need for expert judgments about what tests to use. Individualized approaches allow in-depth assessment of particular

problems, permit the use of new tests as they are developed, and focus on specific deficits more thoroughly. By the same token, each approach has disadvantages. Batteries can be inefficient, since they assess functions that are obviously not disturbed in many patients; also, because of their fixed nature, batteries may become obsolete since it is difficult to incorporate new and perhaps better tests of abilities into them. Individualized approaches require their users to have more training and sophistication; and, because of the different combinations of tests they employ, research comparing different patients is much more difficult.

In the following sections we briefly summarize some of the best-known examples of each approach to neuropsychological assessment.

Batteries. The most widely used battery is the Halstead-Reitan Neuropsychological Test Battery, developed, as you have already learned, by Ward Halstead and later modified by his student Ralph Reitan. The Halstead-Reitan is suitable for persons aged fifteen and older, but there are two other versions that can be used for children aged nine to fourteen and children between five and eight years of age.

A complete Halstead-Reitan for adults consists of the following tests (Boll, 1981):

1. An *MMPI* (see Chapter 5 for a description).
2. A *Wechsler Adult Intelligence Scale* (see Chapter 5 for a description).
3. *The Categories Test,* which consists of 208 slides that require a subject to form correct categori-

zations of the visual stimuli in the slides. Initially the task is simple but later becomes quite difficult. The test measures mental efficiency and the ability to form abstract concepts.

4. *The Tactual Performance Test* consists of a board with spaces into which ten blocks of various shapes can be fitted, somewhat like a big jigsaw puzzle. The subject is blindfolded and then asked to fit the blocks into the spaces as quickly as possible. The subject performs this task three times; first with the preferred hand, next with the nonpreferred hand, and finally with both hands. Following the last trial, the blindfold is removed, the board is removed from view, and the subject is asked to draw the board and blocks in their proper places from memory. This test measures abilities such as motor speed, tactile and kinesthetic perception, and incidental memory.

5. *The Rhythm Test* presents thirty pairs of rhythmic beats. The subject's task is to say whether the rhythms are the same or different. It is a measure of nonverbal auditory perception, attention, and concentration.

6. *The Speech-Sounds Perception Test* requires that the subject match spoken nonsense words to words on written lists. Language processing, verbal auditory perception, attention, and concentration are measured by this task.

7. *The Finger Tapping Test* is a simple test of motor speed in which the subject depresses a small lever with his (her) index finger as fast as possible for ten seconds. Several trials with both hands are used, allowing comparison of lateralized motor speed.

8. *The Trail Making Test* is a kind of "connect-the-dots" task involving a set of numbered circles and a set of circles that are numbered or lettered. The circles must be connected in a consecutive sequence requiring speed, visual scanning, and the ability to use and integrate different sets.

9. *The Strength of Grip Test* gives a right-side versus left-side comparison of strength. The subject simply squeezes a dynamometer twice with each hand.

10. *The Sensory-Perceptual Exam* assesses whether the subject can perceive tactile, auditory, and visual stimulation when presented on each side of the body (unilaterally) and on both sides simultaneously (bilaterally). Each of the three senses is assessed individually

and with standard variations in the location of the stimulation used.

11. *Tactile Perception Tests* employ various methods to assess the subject's ability to identify objects when they are placed in the right and left hand, to perceive touch in different fingers of both hands, and to decipher numbers when they are traced on the fingertips while the subject's eyes are closed.

12. The *Aphasia Screening Test* is a short test that measures several aspects of language usage and recognition, as well as abilities to reproduce geometric forms and pantomime simple actions (see Reitan, 1984, for a thorough discussion of how he uses this test). Examples of twelve tasks from this test (there are a total of thirty-two) are presented in Box 11-8.

Reitan recommended four procedures for evaluating the Halstead-Reitan Battery. These procedures are generally followed by practitioners today, although there are variations in the extent to which each of them is emphasized. First *level of performance* is assessed by comparing the patient's performance to that of normative groups; an impairment index is calculated based on the number of tests for which the patient's performance falls into a clinically deficient range. Second, *patterns of performance* are analyzed. Pattern analysis examines variations in performance on different components of a test; the most common example is the comparison of verbal to performance IQ scores on the WAIS. Third, because of the varying responsibilities of the brain's hemispheres, emphasis is placed on *comparing right-side to left-side performance* and drawing inferences from large comparative differences. Fourth, the neuropsychologist looks for any *pathognomonic* signs. These signs involve specific deficits that are so strongly indicative of organic problems that their presence almost always indicates a disorder.

The Luria-Nebraska Neuropsychological Battery. In an attempt to administer and evaluate the neuropsychological approach pioneered by Luria in a standard-

BOX 11-8 Examples of items from the aphasia screening test

Patient's Task	Examiner's Instructions to the Patient
Copy Square	**First, draw this on your paper** (examiner points to picture of a square). **I want you to do it without lifting your pencil from the paper. Make it about this same size** (points to square).
Name Square	**What is that shape called?**
Spell Square	**Would you spell that word for me?**
Copy Cross	**Draw this on your paper.** (Examiner points to picture of a cross). **Go around the outside like this until you get back to where you started** (examiner draws a finger line around the edge of the stimulus figure). **Make it about this same size** (points to cross).
Name Cross	**What is that shape called?**
Spell Cross	**Would you spell that word for me?**
Name Baby	**What is this?** (examiner points to picture of baby)
Repeat/Explain "He shouted the warning"	**I am going to say something that I want you to say after me. So listen carefully: He shouted the warning. Now you say it. Would you explain what that means?** Sometimes it is necessary to amplify by asking the kind of situation to which the sentence would refer. The patient's understanding is adequately demonstrated when he brings the concept of impending danger into his explanation.
Write "He shouted the warning"	**Now I want you to write that sentence on the paper.** Sometimes it is necessary to repeat the sentence so that the patient understands clearly what he is to write.
Name Key	**What is this?** (examiner points to picture of key)
Demonstrate use of Key	**If you had one of these in your hand, show me how you would use it** (points to key).
Draw Key	**Now I want you to draw a picture that looks just like this. Try to make your key look enough like this one so that I would know it was the same key from your drawing** (points to key).

Source: Filskov & Boll, 1981. (© Copyright 1981. Used by permission of John Wiley & Sons.)

---

ized and reliable manner, Charles Golden and his colleagues at the University of Nebraska (Golden, 1981; Golden, Hammeke & Purisch, 1980) compiled a battery based on Luria's methods but with explicit rules for quantitative scoring of the results. This battery, known as the Luria-Nebraska Neuropsychological Battery, consists of 269 items and can be completed in about two and half hours, roughly half the time it takes to finish the Halstead-Reitan. The items in the test are those that best discriminated control subjects (psychiatric patients and normal subjects) from neurological patients in the original validation studies. The items are organized into eleven content scales: motor functions, rhythm and pitch, tactile and kinesthetic functions, visual functions, receptive language, expressive language, reading, arithmetic, writing, memory, and intelligence. In addition, there is a pathognomonic scale composed of items that are rarely missed by normal subjects but rarely passed by brain-damaged ones, and a left hemisphere scale and a right hemisphere scale that measure motor and sensory functions of the right and left sides of the body, respectively. New scales for localization and lateralization have also been reported but are not as thoroughly validated as the initial scales (e.g., McKay & Golden, 1979).

Each item is given a score of 0 (normal

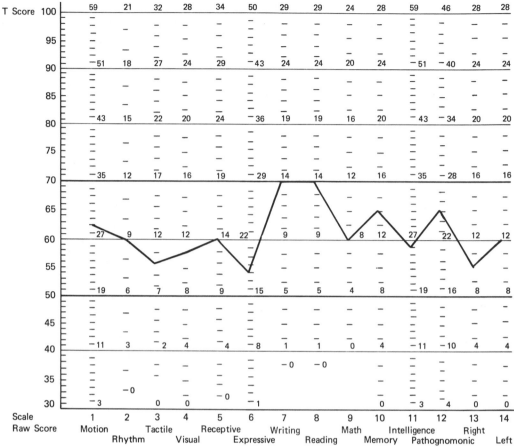

FIGURE 11-2. An example of a Luria-Nebraska profile sheet. This form shows the cutoff points for discriminating between normal and neurological patients on the Luria Battery. (Reproduced from S. B. Filskov & T. J. Boll, eds., *Handbook of Clinical Neuropsychology,* Figure 4, p. 628, by permission of John Wiley & Sons, Inc. Copyright 1981.)

performance), 1 (borderline performance), or 2 (defective performance). The items from each scale are summed, and the sums are converted to T-scores, allowing a profile to be drawn much like an MMPI profile (see Figure 11-2).

In addition to profile analysis, the Luria-Nebraska can be interpreted qualitatively by analyzing patterns of item failures or the presence of pathognomonic signs. T-scores can also be adjusted for age and education,

making the cutoff scores used to assess impairment specific to such characteristics.

Evaluation of Batteries. Both the Halstead-Reitan and the Luria-Nebraska batteries have shown impressive validities in discriminating brain-damaged patients from control subjects (Golden, Hammeke & Purisch, 1978; Reitan, 1955; Vega & Parsons, 1967). The Halstead-Reitan has also demonstrated good validity in detecting the lateralization (Wheeler & Reitan, 1962) and localization (Reitan, 1964) of brain damage, but it does a relatively poor job of discriminating between brain damage and serious psychological disorders such as schizophrenia (Jones & Butters, 1983). Although strong claims are made for the Luria-Nebraska's ability to discriminate brain-damaged from schizophrenic patients, this battery has been severely criticized on the following grounds: flawed test construction, improper analysis of the data, inadequate standardization, and a distortion of Luria's original methods, which simply may not be translatable into items on a battery (Adams, 1980a,b; Golden, 1980; and Spiers, 1980, provide the flavor of this sometimes bitter controversy).

Individualized Approaches. One of the most thorough and best-described individualized approaches is that of Muriel D. Lezak, a psychologist at the Oregon Health Sciences University and the Portland, Oregon, VA Hospital. Lezak's strategy, as described in her book, *Neuropsychological Assessment* (1983), is to perform several standard tests for all patients that assess "major functions in the auditory and visual receptive modalities and the spoken, written, graphic and constructional response modalities" (p. 107). This preliminary battery can take as long as nine hours of testing, although it usually goes more quickly than that. Following the initial battery, Lezak proceeds with what she calls "hypothesis testing." During this part of the examination she shifts the focus of the assessment from one set of functions to another as the data indicate changes in what abilities may be most impaired. "The addition of specialized tests depends on continuing formulation and reformulation of hypotheses as new data answer some questions and raise others. Hypotheses involving differentiation of learning from retrieval, for instance, will dictate the use of techniques for assessing learning when retrieval is impaired . . . every other function can be examined

across modalities and in systematically varied formats. In each case, the examiner can best determine what particular combinations of modality, content, and format are needed to test the pertinent hypothesis" (Lezak, 1983, 110–111).

The other well-known individualized approach to neuropsychological assessment is the strategy developed by the Boston group of Edith Kaplan, Harold Goodglass, and Nelson Butters. Their assessment begins with a core set of eleven tests that measure areas such as intelligence, memory, attention, construction, and sensory-perceptual abilities. Then, depending on the nature of the referral plus the results of the initial testing, additional tests are administered. Special attention is paid to the areas of language, memory, and other cortical functions. According to Jones and Butters (1983), "Attention to the strategies and processes involved in patients' failures and successes in test performance partially determines the selection of tests to be used in addition to those in the core group. Even more importantly, the emphasis on process and strategy contributes to a more than usually detailed analysis of patients' deficits, with the recognition that superficially similar deficits can reflect quite distinctive underlying processes" (p. 388).

Evaluation of Individualized Approaches. Because individualized approaches are tailored to each patient's needs, it is difficult to assess their validity, since the same combination of tests is not given to sufficient numbers of patients to permit large-scale comparisons. Furthermore, individualized approaches depend much more on the skill of the examiner using them than is the case with batteries. It therefore becomes difficult to separate the validity of the tests from the clinical acumen of the examiner. Despite these limitations, individualized approaches have been hailed as a very promising strategy for neuropsychologists to follow when such approaches are based on theoretical models that specify the nature of impairments that one will encounter with various types of brain damage (Satz & Fletcher, 1981). This preference for individualized approaches is based on the fact that they usually reflect a theoretical justification for the use of any particular tests while the typical neuropsychological battery does not; its construction depends only on the ability of its items to empirically differentiate brain-damaged subjects from others. This difference relates to the distinction between empirical verus rational approaches to test construction that we outlined in Chapter 5.

The Future of Neuropsychology

The professional roles for neuropsychologists are evolving quickly and are subject to several forces that suggest the neuropsychology of the future might look very different than it has in the past. For one thing, the development of safe and very accurate neurological methods like the CAT scan and NMR is making the purely diagnostic role of the neuropsychologist less important. Several new activities will probably replace traditional diagnostic tasks for tomorrow's neuropsychologist. Based on existing trends, we foresee six areas where future action in neuropsychology will be the greatest.

1. Deficiencies in current assessment approaches (both batteries and individualized testing) will lead to new systems of interpreting or combining instruments. As part of this work, brief screening batteries will receive particular emphasis (Jones & Butters, (1983).
2. Neuropsychologists will become increasingly involved in the planning and delivery of rehabilitative services for brain-damaged patients (Diller & Gordon, 1981).
3. Greater importance will be given to assessing patients' potential for everyday functioning following brain damage and its treatment (Chelune & Edwards, 1981). Topics such as living arrangements, employment potential, and the need for protective-facilitative environments will become an important part of assessments (Heaton & Pendleton, 1981).
4. Increased attention will be given to assessing the relationship between organic brain dysfunctions and the psychoses (Flor-Henry, 1983).
5. One area destined to become extremely important is the study of neuro-developmental issues, including the assessment of cerebral dysfunction in children (Rutter, 1983) and the elderly (Albert, 1981). The development of norms for brain function in older subjects is a crucial need for neuropsychology.
6. As neuropsychology becomes more theoretically sophisticated, we can expect that there will be increasing cross-fertilization of ideas and methods between scientists studying basic cognitive processes and clinicians responsible for the care of brain-damaged patients (Satz & Fletcher, 1981).

Readers interested in obtaining additional description of neuropsychology can find extensive coverage of the field in Filskov and Boll (1981), Lezak (1983), Kolb and Whishaw (1985), and Heilman and Valenstein (1985).

EXPERIMENTAL PSYCHOPATHOLOGY

A third area in clinical psychology where biological factors are receiving increasingly greater attention is *experimental psychopathology*, which is defined as the study of the causes and characteristics of abnormal behaviors. Clinicians obviously need to be knowledgeable about psychopathology because it has many implications for the way they diagnose and treat mental disorders. In addition, understanding the cause of a condition is usually a necessity for being able to prevent it effectively. As a result of these implications, clinical psychologists have been very interested in developing theories and conducting research that will promote their understanding of psychopathology.

Theories of abnormal behavior tend to fall into three categories: biological, psychological, and social-environmental. *Biological* theories stress genetic, biochemical, or structural problems as the underlying causes of disorders. *Psychological* theories emphasize problems in the psychological processes of thinking, emotion, perception, or motivation as causative agents. However, as Chapter 2 made clear, they differ widely on how these problematic processes themselves originate; some psychologists stress faulty learning experiences (behaviorists), some concentrate on early personality dynamics (psychoanalysts), and some look to current conditions that limit a person's ability to live an authentic, fully actualized life (phenomenologists). *Social-environmental* theories look for the causes of abnormal behavior in the conditions of society (e.g., poverty, discrimination, undereducation) or in environments that do not fit the needs of their inhabitants; they have often been the basis for the interventions of community psychologists, as we described in Chapter 7.

Over the years the relationship between biological, psychological, and social-environmental theories has often been a competitive one. In one sense this competition is healthy because it stimulates new research that can lead to the improvement of all theories. In other cases, competition is less beneficial because it reflects political and financial motives. This problem arises when psychiatrists and psychologists bicker over competing biological and psychological theories of some disorder, believing that whoever is correct will be able to claim priority in treating the disorder. Disputes between advocates of different etiological explanations will always be with us, but in recent years the debate has shifted from framing the issue in terms of psychology versus biology to more balanced analyses of how biological, psychological, and social factors may all be implicated in causing many disorders.

Most important for our interests in this chapter, psychologists have come to recognize that there are several patterns of causation, many involving biological contributions, that underlie serious psychological disorders. Psychologists' greater appreciation of biological etiology is due to several factors. First, improved research strategies have confirmed biological contributions that are hard to ignore. Second, psychologists have come to understand that the ultimate etiology of a disorder does not necessarily mean that only certain treatments can be applied to that disorder. For example, the fact that a person's fear of leaving home may have developed from a collection of faulty learning experiences does not restrict treatment to behavioral techniques, especially if there is a medication that might also help remedy the problem. Likewise, if a child's hyperactivity is traced to some neurological defect, this discovery does not eliminate the possibility that a behaviorally based program could help the child control his behavior. Third, psychologists are becoming more receptive to biological variables because they have come to realize that psychological processes can modify biological ones. As the field of health psychology has demonstrated, the relationship between biology and psychology is truly a reciprocal one, with cause and effect entwined in ways we are just beginning to understand.

Biological causes of disordered behavior can take several forms. First, some conditions can be caused almost entirely by biological abnormalities that exert a *direct influence* on behavior. Drug and alcohol intoxication, degenerative conditions like Alzheimer's disease, and most forms of profound mental retardation involve direct biological causation. A second pattern, suspected in many disorders, is that some aspects or subtypes of a problem are due to biological causes, while other aspects or subtypes are caused by psychological and/or social forces. This pattern, sometimes called *multiple pathways* etiology, is probably at work with subtypes of depression, some anxiety disorders, and perhaps even various personality disorders. The etiological pattern that has received the greatest attention involves biological, psychological, and social factors interacting with one another to cause a clinical disorder. This pattern, often termed the *diathesis-stress* model, involves three basic components:

1. A person has some defect which usually involves a biochemical or structural problem in the central or autonomic nervous system. This defect (or set of defects) is often inherited, but it can be acquired through trauma, infections, or other disease processes.
2. This defect or *diathesis* leaves the person vulnerable to developing a psychological disorder. Persons who carry the diathesis are said to be "at risk," suggesting that they are somehow predisposed to becoming clinically disordered.
3. If at-risk persons are exposed to *pathogenic* (disease-causing) stresses, their predispositions may worsen to the point that they become ill. On the other hand, if at-risk persons are exposed to mostly benign psychological, familial, and social influences, their predisposition may never express itself at a clinical level of disturbance.

Although the diathesis-stress model has been applied to several behavioral disorders, it has received its greatest attention and support in the study of schizophrenia.

The Etiology of Schizophrenia. About three million Americans (one percent of the population) develop schizophrenia in their lifetimes. Schizophrenia is one of the most serious mental disorders, accounting for 100,000 hospitalized patients on any given day, or roughly 50 percent of all the persons in mental hospitals in the United States. It affects young adults, men usually before the age of twenty-five and women usually after the age of twenty-five, and can last a lifetime. Although schizophrenia occurs in all social classes, it is particularly common among the urban poor.

Treatment of schizophrenia was very difficult until the mid-1950s, when the phenothiazines (major tranquilizers) were introduced. These drugs do not cure schizophrenia, but they are effective in controlling most of its more disturbing symptoms in the majority of patients. Nonetheless, the costs of schizophrenia remain enormous. It is estimated that schizophrenia costs society about $30 billion annually in treatment, disability payments, lost productivity and wages, legal expenses, and welfare support.

Schizophrenia is actually a group of disorders in which different combinations of symptoms are observed. DSM-III identifies five subtypes of schizophrenia (disorganized type, catatonic type, paranoid type, undifferentiated type, and residual type). Each of these subtypes presents a different clinical picture, but differentiating between them is not easy because schizophrenics show great variability in their symptoms.

DSM-III lists eight categories of symptoms characteristic of schizophrenics. While at some point in their disorder all schizophrenics either have some type of thought disorder or hallucinations, they typically also show disturbances in several other symptom categories as well. The eight categories of symptoms are as follows:

1. *Content of thought.* The major symptom here is some type of delusion or false belief.
2. *Form of thought.* Formal thought disorder involves abnormalities in the way a person's thought processes are organized. "Loose associations," in which ideas shift from one unrelated topic to another, are a common example of this type of symptom.
3. *Perception.* Hallucinations or the reporting of experiences for which there appear to be no tangible stimuli are the major symptom in this category.
4. *Affect.* This category involves disturbed emotions. Most common are emotions that are blunted, flat, or inappropriate to the situation.
5. *Sense of self.* These symptoms refer to persons' confusion about their identities; they may feel unreal or controlled by forces outside their control.
6. *Volition.* These symptoms involve reduced motivation and interest in pursuing almost any sort of goal. They interfere severely with a person's ability to work.
7. *Relationship to the external world.* Schizophrenics often withdraw from the external world

and become preoccupied with internal fantasies and odd ideas. These symptoms are sometimes called *autistic*.

8. *Psychomotor behavior*. Abnormalities of movement include rocking, pacing, stereotyped actions, and bizarre behavioral rituals. Some schizophrenics become almost totally immobile; others take on a very disheveled look or dress very strangely.

More information about the nature of schizophrenic disorders is contained in textbooks on abnormal psychology (e.g., Davison & Neale, 1986; Price & Lynn, 1986; Rosenhan & Seligman, 1984) and in specialized texts on schizophrenia (Alpert, 1985; Bellack, 1984; Bleuler, 1978; Neale & Oltmanns, 1980).

Because schizophrenia is such a serious disorder and because it affects so many people, research on its causes has been a priority in mental health fields for several years. Progress in understanding the disorder has been slow, so there is still no definitive answer to the question, "What causes schizophrenia?" However, we have gained important knowledge about two potential organic factors in schizophrenia's development—genetics and biochemical abnormalities.

The Genetics of Schizophrenia

Family Studies. It has been known for some time that schizophrenia tends to run in families. This discovery was based on comparisons of the overall incidence of schizophrenia in a population to the incidence of schizophrenia in families where one member has been diagnosed as schizophrenic. Rosenthal (1970) has reviewed the evidence on this question and reports the following figures: (1) The incidence of schizophrenia in the siblings of a schizophrenic ranges from 3.3 to 14.3 percent; (2) the incidence of schizophrenia in the parents of a schizophrenic ranges from .2 percent to 12 percent; and (3) the incidence of schizophrenia in children with two schizophrenic parents is about 35 percent. All

these figures are much greater than the population base rate of 1 percent. These data suggest a genetic basis for schizophrenia, but they do not really settle the issue because families share much more than their genetic inheritance. They also share a similar environment that could lead to schizophrenia; further, schizophrenic parents and siblings might induce schizophrenia in their relatives through repeated, strange interactions they are likely to have with them. A more significant test of the genetic transmission of schizophrenia involves comparison of incidence figures for different types of twins.

Twin Studies. The typical twin study of genetic etiology is based on the following logic: Holding other factors constant, people who are more similar in terms of their genetic makeup should be more similar in terms of displaying genetically carried characteristics. Extending this logic to the inheritance of schizophrenia, a researcher should find that *monozygotic (Mz) twins,* who are genetically identical, will be more likely to be *concordant* (share the same diagnosis) for schizophrenia than *dizygotic (DZ) twins,* who are no more genetically similar than any siblings born at different times (such twins are sometimes called *fraternal*). The results have been consistent in study after study. Concordance rates for monozygotic twins are greater than that for dizygotic twins. If you have an identical twin who is schizophrenic, the risk of developing schizophrenia yourself is about 46 percent, while the risk is only about 14 percent if you have a fraternal twin who is schizophrenic (Gottesman & Shields, 1982).

While these figures lend additional support to the genetic hypothesis, they really raise more questions than they answer. First, in no study has the concordance rate between MZ twins been 100 percent, indicating that nongenetic factors must play some role in the etiology of schizophrenia. Second, as Rosenhan and Seligman (1984) observe, MZ twins share a unique environment involving slower maturation and language development and more frequent identity problems that could help to cause their eventual schizophrenia. However, two lines of evidence suggest that nongenetic explanations of the high concordance rate among MZ twins are probably not correct. First, the rate of schizophrenia among all MZ twins is no greater than the overall population incidence. Second, the results of a third research strategy involving the study of adopted children provides even stronger evidence that there is a genetic component to schizophrenia.

Adoption Studies. The most convincing method for separating the effects of genetics from the confounding effects of similar environments is to compare the offspring of schizophrenic parents who are adopted at an early age to the offspring of nonschizophrenic parents who are adopted at equally early ages. Higher rates of schizophrenia in the first group relative to the general population and to the control group provide evidence for a genetic influence. Another research approach has been to locate a large number of adults who were adopted, identify those who have been diagnosed as schizophrenic, and then determine the incidence of schizophrenia among their biological and adoptive parents. Genetic factors would be implicated if the rate of schizophrenia is higher among the biological parents of the schizophrenics than it is in the general population or in the adoptive parents. Such studies are very time-consuming to conduct, but when they have been accomplished (e.g., Heston, 1966; Kety, Rosenthal, Wender & Schulsinger, 1968) they have always favored a strong role for genetic transmission of schizophrenia.

Even though the role of genetics in the development of schizophrenia seems clear, questions still remain as to how large a role it plays and just what abnormality is inherited that predisposes a person to becoming schizophrenic. We have no final answers to either of these questions, but some promising leads have turned up in the study of children considered at high risk for schizophrenia as a result of being born to mothers who were chronic schizophrenics (Mednick & Schulsinger, 1968). Several indirect clues about abnormalities in biochemical functions have also been found.

A Biochemical Theory of Schizophrenia—The Dopamine Hypothesis

A large number of studies have reported chemical and physical differences in the brains of schizophrenics. For example, in comparison to normal subjects, they show lower birth weights, more abnormal EEG readings, different blood-flow patterns, more difficulty in visually tracking a moving object, stronger galvanic skin responses, a larger number of unusual immune system antibodies, and a host of problems in some of their reflexes and motor responses (see Mirsky & Duncan, 1986, for a review). However, the discovery of these differences does not establish them as causes of schizophrenia. They may be caused by some other as-yet-undetected problem, or they may be by-products of schizophrenia itself. We know that most schizophrenics differ from non-schizophrenics in terms of their exercise, nutrition, drug use, and general health; such factors are more likely to reflect life-style differences than fundamental causes of their disorder. Despite frequent disappointments in isolating a specific biochemical fault underlying schizophrenia, researchers have begun to concentrate on abnormal brain functioning involving one or more neurotransmitters in the brain.

One of the most popular neurotransmitter theories suggests that the symptoms of schizophrenia are caused by overactivity on the part of dopamine, one of about twenty chemicals in the brain responsible for carrying electrical impulses across the synaptic spaces between neurons. Excessive activity in dopaminergic neural circuits is thought to push schizophrenics' brains into abnormally high levels of activation, particularly when they are stressed. The results are the florid symptoms that we associate with schizophrenia—jumbled thoughts, delusional beliefs, and hallucinations.

Evidence for the dopamine theory has been pieced together from three related discoveries that are summarized in Figure 11-3.

As line 1 of Figure 11-3 suggests, many of the symptoms of schizophrenia closely resemble the psychosis that can develop from an overdose of amphetamines (amphetamines will also worsen the symptoms of schizophrenia). There is good evidence that amphetamines induce psychotic symptoms by increasing available dopamine at the synapses. In addition, the phenothiazines, which are effective in controlling the symptoms of schizophrenia, are also effective in calming patients suffering from amphetamine psychosis.

Line 2 of Figure 11-3 shows that Parkinson's disease, which is caused in part by lowered levels of dopamine in the area of the brain called the corpus striatum, can be successfully treated with L-dopa, a drug that increases available dopamine in the brain. The significance of this discovery is revealed by two findings that are depicted in the third line of Figure 11-3.

First, the phenothiazines, so successful in the treatment of schizophrenics' symptoms, exert a specific effect on brain chemistry: They decrease the amount of dopaminergic activity by blocking receptor sites of dopamine in the brain, but do not have as strong an effect on other neurotransmitters. Second, when schizophrenics are treated for long periods with large doses of phenothiazines they often develop symptoms almost identical to those found with Parkinson's disease!

The implication of these findings is that the common mechanism by which amphetamines stimulate psychotic behavior, L-dopa reduces Parkinsonian symptoms, and the phenothiazines calm schizophrenic behavior is the dopamine system, which appears to be underactivated in Parkinson's disease and overactivated in schizophrenia. As you can see, the dopamine theory is based on a clever integration of what has been learned about the dopamine system and its responsiveness to various drugs. However, it remains only a theory about how schizophrenia might develop in some patients. In fact, some recent findings do not fit well with the

FIGURE 11-3. Patterns of evidence supporting the dopamine hypothesis of schizophrenia. (Reproduced from *Abnormal Psychology* by David L. Rosenhan and Martin E. P. Seligman, by permission of W. W. Norton & Company, Inc. Copyright © 1984 by W. W. Norton & Company, Inc.)

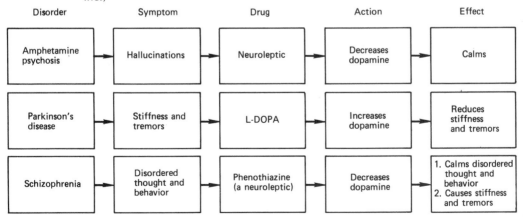

theory. For example, despite the fact that phenothiazines rapidly block dopamine receptors, their therapeutic effect on schizophrenics is quite gradual, sometimes taking weeks before improvement is noted. This is the sort of puzzle that the dopamine theory has yet to solve; until it does and until there is direct evidence that excess dopamine activity precedes schizophrenia, this theory should not be accepted as an adequate causal explanation of schizophrenia.

A Final Word

In this chapter we have reviewed three areas in which clinical psychologists have become increasingly involved in studying relations between biological and psychological variables. The ultimate justification for this interest is that a complete understanding of human behavior requires it, and the scientific training of psychologists should leave them content with nothing less than an understanding of behavior that is as complete as possible. There are many practical advantages to clinicians becoming well-informed about biological influences on behavior, but they are secondary to the most compelling reason—the advancement of scientific knowledge.

The interaction between clinical psychology and biological sciences is, of course, bidirectional. Biologically oriented scientists also have an obligation to understand the influences psychological processes exert on physical phenomena. We are not implying, as is sometimes suggested, that all psychological variables must ultimately be reduced to a physical level before they can be understood. Biological and psychological variables are each legitimate targets of study in their own right. However, human behavior cannot be adequately explained without considering the complex interrelationships between both types of influences.

chapter 12

Professional Issues in Clinical Psychology

If Lightner Witmer were to return from the dead to review the field he founded, we doubt he would recognize many modern clinicians as his colleagues. A few might match his original psychoeducational, child-oriented model. But many others would bewilder Witmer, for they are clinicians who practice something very different from the clinical psychology of the early twentieth century.

Having read the previous eleven chapters, you should be able to sympathize with Witmer's confusion. Clinical psychology is an expanding profession that is becoming more and more difficult to summarize in a single volume. As we saw in Chapter 1, there is a long list of professional roles clinicians now fill. However, no list does full justice to the complexity of clinical psychology, because it does not indicate either the multiple functions required by each job or the new specialties that will emerge in the years

to come within clinical psychology. Struck by an almost geometric growth in the number of clinicians, a proliferation of alternative roles, and increasing specialization, commentators struggle for an apt description of clinical psychology's current status. A favorite summary is that clinical psychology is in "a transitional state."

This claim is an understatement on at least two counts. First, it suggests that transition is a novel era in an otherwise tranquil history. This is, of course, not correct. Clinical psychology has been in constant transition. Witmer would not have had to wait until the 1980s to be surprised by changes in clinical psychology; he would have seen changes by the 1920s.

On the one hand, this state of flux has made clinical psychology a very challenging field with which to be associated. On the other hand, rapid transitions have prevented the profession from developing a "sound fund of tradition" (Guiora & Brandwin, 1968) that could serve as a common reference point for professional identity. It is a little like the child who is forced to become an adult before being an adolescent. Further, the growth of clinical psychology has often been in response to necessity, social demands, and financial opportunities for expansion rather than on the basis of planned development (Shakow, 1978).

The words "transitional state" also underestimate the pace of the changes in clinical psychology. The rate of transition has been accelerating like an object falling through space. Each decade since World War II has seen more extensive changes in the field than any preceding period.

Consider these three examples: (1) In 1947 there were 787 members in APA's Division 12, the Division of Clinical Psychology. In 1964 there were 2883 members (Shakow, 1968). In 1984 the membership of Division 12 stood at more than 5000, approximately seven times its original size. (2) In the first fifty years of clinical psychology there was only one conference on professional training, held in 1949 in Boulder, Colorado. Since that time there have been four national training conferences and many smaller-scale conferences. (3) Early proposals for training in clinical psychology discouraged clinicians from entering private practice; only a handful of psychologists did so. Today approximately 27 percent of APA doctoral-level health-care providers are *primarily* employed in private practice (Stapp, Tucker & VandenBos, 1985). These changes, along with others related to the community mental health movement, health insurance, behavioral medicine, and society's demand for mental health services, suggest that it would be more accurate to portray clinical psychology as being not so much in transition as in an entirely new era.

The first era of clinical psychology extended from its birth in 1896 to World War II. This was the time when clinical psychology appeared as a subfield of scientific psychology and as a contributing member of

the mental health team under the supervision of psychiatry. The forty years since World War II have constituted clinical psychology's second era. During this period the field's unique identity became established and expanded vigorously. This modern era has seen the field largely transformed from an academic discipline into a service profession. It has seen clinical psychology liberate itself from both the opposition of some members of nonclinical psychology and from the domination of psychiatry. It has been an era in which clinicians struggled for autonomy, got it, and became determined to retain it.

The professionalization and current status of clinical psychology are the topics of this last chapter. It is a story that has many subplots because the professionalization of clinical psychology is the result of progress on several overlapping fronts. We focus on the five issues most essential for understanding clinical psychology's struggle for professional recognition:

1. Professional training. What sort of training does one need to become a clinical psychologist, and what are the options for obtaining this training?

2. Professional regulation. What are the mechanisms for insuring that a clinical psychologist possesses certain minimum skills and meets minimum requirements to function professionally?

3. Professional ethics. What principles guide clinicians in determining the ethical standards for their professional activities? How are matters of unethical behavior handled?

4. Professional independence. What should be the relationship between clinical psychology and other mental health professions? Should clinical psychology be an autonomous profession responsible for its own direction and supervision, or should it operate under the supervision of medicine, particularly psychiatry?

5. Perils of professionalization. Has the professionalization of clinical psychology been an asset or a detriment? Has the public benefited? Has the quality of clinical psychology improved?

PROFESSIONAL TRAINING

Throughout the first four decades of the twentieth century, advanced training for clinical psychologists made little progress. For clinicians of that period, experience was not only the best teacher, it was practically the only one. Psychologists were involved increasingly in clinical work during this time, but their training for these activities was unsystematic. Acquisition of the knowledge and experience necessary for competent clinical work was largely self-organized.

A few steps toward formalization of clinical training were taken by the APA during the 1930s and early 1940s, but they had little effect. In 1931 an APA Committee on Standards of Training for Clinical Psychologists was formed, and in 1935 this committee published a report containing several recommendations for clinical training. In 1936 the Psychology Department at Columbia University proposed a training curriculum for clinical psychologists that involved two years of graduate work and a one-year internship (Shakow, 1948). In 1943 a Committee on Training in Clinical Psychology released a report entitled "Proposed Program of Professional Training in Clinical Psychology"; and two years later a report on graduate internship training in psychology was published.

Very little was accomplished with respect to training clinical psychologists until the late 1940s, when the social needs brought about by World War II and the financial support provided by the Veterans Administration and the U.S. Public Health Service combined to offer psychology a unique opportunity for expansion, establishment, and esteem.

The most influential psychologist in the development of clinical training programs was David Shakow, for many years the chief psychologist at Worcester State Hospital in Massachusetts and later an important figure at the National Institute of Mental Health. As early as 1942, Shakow saw the need for a four-year doctoral-level training program in clinical psychology that included an internship during the third year (Shakow, 1942).

Shakow's foresight in this area attracted the attention of Carl Rogers, who was then president of the APA. Rogers asked Shakow to chair a Committee on Training in Clinical Psychology, whose task was to formulate a recommended clinical training program. The committee prepared a report entitled "Recommended Graduate Training in Clinical Psychology" which was accepted by the APA in September 1947 and was published that same year in the *American Psychologist*. The "Shakow report" set the pattern for clinical training and remains, with surprisingly few exceptions, a standard against which modern clinical programs can be evaluated.

Three of the most important recommendations of the Shakow report on clinical training were:

1. A clinical psychologist should be trained first and foremost as a psychologist.
2. Clinical training should be as rigorous as that for nonclinical areas of psychology.
3. Preparation of the clinical psychologist should be broad and directed toward the three areas of assessment, research, and therapy.

In addition to these objectives, several other principles for graduate clinical programs were advocated in the Shakow report:

4. The core content of clinical training programs should involve six areas: general psychology, psychodynamics of behavior, diagnostic methods, research methods, related disciplines, and therapy.
5. The program should offer basic courses in principles as opposed to a large number of courses on special techniques.
6. Training should integrate theory with practice. This emphasis on integrated training was a hallmark of Shakow's plan; mechanisms for integrating theory with practice are suggested in every one of his many articles on training.

7. Throughout the entire graduate program, beginning in the first year, the student should have contact with clinical material.

8. Opportunities should also be provided for contact with "normal" persons who never establish clinical contacts.

9. The training atmosphere should encourage maturity and the continued growth of desirable personality characteristics.

10. The program should promote a sense of responsibility for patients and clients.

11. Representatives of related disciplines should teach clinical trainees, and joint study with students in these related disciplines needs to be arranged.

12. The program must emphasize the research implications of clinical phenomena.

13. Trainees "must acquire the ability to see beyond the responsibilities they owe the individual patient, to those they owe society" (Shakow, 1978, p. 151).

The Shakow report suggested a year-by-year curriculum that would fulfill these criteria. This schedule was not offered as a blueprint for training but as an illustrative model of what an adequate clinical program could look like.

In this model, first-year clinical students would become acquainted with the foundations and the core content of general psychology. They would also be trained in observational techniques. The second year would be devoted primarily to the experimental, diagnostic, and therapeutic content of clinical psychology. In addition to didactic material, students would acquire direct, practical experience through practicum courses and clinical placements.

The third year would be the internship, a year of intensive and extensive experience with clinical phenomena at a hospital, clinic, or medical center. Here the student would have an opportunity to build a "mass of experience which gives concrete meaning to general principles" (Shakow, 1947, p. 551). Shakow regarded the internship as an essential component that engendered the student's sense of professional identity and immersed her or him in practical clinical experience.

Several objectives were to be met during the fourth year. The dissertation would be completed; the student would take a seminar on professional problems and ethics as well as seminars involving related disciplines; and the student would undergo a period of "self-evaluation." Self-evaluation usually meant being a patient in individual psychotherapy, which would help the student uncover biases, attitudes, and personality problems that might interfere with later clinical work.

Many of today's clinical training programs are much like Shakow's prototype. However, it usually takes five rather than four years to complete the entire training sequence (the internship is usually taken in the fourth year). The major reasons for the extra year are that most programs require their students to complete a master's thesis (usually in the second year), and some universities still retain requirements such as a foreign language.

While there are many variations in the curricula of APA-approved programs, the sample schedule in Box 12-1 shows roughly what you might encounter in most Ph.D. programs.

The Shakow report also dealt with issues such as the best ways to select students, the undergraduate background of graduate students, and the means by which professional growth and training could be continued after earning the Ph.D. The greatest impact of the report, however, was that it prescribed that special mix of scientific and professional preparation that has typified most clinical training programs ever since. This recipe for training (which we have already described as the scientist-professional model) was officially endorsed at clinical psychology's first major training conference held in Boulder, Colorado, 1949 (Raimy, 1950).

The Boulder Conference

The Boulder Conference on Training in Clinical Psychology was convened with the financial support of the Veterans Adminis-

BOX 12-1   Sample schedule of Ph.D. program in clinical psychology

Fall Semester	Spring Semester
First year	
Psychological Statistics I Introduction to Interviewing Clinical Assessment I Practicum in Assessment History and Systems of Psychology	Psychological Statistics II Clinical Assessment II Selected Proseminar (Social Psychology, Developmental Psychology, Psychology of Learning, Physiological Psychology) Theories and Research in Personality
Second year	
Psychopathology Selected Proseminar (choose one from list above) Systems of Psychotherapy M.A. research	Psychotherapy Practicum Clinical Seminar (Group Therapy, Behavior Modification, Child and Family Therapy, Community Psychology) M.A. research
Third year	
Psychotherapy Practicum Clinical Seminar (choose one from list above) Clinical Research Seminar (Research in Personality, Psychopathology Research, Research in Psychotherapy) Advanced nonclinical seminar	Advanced nonclinical seminar Clinical or nonclinical research seminar Psychotherapy Practicum

A written qualifying examination is to be taken during the third year of graduate work, but no later than the beginning of the fourth year. Only those students who have completed their M.A. thesis are permitted to register for the qualifying examination.

Fourth year	
Internship	
Fifth year	
Clinical or nonclinical research seminar Advanced nonclinical seminar Research on dissertation	Same

tration and the U.S. Public Health Service, which requested APA to (1) name those universities that offered satisfactory training programs and (2) develop acceptable programs in universities that did not have them.

The Boulder conferees accepted the recommendations of Shakow's committee for a scientist-professional model of training. Clinical psychologists were expected to be proficient in research and professional practice and to have earned a Ph.D. in psychology from a university-based graduate program. A supervised, year-long internship would also be required. Shakow's plan became known as the *Boulder model.*

The Boulder conferees further agreed that some mechanism was necessary for monitoring, evaluating, and officially accrediting clinical training programs and internship facilities. As a result, APA formed an Education and Training Board whose Committee on Accreditation was charged with these tasks. Currently, clinical training sites are visited by an APA accreditation team about every five years. The team consists of three psychologists (selected by the program from a list of potential visitors) who evaluate how well the program is meeting its own training goals and APA's training standards. The most recent version of APA's criteria for accreditation was published in 1986 in the form of an *Accreditation Handbook*.

The results of accreditation site visits are published each year in the APA's official journal, *American Psychologist*. In 1985 there were 131 clinical training programs fully approved by the APA (see Box 12-2) and 275 fully approved internships.[1] In addition, there are several doctoral training programs that function without APA approval, either because the program has not requested a site visit or because approval has not been granted after an accreditation visit.

The Conferences at Stanford, Miami, and Chicago

Although the Boulder model remains the dominant training pattern, some clinicians have expressed discontent with it ever since 1949. This discontent has grown in recent years, and we have now reached a stage where there are two major alternatives to the Boulder model. We will describe each of these later; for now we need to examine the post-Boulder training conferences that set the stage for these alternatives.

Stanford. The Stanford conference, held at Stanford University in 1955 (Strother, 1956), offered no significant new direction for clinical training. It did anticipate some of the effects that the community mental health movement would later have on clinical psychology, and it stressed the need to prepare clinicians for the new professional roles community mental health would offer.

Miami. The Miami Beach training conference was held in 1958 (Roe, Gustad, Moore, Ross & Skodak, 1959). By then, clinical psychology had undergone enough changes to warrant some reevaluation of the scientist-professional model. Although questions were raised about the Ph.D., the conclusion was that the Ph.D. program should be retained as the primary training vehicle, although departments were encouraged to develop programs that best suited their own resources and needs. Emphasis was placed on the need for psychology to continue to train its graduates in the techniques of empirical research.

Chicago. The 1965 Chicago Conference on the Professional Preparation of Clinical Psychologists was the first conference to consider seriously alternative models of clinical training. A theme of this conference was that, while the scientist-professional model should be continued, the value of a purely *professional* model of training should also be appreciated.

The interest in a professional model that stressed training for the delivery of clinical services stemmed from two sources. First, the need for psychological service providers was burgeoning, due in large part to the community mental health movement. Second, only a small percentage of psychologists, probably about 10 percent, publish research in psychology. Critics of the Boulder model argued that too much time was being spent training students for activities that, as professionals, they did not perform. At the same time, research-oriented departments of psychology were accepting increasing numbers of practice-oriented graduate students. The fit was often a bad one.

In place of the scientist-professional model, a professional program was proposed (Zimet & Throne, 1965):

The distinctive feature of this pattern of doctoral training would be the effort to prepare a broadly

---

[1] In an effort to acquaint prospective clinical students with the array of training possibilities, APA publishes a book annually called *Graduate Study in Psychology and Associated Fields*, which lists all graduate programs in psychology along with a brief description of requirements and training features. In addition, almost all clinical programs have a brochure that can be obtained on request. These brochures discuss the program's orientation, faculty interests, requirements, and means of financial support for students (see Appendix).

trained psychological clinician prepared to intervene in a wide variety of settings for the purpose of fostering change and forestalling psychological problems. His training would include psychological science but would stress those areas in which clinical methods find their support. It would also include relevant material from related disciplines such as medicine and sociology. He would be introduced to a variety of diagnostic, remedial, and preventive procedures. His training would include analysis of the manner in which clinical methods are developed with the intent to make him a sophisticated evaluator of new methods developed in the future. Because he would not carry out a doctoral dissertation or learn foreign languages, he would have more time available for professional training and experience. Should he wish to develop the competence of a specialist in specified diagnostic, remedial, or preventive procedures he will need additional training—either on the job or in formal postdoctoral training programs.

We would expect a clinical psychologist trained in this manner to devote full time to professional practice oriented toward treatment, prevention, or both. He would use diagnostic instruments, carry out psychotherapy, engage in milieu therapy, use behavior therapy, consult in community mental health projects, work with groups, organizations, and communities—as the occasion demanded. He would, as far as his limited scientific training would permit, keep abreast of new methods as they developed and critically appraise them prior to adoption. He would contribute to the development of methods of practice by exchanging his professional experience with that of his colleagues. (pp. 21–22)

In the end, the conferees refused to endorse the explicitly professional model, preferring instead a flexible scientist-professional plan that would not shortchange training in clinical activities. Training programs were urged to add faculty who were practicing clinicians and also to broaden their criteria for acceptable research activities.

Diversity in training was encouraged by calling for pilot programs that would experiment with innovative ways of implementing the professional model. Special interest focused on the first Psy.D. (Doctor of Psychol-

ogy) program then under development at the University of Illinois at Urbana-Champaign. The appropriate levels (doctoral and subdoctoral) and locations (department of psychology, medical center, independent professional school) of clinical training were also debated at Chicago.

The importance of the Chicago conference was that professional training models and subdoctoral programs, while not officially endorsed, were gaining support among clinical psychology's leadership. Innovation in doctoral training was being encouraged. Many of the ideas considered for the first time at Chicago were adopted by the participants at psychology's next training conference.

The Vail Conference

The National Conference on Levels and Patterns of Professional Training in Psychology was held in 1973 in Vail, Colorado. Sponsored by a grant from the National Institute of Mental Health (NIMH), the Vail conference included a wide range of psychological specialties, training orientations, graduate students, and minority-group psychologists. Vail was the most ambitious of the post-Boulder conferences. In only five days the conference passed 150 resolutions, some of which introduced sweeping changes in the training of psychologists. These recommendations were organized around the following themes (Korman, 1976):

1 Professional training models. The conference officially recognized professional training as an acceptable model for those programs that defined their mission as the preparation of students for the delivery of clinical services. These "unambiguously professional" programs were to be given status equal to their more traditional scientist-professional counterparts. Professional programs could be housed in a number of settings, including academic psychology departments, medical schools, or specially es-

BOX 12-2 APA-accredited programs in clinical psychology

In addition to the 131 fully approved programs, there are nine clinical programs that have received provisional approval. This is a category for relatively new programs whose development shows promise or for programs that are innovative and consequently do not fit the usual accreditation criteria. For the institutions listed, the training programs are housed in the department of psychology unless otherwise indicated; the majority of training programs still follow Shakow's recommendation that clinical students be trained in an environment that stresses general psychological knowledge. Programs awarding the Psy.D. degree rather than the Ph.D. are noted.

Adelphi University, Institute of Advanced Psychological Studies
University of Alabama
University of Alabama at Birmingham
American University
University of Arizona
Arizona State University
University of Arkansas
Auburn University
Baylor University (Psy.D.)
Biola University, Rosemead School of Psychology (Ph.D., Psy.D.)
Boston University
Bowling Green State University
Brigham Young University
University of California (Berkeley)
University of California (Fresno)
California School of Professional Psychology (Berkeley)
California School of Professional Psychology (Fresno)
California School of Professional Psychology (San Diego)
Case Western Reserve University
Catholic University of America
University of Cincinnati
City College, CUNY, The Psychological Center
Clark University
University of Colorado
Columbia University, Teachers College Department of Clinical Psychology and Psychoeducational Practice
Concordia University
University of Connecticut
University of Delaware
University of Denver

University of Denver, School of Professional Psychology (Psy.D.)
DePaul University
Duke University
Emory University
University of Florida Department of Clinical Psychology
Florida State University
Fordham University
Fuller Theological Seminary Graduate School of Psychology
George Washington University
University of Georgia
Georgia State University
Hahnemann University, Department of Mental Health Sciences (Psy.D.)
University of Hawaii
University of Houston
University of Illinois (Chicago)
University of Illinois (Urbana-Champaign)
Illinois Institute of Technology
Indiana University at Bloomington
University of Iowa
University of Kansas
Kent State University
University of Kentucky
Louisiana State University
University of Louisville
Loyola University of Chicago
University of Maine at Orono
University of Manitoba
University of Maryland
University of Massachusetts
McGill University
Memphis State University
Miami University (Ohio)
University of Miami (Florida)

University of Michigan
Michigan State University
University of Minnesota
University of Mississippi
University of Missouri (Columbia)
University of Missouri (St. Louis)
University of Montana
University of Nebraska (Lincoln)
University of Nevada (Reno)
University of New Mexico
New York University
University of North Carolina (Chapel Hill)
University of North Carolina (Greensboro)
University of North Dakota
North Texas State University
Northern Illinois University
Northwestern University Medical School
  Department of Psychiatry and Behavioral
  Sciences
Nova University
  School of Psychology
Ohio University
Ohio State University
Oklahoma State University
University of Oregon
University of Pennsylvania
Pennsylvania State University
University of Pittsburgh
Purdue University
  Department of Psychological Services
University of Rhode Island
University of Rochester
Rutgers—The State University of New Jersey
Rutgers—The State University of New Jersey, Department of Clinical Psychology (Psy.D.)
St. John's University
St. Louis University
University of South Carolina
University of South Dakota
University of South Florida
University of Southern California

Southern Illinois University
University of Southern Mississippi
State University of New York at Albany
State University of New York at Buffalo
State University of New York at Stony Brook
Syracuse University
Temple University
University of Tennessee
University of Texas at Austin
Texas Tech University
University of Utah
Vanderbilt University
University of Vermont
University of Virginia, Institute of Clinical Psychology
Virginia Commonwealth University
Virginia Consortium for Professional Psychology (Psy.D.)
Virginia Polytechnic Institute and State University
University of Washington
Washington State University
Washington University in St. Louis
University of Waterloo
Wayne State University
West Virginia University
University of Wisconsin (Madison)
University of Wisconsin (Milwaukee)
Wright State University
  School of Professional Psychology (Psy.D.)
University of Wyoming
Yale University
Yeshiva University, Ferkauf Graduate School of Psychology
Hofstra University*
Utah State University*
Vanderbilt University*, Department of Psychology and Human Development, George Peabody College for Teachers
University of Virginia,* Institute of Clinical Psychology

* Fully accredited programs offering training in more than one specialty, one of which is clinical.

tablished professional schools. When emphasis in training was on the delivery and evaluation of professional services, the Psy.D. would be the appropriate degree. When emphasis was on the development of new knowledge in psychology, the Ph.D. would be preferred.

2 Levels of training. The conferees believed that priority should be given to programs that provided multiple levels of training or demonstrated coordination with degree programs at varying levels. They felt that the concept of a *career ladder* should be replaced by the idea of a *career lattice,* a structure that would make possible upward professional mobility through continued, integrated training.

One of the most controversial of the Vail recommendations was that persons trained at the master's level should be considered to be professional psychologists. This sentiment was a reversal of the opinion of previous conferences, all of which envisioned psychology as a doctoral-level profession. The Vail participants, on the other hand, felt that many of the services performed by doctoral psychologists could be performed with equal competence by personnel trained at the master's or submaster's level. The conference called for professional master's programs and full APA membership for the master's-level individual. Soon, universities in several states had developed M.A. training programs in clinical psychology. Today, master's-level clinicians outnumber Ph.D.'s in some of these states.

The M.A. proposal was a dramatic one. It also was short-lived because the tide later turned against the M.A. as a recognized degree for the professional psychologist. In 1977 the APA's Council of Representatives voted that the title "psychologist" should be reserved for those who have completed a *doctoral* training program, a policy that remains in effect today.

The status of the master's-level clinician was also jeopardized by those Vail advocates who, while willing to endorse M.A.-trained

persons as professionals, were unwilling to recommend licensure for them. Another obstacle to full professional standing for the master's-level clinician has been a political one. Quite simply, the status of psychology as a profession vis-à-vis psychiatry is threatened by including the M.A. holder along with the Ph.D. psychologist. Most observers agree that the professional autonomy of psychology is best preserved by defining psychology exclusively as a doctoral-level enterprise. Financial considerations have also exerted pressure against granting full standing to M.A. recipients. Psychologists' eligibility for reimbursement as private practitioners is strengthened by portraying clinical psychology as a profession of persons holding doctoral degrees (we shall return to this topic later).

3 Desirable characteristics of professional training. The Vail conference considered many issues related to the social obligations of psychology, affirmative action, racism and sexism, and the need for continuing professional development. Although those issues are beyond the scope of this chapter, the attention paid to them at Vail is another illustration that this conference, more than any of its predecessors, seriously challenged both the history and the future of professional psychology.

After five national training conferences, several smaller conferences, countless hours of discussion, contention, and argument among clinicians, educators, and students, what is the state of training in clinical psychology? That question allows no easy answer, although we can give some general responses. First, the scientist-professional model has proven to be a tough competitor that is still the "champ" in terms of the number of programs professing it as their training philosophy. This model now comes in an increasing number of different packages. Most programs have increased the amount of time devoted to professional training in psychotherapy, at the expense of courses in psychodiagnostics or general psychology.

Several programs follow a special theoretical model (e.g., behavioral or psychoanalytic) which offers a relatively narrow approach to the field. Other programs emphasize a certain specialty such as child-clinical or community psychology.

The most recent national conference on graduate education in psychology was held in June 1987. This conference discussed *designation*, a new system for evaluating and accrediting training programs. Because of the increasing number of programs purporting to train psychologists outside traditional university settings and because of more frequent legal challenges to eligibility for professional licensure, psychology needs a uniform policy for identifying those programs that adequately educate psychologists for the practice of psychology. Designation by APA or some consortium of organizations is intended to provide this function.

As described earlier, there are other training programs that depart markedly from the scientist-professional formulation. Two alternative models enjoy current popularity: the Psy.D. program and the professional school of psychology.

The Doctor of Psychology (Psy.D.) Degree

The professional training model has a long history (Pottharst, 1976), but the first continuously functioning program was the Psy.D. program begun by the department of psychology at the University of Illinois (Urbana-Champaign) in 1968 (it was discontinued in 1980). Psy.D. programs give students desiring careers in clinical service training that is relevant to that goal. That is, emphasis is placed on the skills necessary for the delivery of competent psychological services. A master's thesis is not required, nor is a research-oriented dissertation, although a written, doctoral-level report of professional quality is a requirement for the Psy.D.

The Psy.D. program at Illinois received APA accreditation in 1973. As of 1985, there were seven fully accredited Psy.D.

programs and four programs with provisional accreditation. Of course, the Psy.D. has not been received enthusiastically by all clinicians. Goldenberg (1973) summarized some early objections to the program:

(1) The Psy.D. program is likely to acquire second-class status in the eyes of faculty, students and the public; (2) the fact that support for the alternate doctorate comes from the unlikely quarter of academic psychology is suspect as being perhaps a device for shunting aside the bothersome problem of professional training in clinical psychology; (3) the profession of clinical psychology is in a state of flux, with new roles and practices emerging, making this a particularly inappropriate time to create a new profession with activities that are only dimly foreseeable at present and whose present clinical skills may soon be obsolete; (4) two parallel programs, producing two different degrees, will tend to separate clinical practice from the rest of psychology even further, thus cutting the profession off from its scientific roots; (5) expert practitioners, necessary in a professional degree program, are likely to find it as difficult to be appointed and later promoted at the university as is the case now of competent clinical professors who do not publish research findings; and (6) future graduates of such programs are likely to be stigmatized because of their different degree and different training. (p. 85)

Comparisons of Ph.D. and Psy.D. graduates suggest that they do about equally well on most evaluative criteria. For example, Peterson and Baron (1975) found that Psy.D. and Ph.D. students at the University of Illinois performed equivalently on qualifying exams and course grades, and showed similar attrition rates. Shemberg and Leventhal (1981) found that internship supervisors did not differentiate the quality of work by Ph.D. versus Psy.D. interns. Although very limited in scope, these data belie some of the gloomy predictions that were made about Psy.D. programs. However, serious reservations about the quality of training in some Psy.D. programs remain (Strickland, 1985), even among proponents of the degree (Peterson, 1985). Large numbers of students trained by small numbers of part-time faculty in settings that do not encourage comprehensive education are characteristic of too many Psy.D. programs.

The Professional School

Professional schools of psychology have formed as "free-standing" clinical training units, independent of university departments of psychology. This arrangement is thought to free clinical psychology from the academic constraints of the university, to allow rewards for professional as well as scholarly achievements, and to provide students with faculty role models who are active, practicing clinicians.

Professional schools of psychology are sometimes associated with a university (e.g., at Rutgers or Yeshiva), but "free-standing" organizations are more common. The earliest example of a "free-standing" school was the California School of Professional Psychology, founded under the auspices of the California Psychological Association in 1969. The school has four campuses (Los Angeles, Berkeley, San Diego, and Fresno) with full or provisional accreditation, and is generally regarded as the leading professional school in the country.

There are now more than forty professional schools operating in the United States, the majority of which are free-standing and award the Psy.D. rather than the Ph.D. degree (Peterson, 1985). It has been estimated that by 1990, half of the doctorates awarded to clinical psychologists will be granted by professional schools (Peterson, 1983). This is because the average entering class of a professional school is about five times larger than the typical first-year class in a university psychology department. Further, professional schools appear to admit a much higher percentage of applicants than do programs in university psychology departments (Peterson, 1985).

The growth of the professional schools stems from several influences. First, well-intentioned, competent psychologists have honest differences about the best way to educate students. Were this not the case, debate about Ph.D.'s and Psy.D.'s would have ended long ago. Second, the curricula of professional schools are intended to reflect the expressed interest of most graduate students, which is to be trained as providers of psychological services rather than as academicians and researchers. Third, economic factors and changing employment opportunities have encouraged more and more psychologists to start independent practices, work in health-care facilities, and take other applied positions for which professional schools promise relevant training. Fourth, many professional schools have admitted the large number of graduates from terminal M.A. programs who, not finding much success in being admitted to traditional programs, have flocked to the professional schools. Finally, professional schools provide a training atmosphere that many students prefer to what they perceive in academic programs. The professional schools' emphasis on clinical practice and their provision of role models whose primary interests are those of the practitioner create a culture more in tune with the applied interests of most of today's clinical students.

Professional schools have revolutionized the nature of clinical training, regardless of whether they become the major producer of clinical psychologists. Should academic psychology departments retain their domination of clinical training, it is certain they will do so only by continuing to take professional training as seriously as the professional school movement forced them to do in the 1970s and 1980s (Peterson, 1985). On the other hand, if the professional schools continue to proliferate as predicted, the clinical psychologist of the twenty-first century is likely to be a more specialized practitioner for whom research is a secondary activity and interest. As a result, clinical psychology may become a better profession, but a poorer science.

Thorough discussions of the merits and demerits of professional and Boulder model training can be found in Barlow, Hayes, and Nelson (1983), Stricker (1975), Perry (1979), and Peterson (1985).

PROFESSIONAL REGULATION

One major responsibility of a human service profession is the establishment of standards of competence which members of the profession must meet before they are authorized to practice. The purpose of such regulation is to protect the public from unauthorized or incompetent practice of psychology by impostors, untrained persons, or psychologists who are unable to function at a minimum level of competence. Though some doubt the value of the regulation enterprise (e.g., Gross, 1978; Hogan, 1983), psychology has developed an active system of professional regulation.

Certification and Licensure

The most important type of regulation lies in state laws that establish requirements for the practice of psychology and/or restrict the use of the term "psychologist" to persons with certain qualifications. This legislative regulation comes in two kinds of statutes: certification and licensure. In both cases the laws are passed at the state level because the Constitution delegates sovereignty over this type of regulation to the states. The legal basis for these laws rests in the right of the state to pass legislation that protects its citizens. Caveat emptor ("let the buyer beware") is thought to be insufficient protection when buyers are not sufficiently informed about the services to know what to beware *of*.

Certification laws restrict the use of the title "psychologist" or "certified psychologist" to people who have met requirements specified in the law. Certification only protects the *title* of psychologist; it does not regulate the actual practice of psychology. In some states a person may be certified without having a doctoral degree.

Licensure, on the other hand, is a more restrictive type of statute. Licensure laws define the practice of psychology by specifying the services that the psychologist is authorized to offer the public. The requirements for licensure are usually more comprehensive than those for certification. In order to distinguish between certification and licensure, remember the following rule of thumb: A certification law would not prevent a nonpsychologist from doing the same things as a certified psychologist; it would only prevent the person from being called a psychologist. A licensure law, on the other hand, would prevent a nonpsychologist from using the term "psychologist," *and* it would also prohibit the person from offering services that the average citizen would believe to be among the professional functions of a psychologist.

Several statutes combine certification and licensure. The first paragraph of Kentucky's Statute 319 reads as follows:

No person not licensed or certified as provided in this chapter shall engage in any practice which the board finds constitutes the practice of psychology as defined in KRS 319.010, and is against the public interest and hold himself out by any title or description of services representing himself as a psychologist which incorporates the words "psychological, Psychologist," or "psychology"; except as such usage of title or description is authorized by this act.

Licensing laws are administered by state boards of psychology, which are charged by legislatures with regulating the practice of psychology in the states. There are two major functions of state boards of psychology: (1) to determine the standards for admission to the profession and administer procedures for the selection and examination of candidates, and (2) to regulate professional practice and conduct disciplinary proceedings involving violators of the professional standards set forth in the law.

Thus, a Ph.D. in clinical psychology does not allow you to hang out a shingle and start to practice psychology. While the steps in-

volved in becoming licensed differ somewhat from state to state, there is enough
uniformity in the procedures of most states
to offer a rough sketch of how the aspiring
clinical psychologist would approach this
task. Box 12-3 outlines the basic steps involved.

In 1945 Connecticut enacted the first
psychology licensing law; Virgina, Kentucky, and Ohio followed suit within five
years (Carlson, 1978). Today, all fifty states,
the District of Columbia, and several Cana-
dian provinces have certification or licensure laws.

As more states passed licensing statutes, a
number of interstate problems began to
emerge. It became obvious that there was a
need for an organization to coordinate the
activities of the state boards of psychology
and to bring about some uniformity in standards and procedures. To answer these
needs, the American Association of State
Psychology Boards (AASPB) was formed in
1961.

In addition to its coordinating efforts, the
AASPB developed a standardized, objective
examination for use by state boards in examining candidates for licensure. First released in 1964 and revised frequently since
then, this Examination for Professional
Practice in Psychology is sometimes called
the *multistate* or *national exam* because it can
be used by all jurisdictions as a part of their
exam procedure. The AASPB also helped
develop a system of *reciprocity,* meaning that
someone licensed in one state can sometimes transfer licensure to another jurisdic-
tion.

Licensure of psychologists has been criticized on several grounds. A major objection
has been that licensure does not assure competence of practitioners because the examination procedures do not adequately assess
professional abilities. Some critics further
contend that licensure may be detrimental
to the public interest because it functions to
curtail competition and increase the cost of
psychologists' services. Legal challenges to
licensure of psychologists involving alleged

due process violations and antitrust considerations have been attempted by disgruntled parties, but the success of these attacks
has been limited (Herbsleb, Sales & Overcast, 1985).

In the 1970s, as part of a general sentiment favoring governmental deregulation
of various activities, psychology licensure
statutes were eliminated in some states (they
have now been reenacted) through a process known as "sunset" legislation (laws requiring unnecessary regulations would be
terminated or have "the sun set" on them).
Today, licensure laws are applauded by a
majority of clinicians and are upheld by
courts if there is a plausible reason to believe
they protect the public.

In 1975 the first edition of the *National
Register of Health Service Providers in Psychology* was published. The *Register* was intended as a listing of psychologists who possessed the necessary training and
experience to be considered a health service
provider, defined as "a psychologist, certi-
fied/licensed at the independent practice
level in his/her state who is duly trained and
experienced in the delivery of direct, preventive, assessment, and therapeutic intervention services to individuals whose
growth, adjustment or functioning is actually impaired or is demonstrably at high risk
of impairment" (Asher, 1975, p. 1). The primary use of the *Register* is to identify psychologists who specialize in delivering
health services and to help various organizations and insurance companies identify
those psychologists who should be eligible
for reinbursement for delivering mental
health services. Over 14,000 psychologists
are now listed in the *Register,* and more than
250 organizations, including many of the
country's largest insurance companies, subscribe to the *Register.*

ABPP Certification

Another type of professional regulation
is certification by the American Board of
Professional Psychology (ABPP). ABPP was

BOX 12-3 "So you want to be a licensed psychologist"

Imagine that you have just received your Ph.D. or Psy.D. from a clinical training program and are now interested in becoming a licensed clinical psychologist. What are the steps you would have to take? The following hurdles will be encountered in obtaining licensure in most states.

First, you must ask that the state board of psychology review your credentials to determine your eligibility for examination. Their decision is based on several criteria.

1. *Administrative Requirements.* You must have reached a certain age, be a U.S. citizen, and have been a resident in the state for some minimum period. There is not too much to be done about these requirements; you either meet them or you do not. One bit of advice: Don't commit any felonies, engage in treason, or libel your governor. Those activities are judged to be indicative of poor moral character and may leave you plenty of time to fantasize about licensure while in prison.

2. *Education.* Almost all states require a doctoral degree in psychology from an accredited university (accreditation in this case refers not to APA approval but to accreditation of the university by a recognized accrediting agency). Official graduate and undergraduate transcripts are required.

3. *Experience.* This will usually amount to one to two years of supervised professional experience in a setting approved by the board. Some of the experience may have to be postdoctoral; letters of reference will be required from your supervisor(s).

If after scrutinizing your credentials the board finds you are eligible for examination, you will be invited for an exam. Here is what to expect:

1. *Examination Fee.* There is a charge for the examination; it is usually between $50 and $100.

2. *The Examination.* Many states will use the national exam. It contains about 200 objective items covering general psychology, methodology, applications of psychology, and professional conduct and ethics. Since many candidates will want to practice a "specialty" like clinical, school, or industrial psychology, most boards also prepare essay examinations in these areas. You can also expect an oral examination by the board in which any material relevant to psychology may be covered.

3. *Reexamination.* If you should fail any part of the exam, you will probably be given another chance at that portion. Most boards feel that twice is enough, however; so if you fail the second time, it might be wise to reconsider the advantages of the family business.

In most states, you will be required to keep your license or certificate up to date only by paying a periodic renewal fee. Some states have also begun to require *continuing professional education* (CPE) as a condition for maintaining licensure. Continuing professional education is usually provided in special postdoctoral institutes, seminars, or workshops conducted by an expert in a particular area. The purpose of this activity is to keep the practicing psychologist abreast of current progress in important professional areas. In states requiring CPE, psychologists must document their participation in a certain number of CPE units of instruction. Although psychology has not yet developed its CPE plan to the level of professions like law or medicine, most psychologists agree that the future will see a strengthening of CPE requirements for their field.

founded in 1947 as a national organization that would certify the professional competence of psychologists. Its certification is signified by the award of a diploma in one of four areas: clinical psychology, counseling psychology, school psychology, or industrial psychology. Diplomate status is awarded in some other newer specialties that have affiliated with ABPP; a recent example is the American Board of Forensic Psychology.

An ABPP diploma is considered more prestigious than licensure, although it carries no legal authority. While licensure signifies a minimal level of competence, diplomate status is an endorsement of professional expertise, an indication that the person possesses a masterful knowledge of the field. Despite this reputation, Schofield (1964) reported that in a 1959 survey of diplomates, only 27 percent of the respondents reported direct material benefit as a result of their status. Being a diplomate is an honor; in a few settings it may have additional financial rewards.

Requirements for the ABPP diploma are more rigorous than for licensure. Five years of postdoctoral experience is a prerequisite to take the ABPP examination, which is conducted by a group of diplomates who observe the candidate dealing directly with clinical phenomena (e.g., testing or interacting with a client). Evaluation concentrates on the candidate's knowledge and expertise in the areas of assessment, therapy, research, theory, and the ethics of psychological practice.

Other Forms of Legal Regulation

An interesting by-product of psychology's professionalization is greater legal scrutiny of the profession. Historically, courts have been disinclined to pass judgment on what constitutes acceptable psychological treatment. More recently, this reluctance has given way to a willingness to evaluate the legality of mental health care. It is apparent that courts are no longer willing to permit what they see as violations of clients' rights, despite the hazards in the non-expert evaluation of treatment methods.

A comprehensive review of the legal status of psychological treatments exceeds our purpose here, but we will highlight three frequently cited legal principles that have been used to challenge some forms of intervention. The first two (right to treatment and informed consent) are usually concerned with institutionalized persons such as mental patients or prison inmates. The third (privileged communication) is particularly relevant to outpatient psychotherapy clients.

Right to Treatment. The concept of the right to treatment for patients committed to psychiatric hospitals found legal support in the landmark *Rouse v. Cameron*[2] decision. Subsequent cases have strengthened this doctrine through due process arguments (*Wyatt v. Stickney*[3]; *Wyatt v. Aderholt*[4]). Recently the Supreme Court concluded that a state cannot confine without treatment non-dangerous individuals who can survive by themselves or with the help of others outside the institution (*O'Connor v. Donaldson*)[5]. Since *O'Connor*, mentally retarded patients also have had their treatment rights strengthened, although not guaranteed as an absolute right (*Youngberg v. Romero*[6]).

The *Wyatt* decision included a ban on involuntary labor by patients unless compensated by the minimum wage and a requirement that the physical and psychological resources to which patients are entitled as constitutional rights be specified. *Wyatt* directed that a patient is entitled to the "least restrictive conditions necessary to achieve the purposes of commitment." The "least restrictive conditions" doctrine was first applied in a case where a mental patient was being involuntarily committed to a hospital

---

[2] 373 F. 2d 451 (D.C. Cir. 1966).

[3] 344 F. Supp. 373 (1972).

[4] 503 F. 2d 1305 (5th Cir. 1974).

[5] 422 U.S. 563 (1975).

[6] 457 U.S. 307 (1982).

(*Lessard v. Schmidt*[7]). This doctrine holds that a state cannot stifle a person's civil liberties any more than is necessary for accomplishing legitimate treatment goals. Whenever less drastic means of effective treatment are available, they should be implemented rather than more drastic means. Like many well-intentioned reforms, the "least restrictive conditions" requirement poses some problems for mental health professionals. An example is the young chronic mental patient whose frequent history of substance abuse and acting out make voluntary care in noninstitutional settings difficult.

The *Wyatt* case also had many implications for the legally acceptable reinforcers that can be used in institutional token economies. While based on principles of reward, reinforcement programs require an initial state of deprivation to insure their motivational potency. *Wyatt* requires, however, the noncontingent availability of the following constitutionally protected rights:

1. Payment of the minimum wage for institutional work;
2. A right to privacy, including a bed, closet, chair, and bedside table;
3. Meals meeting minimum daily dietary requirements;
4. The right to visitors, religious services, and clean personal clothing;
5. Recreational privileges (e.g., television in the day room); and
6. An open ward and ground privileges when clinically acceptable.

Understandably, psychologists viewed *Wyatt* with some concern. Berwick and Morris (1974, p. 436) commented: "The field of law is beginning to step in and demand that mental patients get fair treatment; however, they may inadvertently be undermining attempts to establish adequate treatments." There is no doubt that *Wyatt* jeopardizes traditional token economies. At the same time,

the decision is not incompatible with all possible behavior-modification programs.

Wexler (1973) recommended the contingent use of "idiosyncratic reinforcers," nonbasic items that certain patients particularly prefer (e.g., eating hard-boiled rather than soft-boiled eggs). Token economies utilizing idiosyncratic reinforcers would probably be legally permissible because, by definition, idiosyncratic reinforcers are not the same as general rights. Another alternative (Wexler, 1974) would be to continue to use the *Wyatt* basics as reinforcers, but to require informed consent of all participants in the program (see below). One problem with this solution is that courts have held that informed consent to "drastic therapies" can be revoked at any time. This requirement would permit residents to convert contingent privileges into noncontingent rights whenever they wished, thereby depriving the program of its motivational impact.

Informed Consent. The claim that institutionalized persons have a right to treatment is complicated by the suggestion that they also may have a right to refuse at least some treatments. An individual's control over her or his treatment often takes the form of giving or withholding informed consent. Full informed consent involves several elements, including full specification of the nature of treatment; a description of its purpose, risks, and likely outcomes; notification that consent may be terminated at any time without prejudice to the individual; and demonstration of a capacity to consent. Written informed consent is usually required for treatments of an experimental, intrusive, or aversive nature (e.g., psychosurgery: *Kaimowitz and Doe v. Department of Mental Health*[8]).

As yet there is no legal doctrine allowing a patient to reject all rehabilitation or refuse all but the most preferred mode of treatment, but there is precedent that patients

---

[7] 349 F. Supp. 1078 (E.D. Wis. 1972).

[8] C.A. 73-19434-AW (Cir. Ct. of Wayne, Mich., July 10, 1973).

can disapprove methods which (1) violate their privacy (Spece, 1972), (2) are unduly drastic (Damich, 1974), or (3) are no more than cruel and unusual punishment (*Knecht v. Gillman*).[9]

From a practical perspective, the right to refuse treatment usually involves whether a patient can refuse psychotropic medication, since it is the major treatment for most seriously disturbed patients regardless of whether they are in hospitals. This question is hotly debated by mental health professionals who are responsible for treating such patients and by attorneys who are responsible for insuring the protection of patients' civil rights. The issue has been contested in court (e.g., *Rennie v. Klein*[10]), and there have been proposals for a review system to be utilized when involuntary patients refuse medication and physicians contend that medication should be imposed (Hickman, Resnick & Olson, 1982). In general, it is still the case that professionally recognized treatments can be forced on unwilling patients if an emergency requires such treatment and if sound professional judgment is documented in the use of the treatment.

Privileged Communication. Numerous states have passed laws that establish a psychotherapist-client *privilege*. Privilege is a legal right imposed to protect the client from public disclosure of confidences by the therapist without the client's permission. In function, privilege is like confidentiality. The main difference is that confidentiality is an ethical obligation of a profession, not a legal requirement. Passage of therapist-client privilege statutes is due mainly to the recognition that confidentiality of treatment is essential to the success of psychotherapy.

Just as the law of some states recognizes this type of privilege, it recognizes several exceptions to it, the most common of which are: (1) where a therapist determines that a client needs commitment to a hospital, (2) where a client has undergone a court-ordered examination and a judge has informed the client that his or her communications would not be privileged, (3) where a patient introduces his or her mental condition as an element of a defense against a criminal conviction, and (4) where a therapist believes the client may be engaging in child abuse.

Another area in which violations of confidentiality may be legally mandated is where a client communicates to a therapist the intention to commit harmful acts. This exception presents a dilemma for the psychotherapist who, by the open and trusting character of the therapeutic relationship, encourages verbal expressions of violent impulses from clients. The courts have held that privilege does not apply where its use would conceal information necessary for public safety or the administration of justice.

This brings us to a practical question: Should a therapist who has heard a client threaten to harm another person be required to protect the intended victim? This question was raised in the now-famous case of *Tarasoff v. Regents of University of California*,[11] and the answer—at least in some states—is "yes." In the *Tarasoff* case, a couple sued the University of California, psychotherapists employed by the university, and the campus police to recover damages for the murder of their daughter (a UC coed) by a client of one of the psychotherapists. A lower court sustained the defendants' answers to the suit, but the Supreme Court of California reversed that decision and found for the plaintiffs.

Here are the facts of the case. The client, Prosenjit Poddar, told his psychotherapist, Dr. Lawrence Moore, of his intention to kill a young woman, Tatiana Tarasoff. The therapist informed his superior, Dr. Harvey Powelson, of this threat, and the campus police were called and requested in writing to

---

[9] 488 F. 2d, 1136 (8th Cir. 1973).
[10] 653 F. 2d 836 (3d Cir. 1981).

[11] 529 P. 2d 553 (Col. 1974) *Vac. reheard in bank and affirmed* 131 Cal. Rptr. 14, 551 P. 2d 334 (1976).

confine the client. This they did, but shortly thereafter they released him, concluding that he was rational and believing his promise that he would stay away from the Tarasoff's home. He didn't. After terminating his relationship with his therapist, Poddar killed Tatiana. He was later convicted of murder. No one had warned the woman or her parents of the threat. In fact, Powelson had asked the police to return Moore's letter and further ordered that all copies of the letter and Moore's therapy notes be destroyed and that Poddar not be confined.

In reaching its decision, the court weighed the importance of confidential therapy relationships against society's interest in protecting itself from dangerous persons. The balance was struck in favor of society's protection. The therapist's situation was analogized to that of a physician who would be held liable for the failure to warn persons threatened with a contagious disease: "The protective privilege ends where the public peril begins."

Tarasoff's conclusion that therapists have a duty to protect specific victims from clients that the therapist believes or should believe to be dangerous has been implemented in other states. However, it is not legally binding in all states, a fact that many psychologists misunderstand. For example, in Pennsylvania, which has a statute that reads in part, "in no event (s)hall privileged communication, whether written or oral, be disclosed to anyone without (w)ritten consent," a woman successfully sued her psychotherapist, who had written the women's employer to warn him that the woman was threatening to blow up somebody if she continued to be harrassed at work (*Hopewell v. Adebimpe*[12]). At the same time, some other states have extended "*Tarasoff* liability" to persons other than those specifically threatened; in *Peterson v. State*,[13] the Supreme Court of

Washington held that therapists are responsible "to protect anyone who might foreseeably be endangered" by their clients. One thing is clear: Therapists are responsible for knowing what their state requires regarding protection of third parties.

PROFESSIONAL ETHICS

A code of professional ethics is a set of principles that encourages or forbids certain kinds of professional conduct. Ethics are normative statements that justify certain goals and patterns of behavior. All professions have ethical principles that suggest the proper way for professionals to behave toward the public and toward each other. As psychology moved into its professional era, it needed to articulate the principles that should guide its members.

Psychology's first code of ethics was published in 1953 (APA, 1953). A unique feature of this code was the manner by which it was developed. True to their empirical foundations, psychologists submitted to an APA committee a large number of "critical incidents" involving some ethical dilemma that had occurred in a professional context. By analyzing this real-life material, the committee distilled a comprehensive ethical code, which was summarized in a set of general principles six years later (APA, 1959). After this version had been in use for three years, it was amended and formally adopted (APA, 1963). The Ethical Principles have undergone subsequent revisions; the current version of the Ethical Principles was adopted by APA in 1981.

In 1967 the APA published a *Casebook on Ethical Standards of Psychologists*, which contained a restatement of the 1963 ethical principles as well as actual case material drawn from the discussions of the APA's Committee on Scientific and Professional Ethics and Conduct between 1959 and 1962. The facts of these case decisions were disguised to protect the anonymity of both the innocent and the guilty. The *Casebook* is

---

[12] Court of Common Pleas of Allegheny County, Pennsylvania, Civil Case No. G.D. 78-28756, 130 Pittsburgh Legal Journal 107 (1982).

[13] 100 Wn 2d 421, 671 P.2d 320 (1983).

intended to serve as a guide for how ethical principles are applied to real cases. It is the source most psychologists study in order to educate themselves about the profession's ethical standards. Periodically, summaries of actual ethical cases and their resolutions are published in the *American Psychologist* (Mills, 1984; Sanders, 1979; Sanders & Keith-Spiegel, 1980).

The 1981 Ethical Principles contains a preamble and ten principles covering all the primary psychological activities: research, academic standards, therapy, testing, and diagnosis. All the principles are relevant to clinical psychologists in one way or another.

ETHICAL PRINCIPLES OF PSYCHOLOGISTS

Preamble

Psychologists respect the dignity and worth of the individual and strive for the preservation and protection of fundamental human rights. They are committed to increasing knowledge of human behavior and of people's understanding of themselves and others and to the utilization of such knowledge for the promotion of human welfare. While pursuing these objectives, they make every effort to protect the welfare of those who seek their services and of the research participants that may be the object of study. They use their skills only for purposes consistent with these values and do not knowingly permit their misuse by others. While demanding for themselves freedom of inquiry and communication, psychologists accept the responsibility this freedom requires: competence, objectivity in the application of skills, and concern for the best interests of clients, colleagues, students, research participants, and society. In the pursuit of these ideals, psychologists subscribe to principles in the following areas: 1. Responsibility, 2. Competence, 3. Moral and Legal Standards, 4. Public Statements, 5. Confidentiality, 6. Welfare of the Consumer, 7. Professional Relationships, 8. Assessment Techniques, 9. Research With Human Participants, and 10. Care and Use of Animals.

Acceptance of membership in the American Psychological Association commits the member to adherence to these principles.

Psychologists cooperate with duly constituted committees of the American Psychological Association, in particular, the Committee on Scientific and Professional Ethics and Conduct, by responding to inquiries promptly and completely. Members also respond promptly and completely to inquiries from duly constituted state association ethics committees and professional standards review committees.

Principle 1
RESPONSIBILITY

In providing services, psychologists maintain the highest standards of their profession. They accept responsibility for the consequences of their acts and make every effort to ensure that their services are used appropriately.

Principle 2
COMPETENCE

The maintenance of high standards of competence is a responsibility shared by all psychologists in the interest of the public and the profession as a whole. Psychologists recognize the boundaries of their competence and the limitations of their techniques. They only provide services and only use techniques for which they are qualified by training and experience. In those areas in which recognized standards do not yet exist, psychologists take whatever precautions are necessary to protect the welfare of their clients. They maintain knowledge of current scientific and professional information related to the services they render.

Principle 3
MORAL AND LEGAL STANDARDS

Psychologists' moral and ethical standards of behavior are a personal matter to the same degree as they are for any other citizen, except as these may compromise the fulfillment of their professional responsibilities or reduce the public trust in psychology and psychologists. Regarding their own behavior, psychologists are sensitive to prevailing community standards and to the possible impact that conformity to or deviation from these standards may have upon the quality of their performance as psychologists. Psychologists are also aware of the possible impact of their public behavior upon the ability of colleagues to perform their professional duties.

Principle 4
PUBLIC STATEMENTS

Public statements, announcements of services, advertising, and promotional activities of psychologists serve the purpose of helping the public make informed judgments and choices. Psychologists represent accurately and objectively their professional qualifications, affiliations, and functions, as well as those of the institutions or organizations with which they or the statements may be associated. In public statements providing psychological information or professional opinions or providing information about the availability of psychological products, publications, and services, psychologists base their statements on scientifically acceptable psychological findings and techniques with full recognition of the limits and uncertainties of such evidence.

Principle 5
CONFIDENTIALITY

Psychologists have a primary obligation to respect the confidentiality of information obtained from persons in the course of their work as psychologists. They reveal such information to others only with the consent of the person or the person's legal representative, except in those unusual circumstances in which not to do so would result in clear danger to the person or to others. Where appropriate, psychologists inform their clients of the legal limits of confidentiality.

Principle 6
WELFARE OF THE CONSUMER

Psychologists respect the integrity and protect the welfare of the people and groups with whom they work. When conflicts of interests arise between clients and psychologists' employing institutions, psychologists clarify the nature and direction of their loyalties and responsibilities and keep all parties informed of their commitments. Psychologists fully inform consumers as to the purpose and nature of an evaluative, treatment, educational, or training procedure, and they freely acknowledge that clients, students, or participants in research have freedom of choice with regard to participation.

Principle 7
PROFESSIONAL RELATIONSHIPS

Psychologists act with due regard for the needs, special competencies, and obligations of their colleagues in psychology and other professions. They respect the prerogatives and obligations of the institutions or organizations with which these other colleagues are associated.

Principle 8
ASSESSMENT TECHNIQUES

In the development, publication, and utilization of psychological assessment techniques, psychologists make every effort to promote the welfare and best interests of the client. They guard against the misuse of assessment results. They respect the client's right to know the results, the interpretations made, and the bases for their conclusions and recommendations. Psychologists make every effort to maintain the security of tests and other assessment techniques within limits of legal mandates. They strive to ensure the appropriate use of assessment techniques by others.

Principle 9
RESEARCH WITH HUMAN PARTICIPANTS

The decision to undertake research rests upon a considered judgment by the individual psychologist about how best to contribute to psychological science and human welfare. Having made the decision to conduct research, the psychologist considers alternative directions in which research energies and resources might be invested. On the basis of this consideration, the psychologist carries out the investigation with respect and concern for the dignity and welfare of the people who participate and with cognizance of federal and state regulations and professional standards governing the conduct of research with human participants.

Principle 10
CARE AND USE OF ANIMALS

An investigator of animal behavior strives to advance understanding of basic behavioral principles and/or to contribute to the improvement of human health and welfare. In seeking these ends, the investigator ensures the welfare of animals and treats them humanely. Laws and regulations notwithstanding, an animal's immediate

BOX 12-4   An example of an ethical dilemma

The following case history is drawn from the APA *Casebook* on ethical standards (1967, pp. 29–30). It deals with the difficult issue of a clinician's obligation to protect the welfare of a client on the one hand while remaining sensitive to the social interests inherent in criminal conduct on the other hand. It raises a somewhat different problem than the one involved in the *Tarasoff* case.

Case 6A

A fully trained clinical psychologist in private practice was referred a patient for psychotherapeutic treatment because of a "near nervous breakdown." The background of the patient revealed many stressful and traumatic circumstances. After a few visits the patient admitted to having committed murder, something which weighed heavily on his conscience. The psychologist wrote to the committee for advice, pointing out that no ethical principle fitted the case exactly, the closest being one dealing with situations in which knowledge and intent are revealed but in which an act has not yet been committed. The psychologist wrote further as follows:

I find myself in a very uncomfortable position of not knowing whether accepting him in a treatment basis would be in effect condoning his act. It is possible to understand the internal pressures and the dynamics which led him to behave as he did. Nor am I sure when he says that he thinks he ought to make public what he has done and bear punishment for it that it is my responsibility to encourage this action. Theoretically I know

that I should help him to clarify his own thinking to the point where he can take the course of action which he deems most suitable. However, as he himself states, not only is he involved, but the public knowledge of his act would have to be borne by his wife and daughters. From a psychotherapeutic point of view there is no doubt that this man is in intense psychic pain and regardless of what course he decides to follow I suppose that I could justify seeing him in a professional role in an attempt to make him more comfortable. Yet I do not find it possible to completely encapsulate his act. There is no indication that he is suspected of the act or that he would ever do it again.

I am afraid that my own ethical values and social conscience are being intruded, and in a sense I suppose I am asking whether, in this case, they should not be. I do hope that I have outlined the situation clearly enough that your committee can help me to ascertain my ethical responsibilities as a psychologist.

Opinion

The committee felt the client should be accepted in therapy without condoning his act, but that the decision in such a case rested with the psychologist involved. In reaching such a decision, it is necessary to take into account responsibilities to both the profession and the community, in addition to recognizing the legal considerations as well. Since the laws in the different states vary with respect to privileged communication, the committee recommended as well that the psychologist confronted with such a question consult an attorney as to what his legal obligations might be under the particular circumstances.

protection depends upon the scientist's own conscience.

Most clinicians believe in and are guided by the APA Ethical Principles. As exemplified by the case presented in Box 12-4, they take great pains to deal with complex and ethically ambiguous situations in accordance

with the highest standards of professional conduct. On those rare occasions when, as a fallible human being, a psychologist makes an unwise choice and behaves in a questionable manner, she or he is subject to censure by local, state, and national organizations whose task it is to deal with violations of ethical practice.

Once a complaint of unethical behavior has been brought against an APA member and the appropriate committee has decided that the conduct in question was in fact unethical, the question of punishment must be decided. The most severe APA sanction is to dismiss the offender from the association and to inform the membership of this action. This penalty is embarrassing for most transgressors, humiliating for a few, but seldom devastating for any. In the case of extreme or repeated unethical conduct, a psychologist could be threatened with the loss of his or her license through action of the board of psychology in the state where the psychologist practices.

Other Ethical Standards

Ethical principles 9 and 10 make the psychologist responsible for the welfare of research subjects, both animal and human. Because of increasing public concern, new governmental research regulations, and outrage about the alleged mistreatment of animals in some laboratories, APA has found it necessary to supplement its ethical standards with a more detailed set of guidelines covering research with animals. A copy of these Guidelines for Ethical Conduct in the Care and Use of Animals is available from APA's Office of Scientific Affairs.

Clinical psychologists are responsible for being knowledgeable about other standards that govern their delivery of psychological services. The major sources for these various standards are *Standards for Educational and Psychological Testing* (APA, 1985), *Standards for Providers of Psychological Services* (APA, 1977), and *Specialty Guidelines for the Delivery of Services by Clinical Psychologists* (APA, 1981b).

PROFESSIONAL INDEPENDENCE

The clinical psychologist must consult and collaborate with people from other professions in many aspects of clinical practice. Clinical psychologists often work closely with educators, attorneys, ministers, social workers, nurses, physicians, and other psychologists.

For the most part, psychology's interprofessional relationships are healthy, profitable, and characterized by good will. The most obvious sign of this harmony is the frequency of referrals made across groups. A teacher with a child whose classroom misbehavior is related to a serious emotional problem is likely to suggest that the family consult a psychologist. Psychologists, on the other hand, may encounter clients who are in legal trouble; rather than offer legal advice, they will urge such clients to hire an attorney.

Psychologists have had considerable friction with physicians, particularly psychiatrists. In fact, one of clinical psychology's lingering problems in its efforts at professionalization has been its wary, often stormy relationships with the medical profession. Garfield (1965) observes that as early as 1917, psychiatrists were critical of psychologists, particularly "those who have termed themselves 'clinical psychologists'" and work in "so-called 'psychological clinics'" and provide "so-called expert testimony."

There have been two main sources of friction between clinical psychology and psychiatry. The first of these involved the independent practice of psychotherapy by psychologists. More recently, the squabble has concentrated on psychologists' inclusion in insurance policies covering treatment for mental disorders. Although the two controversies are related, we will look at them individually in order to understand the development of each.

Independent Practice of Psychotherapy

As long as psychologists confined themselves to research, consultation, and testing, physicians did not interfere with them. Psychologists, by the same token, found no problem with the fact that physicians must be the authority on matters of physical disorder or organic treatments such as medication, electroconvulsive therapy, and surgery. Disagreement, when it came, centered on psychotherapy, which both professions (along with several others) offered to the public. When psychologists began to assert their right to engage in the independent practice of psychotherapy, psychiatrists objected and insisted that a psychotherapist must be either a physician or under the supervision of a physician.

The rationale for the psychiatrists' position is that physicians are the experts on the functioning of the *whole person* and that with many types of abnormal behaviors it is essential that the therapist be able to differentiate mental and physical aspects of the disorder and treat both aspects thoroughly. For their part, psychologists contend that the vast majority of mental disorders involve psychological and social processes rather than physical ones, and that they are better trained about these processes than physicians are. In addition, when physical etiology and/or medical treatments are indicated, psychologists are aware of their ethical obligations to refer such clients to physicians. Finally, psychologists point out that many of the most influential therapists over the years have been nonphysicians (e.g., Anna Freud, Carl Rogers, Erich Fromm, Erik Erikson).

However, psychologists themselves were at one time opposed to practicing psychotherapy independently. In 1949 the APA discouraged the practice of psychotherapy by psychologists who were not working in collaboration with psychiatrists (Goldenberg, 1973). Shakow commented on this topic: "The leadership in therapy naturally rests in the hands of the psychiatrist because of his medical background, with its social and legally recognized responsibilities for treatment, and his major concern with this problem" (Shakow, 1948, p. 517).

While psychologists reconsidered their position on the independent practice of psychotherapy (APA, 1958), psychiatrists did not. In fact, the American Medical Association (1954) adopted an official policy that

psychotherapy was a medical procedure to be performed only by medically trained personnel. The strategy of the AMA in this battle was to oppose state certification and licensure of psychologists. This strategy was unsuccessful, a fact for which most clinical psychologists are very grateful.

Relations between psychologists and psychiatrists have improved considerably over the years. Psychiatrists have come to accept psychologists as professionals and are less likely to treat them with the condescension of earlier days. In turn, psychologists have shed some of their defensive armor and are not as prone to feel that they constantly must be on guard against psychiatrists. Both fields have been enhanced by the growing number of well-qualified persons who have entered the two professions, and mutual learning experiences are increasingly likely.

Health Insurance

Having won the battles over licensure and recognition of psychology as an independent profession, clinicians turned in the 1970s and 1980s to struggles involving the economic aspects of mental health care. The focus of these struggles was whether psychologists should be eligible for reimbursement for their services by insurance companies. Physicians opposed psychologists' inclusion because they said it would be too costly to "third-party payers" and consumers. If psychologists were to be included, physicians argued that their services should be reimbursed *only* when they were treating clients referred and supervised by physicians. Because many major health insurance companies (such as Blue Cross/Blue Shield) are run by and for physicians, psychologists were excluded from third-party payments except when billing under a physician's supervision.

Psychologists found this an intolerable situation for a profession that aspired to full autonomy. As a result, in the late 1960s and early 1970s psychologists began to lobby state legislatures to pass what is known as *freedom-of-choice* laws. A freedom-of-choice law mandates that services rendered by qualified mental health professionals licensed to practice in a given state shall be reimbursed by insurance plans covering such services regardless of whether the provider is a physician.

Physicians fought hard against such legislation, frequently using the term "medical psychotherapy" to refer to the services they believed should be reimbursable. This term was interpreted by psychology to be a political maneuver intended to guarantee that physicians would be the only professionals identified as appropriate providers of psychotherapy.

Psychologists argued that in the vast majority of cases there was nothing "medical" about psychotherapy. In addition, psychologists presented data to counter the claims that including them as providers or even including coverage of mental disorders treated by any provider would be too costly for third-party payers. For example, one study showed that a *single session of psychotherapy* reduced subsequent use of medical resources by 60 percent among the recipients, and there was about a 75 percent reduction in medical utilizations by patients receiving two to eight sessions of psychotherapy (Cummings, 1977; see also Olbrisch, 1977). Far from being economically disadvantageous, reimbursing psychotherapy may be cost effective because it saves money that would otherwise be spent for more expensive medical services.[14]

Over the years psychologists have succeeded in having freedom-of-choice laws enacted in most states. By 1983 forty states covering 90 percent of the country's population had passed legislation that provided free choice of licensed psychologists as reimbursable providers of mental health services. In addition, other legislation at the federal level promoted recognition of psychologists as independent clinicians. The Rehabilitation Act of 1973 (PL 93-112) provided parity for psychologists with physicians in both assessment and treatment services. Services provided by clinical psychologists are reimbursable under both the Federal Employee Health Benefits Act (PL 93-363) and the Federal Work Injuries Compensation Program (PL 94-212). Licensed psychologists are also recognized as *independent* providers by CHAMPUS (The Civilian Health and Medical Program of the Uniformed Services), a federal program covering about eight million beneficiaries in all fifty states and the District of Columbia.

In contrast to these gains, psychologists have encountered setbacks in their attempts to be included in major health insurance plans. Neither Medicare nor Medicaid includes psychologists as independent practitioners, despite several attempts to amend the programs to include them. This exclusion is important for at least two reasons. First, Medicare (the federal insurance program for elderly and disabled clients) and Medicaid (the shared federal/state program for the medically needy) are enormous programs, together accounting for 90 percent of the federal health budget (Uyeda & Moldawsky, 1986). Second, these two programs are often used as models for other public and private insurance programs; policy limits, payment plans, benefits, and cost containment provisions employed by Medicare/Medicaid are copied by many other providers. In fact, Medicare/Medicaid "together are the closest representation to a national health insurance program that we have" (Uyeda & Moldawsky, 1986, p. 60). Psychologists' services are reimbursed by these programs only when such services are

---

[14] Not all psychologists approve of psychology being included under health insurance benefits. Albee (1975) argued that reimbursing the cost of psychotherapy services by any profession through health insurance reinforces the incorrect belief that behavior problems are due to an illness and consequently directs resources away from social change and prevention programs (see Meltzer, 1975, for a similar discussion). Albee (1977) has also claimed that since it is the middle and upper classes that most frequently seek psychotherapy, inclusion of this service under any federal insurance plan would require a regressive tax, a subsidy of the rich by the poor (see also Crowell, 1977).

authorized by a physician, a serious limitation on psychology's autonomy.

Another problem concerns enforcement of freedom-of-choice laws. Even though a state passes a freedom-of-choice law, psychologists have discovered that some insurance companies will ignore it unless forced to comply. Resnick (1985) describes the three and a half years of litigation needed to require Blue Cross/Blue Shield of Virginia to comply with that state's freedom-of-choice law. (A related area of litigation lies in antitrust suits against the Joint Commission on the Accreditation of Hospitals and its practice of denying staff privileges to nonphysicians).

The skyrocketing costs of health care (accounting in 1980 for almost 12 percent of the gross national product; Binner, 1986) are currently causing insurance companies to invent new reimbursement plans and various self-insurance packages in order to curtail costs and extent of health care coverage. Many of the newer forms of health insurance, especially the self-insurance packages offered by large corporations, either exclude mental health benefits altogether or put a cap on how much reimbursement is allowed for such services. Psychologists now find themselves facing a situation where the victories they won in the freedom-of-choice legislation may be made obsolete by new insurance plans. Economics determine to a large degree the nature, quality, and extent of health care, a lesson that psychologists have been slow to learn (Cummings, 1986). In the near future, clinical psychology will face at least three important changes in health-care economics that it must be prepared for if it is to remain viable in the health-care marketplace.

1. Debate over the need for national health insurance is sure to continue, and well it should, for national health insurance would have a tremendous impact on the delivery and quality of mental health services in this country. Although the conservative politics of recent administrations have discouraged development of national health insurance (NHI), it is certain that future administrations will promote it as part of their legislative agenda. The two questions involving NHI with the greatest implications for clinical psychologists is whether outpatient mental health services will be covered and whether psychologists will be reimbursed as autonomous professionals or whether Medicare guidelines will be incorporated restricting psychologists' reimbursements to only those services under the supervision of a physician.

One of psychology's most important contributions to a national system of health care would be to help evaluate the consequences of implementing the program itself. As evidence of its commitment to evaluative research, the APA established in 1976 a Task Force on Continuing Evaluation in National Health Insurance that published sixteen principles it believed should guide any health insurance legislation. The sentiment of these principles was expressed in the introduction to the task force report in the April 1978 issue of the *American Psychologist:*

The probable advent of NHI provides psychology and the other health professions with a remarkable opportunity to display professional maturity and leadership in also urging Congress to build into the NHI provisions for systematic evaluation of covered services and reimbursement only for effective treatments and programs. In the vast majority of cases, the only really ethical position lies in providing the public with effective services whose effectiveness is under systematic evaluation. It is unlikely that any health profession would in the long run lose by affirming its confidence in its ability to provide effective services, and the public could only gain. (p. 305)

2. The newest form of health insurance plans is what has been termed the "alphabet soup" packages, including HMOs (Health Maintenance Organizations), PPOs (Preferred Provider Organizations) and IPAs (Independent Practice Associations). Despite various differences, these plans provide health care to subscribers for a fixed, prepaid price in contrast to the traditional fee-for-service management. Thus, these plans offer an incentive for keeping subscribers healthy as opposed to increasing their utilization of services (Tulkin & Frank, 1985).

All federally qualified HMOs are required to provide a subscriber up to twenty outpatient visits for mental health care per year. The number of clinical psychologists currently working in HMOs or PPOs is relatively small, but the potential role for psychologists in these types of health plans is expanding, especially in relation to behavioral medicine and health psychology.

3. In an effort to control the price of medical services, in 1983 the United States Congress implemented a new system for reimbursing hospitals at a predetermined rate for their treatment of Medicare patients. Under this system, payment, is determined on the basis of the diagnosis a patient receives rather than on the basis of the actual cost of treatment (as was the case prior to 1983). Patients are classified into one of 467 *diagnosis-related groups* (known as DRGs), and payment is based on the average cost of treating patients with that diagnosis. Thus, if a hospital treats a patient for less money than the DRG payment provides, it makes a profit; if it spends more than the allocated amount, it loses money.

Currently, several types of settings in which psychologists are employed are exempted from the DRG system because the nature of the disorders treated in these settings makes them inappropriate for DRG classification. Psychiatric hospitals and specialty settings that treat alcoholics, drug abusers, or children are exempt, for example. However, there are new proposals for expanding the DRG system to these settings (Weiss, 1986). Should such an expansion occur, psychologists will encounter powerful restraints on the treatments they deliver to patients in these settings. The DRG system may also influence the diagnosis of patients because it provides an incentive to give patients diagnoses that are associated with larger reimbursements. It is important that the possible effects of expanding the DRG system be studied and understood before being implemented; psychologists might want to take the initiative and be involved in empirical studies of this proposal.

The legal struggles and political combat over the many issues of professional independence have negative effects that clinical psychology must consider. First, litigation is very expensive. Legal costs are usually encumbered by state psychological associations, APA, or other organizations of psychologists. As a result, funds may not be available for other activities (e.g., sponsorship of research or prevention programs) that might be of greater interest to academic or nonclinical psychologists, who are justifiably concerned that clinicians will bankrupt psychological associations by constantly expending their resources in court cases. Clinicians need to take seriously the questions raised by nonpractitioners about the best use of organized psychology's limited resources.

Another risk of some of this litigation is that in its effort to stay competitive in the mental health marketplace, psychologists may be tempted to exaggerate their accomplishments and claims for success, particularly in psychotherapy. The profession will not be served well by promising more than it can deliver, especially when consumers must bear whatever additional costs expanding health-care coverage might bring. Finally, there are disadvantages in maintaining an adversary stance toward psychiatry. As Resnick (1985, p. 983) put it, "today's adversaries are tomorrow's allies." Psychology and psychiatry have mutual interests in several areas that will be jeopardized by continued interprofessional sparring. For example, most proposed forms of national health insurance omit mental health services, an exclusion that both psychology and psychiatry should probably oppose. Members of both professions may find that the most serious threats to mental health care do not come from each other, but from outside forces that require a cooperative and unified response.

PERILS OF PROFESSIONALISM

Have the first four decades of clinical psychology's professional era strengthened the field by making it a better profession, or have they simply made it more of a guild that employs meaningless membership criteria? Has clinical psychology become a better profession by erecting standards of training, competence, and service, or is it merely a more closed profession? We consider such questions in these final pages.

The ultimate justification for the professionalization of any discipline is that the public will benefit from the standards that govern the profession. Of course these restrictions also benefit members of the profession in that they control the profession's size and reduce competition. There is little objection to this latter function when it is a by-product of protecting the public from unqualified practitioners. The problem arises when the priorities of a profession are reversed, so that the promotion of its own members takes precedence over its obligations to the public.

As early as 1951, Fillmore Sanford, then executive secretary of the APA, warned about the perils of professionalization. In an effort to call psychology's attention to its obligations as a profession, Sanford proposed sixteen principles that should be considered "the criteria of a good profession" (Sanford, 1951, p. 667). He hoped that these criteria would guide the development of psychology as a socially useful and responsive profession. Sanford's criteria of a good profession are summarized in Box 12-5.

Sanford's statement remains timely. Although it was written as an idealistic vision of what psychology should strive for, it can be used today as a yardstick for measuring what psychology has become. The first two criteria deal with the need for psychologists to adjust to social needs and changes. At several points we have emphasized that clinical psychology has been responsive to the social and political events surrounding it. The growth of the profession itself was a reaction to social upheaval and virtually unprecedented human needs. In a similar fashion, the evolution of such disparate psychological activities as assessment, psychotherapy, community psychology, and behavior modification had roots in the fact that psychology has always been well-tuned to the current *zeitgeist*.

Several criteria (i.e., 3, 4, 13, and 14) are concerned with professional ethics. Psychologists are justifiably proud of their code of ethics because it remains the only set of professional standards that was developed with explicitly empirical procedures. This pride has not fostered complacency, however, and the code continues to be revised and updated.

Three of the criteria (10, 11, and 15) involve professional training. Clinical psychology is committed to the development of training programs that are most appropriate for the roles clinicians are asked to fill. While value is still placed on the Boulder model of training, it is valued in the context of experimentation with other systems of training intended to prepare psychologists who will deliver clinical services. The one area that has lagged behind is continuing professional education (CPE). Progress is being made on this front, however, and we believe that within the next few years a majority of states will be mandating CPE as a condition for the licensing of psychologists.

The sixth of Sanford's criteria is related to our discussion of interprofessional relationships. This issue, especially as it relates to psychiatrists and clinical psychologists, will continue to be the focus of much attention. An adequate response to our sometimes troubled relations with psychiatry requires a balancing act. On the one hand, clinicians must search for new opportunities to collaborate and cooperate with *all* professions. At the same time, psychology must also be a free profession, unwilling to enter into any Faustian pact where the goodwill of the medical profession is purchased with acquiescence to its domination of psychology.

The greatest number of Sanford's crite-

BOX 12-5   Fillmore Sanford's criteria for a good profession

1. A good profession is motivated by a sense of social responsibility.

2. A good profession is sufficiently perceptive of its place in society to guide its practices and policies so they conform to the best and changing interests of that society.

3. A good profession is continually on guard lest it represent itself as able to render services that are beyond its demonstrable competence.

4. A good profession continually seeks to find its unique pattern of competence and concentrates its efforts on the rendering of the unique service based on its pattern of competencies.

5. A good profession devotes relatively little of its energy to "guild" functions, to the building of its own in-group strength, and relatively much of its energy to the serving of its social function.

6. The good profession engages in rational and non-invidious relations with other professions having related competencies and common purposes.

7. A good profession devotes a proportion of its energies to the discovery of new knowledge.

8. The good profession develops channels of communication between the discoverers of knowledge and the appliers of knowledge.

9. The good profession does not relegate its discoverers of knowledge to positions of second-rate status.

10. The good profession is free of non-functional entrance requirements.

11. The good profession provides preparatory training which is validly related to the ultimate function of the members of the profession.

12. A good profession is one in which the material benefits accruing to its members are proportional to social contributions.

13. The good profession is one whose members are socially and financially accessible to the public.

14. The good profession has a code of ethics designed primarily to protect the client and only secondarily to protect the members of the profession.

15. A good profession facilitates the continuing education and training of all its members.

16. A good profession is continually concerned with the validity of its techniques and procedures.

---

ria discuss the priorities of the profession, the essential contributions it should make to the public. Sanford, like many psychologists before and after him, affirmed research and advancement of new knowledge as psychology's primary activity. The creation of basic knowledge is the one function that separates the professional from the technician, who applies methods based on existing knowledge. This judgment may be most accurate for a new profession like clinical psychology, where "the fewer its techniques of demonstrable utility, the more of its resources it should devote to research" (Sanford, 1951, p. 669).

THE FUTURE OF CLINICAL PSYCHOLOGY

We have reached that point where authors are obliged to become seers who boldly predict the future of their profession. While we cannot completely resist the temptation of trying to tell the future, we hope to avoid the excesses of forecasting that sometimes bedevil the incautious commentator. Our outlook on clinical psychology's future emphasizes the following points:

1. The number of clinicians will continue to increase, although at a slower pace than in recent years.

2. Accompanying this increase will be a broadening of the professional roles clinicians will fill. We refer to this trend as "boundary stretching" and see a continuing tendency for psychologists to involve themselves in a great number of activities.

Three areas are likely to continue as "growth stocks" for clinicians. First, as described in Chapter 11, health psychology and behavioral medicine should remain important specialty areas because of the important contributions psychologists can make to the promotion of physical health. Although these activities pose exciting opportunities for psychologists, we must be realistic in our appraisals and in our claims of success so as not to promise more than our knowledge allows us to deliver (Kaplan, 1984).

A second burgeoning specialty area is forensic psychology. Psychologists are being consulted on a range of topics of relevance to the legal system, including trial strategy and jury selection (Nietzel & Dillehay, 1986), law enforcement procedures (Ellison & Buckhout, 1981), legal decision making (Kassin & Wrightsman, 1985), and expert testimony (Blau, 1984). Box 12-6 summarizes sixteen areas of expert testimony frequently offered by psychologists. For each category of testimony, the ultimate question that the expert is usually asked is identified, and some references describing the testimonial topic are listed. The list of topics in Box 12-6 is not exhaustive. Today's list of subjects will be outdated tomorrow because demand for psychologists' expertise in litigation has expanded dramatically. While this demand is gratifying and potentially lucrative, psychologists must be careful not to testify on matters that exceed their competence and not to exaggerate the scientific support for the conclusions they report. (For criticisms of psychologists' expert testimony, see McCloskey & Egeth, 1983; Morse, 1978; Ziskin, 1981; and the June 1986 issue of *Law & Human Behavior,* which discusses the ethical problems in expert testimony.)

The third specialty area in which clinical psychologists enjoy an increasing demand for services relates to children. Assessment and treatment of childhood disorders have advanced remarkably in the past decade, as has research on basic child development and the etiology of child psychopathology (Achenbach, 1982; Bornstein & Kazdin, 1985; Ollendick & Hersen, 1984; Quay & Werry, 1986). This greater attention to children has generated much knowledge on the unique qualities and problems of children and has led to an emphasis on early interventions with children in order to prevent emotional and academic problems (Rolf, 1985). Another direction that has gained popularity in recent years is the prevention of child-abusing behaviors that have been shown to contribute to several forms of later, severe psychopathology (Rosenberg & Reppucci, 1985).

To resume our enumeration of the salient points of our outlook on clinical psychology's future:

3. Clinical psychology will take on more of a consumer orientation. This trend is apparent in the large number of self-help groups that have been formed, the emphasis on professional accountability to clients, and the expectation that psychologists must develop their own standards as health-service providers. The result of these movements is that clinicians will need to evaluate the effectiveness of their interventions as well as the financial costs of producing certain outcomes (Banta & Saxe, 1983; Newman & Howard, 1986). The psychologist as researcher will always have a place in the future.

BOX 12-6 Topics of expert testimony by psychologists

Areas of Expert Testimony	*Questions Addressed in the Testimony*	*Cases and References*
Insanity defense/criminal responsibility	What is the relationship between the defendant's mental condition at the time of the alleged offense and the defendant's responsibility for the crime with which the defendant is charged? What sort of "personality profile" does the defendant have, and is it consistent with the crimes charged?	*M'Naghten* (1843)[15], *Durham v. United States* (1954)[16]; *U.S. v. Brawner* (1982)[17]; Rogers, Wasyliw & Cavanaugh (1984); Slobogin, Melton & Showalter (1984)
Competence to stand trial	Does the defendant have an adequate understanding of the legal proceedings?	*Dusky v. United States* (1960)[18]; Lipsitt, Lelos & McGarry (1971); Roesch & Golding (1980); McGarry et al. (1973)
Sentencing	What are the prospects for the defendant's rehabilitation? What deterrent effects do certain sentences have?	*Estelle v. Smith* (1981)[19]; Wolfgang (1974)
Eyewitness identification	What are the factors that affect the accuracy of eyewitness identification? How is witness confidence related to witness accuracy?	*United States v. Amaral* (1973)[20]; *Law and Human Behavior* (1980, Vol. 4, No. 4); Loftus (1983); McCloskey & Egeth (1983); Yarmey (1979); Wells & Loftus (1983)
Trial procedure	What effects are associated with variations in pretrial and/or trial procedures?	*Hovey v. Superior Court of Alameda County* (1980)[21]; Haney (1984); Grisso (1981)
Civil commitment	Does a mentally ill person present an immediate danger or threat of danger to self or others which requires treatment no less restrictive than hospitalization?	*Lessard v. Schmidt* (1972)[22]; *Addington v. Texas* (1979)[23]; Monahan (1981); Robinson (1980)
Psychological damages in civil cases	What psychological consequences has an individual suffered as a result of tortuous conduct? How treatable are these consequences? To what extent are the psychological problems attributable to a preexisting condition?	*Hidden v. Mutual Life Insurance Co.* (1954)[24]; *Reese v. Naylor* (1969)[25]; Gaines (1956)
Psychological autopsies	In equivocal cases, do the personality and circumstances under which a person died indicate a likely mode of death?	*Biro v. Prudential Insurance Co.* (1970)[26]; Widman (1980); Selkin & Loya (1979)

(Continued)

[15] *M'Naghten's Case,* 8 Eng. Rep. 718 (1843).

[16] 214 F. 2d 862 (D.C. Cir. 1954).

[17] 471 F. 2d 969 (D.C. Cir. 1972).

[18] 362 U.S. 402 (1960).   [19] 451 U.S. 454 (1981).

[20] 488 F. 2d 1148 (9th Cir. 1973).

[21] 28 Cal. 3dI, 168 Cal. Rptr. 128, 616 P. 2d 1301

(1980).

[22] 349 F. Supp. 1078 (E.D. Wis. 1972).

[23] 441 U.S. 418 (1979).

[24] 217 F. 2d 818 (4th Cir. 1954).

[25] 222 So. 2d 487 (Fla. Dist. Ct. App. 1969).

[26] 110 N.J. Super 391, 265 Azd 830 (Super. Ct. App. Div. 1970).

Areas of Expert Testimony	Questions Addressed in the Testimony	Cases and References
Negligence and product liability	How do environmental factors and human perceptual abilities affect an individual's use of a product or ability to take certain precautions in its use?	*Seaboard Coastline R. R. v. Hill* (1971)[27]; Gass (1979, pp. 544–550); Levitt (1969)
Trademark litigation	Is a certain product name or trademark confusingly similar to a competitor's? Are advertising claims likely to mislead consumers?	*Anti-Monopoly, Inc. v. General Mills Fun Group, Inc.* (1982)[28]; Zeisel (1983)
Class action suits	What psychological evidence is there that effective treatment is being denied or that certain testing procedures are discriminatory against minorities in the schools or in the workplace?	*Larry P. v. Riles* (1979)[29]; *Griggs v. Duke Power Co.* (1971)[30]; *Wyatt v. Stickney* (1972)[31]; Bersoff (1981); Loh (1984, pp. 107–191)
Guardianship and conservatorship	Does an individual possess the necessary mental ability to make decisions concerning living conditions, financial matters, health, etc.?	Hafemeister & Sales (1984); Sales, Powell & Van Duizend (1982)
Child custody	What psychological factors will affect the best interests of the child whose custody is in dispute? What consequences are these factors likely to have on the family?	*Painter v. Bannister* (1966)[32]; Okpaku (1976); Litwack, Gerber & Fenster (1979–1980); Swenson, Nash & Roos (1984)
Adoption and termination of parental rights	What psychological factors affect the best interests of a child whose parents' disabilities may render them unfit to raise and care for the child?	*In re David B.* (1979)[33]; Shapiro (1984, pp. 108–118)
Professional malpractice	Did defendant's professional conduct fail to meet the standard of care owed to plaintiff?	*Hammer v. Rosen* (1960)[34]; Deleon & Borreliz (1978)
Social issues in litigation	What are the effects of pornography, televised aggression, spouse abuse, etc., on the behavior of a defendant who claims that his or her misconduct was due in part to one of these influences?	*Hawthorne v. Florida* (1982)[35]; Fiora-Gormally (1978); Walker (1984)

Source: Nietzel & Dillehay (1986). Copyright 1986 by Pergamon Press.

[27] 250 So. 2d 311, 314-315 (Fla. Dist. Ct. App. 1971)
[28] 684 F. 2d 1316 (9th Cir. 1982).
[29] 495 F. Supp. 926 (N.D. Ca. 1979).
[30] 401 U.S. 424 (1971).
[31] 344 F. Supp. 387 (M.D. Ala. 1972) *aff'd in part* 503 F. 2d 1305 (5th Cir. 1974).
[32] 258 Iowa 1390, 140 N.W. 2d 152 (1966).

[33] 5 Fam. L. Rep. 2531 (Cal. 5th Dist. Ct. of Appeals, March 28, 1979).

[34] 198 N.Y.S. 2d 803, 165 N.E. 2d 756 (New York Court of Appeals 1960).

[35] 408 So. 2d 801 (Fla. 1st DCA), Cert. Denied, 415 So. 2d 1361 (Fla. 1982).

4. The question of how best to train clinical psychologists will continue to be controversial in the next decade. Currently, there is considerable enthusiasm for preparing clinicians to work with specialty problems and/or groups such as the chronically mentally ill, children and youth, rural populations, substance abusers, and older patients. NIMH has concentrated much of its training grant money on these priorities (sometimes designated as "underserved groups"), and they will probably remain a focus for some clinical programs in the near future.

Along with more specialty training, there is bound to be continuing pressures and proposals for revamping the way clinical psychologists are trained. For example, Fox, Kovacs, and Graham (1985) suggested a set of twenty recommendations that, if adopted, would radically change clinical training. Among their most controversial proposals are the following: (1) training of professional psychologists should be conducted in "schools of psychology affiliated with accredited universities"; (2) the Psy.D. degree should be recognized as the degree for professional psychologists; (3) the doctoral curriculum should be generic rather than specialty oriented, with specialty training taking place in postdoctoral programs; and (4) a preprofessional psychology major should be created at the undergraduate level for students who want to become professional psychologists.

5. The growing emphasis on evaluation may be accompanied by abandonment of a "brand name" approach to psychotherapy. As research indicates the effectiveness of behavior-change techniques, regardless of their theoretical origins, clinicians will find little advantage in identifying themselves as "behaviorists," "gestaltists," or "analysts." Some form of general systems theory may come to replace the narrower, pathology-oriented theories that clinicians have embraced in the past, thereby leading to a further breakdown of psychotherapy "schools."

6. Psychologists will continue to estab-

lish the freedom of their profession. Organized psychology is likely to intensify its political efforts for freedom-of-choice legislation. Individual psychologists will need to keep abreast of the most modern clinical techniques so that they can continue to offer top-quality services. A vigorous program of continuing professional education would be an excellent mechanism for achieving this end.

Of course, none of these projections tells us what clinical psychology should strive for and what it should avoid. For this wisdom we will rely on the ideas of a clinical psychologist who has given the question a career's worth of serious attention:

Clinical psychology, after a long period spent as part of an academic discipline, is in the early stages of becoming a profession. It is going through the natural disturbances and difficulties which attend a growth process of this kind. However, if it selects its students carefully, for personality as well as intellect; if it trains thoroughly, in spirit as well as letter; if it trains broadly, recognizing that "specialists" . . . are not clinical psychologists; if it remains flexible about its training and encourges experimentation; if it does not become overwhelmed by immediate needs at the cost of important remoter goals; if it maintains its contact with its scientific background, remaining aware of the importance of theory as well as practice; if it remains modest in the face of the complexity of its problems, rather than becoming pretentious—in other words, if it finds good people and gives them good training—these disturbances and difficulties need not be of serious concern. Its future, both for itself as a profession and for society in the contribution it can make, is then assured. Fortunately, there are many reasons for believing that these are the prevailing aspirations in clinical psychology.

These words were written by David Shakow in 1948. They are as true today as they were then, and they provide sage advice for a profession whose accomplishments in the future should outshine the achievements of a distinguished past. We hope this book plays a role in moving some of you to join in the creation of that future.

appendix

Getting into Graduate School in Clinical Psychology

John P. Fiore, M.Ed.

Assistant Head for Undergraduate Affairs,
University of Illinois, Urbana-Champaign

As noted in Chapter 1, gaining admission to graduate school in clinical psychology is a competitive endeavor. Here are some questions and answers that are most relevant to the application enterprise.

GENERAL ISSUES

I Have Decided to Apply to Graduate School in Clinical Psychology. What Should I Do First?

In choosing graduate programs, you will want to make sure they provide the training and professional environment that will meet your needs. Therefore, you should clarify your personal goals, objectives, and plans. Are you most interested in research, balanced training in clinical practice and research, or primarily in clinical practice? Are you interested in doctoral-level or master's-level programs? Do you have an interest in a

specific client population? Do you have preferences related to types and/or locations of future employment? These are a few of the questions you should be asking yourself before the application process begins. You will not have definitive answers for all possible questions, but you will have some, and these will probably indicate what is most important to you in choosing a graduate program.

Should I Apply to a Master's Degree Program and Complete It Before I Apply to a Doctoral Program?

There are different routes one can take to earn the doctorate in clinical psychology. A number of graduate programs provide master's degree training only. Many graduates from these programs terminate their formal education at the M.A.; others apply to doctoral programs.

Some graduate schools have separate

training programs at the master's and doctoral levels and accept students for each. The master's program in these schools sometimes serves as a "feeder" to the doctoral program. However, each program is separate, so that the student who does not enter the doctoral program will have completed training similar to that offered at "master's only" schools.

Other programs are designed to prepare doctoral-level clinicians only. They may award the master's degree after a minimum number of credits and a master's thesis have been completed, but it is important to recognize that these departments accept applicants for the doctoral degree only.

If I Earn a Master's Degree, Are My Chances for Then Being Admitted to a Doctoral Program Better or Worse?

Generally, the possession of a master's degree has little impact on a student's application. Graduate schools are interested in the best candidates they can find. If your credentials are excellent, your chances for being admitted to a doctoral program are good. Some students who feel they need to improve their credentials may find master's degree work helpful in achieving that goal, but doctoral admission committees consider all academic work when making their decision. A mediocre undergraduate academic record is not disregarded because it has been supplemented with a master's degree and good graduate school grades, but these graduate credentials can improve a student's chances for being considered seriously.

If I Chose to Terminate My Training After Earning a Master's Degree, Will My Opportunities for Doing Clinical Work Be Limited?

Though there are many good clinicians whose highest academic degree is the master's, the doctorate is the standard of the profession. The following resolution was adopted by the American Psychological Association Council of Representatives.

The title "Professional Psychologist" has been used so widely and by persons with such a wide variety of training and experience that it does not provide the information the public deserves.

As a consequence, the APA takes the position and makes it a part of its policy that the use of the titles "Professional Psychologist," "School Psychologist," and "Industrial Psychologist" is reserved for those who have completed a doctoral training program in psychology in a university, college, or professional school of psychology that is APA or regionally accredited. In order to meet this standard, a transition period will be acknowledged for the use of the title "School Psychologist," so that ways may be sought to increase opportunities for doctoral training and to improve the level of the educational codes pertaining to the title.

The APA further takes the position and makes part of its policy that only those who have completed a doctoral training program in professional psychology in a university, college, or professional school of psychology that is APA or regionally accredited are qualified to independently provide unsupervised direct delivery of professional services including preventive, assessment, and therapeutic services. The exclusions mentioned above pertaining to school psychologists do not apply to the independent, unsupervised, direct delivery of professional services discussed in this paragraph.

Licensed or certified master's-level psychologists, having met earlier standards of the profession (i.e., were accorded grandmother/grandfather recognition) are to be regarded as comparably qualified through education, experience, examination, and the test of time, as are present and future doctoral psychologists, and shall be entitled under APA guidelines to include as part of their title the word "psychologist." (APA, 1984, p. x)

Another fact that needs to be considered is that all states employ some form of licensing or certification for psychologists (see Chapter 12). Though requirements vary from state to state, an earned doctorate is a prerequisite in most of them. Before you decide to prepare for clinical work by earning a master's degree, be certain your career expectations can be met with this degree.

Are All Doctoral Programs in Clinical Psychology Research-Oriented?

All university-based Ph.D. programs in clinical psychology provide training in research as well as in clinical functions, but there are differences in emphasis from one institution to another. It is worth your effort to learn of each program's emphasis when you are securing other information about the program. Programs that are strictly research-oriented make this fact clear in their information and refrain from using "clinical psychology" as a title (experimental psychopathology is a common substitute). Some graduate programs offer a Doctor of Psychology (Psy.D.) degree in addition to, or instead of, a traditional Ph.D. This degree puts the emphasis on clinical training while reducing the emphasis on research. These programs still require their students to acquire knowledge of research tools, but do not require students to do basic research. In other words, students still develop their knowledge of statistics and research methods but are not required to do a thesis or dissertation.

How Does One Identify "Good" Graduate Programs?

It is difficult to label graduate programs as "good" and "bad." The question to be answered is whether a specific program fits a particular student's needs. A "research" versus "clinical" emphasis has already been discussed and can be ascertained for a specific program by corresponding with current graduate students and faculty at the particular school. If you can identify graduates of particular programs, ask them for their evaluation. Other things to consider include the size of the department and the program, the student/faculty ratio, opportunities for a variety of practicum experiences, the size and location of the campus and the commu-

nity, the type and extent of department resources, and the particular philosophical school of thought which may be dominant in the program. Any of the above that is important to *you* should be considered when you attempt to identify "good" programs.

One final caution concerns generalizing the quality of the department to the program. There are some psychology departments considered to be the best by many psychologists. Since your interest is in clinical psychology, do not assume that the clinical program is one of the best because the department is considered one of the best. Identify what is the best for *you* and judge each program against *your* criteria.

What Does American Psychological Association (APA) Accreditation of a Clinical Psychology Graduate Program Mean?

APA accreditation means the program has met a minimum standard of quality (see Chapter 12). The APA publication *Graduate Study in Psychology and Associated Fields* explains that APA accreditation should be interpreted to mean:

1. The program is recognized and publicly labeled as a doctoral program in clinical, counseling, or school psychology (or combination thereof). It is located in and supported by an institution of higher education, which itself is accredited by one of six regional accrediting bodies also recognized by COPA.

2. The program voluntarily applied for accreditation and, in so doing, engaged in extensive self-study of its program objectives, educational and training practices, its resource support base, and its faculty, students, and graduates. The program also participated in a peer review of its operations by a site-visit team of distinguished professional colleagues.

3. The program was thoroughly evaluated by the APA Committee on Accreditation (comprised of professional and public members) and judged to be in sufficient compliance with the APA Criteria for Accreditation to warrant accreditation status. Those criteria against which a program is evaluated include institutional sup-

port; sensitivity to cultural and individual differences; training models and curricula; faculty; students; facilities; and practicum and internship training.

Accreditation, in summary, applies to educational institutions and programs, not to individuals. It does not guarantee jobs or licensure for individuals, though being a graduate of an accredited program may facilitate such achievement. It does speak to the manner and quality by which an educational institution or program conducts its business. It speaks to a sense of public trust, as well as professional quality. (APA, 1986, p. xiii)

Students should be aware that there may be excellent departments that have not applied for accreditation or that have not had a doctoral program in clinical psychology long enough to be eligible for approval.

APPLICATION PROCEDURES

How Do I Get Initial Information About Graduate Schools?

There are several sources of information; you should use *all* of them. Some of the best informants are psychology faculty, especially those who are clinical psychologists. Preparing for courses, doing research, and keeping current for clinical practice requires review of new ideas and research as well as participation at professional meetings and workshops. This exposure to the field helps faculty know about various schools, training and research staff, the nature and philosophies of different programs, recent changes in certain departments, and other pertinent information. Though it is not reasonable to expect the faculty to know about all or even most doctoral programs, they will be able to provide you with good information about many of them.

Professional journals and related publications are information sources that are often overlooked. An excellent way to find programs that meet your needs is to use these sources to identify faculty who are studying topics which interest you. A thorough search of the literature will highlight programs that have several faculty with whom you might like to study. Find out where they are teaching by consulting the APA membership directory (most psychology departments have a recent edition).

Some colleges or undergraduate departments have a special advising staff for their students. The advisors or counselors may or may not be faculty, but if part of their job is to help with graduate school applications, you can benefit from their experience with former students. Even if this source of information does not exist at your school, all department offices receive pamphlets, notices, and general information brochures from many graduate psychology programs in the United States and Canada. Use this information; it may answer some of your questions and inform you of new programs.

There are numerous books that list graduate schools and programs. The best of these for psychology is published by the American Psychological Association. It is called *Graduate Study in Psychology and Associated Fields*. This book is revised semi-annually and has over 500 pages of information, including application addresses, types of programs and degrees offered by each institution, size of faculty, financial aid information, tuition, degree requirements, admission requirements, average grades and entrance test scores for students admitted the previous year, comments about the program, and other valuable information. You may purchase a copy of this publication from the American Psychological Association, 1200 Seventeenth Street N.W., Washington, D.C. 20036. The cost of *Graduate Study in Psychology and Associated Fields* for 1986 was $18.50.

Finally, your library should have catalogs from most universities. Once you have identified clinical programs that interest you, look at the graduate catalog for the university to get some idea of general university structure and requirements. If course descriptions are listed, you may be able to identify a particular program's emphasis.

How Many Potential Programs in Clinical Psychology Should Be on My Initial List?

Your *initial* list should include as many programs as possible. The APA's *Graduate Study in Psychology and Associated Fields* lists almost every clinical psychology program in the United States and Canada. As you use the various sources of information mentioned above and decide about location and degree preferences, you will begin to eliminate programs from your initial list. Once you have eliminated as many programs as possible by using the information you have compiled, you should write to each remaining program to request descriptions. This will allow you to continue to reduce the list on the basis of new information.

When Should I Write to Graduate Programs for Information?

You should request information in August and September, approximately a year before the projected admission date (e.g., September 1987 for Fall 1988 admission). Requesting material earlier than this sometimes gets you old information or places you on a waiting list until material is available. If you make a request too late, the material may not arrive in time for you to make effective use of it. Remember, you may have questions which arise from your reading of the material and you may wish to correspond with some departments before a final decision is made about whether to apply to them. This all requires time—give yourself plenty!

When Writing for Application Information, What Should I Ask for and What Format Should I Use?

At minimum, you should ask for information about the clinical psychology program, appropriate department and graduate school application forms, a graduate

school program and course catalog, financial aid information, financial aid application forms, and a list of faculty and their research interests.

Your request for information need not be elaborate. A postcard or form letter addressed to the department's graduate admission committee can be used, but be sure it includes a request for all the information you will need.

When Should I Apply?

Department application deadlines vary, but most are from February 1 through 15. A few come as early as December, while others (mostly for master's degree programs) run as late as August. A rule of thumb is to use February 1 as an application deadline except for schools having earlier dates. Some schools which use later deadlines are often selecting students as applications are being processed. Therefore, it is to your advantage to submit your application early to these schools.

Submitting *very* early applications (September or October) is usually of no particular value since departments are not "tooled up" for the admission process. Also, required test scores (to be discussed later) are usually not available this early in the school year.

How Many Programs Should I Apply to?

It is difficult to identify a specific number of applications appropriate for all students. I am reminded of two cases: One student applied to six schools and was admitted to all of them, while another applied to twenty-seven and was admitted to one. The general rule is apply to as many programs as you can reasonably afford. The larger the number of applications, the better your chances of being accepted.

Once you have decided on a final list of schools, ask yourself what you will do if you are not accepted by any of them. Perhaps at this point you may want to add one or two "safety valve" programs to fall back on.

However, do not apply to programs that are really not acceptable to you. Such applications waste admission committee time, your time (and money), and may prevent a serious applicant from being admitted.

How Much Does Applying Cost?

Total testing costs can range from $15 to $60. Application fees usually vary from nothing to $25. Transcript costs (usually $2 each), additional test report fees, postage, and phone calls add up quickly. A total cost of $30 per application is about average.

QUALIFICATIONS AND CREDENTIALS

What Kinds of Courses and Experiences Will Help My Application?

Your undergraduate department will have designed a graduate preparatory major to meet your course needs. This will probably include a core program of introductory psychology, statistics, and experimental psychology (including a laboratory). These are the minimum requirements for most graduate programs, regardless of specialization area. In addition to these core courses and some breadth in psychology, Ph.D. programs often look for course work in mathematics, laboratory work in other sciences, and computer science courses. Remember, graduate programs are looking for the best students they can find, so a strong academic preparation is essential.

In addition to standard course work, independent research such as a bachelor's thesis and/or experience as an assistant to faculty who are involved in research is very helpful. This not only provides you with desired experience, but also allows faculty supervisors to observe your potential for scholarly endeavors and to include their evaluations and impressions in letters of recommendation.

Psychology departments will not expect you to enter their programs as a trained clinician, but they will look for evidence of experience in "helping relationships." Practica and relevant volunteer work will assist in establishing that your career decision is based in part on some firsthand knowledge of the field. Remember, impressions of what it is like to work in a field and actual working experiences are often very different. It is important that you know what you are getting into when you choose clinical psychology as a career.

What Grade Average Is Necessary in Order to Be Accepted?

Grade average requirements will vary across programs, degrees, and institutions. Some admissions committees will be concerned with a four-year average, while others will consider the last two years only. For clinical psychology doctoral programs, a 3.5 grade average (on a 4-point system) is generally considered *minimum*. At highly competitive schools a 3.7 grade average may be more common, but other criteria are also taken into consideration. It is not unusual for a department to select a student with a 3.5 grade average over a student with a 4.0 grade average when other admissions data (test scores, research experience, course selection, and the like) are more in line with the program's goals, requirements, and orientation.

Admission to master's degree programs is less competitive than for doctoral programs. Many master's programs have a minimum grade average requirement of B− (approximately 2.75), though the typical student admitted to such programs is likely to have a solid B (3.25) grade average.

What Testing Is Involved in Applying to Graduate School?

Most graduate schools use standardized tests to assist them in evaluating applicants. The most common are the Graduate Record Examination (GRE) and the Miller Analogies Test (MAT).

The GRE General Test is described in the 1985-86 *GRE Information Bulletin* as follows:

The GRE General Test measures certain developed verbal, quantitative, and analytical abilities that are important for academic achievement. In doing so, the test necessarily reflects the opportunities and efforts that have contributed to the development of those abilities.

As has been stated earlier, the General Test is only one of several means of evaluating likely success in graduate school. It is not intended to measure inherent intellectual capacity or intelligence. Neither is it intended to measure creativity, motivation, perseverance, or social worth. The test does, however, make it possible to compare students with different backgrounds. A GRE score of 500, for example, has the same meaning whether earned by a student at a small, private liberal arts college or by a student at a large public university.

Because several different forms (or editions) of the test are in active use, all students do not receive exactly the same test edition. However, all editions measure the same skills and meet the same specifications for content and difficulty. The scores from different editions are made comparable to one another by a statistical procedure known as equating. This process makes it possible to assure that all reported scores of a given value denote the same level of developed ability regardless of which edition of the test is taken.

Since students have wide-ranging backgrounds, interests, and skills, the *verbal sections* of the General Test use questions from diverse areas of experience. The areas tested range from the activities of daily life to broad categories of academic interest such as the sciences, social studies, and the humanities. Knowledge of high school level arithmetic, plane geometry, and algebra provides adequate preparation for the *quantitative sections* of the test. Questions in the *analytical sections* measure analytical skills developed in virtually all fields of study. No formal training in logic or methods of analysis is needed to do well in these sections. (ETS, 1985, p. 31)

The GRE Subject Test in Psychology is described in the 1985-86 information booklet as follows:

The questions in the Psychology Test are drawn from courses of study most commonly offered within the broadly defined field of psychology. Questions often require the student to identify psychologists associated with particular theories or conclusions and to recall information from psychology courses. In addition, some questions require analyzing relationships, applying principles, drawing conclusions from experimental data, and evaluating experiments.

The Psychology Test yields two subscores in addition to the total score. Although the test offers only two subscores, there are questions in three content categories:

1. Experimental or natural science oriented. About half the questions in this category are concerned with learning, cognition, and perception; the other half are concerned with ethology and comparative psychology, and sensation and physiology. These questions contribute to the experimental psychology subscore.

2. Social or social science oriented. These questions are about equally distributed among the fields of personality, clinical and abnormal, developmental, and social psychology. They contribute to the social psychology subscore.

3. General. This category includes historical and applied psychology, measurement, and statistics. The questions contribute to the total score, but are not included in a subscore. (ETS, 1985, p. 4)

The General Test is given in the morning on each testing date, while the Subject Test is given in the afternoon. Each test requires about three hours.

The GRE Information Bulletin includes all application material and is available at most colleges and universities. You may also receive a copy by writing to:

Graduate Record Examinations
Educational Testing Service
Princeton, New Jersey 08541

The basic fees for 1985-86 were $29 for the General Test and $29 for the Subject Test.

The Miller Analogies Test (MAT) consists of one hundred very difficult verbal analogy items. Though the MAT is not as widely used as the GRE, a substantial number of programs require MAT scores. As with the GRE, testing is often available on college and university campuses. Further information about the MAT and testing locations can be obtained by writing to:

Psychological Corporation
304 East 45th Street
New York, New York 10017

Should I Take Both the GRE General Test and the GRE Subject Test?

Since the General Test is almost always required, there is no choice but to take it. As for the Subject Test, your decision will be determined, in part, by your choice of schools. If you have decided on the graduate programs to which you will apply, the application information from these schools will indicate whether the Subject Test is required. If you have not decided on a specific list of schools, you had better take both the General Test and the Subject Test. If you wish to send only General Test results or only Subject Test results to a particular school, Educational Testing Service will honor your request.

When Should I Take the Graduate Record Exam?

Most students take the exam on the October test date in the fall of their senior year. The results of this test are usually in the mail to the student and to all schools designated by the student by the end of November.

There are six test dates scheduled each year. Educational Testing Service reports that it takes approximately six weeks to score tests and have the results in the mail. Therefore, the latest you can take the exam is on a scheduled date that is at least six weeks before the application deadline for a given institution. If February 1 is the deadline date, only October and December tests in the school year will meet the deadline.

When selecting test dates keep in mind that you are likely to be taking both the General Test and the Subject Test. Three hours of testing in the morning and three more hours in the afternoon can be tiring, so many students take the General Test on one test date and the Subject Test on another.

Another consideration in selecting test dates is whether you wish to use the results in making decisions about where to apply. If you choose test dates that are sufficiently early, you will be able to look over your scores, consult advisors, and review resource material. For example, the APA's *Graduate Study in Psychology and Associated Fields* lists average GRE scores for students admitted to specific schools. Students who apply to graduate programs without knowing their GRE scores are taking a chance. Scores at the 90th percentile permit application to a different set of schools than do scores at the 60th percentile. Being fully informed when you apply will save time and money, as well as increase your chances of being admitted to a clinical psychology program.

One test-scheduling strategy that has worked well for some students is to take the General Test in June, at the end of the junior year. The summer is then spent reviewing for the Subject Test in Psychology, which is taken in October of the senior year. This allows time for retaking tests if necessary and using the results for choosing schools.

Can I Study for the Tests?

There are several "how to prepare" books on the market. Generally, they provide a mathematics and vocabulary review, give tips on test taking, and provide sample GRE test items. The *GRE Information Bulletin* provides a sample GRE. Educational Testing Services sells practice material, including GRE General Tests and Subject Tests actually administered in the previous year. These sources can be helpful in familiarizing yourself with the types and forms of questions you are likely to encounter and can give you practice at pacing yourself during an examination.

One can review for the quantitative portion of the General Test, especially if you have been away from mathematics for a while. Brushing up on basic algebra and geometry will help you during the exam by reducing the time needed to recall how to solve particular problems. Students report that the quantitative portion of the test is not difficult, but that it is fast paced. Know your basic math "cold," so you can work quickly and accurately.

Some of the sources frequently used by students in preparing for the GRE Aptitude Test include:

BROWNSTEIN, S., AND M. WEINER, *Barron's How to Prepare for the Graduate Record Examination* (7th ed.). Woodbury, NY: Barron's Educational Series, 1985.

CROCETTI, GINO. *Graduate Record Examination General (Aptitude) Test.* New York: Arco, 1983.

JANA, PATRICIA O'DOWD. *Lovejoy's Preparation for the GRE.* New York: Monarch Press, 1984.

As for the Subject Test in psychology, remember that it covers all areas of psychology. Names, theories, and definitions are likely to be a part of the test, as are basic concepts. no one is expected to know every area, so if you have not been exposed to certain aspects of psychology, you will no doubt have trouble with some questions. You can prepare for the Subject Test in psychology by thoroughly reviewing a comprehensive text book in introductory psychology, such as:

GLEITMAN, H. *Psychology* (2nd ed.). New York: Norton & Co., 1986.

HILGARD, E. R., R. E. ATKINSON, AND R. L. ATKINSON, *Introduction to Psychology* (8th ed.). New York: Harcourt, Brace, Jovanovich, 1983.

ZIMBARDO, P. G. *Psychology and Life* (11th ed.). Glenview, IL.: Scott, Foresman, 1985.

Books covering history and systems in psychology will also be helpful in preparing for the exam. Some sources include:

CHAPLIN, J. P., AND T. S. KRAWIEC, *Systems and Theories of Psychology* (4th ed.). New York: Holt, Rinehart, Winston, 1979.

MARX, M. H., AND W. S. HILLIX, *Systems and Theories in Psychology* (3rd ed.). New York: McGraw-Hill, 1979.

Other preparation sources for the GRE Advanced Test in psychology include:

PALMER, E. L. *Barron's How to Prepare for the Graduate Record Examination—The Psychology Test.* New York: Barron's Educational Series, Inc., 1984.

RUDMAN, JACK. *Rudman's Questions and Answers on the Graduate Record Advanced Test in Psychology.* Syosset, NY: National Learning Corporation, 1985.

Preparation sources for the MAT include:

GRUBER, G. K., AND E. G. GRUBER, *Preparation for the Miller's Analogies Test.* New York: Monarch Press, 1976.

STEINBERG, R. J. *Barron's How to Prepare for the Miller's Analogies Test* (4th ed.). New York: Barron's Educational Series, Inc., 1986.

Will I Need Letters of Recommendation for Graduate School Application? If So, How Many and from Whom?

Three letters of recommendation are required by the majority of graduate programs in clinical psychology. At least two letters should be from psychology faculty who are familiar with your academic ability. If faculty from other disciplines can provide a better picture of your academic achievement and potential for graduate study, use them. The quality of the recommendation could be more important than whether the writer is a psychologist.

Letters from practicum or (relevant) job supervisors can also be helpful, since they help establish your success at working within the mental health field. Letters from "important people" such as senators, governors, and other political figures do not help your application. Generally, these say nothing more than "I've been asked to write . . ." and "Please give this student full consideration." Such letters are likely to leave the impression that the student feels incapable of making it on his or her own. Unless the writer is in a position to judge the candidate's potential as a graduate student or a clinician, such "prestige" letters should not be submitted.

What Should I Know About Asking for Letters of Recommendation?

First, ask permission before you use someone's name as a reference. Many faculty will want to talk with you about your academic and career objectives before agreeing to write a letter. Some will ask you to provide additional written information about yourself and may want to discuss this information with you. Be prepared to do this.

It is appropriate for you to provide faculty with information about yourself. Faculty with many students can easily forget individual students' work, when they took courses, and other details. Also, it is not unusual for faculty to know little about a student other than what has been observed in the classroom setting. General knowledge of the student's activities, accomplishments, and jobs can supplement classroom contacts in a way which enhances a reference letter.

Here is a list of information items you should provide faculty who are writing letters of reference for you:

1. Your full name.
2. Major, minor, curriculum, and specialization.
3. A computation of grade average in your major, in all college work, and in work since the end of the sophomore year.
4. A transcript of your college courses and grades.
5. A list of the psychology laboratory courses you have had.
6. A description of other research experiences, including comments on the full extent of your participation (include a copy of any major research papers).
7. A list of honor societies, clubs, and organizations to which you belong, along with com-

ments on your participation (be sure to include positions of responsibility you held).
8. A brief discussion of jobs you have held and volunteer work you have done. Some students carry heavy work loads while being enrolled as full-time students in order to pay for their education. This type of information should be included.
9. An outline of your personal and professional plans and goals.
10. Any other information which it might be appropriate for this person to know as she or he writes a letter of recommendation.

Be sure to ask for letters and provide appropriate recommendation materials early. Faculty often write letters for several students; give them plenty of time to prepare yours. To reduce the possibility of error and to speed the process:

1. Include a stamped, addressed envelope for each program for which a recommendation is being sent.
2. When forms are included, *your name* and other information which is not part of the formal recommendation should be *typed* in the appropriate space. *Do not hand blank forms to the recommender.*
3. Include a list of all the schools to which a recommendation is to be sent. Indicate which have forms to be completed and those that did not provide forms. This can later be used by the writer as a checklist against which actual references can be compared.

Will I Be Able to See My Recommendation?

Letters of reference are not confidential unless you waive your right to see them. You are encouraged to consider doing so since some readers feel that the recommendation is more likely to be a candid assessment of the student if the writer knows the student will not see the letter. If you are concerned about what the letter might include, ask the writer if he or she can write a letter *supporting* your application.

Are Personal Interviews Required?

When interviews are part of the admissions procedure, they are likely to come only after the admission committee has considerably narrowed the number of applicants. Interviews are usually held on the school's campus, but when a visit requires long-distance travel, a representative of the school may interview applicants at a location closer to their residences. Telephone interviews are sometimes used, but they are the exception rather than the rule. On the other hand, a student who has already been interviewed in person should be prepared for a follow-up telephone call. When final decisions are being made, the committee may want to ask some candidates a few more questions.

One bit of strategy used by one successful applicant might be considered. He kept information about the programs to which he had applied (e.g., who was on the faculty, particular emphases and strengths), along with notes about his interests and goals near his telephone. He felt that if he received a call, this preparation would reduce his anxiety about the conversation and help him organize his responses so that the emphasis would be appropriate for each institution. This also assured that he would include all the points he wanted to make so that he could avoid blaming himself later for not remembering to mention something important. He did receive a call and the strategy worked.

It is appropriate for an applicant to visit various schools and talk with department representatives and graduate students about their programs. These conversations can be of assistance in deciding whether to apply or whether to accept an offer of admission. It is *not* appropriate to show up unannounced and expect department representatives to be available. Make an appointment ahead of time by calling the director of clinical training and asking to meet with members of the clinical psychology program and with graduate students.

Be prepared to outline in brief the nature of your questions, and have a number of alternate dates in mind before you call.

Are My College Transcripts Required?

Most programs will ask for a transcript of your college work from each institution at which you have studied. Transfer work summarized on the transcript from the last school you attended is not usually accepted—separate transcripts are required. You should call the schools you have attended to find out about transcript charges. Once that has been determined, send a letter to the director of student records at each school, enclosing a list of institutions to which a copy of your transcript is to be sent. Include a check to cover the cost.

FINANCIAL AID

What Kind of Financial Aid Is Available for Graduate Study?

Financial aid comes in three forms: loans, grants, and work programs. The major sources of all financial aid are the universities themselves. This aid is, of course, limited to their own students. Other sources include guaranteed loan programs (many of which are government sponsored) and national awards which are competitive and have specific criteria for application. These are awarded directly to the student for use at the school of her or his choice. One example of this type of aid is the Danforth graduate fellowship, which provides support for four years. It is awarded to seniors who intend to obtain the highest degree in their fields and who have a serious interest in college teaching. Students applying to clinical programs with the intention of teaching in colleges or universities are eligible.

Since the availability of awards and loans changes regularly, you are encouraged to check for current information with the financial aid officer at your college or at the institution to which you are applying.

Since financial support is usually received through the program to which you are admitted, the aid information you will receive with your application material is very important—read it carefully!

Loan programs exist on most campuses as a way of assisting students to invest in their own future. They usually carry a low interest rate with payments beginning after the students leave graduate school.

Fellowships and scholarships are given on many campuses as outright grants to support and encourage very bright students with excellent potential. These are few in number and highly competitive in nature.

Assistantships come in two forms: research assistantships and teaching assistantships. Both are *jobs* in the university which require graduate students to assist faculty in research projects or in teaching responsibilities (e.g., as discussion leaders, laboratory instructors, or paper graders). Assistantships usually require ten to twenty hours of work each week.

Some programs have received grants from the federal government to provide *traineeships* in clinical psychology. As a result, there may be training grant funds available for a limited number of students at some institutions. Like fellowships, these are usually outright gifts, but do require that you carry a full academic load. They, too, are few in number, and competition for them is keen.

Not all types of aid are offered at all schools. Be sure you understand what is available at each school and at each level of graduate standing by carefully reading the financial aid information you receive.

Are There Assistantships Available from Departments Other Than the One to Which I Have Applied?

Assistantships of various types may be available on a campus. If you are accepted to a program with little or no financial aid, it is well worth your time to check on the availability of assistantships in other departments. For example, administrators of residence halls may hire graduate students to serve as hall counselors. Departments with large enrollments in undergraduate courses may have more teaching assistantships than graduate students in their programs and thus "import" assistants from related areas. Identify your skills and experiences and seek out jobs that fit them.

Do All Financial Aid Packages Involve About the Same Amount of Money?

Financial aid will vary from campus to campus and between departments on the same campus. For example, one school may give more money, but recipients are required to pay their own tuition. Others will give a smaller sum of money, but also pay tuition and fees. Some residence hall assistantships provide room and board only; others provide room, board, tuition, and fees. If the amount of financial aid is an important factor in your selection of a graduate program, be sure you know both the amount you will receive and the costs you will incur before you make a final decision to accept or reject an offer of admission.

Are Separate References Required When Applying for Financial Aid?

Sometimes, separate application deadlines and reference letters are involved for financial aid consideration. Usually the letters of reference, when required, are copies of those used by departments in the admission process. The reference letters are usually used to assess the student's academic potential, not financial need. Read your application material carefully to determine just what is required in order to apply for financial aid, and remember that *deadlines for financial aid applications are sometimes earlier than deadlines for applying to clinical psychology graduate programs.*

Graduate Admissions Committee
Department of Psychology
University of Illinois
Champaign, Illinois 61820

To Whom It May Concern:

    I have applied to your graduate program in clinical psychology. Since I am very interested in being accepted to your program, I would like to verify that my application file is complete. I have enclosed a checklist and a self-addressed, stamped envelope to assist you in providing me with that information. Thank you for your cooperation.

                          Sincerely,

                          Mary Smith

                          Mary Smith

Date:_____   (PLEASE CHECK APPROPRIATE LINES)

                                Received

Application for Admission
Application for Financial Aid   _____
GRE General Test Scores   _____
GRE Subject Test Scores   _____
Miller Analogies Test Score   _____
Recommendation letters from:
  Professor Abigail Jones   _____
  Professor Herbert Long   _____
  Mr. Ben Wright   _____
Transcripts from:
  City Junior College
  University of Colorado   _____

Are there other required materials which have not been received?

_____

_____

_____

    (PLEASE RETURN IN ENCLOSED STAMPED AND ADDRESSED ENVELOPE.)

FIGURE A-1. An example of a brief note and checklist to send to the admissions committee when applying to a graduate program in clinical psychology.

OTHER IMPORTANT QUESTIONS

Are There Any Last-Minute Things I Need to Do When Applying?

Once your applications are sent out, you are encouraged to check with each department to which you have applied for the purpose of assuring that your application is complete. Each year, some applications are not considered because the students were unaware that they were incomplete. Some departments notify students when letters of reference or GRE scores are missing, but many do not. To eliminate this potential problem, ask each department to verify that your application is complete. Be sure to enclose a stamped, self-addressed envelope for their response. The brief note and checklist shown in Figure A-1 provide examples of what might be sent.

When I Am Admitted to a Program, How Long Will I Have to Make a Decision About Whether to Accept?

Most offers are made with a specific deadline for accepting or rejecting them. For doctoral programs, this is usually April 15. This date was adopted by the APA Council of Graduate Schools to protect students from being pressured to make decisions before having full information about their alternatives. The council's statement reads as follows:

Acceptance of an offer of financial aid (such as graduate scholarship, fellowship, traineeship, or assistantship) for the next academic year by an actual or prospective graduate student completes an agreement which both student and graduate school expect to honor. In those instances in which the student accepts the offer before April 15 and subsequently desires to withdraw, the student may submit in writing a resignation of the appointment at any time through April 15. However, an acceptance given or left in force after April 15 commits the student not to accept another offer without first obtaining a written release from the institution to which a commitment has been made. Similarly, an offer by an institution after April 15 is conditional on presentation by the student of the written release from any previously accepted offer. It is further agreed by the institutions and organizations subscribing to the above Resolution that a copy of this Resolution should accompany every scholarship, fellowship, traineeship, and assistantship offer. (APA, 1986, p. xii)

However, the resolution was modified by the Counsel of Graduate Departments of Psychology to read:

An acceptance given or left in force after April 15 commits the student not to solicit or accept another offer. Offers made after April 15 must include the proviso that the offer is void if acceptance of a previous offer from a department accepting this resolution is in force on that date. These rules are binding on all persons acting on the behalf of the offering institution. (APA, 1986, p. xii)

If financial aid as described in this statement is not involved, the student is not under the same obligation. In such cases, however, courtesy dictates that you inform the department of your decision as soon as possible. This will be appreciated by the department and may provide space for another student. If you do not receive an acceptance letter in April, you may receive one later because space sometimes becomes available as students decline offers.

References

ABEL, G. G. (1976). Assessment of sexual deviation in the male. In M. Hersen & A. S. Bellack (Eds.), *Behavioral assessment: A practical handbook* (pp. 437–457). New York: Pergamon Press.

ABEL, G. G., BLANCHARD, E. B., BARLOW, D. H., & MAVISSAKALIAN, M. (1975). Identifying specific erotic cues in sexual deviations by audiotaped descriptions. *Journal of Applied Behavior Analysis, 8,* 247–260.

ABELS, B. S. & BRANDSMA, J. M. (1977). *Therapy for couples.* San Francisco: Jossey-Bass Publishers.

ABOOD, L. G. (1960). A chemical approach to the problem of mental illness. In D. D. Jackson (Ed.), *The etiology of schizophrenia* (pp. 91–119). New York: Basic Books.

ABRAMOWITZ, S. I., ABRAMOWITZ, C. V., JACKSON, C., & GOMES, B. (1973). The politics of clinical judgment: What nonliberal examiners infer about women who do not stifle themselves. *Journal of Consulting and Clinical Psychology, 41,* 385–391.

ACHENBACH, T. M. (1982). *Developmental psychopathology* (2nd ed.). New York: John Wiley.

ACHTERBERG-LAWLIS, J. (1982). The psychological dimensions of arthritis. *Journal of Consulting and Clinical Psychology, 50,* 984–992.

ACKERMAN, N. W. (1958). *The psychodynamics of family life.* New York: Basic Books.

ADAMS, H. E., DOSTER, J. A., & CALHOUN, K. S. (1977). A psychologically based system of response classification. In A. R. Ciminero, K. S. Calhoun, and H. E. Adams (Eds.), *Handbook of behavioral assessment* (pp. 47–78). New York: John Wiley.

ADAMS, K. M. (1980a). In search of Luria's battery: A false start. *Journal of Consulting and Clinical Psychology, 48,* 511–516.

ADAMS, K. M. (1980b). An end of innocence for behavioral neurology? Adams replies. *Journal of Consulting and Clinical Psychology, 48,* 522–524.

ADLER, A. (1963). *The practice and theory of individual psychology.* Paterson, NJ: Littlefield.

ADLER, A. (1964). *Problems of neurosis.* New York: Harper & Row.

AGRAS, W. S., KAZDIN, A. E., & WILSON, G. T. (1979). *Behavior therapy: Towards an applied clinical science.* San Francisco: W. H. Freeman & Company.

AGUILERA, D. C. & MESSICK, J. M. (1982). *Crisis intervention: Therapy and methodology,* (4th ed.). St. Louis: C. V. Mosby.

ALBEE, G. W. (1959). *Mental health manpower trends.* New York: Basic Books.

ALBEE, G. W. (1975). To thine ownself be true. Comments on "insurance reimbursement." *American Psychologist, 30,* 1156–1158.

ALBEE, G. W. (1977). Does including psychotherapy in health insurance represent a subsidy to the rich from the poor? *American Psychologist, 32,* 719–721.

ALBERT, M. S. (1981). Geriatric neuropsychology. *Journal of Consulting and Clinical Psychology, 49,* 835–850.

ALBERTI, R. E. & EMMONS, M. L. (1974). *Your perfect right: A guide to assertive behavior.* San Luis Obispo, CA: Impact Publishers.

ALEXANDER, F. M. (1937). *The medical value of psychoanalysis.* New York: W. W. Norton & Co.

ALEXANDER, F. M. (1956). *Psychoanalysis and psychotherapy.* New York: W. W. Norton & Co.

ALEXANDER, F. M. (1963). *Fundamentals of psychoanalysis.* New York: W. W. Norton & Co.

ALEXANDER, F. M. & FRENCH, T. M. (1946). *Psychoanalytic therapy.* New York: Ronald Press Co.

ALEXANDER, J. F. & PARSONS, B. V. (1973). Short-term behavioral intervention with delinquent families: Impact on family process and recidivism. *Journal of Abnormal Psychology, 81,* 219–225.

ALLEN, G. J. (1971). The effectiveness of study counseling and desensitization in alleviating test anxiety in college students. *Journal of Abnormal Psychology, 77,* 282–289.

ALLEN, G. J. & CONDON, T. J. (1982). Whither subliminal psychodynamic activation? A reply to Silverman. *Journal of Abnormal Psychology, 91,* 131–133.

ALLPORT, F. H. (1924). *Social psychology.* Cambridge, MA: Riverside Press.

ALLPORT, G. W. (1942). The use of personal documents in psychological science. *Social Science Research Council Bulletin* (No. 49).

ALLPORT, G. W. (1961). *Pattern and growth in personality.* New York: Holt, Rinehart & Winston.

ALLPORT, G. W., VERNON, C. E., & LINDZEY, G. (1970). *Study of values* (revised manual). Boston: Houghton-Mifflin.

ALPERT, M. (Ed.) (1985). *Controversies in schizophrenia: Changes and constancies.* New York: The Guilford Press.

AMERICAN MEDICAL ASSOCIATION (1954). Report of committee on mental health. *Journal of the American Medical Association, 156,* 72.

AMERICAN PSYCHIATRIC ASSOCIATION (1980). *Diagnostic and statistical manual of mental disorders* (3rd ed.). Washington, DC: American Psychiatric Association.

AMERICAN PSYCHOLOGICAL ASSOCIATION (1947). Recommended graduate training programs in clinical psychology. *American Psychologist, 2,* 539–558.

AMERICAN PSYCHOLOGICAL ASSOCIATION (1953). *Ethical standards of psychologists.* Washington, DC: American Psychological Association.

AMERICAN PSYCHOLOGICAL ASSOCIATION (1958). Committee on Relations with Psychiatry, Annual Report. *American Psychologist, 13,* 761–763.

AMERICAN PSYCHOLOGICAL ASSOCIATION (1959). Ethical standards of psychologists. *American Psychologist, 14,* 279–282.

AMERICAN PSYCHOLOGICAL ASSOCIATION (1963). Ethical standards of psychologists. *American Psychologist, 18,* 56–60.

AMERICAN PSYCHOLOGICAL ASSOCIATION (1967). *Casebook on ethical standards of psychologists.* Washington, DC: American Psychological Association.

AMERICAN PSYCHOLOGICAL ASSOCIATION (1977). *Standards for providers of psychological services* (Rev. ed.). Washington, DC: American Psychological Association.

AMERICAN PSYCHOLOGICAL ASSOCIATION (1978). Task Force on Continuing Education in National Health Insurance: Continuing evaluation and accountability controls for a national health insurance program. *American Psychologist, 33,* 305–313.

AMERICAN PSYCHOLOGICAL ASSOCIATION (1981a). Ethical principles of psychologists. *American Psychologist, 36,* 633–638.

AMERICAN PSYCHOLOGICAL ASSOCIATION (1981b). *Specialty guidelines for the delivery of services by clinical psychologists*. Washington, DC: American Psychological Association.

AMERICAN PSYCHOLOGICAL ASSOCIATION (1985). *Standards for educational and psychological testing*. Washington, DC: American Psychological Association.

AMERICAN PSYCHOLOGICAL ASSOCIATION (1986, March). 1985–86 faculty salary survey. *APA Monitor* (p. 37).

AMRINE, M. (1965). The 1965 congressional inquiry into testing: A commentary. *American Psychologist, 20*, 859–870.

AMUNDSON, M. E., HART, C. A., & HOLMES, T. H. (1986). *Manual for the schedule of recent experience*. Seattle: University of Washington Press.

ANASTASI, A. (1982). *Psychological testing* (5th ed.). New York: Collier Macmillan.

ANDERSON, K. O., BRADLEY, L. A., YOUNG, L. D., McDANIEL, L. K., & WISE, C. M. (1985). Rheumatoid arthritis: Review of psychological factors related to etiology. *Psychological Bulletin, 98*, 358–387.

ANDREWS, G. & HARVEY, R. (1981). Does psychotherapy benefit neurotic patients? A re-analysis of the Smith, Glass, and Miller data. *Archives of General Psychiatry, 38*, 1203–1208.

ARENA, J. G., BLANCHARD, E. B., ANDRASIK, F., & DUDEK, B. (1982). The Headache Symptom Questionnaire: Discriminant classificatory ability and headache syndromes suggested by a factor analysis. *Journal of Behavioral Assessment, 4*, 55–69.

ARKES, H. A. (1981). Impediments to accurate clinical judgment and possible ways to minimize their impact. *Journal of Consulting and Clinical Psychology, 49*, 323–330.

ARKOWITZ, H. (1981). Assessment of social skills. In M. Hersen & A. S. Bellack (Eds.), *Behavioral assessment: A practical handbook* (2nd ed.). (pp. 296–327). New York: Pergamon Press.

ARKOWITZ, H. & MESSER, S. B. (Eds.) (1984). *Psychoanalytic therapy and behavior therapy: Is integration possible?* New York: Plenum.

ARRINGTON, R. E. (1932). *Interrelations in the behavior of young children*. New York: Columbia University Press.

ASH, P. (1949). The reliability of psychiatric diagnosis. *Journal of Abnormal and Social Psychology, 44*, 272–276.

ASHER, J. (1975). First edition of national register due: 7000 psychologists to be included. *APA Monitor* (May, p. 1).

ASSOCIATION FOR THE ADVANCEMENT OF BEHAVIOR THERAPY (1977). Ethical issues for human services. *AABT Newsletter, 4*, 11.

ATKINSON, J. W. (1981). Studying personality in the context of an advanced motivational psychology. *American Psychologist, 36*, 117–128.

AULD, F., JR. & MURRAY, E. J. (1955). Content-analysis studies of psychotherapy. *Psychological Bulletin, 52*, 377–395.

AUERBACH, A. H. & JOHNSON, M. (1977). Research on the therapist's level of experience. In A. S. Gurman & A. M. Razin (Eds.), *Effective psychotherapy: A handbook of research* (pp. 84–102). New York: Pergamon Press.

AVERY-CLARK, C. A. & LAWS, D. R. (1984). Differential erection response patterns of sexual child abusers to stimuli describing activities with children. *Behavior Therapy, 15*, 71–83.

AYLLON, T. & AZRIN, N. H. (1965). The measurement and reinforcement of behavior of psychotics. *Journal of the Experimental Analysis of Behavior, 8*, 357–383.

BALES, R. F. (1950). *Interaction process analysis*. Cambridge, MA: Addison-Wesley.

BANDURA, A. (1969). *Principles of behavior modification*. New York: Holt, Rinehart and Winston.

BANDURA, A. (1977). Self-efficacy: Toward a unifying theory of behavioral change. *Psychological Review, 84*, 191–215.

BANDURA, A. (1978). The self system in reciprocal determinism. *American Psychologist, 33*, 344–358.

BANDURA, A. (1982). Self-efficacy mechanism in human agency. *American Psychologist, 37*, 122–147.

BANDURA, A. (1986). *Social foundations of thought and action: A social cognitive theory*. Englewood Cliffs, NJ: Prentice-Hall.

BANDURA, A., BLANCHARD, E. B., & RITTER, B. (1969). The relative efficacy of desensitization and modeling approaches for inducing behavioral, affective, and attitudinal changes. *Journal of Personality and Social Psychology, 13*, 173–199.

BANDURA, A., JEFFERY, R. W., & WRIGHT, C. L. (1974). Efficacy of participant modeling as a function of response induction aids. *Journal of Abnormal Psychology, 83*, 56–64.

BANDURA, A., Ross, D., & Ross, S. A. (1963). Imitation of film-mediated aggressive models.

Journal of Abnormal and Social Psychology, 66, 3–11.

BANTA, H. D. & SAXE, L. (1983). Reimbursement for psychotherapy: Linking efficacy research and public policymaking. *American Psychologist, 38,* 918–923.

BARKER, R. G., DEMBO, T., & LEWIN, K. (1941). Frustration and regression: An experiment with young children. *University of Iowa Student Child Welfare, 18,* No. 1.

BARKER, R. G., SCHOGGEN, M. F., & BARKER, L. S. (1955). Hemerography of Mary Ennis. In A. Burton & R. E. Harris (Eds.), *Clinical studies of personality* (pp. 768–808). New York: Harper & Row.

BARKER, R. G. & WRIGHT, H. F. (1951). *One boy's day.* New York: Harper.

BARKER, R. G. & WRIGHT, H. F. (1955). *Midwest and its children: The psychological ecology of an American town.* New York: Row, Peterson.

BARLOW, D. H. (1980). Behavior therapy: The next decade. *Behavior Therapy, 11,* 315–328.

BARLOW, D. H. (1981). *Behavioral assessment of adult disorders.* New York: Guilford Press.

BARLOW, D. H., HAYES, S. C., & NELSON, R. O. (1983). *The scientist-practitioner: Research and accountability in clinical and educational settings.* New York: Pergamon Press.

BARLOW, D. H. & HERSEN, M. (1984). *Single-case experimental designs: Strategies for studying behavior* (2nd ed.). New York: Pergamon Press.

BARLOW, D. H., O'BRIEN, G. T., & LAST, C. G. (1984). Couples treatment of agoraphobia. *Behavior Therapy, 15,* 41–58.

BARLOW, D. H. & WADDELL, M. T. (1985). Agoraphobia. In D. H. Barlow (Ed.), *Clinical handbook of psychological disorders* (pp. 1–68). New York: Guilford Press.

BARLOW, D. H. & WOLFE, B. (1981). Behavioral approaches to anxiety disorders: A report on the NIMH-SUNY, Albany, research conference. *Journal of Consulting and Clinical Psychology, 49,* 448–454.

BARTHELL, C. N. & HOLMES, D. S. (1968). High school yearbooks: A nonreactive measure of social isolation in graduates who later became schizophrenic. *Journal of Abnormal Psychology, 73,* 313–316.

BARTLETT, C. J. & GREEN, C. G. (1966). Clinical prediction: Does one sometimes know too much? *Journal of Counseling Psychology, 13,* 267–270.

BARTON, A. (1974). *Three worlds of therapy: An existential-phenomenological study of the therapies of Freud, Jung, and Rogers.* Palo Alto, CA: National Press Books.

BATESON, C., JACKSON, D. D., HALEY, J., & WEAKLAND, J. H. (1956). Toward a theory of schizophrenia. *Behavioral Science, 1,* 251–264.

BAUM, C. G., FOREHAND, R., & ZEIGOB, L. E. (1979). A review of observer reactivity in adult-child interactions. *Journal of Behavioral Assessment, 1,* 167–178.

BAYLEY, N. (1965). Comparisons of mental and motor test scores for ages 1–15 months by sex, birth order, race, geographic location, and education of parents. *Child Development, 36,* 379–411.

BECK, A. T., WARD, C. H., MENDELSON, M., MOCK, J., & ERBAUGH, J. (1961). An inventory for measuring depression. *Archives of General Psychiatry, 4,* 561–571.

BECK, J. G., BARLOW, D. H., & SAKHEIM, D. K. (1983). The effects of attentional focus and partner arousal on sexual responding in functional and dysfunctional men. *Behaviour Research and Therapy, 21,* 1–8.

BECKER, M. H. & MAIMAN, L. A. (1975). Sociobehavioral determinants of compliance with health and medical care recommendations. *Medical Care, 13,* 10–24.

BEDNAR, R. L. & KAUL, T. J. (1978). Experiential group research: Current perspectives. In S. L. Garfield & A. E. Bergin (Eds.), *Handbook of psychotherapy and behavior change: An empirical analysis* (2nd ed.) (pp. 769–815). New York: John Wiley.

BEGELMAN, C. A. (1976). Behavioral classification. In M. Hersen & A. S. Bellack (Eds.), *Behavioral assessment: A practical handbook.* New York: Pergamon Press.

BEIDEL, D. C. & TURNER, S. M. (1986). A critique of the theoretical base of cognitive-behavioral theories and therapy. *Clinical Psychology Review, 6,* 177–197.

BEIDEL, D. C., TURNER, S. M., & DANCU, C. V. (1985). Physiological, cognitive, and behavioral aspects of social anxiety. *Behaviour Research and Therapy, 23,* 109–118.

BELLACK, A. S. (1983). Recurrent problems in the behavioral assessment of social skill. *Behaviour Research and Therapy, 21,* 29–42.

BELLACK, A. S. (1984). *Schizophrenia: Treatment, management, and rehabilitation.* Orlando, FL: Grune & Stratton.

BELLACK, A. S., HERSEN, M., & HIMMELHOCH, J. M. (1983). A comparison of social skills training, pharmacotherapy and psychotherapy for depression. *Behaviour Research and Therapy, 21,* 101–107.

BELLAK, L. (1986). *The thematic apperception test, the children's apperception test, and the senior apperception technique in clinical use* (4th ed.). New York: Grune & Stratton.

BENDER, L. A. (1938). A visual motor Gestalt test and its clinical use. *American Orthopsychiatric Association Research Monograph, No. 3.*

BENNETT, C. C. (1965). Community psychology: Impressions of the Boston conference on the education of psychologists for community mental health. *American Psychologist, 20,* 832–835.

BENNEY, M., RIESMAN, D., & STAR, S. A. (1956). Age and sex in the interview. *American Journal of Sociology, 62,* 143–152.

BENTON, A. L. (1974). *Revised visual retention test: Clinical and experimental applications* (4th ed.). New York: Psychological Corporation.

BENTON, A. L., HAMSHER, K., VARNEY, N. R., & SPREEN, O. (1983). *Contributions to neuropsychological assessment: A clinical manual.* New York: Oxford University Press.

BERG, I. A. (1955). Response bias and personality: The deviation hypothesis. *Journal of Psychology, 40,* 61–71.

BERGIN, A. E. (1971). The evaluation of therapeutic outcomes. In A. E. Bergin & S. L. Garfield (Eds.), *Handbook of psychotherapy and behavior change: An empirical analysis.* New York: John Wiley.

BERGIN, A. E. & LAMBERT, M. J. (1978). The evaluation of therapeutic outcomes. In S. L. Garfield & A. E. Bergin (Eds.), *Handbook of psychotherapy and behavior change: An empirical analysis* (2nd ed.). New York: John Wiley.

BERMAN, J. S. & NORTON, N. C. (1985). Does professional training make a therapist more effective? *Psychological Bulletin, 98,* 401–406.

BERNARDONI, L. C. (1964). A culture fair intelligence test for the ugh, no, and oo-la-la cultures. *Personnel and Guidance Journal, 42,* 554–557.

BERNSTEIN, D. A. (1973). Behavioral fear assessment: Anxiety or artifact? In H. Adams & P. Unikel (Eds.), *Issues and trends in behavior therapy* (pp. 225–267). Springfield, IL: Chas. C Thomas.

BERNSTEIN, D. A. & BORKOVEC, T. D. (1973). *Progressive relaxation training.* Champaign, IL: Research Press.

BERNSTEIN, D. A. & NIETZEL, M. T. (1973). Procedural variation in behavioral avoidance tests. *Journal of Consulting and Clinical Psychology, 41,* 165–174.

BERNSTEIN, D. A. & NIETZEL, M. T. (1977). Demand characteristics in behavior modification: A natural history of a "nuisance." In M. Hersen, R. M. Eisler, & P. M. Miller (Eds.), *Progress in behavior modification* (Vol. 4, pp. 119–162). New York: Academic Press.

BERNSTEIN, D. A. & PAUL, G. L. (1971). Some comments on therapy analogue research with small animal "phobias." *Journal of Behavior Therapy and Experimental Psychiatry, 2,* 225–237.

BERNSTEIN, L. (1956). The examiner as an inhibiting factor in clinical testing. *Journal of Consulting Psychology, 20,* 287–290.

BERNSTEIN, L., BERNSTEIN, R. S., & DANA, R. H. (1974). *Interviewing: A guide for health professionals* (2nd ed.). New York: Appleton-Century-Crofts.

BERSOFF, D. N. (1973). Silk purses into sow's ears: The decline of psychological testing and a suggestion for its redemption. *American Psychologist, 28,* 892–899.

BERSOFF, D. N. (1981). Testing and the law. *American Psychologist, 36,* 1047–1056.

BERSOFF, D. N. (1982). The legal regulation of school psychology. In C. R. Reynolds & T. B. Gutkin (Eds.), *The handbook of school psychology.* New York: John Wiley.

BERWICK, P. & MORRIS, L. A. (1974). Token economies: Are they doomed? *Professional Psychology, 5,* 434–439.

BERZINS, J. I. (1977). Therapist-patient matching. In A. S. Gurman & A. M. Razin (Eds.), *Effective psychotherapy: A handbook of research.* New York: Pergamon Press.

BERZINS, J. I., WELLING, M. A., & WETTER, R. E. (1978). A new measure of psychological androgyny based on The Personality Research Form. *Journal of Consulting and Clinical Psychology, 46,* 126–138.

BIERI, J., ATKINS, A. L., BRIAR, S., LEAMAN, R. L., MILLER, H., & TRIPOLDI, T. (1966). *Clinical and social judgment: The discrimination of behavioral information.* New York: John Wiley.

BIJOU, S. W., PETERSON, R. F., & AULT, M. H. (1968). A method to integrate descriptive and experimental field studies at the level of data and empirical concepts. *Journal of Applied Behavior Analysis, 1,* 175–191.

BINET, A. & SIMON, T. (1905). Application des methodes nouvelles au diagnostic du niveau intellectuel chez des enfants normaux et anormaux d'hospice et d'ecole primaire. *L'Annee Psychologique, 11,* 245–336.

BINGHAM, W. V. D., MOORE, B. V., & GUSTAD, J. W. (1959). *How to interview.* New York: Harper & Row.

BINNER, P. R. (1986). DRGs and the administration of mental health services. *American Psychologist, 41,* 64–69.

BIRNBAUMER, N. (1977). Biofeedback training: A critical review of its clinical applications and some possible future directions. *European Journal of Behavioral Analysis and Modification, 1,* 235–251.

BLAKE, B. G. (1965). The application of behaviour therapy to the treatment of alcoholism. *Behaviour Research and Therapy, 3,* 75–85.

BLANCHARD, E. B. & ANDRASIK, F. (1985). *Management of chronic headaches: A psychological approach.* New York: Pergamon Press.

BLANCHARD, E. B. & EPSTEIN, L. H. (1978). *A biofeedback primer.* Reading, MA: Addison-Wesley.

BLANCK, G. (1976). Psychoanalytic technique. In B. B. Wolman (Ed.), *The therapist's handbook: Treatment methods of mental disorders* (pp. 61–86). New York: Van Nostrand Reinhold.

BLATT, S. J. & LERNER, H. (1983). Psychodynamic perspectives on personality theory. In M. Hersen, A. E. Kazdin, & A. S. Bellack (Eds.), *The clinical psychology handbook* (pp. 87–106). New York: Pergamon Press.

BLAU, T. H. (1984). *The psychologist as expert witness.* New York: John Wiley.

BLECHMAN, E. A. & BROWNELL, K. D. (Eds.) (1986). *Behavioral medicine for women.* New York: Pergamon Press.

BLEULER, M. (1978). *The schizophrenic disorders: Long-term patient and family studies.* New Haven: Yale University Press (translated by Siegfried M. Clemens).

BLOOM, B. L. (1973). The domain of community psychology. *American Journal of Community Psychology, 1,* 8–11.

BLOUNT, R. L., BAER, R. A., & COLLINS, F. L. (1984). Improving visual acuity in a myopic child: Assessing compliance and effectiveness. *Behaviour Research and Therapy, 22,* 53–58.

BOCZKOWSKI, J. A., ZEICHNER, A., & DeSANTO, N. (1985). Neuroleptic compliance among chronic schizophrenic outpatients: An intervention outcome report. *Journal of Consulting and Clinical Psychology, 53,* 666–671.

BOLGAR, H. (1965). The case study method. In B. B. Wolman (Ed.), *Handbook of clinical psychology* (pp. 28–39). New York: McGraw-Hill.

BOLL, T. J. (1981). The Halstead-Reitan Neuropsychology Battery. In S. B. Filskov & T. J. Boll (Eds.), *Handbook of clinical neuropsychology* (pp. 577–607). New York: John Wiley.

BONIME, W. (1962). *The clinical use of dreams.* New York: Basic Books.

BORDIN, E. S. (1955). Ambiguity as a therapeutic variable. *Journal of Consulting Psychology, 19,* 9–15.

BORGATTA, E. F. (1955). Analysis of social interaction: Actual, role playing, and projective. *Journal of Abnormal and Social Psychology, 51,* 394–405.

BORING, E. G. (1950). *A history of experimental psychology* (2nd ed.). New York: Appleton-Century-Crofts.

BORKOVEC, T. D. & O'BRIEN, G. T. (1976). Methodological and target behavior issues in analogue therapy outcome research. In M. Hersen, R. M. Eisler, & P. M. Miller (Eds.), *Progress in behavior modification* (pp. 133–172). New York: Academic Press.

BORKOVEC, T. D., STONE, N. M., O'BRIEN, G. T., & KALOUPEK, D. G. (1974). Evaluation of a clinically relevant target behavior for analogue outcome research. *Behavior Therapy, 5,* 504–514.

BORNSTEIN, P. H. & KAZDIN, A. E. (Eds.) (1985). *Handbook of clinical behavior therapy with children.* Homewood, IL: Dorsey Press.

BOROFSKY, G. L. (1974). Issues in the diagnosis and classification of personality functioning. In A. I. Rabin (Ed.), *Clinical psychology: Issues of the seventies* (pp. 24–48). East Lansing, MI: Michigan State University Press.

BOUDIN, H. (1972). Contingency contracting as a therapeutic tool in the deceleration of amphetamine use. *Behavior Therapy, 3,* 604–608.

BOURNE, L. E. & EKSTRAND, B. R. (1976). *Psychology: Its principles and meanings* (2nd ed.). New York: Holt, Rinehart & Winston.

BRAGINSKY, B. M., BRAGINSKY, D. D., & RING, K. (1969). *Methods of madness: The mental hospital as a last resort.* New York: Holt, Rinehart & Winston.

BRAGINSKY, B. M., GROSSE, M., & RING, K. (1966). Controlling outcomes through impression management: An experimental study of the manipulative tactics of mental patients. *Journal of Consulting Psychology, 30,* 295–300.

BREGER, L. & McGAUGH, J. L. (1965). Critique and reformulation of "learning theory" approaches to psychotherapy and neurosis. *Psychological Bulletin, 63,* 338–358.

BRENNER, C. (1974). *An elementary textbook of psychoanalysis.* New York: Anchor Books.

BRESLOW, L. (1979). A positive strategy for the nation's health. *Journal of the American Medical Association, 242,* 2093–2094.

BRILL, A. A. (1938). *The basic writings of Sigmund Freud.* New York: Random House.

BRITTAIN, H. L. (1907). A study in imagination. *Pedagogical Seminary and Journal of Genetic Psychology, 14,* 137–207.

BROTEMARKLE, B. A. (1947). Fifty years of clinical psychology: Clinical psychology 1896–1946. *Journal of Consulting Psychology, 11,* 1–4.

BROVERMAN, I. K., BROVERMAN, D. M., CLARKSON, F. E., ROSENKRANTZ, P. S., & VOGEL, S. R. (1970). Sex role stereotypes and clinical judgments of mental health. *Journal of Consulting and Clinical Psychology, 34,* 1–7.

BROWN, E. (1972). Assessment from a humanistic perspective. *Psychotherapy: Theory, Research, and Practice, 9,* 103–106.

BROWN, G. W. & HARRIS, T. (1978). *The social origins of depression.* New York: Free Press.

BROWN, R. & HERRNSTEIN, R. J. (1975). *Psychology.* Boston: Little, Brown.

BROWNELL, K. D. (1981). Assessment of eating disorders. In D. H. Barlow (Ed.), *Behavioral assessment of adult disorders.* New York: Guilford Press.

BROWNELL, K. D. (1982). Obesity: Understanding and treating a serious, prevalent, and refractory disorder. *Journal of Consulting and Clinical Psychology, 50,* 820–840.

BROWNELL, K. D. & FOREYT, J. P. (1985). Obesity. In D. H. Barlow (Ed.), *Clinical handbook of psychological disorders* (pp. 299–343). New York: Guilford Press.

BRUININK, S. A. & SCHROEDER, H. E. (1979). Verbal therapeutic behavior of expert psychoanalytically oriented, Gestalt, & behavior therapists. *Journal of Consulting and Clinical Psychology, 47,* 567–574.

BRUNSWICK, E. (1947). *Systematic and representative design of psychological experiments with results in physical and social perception.* Berkeley: University of California Press.

BRY, B. H. (1982). Reducing the incidence of adolescent problems through preventive intervention: One- and five-year follow-up. *American Journal of Community Psychology, 10,* 265–276.

BRY, B. H. & GEORGE, F. E. (1980). The preventive effects of early intervention on the attendance and grades of urban adolescents. *Professional Psychology, 11,* 252–260.

BRYNTWICK, S. & SOLYOM, L. (1973). A brief treatment of elevator phobia. *Journal of Behavior Therapy and Experimental Psychiatry, 4,* 355–356.

BUCK, J. N. (1948). The H-T-P technique: A qualitative and quantitative scoring manual. *Journal of Clinical Psychology, 4,* 319–396.

BUGENTAL, J. F. T. (1978). *Psychotherapy and process: The fundamentals of an existential-humanistic approach.* Reading, MA: Addison-Wesley.

BUGENTAL, J. F. T. & ZELEN, S. (1950). Investigations into the "self-concept." I. The W-A-Y technique. *Journal of Personality, 18,* 483–498.

BURCHARD, J. D. (1967). Systematic socialization: A programmed environment for the habilitation of antisocial retardates. *Psychological Record, 17,* 461–476.

BURGESS, A. W. & HOLMSTROM, L. L. (1979). Adaptive strategies and recovery from rape. *American Journal of Psychiatry, 131,* 981–986.

BURISCH, M. (1984). Approaches to personality inventory construction: A comparison of merits. *American Psychologist, 39,* 214–227.

BUROS, O. K. (Ed.) (1938). *The 1940 mental measurements yearbook.* Highland Park, NJ: Gryphon Press.

BUSS, D. M. & CRAIK, K. H. (1983). The act frequency approach to personality. *Psychological Review, 90,* 105–126.

BUTCHER, J. N. (1978). Computerized MMPI scoring and interpreting services. In O. K. Buros (Ed.), *Eighth mental measurements yearbook* (Vol. 1, pp. 942–945). Highland Park, NJ: Gryphon Press.

BUTCHER, J. N. & KELLER, L. S. (1984). Objective personality assessment. In G. Goldstein & M. Hersen (Eds.), *Handbook of psychological assessment* (pp. 307–331). New York: Pergamon Press.

BUTCHER, J. N., KELLER, L. S., & BACON, S. F. (1985). Current developments and future directions in computerized personality assessment. *Journal of Consulting and Clinical Psychology, 53,* 803–815.

BUTCHER, J. N. & KOSS, M. P. (1978). Research on brief and crisis-oriented psychotherapies. In S. L. Garfield & A. E. Bergin (Eds.), *Handbook of psychotherapy and behavior change: An empirical analysis* (2nd ed.) (pp. 725–767). New York: John Wiley.

CAMPBELL, D. P. & HANSEN, J. C. (1981). *Manual for the SVIB-SCII* (3rd ed.). Palo Alto, CA: Stanford University Press.

CAMPBELL, D. T. & FISKE, D. W. (1959). Convergent and discriminant validation by the multitrait-multimethod matrix. *Psychological Bulletin, 56,* 81–105.

CAPLAN, G. (1961). *An approach to community mental health.* New York: Grune & Stratton.

CAPLAN, G. (1964). *Principles of preventive psychiatry.* New York: Basic Books.

CAPLAN, G. (1970). *The theory and practice of mental health consultation.* New York: Basic Books.

CAPLAN, G. (1974). *Support systems and community mental health.* New York: Behavioral Publications.

CARLSON, H. S. (1978). The AASPB Story: The beginnings and first 16 years of the American Association of State Psychology Boards, 1961–1977. *American Psychologist, 33,* 486–495.

CARTWRIGHT, R. A. (1966). A comparison of the response to psychoanalytic and client-centered therapy. In L. A. Gottschalk & A. H. Auerbach (Eds.), *Methods of research in psychotherapy* (pp. 517–529). New York: Appleton-Century-Crofts.

CATTELL, R. B. & EBER, H. W. (1962). *Manual for forms A and B of the Sixteen Personality Factor Questionnaire.* Champaign, IL: Institute for Personality and Ability Testing.

CAUTELA, J. R. (1966). Treatment of compulsive behavior by covert sensitization. *Psychological Record, 86,* 33–41.

CAUTELA, J. R. (1977). *Behavior analysis forms for clinical intervention.* Champaign, IL: Research Press.

CAUTELA, J. R. & KASTENBAUM, R. A. (1967). A reinforcement survey schedule for use in therapy, training, and research. *Psychological Reports, 20,* 1115–1130.

CAUTELA, J. R. & ROSENSTIEL, A. K. (1975). Use of covert sensitization in treatment of drug abuse. *The International Journal of the Addictions, 10,* 277–303.

CHAMBLESS, D. & GOLDSTEIN, A. (1980). The treatment of agoraphobia. In A. Goldstein & E. B. Foa (Eds.), *Handbook of behavioral interventions: A clinical guide* (pp. 322–414). New York: John Wiley.

CHAPMAN, L. J. & CHAPMAN, J. P. (1967). The genesis of popular but erroneous psychodiagnostic observations. *Journal of Abnormal Psychology, 72,* 193–204.

CHELUNE, G. J. & EDWARDS, P. (1981). Early brain lesions: Ontogenetic-environmental considerations. *Journal of Consulting and Clinical Psychology, 49,* 777–790.

CHESS, S., THOMAS, A., & BIRCH, H. G. (1966). Distortions in developmental reporting made by parents of behaviorally disturbed children. *Journal of the American Academy of Child Psychiatry, 5,* 226–231.

CHINSKY, J. M. & RAPPAPORT, J. (1970). Brief critique of meaning and reliability of "accurate empathy" ratings. *Psychological Bulletin, 73,* 379–382.

CHUN, KI-TAEK, COBB, S., & FRENCH, J. R. R., JR. (1975). *Measures for psychological assessment: A guide to 3000 original sources and their applications.* Ann Arbor, MI: Institute of Social Research.

CIMINERO, A. R., CALHOUN, K. S., & ADAMS, H. E. (1986). *Handbook of behavioral assessment* (2nd ed.). New York: John Wiley.

CLARK, R. W. (1980). *Freud: The man and the cause.* New York: Random House.

CLINE, V. B. & RICHARDS, J. M., JR. (1961). The generality of accuracy of interpersonal perception. *Journal of Abnormal and Social Psychology, 62,* 446–449.

COATES, T. J., KILLEN, J. D., GEORGE, J., MAR-CHINI, E., SILVERMAN, S., & THORESEN, C. (1982). Estimating sleep parameters: A multi-trait-multimethod analysis. *Journal of Consulting and Clinical Psychology, 50*, 345–352.

COBB, S. (1976). Social support as a moderator of life stress. *Psychosomatic Medicine, 38*, 300–314.

COHEN, F. & LAZARUS, R. S. (1973). Active coping processes, coping dispositions, and recovery from surgery. *Psychosomatic Medicine, 35*, 375–389.

COHEN, H. L. (1968). Educational therapy: The design of learning environments. *Research in Psychotherapy, 3*, 21–58.

COHEN, L. H., SARGENT, M. M., & SECHREST, L. B. (1986). Use of psychotherapy research by professional psychologists. *American Psychologist, 41*, 198–206.

COHEN, S. & WILLS, T. A. (1985). Stress, social support, and the buffering hypothesis. *Psychological Bulletin, 98*, 310–357.

COLE, N. S. (1981). Bias in testing. *American Psychologist, 36*, 1067–1077.

COLLINS, F. L. & GILL, K. M. (1983). Behavioral approaches to visual disorders. In S. Rachman (Ed.), *Contributions to medical psychology* (Vol. 3). New York: Pergamon Press.

COLLINS, R. L., PARKS, G. A., & MARLATT, G. A. (1985). Social determinants of alcohol consumption: The effects of social interactions and model status on the self-administration of alcohol. *Journal of Consulting and Clinical Psychology, 53*, 189–200.

COLMEN, J. G., KAPLAN, S. J., & BOULGER, J. R. (1964, August). *Selection and selecting research in the Peace Corps.* (Peace Corps Research Note No. 7).

CONE, J. D. (1981). Psychometric considerations. In M. Hersen & A. S. Bellack (Eds.), *Behavioral assessment: A practical handbook* (2nd ed.) (pp. 38–68). New York: Pergamon Press.

CONE, J. D. & FOSTER, S. L. (1982). Direct observation in clinical psychology. In P. C. Kendall & J. N. Butcher (Eds.), *Handbook of research methods in clinical psychology* (pp. 311–354). New York: John Wiley.

CONE, J. D. & HAWKINS, R. P. (Eds.) (1977). *Behavioral assessment: New directions in clinical psychology.* New York: Bruner-Mazel.

COOK, T. D. & CAMPBELL, D. T. (1979). *Quasi-experimentation: Design and analysis issues for field settings.* Chicago: Rand-McNally.

CORMIER, W. H. & CORMIER, L. S. (1979). *Interviewing strategies for helpers: A guide to assessment, treatment, and evaluation.* Monterey, CA: Brooks/Cole Publishing Co.

COSTELLO, A. J., EDELBROCK, C., KALAS, R., KESSLER, M. D., & KLARIC, S. (1982). *The NIMH Diagnostic Interview Schedule for Children (DISC).* Pittsburgh: Author.

COVNER, B. J. (1942). Studies in phonographic recordings. I. The use of phonographic recordings in counseling practice and research. *Journal of Consulting Psychology, 6*, 105–113.

COVNER, B. J. (1944). Studies in phonographic recordings of verbal material. III. The completeness and accuracy of counseling interview reports. *Journal of General Psychology, 30*, 181–203.

COWEN, E. L. (1973). Social and community intervention. *Annual Review of Psychology, 24*, 423–472.

COWEN, E. L. (1977). Psychologists in primary prevention: Blowing the cover story. An editorial. *American Journal of Community Psychology, 5*, 481–490.

COWEN, E. L. (1980). The wooing of primary prevention. *American Journal of Community Psychology, 8*, 258–284.

COWEN, E. L. (1982). Help is where you find it: Four informal helping groups. *American Psychologist, 37*, 385–395.

COWEN, E. L. (1983). Primary prevention in mental health: Past, present and future. In R. D. Felner, L. A. Jason, J. N. Moritsugu, & S. S. Farber (Eds.), *Preventive psychology: Theory, research and practice.* New York: Pergamon Press.

COWEN, E. L., GESTEN, E. L., & WILSON, A. B. (1979). The primary mental health project (PMHP): Evaluation of current program effectiveness. *American Journal of Community Psychology, 7*, 293–303.

CREER, T. L. (1982). Asthma. *Journal of Consulting and Clinical Psychology, 50*, 912–921.

CRITELLI, J. W. & NEUMANN, K. F. (1984). The placebo: Conceptual analysis of a construct in transition. *American Psychologist, 39*, 32–39.

CROCKETT, D., CLARK, C., & KLONOFF, H. (1981). Introduction—an overview of neuropsychology. In S. B. Filskov & T. J. Boll (Eds.), *Handbook of clinical neuropsychology* (pp. 1–37). New York: John Wiley.

CRONBACH, L. J. (1946). Response sets and test validity. *Educational and psychological measurement, 6,* 475–494.

CRONBACH, L. J. (1960). *Essentials of psychological testing* (2nd ed.). New York: Harper & Row.

CRONBACH, L. J. (1970). *Essentials of psychological testing* (3rd ed.). New York: Harper & Row.

CRONBACH, L. J. (1975). Five decades of public controversy over mental testing. *American Psychologist, 30,* 1–14.

CRONBACH, L. J. (1984). *Essentials of psychological testing* (4th ed.). New York: Harper & Row.

CRONBACH, L. J. & GLESER, G. C. (1965). *Psychological tests and personnel decisions* (2nd ed.). Urbana, IL: University of Illinois Press.

CRONBACH, L. J., GLESER, G. C., NANDA, H., & RAJARATNAM, N. (1972). *The dependability of behavioral measurements.* New York: John Wiley.

CRONBACH, L. J. & MEEHL, P. E. (1955). Construct validity in psychology tests. *Psychological Bulletin, 52,* 281–302.

CROSS, D. G., SHEEHAN, P. W., & KHAN, J. A. (1980). Alternative advice and counsel in psychotherapy. *Journal of Consulting and Clinical Psychology, 48,* 615–625.

CROW, W. J. & HAMMOND, K. R. (1957). The generality of accuracy and response sets in interpersonal perception. *Journal of Abnormal and Social Psychology, 54,* 384–390.

CROWELL, E. (1977). Redistributive aspects of psychotherapy's inclusion in national health insurance: A summary. *American Psychologist, 32,* 731–737.

CRUMBAUGH, J. C. (1968). Cross-validation of the Purpose in Life test based on Frankl's concepts. *Journal of Individual Psychology, 24,* 74–81.

CUCA, J. (1975, January). Clinicians compose 36 percent of APA. *APA Monitor* (p. 4).

CUMMINGS, N. A. (1977). The anatomy of psychotherapy under national health insurance. *American Psychologist, 32,* 711–718.

CUMMINGS, N. A. (1986). The dismantling of our health system: Strategies for the survival of psychological practice. *American Psychologist, 41,* 426–431.

CUTRONA, C. E. (1984). Social support and stress in the transition to parenthood. *Journal of Abnormal Psychology, 93,* 378–390.

DAHLSTROM, W. G. & WELSH, G. S. (1960). *An MMPI handbook: A guide to use in clinical practice and research.* Minneapolis: University of Minnesota Press.

DAHLSTROM, W. G., WELSH, G. S., & DAHLSTROM, L. E. (1972). *An MMPI handbook, Vol. 1, Clinical interpretation* (Rev. ed.). Minneapolis: University of Minnesota Press.

DAILEY, C. A. (1952). The effects of premature conclusions upon the acquisition of understanding a person. *Journal of Psychology, 33,* 133–152.

DAILEY, C. A. (1953). The practical utility of the clinical report. *Journal of Consulting Psychology, 17,* 297–302.

DAMICH, E. (1974). The right against treatment: Behavior modification and the involuntarily committed. *Catholic University Law Review, 23,* 774–787.

DANA, R. H. (1959). The perceptual organization TAT score, number, order, and frequency. *Journal of Projective Techniques, 23,* 307–310.

DANA, R. H. & LEECH, S. (1974). Existential assessment. *Journal of Personality Assessment, 38,* 428–435.

DAVES, C. W. (Ed.) (1984). *The uses and misuses of tests: Examining current issues in educational and psychological testing.* San Francisco: Jossey-Bass.

DAVIDSON, W. S. (1974). Studies of aversive conditioning for alcoholics: A critical review of theory and research methodology. *Psychological Bulletin, 81,* 571–581.

DAVIS, J. D. (1971). *The interview as arena.* Stanford, CA: Stanford University Press.

DAVISON, G. C. & NEALE, J. M. (1986). *Abnormal psychology: The experimental clinical approach* (4th ed.). New York: John Wiley.

DAVISON, G. C. & WILSON, G. T. (1973). Processes of fear reduction in systematic desensitization: Cognitive and social reinforcement factors in humans. *Behavior Therapy, 4,* 1–21.

DAWE, H. C. (1934). An analysis of two-hundred quarrels of pre-school children. *Child Development, 5,* 139–157.

DELEON, P. H. & BORRELIZ, M. (1978). Malpractice: Professional liability and the law. *Professional Psychology, 9,* 467–477.

DELMONTE, M. M. (1985). Meditation and anxiety reduction: A literature review. *Clinical Psychology Review, 5,* 91–102.

DENNIS, W. (1948). *Readings in the history of psychology.* New York: Appleton-Century-Crofts.

DEUTSCH, F. & MURPHY, W. F. (1955). *The clinical interview.* New York: International Universities Press.

DIGIUSEPEE, R. A. & MILLER, N. J. (1977). A review of outcome studies on rational-emotive therapy. In A. Ellis & R. Grieger (Eds.), *Handbook of rational-emotive therapy* (pp. 72–95). New York: Springer Publishing Co.

DILLEHAY, R. C. (1973). On the irrelevance of the classical negative evidence concerning the effect of attitudes on behavior. *American Psychologist, 28,* 887–891.

DILLER, L. & GORDON, W. A. (1981). Interventions for cognitive deficits in brain-injured adults. *Journal of Consulting and Clinical Psychology, 49,* 822–834.

DINARDO, P. A. (1975). Social class and diagnostic suggestion as variables in clinical judgment. *Journal of Consulting and Clinical Psychology, 43,* 363–368.

DINARDO, P. A., O'BRIEN, G. T., BARLOW, D. H., WADDELL, M. T., & BLANCHARD, E. B. (1983). Reliability of DSM-III anxiety disorder categories using a new structural interview. *Archives of General Psychiatry, 40,* 1070–1075.

DODGE, K. A., McCLASKEY, C. L., & FELDMAN, E. (1985). Situational approach to the assessment of social competence in children. *Journal of Consulting and Clinical Psychology, 53,* 344–353.

DOHRENWEND, B. S. (1978). Social stress and community psychology. *American Journal of Community Psychology, 6,* 1–14.

DOHRENWEND, B. S. & DOHRENWEND, B. P. (Eds.) (1981). *Stressful life events and their contexts.* New Brunswick, NJ: Rutgers University Press.

DOHRENWEND, B. S., DOHRENWEND, B. P., DODSON, M., & SHROUT, P. E. (1984). Symptoms, hassles, social supports, and life events: Problem of confounding measures. *Journal of Abnormal Psychology, 93,* 222–230.

DOHRENWEND, B. S., KRASNOFF, L., ASKENASY, A. R., & DOHRENWEND, B. P. (1978). Exemplification of a method for scaling life events: The PERI life events scale. *Journal of Health and Social Behavior, 19,* 205–229.

DOLLARD, J. & MILLER, N. E. (1950). *Personality and psychotherapy: An analysis in terms of learning, thinking and culture.* New York: McGraw-Hill.

DRAKE, L. E. & OETTING, E. R. (1959). *An MMPI codebook for counselors.* Minneapolis: University of Minnesota Press.

DREIKURS, R. (1954). The psychological interview in medicine. *American Journal of Individual Psychology, 10,* 99–122.

DUBOIS, P. H. (1970). *A history of psychological testing.* Boston: Allyn & Bacon.

DULANY, D. E. (1968). Awareness, rules, and propositional control: A confrontation with S-R behavior theory. In T. R. Dixon & D. L. Horton (Eds.), *Verbal behavior and general behavior theory* (pp. 340–387). Englewood Cliffs, NJ: Prentice-Hall.

DUNHAM, H. W. (1965). Community psychiatry: The newest therapeutic bandwagon. *Archives of General Psychiatry, 12,* 303–313.

DUNLAP, G., KOEGEL, R. L., & O'NEILL, R. (1985). Pervasive developmental disorders. In P. H. Bornstein & A. E. Kazdin (Eds.), *Handbook of clinical behavior therapy with children* (pp. 499–540). Homewood, IL: Dorsey Press.

DURLAK, J. (1979). Comparative effectiveness of paraprofessional and professional helpers. *Psychological Bulletin, 86,* 80–92.

DUSH, D. M., HIRT, M. L., & SCHROEDER, H. (1983). Self-statement modification with adults: A meta-analysis. *Psychological Bulletin, 94,* 408–422.

EAGLE, M. (1984). *Recent developments in psychoanalysis: A critical evaluation.* New York: McGraw-Hill.

EARLS, C. M. & QUINSEY, V. L. (1985). What is to be done? Future research on the assessment and behavioral treatment of sex offenders. *Behavioral Sciences and the Law, 3,* 377–390.

EDELSTEIN, B. A. & EISLER, R. M. (1976). Effects of modeling and modeling with instructions and feedback on the behavioral components of social skills. *Behavior Therapy, 7,* 382–389.

EDWARDS, A. L. (1957). *The social desirability variable in personality assessment and research.* New York: Dryden.

EDWARDS, A. L. (1959). *Edwards Personal Preference Schedule.* New York: Psychological Corporation.

EINHORN, H. J. & HOGARTH, R. M. (1978). Confidence in judgment: Persistence of the illusion of validity. *Psychological Review, 85,* 395–416.

ELKINS, R. (1975). Aversion therapy for alcoholism: Chemical, electrical, or verbal imagery. *The International Journal of the Addictions, 10,* 157–209.

ELLENBERGER, H. F. (1972). The story of "Anna O.": A critical review with new data. *Journal of the History of the Behavioural Sciences, 8,* 267–279.

ELLIS, A. (1962). *Reason and emotion in psychotherapy.* New York: Lyle Stuart.

ELLIS, A. (1973). Rational-emotive therapy. In R. Corsini (Ed.), *Current psychotherapies.* Itasca, IL: F. E. Peacock Publishers.

ELLIS, A. & BERNARD, M. E. (Eds.) (1985). *Clinical applications of rational-emotive therapy.* New York: Plenum.

ELLIS, A. & GRIEGER, R. (Eds.) (1977). *Handbook of rational-emotive therapy.* New York: Springer Publishing Co.

ELLISON, K. W. & BUCKHOUT, R. (1981). *Psychology and criminal justice.* New York: Harper & Row.

EMMELKAMP, P. M. G. & FELTEN, M. (1985). The process of exposure *in vivo:* Cognitive and physiological changes during treatment of acrophobia. *Behaviour Research and Therapy, 23,* 219–224.

EMMELKAMP, P. M. G., VAN DER HOUT, A., & DEVRIES, K. (1983). Assertive training for agoraphobics. *Behaviour Research and Therapy, 21,* 63–68.

ENDICOTT, J. & SPITZER, R. L. (1978). A diagnostic interview: The schedule for affective disorders and schizophrenia. *Archives of General Psychiatry, 35,* 837–844.

ENGLEMANN, S. (1974). The effectiveness of direct verbal instruction on IQ performance and achievement in reading and arithmetic. In R. Ulrich, T. Stachnik, & J. Mabry (Eds.). *Control of human behavior* (Vol. 3, pp. 69–84). Glenview, IL: Scott, Foresman.

ENGLISH, H. B. (1929). Three cases of the conditioned fear response. *Journal of Abnormal and Social Psychology, 24,* 221–225.

ERDBERG, P. & EXNER, J. E. (1984). Rorschach assessment. In G. Goldstein & M. Hersen (Eds.), *Handbook of psychological assessment* (pp. 332–347). New York: Pergamon Press.

ERDMAN, H. P., KLEIN, M. H., & GREIST, J. H. (1985). Direct patient computer interviewing. *Journal of Consulting and Clinical Psychology, 53,* 760–773.

ERIKSON, E. H. (1946). Ego development and historical change. *The psychoanalytic study of the child* (Vol. 2, pp. 359–396). New York: International Universities Press.

ERIKSON, E. H. (1959). Identity and the life cycle. *Psychological Issues,* Monograph 1, New York: International Universities Press.

ERIKSON, E. H. (1963). *Childhood and society* (Rev. ed.). New York: W. W. Norton & Co.

ERLICH, J. & RIESMAN, D. (1961). Age and authority in the interview. *Public Opinion Quarterly, 25,* 39–56.

ERON, L. D. (1950). A normative study of the thematic apperception test. *Psychological Monographs, 64*(9).

ERVIN, S. J., JR. (1965). Why senate hearings on psychological tests. *American Psychologist, 20,* 879–880.

EXNER, J. E. (1973). The self-focus sentence completion: A study of egocentricity. *Journal of Personality Assessment, 37,* 437–455.

EXNER, J. E. (1976). Projective techniques. In I. B. Weiner (Ed.), *Clinical methods in psychology* (pp. 61–121). New York: John Wiley.

EXNER, J. E. (1978). *The Rorschach: A comprehensive system, Vol. 2: Current research and advanced interpretation.* New York: John Wiley.

EXNER, J. E. (1985). *The Rorschach: A comprehensive system,* (Vol. 1, 2nd ed.). New York: John Wiley.

EYSENCK, H. J. (1952). The effects of psychotherapy: An evaluation. *Journal of Consulting Psychology, 16,* 319–324.

EYSENCK, H. J. (1959). Learning theory and behaviour therapy. *Journal of Mental Science, 105,* 61–75.

EYSENCK, H. J. (Ed.) (1960). *Behaviour therapy and the neuroses: Readings in modern methods of treatment derived from learning theory.* New York: Pergamon Press.

EYSENCK, H. J. (1966). *The effects of psychotherapy.* New York: International Science Press.

EYSENCK, H. J. (1978). An exercise in mega-silliness. *American Psychologist, 33,* 517.

EYSENCK, H. J. (1982). Neobehavioristic (S-R) theory. In G. T. Wilson & C. M. Franks (Eds.).

Contemporary behavior therapy: Conceptual and empirical foundations (pp. 205–276). New York: Guilford Press.

EYSENCK, H. J. (1985). *The decline and fall of the Freudian empire.* London: Allen Lane.

EYSENCK, H. J., WAKEFIELD, J. A., & FRIEDMAN, A. F. (1983). Diagnosis and clinical assessment: The DSM-III. *Annual Review of Psychology, 34,* 167–193.

FAIRBAIRN, W. R. D. (1952). *Psychoanalytic studies of the personality.* London: Tavistock Publications/Routledge & Kegan Paul.

FAIRWEATHER, G. W. (1980). *New directions for mental health services: The Fairweather lodge: A twenty-five year retrospective.* San Francisco: Jossey-Bass.

FAIRWEATHER, G. W., SANDERS, D. H., & TORNATZKY, L. G. (1974). *Creating change in mental health organizations.* New York: Pergamon Press.

FANCHER, R. E. (1973). *Psychoanalytic psychology: The development of Freud's thought.* New York: W. W. Norton & Co.

FARKAS, G. M. (1980). An ontological analysis of behavior therapy. *American Psychologist, 35,* 364–374.

FAST, J. (1970). *Body language.* New York: M. Evans.

FELDMAN, S. S. (1959). *Mannerisms of speech and gestures in everyday life.* New York: International Universities Press.

FELNER, R. D. (1985). Prevention. *The Community Psychologist, 19,* 31–34.

FELNER, R. D., JASON, L. A., MORITSUGU, J. N., & FARBER, S. S. (Eds.) (1983). *Preventive psychology: Theory, research and practice.* New York: Pergamon Press.

FERGUSON, J. M. & TAYLOR, L. B. (Eds.) (1981). *The comprehensive handbook of behavioral medicine.* New York: Spectrum Pub.

FEUERSTEIN, M., LABBE, E. E., & KUCZMIERCZYK, A. R. (1986). *Health psychology: A psychobiological perspective.* New York: Plenum.

FIDLER, D. S. & KLEINKNECHT, R. E. (1977). Randomized response versus direct questioning: Two data-collection methods for sensitive information. *Psychological Bulletin, 84,* 1045–1049.

FIEDLER, F. E. (1950). A comparison of therapeutic relationships in psychoanalytic, nondirective, and Adlerian therapy. *Journal of Consulting Psychology, 14,* 436–445.

FILSKOV, S. B. & BOLL, T. J. (Eds.) (1981). *Handbook of clinical neuropsychology.* New York: John Wiley.

FILSKOV, S. B., GRIMM, B. H., & LEWIS, J. A. (1981). Brain-behavior relationships. In S. B. Filskov & T. J. Boll (Eds.), *Handbook of clinical neuropsychology* (pp. 39–73). New York: John Wiley.

FINE, R. (1971). *The healing of the mind: The technique of psychoanalytic psychotherapy.* New York: David McKay.

FIORA-GORMALLY, N. (1978). Battered wives who kill: Double standard out of court, single standard in. *Law and Human Behavior, 2,* 133–166.

FISCHER, C. T. (1979). Individualized assessment and phenomenological psychology. *Journal of Personality Assessment, 43,* 115–122.

FISCHER, C. T. (1985). *Individualizing psychological assessment.* Monterey, CA: Brooks/Cole.

FISCHER, C. T. & FISCHER, W. F. (1983). Phenomenological-existential psychotherapy. In M. Hersen, A. E. Kazdin, & A. S. Bellack (Eds.), *The clinical psychology handbook* (pp. 489–505). New York: Pergamon Press.

FISHER, S. & FISHER, R. (1950). Test of certain assumptions regarding figure drawing analysis. *Journal of Abnormal and Social Psychology, 45,* 727–732.

FISHER, S. & GREENBERG, R. P. (1977). *The scientific credibility of Freud's theories and therapy.* New York: Basic Books.

FLOR-HENRY, P. (Ed.) (1983). *Cerebral basis of psychopathology.* Boston: John Wright PSG, Inc.

FOLKMAN, S. & LAZARUS, R. S. (1980). An analysis of coping in a middle-aged community sample. *Journal of Health and Social Behavior, 21,* 219–239.

FORD, D. H. & URBAN, H. B. (1963). *Systems of psychotherapy: A comparative study.* New York: John Wiley.

FOREHAND, R., LAUTENSCHLAGER, G. J., FAUST, J., & GRAZIANO, W. G. (1986). Parent perceptions and parent-child interactions in clinic-referred children: A preliminary investigation of the effects of maternal depressive moods. *Behaviour Research and Therapy, 24,* 73–76.

FOWLER, R. D. (1985). Landmarks in computer-assisted psychological assessment. *Journal of Consulting and Clinical Psychology, 53,* 748–759.

FOX, L. H. & ZIRKIN, B. (1984). Achievement tests. In G. Goldstein & M. Hersen (Eds.),

Handbook of psychological assessment (pp. 119–131). New York: Pergamon Press.

Fox, R. E., Kovacs, A. L., & Graham, S. R. (1985). Proposals for a revolution in the preparation and regulation of professional psychologists. *American Psychologist, 40,* 1042–1050.

Foy, D. W., Nunn, L. B., & Rychtarik, R. G. (1984). Broad-spectrum behavioral treatment for chronic alcoholics: Effects of training controlled drinking skills. *Journal of Consulting and Clinical Psychology, 52,* 218–230.

Framo, J. L. (1982). *Explorations in marital and family therapy.* New York: Springer Publishing Co.

Frances, A. (1980). The DSM-III personality disorders section: A commentary. *American Journal of Psychiatry, 137,* 1050–1054.

Francis, V., Korsch, B. M., & Morris, M. J. (1969). Gaps in doctor-patient communications. *New England Journal of Medicine, 280,* 535–540.

Frank, J. D. (1957). Some determinants, manifestations, and effects of cohesiveness in therapy groups. *International Journal of Group Psychotherapy 7,* 53–63.

Frank, J. D. (1973). *Persuasion and healing* (Rev. ed.). Baltimore: The Johns Hopkins University Press.

Frank, L. K. (1939). Projective methods for the study of personality. *Journal of Psychology, 8,* 343–389.

Frankl, V. (1963). *Man's search for meaning.* New York: Washington Square Press.

Frankl, V. (1965). *The doctor and the soul.* New York: Knopf.

Frankl, V. (1967). *Psychotherapy and existentialism: Selected papers on logotherapy.* New York: Washington Square Press.

Franks, C. M. (1964). *Conditioning techniques in clinical practice and research.* New York: Springer Publishing Co.

Franks, C. M. (1976). Forward. In E. J. Mash & L. G. Terdal (Eds.), *Behavior therapy assessment* (XI-XIII). New York: Springer Publishing Co.

Freud, A. (1946). *The ego and mechanisms of defense.* New York: International Universities Press.

Freud, S. (1900). In J. Strachey (Ed.), *The standard edition of the complete psychological works of Sigmund Freud.* London: Hogarth Press, 1953–1964.

Freud, S. (1901). *The psychopathology of everyday life.* New York: Macmillan.

Freud, S. (1904). *On psychotherapy.* Lecture delivered before the College of Physicians in Vienna. Reprinted in S. Freud, *Therapy and technique.* New York: Collier Books, 1963.

Freud, S. (1905). Jokes and their relation to the unconscious. In the *Standard edition of the complete psychological works of Sigmund Freud* (Vol. 8). London: Hogarth Press, 1953–1964.

Freud, S. (1912). Recommendations for physicians on the psychoanalytic method of treatment. *Zentralblatt,* DS. II. Reprinted in S. Freud, *Therapy and technique.* New York: Collier Books, 1963.

Freud, S. (1915). Further recommendations in the technique of psychoanalysis. *Zeitschrift,* BD. III. Reprinted in S. Freud, *Therapy and technique.* New York: Collier Books, 1963.

Freud, S. (1949). *An outline of psychoanalysis* (J. Strachey, trans.). New York: W. W. Norton.

Freud, S. (1953–1964). *The standard edition of the complete psychological works of Sigmund Freud* (24 vols.). London: Hogarth Press.

Friedman, M. & Rosenman, R. H. (1974). *Type A behavior and your heart.* New York: Knopf.

Frykholm, B., Gunne, M., & Hursfeldt, B. (1976). Prediction of outcome in drug dependence. *Addictive Behaviors, 1,* 103–110.

Gaffney, L. R. & McFall, R. M. (1981). A comparison of social skills in delinquent and nondelinquent girls using a behavioral role-playing inventory. *Journal of Consulting and Clinical Psychology, 49,* 959–967.

Gaines, I. D. (1956). The psychologist as an expert witness in a personal injury case. *Marquette Law Review, 39,* 239–244.

Gallessich, J. (1982). *The profession and practice of consultation.* San Francisco, CA: Jossey-Bass.

Galton, F. (1883). *Inquiries into human faculty and its development.* London: Macmillan.

Ganzer, V. J. & Sarason, I. G. (1964). Interrelations among hostility, experimental conditions, and verbal behavior. *Journal of Abnormal and Social Psychology, 68,* 79–84.

Garb, H. N. (1984). The incremental validity of information used in personality assessment. *Clinical Psychology Review, 4,* 641–656.

Garcia, J., McGowan, B., & Green, K. (1971). Sensory quality and integration: Constraints

on conditioning. In A. H. Block & W. F. Pro-
kasky (Eds.), *Classical conditioning*. New York:
Appleton-Century-Crofts.

GARFIELD, S. L. (1965). Historical introduction.
In B. B. Wolman (Ed.), *Handbook of clinical
psychology* (pp. 125–140). New York: McGraw-
Hill.

GARFIELD, S. L. (1974). *Clinical psychology: The
study of personality and behavior*. Chicago: Aldine.

GARFIELD, S. L. (1986). Research on client variables in psychotherapy. In S. L. Garfield & A.
E. Bergin (Eds.), *Handbook of psychotherapy and
behavior change* (3rd ed.) (pp. 213–256). New
York: John Wiley.

GARFIELD, S. L., & KURTZ, R. (1976). Clinical psychologists in the 1970s. *American Psychologist,
31*, 1–9.

GARNER, A. M. & SMITH, G. M. (1976). An experimental videotape technique for evaluating
trainee approaches to clinical judging. *Journal
of Consulting and Clinical Psychology, 44*, 945–
950.

GARNER, D. M., OLMSTEAD, M. P., & POLIVY, J.
(1983). Development and validation of a multidimensional eating disorder inventory for
anorexia nervosa and bulimia. *International
Journal of Eating Disorders, 2*, 15–35.

GARNER, H. H. (1970). *Psychotherapy*. St. Louis:
Warren H. Green.

GASS, R. (1979). The psychologist as expert witness: Science in the courtroom. *Maryland Law
Review, 38*, 539–631.

GEER, J. H. (1965). The development of a scale to
measure fear. *Behaviour Research and Therapy,
3*, 45–53.

GENTILE, J. R., RODEN, A. H., & KLEIN, R. D.
(1972). An analysis of variance model for the
intrasubject replication design. *Journal of Applied Behavior Analysis, 5*, 193–198.

GILBERSTADT, H. & DUKER, J. (1965). *A handbook
for clinical and actuarial MMPI interpretation*.
Philadelphia: Saunders.

GILL, M. M. & HOFFMAN, I. Z. (1982). A method
of studying the analysis of aspects of the patient's experience of the relationship in psychoanalysis and psychotherapy. *Journal of The
American Psychoanalytic Association, 30*, 137–
167.

GLASER, D. (1964). *The effectiveness of a prison and
parole system*. Indianapolis: Bobbs-Merrill.

GLASS, G. V. & KLIEGL, R. M. (1983). An apology
for research integration in the study of psychotherapy. *Journal of Consulting and Clinical
Psychology, 51*, 28–41.

GLASS, G. V., WILSON, V. L., & GOTTMAN, J. M.
(1975). *Design and analysis of time-series experiments*. Boulder, CO: Colorado Associated University Press.

GLENWICK, D. & JASON, L. A. (Eds.) (1980). *Behavioral community psychology*. New York:
Praeger.

GOFFMAN, E. (1959). *The presentation of self in everyday life*. Garden City, NY: Doubleday.

GOFFMAN, E. (1961). *Asylums*. New York: Doubleday.

GOLDBERG, L. R. (1959). The effectiveness of clinicians' judgments: The diagnosis of organic
brain damage from the Bender-Gestalt
test. *Journal of Consulting Psychology, 23*, 25–
33.

GOLDBERG, L. R. (1968). Simple models or simple
processes? Some research on clinical judgments. *American Psychologist, 23*, 483–496.

GOLDBERG, P. A. (1965). A review of sentence
completion methods in personality assessment. *Journal of Projective Techniques and Personality Assessment, 29*, 12–45.

GOLDEN, C. J. (1980). In reply to Adams' "In
search of Luria's battery: A false start." *Journal of Consulting and Clinical Psychology, 48*,
517–521.

GOLDEN, C. J. (1981). A standardized version of
Luria's neuropsychological tests: A quantitative and qualitative approach to neuropsychological evaluation. In S. B. Filskov & T. J. Boll
(Eds.), *Handbook of clinical neuropsychology* (pp.
608–642). New York: John Wiley.

GOLDEN, C. J., HAMMEKE, T., & PURISCH, A.
(1978). Diagnostic validity of the Luria-Nebraska Neuropsychological battery. *Journal of
Consulting and Clinical Psychology, 46*, 1258–
1265.

GOLDEN, C. J., HAMMEKE, T., & PURISCH, A.
(1980). *The Luria-Nebraska Neuropsychological
Battery: Manual (Revised)*. Los Angeles: Western Psychological Services.

GOLDEN, C. J., SAWICKI, R. F., & FRANZEN, M. D.
(1984). Test construction. In G. Goldstein &
M. Hersen (Eds.), *Handbook of psychological assessment* (pp. 19–37). New York: Pergamon
Press.

GOLDEN, M. (1964). Some effects of combining psychological tests on clinical inferences. *Journal of Consulting Psychology, 28*, 440–446.

GOLDENBERG, H. (1973). *Contemporary clinical psychology.* Monterey, CA: Brooks/Cole.

GOLDFRIED, M. R. (1980). Toward the delineation of therapeutic change principles. *American Psychologist, 35*, 991–999.

GOLDFRIED, M. R. & DAVISON, G. C. (1976). *Clinical behavior therapy.* New York: Holt, Rinehart & Winston.

GOLDFRIED, M. R., DECENTECEO, E. T., & WEINBERG, L. (1974). Systematic rational restructuring as a self control technique. *Behavior Therapy, 5*, 247–254.

GOLDFRIED, M. R. & D'ZURILLA, T. J. (1969). A behavior-analytic model for assessing competence. In C. D. Spielberger (Ed.), *Current topics in clinical and community psychology* (Vol. 1, pp. 151–196). New York: Academic Press.

GOLDFRIED, M. R. & SPRAFKIN, J. N. (1974). *Behavioral personality assessment.* Morristown, NJ: General Learning Press.

GOLDFRIED, M. R., STRICKER, G., & WEINER, I. B. (1971). *Rorschach handbook of clinical and research applications.* Englewood Cliffs, NJ: Prentice-Hall.

GOLDING, S. L. & RORER, L. G. (1972). Illusory correlation and subjective judgment. *Journal of Abnormal Psychology, 80*, 249–260.

GOLDMAN, B. A. & BUSCH, J. C. (Eds.) (1978). *Directory of unpublished experimental mental measures* (Vol. 1). New York: Human Sciences Press.

GOLDSCHMID, M. L., STEIN, D. D., WEISSMAN, H. N., & SORRELS, J. A. (1969). A survey of the training and practices of clinical psychologists. *The Clinical Psychologist, 22*, 89–94, 107.

GOLDSMITH, J. B. & McFALL, R. M. (1975). Development and evaluation of an interpersonal skill-training program for psychiatric inpatients. *Journal of Abnormal Psychology, 84*, 51–58.

GOLDSTEIN, A. J. (1973). Behavior therapy. In R. Corsini (Ed.), *Current psychotherapies.* Itaska, IL: F. E. Peacock Publishers, Inc.

GOLDSTEIN, A. J. & CHAMBLESS, D. L. (1978). A reanalysis of agoraphobia. *Behavior Therapy, 9*, 47–59.

GOLDSTEIN, A. P. (1971). *Psychotherapeutic attraction.* New York: Pergamon Press.

GOLDSTEIN, A. P. (1976). Relationship-enchancement methods. In F. H. Kanfer & A. P. Goldstein (Eds.), *Helping people change* (pp. 15–49). New York: Pergamon Press.

GOLDSTEIN, G. & HERSEN, M. (Eds.) (1984). *Handbook of psychological assessment.* New York: Pergamon Press.

GOODENOUGH, F. L. (1926). *Measurement of intelligence by drawing.* Yonkers, NY: World Book.

GOODENOUGH, F. L. (1949). *Mental testing.* New York: Rinehart.

GOODMAN, E. S., & MAULTSBY, M. C. (1974). *Emotional well being through rational behavior training.* Springfield, IL: Charles C Thomas.

GORDEN, R. L. (1969). *Interviewing: Strategy, techniques, and tactics.* Homewood, IL: Dorsey Press.

GOTTESMAN, I. I. & SHIELDS, J. (1982). *Schizophrenia: The epigenetic puzzle.* Cambridge: Cambridge University Press.

GOTTMAN, J. M. (1979). *Marital interaction: Experimental investigations.* New York: Academic Press.

GOTTMAN, J. M. & MARKMAN, H. J. (1978). Experimental designs in psychotherapy research. In S. Garfield & A. Bergin (Eds.), *Handbook of psychotherapy and behavior change* (2nd ed.) (pp. 12–62). New York: John Wiley.

GOTTMAN, J. M., MARKMAN, H. J., & NOTARIUS, C. (1977). The topography of marital conflict: A sequential analysis of verbal and nonverbal behavior. *Journal of Marriage and the Family, 39*, 461-477.

GOUGH, H. G. (1957). *California Psychological Inventory: Manual.* Palo Alto, CA: Consulting Psychologists Press.

GOUGH, H. G. (1975). *California Psychological Inventory (revised manual).* Palo Alto, CA: Consulting Psychologists Press.

GRAHAM, F. K. & KENDALL, B. S. (1960). Memory-for-designs test: Revised general manual. *Perceptual and Motor Skills, 11*, 147–188.

GRAHAM, J. R. (1977). *The MMPI: A practical guide.* New York: Oxford University Press.

GRANTHAM, R. J. (1973). Effects of counselor sex, race, and language style on black students in initial interviews. *Journal of Counseling Psychology, 20*, 553–559.

GREENBLATT, M. (1959). Discussion of papers by Saslow, Matarazzo, & Lacey. In E. A. Rubinstein & M. B. Parloff (Eds.), *Research in psycho-*

therapy (Vol. 1, pp. 209–220). Washington, DC: American Psychological Association.

GREENSON, R. R. (1967). *The technique and practice of psychoanalysis.* New York: International Universities Press.

GREENSPOON, J. (1962). Verbal conditioning and clinical psychology. In A. J. Bachrach (Ed.), *Experimental foundations of clinical psychology* (pp. 510–553). New York: Basic Books.

GRISSO, T. (1981). *Juveniles' waiver of rights: Legal and psychological competence.* New York: Plenum Press.

GROSS, M. L. (1962). *The brain watchers.* New York: Random House.

GROSS, S. J. (1978). The myth of professional licensing. *American Psychologist, 33,* 1009–1016.

GROSSBERG, J. M. & GRANT, B. F. (1978). Clinical psychophysics: Applications of ratio scaling and signal detection methods to research on pain, fear, drugs, and medical decision making. *Psychological Bulletin, 85,* 1154–1176.

GROTH-MARNAT, G. (1984). *Handbook of psychological assessment.* New York: Van Nostrand Reinhold.

GROTJAHN, M. (1957). *Beyond laughter: Humor and the subsconscious.* New York: McGraw-Hill.

GUERNEY, B. G. (Ed.) (1969). *Psychotherapeutic agents: New roles for nonprofessionals, parents, and teachers.* New York: Holt, Rinehart & Winston.

GUIORA, A. Z. & BRANDWIN, M. A. (1968). *Perspectives in clinical psychology.* Princeton, NJ: D. Van Nostrand Co.

GUNTRIP, H. (1973). *Psychoanalytic theory, therapy, and the self.* New York: Basic Books.

GURIN, G., VEROFF, J., & FELD, S. (1960). *Americans view their mental health.* New York: Basic Books.

GURMAN, A. S. (1985). *Casebook of marital therapy.* New York: Guilford Press.

GURMAN, A. S. & KNISKERN, D. P. (Eds.) (1981). *Handbook of family therapy.* New York: Bruner/Mazel.

GURMAN, A. S. & RAZIN, A. M. (1977). *Effective psychotherapy: A handbook of research.* New York: Pergamon Press.

GUTHRIE, E. R. (1935). *The psychology of learning.* New York: Harper & Row.

HAFEMEISTER, T. & SALES, B. D. (1984). Interdisciplinary evaluations for guardianship and conservatorship. *Law and Human Behavior, 8,* 335–354.

HAHLWEG, K., REVENSTORF, D., & SCHINDLER, L. (1984). Effects of behavioral marital therapy on couples' communication and problem-solving skills. *Journal of Consulting and Clinical Psychology, 52,* 553–566.

HALE, R. L. (1983). Intellectual assessment. In M. Hersen, A. E. Kazdin, & A. S. Bellack (Eds.), *The clinical psychology handbook* (pp. 345–376). New York: Pergamon Press.

HALL, C. S., & LINDZEY, G. (1985). *Introduction to theories of personality.* New York: John Wiley.

HALL, S. M., LOEB, P., COYNE, K., & COOPER, J. (1981). Increasing employment in ex-heroin addicts I: Criminal justice sample. *Behavior Therapy, 12,* 443–452.

HALL, S. M., LOEB, P., LeVOIS, M., & COOPER, J. (1981). Increasing employment in ex-heroin addicts II: Methadone maintenance sample. *Behavior Therapy, 12,* 453–460.

HALLECK, S. L. (1969). Community psychiatry: Some troubling questions. In L. M. Roberts, S. L. Halleck, & M. B. Loeb (Eds.), *Community psychiatry.* Garden City, NY: Doubleday, Anchor Books.

HAMMER, E. F. (1968). Projective drawings. In A. I. Rabin (Ed.), *Projective techniques in personality assessment* (pp. 366–393). New York: Springer Publishing Co.

HAMMOND, K. R. & ALLEN, J. M. (1953). *Writing clinical reports.* Englewood Cliffs, NJ: Prentice-Hall.

HANDLER, L. (1974). Psychotherapy, assessment, and clinical research: Parallels and similarities. In A. I. Rabin (Ed.), *Clinical psychology: Issues of the seventies* (pp. 49–62). East Lansing, MI: Michigan State University Press.

HANEY, C. (1984). Examining death qualification: Further analysis of the process effect. *Law and Human Behavior, 8,* 133–152.

HANSEN, D. J., ST. LAWRENCE, J. S., & CHRISTOFF, K. A. (1985). Effects of interpersonal problem-solving training with chronic aftercare patients on problem-solving component skills and effectiveness of solutions. *Journal of Consulting and Clinical Psychology, 53,* 167–174.

HANSEN, J. C. (1984). Interest inventories. In G. Goldstein & M. Hersen (Eds.), *Handbook of psychological assessment* (pp. 157–177). New York: Pergamon Press.

HARE, R. D. (1985). Comparison of procedures for the assessment of psychopathy. *Journal of Consulting and Clinical Psychology, 53*, 7–16.

HARPER, R. A. (1959). *Psychoanalysis and psychotherapy: Thirty-six systems.* Englewood Cliffs, NJ: Prentice-Hall.

HARPER, R. G., WIENS, A. N., & MATARAZZO, J. D. (1978). *Nonverbal communication: The state of the art.* New York: John Wiley.

HARRIS, F. C. & LAHEY, B. B. (1982a). Recording system bias in direct observational methodology: A review and critical analysis of factors causing inaccurate coding behavior. *Clinical Psychology Review, 2*, 539–556.

HARRIS, F. C. & LAHEY, B. B. (1982b). Subject reactivity in direct observational assessment: A review and critical analysis. *Clinical Psychology Review, 2*, 523–538.

HARRIS, J. G. (1984). Prognosis in schizophrenia. In A. S. Bellack (Ed.), *Schizophrenia: Treatment, management and rehabilitation* (pp. 79–112). Orlando, FL: Grune & Stratton.

HARRIS, V. W. & SHERMAN, J. A. (1973). Effects of peer tutoring and consequences on the math performance of elementary classroom students. *Journal of Applied Behavior Analysis, 6*, 587–598.

HARRISON, R. (1965). Thematic apperceptive methods. In B. B. Wolman (Ed.), *Handbook of clinical psychology* (pp. 562–620). New York: McGraw-Hill.

HARROWER, M. R. (1945). *Psychodiagnostic inkblots.* New York: Grune & Stratton.

HARROWER, M. R. (1961). *The practice of clinical psychology.* Springfield, IL: Charles C Thomas.

HARROWER, M. R. (1965). Clinical psychologists at work. In B. B. Wolman (Ed.), *Handbook of clinical psychology* (pp. 1443–1458). New York: McGraw-Hill.

HARROWER, M. R. & STEINER, M. (1945). *Large scale Rorschach techniques.* Springfield, IL: Charles C Thomas.

HARTMANN, D. P. (1974). Forcing square pegs into round holes: Some comments on "An analysis of variance model for the intrasubject replication design." *Journal of Applied Behavior Analysis, 7*, 635–638.

HARTMANN, H. (1939). Psychoanalysis and the concept of health. *International Journal of Psychoanalysis, 20*, 308–321.

HARTMANN, H. (1958). *Ego psychology and the problem of adaptation.* New York: International Universities Press.

HARTSHORNE, H. & MAY, M. A. (1928). *Studies in deceit.* New York: Macmillan.

HATCHER, C. & HIMMELSTEIN, P. (Eds.) (1976). *The handbook of Gestalt therapy.* New York: Jason Aronson.

HATHAWAY, S. R. (1958). A study of human behavior: The clinical psychologist. *American Psychologist, 13*, 255–265.

HATHAWAY, S. R. & McKINLEY, J. C. (1967). *The Minnesota Multiphasic Personality Inventory Manual.* New York: Psychological Corporation.

HAWKINS, R. C., FREMOUW, W. J., & CLEMENT, P. F. (Eds.) (1984). *The binge-purge syndrome: Diagnosis, treatment, and research.* New York: Springer Publishing Co.

HAWKINS, R. P. (1975). Who decided that was the problem? Two stages of responsibility for applied behavior analysis. In W. S. Wood (Ed.), *Issues in evaluating behavior modification* (pp. 195–214). Champaign, IL: Research Press.

HAWKINS, R. P. & DOBES, R. W. (1977). Behavioral definitions in applied behavior analysis: Explicit or implicit. In B. C. Etzel, J. M. LeBlanc, & D. M. Baer (Eds.), *New Developments in behavioral research: Theory, method and application* (pp. 167–188). Hillsdale, NJ: Lawrence Erlbaum Assoc.

HAYES, S. C. (1983). The role of the individual case in the production and consumption of clinical knowledge. In M. Hersen, A. E. Kazdin, & A. S. Bellack (Eds.), *The clinical psychology handbook* (pp. 181–195). New York: Pergamon Press.

HAYNES, R. B. (1982). Improving patient compliance: An empirical view. In R. B. Stuart (Ed.), *Adherence, compliance, and generalization in behavioral medicine* (pp. 56–78). New York: Bruner/Mazel.

HAYNES, S. G., LEVINE, S., SCOTCH, N., FEINLEIB, M., & KANNEL, W. B. (1978). The relationship of psychosocial factors to coronary heart disease in the Framingham study: I. Methods and risk factors. *American Journal of Epidemiology, 107*, 362–383.

HAYNES, S. N. (1978). *Principles of behavioral assessment.* New York: Gardner Press.

HAYNES, S. N. (1984). Behavioral assessment of adults. In G. Goldstein & M. Hersen (Eds.), *Handbook of psychological assessment* (pp. 369–401). New York: Pergamon Press.

HEATON, R. K. & PENDLETON, M. G. (1981). Use of neuropsychological tests to predict adult patients' everyday functioning. *Journal of Consulting and Clinical Psychology, 49,* 807–821.

HEILMAN, K. M. & VALENSTEIN, E. (Eds.) (1985). *Clinical neuropsychology* (2nd ed.). New York: Oxford University Press.

HEINRICH, R. L. & SCHAG, C. C. (1985). Stress and activity management: Group treatment for cancer patients and spouses. *Journal of Consulting and Clinical Psychology, 53,* 439–446.

HEITLER, J. B. (1976). Preparatory techniques in initiating expressive psychotherapy with lower-class, unsophisticated patients. *Psychological Bulletin, 83,* 339–352.

HELLER, K. (1971). Laboratory interview research as analogue to treatment. In A. E. Bergin & S. L. Garfield (Eds.), *Handbook of psychotherapy and behavior change* (pp. 126–153). New York: John Wiley.

HELLER, K. (1972). Interview structure and interviewer style in initial interviews. In A. W. Siegman & B. Pope (Eds.), *Studies in dyadic communication* (pp. 9–28). New York: Pergamon Press.

HELLER, K., DAVIS, J. D., & MYERS, R. A. (1966). The effects of interviewer style in a standardized interview. *Journal of Consulting Psychology, 30,* 501–508.

HELLER, K., HOLTZMAN, W., & MESSICK, S. (Eds.) (1982). *Placing children in special education: A strategy for equity.* Washington, DC: National Academy Press.

HELLER, K., MYERS, R. A., & KLINE, L. V. (1963). Interviewer behavior as a function of standardized client roles. *Journal of Consulting Psychology, 27,* 117–122.

HELLER, K. PRICE, R. H., REINHARZ, S., RIGER, S., & WANDERSMAN, A. (1984). *Psychology and community change* (2nd ed.). Homewood, IL: Dorsey.

HENRY, W. E. (1956). *The analysis of fantasy: The thematic apperception technique in the study of personality.* New York: John Wiley.

HERBSLEB, J. D., SALES, B. D., & OVERCAST, T. D. (1985). Challenging licensure and certification. *American Psychologist, 40,* 1165–1178.

HERGENHAHN, B. R. (1984). *An introduction to theories of personality* (2nd ed.). Englewood Cliffs, NJ: Prentice-Hall.

HERINK, R. (Ed.) (1980). *The psychotherapy handbook: The A to Z guide to more than 250 different therapies in use today.* New York: New American Library.

HERMANN, B. P. & WHITMAN, S. (1984). Behavioral and personality correlates of epilepsy: A review, methodological critique, and conceptual model. *Psychological Bulletin, 95,* 451–497.

HERSEN, M. (1981). Complex problems require complex solutions. *Behavior Therapy, 12,* 15–29.

HERSEN, M. & BELLACK, A. S. (Eds.) (1985). *Handbook of clinical behavior therapy with adults.* New York: Plenum.

HERSEN, M. & BELLACK, A. S. (Eds.) (in press). *Behavioral assessment: A practical handbook* (3rd ed.). New York: Pergamon Press.

HERSEN, M. & TURNER, S. M. (Eds.) (1985). *Diagnostic interviewing.* New York: Plenum.

HESTON, L. L. (1966). Psychiatric disorders in foster home reared children of schizophrenic mothers. *British Journal of Psychiatry, 112,* 819–825.

HICKMAN, F. J., RESNICK, P. J., & OLSON, K. B. (1982). Right to refuse psychotropic medication: An interdisciplinary proposal. *Mental Disability Law Reporter, 6,* 122–130.

HILGARD, E. R. (1969). Pain as a puzzle for psychology and physiology. *American Psychologist, 24,* 103–114.

HOCH, E. L. (1971). *Experimental contributions to clinical psychology.* Belmont, CA: Brooks/Cole.

HODGSON, R. J. & RACHMAN, S. (1977). Obsessional-compulsive complaints. *Behaviour Research and Therapy, 15,* 389–395.

HOELSCHER, T. J., LICHSTEIN, K. L., & ROSENTHAL, T. L. (1986). Home relaxation practice in hypertension treatment: Objective assessment and compliance induction. *Journal of Consulting and Clinical Psychology, 54,* 217–221.

HOFFMAN, B. (1962). *The tyranny of testing.* New York: Crowell-Collier.

HOFFMAN, P. J. (1960). The paramorphic representation of clinical judgment. *Psychological Bulletin, 57,* 116–131.

HOFFMAN, R. S. (1973). The varieties of psychotherapeutic experience. *Journal of Irreproducible Results, 19,* 76–77.

HOGAN, D. B. (1983). The effectiveness of licensing: History, evidence, and recommendations. *Law and Human Behavior, 7,* 117–138.

HOLLAND, J. L. (1978). *Manual for the Vocational Preference Inventory* (3rd ed.). Palo Alto, CA: Consulting Psychologists Press.

HOLMES, M. R., HANSEN, D. J., & ST. LAWRENCE, J. S. (1984). Conversational skills training with aftercare patients in the community: Social validation and generalization. *Behavior Therapy, 15,* 84–100.

HOLMES, T. H. & MASUDA, M. (1974). Life change and illness susceptibility. In B. S. Dohrenwend & B. P. Dohrenwend (Eds.), *Stressful life events: Their nature and effects* (pp. 45–72). New York: John Wiley.

HOLT, R. R. (1958). Formal aspects of the TAT: A neglected resource. *Journal of Projective Techniques, 22,* 163–172.

HOLT, R. R. (1971). *Assessing personality.* New York: Harcourt Brace Jovanovich.

HOLT, R. R. (1978). *Methods in clinical psychology: Projective assessment* (Vol. 1). New York: Plenum.

HOLT, R. R. & LUBORSKY, L. (1958). *Personality patterns of psychiatrists: A study of methods for selecting residents* (Vol. 1). New York: Basic Books.

HOLTZMAN, W. H., THORPE, J. W., SWARTZ, J. D., & HERRON, E. W. (1961). *Inkblot perception and personality: Holtzman Inkblot Technique.* Austin: University of Texas Press.

HOLZMAN, A. D. & TURK, D. C. (1986). *Pain management: A handbook of psychological treatment approaches.* New York: Pergamon Press.

HOON, P. W., FEUERSTEIN, M., & PAPCIAK, A. S. (1985). Evaluation of the chronic low back pain patient: Conceptual and clinical considerations. *Clinical Psychology Review, 5,* 377–401.

HOUSE, J. S., ROBBINS, C., & METZNER, H. L. (1982). The association of social relationships and activities with mortality: Prospective evidence from the Tecumseh Community Health Study. *American Journal of Epidemiology, 116,* 123–140.

HOVANCIK, J. R. (1985). The new odds are at odds with the laws of probability. *American Psychologist, 40,* 852–853.

HULL, C. L. (1943). *Principles of behavior.* New York: Appleton.

HUMPHREY, L. L., APPLE, R. F., & KIRSCHENBAUM, D. S. (1986). Differentiating bulimic-anorexic from normal families using interpersonal and behavioral observational systems. *Journal of Consulting and Clinical Psychology, 54,* 190–195.

HUNT, W. A. & JONES, N. F. (1962). The experimental investigation of clinical judgment. In A. J. Bachrach (Ed.), *Experimental foundations of clinical psychology* (pp. 26–51). New York: Basic Books.

HUTT, C. & HUTT, S. J. (1968). Stereotypy, arousal and autism. *Human Development, 11,* 277–286.

INSTITUTE OF PERSONALITY ASSESSMENT AND RESEARCH. (1970). *Annual report: 1969-1970.* Berkeley, CA: University of California.

INUI, T., YOURTEE, E., & WILLIAMSON, J. (1976). Improved outcomes in hypertension after physician tutorials. *Annals of Internal Medicine, 84,* 646–651.

ISCOE, I. & HARRIS, L. C. (1984). Social and community interventions. *Annual Review of Psychology, 35,* 333–360.

JACKSON, D. N. (1967). *Personality Research Form manual.* Goshen, NY: Research Psychologists Press.

JACKSON, D. N. (1975). The relative validity of scales prepared by naive item writers and those based on empirical methods of personality scale construction. *Educational and Psychological Measurement, 35,* 361–370.

JACKSON, D. N. & MESSICK, S. (1958). Content and style in personality assessment. *Psychological Bulletin, 55,* 243–252.

JACKSON, D. N. & MESSICK, S. (1961). Acquiescence and desirability as response determinants on the MMPI. *Educational and Psychological Measurement, 21,* 771–790.

JACOBSON, N. S., FOLLETTE, W. C., & REVENSTORF, D. (1984). Psychotherapy outcome research: Methods for reporting variability and evaluating clinical significance. *Behavior Therapy, 15,* 336–352.

JANSSON, L. & OST, L. G. (1982). Behavioral treatments for agoraphobia: An evaluative review. *Clinical Psychology Review, 2,* 311–336.

JEMMOTT, J. B. & LOCKE, S. E. (1984). Psychosocial factors, immunologic mediation, and human susceptibility to infectious diseases: How much do we know? *Psychological Bulletin, 95,* 52–77.

JENKINS, C. D., ZYZANSKI, S. J., & ROSENMAN, R. H. (1971). Progress toward validation of a computer-scored test for the Type A coronary-prone behavior pattern. *Psychosomatic Medicine, 33,* 193–202.

JENSEN, A. R. (1980). *Bias in mental testing.* New York: The Free Press.

JOHNSON, M. L. (1953). Seeing's believing. *New Biology, 15,* 60–80.

JOHNSON, S. M. & BOLSTAD, O. D. (1973). Methodological issues in naturalistic observation: Some problems and solutions for field research. In L. A. Hamerlynck, L. C. Handy, & E. J. Mash (Eds.), *Behavior change: Methodology, concepts and practice.* Champaign, IL: Research Press.

JOHNSON, S. M. & LOBITZ, G. K. (1974). Parental manipulation of child behavior in home observations. *Journal of Applied Behavior Analysis, 7,* 23–32.

JONES, B. P. & BUTTERS, N. (1983). Neuropsychological assessment. In M. Hersen, A. E. Kazdin, & A. S. Bellack (Eds.), *The clinical psychology handbook* (pp. 377–396). New York: Pergamon Press.

JONES, E. (1953, 1955, 1957). *The life and work of Sigmund Freud* (Vol. 1, 2, and 3). New York: Basic Books.

JONES, H. E. et al. (1943). *Development in adolescence.* New York: Appleton-Century.

JONES, M. C. (1924a). The elimination of children's fears. *Journal of Experimental Psychology, 7,* 382–390.

JONES, M. C. (1924b). A laboratory study of fear: The case of Peter. *Pedagogical Seminary and Journal of Genetic Psychology, 31,* 308–315.

JONES, R. R., REID, J. B., & PATTERSON, G. R. (1975). Naturalistic observation in clinical assessment. In P. McReynolds (Ed.), *Advances in psychological assessment* (Vol. 3, pp. 42–95). San Francisco: Jossey-Bass.

JOURILES, E. N. & O'LEARY, K. D. (1985). Interspousal reliability of reports of marital violence. *Journal of Consulting and Clinical Psychology, 53,* 419–421.

JURJEVICH, R. M. (1974). *The hoax of Freudism.* Philadelphia: Dorrence & Co.

KAGAN, N. (1974). Influencing human interaction—Eleven years with IPR. In B. A. Jacobs,

R. K. Buschman, R. F. Dency, D. T. Schaeffer, & J. Stieber (Eds.), *Counselor training* (pp. 329–346). Arlington, VA: National Drug Abuse Training Center.

KAHN, E. (1985). Heinz Kohut and Carl Rogers: A timely comparison. *American Psychologist, 40,* 893–904.

KAHN, T. C. (1955). Personality projection on culturally structured symbols. *Journal of Projective Techniques, 19,* 431–442.

KAHNEMAN, D. & TVERSKY, A. (1979). Intuitive prediction: Biases and corrective procedures. *TIMS Studies in the Management Sciences, 12,* 313–327.

KANFER, F. H. (1968). Verbal conditioning: A review of its current status. In T. R. Dixon & D. L. Horton (Eds.), *Verbal behavior and general behavior theory* (pp. 245–290). Englewood Cliffs, NJ: Prentice-Hall.

KANFER, F. H. & MCBREARTY, J. F. (1962). Minimal social reinforcement and interview content. *Journal of Clinical Psychology, 18,* 210–215.

KANFER, F. H. & SASLOW, G. (1969). Behavioral diagnosis. In C. M. Franks (Ed.), *Behavior therapy: Appraisal and status* (pp. 210–215). New York: McGraw-Hill.

KANNER, A. D., COYNE, J. C., SCHAEFER, C., & LAZARUS, R. S. (1981). Comparison of two modes of stress measurement: Daily hassles and uplifts versus major life events. *Journal of Behavioral Medicine, 14,* 1–39.

KAPLAN, A. (1964). *The conduct of inquiry.* San Francisco: Chander.

KAPLAN, M. (1983). A woman's view of DSM-III. *American Psychologist, 38,* 786–792.

KAPLAN, R. M. (1984). The connection between clinical health promotion and health status: A critical overview. *American Psychologist, 39,* 755–765.

KASL, S. V. (1980). Cardiovascular risk reduction in a community setting: Some comments. *Journal of Consulting and Clinical Psychology, 48,* 143–149.

KASSIN, S. M. & WRIGHTSMAN, L. S. (Eds.) (1985). *The psychology of evidence and trial procedure.* Beverly Hills, CA: Sage.

KAUFMAN, A. S. & KAUFMAN, N. L. (1983). *K-ABC: Kaufman Assessment Battery for Children.* Circle Pines, MN: American Guidance Service.

KAZDIN, A. E. (1973). Covert modeling and reduction of avoidance behavior. *Journal of Abnormal Psychology, 81,* 87–95.

KAZDIN, A. E. (1974). Self-monitoring and behavior change. In M. J. Mahoney & C. E. Thoresen (Eds.), *Self-control: Power to the person* (pp. 218–246). Monterey, CA: Brooks/Cole.

KAZDIN, A. E. (1978). *History of behavior modification: Experimental foundations of contemporary research.* Baltimore: University Park Press.

KAZDIN, A. E. (1982a). *Single-case research designs: Methods for clinical and applied settings.* New York: Oxford University Press.

KAZDIN, A. E. (1982b). Single-case experimental designs. In P. C. Kendall & J. N. Butcher (Eds.), *Handbook of research methods in clinical psychology* (pp. 461–490). New York: John Wiley.

KAZDIN, A. E. (1984). *Behavior modification in applied settings* (3rd ed.). Homewood, IL: Dorsey Press.

KAZDIN, A. E. (1985). *Treatment of antisocial behavior in children and adolescents.* Homewood, IL: Dorsey Press.

KAZDIN, A. E., ESVELDT-DAWSON, K., & MATSON, J. L. (1983). The effects of instructional set on social skills performance among psychiatric inpatient children. *Behavior Therapy, 14,* 413–423.

KAZDIN, A. E. & KLOCK, J. (1973). The effect of nonverbal teacher approval on student attentive behavior. *Journal of Applied Behavior Analysis, 6,* 643–654.

KAZDIN, A. E. & KOPEL, S. A. (1975). On resolving ambiguities of the multiple baseline design: Problems and recommendations. *Behavior Therapy, 6,* 601–608.

KAZDIN, A. E., MATSON, J. L., & ESVELDT-DAWSON, K. (1984). The relationship of role-play assessment of children's social skills to multiple measures of social competence. *Behaviour Research and Therapy, 22,* 129–140.

KAZDIN, A. E. & WILCOXON, L. A. (1976). Systematic desensitization and nonspecific treatment effects: A methodological evaluation. *Psychological Bulletin, 83,* 729–758.

KAZDIN, A. E. & WILSON, G. T. (1978). *Evaluation of behavior therapy: Issues, evidence and research strategies.* Cambridge, MA: Ballinger.

KEEFE, F. J., KOPEL, S. A., & GORDON, S. B. (1978). *A practical guide to behavioral assessment.* New York: Springer Publishing Co.

KEELEY, S. M., SHEMBERG, K. M., & CARBONELL, J. (1976). Operant clinical intervention: Behavior management or beyond? Where are the data? *Behavior Therapy, 7,* 292–305.

KELLY, E. L. (1961). Clinical psychology–1960: A report of survey findings. *Newsletter, Division of Clinical Psychology of APA, 14,* 1–11.

KELLY, E. L. & FISKE, D. W. (1951). *The prediction of performance in clinical psychology.* Ann Arbor, MI: University of Michigan Press.

KELLY, G. A. (1955). *The psychology of personal constructs.* New York: W. W. Norton.

KELLY, G. A. (1958). The theory and technique of assessment. *Annual review of psychology* (Vol. 9, pp. 323–352). Palo Alto, CA: Annual Reviews, Inc.

KELLY, J. A. (1982). *Social skills training: A practical guide for interventions.* New York: Springer Publishing Co.

KEMPLER, W. (1973). Gestalt therapy. In R. Corsini (Ed.), *Current psychotherapies* (pp. 251–286). Itasca, IL: F. E. Peacock Publishers.

KENDALL, P. C. (1984). Behavioral assessment and methodology. In G. T. Wilson, C. M. Franks, K. D. Brownell, & P. C. Kendall (Eds.), *Annual Review of Behavior Therapy* (Vol. 9, pp. 123–163). New York: Guilford Press.

KENDALL, P. C. & BRASWELL, L. (1985). *Cognitive-behavioral modification with impulsive children.* New York: Guilford Press.

KENDALL, P. C. & HOLLON, S. D. (Eds.) (1979). *Cognitive-behavioral interventions: Theory, research, and procedures.* New York: Academic Press.

KENDALL, P. C. & ZUPAN, B. A. (1981). Individual versus group application of cognitive-behavioral self-control procedures with children. *Behavior Therapy, 12,* 344–359.

KENT, R. N. & FOSTER, S. L. (1977). Direct observational procedures: Methodological issues in naturalistic settings. In A. R. Ciminero, K. S. Calhoun, & H. E. Adams (Eds.), *Handbook of behavioral assessment* (pp. 279–328). New York: John Wiley.

KERN, J. M. (1982). The comparative external and concurrent validity of three role-plays for assessing heterosocial performance. *Behavior Therapy, 13,* 666–680.

KERN, J. M., CAVELL, T. A., & BECK, B. (1985). Predicting differential reactions to males' versus females' assertions, empathic-assertions, and non-assertions. *Behavior Therapy, 16,* 63–75.

KERN, J. M., MILLER, C., & EGGERS, J. (1983). Enhancing the validity of role-play tests: A comparison of three role-play methodologies. *Behavior Therapy, 14*, 482–492.

KERNBERG, O. (1976). *Object relations, theory and clinical psychoanalysis.* New York: Jason Aronson.

KESSLER, R. C., PRICE, R. H., & WORTMAN, C. B. (1985). Social factors in psychopathology: Stress, social support, and coping processes. *Annual Review of Psychology, 36*, 531–572.

KETY, S. S., ROSENTHAL, D., WENDER, P. H., & SCHULSINGER, F. (1968). The types and prevalence of mental illness in the biological and adoptive families of adopted schizophrenics. In D. Rosenthal & S. S. Kety (Eds.), *The transmission of schizophrenia* (pp. 345–362). Oxford: Pergamon Press.

KILBURG, R. R. (1984). Psychologists in management: The unseen career path in psychology. *Professional psychology: Research and practice, 15*, 613–625.

KIRCHNER, E. P., & DRAGUNS, J. G. (1979). Assertion and aggression in adult offenders. *Behavior Therapy, 10*, 452–471.

KLEIN, M. (1960). *The psychoanalysis of children.* New York: Grove Press.

KLEIN, M. (1975). *The writings of Melanie Klein* (Vol. III). London: Hogarth Press.

KLEIN, R. H. (1983). Group treatment approaches. In M. Hersen, A. E. Kazdin, & A. S. Bellack (Eds.), *The clinical psychology handbook* (pp. 593–610). New York: Pergamon Press.

KLEINKNECHT, R. A. & BERNSTEIN, D. A. (1978). Assessment of dental fear. *Behavior Therapy, 9*, 626–634.

KLEINMUNTZ, B. (1963). MMPI decision rules for the identification of college maladjustment: A digital computer approach. *Psychological Monographs, 77*(14, Whole No. 477).

KLEINMUNTZ, B. (1969). Personality test interpretation by computer and clinician. In J. N. Butcher (Ed.), *MMPI: Research developments and clinical applications.* New York: John Wiley.

KLEINMUNTZ, B. (1982). *Personality and psychological assessment.* New York: St. Martin's Press.

KLEINMUNTZ, B. (1984). The scientific study of clinical judgment in psychology and medicine. *Clinical Psychology Review, 4*, 111–126.

KLOPFER, B. & KELLEY, D. M. (1937). The techniques of the Rorschach performance. *Rorschach Research Exchange, 2*, 1–14.

KLOPFER, B. & KELLEY, D. M. (1942). *The Rorschach technique.* New York: Harcourt, Brace & World.

KLOPFER, W. G. (1960). *The psychological report.* New York: Grune & Stratton.

KOFFKA, K. (1935). *Principles of Gestalt psychology.* New York: Harcourt, Brace & Co.

KOHLER, W. (1925). *The mentality of apes.* New York: Harcourt, Brace & Co.

KOHUT, H. (1971). *The analysis of self.* New York: International Universities Press.

KOHUT, H. (1977). *The restoration of the self.* New York: International Universities Press.

KOHUT, H. (1983). Selected problems of self-psychological theory. In J. D. Lichtenberg & S. Kaplan (Eds.)., *Reflections on self psychology* (pp. 387–416). Hillsdale, NJ: Lawrence Erlbaum Associates.

KOLB, B. & WHISHAW, I. Q. (1985). *Fundamentals of human neuropsychology* (2nd ed.). New York: W. H. Freeman & Company.

KOLEVZON, M. S. & GREEN, R. G. (1985). *Family therapy models: Convergence and divergence.* New York: Springer Publishing Co.

KOLKO, D. J., KAZDIN, A. E., & MEYER, E. C. (1985). Aggression and psychopathology in childhood firesetters: Parent and child report. *Journal of Consulting and Clinical Psychology, 53*, 377–385.

KOLOTKIN, R. H. (1980). Situation specificity in the assessment of assertion: Considerations for the measurement of training and transfer. *Behavior Therapy, 11*, 651–661.

KORCHIN, S. J. (1976). *Modern clinical psychology: Principles of intervention in the clinic and community.* New York: Basic Books.

KORIAT, A., LICHTENSTEIN, S., & FISCHHOFF, B. (1980). Reasons for confidence. *Journal of Experimental Psychology: Human Learning and Memory, 6*, 107–118.

KORMAN, M. (1974). National conference on levels and patterns of professional training in psychology: The major themes. *American Psychologist, 29*, 441–449.

KORMAN, M. (Ed.) (1976). *Levels and patterns of professional training in psychology.* Washington, DC: American Psychological Association.

KORN, J. H. (1984). New odds on acceptance into Ph.D. programs in psychology. *American Psychologist, 39*, 179–180.

KORSCH, B. M. & NEGRETE, V. F. (1972). Doctor-patient communication. *Scientific American, 227*, 66–74.

KOSTLAN, A. (1954). A method for the empirical study of psychodiagnosis. *Journal of Consulting Psychology, 18*, 83–88.

KOVACS, M. (1981). Rating scales to assess depression in school aged children. *Acta Paedopsychiatrica, 46*, 305–315.

KOVACS, M., RUSH, A. J., BECK, A. T., & HOLLON, S. D. (1981). Depressed outpatients treated with cognitive therapy or pharmacotherapy: A one-year follow-up. *Archives of General Psychiatry, 38*, 33–39.

KRAEMER, H. D. (1981). Coping strategies in psychiatric clinical research. *Journal of Consulting and Clinical Psychology, 49*, 309–319.

KRANTZ, D. S., GRUNBERG, N. E., & BAUM, A. (1985). Health psychology. *Annual Review of Psychology, 36*, 349–383.

KRASNER, L. (1965). Verbal conditioning and psychotherapy. In L. Krasner & L. P. Ullmann (Eds.), *Research in behavior modification: New developments and implications* (pp. 211–228). New York: Holt, Rinehart & Winston.

KRASNER, L. & ULLMANN, L. P. (Eds.) (1965). *Research in behavior modification: New developments and implications*. New York: Holt, Rinehart & Winston.

KRASNER, L. & ULLMANN, L. P. (1973). *Behavior influence and personality*. New York: Holt, Rinehart & Winston.

KROGER, R. O. & TURNBULL, W. (1975). Invalidity of validity scales: The case of the MMPI. *Journal of Consulting and Clinical Psychology, 43*, 48–55.

KUDER, G. F. (1948). *Kuder Preference Record-Form C (Vocational)*. Chicago: Science Research Associates.

KUIPER, N. A. & MACDONALD, M. R. (1983). Reason, emotion, and cognitive therapy. *Clinical Psychology Review, 3*, 297–316.

KUTASH, S. B. (1976). Modified psychoanalytic therapies. In B. B. Wolman (Ed.), *The therapist's handbook* (pp. 87–116). New York: Van Nostrand Reinhold.

L'ABATE, L. (1964). *Principles of clinical psychology*. New York: Grune & Stratton.

L'ABATE, L. (1969). Introduction. In L. L'Abate (Ed.), *Models of clinical psychology*. Research paper number 22. Atlanta, GA: Georgia State College.

LACHAR, D. (1974). *The MMPI: Clinical assessment and automated interpretation*. Los Angeles, CA: Western Psychological Services.

LACHAR, D. & GDOWSKI, C. L. (1979). *Actuarial assessment of child and adolescent personality: An interpretive guide for the Personality Inventory for Children profile*. Los Angeles: Western Psychological Services.

LAING, R. D. (1967). *The politics of experience*. New York: Pantheon.

LAMB, H. R. & ZUSMAN, J. (1981). Primary prevention in perspective. *American Journal of Psychiatry, 9*, 1–26.

LAMBERT, N. M., COX, H. W., & HARTSOUGH, C. S. (1970). The observability of intellectual functioning of first graders. *Psychology in the Schools*, 74–85.

LANDMAN, J. T. & DAWES, R. (1982). Experimental outcome: Smith and Glass' conclusions stand up under scrutiny. *American Psychologist, 37*, 504–516.

LANG, P. J. & LAZOVIK, A. D. (1963). Experimental desensitization of a phobia. *Journal of Abnormal and Social Psychology, 66*, 519–525.

LANGER, E. J. & ABELSON, R. (1974). A patient by any name: Clinician group differences in labeling bias. *Journal of Consulting and Clinical Psychology, 42*, 4–9.

LANYON, R. I. (1984). Personality assessment. *Annual Review of Psychology, 35*, 667–701.

LANYON, R. I. & GOODSTEIN, L. D. (1982). *Personality assessment* (2nd ed.). New York: John Wiley.

LATIMER, P. R. (1983). *Functional gastrointestinal disorders: A behavioral medicine approach*. New York: Springer Publishing Co.

LAWLIS, G. F. (1971). Response styles of a patient population on the Fear Survey Schedule. *Behaviour Research and Therapy, 9*, 95–102.

LAZARUS, A. A. (1976). *Multimodal behavior therapy*. New York: Springer Publishing Co.

LAZARUS, A. A. (1977). Has behavior therapy outlived its usefulness? *American Psychologist, 32*, 550–554.

LAZARUS, A. A. (1981). *The practice of multimodal therapy*. New York: McGraw-Hill.

LAZARUS, A. A. (1985). *Casebook of multimodal therapy.* New York: Guilford Press.

LEAHEY, T. H. (1980). *A history of psychology.* Englewood Cliffs, NJ: Prentice-Hall.

LEARY, T. & GILL, M. (1959). The dimensions and a measure of the process of psychotherapy: A system for the analysis of the content of clinical evaluations and patient-therapist verbalizations. In E. A. Rubinstein & M. B. Parloff (Eds.), *Research in psychotherapy* (Vol. 1, pp. 62–95). Washington, DC: American Psychological Association.

LEDERER, W. J. & JACKSON, D. D. (1968). *The mirages of marriage.* New York: W. W. Norton.

LEDVINKA, J. (1971). Race of interviewer and the language elaboration of black interviewees. *Journal of Social Issues, 27,* 185–197.

LEDWIDGE, B. (1978). Cognitive behavior modification: A step in the wrong direction? *Psychological Bulletin, 85,* 353–375.

LEE, S. D. & TEMERLIN, M. K. (1970). Social class, diagnosis, and prognosis for psychotherapy. *Psychotherapy: Theory, Research, and Practice, 7,* 181–185.

LEFEBVRE, R. C. (1986). Primary prevention of coronary heart disease. In M. Hersen, R. M. Eisler, & P. M. Miller (Eds.), *Progress in behavior modification.* Beverly Hills, CA: Sage.

LEHRER, P. M. & WOOLFOLK, R. L. (1982). Self-report assessment of anxiety: Somatic, cognitive, and behavioral modalities. *Behavioral Assessment, 4,* 167–177.

LEITENBERG, H., AGRAS, W. S., BARLOW, D. H., & OLIVEAU, D. C. (1969). Contribution of selective positive reinforcement and therapeutic instructions to systematic desensitization therapy. *Journal of Abnormal Psychology, 74,* 113–118.

LENNARD, H. L. & BERNSTEIN, A. (1960). *The anatomy of psychotherapy: Systems of communication and expectation.* New York: Columbia University Press.

LENROW, P. & COWDEN, P. (1980). Human services, professionals, and the paradox of institutional reform. *American Journal of Community Psychology, 8,* 463–484.

LERNER, P. M. (1985). Current psychoanalytic perspectives on the borderline and narcissistic concepts. *Clinical Psychology Review, 5,* 199–214.

LEVENBERG, S. B. (1975). Professional training, psychodiagnostic skill, and kinetic family drawings. *Journal of Personality Assessment, 39,* 389–393.

LEVENTHAL, H., SAFER, M. A., CLEARY, P. D., & GUTMANN, M. (1980). Cardiovascular risk modification by community-based programs for life-style change: Comments on the Stanford Study. *Journal of Consulting and Clinical Psychology, 48,* 150–158.

LEVIN, R. B. & GROSS, A. M. (1985). The role of relaxation in systematic desensitization. *Behaviour Research and Therapy, 23,* 187–196.

LEVINE, F. J. (1985). Self-psychology and the new narcissism in psychoanalysis. *Clinical Psychology Review, 5,* 215–230.

LEVITSKY, A. & PERLS, F. S. (1970). The rules and games of gestalt therapy. In J. Fagan & I. L. Shepherd (Eds.), *Gestalt therapy now.* Palo Alto, CA: Science and Behavior Books.

LEVITT, E. E. (1969). The psychologist: A neglected legal source. *Indiana Law Journal, 45,* 82–89.

LEVY, L. H. (1963). *Psychological interpretation.* New York: Holt, Rinehart & Winston.

LEVY, L. H. (1984). The metamorphosis of clinical psychology: Toward a new charter as human services psychology. *American Psychologist, 39,* 486–494.

LEVY, N. B. (Ed.), MATTERN, W., & FREEDMAN, A. M. (Asst. Eds.) (1983). *Psychonephrology 2: Psychological problems in kidney failure and their treatment.* New York: Plenum.

LEWINSOHN, P. M. & SHAFFER, M. (1971). Use of home observations as an integral part of the treatment of depression: Preliminary report and case studies. *Journal of Consulting and Clinical Psychology, 37,* 87–94.

LEY, P., BRADSHAW, P. W., EAVES, D. E., & WALKER, C. M. (1973). A method for increasing patient recall of information presented to them. *Psychological Medicine, 3,* 217–220.

LEZAK, M. D. (1983). *Neuropsychological assessment* (2nd ed.). New York: Oxford University Press.

LIBBY, W. (1908). The imagination of adolescents. *American Journal of Psychology, 19,* 249–252.

LIBET, J. M. & LEWINSOHN, P. M. (1973). Concept of social skill with special reference to the behavior of depressed persons. *Journal of Consulting and Clinical Psychology, 40,* 304–312.

LICHTENSTEIN, E. (1982). The smoking problem: A behavioral perspective. *Journal of Consulting and Clinical Psychology, 50,* 804–819.

LICK, J. R. (1977). The effects of pretreatment demand characteristics on verbally reported fear. *Behavior Therapy, 8,* 727–730.

LIDZ, R. W. & LIDZ, T. (1949). The family environment of schizophrenic patients. *American Journal of Psychiatry, 106,* 332–345.

LIEBERT, R. M. & SPIEGLER, M. D. (1982). *Personality: Strategies and issues* (4th ed.). Homewood, IL: Dorsey.

LINDEMANN, E. (1944). Symptomology and management of acute grief. *American Journal of Psychology, 101,* 141–148.

LINDEMANN, J. E. & MATARAZZO, J. D. (1984). Intellectual assessment of adults. In G. Goldstein & M. Hersen (Eds.), *Handbook of psychological assessment* (pp. 77–99). New York: Pergamon Press.

LINDESMITH, A. R. & STRAUSS, A. (1950). A critique of culture-personality writings. *American Sociological Review, 15,* 587–600.

LINDNER, R. (1954). *The fifty minute hour.* New York: Rinehart.

LINDSLEY, O. R., SKINNER, B. F., & SOLOMON, H. C. (1953). *Studies in behavior therapy. Status report 1.* Waltham, MA: Metropolitan State Hospital.

LINDZEY, G. (1952). The thematic apperception test: Interpretive assumptions and related empirical evidence. *Psychological Bulletin, 49,* 1–25.

LINDZEY, G. (1961). *Projective techniques and cross-cultural research.* New York: Appleton-Century-Crofts.

LINDZEY, G., BRADFORD, J., TEJESSY, C., & DAVIDS, A. (1959). Thematic apperception test: An interpretive lexicon. *Journal of Clinical Psychology Monograph Supplement,* No. 12.

LINEHAN, M. M. (1984). *Dialectical behavior therapy for treatment of parasuicidal women: Treatment manual.* Seattle: University of Washington, Psychology Department.

LINEHAN, M. M. & NIELSEN, S. L. (1983). Social desirability: Its relevance to the measurement of hopelessness and suicidal behavior. *Journal of Consulting and Clinical Psychology, 51,* 141–143.

LIPINSKI, D. P., BLACK, J. L., NELSON, R. O., & CIMINERO, A. R. (1975). The influence of motivational variables on the reactivity and reliability of self-recording. *Journal of Consulting and Clinical Psychology, 43,* 637–646.

LIPSITT, P. D., LELOS, D., & McGARRY, A. L. (1971). Competency for trial: A screening instrument. *American Journal of Psychiatry, 128,* 105–109.

LITTLE, K. B. & SHNEIDMAN, E. S. (1959). Congruences among interpretations of psychological test and anamnestic data. *Psychological Monographs, 73* (Whole No. 476).

LITTLE, L. M. & CURRAN, J. P. (1978). Covert sensitization: A clinical procedure in need of some explanation. *Psychological Bulletin, 85,* 513–531.

LITWACK, T. R., GERBER, G. L., & FENSTER, C. A. (1979–1980). The proper role of psychology in child custody disputes. *Journal of Family Law, 18,* 269–300.

LOEBER, R. & DISHION, T. (1983). Early predictors of male delinquency: A review. *Psychological Bulletin, 94,* 68–99.

LOEVINGER, J. (1965). Measurement in clinical psychology. In B. B. Wolman (Ed.), *Handbook of clinical psychology* (pp. 78–94). New York: McGraw-Hill.

LOFTUS, E. F. (1983). Silence is not golden. *American Psychologist, 38,* 564–572.

LOH, W. D. (1984). *Social research in the judicial process: Cases, readings, and text.* New York: Russell Sage Foundation.

LORR, M., KLETT, J., & McNAIR, D. M. (1963). *Syndromes of psychosis.* New York: Macmillan.

LOUTTIT, C. M. & BROWNE, C. G. (1947). Psychometric instruments in psychological clinics. *Journal of Consulting Psychology, 11,* 49–54.

LUBIN, B., LARSEN, R. M., & MATARAZZO, J. D. (1984). Patterns of psychological test usage in the United States: 1935–1982. *American Psychologist, 39,* 451–454.

LUBIN, B., LARSEN, R. M., MATARAZZO, J. D., & SEEVER, M. (1985). Psychological test usage patterns in five professional settings. *American Psychologist, 40,* 857–861.

LUBIN, B., WALLIS, R. R., & PAINE, C. (1971). Patterns of psychological test usage in the United States: 1935–1969. *Professional Psychology, 2,* 70–74.

LUBORSKY, L. (1984). *Principles of psychoanalytic psychotherapy: A manual for supportive-expressive treatment.* New York: Basic Books.

LUBORSKY, L., CRITS-CHRISTOPH, P., & MELLON, J. (1986). Advent of objective measures of the transference concept. *Journal of Consulting and Clinical Psychology, 54,* 39–47.

LUBORSKY, L. & SPENCE, D. P. (1978). Quantitative research on psychoanalytic therapy. In S. L. Garfield & A. E. Bergin (Eds.), *Handbook of psychotherapy and behavior change* (2d ed., pp. 331–368). New York: John Wiley.

LUBORSKY, L., SINGER, B., & LUBORSKY, L. (1975). Comparative studies of psychotherapies: Is it true that "Everyone has won and all must have prizes"? *Archives of General Psychiatry, 32,* 995–1008.

LYMAN, R. D. (1984). The effect of private and public goal setting on classroom on-task behavior of emotionally disturbed children. *Behavior Therapy, 15,* 395–402.

MACDONALD, M. L. (1978). Measuring assertion: A model and method. *Behavior Therapy, 9,* 889–899.

MACHOVER, K. (1949). *Personality projection in the drawing of the human figure.* Springfield, IL: Charles C Thomas.

MACKINNON, R. A. (1980). Psychiatric interview. In H. I. Kaplan, A. M. Freedman, & B. J. Sadock (Eds.), *Comprehensive textbook of psychiatry, Vol. III.* Baltimore: Williams & Wilkins.

MACPHILLAMY, D. J. & LEWINSOHN, P. M. (1972). Measuring reinforcing events. *Proceedings of the 80th Annual Convention,* American Psychological Association.

MAGARET, A. (1952). Clinical methods: Psychodiagnostics. *Annual Review of Psychology, 3,* 283–320.

MAGRAB, P. & PAPADOPOULOU, Z. L. (1977). The effect of a token economy on dietary compliance for children on hemodialysis. *Journal of Applied Behavioral Analysis, 10,* 573–578.

MAHL, G. F. (1959). Exploring emotional states by content analysis. In I. Pool (Ed.), *Trends in content analysis* (pp. 89–130). Urbana, IL: University of Illinois Press.

MAHLER, M. S. (1965). On the significance of the normal separation-individuation phase: With reference to research in symbiotic child psychosis. In M. Schur (Ed.), *Drives, affects, behavior* (Vol. 2, pp. 161–169). New York: International Universities Press.

MAHLER, M. S., PINE, F., & BERGMAN, A. (1975). *The psychological birth of the human infant.* New York: Basic Books.

MAHONEY, M. J. (1974a). *Cognition and behavior modification.* Cambridge, MA: Ballinger.

MAHONEY, M. J. (1974b). Self-reward and self-monitoring techniques for weight control. *Behavior Therapy, 5,* 48–57.

MAHONEY, M. J. & FREEMAN, A. (Eds.) (1985). *Cognition and psychotherapy.* New York: Plenum.

MAHRER, A. R. (Ed.) (1970). *New approaches to personality classification.* New York: Columbia University Press.

MAISTO, S. A. & MAISTO, C. A. (1983). Institutional measures of treatment outcome. In M. J. Lambert, E. R. Christensen, & S. S. DeJulio (Eds.), *The assessment of psychotherapy outcome* (pp. 603–625). New York: John Wiley.

MALMO, R. B., SHAGASS, C., & DAVIS, F. H. (1950). Symptom specificity and bodily reactions during psychiatric interviews. *Psychosomatic Medicine, 12,* 362–376.

MALONEY, M. P. & WARD, M. P. (1976). *Psychological assessment: A conceptual approach.* New York: Oxford University Press.

MANN, P. A. (1978). *Community psychology: Concepts and applications.* New York: The Free Press.

MARKS, I. (1975). Behavioral treatments of phobic and obsessive compulsive disorders: A critical appraisal. In M. Hersen, R. M. Eisler, & P. M. Miller (Eds.), *Progress in behavior modification: Vol. I.* New York: Academic Press.

MARTIN, G. & PEAR, J. (1983). *Behavior modification: What it is and how to do it.* Englewood Cliffs, NJ: Prentice-Hall.

MARX, M. B., GARRITY, T. F., & BOWERS, F. R. (1975). The influence of recent life experience on the life of college freshmen. *Journal of Psychosomatic Research, 19,* 87–98.

MASH, E. J. & McELWEE, J. D. (1974). Situational effects on observer accuracy: Behavior predictability, prior experience, and complexity of coding categories. *Child Development, 45,* 367–377.

MASH, E. J. & TERDAL, L. G. (Eds.) (1976). *Behavior therapy assessment.* New York: Springer Publishing Co.

MASH, E. J. & TERDAL, L. G. (1981). *Behavioral assessment of childhood disorders.* New York: Guilford Press.

MASLING, J. (1960). The influence of situational and interpersonal variables in projective testing. *Psychological Bulletin, 57,* 65–68.

MASLING, J. (1966). Role-related behavior of the subject and psychologist and its effect upon psychological data. In D. Levine (Ed.), *Nebraska symposium on motivation* (pp. 67–103). Lincoln, NE: University of Nebraska Press.

MASLING, J. (Ed.) (1982). *Empirical studies of psychoanalytical theories* (Vol. 1). Hillsdale, NJ: Lawrence Erlbaum Associates.

MASLOW, A. H. (1954). *Motivation and personality.* New York: Harper.

MASLOW, A. H. (1962). *Toward a psychology of being.* Princeton, NJ: D. Van Nostrand.

MASLOW, A. H. (1967). Self-actualization and beyond. In J. F. T. Bugental (Ed.), *Challenges of humanistic psychology.* New York: McGraw-Hill.

MASLOW, A. H. (1968). *Toward a psychology of being* (2nd ed.). New York: Van Nostrand Reinhold.

MASLOW, A. H. (1971). *The farther reaches of human nature.* New York: Viking Press.

MASSERMAN, J. H. (1943). *Behavior and neurosis: An experimental psycho-analytic approach to psychobiologic principles.* Chicago: University of Chicago Press.

MASSEY, R. F. (1981). *Personality theories: Comparisons and syntheses.* New York: Van Nostrand.

MASSON, J. M. (1983). *The assault on the truth: Freud's suppression of the seduction theory.* New York: Farrar, Straus & Giroux.

MASUR, F. T. (1981). Adherence to health care regimens. In C. K. Prokop & L. A. Bradley (Eds.), *Medical psychology: Contributions to behavioral medicine* (pp. 442–470). New York: Academic Press.

MATARAZZO, J. D. (1965). The interview. In B. B. Wolman (Ed.), *Handbook of clinical psychology* (pp. 403–450). New York: McGraw-Hill.

MATARAZZO, J. D. (1986). Computerized clinical psychological test interpretations: Unvalidated plus all mean and no sigma. *American Psychologist, 41,* 14–24.

MATARAZZO, J. D. & CARMODY, T. P. (1983). Health psychology. In M. Hersen, A. E. Kazdin, & A. S. Bellack (Eds.), *The clinical psychology handbook* (pp. 657–682). New York: Pergamon Press.

MATARAZZO, J. D., MILLER, N. E., WEISS, S. M., HERD, J. A., & WEISS, S. M. (Eds.) (1984). *Behavioral health: A handbook of health enhancement and disease prevention.* New York: John Wiley.

MATARAZZO, J. D., WIENS, A. N., MATARAZZO, R. G., & SASLOW, G. (1968). Speech and silence behavior in clinical psychotherapy and its laboratory correlates. In J. M. Shlien, H. F. Hunt, J. D. Matarazzo, & C. Savage (Eds.), *Research in psychotherapy.* Washington, DC: American Psychological Association.

MATARAZZO, J. D., WIENS, A. N., SASLOW, G., DUNHAM, R. M., & VOAS, R. B. (1964). Speech durations of astronaut and ground communicator. *Science, 143,* 148–150.

MATARAZZO, J. D., WEITMAN, M., SASLOW, G., & WIENS, A. N. (1963). Interviewer influence on durations of interviewee speech. *Journal of Verbal Learning and Verbal Behavior, 1,* 451–458.

MATTHEWS, K. A. (1982). Psychological perspectives on the Type A behavior pattern. *Psychological Bulletin, 91,* 293–323.

MAY, R. (1969). *Love and will.* New York: Norton.

MAY, R., ANGEL, E., AND ELLENBERGER, H. F. (Eds.) (1958). *Existence: A new dimension in psychiatry and psychology.* New York: Basic Books.

MCARTHUR, C. C. (1956). Clinical vs. statistical prediction. *Proceedings of the 1955 Invitational Conference on Testing Problems* (pp. 99–106). Princeton, NJ: Educational Testing Service.

MCCARTHY, D. (1972). *Manual for the McCarthy Scale of Children's Abilities.* New York: Psychological Corporation.

MCCLELLAND, D. C., ATKINSON, J. W., CLARK, R. A., & LOWELL, E. L. (1953). *The achievement motive.* New York: Appleton-Century-Crofts.

MCCLOSKEY, M. & EGETH, H. E. (1983). Eyewitness identification: What can a psychologist tell a jury. *American Psychologist, 38,* 550–563.

MCCOY, S. A. (1976). Clinical judgments of normal childhood behavior. *Journal of Consulting and Clinical Psychology, 44,* 710–714.

MCCRAE, R. R. & COSTA, P. T. (1983). Social desirability scales: More substance than style. *Journal of Consulting and Clinical Psychology, 51,* 882–888.

MCFALL, R. M. & LILLESAND, D. B. (1971). Behavior rehearsal with modeling and coaching in assertion training. *Journal of Abnormal Psychology, 77,* 313–323.

MCFALL, R. M. & TWENTYMAN, C. T. (1973). Four experiments on the relative contributions of rehearsal, modeling, and coaching to assertion training. *Journal of Abnormal Psychology, 81,* 199–218.

McGarry, A. L., et al. (1973). *Competency to stand trial and mental illness.* Washington, DC: U. S. Government Printing Office, Publication HSM 73-9105.

McGee, R. K. (1983). Crisis intervention and brief psychotherapy. In M. Hersen, A. E. Kazdin, & A. S. Bellack (Eds.), *The clinical psychology handbook* (pp. 759–781). New York: Pergamon Press.

McGlynn, F. D., Mealiea, W. L., & Landau, D. L. (1981). The current status of systematic desensitization. *Clinical Psychology Review, 1,* 149–180.

McIntyre, T. J., Bornstein, P. H., Isaacs, C. D., Woody, D. J., Bornstein, M. T., Clucas, T. J., & Long, G. (1983). Naturalistic observation of conduct-disordered children: An archival analysis. *Behavior Therapy, 14,* 375–385.

McKay, S. & Golden, C. J. (1979). Empirical derivation of neuropsychological scales for the lateralization of brain damage using the Luria-Nebraska Neuropsychological Battery. *Clinical Neuropsychology, 1,* 1–5.

McKim, B. J., Weissberg, R. P., Cowen, E., Gesten, E., & Rapkin, B. D. (1982). A comparison of the problem-solving ability and adjustment of suburban and urban third-grade children. *American Journal of Community Psychology, 10,* 155–170.

McLemore, C. W. & Benjamin, L. S. (1979). Whatever happened to interpersonal diagnosis: A psychosocial alternative to DSM-III. *American Psychologist, 34,* 17–34.

McReynolds, P. (1975). Historical antecedents of personality assessment. In P. McReynolds (Ed.), *Advances in psychological assessment* (Vol. 3, pp. 477–532). San Francisco: Jossey-Bass.

Mead, M. (1928). *Coming of age in Samoa.* New York: Morrow.

Mead, M. (1939). *From the South Seas.* New York: Morrow.

Meador, B. D. & Rogers, C. R. (1973). Client-centered therapy. In R. Corsini (Ed.), *Current psychotherapies* (pp. 119–165). Itasca, IL: F. E. Peacock Publishers.

Mednick, S. A. & Schulsinger, F. (1968). Some premorbid characteristics related to breakdown in children with schizophrenic mothers. In D. Rosenthal and S. S. Kety (Eds.), *The transmission of schizophrenia.* Oxford: Pergamon Press.

Meehl, P. E. (1954). *Clinical versus statistical prediction.* Minneapolis: University of Minnesota Press.

Meehl, P. E. (1956). Wanted—A good cookbook. *American Psychologist, 11,* 263–272.

Meehl, P. E. (1957). When shall we use our heads instead of the formula? *Journal of Counseling Psychology, 4,* 268–273.

Meehl, P. E. (1960). The cognitive activity of the clinician. *American Psychologist, 15,* 19–27.

Meehl, P. E. (1965). Seer over sign: The first good example. *Journal of Experimental Research in Personality, 1,* 27–32.

Meehl, P. E. (1972). Reactions, reflections, projections. In J. N. Butcher (Ed.), *Objective personality assessment* (pp. 131–189). New York: Academic Press.

Meehl, P. E. & Rosen, A. (1955). Antecedent probability and the efficiency of psychometric signs, patterns, and cutting scores. *Psychological Bulletin, 52,* 194–216.

Meichenbaum, D. H. (1971). Examination of model characteristics in reducing avoidance behavior. *Journal of Personality and Social Psychology, 17,* 298–307.

Meichenbaum, D. H. (1972). Cognitive modification of test anxious college students. *Journal of Consulting and Clinical Psychology, 39,* 370–380.

Meichenbaum, D. H. (1975). A self-instructional approach to stress management: A proposal for stress inoculation training. In C. Spielberger & I. Sarason (Eds.), *Stress and anxiety* (Vol. 2). New York: John Wiley.

Meichenbaum, D. H. (1977). *Cognitive-behavior modification.* New York: Plenum.

Meier, M. J. (1981). Education for competency assurance in human neuropsychology: Antecedents, models, and directions. In S. B. Filskov & T. J. Boll (Eds.), *Handbook of clinical neuropsychology* (pp. 754–781). New York: John Wiley.

Melton, A. W. (Ed.) (1947). *Apparatus tests.* Washington: Government Printing Office.

Meltzer, M. L. (1975). Insurance reimbursement: A mixed blessing. *American Psychologist, 30,* 1150–1156.

Meltzoff, J. & Kornreich, M. (1970). *Research in psychotherapy.* New York: Atherton Press.

Mendel, W. M. & Rapport, S. (1969). Determinants of the decision for psychiatric hospitalization. *Archives of General Psychiatry, 20,* 321–328.

MENNINGER, K. (1958). *The theory of psychoanalytic technique.* New York: Basic Books.

MERCATORIS, M. & CRAIGHEAD, W. E. (1974). The effects of non-participant observation on teacher and pupil classroom behavior. *Journal of Educational Psychology, 66,* 512–519.

MERMELSTEIN, R., LICHTENSTEIN, E., & McINTYRE, K. (1983). Partner support and relapse in smoking-cessation programs. *Journal of Consulting and Clinical Psychology, 51,* 331–337.

MESSER, S. B. & WINOKUR, M. (1980). Some limits to the integration of psychoanalytic and behavior therapy. *American Psychologist, 35,* 818–827.

MEYER, A. J., NASH, J. D., McALISTER, A. L., MACCOBY, N., & FARQUHAR, J. W. (1980). Skills training in a cardiovascular education campaign. *Journal of Consulting and Clinical Psychology, 48,* 129–142.

MEYER, M. L. & GERRARD, M. (1977). Graduate training in community psychology. *American Journal of Community Psychology, 5,* 155–164.

MEYERS, J. (1975). Consultee centered consultation with a teacher as a technique in behavior management. *American Journal of Community Psychology, 3,* 111–122.

MICHELSON, L. & EDELSTEIN, B. A. (Eds.) (1986). *Handbook of prevention.* New York: Plenum.

MILICH, R. & FITZGERALD, G. (1985). Validation of inattention/overactivity and aggression ratings with classroom observations. *Journal of Consulting and Clinical Psychology, 53,* 139–140.

MILICH, R., LONEY, J., & LANDAU, S. (1982). Independent dimensions of hyperactivity and aggression: A validation with playroom observation data. *Journal of Abnormal Psychology, 91,* 183–198.

MILLER, B. V. & BERNSTEIN, D. A. (1972). Instructional demand in a behavioral avoidance test for claustrophobic fear. *Journal of Abnormal Psychology 80,* 206–210.

MILLER, L. K. & MILLER, O. (1970). Reinforcing self help group activities of welfare recipients. *Journal of Applied Behavior Analysis, 3,* 57–64.

MILLER, N. E. (1951). Learnable drives and rewards. In S. S. Stevens (Ed.), *Handbook of experimental psychology* (pp. 435–472). New York: John Wiley.

MILLER, N. E. (1969). Learning of visceral and glandular responses. *Science, 163,* 434–445.

MILLER, N. E. (1983). Behavioral medicine: Symbiosis between laboratory and clinic. *Annual Review of Psychology, 34,* 1–31.

MILLER, N. E. & DOLLARD, J. (1941). *Social learning and imitation.* New Haven, CT: Yale University Press.

MILLER, R. C. & BERMAN, J. S. (1983). The efficacy of cognitive behavior therapies: A quantitative review of the research evidence. *Psychological Bulletin, 94,* 39–53.

MILLER, W. R. & DiPILATO, M. (1983). Treatment of nightmares via relaxation and desensitization: A controlled evaluation. *Journal of Consulting and Clinical Psychology, 51,* 870–877.

MILLON, T. (1981). *Disorders of personality: DSM-III, Axis II.* New York: John Wiley.

MILLON, T. (1982). *Millon Clinical Multiaxial Inventory Manual.* Minneapolis, MN: National Computer Systems.

MILLS, D. H. (1984). Ethics education and ajudication within psychology. *American Psychologist, 39,* 669–675.

MIRSKY, A. F. & DUNCAN, C. C. (1986). Etiology and expression of schizophrenia: Neurobiological and psychosocial factors. *Annual Review of Psychology, 37,* 291–319.

MISCHEL, W. (1968). *Personality and assessment.* New York: John Wiley.

MISCHEL, W. (1971). *Introduction to personality.* New York: Holt, Rinehart & Winston.

MISCHEL, W. (1984). Convergences and challenges in the search for consistency. *American Psychologist, 39,* 351–364.

MISCHEL, W. (1986). *Introduction to personality* (4th ed.). New York: Holt, Rinehart & Winston.

MITCHELL, J. V. (Ed.) (1985). *The ninth mental measurements yearbook.* Lincoln, NE: Buros Institute of Mental Measurements, University of Nebraska.

MITCHELL, R. E., BILLINGS, A. G., & MOOS, R. H. (1982). Social support and well-being: Implications for prevention programs. *Journal of Primary Prevention, 3,* 77–98.

MITCHELL, S. K. (1979). Interobserver agreement, reliability, and generalizability of data collected in observational studies. *Psychological Bulletin, 86,* 376–390.

MONAHAN, J. (1981). *Predicting violent behavior: An assessment of clinical techniques.* Beverly Hills, CA: Sage.

MOON, J. R. & EISLER, R. M. (1983). Anger control: An experimental comparison of three behavioral treatments. *Behavior Therapy, 14,* 493–505.

MOOS, R. H. & BILLINGS, A. G. (1982). Conceptualizing and measuring coping resources and processes. In L. Goldenberger & S. Breznitz (Eds.), *Handbook of stress: Theoretical and clinical aspects.* New York: Macmillan.

MORENO, J. L. (1946). *Psychodrama.* New York: Beacon House.

MORGAN, C. & MURRAY, H. A. (1935). A method for investigating phantasies: The thematic apperception test. *Archives of Neurology and Psychiatry, 34,* 289–306.

MORGAN, H. & COGGER, J. (1972). *The interviewer's manual.* New York: Psychological Corporation.

MORGANSTERN, K. P. & TEVLIN, H. E. (1981). Behavioral interviewing. In M. Hersen & A. S. Bellack (Eds.), *Behavioral assessment: A practical handbook* (2nd ed., pp. 71–100). New York: Pergamon Press.

MORRIS, D. (1977). *Manwatching: A field guide to human behavior.* New York: Harry N. Abrams.

MORSE, S. J. (1978). Law and mental health professionals: The limits of expertise. *Professional Psychology, 9,* 389–399.

MOSAK, H. H. & DREIKURS, R. (1973). Adlerian psychotherapy. In R. Corsini (Ed.), *Current psychotherapies* (pp. 35–83). Itasca, IL: F. E. Peacock Publishers.

MOSAK, H. H. & GUSHURST, R. S. (1972). Some therapeutic uses of psychological testing. *American Journal of Psychotherapy, 26,* 539–546.

MOWRER, O. H. (1939). A stimulus-response analysis of anxiety and its role as a reinforcing agent. *Psychological Review, 46,* 553–565.

MOWRER, O. H. (1960). *Learning theory and behavior.* New York: John Wiley.

MRFIT (MULTIPLE RISK FACTOR INTERVENTION TRIAL RESEARCH GROUP). (1982). Multiple risk factor intervention trial: Risk factor changes and mortality results. *Journal of the American Medical Association, 248,* 1465–1477.

MULLAHY, P. (1965). Non-Freudian analytic theories. In B. B. Wolman (Ed.), *Handbook of clinical psychology* (pp. 341–377). New York: McGraw-Hill.

MULLEN, B. & SULS, J. (1982). The effectiveness of attention and rejection as coping styles. *Journal of Psychosomatic Research, 26,* 43–49.

MUNROE, R. (1955). *Schools of psychoanalytic thought.* New York: Dryden Press.

MURRAY, H. A. (1938). *Explorations in personality.* Fairlawn, NJ: Oxford University Press.

MURRAY, H. A. (1943). *Thematic Apperception Test.* Cambridge: Harvard University Press.

MURRELL, S. A. (1973). *Community psychology and social systems.* New York: Behavioral Publications.

MURSTEIN, B. I. (1963). *Theory and research in projective techniques (emphasizing the TAT).* New York: John Wiley.

MURSTEIN, B. I. (1965). Assumptions, adaptation level, and projective techniques. In B. I. Murstein (Ed.), *Handbook of projective techniques* (pp. 49–69). New York: Basic Books.

MURSTEIN, B. I. (1972). Normative written TAT responses for a college sample. *Journal of Personality Assessment, 36,* 109–147.

MUSSEN, P. H. & SCODEL, A. (1955). The effects of sexual stimulation under varying conditions on TAT sexual responsiveness. *Journal of Consulting Psychology, 19,* 90.

NAPOLI, P. J. (1947). Interpretative aspects of finger painting. *Journal of Psychology, 23,* 93–132.

NAY, W. R. (1979). *Multimethod clinical assessment.* New York: Gardner Press.

NEALE, J. M. & OLTMANNS, T. F. (1980). *Schizophrenia.* New York: John Wiley.

NELSON, R. O. (1977). Assessment and therapeutic functions of self-monitoring. In M. Hersen, R. M. Eisler, & P. M. Miller (Eds.), *Progress in behavior modification* (pp. 264–308). New York: Academic Press.

NELSON, R. O., & HAYES, S. C. (1981). Nature of behavioral assessment. In M. Hersen & A. S. Bellack (Eds.), *Behavioral assessment: A practical handbook* (2nd ed., pp. 3–37). New York: Pergamon Press.

NELSON, R. O. & HAYES, S. C. (Eds.) (1986). *Conceptual foundations of behavioral assessment.* New York: Guilford Press.

NELSON, R. O., HAYES, S. C., FELTON, J. L., & JARRETT, R. B. (1985). A comparison of data produced by different behavioral assessment techniques with implications for models of social-skills adequacy. *Behaviour Research and Therapy, 23,* 1–12.

NEUMAN, P. A. & HALVORSON, P. A. (1983). *Anorexia nervosa and bulimia: A handbook for counselors and therapists.* New York: Van Nostrand Reinhold.

NEWMAN, F. L. & HOWARD, K. I. (1986). Therapeutic effort, treatment outcome, and national health policy. *American Psychologist, 41,* 181–187.

NEWMARK, C. S. (1985). *Major psychological assessment instruments.* Rockleigh, NJ: Allyn & Bacon.

NIETZEL, M. T. & BANKS, K. (1983). Behavioral community psychology: A negative virtue analysis. *Behavioral Counseling and Community Interventions, 3,* 12–27.

NIETZEL, M. T. & BERNSTEIN, D. A. (1976). The effects of instructionally mediated demand upon the behavioral assessment of assertiveness. *Journal of Consulting and Clinical Psychology, 44,* p. 500.

NIETZEL, M. T. & BERNSTEIN, D. A. (1981). Assessment of anxiety and fear. In M. Hersen & A. S. Bellack (Eds.), *Behavioral assessment: A practical handbook* (2nd ed., pp. 215–245). New York: Pergamon Press.

NIETZEL, M. T., BERNSTEIN, D. A., & RUSSELL, R. L. (in press). Assessment of anxiety and fear. In M. Hersen & A. S. Bellack (Eds.), *Behavioral assessment: A practical handbook* (3rd ed.). New York: Pergamon Press.

NIETZEL, M. T. & DILLEHAY, R. C. (1986). *Psychological consultation in the courtroom.* New York: Pergamon Press.

NIETZEL, M. T. & FISHER, S. G. (1981). Effectiveness of professional and paraprofessional helpers: A reply to Durlak. *Psychological Bulletin, 89,* 555–565.

NIETZEL, M. T. & HIMELEIN, M. J. (1986). Prevention of crime and delinquency. In L. Michelson & B. Edelstein (Eds.), *Handbook of prevention* (pp. 195–221). New York: Plenum.

NIETZEL, M. T., MARTORANO, R., & MELNICK, J. (1977). The effects of covert modeling with and without reply training on the development and generalization of assertive responses. *Behavior Therapy, 8,* 183–192.

NIETZEL, M. T., RUSSELL, R. L., HEMMINGS, K. A., & GRETTER, M. L. (in press). The clinical significance of psychotherapy for unipolar depression: A meta-analytic approach to social comparison. *Journal of Consulting and Clinical Psychology.*

NIETZEL, M. T., WINETT, R. A., MacDONALD, M. L., & DAVIDSON, W. S. (1977). *Behavioral approaches to community psychology.* New York: Pergamon Press.

NISBETT, R. E. & ROSS, L. (1980). *Human inference: Strategies and shortcomings of social judgment.* Englewood Cliffs, NJ: Prentice-Hall.

NISBETT, R. E. & WILSON, T. D. (1977). Telling more than we can know: Verbal reports on mental processes. *Psychological Review, 84,* 231–259.

NORCROSS, J. C. & PROCHASKA, J. O. (1982). A national survey of clinical psychologists: Characteristics and activities. *The Clinical Psychologist, 38,* 1, 5–8.

NORCROSS, J. C. & PROCHASKA, J. O. (1983). Psychotherapists in independent practice: Some findings and issues. *Professional Psychology: Research and Practice, 14,* 869–881.

NOVACO, R. W. & MONAHAN, J. (1980). Research in community psychology: An analysis of works published in the first six years of the *American Journal of Community Psychology. American Journal of Community Psychology, 8,* 131–145.

NYE, R. D. (1975). *Three views of man: Perspectives from Sigmund Freud, B. F. Skinner, and Carl Rogers.* Monterey, CA: Brooks/Cole.

NYMAN, L. (1973). Some odds on getting into Ph.D. programs in clinical psychology and counseling psychology. *American Psychologist, 28,* 934–935.

OFFICE OF STRATEGIC SERVICES ASSESSMENT STAFF (1948). *Assessment of men.* New York: Rinehart.

OKPAKU, S. (1976). Psychology: Impediment or aid in child custody cases. *Rutgers Law Review, 29,* 1117–1153.

OLBRISCH, M. E. (1977). Psychotherapeutic interventions in physical health: Effectiveness and economic efficiency. *American Psychologist, 32,* 761–777.

O'LEARY, K. D. & BECKER, W. C. (1967). Behavior modification of an adjustment class: A token reinforcement program. *Exceptional Children, 33,* 637–642.

O'LEARY, K. D. & KENT, R. (1973). Behavior modification for social action: Research tactics and problems. In L. A. Hamerlynck, L. C. Handy, & E. J. Mash (Eds.), *Behavior change: Methodology, concepts, and practice* (pp. 69–96). Champaign, IL: Research Press.

O'LEARY, K. D. & O'LEARY, S. G. (Eds.) (1972). *Classroom management.* New York: Pergamon Press.

O'LEARY, K. D. & WILSON, G. T. (1975). *Behavior therapy: Application and outcome.* Englewood Cliffs, NJ: Prentice-Hall.

OLIVE, H. (1972). Psychoanalysts' opinions of psychologists' reports: 1952 and 1970. *Journal of Clinical Psychology, 28,* 50–54.

OLLENDICK, T. H. (1983). Reliability and validity of the Revised-Fear Survey Schedule for Children (FSSC-R). *Behaviour Research and Therapy, 21,* 685–692.

OLLENDICK, T. H. & HERSEN, M. (1984). *Child behavioral assessment: Principles and procedures.* New York: Pergamon Press.

OLLENDICK, T. H. & MEADOR, A. E. (1984). Behavioral assessment of children. In G. Goldstein & M. Hersen (Eds.), *Handbook of psychological assessment* (pp. 351–368). New York: Pergamon Press.

O'NEILL, P. & TRICKETT, E. J. (1982). *Community consultation.* San Francisco: Jossey-Bass.

ORBACH, C. E., & TALLENT, N. (1965). Modification of perceived body and body concepts following the construction of a colostomy. *Archives of General Psychiatry, 12,* 126–135.

ORNE, M. T. (1962). On the social psychology of the psychological experiment: With particular reference to demand characteristics and their implications. *American Psychologist, 17,* 776–783.

ORNE, M. T. & SCHEIBE, K. E. (1964). The contribution of nondeprivation factors in the production of sensory deprivation effects: The psychology of the panic button. *Journal of Abnormal and Social Psychology, 68,* 3–12.

ORNE, M. T. & WENDER, P. (1968). Anticipatory socialization for psychotherapy: Method and rationale. *American Journal of Psychiatry, 124,* 88–98.

OSKAMP, S. (1965). Overconfidence in case-study judgments. *Journal of Consulting Psychology, 29,* 261–265.

OSSIP-KLEIN, D. J., MARTIN, J. E., LOMAX, B. D., PRUE, D. M., & DAVIS, C. J. (1983). Assessment of smoking topography generalization across laboratory, clinical, and naturalistic settings. *Addictive Behaviors, 8,* 11–17.

PARLOFF, M. B., WASKOW, I. E., & WOLFE, B. E. (1978). Research on therapist variables in relation to process and outcome. In S. L. Garfield and A. E. Bergin (Eds.), *Handbook of psychotherapy and behavior change* (pp. 233–282). New York: John Wiley.

PATTERSON, C. H. (1973). *Theories of counseling and psychotherapy* (2nd ed.). New York: Harper & Row.

PATTERSON, D. & SECHREST, L. B. (1983). Nonreactive measures in psychotherapy outcome research. *Clinical Psychology Review, 3,* 391–416.

PATTERSON, G. R. (1974). Interventions for boys with conduct problems: Multiple settings, treatments, and criteria. *Journal of Consulting and Clinical Psychology, 42,* 471–481.

PATTERSON, G. R. (1982). *Coercive family process.* Eugene, OR: Castalia.

PATTERSON, G. R., RAY, R. S., SHAW, D. A., & COBB, J. A. (1969). *Manual for coding of family interactions* (Document No. 01234). Available from ASIS/NAPS, c/o Microfiche Publications, 305 East 46th St., New York, NY 10017

PAUL, G. L. (1966). *Insight versus desensitization in psychotherapy: An experiment in anxiety reduction.* Stanford, CA: Stanford University Press.

PAUL, G. L. (1969a). Behavior modification research: Design and tactics. In C. M. Franks (Ed.), *Behavior therapy: Appraisal and status.* New York: McGraw-Hill.

PAUL, G. L. (1969b). Outcome of systematic desensitization, II. In C. M. Franks (Ed.), *Behavior therapy: Appraisal and status.* New York: McGraw-Hill.

PAUL, G. L. & LENTZ, R. J. (1977). *Psychosocial treatment of chronic mental patients: Milieu versus social-learning programs.* Cambridge, MA: Harvard University Press.

PAVLOV, I. P. (1927). *Conditioned reflexes.* New York: Oxford University Press.

PAYNE, A. F. (1928). *Sentence completions.* New York: New York Guidance Clinic.

PEARLIN, L. I. & SCHOOLER, C. (1978). The structure of coping. *Journal of Health and Social Behavior, 22,* 337–356.

PECK, C. P. & ASH, E. (1964). Training in the Veterans Administration. In L. Blank & H. P. David (Eds.), *Sourcebook for training in clinical psychology* (pp. 61–81). New York: Springer Publishing Co.

PEELE, S. (1981). Reductionism in the psychology of the eighties: Can biochemistry eliminate addiction, mental illness, and pain. *American Psychologist, 36*, 807–818.

PERLS, F. S. (1947). *Ego, hunger and aggression: A revision of Freud's theory and method.* New York: Random House.

PERLS, F. S. (1965). Gestalt therapy, Film no. 2. In Everett Shostrom (Ed.), *Three approaches to psychotherapy.* (Three 16 mm color motion pictures). Santa Ana, CA: Psychological Films.

PERLS, F. S. (1969). *Gestalt therapy verbatim.* Lafayette, CA: Real People Press.

PERLS, F. S. (1970). Four lectures. In J. Fagan & I. L. Shepherd (Eds.), *Gestalt therapy now* (pp. 14–38). Palo Alto, CA: Science and Behavior Books.

PERLS, F. S., HEFFERLINE, R. F., & GOODMAN, P. (1951). *Gestalt therapy.* New York: Julian Press.

PERRY, N. W. (1979). Why clinical psychology does not need alternative training models. *American Psychologist, 34*, 603–611.

PETERSON, C., SEMMEL, A., METALSKY, G., ABRAMSON, L., VON BAEYER, C., & SELIGMAN, M. E. P. (1982). The Attributional Style Questionnaire. *Cognitive Therapy and Research, 6*, 287–300.

PETERSON, D. R. (1968). *The clinical study of social behavior.* New York: Appleton-Century-Crofts.

PETERSON, D. R. (1983). The case for the Psy.D. In S. Walfish & G. Sumprer (Eds.), *Clinical counseling, and community psychology.* New York: Irvington.

PETERSON, D. R. (1985). Twenty years of practitioner training in psychology. *American Psychologist, 40*, 441–451.

PETERSON, D. R. & BARON, A. (1975). Status of the University of Illinois doctor of psychology program, 1974. *Professional Psychology, 6*, 88–95.

PETZELT, J. T. & CRADDICK, R. (1978). Present meaning of assessment in psychology. *Professional Psychology, 9*, 587–591.

PIAGET, J. (1947). *The psychology of intelligence.* London: Kegan Paul.

PIKOFF, H. (1984). A critical review of autogenic training in America. *Clinical Psychology Review, 4*, 619–640.

PIOTROWSKI, C., SHERRY, D., & KELLER, J. W. (1985). Psychodiagnostic test usage: A survey of the society for personality assessment. *Journal of Personality Assessment, 49*, 115–119.

PIOTROWSKI, Z. (1972). Psychological testing of intelligence and personality. In A. M. Freedman & H. I. Kaplan (Eds.), *Diagnosing mental illness: Evaluation in psychiatry and psychology* (pp. 41–85). New York: Atheneum.

PIPER, W. E., DEBBANE, E. G., BIENVENU, J. P., & GARANT, J. (1984). A comparative study of four forms of psychotherapy. *Journal of Consulting and Clinical Psychology, 52*, 268–279.

PITTENGER, R. E., HOCKETT, C. F., & DANEHY, J. J. (1960). *The first five minutes: A sample of microscopic interview analyses.* Ithaca, NY: Paul Martineau.

POLSTER, E. & POLSTER, M. (1973). *Gestalt therapy integrated: Contours of theory and practice.* New York: Brunner/Mazel.

POLYSON, J., NORRIS, D., & OTT, E. (1985). The recent decline in TAT research. *Professional Psychology, 16*, 26–28.

POMERANZ, D. M. & GOLDFRIED, M. R. (1970). An intake report outline for behavior modification. *Psychological Reports, 26*, 447–450.

POMERLEAU, O. F. & POMERLEAU, C. S. (1977). *Break the smoking habit.* Champaign, IL: Research Press.

POPE, B., NUDLER, S., VONKORFF, M. R., & McGHEE, J. P. (1974). The experienced professional interviewer versus the complete novice. *Journal of Consulting and Clinical Psychology, 42*, 680–690.

PORTER, E. H., JR. (1943). The development and evaluation of a measure of counseling interview procedures. *Educational and Psychological Measurement, 3*, 105–126.

POTTHARST, K. E. (1976). A brief history of the professional model of training. In M. Korman (Ed.), *Levels and patterns of professional training in psychology* (pp. 33–40). Washington, DC: American Psychological Association.

PRICE, R. H. & LYNN, S. J. (1986). *Abnormal psychology* (2nd ed.). Chicago: The Dorsey Press.

PROCHASKA, J. O. & DiCLEMENTE, C. C. (1984). *The transtheoretical approach: Crossing traditional boundaries of therapy.* Homewood, IL: Dow Jones-Irwin.

QUAY, H. C. & WERRY, J. S. (Eds.) (1986). *Psychopathological disorders of childhood* (3rd ed.). New York: John Wiley.

RABIN, A. I. & HAWORTH, M. R. (Eds.) (1960). *Projective techniques with children.* New York: Grune & Stratton.

RABKIN, J. G. & STRUENING, E. L. (1976). Life events, stress and illness. *Science, 194,* 1013–1020.

RACHMAN, S. J. & WILSON, G. T. (1980). *The effects of psychological therapy.* Oxford: Pergamon Press.

RAHE, R. H. (1975). Epidemiological studies of life change and illness. *International Journal of Psychiatry in Medicine, 6,* 133–146.

RAIMY, V. C. (1950). *Training in clinical psychology.* New York: Prentice-Hall.

RAINES, G. N. & ROHRER, J. H. (1955). The operational matrix of psychiatric practice, I. Consistency and variability in interview impressions of different psychiatrists. *American Journal of Psychiatry, 111,* 721–733.

RAINES, G. N. & ROHRER, J. H. (1960). The operational matrix of psychiatric practice, II. Variability in psychiatric impressions and the projection hypothesis. *American Journal of Psychiatry, 117,* 133–139.

RAPAPORT, D. (1951). *Organization and pathology of thought.* New York: Columbia University Press.

RAPAPORT, D., GILL, M. M., & SCHAFER, R. (1945). *Diagnostic psychological testing* (Vol. 1). Chicago: Yearbook.

RAPAPORT, D., GILL, M. M., & SCHAFER, R. (1946). *Diagnostic psychological testing* (Vol. 2). Chicago: Yearbook.

RAPP, D. W. (1965). *Detection of observer bias in the written record.* Unpublished manuscript, University of Georgia.

RAPPAPORT, J. (1977). *Community psychology: Values, research and action.* New York: Holt, Rinehart & Winston.

RAPPAPORT, J. (1981). In praise of paradox: A social policy of empowerment over prevention. *American Journal of Community Psychology, 9,* 1–25.

RAPPAPORT, J. & CHINSKY, J. M. (1972). Accurate empathy: Confusion of a construct. *Psychological Bulletin, 77,* 400–404.

RAPPAPORT, J. & CHINSKY, J. M. (1974). Models for delivery of services from a historical and conceptual perspective. *Professional Psychology, 5,* 42–50.

RATHUS, S. A. (1973). A 30-item schedule for assessing assertive behavior. *Behavior Therapy, 4,* 398–406.

RAUSCH, H. L. & BORDIN, E. S. (1957). Warmth in personality development and in psychotherapy. *Psychiatry, 20,* 351–363.

RAY, W. J., COLE, H. W., & RACZYNSKI, J. M. (1983). Psychophysiological assessment. In M. Hersen, A. E. Kazdin, & A. S. Bellack (Eds.), *The clinical psychology handbook* (pp. 427–453). New York: Pergamon Press.

RAYMOND, M. J. (1956). Case of fetishism treated by aversion therapy. *British Medical Journal, 2,* 854–857.

REDD, W. H. & HENDLER, C. S. (1983). Behavioral medicine in comprehensive cancer treatment. *Journal of Psychosocial Oncology, 1,* 3–17.

REDD, W. H., PORTERFIELD, A. L., & ANDERSEN, B. L. (1979). *Behavior modification: Behavioral approaches to human problems.* New York: Random House.

REHM, L. P., KORNBLITH, S. J., O'HARA, M. W., LAMPARSKI, D. J., ROMANO, J. M., & VOLKIN, J. I. (1981). An evaluation of major components in a self-control therapy program for depression. *Behavior Modification, 5,* 459–489.

REHM, L. P. & MARSTON, A. R. (1968). Reduction of social anxiety through modification of self-reinforcement: An instigation therapy technique. *Journal of Consulting and Clinical Psychology, 32,* 565–574.

REID, J. B. (Ed.) (1978). *A social learning approach to family intervention: Observation in home settings* (Vol. 2). Eugene, OR: Castalia Publishing.

REIK, T. (1948). *Listening with the third ear.* New York: Farrar, Straus & Giroux.

REISMAN, J. M. (1976). *A history of clinical psychology.* Irvington.

REITAN, R. M. (1955). An investigation of the validity of Halstead's measure of biological intelligence. *Archives of Neurology and Psychiatry, 73,* 28–35.

REITAN, R. M. (1964). Psychological deficits resulting from cerebral lesions in man. In J. M. Warren & K. Akert (Eds.), *The frontal granular cortex and behavior.* New York: McGraw-Hill.

REITAN, R. M. (1984). *Aphasia and sensory-perceptual deficits in adults.* Tucson, AZ: Reitan Neuropsychology Laboratories.

RESCHLY, D. J. (1984). Aptitude tests. In G. Goldstein & M. Hersen (Eds.), *Handbook of psychological assessment* (pp. 132–156). New York: Pergamon Press.

RESNICK, R. J. (1985). The case against the Blues: The Virginia challenge. *American Psychologist, 40,* 975–983.

REYNOLDS, C. R. (1982). The problem of bias in psychological assessment. In C. R. Reynolds & T. B. Gutkin (Eds.), *The handbook of school psychology.* New York: John Wiley.

REYNOLDS, W. M. (1979). Psychological tests: Clinical usage versus psychometric quality. *Professional Psychology, 10,* 324–329.

RICE, L. & GREENBERG, L. (1984). *Patterns of change: Intensive analysis of psychotherapy process.* New York: Guilford Press.

RICE, S. A. (1929). Contagious bias in the interview: A methodological note. *American Journal of Sociology, 35,* 420–423.

RICHARDSON, F. C. & TASTO, D. L. (1976). Development of factor analysis of a social anxiety inventory. *Behavior Therapy, 7,* 453–462.

RIEU, E. V. (Trans.) (1950). *Homer: The Iliad.* Hammondsworth, Middlesex: Penguin.

ROBBINS, L. C. (1963). The accuracy of parental recall of child development and of child rearing practices. *Journal of Abnormal and Social Psychology, 66,* 261–270.

ROBINS, L. N. & HELZER, J. E. (1986). Diagnosis and clinical assessment: The current state of psychiatric diagnosis. *Annual Review of Psychology, 37,* 409–432.

ROBINS, L. N., HELZER, J. E., RATCLIFF, K. S., & SEYFRIED, W. (1982). Validity of the diagnostic interview schedule, version II: DSM-III diagnoses. *Psychological Medicine, 12,* 855–870.

ROBINSON, D. N. (1980). *Psychology and law: Can justice survive the social sciences?* New York: Oxford University Press.

RODGERS, D. A. (1972). Minnesota Multiphasic Personality Inventory. In O. K. Buros (Ed.), *The seventh mental measurements yearbook* (Vol. 1, pp. 245–250). Highland Park, NJ: The Gryphon Press.

RODRIGUEZ, R., NIETZEL, M. T., & BERZINS, J. I. (1980). Sex role orientation and assertiveness among female college students. *Behavior Therapy, 11,* 353–366.

ROE, A., GUSTAD, J. W., MOORE, B. V., ROSS, S., & SKODAK, M. (Eds.) (1959). *Graduate education in psychology.* Washington, DC: American Psychological Association.

ROESCH, R. & GOLDING, S. L. (1980). *Competency to stand trial.* Champaign, IL: University of Illinois Press.

ROGERS, C. R. (1939). *The clinical treatment of the problem child.* Boston: Houghton Mifflin.

ROGERS, C. R. (1942). *Counseling and psychotherapy.* Boston: Houghton Mifflin.

ROGERS, C. R. (1951). *Client-centered therapy.* Boston: Houghton Mifflin.

ROGERS, C. R. (1954). *Psychotherapy and personality change.* Chicago: University of Chicago Press.

ROGERS, C. R. (1959). A theory of therapy, personality, and interpersonal relationships as developed in the client-centered framework. In S. Koch (Ed.), *Psychology: A study of a science,* Vol. III, *Formulations of the person and the social context* (pp. 184–256). New York: McGraw-Hill.

ROGERS, C. R. (1961). *On becoming a person.* Boston: Houghton Mifflin.

ROGERS, C. R. (1965). Client-centered therapy, Film no. 1. In Everett Shostrom (Ed.), *Three approaches to psychotherapy* (three 16 mm. color motion pictures). Santa Ana, CA: Psychological Films.

ROGERS, C. R. (Ed.) (1967). *The therapeutic relationship and its impact: A study of psychotherapy with schizophrenics.* With E. T. Gendlin, D. J. Kiesler, and C. Louax. Madison, WI: University of Wisconsin Press.

ROGERS, C. R. (1969). *Freedom to learn.* Columbus, OH: Merrill.

ROGERS, C. R. (1970). *Carl Rogers on encounter groups.* New York: Harper & Row.

ROGERS, C. R. (1972). *On becoming partners: Marriage and its alternatives.* New York: Delacourte.

ROGERS, C. R. (1974). Remarks on the future of client-centered therapy. In D. A. Wexler & L. N. Rice (Eds.), *Innovations in client-centered therapy* (pp. 7–13). New York: John Wiley.

ROGERS, C. R. (1980). *A way of being.* Boston: Houghton Mifflin.

ROGERS, R., WASYLIW, O. E., & CAVANAUGH, J. L. (1984). Evaluating insanity: A study of construct validity. *Law and Human Behavior, 8,* 293–304.

ROLF, J. E. (1985). Evolving adaptive theories and methods for prevention research with children. *Journal of Consulting and Clinical Psychology, 53,* 631–646.

ROMANCZYK, R. G., KENT, R. N., DIAMENT, C., & O'LEARY, K. D. (1973). Measuring the reliability of observational data: A reactive process. *Journal of Applied Behavior Analysis, 6,* 175–184.

RORER, L. G. (1965). The great response style myth. *Psychological Bulletin, 63,* 129–156.

RORER, L. G. & WIDIGER, T. A. (1983). Personality structure and assessment. *Annual Review of Psychology, 34,* 431–463.

ROSEN, R. C. & KOPEL, S. A. (1977). Penile plethysmography and biofeedback in the treatment of a transvestite-exhibitionist. *Journal of Consulting and Clinical Psychology, 45,* 908–916.

ROSENBERG, M. S. & REPPUCCI, N. D. (1985). Primary prevention of child abuse. *Journal of Consulting and Clinical Psychology, 53,* 576–585.

ROSENBLATT, D. (1975). *Opening doors: What happens in Gestalt therapy.* New York: Harper & Row.

ROSENHAN, D. L. (1973). On being sane in insane places. *Science, 179,* 250–258.

ROSENHAN, D. L. & SELIGMAN, M. E. P. (1984). *Abnormal psychology.* New York: W. W. Norton.

ROSENMAN, R. H. (1978). The interview method of assessment of the coronary-prone behavior pattern. In T. M. Dembroski, S. M. Weiss, J. L. Shields, S. G. Haynes, & M. Feinleib (Eds.), *Coronary-prone behavior.* New York: Springer-Verlag.

ROSENSTOCK, I. M. (1966). Why people use health services. *Milbank Memorial Fund Quarterly, 44,* 94–127.

ROSENTHAL, D. (1970). *Genetic theory and abnormal behavior.* New York: McGraw-Hill.

ROSENTHAL, H. R. (1959). The final dream: A criterion for the termination of therapy. In A. Adler & D. Deutsch (Eds.), *Essays in individual psychology* (pp. 400–409). New York: Grove Press.

ROSENTHAL, R. (1966). *Experimenter effects in behavioral research.* New York: Appleton-Century-Crofts.

ROSENTHAL, R. (1983). Assessing the statistical and social importance of the effects of psycho-

therapy. *Journal of Consulting and Clinical Psychology, 51,* 4–13.

ROSENTHAL, T. L. (1982). Social learning theory. In G. T. Wilson & C. M. Franks (Eds.), *Contemporary behavior therapy: Conceptual and empirical foundations* (pp. 339–363). New York: Guilford Press.

ROSENZWEIG, S. (1949). Apperceptive norms for the Thematic Apperception Test. I. The problem of norms in projective methods. *Journal of Personality, 17,* 475–482.

ROSENZWEIG, S. & FLEMING, E. E. (1949). Apperceptive norms for the Thematic Apperception Test. II. An empirical investigation. *Journal of Personality, 17,* 483–503.

ROSS, A. O. (1985). To form a more perfect union: It is time to stop standing still. *Behavior Therapy, 16,* 195–204.

ROTTER, J. B. (1954). *Social learning and clinical psychology.* Englewood Cliffs, NJ: Prentice-Hall.

ROTTER, J. B. (1971). *Clinical psychology* (2nd ed.). Englewood Cliffs, NJ: Prentice-Hall.

ROTTER, J. B. & RAFFERTY, J. E. (1950). *The Rotter Incomplete Sentences Test.* New York: Psychological Corporation.

ROUTH, D. K. & KING, K. M. (1972). Social class bias in clinical judgment. *Journal of Consulting and Clinical Psychology, 38,* 202–207.

RUDERMAN, A. J. & CHRISTENSEN, H. (1983). Restraint theory and its applicability to overweight individuals. *Journal of Abnormal Psychology, 92,* 210–215.

RUSH, A. J., BECK, A. T., KOVACS, M., & HOLLON, S. D. (1977). Comparative efficacy of cognitive therapy and pharmocotherapy in the treatment of depressed outpatients. *Cognitive Therapy and Research, 1,* 17–38.

RUSSELL, R. L. (1986). The inadvisability of admixing psychoanalysis with other forms of psychotherapy. *Journal of Contemporary Psychotherapy, 16,* 76–86.

RUTTER, M. (1983) (Ed.). *Developmental neuropsychiatry.* New York: Guilford Press.

RYCHLAK, J. F. (1970). *Introduction to personality and psychotherapy: A theory-construction approach.* Boston: Houghton Mifflin.

SACKS, O. (1985). *The man who mistook his wife for a hat.* New York: Summit Books.

SALES, B. D., POWELL, D. M., VAN DUIZEND, R., & ASSOCIATES (1982). *Disabled persons and the law.* New York: Plenum.

SALTER, A. (1949). *Conditioned reflex therapy: The direct approach to the reconstruction of personality.* New York: Creative Age Press.

SALZINGER, K. (1959). Experimental manipulation of verbal behavior: A review. *Journal of Genetic Psychology, 61,* 65–95.

SAMUDA, R. J. (1975). *Psychological testing of American minorities: Issues and consequences.* New York: Dodd, Mead.

SANDERS, J. R. (1979). Complaints against psychologists adjudicated informally by APA's Committee on Scientific and Professional Ethics and Conduct. *American Psychologist, 34,* 1139–1144.

SANDERS, J. R. & KEITH-SPIEGEL, P. (1980). Formal and informal adjudication of ethics complaints against psychologists. *American Psychologist, 35,* 1096–1105.

SANDS, W. L. (1972). Psychiatric history and mental status. In A. M. Freedman & H. I. Kaplan (Eds.), *Diagnosing mental illness* (pp. 20–40). New York: Atheneum.

SANFORD, F. H. (1951). Annual report of the executive secretary. *American Psychologist, 6,* 664–670.

SANTOSTEFANO, S. (1962). Performance testing of personality. *Merrill-Palmer Quarterly, 8,* 83–97.

SARASON, I. G. (1973). The evolution of community psychology. *American Journal of Community Psychology, 1,* 91–97.

SARASON, I. G., JOHNSON, J. H., & SIEGEL, J. M. (1978). Assessing the impact of life changes: Development of the life experiences survey. *Journal of Consulting and Clinical Psychology, 46,* 932–946.

SARASON, S. B. (1954). *The clinical interaction, with special reference to the Rorschach.* New York: Harper.

SARASON, S. B. (1974). *The psychological sense of community: Prospects for community psychology.* San Francisco: Jossey-Bass.

SARBIN, T. R., TAFT, R., & BAILEY, D. E. (1960). *Clinical inference and cognitive theory.* New York: Holt, Rinehart & Winston.

SASLOW, G. & MATARAZZO, J. D. (1959). A technique for studying changes in interview behavior. In E. A. Rubinstein & M. B. Parloff (Eds.), *Research in psychotherapy* (Vol. 1, pp. 125–159). Washington, DC: American Psychological Association.

SATIR, V. (1967). *Conjoint family therapy* (Rev. ed.). Palo Alto, CA: Science and Behavior Books.

SATTLER, J. M. (1982). *Assessment of children's intelligence and special abilities* (2nd ed.). Rockleigh, NJ: Allyn & Bacon.

SATZ, P. & FLETCHER, J. M. (1981). Emergent trends in neuropsychology: An overview. *Journal of Consulting and Clinical Psychology, 49,* 851–865.

SAWYER, J. (1966). Measurement and prediction, clinical and statistical. *Psychological Bulletin, 66,* 178–200.

SCHAAR, K. (1978). Vermont: Getting through the adult years. *APA Monitor, 9,* 7.

SCHACT, T. & NATHAN, P. E. (1977). But is it good for the psychologists? Appraisal and status of DSM-III. *American Psychologist, 32,* 1017–1025.

SCHAEFER, H. H. & MARTIN, P. L. (1975). *Behavior therapy* (2nd ed.). New York: McGraw-Hill.

SCHAFER, R. (1967). *Projective testing and psychoanalysis.* New York: International Universities Press.

SCHEFF, T. J. (1966). *Being mentally ill.* Chicago: Aldine.

SCHMIDT, H. O. & FONDA, C. P. (1956). The reliability of psychiatric diagnosis: A new look. *Journal of Abnormal and Social Psychology, 52,* 262–267.

SCHNEIDER, S. F. (1985). Behavioral training in clinical psychology. *The Behavior Therapist, 8,* 89–92.

SCHOFIELD, W. (1964). Standards for clinical psychology: Origins and evaluation. In L. Blank and H. P. David (Eds.), *Sourcebook for training in clinical psychology.* New York: Springer Publishing Co.

SCHRADLE, S. B. & DOUGHER, M. J. (1985). Social support as a mediator of stress: Theoretical and empirical issues. *Clinical Psychology Review, 5,* 641–662.

SCHULBERG, H. C. & JERRELL, J. M. (1983). Consultation. In M. Hersen, A. E. Kazdin, & A. S. Bellack (Eds.), *The clinical psychology handbook* (pp. 783–796). New York: Pergamon Press.

SCHULBERG, H. C. & KILLILEA, M. (Eds.) (1982). *The modern practice of community mental health: A volume in honor of Gerald Caplan.* San Francisco: Jossey-Bass.

SCHWARTZ, L. A. (1932). Social-situation pictures in the psychiatric interview. *American Journal of Orthopsychiatry, 2,* 124–135.

SCHWARTZ, R. M. (1982). Cognitive-behavior modification: A conceptual review. *Clinical Psychology Review, 2,* 267–293.

SCHWITZGEBEL, R. K. & KOLB, D. A. (1974). *Changing human behavior.* New York: McGraw-Hill.

SECHREST, L. B. (1963). Incremental validity: A recommendation. *Educational and Psychological Measurement, 23,* 153–158.

SEEMAN, J. A. (1949). A study of the process of nondirective therapy. *Journal of Consulting Psychology, 13,* 157–168.

SEIDMAN, E. (Ed.) (1983). *Handbook of social intervention.* Beverly Hills: Sage.

SEIDMAN, E. & RAPKIN, B. (1983). Economics and psychosocial dysfunction: Toward a conceptual framework and prevention strategies. In R. D. Felner, L. A. Jason, J. N. Moritsugu, & S. S. Farber (Eds.), *Preventive Psychology.* New York: Pergamon Press.

SELKIN, J. & LOYA, F. (1979). Issues in the psychological autopsy of a controversial public figure. *Professional Psychology, 10,* 87–92.

SELYE, H. (1956). *The stress of life.* New York: McGraw-Hill.

SHADEL, C. A. (1944). Aversion treatment of alcohol addiction. *Quarterly Journal of Studies of Alcohol, 5,* 216–228.

SHAFFER, G. W. & LAZARUS, R. S. (1952). *Fundamental concepts in clinical psychology.* New York: McGraw-Hill.

SHAKOW, D. (1942). The training of the clinical psychologist. *Journal of Consulting Psychology, 6,* 277–288.

SHAKOW, D. (1947). Recommended graduate training program in clinical psychology. *American Psychologist, 2,* 539–558.

SHAKOW, D. (1948). Clinical psychology: An evaluation. In L. G. Lowrey & V. Sloane (Eds.), *Orthopsychiatry, 1923–1948: Retrospect and prospect.* New York: American Orthopsychiatric Association, Inc.

SHAKOW, D. (1965). Seventeen years later: Clinical psychology in the light of the 1947 CTCP report. *American Psychologist, 20,* 353–362.

SHAKOW, D. (1968). Clinical psychology. In D. L. Sills (Ed.), *International encyclopedia of the social sciences.* London: Collier Macmillan.

SHAKOW, D. (1969). *Clinical psychology as science and profession.* Chicago: Aldine.

SHAKOW, D. (1978). Clinical psychology seen some 50 years later. *American Psychologist, 33,* 148–158.

SHANNON, D. & WEAVER, W. (1949). *The mathematical theory of communication.* Urbana, IL: University of Illinois Press.

SHAPIRO, A. K. (1971). Placebo effects in medicine, psychotherapy, and psychoanalysis. In A. E. Bergin & S. L. Garfield (Eds.), *Handbook of psychotherapy and behavior change: An empirical analysis.* New York: John Wiley.

SHAPIRO, D. A. & SHAPIRO, D. (1982). Meta-analysis of comparative therapy outcome research: A critical appraisal. *Behavioral Psychotherapy, 10,* 4–25.

SHAPIRO, D. L. (1984). *Psychological evaluation and expert testimony: A practical guide to forensic work.* New York: Van Nostrand Reinhold.

SHAPIRO, D. & GOLDSTEIN, I. B. (1982). Biobehavioral perspectives on hypertension. *Journal of Consulting and Clinical Psychology, 50,* 841–858.

SHAPIRO, E. S. (1984). Self-monitoring. In T. H. Ollendick & M. Hersen (Eds.), *Child behavioral assessment: Principles and procedures.* New York: Pergamon Press.

SHEMBERG, K. M. & LEVENTHAL, D. B. (1978). A survey of activities of academic clinicians. *Professional Psychology, 9,* 580–586.

SHEMBERG, K. M. & LEVENTHAL, D. B. (1981). Attitudes of internship directors toward preinternship training and clinical training models. *Professional Psychology, 12,* 639–646.

SHEPARD, L. A. (1982). Definitions of bias. In R. A. Berk (Ed.), *Handbook of methods for detecting item bias.* Baltimore, MD: The Johns Hopkins University Press.

SHERMAN, M., TRIEF, P., & SPRAFKIN, R. (1975). Impression management in the psychiatric interview: Quality, style, and individual differences. *Journal of Consulting and Clinical Psychology, 43,* 867–871.

SHNEIDMAN, E. S. (1949). *The make-a-picture-story test.* New York: Psychological Corporation.

SHNEIDMAN, E. S. (1965). Projective techniques. In B. B. Wolman (Ed.), *Handbook of clinical psychology* (pp. 498–521). New York: McGraw-Hill.

SHOHAM-SALOMON, V. (1985). Are schizophrenics' behaviors schizophrenic? What medically versus psychosocially oriented therapists attribute to schizophrenic persons. *Journal of Abnormal Psychology, 94,* 443–453.

SHOSTROM, E. L. (1968). *Personal orientation inventory: An inventory for the measurement of self-actualization.* San Diego, CA: Educational and Industrial Testing Service.

SHURE, M. B. & SPIVACK, G. (1982). Interpersonal problem-solving in young children: A cognitive approach to prevention. *American Journal of Community Psychology, 10,* 341–356.

SHWEDER, R. A. (1982). Fact and artifact in trait perception: The systematic distortion hypothesis. *Progress in Experimental Personality Research, 11,* 65–100.

SIASSI, I. (1984). Psychiatric interviews and mental status examinations. In G. Goldstein & M. Hersen (Eds.), *Handbook of psychological assessment* (pp. 259–275). New York: Pergamon Press.

SIEGMAN, A. W. (1972). Do interviewer mm-hmm's reinforce interviewee verbal productivity? *Proceedings of the 80th Annual Convention of the American Psychological Association, 7,* 323–324.

SIEGMAN, A. W. (1974). The gain-loss principle and interpersonal attraction in the interview. *Proceedings of the Division of Personality and Social Psychology,* pp. 83–85.

SIEGMAN, A. W. (1976). Do noncontingent interviewer mm-hmm's facilitate interviewee productivity? *Journal of Consulting and Clinical Psychology, 44,* 171–182.

SILVERMAN, L. H., LACHMANN, F. M., & MILICH, R. H. (1982). *The search for oneness.* New York: International Universities Press.

SILVERMAN, L. H. & WEINBERGER, J. (1985). Mommy and I are one: Implications for psychotherapy. *American Psychologist, 40,* 1296–1308.

SINES, L. K. (1959). The relative contribution of four kinds of data to accuracy in personality assessment. *Journal of Consulting Psychology, 23,* 483–492.

SKINNER, B. F. (1948). *Verbal behavior.* Cambridge, MA: Harvard University Press.

SKINNER, B. F. (1953). *Science and human behavior.* New York: Macmillan.

SKINNER, B. F. (1957). *Verbal behavior.* New York: Appleton-Century-Crofts.

SKINNER, B. F. (1971). *Beyond freedom and dignity.* New York: Knopf.

SLIPP, S. (Ed.) (1981). *Curative factors in psychodynamic therapy.* New York: McGraw-Hill.

SLOANE, R. B., STAPLES, F. R., CRISTOL, A. H., YORKSTON, N. J., & WHIPPLE, K. (1975). *Psychotherapy versus behavior therapy.* Cambridge, MA: Harvard University Press.

SLOBOGIN, C., MELTON, G. B., & SHOWALTER, C. R. (1984). The feasibility of a brief evaluation of mental state at the time of the offense. *Law and Human Behavior, 8,* 305–320.

SMITH, D. (1982). Trends in counseling and psychotherapy. *American Psychologist, 37,* 802–809.

SMITH, M. L., GLASS, G. V., & MILLER, T. I. (1980). *The benefits of psychotherapy.* Baltimore, MD: Johns Hopkins University Press.

SNOWDEN, L. (Ed.). (1982). *Reaching the underserved: Mental health needs of neglected populations.* Beverly Hills: Sage.

SNYDER, D. K. (1981). *Marital Satisfaction Inventory: Manual.* Los Angeles: Western Psychological Services.

SNYDER, W. V. (1945). An investigation of the nature of nondirective psychotherapy. *Journal of General Psychology, 33,* 193–232.

SNYDER, W. V. (Ed.) (1953). *Group report of a program of research in psychotherapy.* State College, PA: Department of Psychology, Pennsylvania State University.

SNYDER, W. V. (1954). Client-centered therapy. In L. A. Pennington & I. A. Berg (Eds.), *An introduction to clinical psychology* (pp. 529–556). New York: Ronald.

SOBELL, L. C. & SOBELL, M. B. (1975). Outpatient alcoholics give valid self-reports. *Journal of Nervous and Mental Disease, 161,* 32–42.

SOBELL, M. B., SOBELL, L. C., & SAMUELS, F. H. (1974). Validity of alcohol-related arrests by alcoholics. *Quarterly Journal of Studies on Alcohol, 35,* 276–280.

SOLLOD, R. N. (1978). Carl Rogers and the origins of client-centered therapy. *Professional Psychology, 9,* 93–104.

SOLOMON, R. L., KAMIN, L. J., & WYNNE, L. C. (1953). Traumatic avoidance learning: The outcomes of several extinction procedures with dogs. *Journal of Abnormal and Social Psychology, 49,* 291–302.

SOSKIN, W. F. (1954). Bias in postdiction from projective tests. *Journal of Abnormal and Social Psychology, 49,* 69–74.

SPANOS, N. P. (1978). Witchcraft in histories of psychiatry: A critical analysis and an alternative conceptualization. *Psychological Bulletin, 85*, 417–439.

SPECE, R. (1972). Conditioning and other techniques used to "treat?," "rehabilitate?," "demolish?" prisoners and mental patients. *Southern California Law Review, 45*, 616–684.

SPENCE, K. W. (1956). *Behavior theory and conditioning.* New Haven, CT: Yale University Press.

SPIEGLER, M. D. (1983). *Contemporary behavioral therapy.* Palo Alto, CA: Mayfield Publishing Company.

SPIELBERGER, C. D. & BUTCHER, J. N. (1982). *Advances in personality assessment* (Vol. 1). Hillsdale, NJ: Lawrence Erlbaum Associates.

SPIELBERGER, C. D., GORSUCH, R. L., LUSHENE, R., VAGG, P. R., & JACOBS, G. A. (1983). *Manual for the State-Trait Anxiety Inventory.* Palo Alto, CA: Consulting Psychologists Press.

SPIERS, P. A. (1980). Have they come to praise Luria or to bury him? The Luria-Nebraska controversy. *Journal of Consulting and Clinical Psychology, 49*, 331–341.

SPIKER, D. G. & EHLER, J. G. (1984). Structured psychiatric interviews for adults. In G. Goldstein & M. Hersen (Eds.), *Handbook of psychological assessment* (pp. 291–304). New York: Pergamon Press.

SPITZER, R. L., ENDICOTT, J., FLEISS, J. L., & COHEN, J. (1970). The Psychiatric Status Schedule: A technique for evaluating psychopathology and impairment in role functioning. *Archives of General Psychiatry, 23*, 41–55.

SPITZER, R. L., FLEISS, J. L., BURDOCK, E. I., & HARDESTY, A. S. (1964). The mental status schedule: Rationale, reliability, and validity. *Comprehensive Psychiatry, 5*, 384–394.

SPIVACK, G. & CIANCI, N. (1983). *High risk early behavior pattern and later delinquency.* Paper presented to the Vermont Conference on the Primary Prevention of Psychopathology.

SPIVACK, G., PLATT, J. J., & SHURE, M. B. (1976). *The problem solving approach to adjustment.* San Francisco: Jossey-Bass.

SPROCK, J. & BLASHFIELD, R. K. (1983). Classification and nosology. In M. Hersen, A. E. Kazdin, & A. S. Bellack (Eds.), *The clinical psychology handbook* (pp. 289–307). New York: Pergamon Press.

STAMPFL, T. G. & LEVIS, D. J. (1973). *Implosive therapy: Theory and technique.* Morristown, NJ: General Learning Press.

STAPP, J. & FULCHER, R. (1983). The employment of APA members. *American Psychologist, 38*, 1298–1320.

STAPP, J., FULCHER, R., & WICHERSKI, M. (1984). The employment of 1981 and 1982 doctorate recipients in psychology. *American Psychologist, 39*, 1408–1423.

STAPP, J., TUCKER, A. M., & VANDENBOS, G. R. (1985). Census of psychological personnel: 1983. *American Psychologist, 40*, 1317–1351.

STEIN, D. M. & LAMBERT, M. J. (1984). On the relationship between therapist experience and psychotherapy outcome. *Clinical Psychology Review, 4*, 127–142.

STEIN, D. M. & POLYSON, J. (1984). The Primary Mental Health Project reconsidered. *Journal of Consulting and Clinical Psychology, 52*, 940–945.

STEKETEE, G. & FOA, E. B. (1985). Obsessive-compulsive disorders. In D. H. Barlow (Ed.), *Clinical handbook of psychological disorders* (pp. 69–144). New York: The Guilford Press.

STERNBERG, R. J. (1985). *Beyond IQ: A triarchic theory of human intelligence.* New York: Cambridge University Press.

STEVENS, M. R. & REILLY, R. R. (1980). MMPI short forms: A literature review. *Journal of Personality Assessment, 44*, 368–376.

STEWART, D. J. & PATTERSON, M. L. (1973). Eliciting effects of verbal and nonverbal cues on projective test responses. *Journal of Consulting and Clinical Psychology, 41*, 74–77.

STONE, A. A. & NEALE, J. M. (1984). New measures of daily coping: Developments and preliminary results. *Journal of Personality and Social Psychology, 46*, 892–906.

STONE, G. C. (1983). Summary of recommendations of the National Working Conference on Education and Training in Health Psychology. *Health Psychology, 2*, 15–18.

STONE, G. C., COHEN, F., & ADLER, N. E. (1979). *Health psychology: A handbook.* San Francisco: Jossey-Bass.

STRICKER, G. (1975). On professional schools and professional degrees. *American Psychologist, 30*, 1062–1066.

STRICKLAND, B. R. (1985). Over the Boulder(s) and through the Vail. *The Clinical Psychologist*, 52–56.

STROTHER, C. R. (1956). *Psychology and mental health*. Washington, DC: American Psychological Association.

STRUPP, H. H. (1960). *Psychotherapists in action: Explorations of the therapist's contribution to the treatment process*. New York: Grune & Stratton.

STRUPP, H. H. (1972). Freudian analysis today. *Psychology Today, 6*(2), 33–40.

STRUPP, H. H. & BLOXOM, A. L. (1973). Preparing lower-class patients for group psychotherapy: Development and evaluation of a role-induction film. *Journal of Consulting and Clinical Psychology, 41*, 373–384.

STRUPP, H. H. & HADLEY, S. W. (1977). A tripartite model of mental health and therapeutic outcomes. *American Psychologist, 32*, 187–196.

STRUPP, H. H. & HADLEY, S. W. (1979). Specific vs. nonspecific factors in psychotherapy. *Archives of General Psychiatry, 36*, 1125–1137.

STUART, R. B. (1971). Behavioral contracting within the families of delinquents. *Journal of Behavior Therapy and Experimental Psychiatry, 2*, 1–11.

SUINN, R. M. (1982). Intervention with Type A behaviors. *Journal of Consulting and Clinical Psychology, 50*, 797–803.

SULLIVAN, H. S. (1953). *The interpersonal theory of psychiatry*. New York: W. W. Norton.

SULLIVAN, H. S. (1954). *The psychiatric interview*. New York: W. W. Norton.

SULZER, E. (1965). Behavior modification in adult psychiatric patients. In L. P. Ullmann & L. Krasner (Eds.), *Case studies in behavior modification*. New York: Holt, Rinehart & Winston.

SUNDBERG, N. D. (1961). The practice of psychological testing in clinical services in the United States. *American Psychologist, 16*, 79–83.

SUNDBERG, N. D. (1977). *Assessment of persons*. Englewood Cliffs, NJ: Prentice-Hall.

SUNDBERG, N. D., TAPLIN, J. R., & TYLER, L. E. (1983). *Introduction to clinical psychology: Perspectives, issues, and contributions to human service*. Englewood Cliffs, NJ: Prentice-Hall.

SUNDBERG, N. D. & TYLER, L. E. (1962). *Clinical psychology: An introduction to research and practice*. New York: Appleton-Century-Crofts.

SUNDBERG, N. D., TYLER, L. E., & TAPLIN, J. R. (1973). *Clinical psychology: Expanding horizons* (2nd ed.). Englewood Cliffs, NJ: Prentice-Hall.

SURWIT, R. S. (1982). Behavioral treatment of Raynaud's syndrome in peripheral vascular disease. *Journal of Consulting and Clinical Psychology, 50*, 922–932.

SWAIN, M. A. & STECKEL, S. B. (1981). Influencing adherence among hypertensives. *Research Nursing and Health, 4*, 213–218.

SWEET, A. A. (1984). The therapeutic relationship in behavior therapy. *Clinical Psychology Review, 4*, 253–272.

SWEETLAND, R. C. & KEYSER, D. J. (Eds.). (1983). *Tests*. Kansas City, MO: Test Corporation of America.

SWENSON, R. A., NASH, D. L., & ROOS, D. C. (1984). Source credibility and perceived expertness of testimony in a simulated child-custody case. *Professional Psychology: Research and Practice, 15*, 891–898.

SZASZ, T. S. (1960). The myth of mental illness. *American Psychologist, 15*, 113–118.

SZONDI, L., MOSER, U., & WEBB, M. W. (1959). *The Szondi test in diagnosis, prognosis and treatment*. Philadelphia: Lippincott.

TAFT, J. (1951). *The dynamics of therapy in a controlled relationship*. New York: Harper.

TAFT, R. (1955). The ability to judge people. *Psychological Bulletin, 52*, 1–23.

TALLENT, N. (1958). On individualizing the psychologist's clinical evaluation. *Journal of Clinical Psychology, 14*, 243–244.

TALLENT, N. (1976). *Psychological report writing*. Englewood Cliffs, NJ: Prentice-Hall.

TALLENT, N. & REISS, W. J. (1959). Multidisciplinary views on the preparation of written, psychological reports, III. The trouble with psychological reports. *Journal of Clinical Psychology, 15*, 444–446.

TAPLIN, P. S. & REID, J. B. (1973). Effects of instructional set and experimenter influence on observer reliability. *Child Development, 44*, 547–554.

TARDE, G. (1903). *The laws of imitation*. New York: Holt.

TELCH, C. F. & TELCH, M. J. (1985). Psychological approaches for enhancing coping among cancer patients: A review. *Clinical Psychology Review, 5*, 325–344.

TEMERLIN, M. K. (1968). Suggestion effects in psychiatric diagnosis. *Journal of Nervous and Mental Disease, 147*, 349–353.

TENDLER, A. D. (1930). A preliminary report on a test for emotional insight. *Journal of Applied Psychology, 14,* 123–136.

THOITS, P. A. (1982). Conceptual, methodological, and theoretical problems in studying social support as a buffer against life stress. *Journal of Health and Social Behavior, 23,* 145–159.

THOMAS, D. S. (1929). *Some new techniques for studying social behavior.* New York: Columbia University.

THOMAS, E. J. (1973). Bias of therapist influence in behavioral assessment. *Journal of Behavior Therapy and Experimental Psychiatry, 4,* 107–111.

THORNDIKE, E. L. (1911). *Animal intelligence.* New York: Macmillan.

THORNE, F. C. (1948). Theoretical foundations of directive psychotherapy. *Current Trends in Clinical Research, 49,* 867–928.

THORNE, F. C. (1967). *Integrative psychology.* Brandon, VT: Clinical Psychology Publishing Co.

THORNE, F. C. (1972). Clinical judgment. In R. H. Woody & J. D. Woody (Eds.), *Clinical assessment in counseling and psychotherapy* (pp. 30–85). Englewood Cliffs, NJ: Prentice-Hall.

THORNE, F. C. (1973). Eclectic psychotherapy. In R. Corsini (Ed.), *Current psychotherapies.* Itasca, IL: F. E. Peacock Publishers.

THORTON, E. M. (1983). *Freud and cocaine: The Freudian fallacy.* London: Blond & Briggs.

THRASH, W. J., MARR, J. N., & BOONE, S. E. (1982). Continuous self-monitoring of discomfort in the dental chair and feedback to the dentist. *Journal of Behavioral Assessment, 4,* 273–284.

TITTLE, C. R., VILLENCE, W. J., & SMITH, D. A. (1978). The myth of social class and criminality: An empirical assessment of the empirical evidence. *American Sociological Review, 43,* 643–656.

TOLMAN, E. C. (1932). *Purposive behavior in animals and men.* New York: Naiburg.

TRYON, W. W. (1976). A system of behavioral diagnosis. *Professional Psychology, 7,* 495–506.

TULKIN, S. R. & FRANK, G. W. (1985). The changing role of psychologists in health maintenance organizations. *American Psychologist, 40,* 1125–1130.

TURKINGTON, C. (1985, April). Psychology fees top non-MD's. *APA Monitor,* p. 18.

TURNER, R. M. (1986). Behavioral self-control procedures for disorders of initiating and maintaining sleep (DIMS). *Clinical Psychology Review, 6,* 27–38.

TWENTYMAN, C. T., JENSEN, M., & KLOSS, J. D. (1978). Social skills training for the complex offender: Employment seeking skills. *Journal of Clinical Psychology, 34,* 320–326.

ULLMANN, L. P. & HUNRICHS, W. A. (1958). The role of anxiety in psychodiagnosis: Replication and extension. *Journal of Clinical Psychology, 14,* 276–279.

ULLMANN, L. P. & KRASNER, L. (Eds.) (1965). *Case studies in behavior modification.* New York: Holt, Rinehart and Winston.

ULLMANN, L. P. & KRASNER, L. (1975). *A psychological approach to abnormal behavior.* Englewood Cliffs, NJ: Prentice-Hall.

UYEDA, M. K. & MOLDAWSKY, S. (1986). Prospective payment and psychological services: What difference does it make? Psychologists aren't in Medicare anyway. *American Psychologist, 41,* 60–63.

VANDENBOS, G. R. & STAPP, J. (1983). Service providers in psychology: Results of the 1982 APA human resources survey. *American Psychologist, 38,* 1330–1352.

VANE, J. R. (1981). The Thematic Apperception Test: A review. *Clinical Psychology Review, 1,* 319–336.

VANE, J. R. & MOTTA, R. W. (1984). Group intelligence tests. In G. Goldstein & M. Hersen (Eds.), *Handbook of psychological assessment* (pp. 100–116). New York: Pergamon Press.

VAUGHN, C. L. & REYNOLDS, W. A. (1951). Reliability of personal interview data. *Journal of Applied Psychology, 35,* 61–63.

VEGA, A. & PARSONS, O. A. (1967). Cross-validation of the Halstead-Reitan tests for brain damage. *Journal of Consulting Psychology, 31,* 619–625.

VERNY, T. R. (1974). *Inside groups: A practical guide to encounter groups and group therapy.* New York: McGraw-Hill.

WACHTEL, P. L. (1977). *Psychoanalysis and behavior therapy.* New York: Basic Books.

WADE, T. C. & BAKER, T. B. (1977). Opinions and use of psychological tests: A survey of clinical psychologists. *American Psychologist, 32,* 874–882.

WALKER, C. E., HEDBERG, A., CLEMENT, P. W., & WRIGHT, L. (1981). *Clinical procedures for behavior therapy.* Englewood Cliffs, NJ: Prentice-Hall.

WALKER, L. E. A. (1984). Battered women, psychology, and public policy. *American Psychologist, 39,* 1178–1182.

WALKER, R. S. & WALSH, J. A. (1969). As others see us? The Medieval Multi-Purpose Inquiry. *Perceptual and Motor Skills, 28,* p. 414.

WALLEN, R. W. (1956). *Clinical psychology: The study of persons.* New York: McGraw-Hill.

WALLERSTEIN, R. S. & SAMPSON, H. (1971). Issues in research in the psychoanalytic process. *International Journal of Psychoanalysis, 52,* 11–50.

WALSH, W. B. (1967). Validity of self-report. *Journal of Counseling Psychology, 14,* 18–23.

WATERHOUSE, G. J. & STRUPP, H. H. (1984). The patient-therapist relationship: Research from the psychodynamic perspective. *Clinical Psychology Review, 4,* 77–92.

WATKINS, C. E. (1985). Counseling psychology, clinical psychology, and human services psychology: Where the twain shall meet. *American Psychologist, 40,* 1054–1056.

WATLEY, D. J. (1968). Feedback training and improvement of clinical forecasting. *Journal of Counseling Psychology, 15,* 167–171.

WATSON, D. & FRIEND, R. (1969). Measurement of social-evaluative anxiety. *Journal of Consulting and Clinical Psychology, 33,* 448–457.

WATSON, D. L. & THARP, R. G. (1972). *Self-directed behavior: Self-modification for personal adjustment.* Monterey, CA: Brooks/Cole.

WATSON, J. B. (1913). Psychology as the behaviorist views it. *Psychological Review, 20,* 158–177.

WATSON, J. B. (1924). *Behaviorism.* New York: W. W. Norton.

WATSON, J. B. (1930). *Behaviorism* (Rev. ed.). New York: W. W. Norton.

WATSON, J. B. & RAYNER, R. (1920). Conditioned emotional reactions. *Journal of Experimental Psychology, 3,* 1–14.

WATSON, R. I. (1951). *The clinical method in psychology.* New York: Harper.

WATSON, R. I. (1953). A brief history of clinical psychology. *Psychological Bulletin, 50,* 321–346.

WEBB, E., CAMPBELL, D. T., SCHWARTZ, R. D., & SECHREST, L. B. (1966). *Unobtrusive measures: Nonreactive research in the social sciences.* Chicago: Rand-McNally.

WECHSLER, D. (1967). *Manual for the WPPSI.* New York: Psychological Corporation.

WECHSLER, D. (1981). *Wechsler Adult Intelligence Scale-Revised.* New York: The Psychological Corporation.

WEICK, K. E. (1968). Systematic observational methods. In G. Lindzey & E. Aronson (Eds.), *Handbook of social psychology* (Vol. 2, pp. 357–451) (2nd ed.). Reading, MA: Addison-Wesley.

WEISS, J. H. (1963). The effect of professional training and amount and accuracy of information on behavioral prediction. *Journal of Consulting Psychology, 27,* 257–262.

WEISS, T. (1986). A legislative view of Medicare and DRGs. *American Psychologist, 41,* 79–82.

WEISSBERG, R. P., COWEN, E. L., LOTYCZEWSKI, B. S., & GESTEN, E. L. (1983). The Primary Mental Health Project: Seven consecutive years of outcome research. *Journal of Consulting and Clinical Psychology, 51,* 100–107.

WEISSBERG, R. P., GESTEN, E. L., CARNRIKE, C. L., TORO, P. A., RAPKIN, B. D., DAVIDSON, E., & COWEN, E. L. (1981). Social problem-solving skills training: A competence-building intervention with second- to fourth-grade children. *American Journal of Community Psychology, 9,* 411–424.

WELLS, G. L. & LOFTUS, E. F. (Eds.) (1983). *Eyewitness testimony: Psychological perspectives.* London: Cambridge University Press.

WENAR, C. & COULTER, J. B. (1962). A reliability study of developmental histories. *Child Development, 33,* 453–462.

WERNICK, R. (1956). *They've got your number.* New York: W. W. Norton.

WERTHEIMER, M. (1923). Studies in the theory of Gestalt psychology. *Psychological Forschung, 4,* 300–350.

WEXLER, D. B. (1973). Token and taboo: Behavior modification, token economies and the law. *California Law Review, 61,* 81–109.

WEXLER, D. B. (1974). Of rights and reinforcers. *San Diego Law Review, 11,* 957–971.

WHEELER, D. R. (1938). Imaginal productivity tests: Beta inkblot test. In H. A. Murray (Ed.),

Explorations in Personality (pp. 111–150). New York: Oxford University Press.

WHEELER, L. & REITAN, R. M. (1962). The presence and laterality of brain damage predicted from responses to a short aphasia screening test. *Perceptual and Motor Skills, 15,* 783–799.

WHITE, L. & TURSKY, B. (Eds.) (1982). *Clinical biofeedback: Efficacy and mechanisms.* New York: Guilford Press.

WHITE, R. F. & WATT, N. F. (1973). *The abnormal personality* (4th ed.). New York: Ronald Press.

WHITEHEAD, W. E. & SCHUSTER, M. M. (1985). *Gastrointestinal disorders: Behavioral and physiological basis for treatment.* Orlando, FL: Academic Press.

WICKER, A. W. (1969). Attitudes versus actions: The relationship of verbal and overt behavioral responses to attitude objects. *Journal of Social Issues, 25,* 41–78.

WIDIGER, T. A. (1985). Review of Millon Clinical Multiaxial Inventory. In J. V. Mitchell (Ed.), *The ninth mental measurements yearbook* (pp. 986–988). Lincoln, NE: Buros Institute of Mental Measurements, University of Nebraska.

WIDIGER, T. A. & KELSO, K. (1983). Psychodiagnosis of Axis II. *Clinical Psychology Review, 3,* 491–510.

WIDIGER, T. A. & RORER, L. G. (1984). The responsible psychotherapist. *American Psychologist, 39,* 503–515.

WIDMAN, E. H. (1980). The use of a suicidologist in accidental death litigation. *Insurance Counsel Journal, 47,* 219–223.

WIENS, A. N. & MATARAZZO, J. D. (1983). Diagnostic interviewing. In M. Hersen, A. E. Kazdin, & A. S. Bellack (Eds.), *The clinical psychology handbook* (pp. 309–328). New York: Pergamon Press.

WIGDOR, A. K. & GARNER, W. R. (Eds.) (1982). *Ability testing: Uses, consequences, and controversies.* Washington, DC: National Academy Press.

WIGGINS, J. S. (1973). *Personality and prediction: Principles of personality assessment.* Reading, MA: Addison-Wesley.

WIGGINS, J. S. (1981). Clinical and statistical prediction: Where are we and where do we go from here? *Clinical Psychology Review, 1,* 3–18.

WILCOX, B. L. (1981). Social support, life stress, and psychological adjustment: A test of the buffering hypothesis. *American Journal of Community Psychology, 9,* 371–386.

WILDMAN, B. G. & ERICKSON, M. T. (1977). Methodological problems in behavioral observation. In J. D. Cone & R. P. Hawkins (Eds.), *Behavioral assessment: New directions in clinical psychology* (pp. 255–273). New York: Brunner/Mazel.

WILKINS, W. (1971). Desensitization: Social and cognitive factors underlying the effectiveness of Wolpe's procedure. *Psychological Bulletin, 76,* 311–317.

WILKINS, W. (1979). Expectancies in therapy research: Discriminating among heterogeneous nonspecifics. *Journal of Consulting and Clinical Psychology, 47,* 837–845.

WILKINS, W. (1984). Psychotherapy: The powerful placebo. *Journal of Consulting and Clinical Psychology, 52,* 570–573.

WILLIAMS, C. L., ARNOLD, C. B., & WYNDER, E. L. (1977). Primary prevention of chronic disease beginning in childhood: The Know Your Body Program: Design of study. *Preventive Medicine, 6,* 344–357.

WILLIAMS, R. L. (1972). *The Black Intelligence Test of Cultural Homogeneity (BITCH)—A culture-specific test.* Paper presented at the American Psychological Association meeting, Honolulu.

WILLIAMS, T. R. (1967). *Field methods in the study of culture.* New York: Holt, Rinehart & Winston.

WILLIAMSON, D. H., MOODY, S. C., GRANBERRY, S. W., LETHERMON, V. K., & BLOUIN, D. C. (1983). Criterion-related validity of a role-play social skills test for children. *Behavior Therapy, 14,* 466–481.

WILLIS, J. & GILES, D. (1978). Behaviorism in the twentieth century: What we have here is a failure to communicate. *Behavior Therapy, 9,* 15–27.

WILSON, G. T. (1978). On the much discussed term "behavior therapy." *Behavior Therapy, 9,* 89–98.

WILSON, G. T. (1982). Psychotherapy process and procedure: The behavioral mandate. *Behavior Therapy, 13,* 291–312.

WILSON, G. T. (1985). Limitations of meta-analysis in the evaluation of the effects of psychological therapy. *Clinical Psychology Review, 5,* 35–47.

WILSON, G. T. & RACHMAN, S. J. (1983). Meta-analysis and the evaluation of psychotherapy outcome: Limitations and liabilities. *Journal of Consulting and Clinical Psychology, 51,* 54–64.

WILSON, M. L. & RAPPAPORT, J. (1974). Personal self-disclosure: Expectancy and situational effects. *Journal of Consulting and Clinical Psychology, 42,* 901–908.

WING, J. K., COOPER, J. E., & SARTORIUS, N. (1974). *The measurement and classification of psychiatric symptoms.* London: Cambridge University Press.

WING, R., EPSTEIN, L. H., NOWALK, M. P., & LAMPARSKI, D. M. (1986). Behavioral self-regulation in the treatment of patients with diabetes mellitus. *Psychological Bulletin, 99,* 78–89.

WINNICOTT, D. W. (1965). *The maturational processes and the facilitating environment.* New York: International Universities Press.

WIRT, R. D., LACHAR, D., KLINEDINST, J. K., & SEAT, P. D. (1984). *Multidimensional description of child personality: A manual for the Personality Inventory for Children.* Los Angeles: Western Psychological Services.

WOLBERG, L. R. (1967). *The technique of psychotherapy* (2nd ed.). New York: Grune & Stratton.

WOLF, M. M. (1978). Social validity: The case of subjective measurement or how applied behavior analysis is finding its heart. *Journal of Applied Behavior Analysis, 11,* 203–214.

WOLFGANG, M. E. (1974). The social scientist in court. *The Journal of Criminal Law and Criminology, 65,* 239–247.

WOLPE, J. (1958). *Psychotherapy by reciprocal inhibition.* Stanford, CA: Stanford University Press.

WOLPE, J. (1982). *The practice of behavior therapy* (3rd ed.). New York: Pergamon Press.

WOLPE, J. (1984). Behavior therapy according to Lazarus. *American Psychologist, 39,* 1326–1327.

WOLPE, J. & LANG, P. J. (1969). *Fear Survey Schedule.* San Diego, CA: Educational and Industrial Testing Service.

WOLPE, J. & LAZARUS, A. A. (1966). *Behavior therapy techniques: A guide to the treatment of neuroses.* New York: Pergamon Press.

WOLTMANN, A. G. (1951). The use of puppetry as a projective method in therapy. In H. H. Anderson & G. L. Anderson (Eds.), *An introduction to projective techniques* (pp. 606–638). Englewood Cliffs, NJ: Prentice-Hall.

WOOD, L. F. & JACOBSON, N. S. (1985). Marital distress. In D. Barlow (Ed.), *Clinical handbook of psychological disorders* (pp. 344–416). New York: Guilford Press.

WOODS, P. A., HIGSON, P. J., & TANNAHILL, M. M. (1984). Token-economy programmes with chronic psychotic patients: The importance of direct measurement and objective evaluation for long-term maintenance. *Behaviour Research and Therapy, 22,* 41–51.

WOODWORTH, R. S. (1920). *Personal data sheet.* Chicago: Stoelting.

WYATT, F. (1968). What is clinical psychology? In A. Z. Guiora & M. A. Brandwin (Eds.), *Perspectives in clinical psychology* (pp. 222–238). Princeton, NJ: D. Van Nostrand.

YALOM, I. D. (1985). *The theory and practice of group psychotherapy* (3rd ed.). New York: Basic Books.

YARMEY, A. D. (1979). *The psychology of eyewitness testimony.* New York: The Free Press.

YARROW, M. R., CAMPBELL, J. D., & BURTON, R. V. (1968). *Child-rearing: An inquiry into research and methods.* San Francisco: Jossey-Bass.

ZAJONC, R. B. (1980). Feeling and thinking: Preferences need no inferences. *American Psychologist, 35,* 151–175.

ZAX, M. & SPECTER, G. A. (1974). *An introduction to community psychology.* New York: John Wiley.

ZEGIOB, L. E., ARNOLD, S., & FOREHAND, R. (1975). An examination of observer effects in parent-child interactions. *Child Development, 46,* 509–512.

ZEINER, A. R., BENDELL, D., & WALKER, C. E. (Eds.) (1985). *Health psychology: Treatment and research issues.* New York: Plenum.

ZEISEL, H. (1983). The surveys that broke Monopoly. *University of Chicago Law Review, 50,* 896–909.

ZETTLE, R. D. & HAYES, S. C. (1980). Conceptual and empirical status of rational-emotive therapy. In M. Hersen, R. M. Eisler, & P. M. Miller (Eds.), *Progress in behavior modification* (Vol. 9, pp. 125–162). Orlando, FL: Academic Press.

ZIFFERBLATT, S. M. (1975). Increasing compliance through the applied analysis of behavior. *Preventive Medicine, 4,* 173–182.

ZILBOORG, G. & HENRY, G. W. (1941). *A history of medical psychology.* New York: W. W. Norton.

ZIMET, C. N. & THRONE, F. M. (1965). *Preconference materials.* Conference on the Professional Preparation of Clinical Psychologists. Washington, DC: American Psychological Association.

ZIMMERMAN, I. L. & WOO-SAM, J. M. (1984). Intellectual assessment of children. In G. Goldstein & M. Hersen (Eds.), *Handbook of psychological assessment* (pp. 57–76). New York: Pergamon Press.

ZIMMERMAN, M. (1983). Methodological issues in the assessment of life events: A review of issues and research. *Clinical Psychology Review, 3,* 339–370.

ZISKIN, J. (1981). *Coping with psychiatric and psychological testimony* (3rd ed.). Venice, CA: Law and Psychology Press.

ZITRIN, C. M., KLEIN, D. F., & WOERNER, M. G. (1980). Treatment of agoraphobia with group exposure in vivo and imipramine. *Archives of General Psychiatry, 37,* 63–72.

ZLUTNIK, S., MAYVILLE, W., & MOFFAT, S. (1975). Modification of seizure disorders: The interruption of behavioral chains. *Journal of Applied Behavior Analysis, 8,* 1–12.

ZUBIN, J. (1969). The role of models in clinical psychology. In L. L'Abate (Ed.), *Models of clinical psychology* (pp. 5–12). Atlanta, GA: Georgia State College.

ZUBIN, J. (1978). Research in clinical diagnosis. In B. Wolman (Ed.), *Clinical diagnosis of mental disorders.* New York: Plenum Press.

ZUBIN, J., ERON, L. D., & SCHUMER, F. (1965). *An experimental approach to projective techniques.* New York: John Wiley.

ZUCKERMAN, M. & LUBIN, B. (1965). *Manual for the multiple affect adjective checklist.* San Diego, CA: Educational and Industrial Testing Service.

ZWANG, G. (1985). *La statue de Freud.* Paris: Robert Lafont.

Index

SUBJECTS